PRO-POOR DEVELOPMENT POLICIES

The **ISEAS – Yusof Ishak Institute** (formerly Institute of Southeast Asian Studies) is an autonomous organization established in 1968. It is a regional centre dedicated to the study of socio-political, security and economic trends and developments in Southeast Asia and its wider geostrategic and economic environment. The Institute's research programmes are grouped under Regional Economic Studies (RES), Regional Strategic and Political Studies (RSPS), and Regional Social and Cultural Studies (RSCS). The Institute is also home to the ASEAN Studies Centre (ASC), the Singapore APEC Study Centre, and the Temasek History Research Centre (THRC).

ISEAS Publishing, an established academic press, has issued more than 2,000 books and journals. It is the largest scholarly publisher of research about Southeast Asia from within the region. ISEAS Publishing works with many other academic and trade publishers and distributors to disseminate important research and analyses from and about Southeast Asia to the rest of the world.

The **Southeast Asian Regional Center for Graduate Study and Research in Agriculture** (SEARCA) is one of the 24 regional centres of excellence of the Southeast Asian Ministers of Education Organization (SEAMEO). Founded on 27 November 1966, SEARCA is mandated to strengthen institutional capacities in agricultural and rural development in Southeast Asia through graduate scholarship, research and development, and knowledge management. It serves the 11 SEAMEO member countries, namely, Brunei Darussalam, Cambodia, Indonesia, Lao People's Democratic Republic, Malaysia, Myanmar, the Philippines, Singapore, Thailand, Vietnam and Timor-Leste. SEARCA is hosted by the Government of the Philippines on the campus of the University of the Philippines Los Baños in Laguna, Philippines. It is supported by donations from SEAMEO members and associate member states, other governments and various international donor agencies.

PRO-POOR DEVELOPMENT POLICIES
LESSONS FROM THE PHILIPPINES AND EAST ASIA

EDITED BY
HAL HILL
MAJAH-LEAH V. RAVAGO
JAMES A. ROUMASSET

First published jointly in Singapore in 2022 by

ISEAS Publishing
30 Heng Mui Keng Terrace
Singapore 119614
E-mail: publish@iseas.edu.sg
Website: http://bookshop.iseas.edu.sg

and

SEAMEO SEARCA
College, Los Baños 4031
Laguna, Philippines

E-mail: akru@searca.org
Website: www.searca.org

All rights reserved. No part of this publication may be reproduced, translated, stored in a retrieval system, or transmitted in any form or by any means, electronic, mechanical, photocopying, recording or otherwise, without the prior permission of the ISEAS – Yusof Ishak Institute.

© 2022 ISEAS – Yusof Ishak Institute, Singapore

The responsibility for facts and opinions in this publication rests exclusively with the authors and their interpretations do not necessarily reflect the views or the policy of the publishers or their supporters.

ISEAS Library Cataloguing-in-Publication Data

Names: Balisacan, A. M., honoree. | Hill, Hal, 1948-, editor. | Ravago, Majah-Leah V., editor. | Roumasset, James A., editor.
Title: Pro-poor development policies : lessons from the Philippines and East Asia / edited by Hal Hill, Majah-Leah V. Ravago, James A. Roumasset.
Description: Singapore : ISEAS-Yusof Ishak Institute : SEARCA, 2022. | Includes bibliographical references and index.
Identifiers: ISBN 9789815011050 (soft cover) | ISBN 9789815011067 (pdf) | ISBN 9789815011074 (epub)
Subjects: LCSH: Philippines—Economic policy. | Economic development—Philippines. | Economic development—East Asia. | Agriculture—Economic aspects—Asia. | Equality—Philippines.
Classification: LCC HC453 P962

Cover photo: Fredelon B. Sison and Lester

Book cover designed by Kalikasan C. Cuevas
Copyedited by Lily Tallafer
Typeset by Kalikasan C. Cuevas
Indexed by Kalikasan C. Cuevas
Printed in Singapore by Mainland Press Pte Ltd

*For Arsenio Molina Balisacan
Outstanding economist, professor, public servant, colleague,
mentor and friend*

Contents

Tables, Figures and Boxes		xi
Foreword by Gerardo P. Sicat		xxvi
Foreword by C. Peter Timmer		xxix
Message by Glenn B. Gregorio		xxxii
Preface and Acknowledgements		xxxiv
About the Editors		xxxvi
About the Contributors		xxxviii
Acronyms		li

PART 1   INTRODUCTION AND SYNTHESIS   1

1. From Agriculture to Competition: Overview and Lessons from the Philippine and Asia for Pro-poor Development   3
   Hal Hill, Majah-Leah V. Ravago and James A. Roumasset

2. Philippine Economic Development in Comparative Perspective: An Interpretative Essay   29
   Hal Hill, Arsenio M. Balisacan and Russel Matthew dela Cruz

PART 2 AGRICULTURAL AND ECONOMIC DEVELOPMENT — 73

3   Trade Distortions as Constraints to Agricultural Development in East Asia — 75
    Kym Anderson

4   Beyond Krugman: The Importance of Agriculture for East Asian Growth — 95
    Peter Warr

5   The Role of Agricultural and Structural Transformations in Rural Poverty Reduction — 116
    Jikun Huang

6   The Changing Relationship between Farm Size and Productivity: Asia and the Philippines — 133
    Keijiro Otsuka

7   The Political Economy of Rice Policy in the Philippines — 157
    V. Bruce J. Tolentino and Beulah Maria de la Peña

8   Adapting Philippine Agriculture to Climate Change — 190
    *Mark W. Rosegrant and Mercedita A. Sombilla
    with Nicostrato Perez, Angga Pradesha
    and Timothy Thomas*

PART 3 ECONOMIC POLICIES FOR ACHIEVING TARGETED LEVELS OF LIVING IN THE PHILIPPINES — 221

9   Low Income Traps and Philippine Poverty Incidence — 223
    Raul V. Fabella and Geoffrey M. Ducanes

10 The Philippines in Global Manufacturing Value Chains: A Tale of Arrested Growth — 246
    Prema-chandra Athukorala

11	The Limits of Trade Policy Liberalization in the Philippines *Fernando T. Aldaba, Alvin Ang and Cielito F. Habito*	280
12	Reaching for the Demographic Dividend to Achieve Inclusive Economic Growth *Dennis S. Mapa, Ernesto M. Pernia and Lisa Grace S. Bersales*	311
13	Collateralizing Wages: The Case of *Sangla* ATM *Nobuhiko Fuwa, Kei Kajisa, Eduardo Lucio, Sharon Faye Piza and Yasuyuki Sawada*	339

PART 4 INEQUALITY AND ECONOMIC DEVELOPMENT — 359

14	An Essay on Markets, Distributive Justice and Social Safety Nets *Dante B. Canlas*	361
15	Convergence of Philippine Spatial Inequality during the American Colonial Period *Jan Carlo B. Punongbayan, Jeffrey G. Williamson and Karl Robert L. Jandoc*	390
16	Social Differentiation: The Middle Class and Its Discontents *Emmanuel S. de Dios and Philip Arnold P. Tuaño*	414
17	Redistributive Preferences and Prospects for Intergenerational Mobility in Southeast Asia *Joseph J. Capuno*	460

PART 5 COMPETITION LAW AND POLICY — 493

18	Adopting and Adapting Competition Policy: Asian Illustrations *Majah-Leah V. Ravago, James A. Roumasset and Arsenio M. Balisacan*	495

19	Competition and Employment Growth in the Philippines: A Baseline Assessment *Stella A. Quimbo, Meg L. Regañon, Eina Izabela Z. Concepcion and Cara T. Latinazo*	546
20	Buyer Power and Late Payment Behaviour in the Shoe Capital of the Philippines *Tetsushi Sonobe*	574
21	Regulation, Market Evolution and Competition in the Philippine Microfinance Sector *Jan Carlo B. Punongbayan, Gilberto M. Llanto and Emmanuel F. Esguerra*	595
22	Tariffication and Market Structure: The Case of the Philippine Rice Industry *Ramon L. Clarete*	633
23	The Role of Government Subsidies in Philippine Agricultural Competition *Arlene B. Inocencio and Agnes C. Rola*	665

PART 5 INTERNATIONAL DIMENSIONS   695

24	Modernization of the Global Rice Market *Suthad Setboonsarng*	697
25	International Cooperation for Development: Learning from Trade and Tax Policies *Marilou Uy*	727

INDEX   750

Figures, Tables and Boxes

FIGURES

2.1	Philippine economic growth and per capita GDP (1960–2020)	35
2.2	Comparative headcount poverty estimates (2000–2019)	42
2.3	Comparison of BPO revenues and OFW remittances (2006–18)	47
2.4	Comparative COVID-19 stimulus spending	51
2.5	Change in employment in high-contact sectors vs. low-contact sectors (January 2020 and January 2021)	51
2.6	Long-term COVID-19 vulnerability index	52
2.7	Comparative ASEAN governance indicators (1996–2019)	58
3.1	Nominal and relative rates of government assistance to agriculture in China, Japan, Korea and Taiwan (1955–2016, %)	82
3.2	Nominal rates of government assistance to agriculture in China, Indonesia, Philippines and OECD countries (1980–2019, %)	83
3.3	Share of rural households with a bank or mobile-money account or equivalent in Asian developing economies and high-income countries (2011 and 2017, %)	91

4.1	GDP shares by sector (Thailand, 1981–2017)	101
4.2	GDP shares by sector (Indonesia, 1981–2017)	102
4.3	Employment shares by sector (Thailand, 1981–2017)	103
4.4	Employment shares by sector (Indonesia, 1981–2017)	103
4.5	Labour productivity by sector (Thailand, 1981–2017)	104
4.6	Labour productivity by sector (Indonesia, 1981–2017)	105
4.7	Productivity growth and structural change (Thailand, 1981–2017)	109
4.8	Productivity growth and structural change (Indonesia, 1981–2017)	109
4.9	Productivity growth and percentage contribution from structural change (Thailand and Indonesia, 1981–2017)	110
5.1	Convergence of agricultural shares in GDP and employment in China and selected Southeast Asian countries (1980s, 2000 and 2019)	119
5.2	Output value share of non-cereal products in agriculture (crop and livestock) in China and selected Southeast Asian countries (1981–2018)	121
5.3	Agricultural labour productivity in China and selected Southeast Asian countries (1991–2019)	122
5.4	Share of rural population under poverty in China and selected Southeast Asian countries (1987–2012)	123
5.5	Average annual change in share of agricultural GDP (or employment) and average annual reduction in rural poverty incidence in the period indicated in China and selected Southeast Asian countries	125
5.6	Average annual change of non-cereal output value share in agriculture and average annual reduction in rural poverty incidence in the period indicated in China and selected Southeast Asian countries	126

5.7	Average annual growth of agricultural labour productivity and average annual reduction in rural poverty incidence in the period indicated in China and selected Southeast Asian countries	127
6.1	Illustration of the inverse relationships between farm size and productivity measured by gross value of production, net value of production and profit per unit of land	140
6.2	Conceptual relationships between farm size and productivity under labour- and capital-intensive farming systems	141
6.3	Changes in average farm sizes (ha) in selected East Asian countries	143
6.4	Changes in grain self-sufficiency ratios in selected East Asian countries	145
6.5	Changes in family and hired labour use (person-days/ha) for care-intensive and other activities during the wet season in Central Luzon (1966–2015)	148
6.6	Tractorization in land preparation and use of combine harvesters during the wet season in Central Luzon (1966–2015)	149
7.1	Rice production, estimated food use and population (production and use in thousand mt rice terms, population in 10,000)	161
7.2	Comparative paddy yields (1990 = 100)	162
7.3	Comparative paddy production (1990 = 100)	162
7.4	Comparative rice prices (Jan 2000–Oct 2020)	163
7.5	Monthly headline and rice inflation (2016–20)	178
8.1	Interlinked modelling system used to assess the agricultural impacts of climate change on the Philippine economy	192
8.2	Impact of climate change on indicators of economic welfare (2050)	197

8.3	Impact of climate change on Philippine GDP by sector (2050)	203
8.4	Impact of climate change on demand for labour by sector and type of labour (2050)	204
8.5	Impact of climate change on GDP through demand for agricultural labour (2011–50)	204
8.6	Impact of three adaptation strategies on net welfare (with and without NFA rice subsidy, 2011–50)	206
10.1	Real exchange rate (RER) and manufacturing share in GDP (%) in the Philippines (2000–2020)	258
10.2	Share in world exports of GMVC products of the Philippines and other ASEAN countries (1976–2019, %)	259
10.3	Value-added share in gross output in computer, electronics and electrical equipment industries in Southeast Asian countries (%)	269
10.4	Total domestic value added of exports in computer, electronics and electrical equipment industries	270
10.5	Political stability: Selected Southeast Asian countries	273
10.6	Rule of law: Selected Southeast Asian countries	273
11.1	Selected indicators as per cent of GDP (1983–2000)	289
11.2	Composition of export goods (1990–2000)	289
11.3	Comparative shares in exports, GDP and employment (2010–20)	294
11.4	Number of OFWs and poverty rates (2009)	295
11.5	Number of OFWs and poverty rates (2018)	296
11.6	Changes in food security index in the ASEAN countries (2012–20)	304
12.1	Declining mortality, declining fertility and the demographic transition	312
12.2	Phase 1 of demographic transition (Philippines, 2000)	313
12.3	Phase 2 of demographic transition (Thailand, 2000)	313

12.4	Phase 3 of demographic transition (Japan, 2000)	314
12.5	Crude birth rates in the Philippines (2010–20)	330
12.6	Labour force participation rate (LFPR) in the Philippines (male and female, 2nd quarter 2005 to 4th quarter 2020)	331
12.7	Unemployment rate of male and female workers in the Philippines (2nd quarter 2005 to 4th quarter 2020)	332
12.8	Youth unemployment rate in the Philippines (2nd quarter 2005 to 4th quarter 2020)	333
15.1	GDP and per capita GDP growth of the Philippines (by decade)	391
15.2	Development index (absolute vs. relative levels, 1903–39)	395
15.3	Population density across regions	397
15.4	Literacy rates across regions	398
15.5	Infant mortality rate across regions	399
15.6	Shares of agriculture, industry and services in GDP	401
15.7	Growth in agriculture and its components	402
15.8	Land area planted to leading crops	402
15.9	Per cent regional share of agricultural produce (in ha)	403
15.10	Contribution to industrial growth of various sectors	405
15.11	Number of enrolled students in the primary and secondary levels	408
16.1	Shares of poor, vulnerable and middle-class households (in %, 1997–2018)	419
16.2	Number of poor, vulnerable and middle-class households (1997–2018)	421
16.3	Shares in unemployment by attained level of education (in %, January 2020 to May 2021)	427
16.4	Share of Philhealth benefits enjoyed by quintile (2016, in %)	433

16.5	Proportion of households provided with social services (by income quintile, 2013 and 2017)	437
16.6	Reducing poverty and fighting criminality as urgent national concerns (responses by socio-economic class, percentage of survey respondents citing, 2000–2019)	447
17.1	Total samples (by country)	467
17.2	Distribution of respondents in their views about government's role to reduce income differences between people with high income and those with low income (by country)	468
17.3	Distribution of respondents by self-assessed socio-economic status (by country)	470
17.4	Marginal effects of serious income loss, own status lower than children's and own status same as children's (Cambodia, Indonesia, Myanmar and Singapore)	485
17.5	Marginal effects of serious income loss, own status lower than children's and own status same as children's (Malaysia, the Philippines, Thailand and Vietnam)	486
18.1	Competition promotes innovation up to a point	505
18.2	The Williamson trade-off: Should efficiency-enhancing mergers be allowed?	509
18.3	Income growth and adoption of competition law	517
18.4	Timeline of enactment of competition law in Asia	531
19.1	Employment growth and import growth (Philippines, 1957–2016)	548
21.1	Philippine MFIs by last known legal status (1999–2018)	610
21.2	Average number of active borrowers by MFI type	613
21.3	Average gross loan portfolio (in million PHP) by MFI type	613
21.4	Average assets (in million PHP) by MFI type	614

21.5	Average efficiency (%) by MFI type	615
21.6	Average cost per borrower (PHP) by MFI type	616
21.7	Average portfolio at risk, > 30 days (%) by MFI type	616
21.8	Average portfolio at risk, > 90 days (%) by MFI type	617
21.9	Average debt-equity ratio by MFI type	618
21.10	Average return on assets (%) by MFI type	618
21.11	Average return on equity (%) by MFI type	619
21.12	Average real yield on gross portfolio (%) by MFI type	619
21.13	HHI values across banks (including rural banks), NGOs and all types	622
21.14	Boone indicator over time	627
21A	Number of banks with microfinance operations	629
21B	Amount of microfinance loans and number of borrowers	360
22.1	Annual rice and palay prices (National Capital Region and Philippines, 2000–2019, in PHP/kg)	642
22.2	Equilibrium in the rice market with heterogeneous importers	651
22.3	Equilibrium without tariff distortions in the rice market with heterogeneous importers	652
22.4	Rice stocks, by market players (1991–2019, in thousand mt)	654
23.1	Subsidies to the agriculture sector (2010–15)	666
24.1	Top ten rice-importing countries	699
24.2	Top ten rice-exporting countries	700
24.3	Ending stocks of rice	702
24.4	Five-year moving average of rice yields in major production areas	703
24.5	Grains price index	704
24.6	Rice consumption per capita in major consuming countries	706

24.7	Consumer preference for the different characteristics of rice	707
24.8	Google search index for Basmati and Jasmin rice	715
24.9	Import tariff of wheat, rice and soybean (2012–15)	718
25.1	Average growth of trade and GDP	730
25.2	Increasing and deepening trade agreements	732
25.3	Statutory corporate tax rates (1980–2020)	735
25.4	Source taxing rights with common treaty partners	737

TABLES

2.1	Comparative Asian economic performance (1940–2010)	33
2.2	Comparative Asian growth rates (1960–2019)	34
2.3	Comparative ASEAN manufactures export performance (1990–2019)	44
2.4	Comparative headcount poverty estimates (2019–21)	48
2.5	Comparative impacts of the COVID-19 pandemic	50
2.6	Comparative economic openness (2019)	56
2.7	Comparative ASEAN internet statistics	61
2.8	Comparative ASEAN health indicators	63
2.9	Comparative ASEAN education indicators	64
2.10	Comparative social assistance —coverage, extent and targeting	67
4.1	Agriculture's contraction and industrialization component (1981–2017)	101
4.2	Labour productivity growth by sector (1981–2017)	106
4.3	Contribution of structural change to aggregate productivity growth (1981–2017)	107
4.4	Structural change and productivity growth rate: Regression results (Thailand and Indonesia, 1981–2017)	111

5.1	Categories of inclusive agricultural transformation (AT) based on the speeds of structural transformation (ST) and AT	128
6.1	Average farm size (ha), paddy yield (t/ha) and labour use (person-days/ha) during the wet season in Central Luzon (1966–2015)	147
7.1	Rice imports (% of domestic supply, 1970–2019)	160
7.2	Officials in key posts relative to the Grain Sector Development Program (pre- and post-January 2001)	167
7.3	Department of Agriculture leadership (1971–2003)	169
7.4	Financial status of 2020 RCEF (as of 27 Oct 2020)	177
7.5	Prices of rice and palay (PHP/kg, % change from year ago)	180
7.6	Estimated losses and benefits from Rice Tariffication Law (Apr 2019–Mar 2020, in billion PHP)	183
8.1	Summary of crop model results in major crop yields due to climate change (2000–2050)	194
8.2	Projected improvements in rainfed maize yields from various technologies (2050)	199
8.3	Projected improvements in irrigated rice yields from various technologies (2050)	200
8.4	Projected improvements in rainfed rice yields from various technologies (2050)	201
8.5	Average net yearly impact of adaptation strategies on household welfare by income group (with and without NFA subsidy, 2011–50)	208
9.1	Sectoral gross value-added growth (2001–15, in %)	227
9.2	Poverty incidence among the employed by sector of employment (2015)	228
9.3	Educational attainment of employed workers by sector (2015, in %)	229
9.4	Average basic pay per day among the employed by sector of employment (2015, in PHP)	230

9.5	Fixed effects model: Household poverty incidence as a function of employment in different economic sectors (region-urban/rural level data, 2009–15)	234
9A	Regional poverty thresholds used in the analysis	238
9B	Poverty incidence by region-area type (2009–15, in %)	239
9C	Share of working-age population employed in agriculture and services	241
9D	Share of working-age population employed in industry and manufacturing	242
10.1	The Philippines: Key indicators of global production sharing and export performance	257
10.2	Composition of GMVC exports from the Philippines (1979–2019, %, US$ million)	261
10.3	Composition of GMVC exports from the Philippines and other ASEAN (2018–19, %, US$ million)	263
10.4	Key indicators of GMVC participation in manufacturing in the Philippines (2012)	266
10.5	Geographical profile of GMVC manufacturing in the Philippines: Employment and gross output (%)	267
10.6	Nominal average monthly earnings in the manufacturing sector (US$)	272
11.1	Shares of specific goods in total export and total import (1995 vs. 2015)	291
11.2	Agriculture and fisheries export values and shares in total exports	297
11.3	Trade-openness index (1990–2012)	298
11.4	Poverty, under-5 stunting and mortality across the ASEAN	301
11.5	Food security index (2020, ASEAN member countries)	303
12.1	Total fertility rate (TFR) in the ASEAN and South Korea (1960–2017)	318
12.2	Total fertility rate (TFR) by wealth quintile (2008, 2013 and 2017)	319

12.3	Total fertility rate (TFR) by region (1998, 2003, 2008, 2013 and 2017)	320
12.4	Econometric models for total children ever born (TFR) (provincial panel data, 1993–2013)	328
13.1	Rank of informal money lender as source of financing	342
13.2	Characteristics of the respondents (factory workers, *Sangla* ATM Survey)	344
13.3	Mode of salary payment and access to bank accounts (*Sangla* ATM Survey)	345
13.4	Utilization of *Sangla* ATM	347
13.5	Characteristics of households with multipurpose cash loans (2009 Consumer Finance Survey)	350
13.6	Access to bank account (2009 Consumer Finance Survey)	351
13.7	Sources and uses of multipurpose cash loan (2009 Consumer Finance Survey)	351
13.8	Logit regression results on the determinants of borrowing via *Sangla* ATM (marginal effects)	353
14.1	Gini coefficient (2000–2018)	373
14.2	Mean income by decile (2012 and 2015, in PHP)	374
14.3	Difference in mean income between top- and low-income decile (2012 and 2015, in PHP)	375
14.4	Labour force, employed and unemployed (2016, in '000 and %)	378
14.5	Unemployment by age group (2016, in %)	378
14.6	Unemployment rate by educational attainment (2012 and 2016, in '000 and %)	379
15.1	Goalposts used in the analysis	394
15.2	Industrial establishments (ranked by value of production, 1902)	406
15.3	Total government expenditure per capita in Southeast Asia (in US$)	407

15.4	Primary school enrolment rates in Southeast Asia (% of school-aged children)	408
15.5	Per pupil educational expenditures for current expenses (in PHP)	409
16.1	Share of families by socio-economic (expenditure) category (1997–2018), in per cent of total	418
16.2	Characteristics of the economically secure and upper middle-income class categories (1997 and 2018)	423
16.3	Transition matrix (2003 and 2009)	425
16.4	Government fund releases for programmes under the Bayanihan 1 and 2 (in million PHP)	438
16.5	Differing socio-economic groups and critical government programmes	452
17.1	Selected development indicators (2013–17)	463
17.2	Regression variables: definitions and summary statistics (N = 7,943)	474
17.3	Marginal effects of selected covariates of preference for redistribution (full sample, N = 7,943)	477
17.4	Marginal effects of selected covariates of preference for redistribution (1st & 2nd income quintiles, N = 4,165)	480
17.5	Marginal effects of the covariates of preference for redistribution (3rd–5th income quintiles, N = 3,778)	482
18.1	Number of countries that adopted competition law in our data	516
18.2	Average growth rates of GDP per capita (1975–2015)	516
18.3	Summary statistics for all countries	520
18.4	Summary statistics for adopting vs non-adopting countries	522
18.5	Parameter estimates of adoption of competition law and growth equations	524

18.6	Conditional expectation, treatment and heterogeneity (average decadal growth of GDP per capita as dependent varible)	528
19.1	Summary statistics: Subclass variables	558
19.2	Average top four concentration ratio (CR4) for major industries	559
19.3	Regression results using HHI Dependent variable: Log total employment	561
19.4	Regression results using CR4 Dependent variable: Log total employment	563
19.5	Regression results using PCM Dependent variable: Log total employment	565
19.6	Employment effects of increased competition via different pathways	567
19.7	Predicted employment effects under increased competition scenarios	568
20.1	Price, quantity, margin and machinery (1998, 2003)	578
20.2	Employment and wage (2003)	580
20.3	Attributes of entrepreneurs	582
20.4	Sales routes and payment practices as percentage of revenue (2003)	583
20.5	Regression summarizing the data (between estimator) (1998, 2001, 2003)	587
20.6	Regressions summarizing the data (fixed-effects estimator) (1998, 2001, 2003)	590
21.1	Top MFI players in 2018	611
21.2	Selected MFI indicators (2018)	614
21.3	Summary statistics	623
21.4	PRH statistic; dependent variable = log of financial revenue	624
21.5	Translog cost function estimation	625
21.6	Boone scores for Philippine MFIs	627

22.1	Estimated implicit tariff protection on rice production (2015–19)	637
22.2	Comparison of the estimated trade-off gains and losses from the Rice Tariffication Law (in billion PHP)*	640
22.3	Standard deviations and correlation coefficients of rice prices and their yearly fluctuations (2000–2019, in PHP/kg)	643
22.4	Estimated average income and own-price elasticities of rice (2018 and 2019)	645
22.5	Actual versus predicted year-on-year changes in rice retail price in 2019	645
23.1	Subsidy, ratios to value added and concentrations of subsidy (2012)	670
23.2	Subsidy, ratios to value added and concentrations of subsidy (2015)	673
23.3	Market concentrations of agriculture sub-sectors (2010–15)	675
23.4	Price-cost margin by market concentration (2010–15)	679
23.5	Impact of subsidies on market concentration	681
23.6	Impact of subsidies on market power	684
23.7	Laws and provisions affecting market competition in the agriculture and fisheries sector of the Philippines	685
23.8	Amounts and nature of subsidies to GOCCs in agriculture (2015–18, PHP million)	687
24.1	Population growth and urbanization	710
24.2	Effects of urbanization and income on per capita rice consumption	713
24.3	Summary of the impacts of key drivers	719

BOXES

8.1	Early gains of the Rice Tariffication Law: Softening the impacts of typhoons and the COVID-19 pandemic	214
21.1	BSP regulations fostering microfinance	600
24.1	Why India's rice export increases despite a fast population growth, and China's rice import increases despite a slowing population growth: The supply side story	712

Foreword

I am very pleased to be drawn into this gentle conspiracy to surprise the honoree, Dr. Arsenio Balisacan, with a Festschrift on the occasion of his sixty-fifth birth anniversary.

Arsi, as he is known to friends, is an economist, teacher, research scholar, anti-poverty activist and public servant, all rolled into one. In his journey of achievement, he has experienced a difficult tale of passage from poor rural surroundings in the Ilocos region of northern Luzon, through disciplined work in the pursuit of his chosen professional dream. Today, he is one of the nation's foremost economists, respected by peers and admired by younger ones in the academe and in government, some of whom he had mentored. Importantly too, he holds a high position of influence that can improve the country's economic future.

I met Arsi in Washington, DC, in 1986, as he was about to head for home. He had just completed his participation as a young research intern in the World Bank's study of agriculture and economic development. I suggested to him then that he join the School of Economics at the University of the Philippines in Diliman. I sent an encouraging word about him to Dean Jose Encarnacion.

At that time, Arsi reminded me that we had actually first met in the early 1970s in Baguio, the country's summer capital, when he was a much younger man. He was then a delegate to a national conference of young public high school leaders that I happened to address as inspirational speaker. He was a young student from a poor family possessed by high educational aspirations. In that situation, success depended mainly on the thin and uncertain thread of scarce financial scholarships to support his study. He succeeded in turning small attainments into opportunities. Eventually, he made them into golden steps. Through scholarships he moved from a rural Ilocos state-supported university to the graduate programme in agricultural economics of the University of the Philippines Los Baños and then a PhD in economics with a teaching assistantship at the University of Hawaii and later a doctoral internship at the East-West Center.

When he joined the UP School of Economics, he intensified his research on important issues affecting the country—poverty alleviation, food policy and rural development. This work raised his profile within the economics profession and more broadly into the public spheres of recognition.

This led to his being appointed to the post of undersecretary in the Department of Agriculture. When he suspected that public governance issues hovered over the proper performance of public duties, he resigned his post and returned to the School. But new occasions for public service immediately kept opening for him. He became the director of SEARCA (Southeast Asian Regional Center for Graduate Study and Research in Agriculture) based in Los Baños. After that, he became dean of the UP School of Economics.

Even when he took on important administrative duties, his own research and scholarship did not suffer because he managed his time well. As an administrator he helped to expand the research opportunities of his colleagues. His deanship was interrupted by another call of government to lead the National Economic and Development Authority (NEDA) as director general and concurrent secretary of socio-economic planning.

After almost four years in this position and after the enactment of the Philippine Competition Commission (PCC) law, he was harnessed to take a full hand in organizing this new institution, becoming its founding chairperson. Among the specific functions of this regulatory body is to prohibit anticompetitive mergers and acquisitions.

The head of the competition commission is in a position to remind national policymakers that the economy thrives better where the markets in goods, labour, land and capital are allowed to move with more rather than less flexibility in order to achieve a more globally competitive economy.

In the course of decades of economic development in the past, economic restrictions have continuously hampered the country's fuller participation in the global economy, many of them instigated by the political constitutional framework. Only lately this year, major economic reforms were passed by legislation to liberalize important legal restrictions that have served as barriers against foreign investment in the economy. These promising developments are likely to play a role in permitting better economic recovery from the pandemic. A regulatory body can protect the guard rails of competition when more beneficial prospects for economic developments are in place than when barriers are stifling progress.

In this Festschrift, some of his intellectual friends contribute their studies on several important issues of economic and social development.

Gerardo P. Sicat, PhD
Founding Director-General
of the National Economic and Development Authority (NEDA)
and concurrent Minister of Economic Planning

Foreword

A Festschrift is intended to review the origins, depth and breadth of the academic works by a noted scholar in the twilight of their career. From this perspective, writing a foreword to a Festschrift for Arsenio M. Balisacan is a strange task for me. Academically speaking, I think of Arsi as my grandson. His promise as a scholar was noted by Professor Cristina Crisostomo David when he enrolled in the master's programme in agricultural economics at the University of the Philippines Los Baños in 1979. Tina was my PhD student in the early 1970s at the Food Research Institute at Stanford University, where she documented the striking role of fertilizer and rice prices in the political economy of Asian countries. Arsi continued this work at the University of the Philippines Los Baños under Tina's direction, and then generalized the results into a conceptual approach to positive political economy in his PhD dissertation at the University of Hawaii, under the mentorship of Professor James A. Roumasset.

My first involvement with agricultural policy in the Philippines came in the early 1970s, when Arsi was still in high school. As part of the Stanford project on "the political economy of rice in Asia" that Tina David worked on, Wally Falcon and I commissioned eight country studies in East and Southeast Asia (including one on the United States by Leon Mears, a familiar name in the Philippines' food policy circles). I worked closely with Mahar Mangahas on the Philippine study, so became acutely aware by 1975 just how complex the Philippines' story was. I had drafted the Indonesian country study as a prototype for other country authors and worked closely with all of them right through the publication stage.[1]

This earlier work on the region's political economy of rice set me up for understanding Arsi's work. My engagement with his work started with rice policy, but extended more broadly to the fields of agricultural development and the nature of pro-poor economic growth. Both fields are well represented in this Festschrift, via contributions from major authors in the field and through the inclusion of Arsi's own path-breaking research in both fields.

These two fields, and especially the economic and policy links *between* them, are very difficult territory for a scholar-practitioner in the Philippines. On two separate occasions, under two different presidents, I failed miserably to make any progress. The combination of an entrenched landed elite and the capture of most agricultural marketing enterprises by deeply vested interests stymied my efforts—after the People Power Revolution in early 1986 forced President Ferdinand Marcos from power—to help revamp the mandate of the National Food Authority to pursue stable rice prices without high protection.

A later effort to connect smallholder farmers to a more inclusive growth process also failed, despite high hopes in the development profession as President Gloria Macapagal-Arroyo had a PhD in economics from the University of the Philippines (she also studied at Georgetown University for two years, where she and Bill Clinton became friends). Over the years, I was able to work successfully with the International Rice Research Institute and the Asian Development Bank, and I enjoyed interacting with my Philippine colleagues and former students on each visit, but I could never make any progress with the government.

Thus, I am simply in awe of how successful Arsi has been as a scholar-practitioner at the very highest levels of the profession. His service at cabinet level in four different presidential administrations, while also serving with great distinction—as professor and dean of the faculty—in the best economics department in Southeast Asia, is without precedent.

My closest personal engagement with Arsi has been through his leadership of the Southeast Asian Regional Center for Graduate Study

---

[1] See volume XIV, nos. 3 and 4, *Food Research Institute Studies*, 1975.

and Research in Agriculture (SEARCA), and through the journal Arsi founded while at SEARCA, the *Asian Journal of Agricultural Development (AJAD)*. I have served on the editorial board of *AJAD* since its founding because I believe deeply in its mission: to highlight the importance of agriculture to the development of Asian economies, and to publish manuscripts by regional scholars that document this role.

I also benefited from Arsi's term as president of the Asian Society of Agricultural Economics (ASAE). In that role he invited me to Manila in August 2008 to give the keynote address at the sixth triennial meeting of the ASAE. I used the occasion to reflect on the twenty-fifth anniversary of the publication of *Food Policy Analysis*.[2] The cross-sectoral perspective developed in that volume remains essential to solving today's problems of poverty and hunger.[3]

This Festschrift is a fitting tribute to Arsi. His creativity, insights and just plain hard work illuminate every chapter. And he is just beginning...

C. Peter Timmer

---

[2] C. Peter Timmer, Walter P. Falcon, and Scott R. Pearson. 1983. *Food Policy Analysis*. Baltimore, MD: Johns Hopkins University Press for the World Bank.

[3] C. Peter Timmer. 2010. "International Best Practice in Food Policy: Reflections on *Food Policy Analysis*". *Asian Journal of Agriculture and Development* 7, no. 1: 1–10.

Message

SEARCA is glad to have played a key role in the formative years of Dr. Arsenio M. Balisacan as a young researcher, providing him a scholarship grant to pursue his master's in agricultural economics. We take pride in his significant contributions to research, policy and actions towards securing food and reducing poverty in Southeast Asia. Appointed to the helm of SEARCA in 2003, Dr. Balisacan reinforced the Centre's efforts towards poverty reduction and food security with a keen focus on agricultural competitiveness and natural resource management, through SEARCA's Eighth Five-Year Plan (2004–9), whose crafting and implementation he closely supervised. Now more than a decade later, SEARCA continues to pursue programmes that contribute to overcoming malnutrition, hunger, poverty and inequality in Southeast Asia. The Centre's Eleventh Five-Year Plan (2020–25), with its focus on "Accelerating Transformation through Agricultural Innovation" (ATTAIN), aims to elevate the quality of life of agricultural families through sustainable livelihoods and access to modern networks and innovative markets.

It thus gives us great pleasure to be part of this Festschrift that honours Dr. Balisacan and his remarkable academic, research and policy work. We see this book as an important influence in continuing the discourse and actions to empower agricultural institutions and communities. As an instrument of knowledge and co-creation, it contains lessons from Asian countries that bring to the fore not only the experience, but also the reforms in economic policies, competition law, inequalities and agricultural development across countries.

We join the authors and the ISEAS–Yusof Ishak Institute in recommending this book, with the hope that it will inspire its readers to contribute to the development of and innovations in the agriculture sector in Asia and beyond.

Glenn B. Gregorio
Director
SEAMEO SEARCA

Preface and Acknowledgements

This volume is a Festschrift for Arsenio Molina Balisacan – economist, professor, public servant, colleague, mentor and friend. It pays tribute to his work and honours him as an outstanding economist and public servant. Its themes reflect his research and policy interests over his professional career. These interests are central to understanding the development dynamics in the Philippines and elsewhere in Asia. The overarching theme is overcoming poverty through agricultural and rural development and complementary policies that engender a robust and sustainable structural transformation. Competition policy plays a particularly key role in combating cronyism and rent-seeking that impede that development path.

This project was conceived in November 2018 when the editors and the honouree attended the back-to-back Philippine Economic Society (PES) and the Federation of ASEAN Economic Associations (FAEA) conference held in Cubao, Quezon City, Philippines. We planned the surprise launch of this volume in time for his sixty-fifth birthday on 8 November 2022. In the Philippines, this age also marks an individual's retirement from government service. Thus began the three-year "gentle conspiracy", as Gerry Sicat aptly describes the project, among the editors, contributors, SEARCA and ISEAS – Yusof Ishak Institute towards the realization of this volume.

This book came to fruition with the help of many people and organizations whose tremendous support we wish to acknowledge. The enthusiastic responses from our forty-six authors from many countries are testimony to the high esteem and affection for Arsi. We thank our contributors for their fine papers and their collaboration as we worked through the refereeing and editorial production processes.

We thank Peter Timmer and Gerardo Sicat for readily accepting our request to write the forewords. Special thanks to Anne Krueger for the back-cover endorsement.

A huge thank you to the Southeast Asian Regional Center for Graduate Study and Research in Agriculture (SEARCA), led by Director Glenn Gregorio, for the funding support for this volume. Many thanks to the SEARCA team for facilitating the physical production of this book, especially Benedict Juliano and Arlene Nadres. Thanks to Lily Tallafer, our excellent and meticulous copyeditor who also happens to be one of Arsi's long-time associates. She not only did a very good job but also helped us move things along promptly. Thanks to our layout artist, Kei Cuevas, who gave a clean finish to the book. We also thank Shereena Salas who assisted in the early stage of the project.

We thank our publisher, ISEAS Publishing, Ng Kok Kiong, Rahilah Yusuf and the rest of the publication team for making the publication of this book possible.

Hal Hill, Majah-Leah V. Ravago and James A. Roumasset
Canberra, Manila and Honolulu

About the Editors

Hal Hill (Australian National University)
Hal Hill is the H. W. Arndt Professor Emeritus of Southeast Asian Economies at the Australian National University. He has written/edited twenty books and about 160 journal articles and book chapters. His books since 2000 include *The Indonesian Economy*, *The Philippine Economy* (co-edited with Arsenio Balisacan), *Malaysian Development Challenges* and *Regional Dynamics in a Decentralized Indonesia*. He serves on various boards and committees, including the *Dewan Kehormatan* of the Bank Indonesia Institute, the Council of the East Asian Economic Association (of which he is currently president), and several university boards. He is a member of the editorial board of fourteen academic journals. He has consulted extensively for various governments and international agencies. He is a fellow of the Academy of Social Sciences of Australia. In 2020, he was appointed an Officer of the Order of Australia (AO).

Majah-Leah V. Ravago (Ateneo de Manila University)
Majah-Leah V. Ravago is an associate professor at the Economics Department of the Ateneo de Manila University. She co-edited *Sustainable Economic Development* (with Arsenio Balisacan and Ujjayant Chakravorty), a volume published by Elsevier in 2015, and *Powering the Philippine Economy* in 2018 (with James Roumasset and Rolando Danao), a UP Press publication that won the 2020 Outstanding Book Award of the National Academy of Science and Technology (NAST). She was the programme director of the 2014–18 Energy Policy and Development Program, funded by the US Agency for International Development. She served as president of the Philippine Economic Society in 2018. In 2016, she received the NAST Outstanding Young Scientist Award in economics. She earned her BS in business economics and MA in

economics from the University of the Philippines, and her PhD in economics from the University of Hawaii in 2012 under the East-West Center Graduate Degree Fellowship Program. She is a former student, close associate and colleague of Arsenio Balisacan.

James A. Roumasset (University of Hawaii)
James A. Roumasset is a professor emeritus in the Economics Department and UHERO research fellow, both at the University of Hawaii, Manoa. His research centres on applications of public policy, including behaviour and organization in agriculture, sustainable economic development, energy and water economics, ecological resource economics, and competition policy. He is extremely proud of the careers and dedication of his former graduate students from the Philippines, Thailand and other countries.

About the Contributors

Fernando T. Aldaba (Ateneo de Manila University)
Fernando T. Aldaba is a professor of economics at the Ateneo de Manila University (ADMU). He served as dean of ADMU's School of Social Sciences from 2015 to 2021. His areas of specialization include labour economics, development economics and macroeconomics. He obtained his PhD in economics from the University of the Philippines Diliman, and his BS in management engineering degree (cum laude) from the ADMU.

Kym Anderson (University of Adelaide)
Kym Anderson is the George Gollin Professor Emeritus in the School of Economics, University of Adelaide (where he has been affiliated since 1984) and an honorary professor in the Arndt-Cordon Department of Economics at the Australian National University's Crawford School of Public Policy (where he was a research fellow in 1977–83 and a part-time professor of economics in 2012–18). In two periods of extended leave, he served as deputy head of economic research at the GATT Secretariat (now the World Trade Organization) in Geneva (1990–92) and as lead economist (Trade Policy) at the World Bank in Washington, DC (2004–7).

Alvin Ang (Ateneo de Manila University)
Alvin Ang is a professor at the Economics Department of the Ateneo de Manila University and a senior fellow of the Ateneo Eagle Watch. He served as president of the Philippine Economic Society in 2013. He finished his BA in economics at the University of Santo Tomas, master's in public policy at the National University of Singapore, and PhD in applied economics at Osaka University.

Prema-chandra Athukorala (Australian National University)
Prema-chandra Athukorala is a professor emeritus of economics in the Crawford School of Public Policy at the Australian National University, and fellow of the Academy of Social Science of Australia. His research interests are in trade and development, and development macroeconomics. His publications in these fields include ten books and over two hundred papers in scholarly journals and multi-author volumes. At various times, he has served as a consultant to the World Bank, Asian Development Bank and several United Nations organizations.

Arsenio M. Balisacan (Philippine Competition Commission)
Arsenio M. Balisacan has been serving as the first chairperson of the Philippine Competition Commission since 2016. He also served as socio-economic planning secretary and concurrent director-general of the National Economic and Development Authority from 2012 to 2016. He was a professor and dean of the School of Economics of the University of the Philippines Diliman, director of the Southeast Asian Regional Center for Graduate Study and Research in Agriculture (SEARCA), and undersecretary of the Philippine Department of Agriculture. He is a lifetime Academician of the National Academy of Science and Technology (NAST), recognized for his outstanding contributions to science and technology. His numerous publications cover wide areas of economic development, including poverty, inequality, human development, agricultural and rural development, antitrust (competition policy), and the political economy of policy reforms.

Lisa Grace S. Bersales (University of the Philippines)
Lisa Grace S. Bersales is a professor in the School of Statistics of the University of the Philippines (UP) in Diliman and vice president for planning and finance of the UP System. She has held various posts in UP Diliman, including director of graduate studies and dean of the School of Statistics. She was the first national statistician of the Philippines and led the implementation of the Philippine Statistics Act of 2013 by setting up the Philippine Statistics Authority in 2014. She earned her bachelor's degree (cum laude), MA and PhD in statistics from UP.

Dante B. Canlas (University of the Philippines)
Dante B. Canlas is a professor emeritus at the School of Economics of the University of the Philippines (UP). He served as socio-economic planning secretary and concurrent director-general of the National Economic and Development Authority in 2001–2. He was the executive director of the

Asian Development Bank (ADB) for Kazakhstan, Maldives, Marshall Islands, Mongolia, Pakistan, and the Philippines from 2003 to 2004. He earned his BS in mathematics and MA and PhD in economics from UP. He was a visiting professor at Northern Illinois University in De Kalb, Illinois, a research fellow at Princeton University in New Jersey, and a visiting research fellow at the Institute of Developing Economies in Tokyo.

Joseph J. Capuno (University of the Philippines)
Joseph J. Capuno is a professor at the School of Economics of the University of the Philippines, where he got his BA (cum laude), MA and PhD degrees. His specialties are public economics, development economics and health economics. His researches on fiscal decentralization, local political economy, local and regional development, health financing and impact evaluation have been published. In 2012 and 2015, his co-authored papers won the Outstanding Scientific Paper Award of the National Academy of Science and Technology of the Philippines.

Ramon L. Clarete (University of the Philippines)
Ramon L. Clarete is presently chief of party of the US Department of Agriculture B-SAFE project in the Philippines. Before this, he served as professor at the School of Economics of the University of the Philippines, specializing in food policy and international economics since 1989, and as dean from 2012 to 2015. He managed trade capacity-building projects for the US Agency for International Development in the Philippines. He also worked on a technical assistance assignment for the Asian Development Bank on ASEAN rice policy (2010–13). He co-authored *Trusting Trade and the Private Sector for Food Security in Southeast Asia*, a World Bank publication. He was with the Economics Department Faculty of the University of Western Ontario (1985–88). He obtained his PhD in economics at the University of Hawaii in 1984.

Eina Izabela Z. Concepcion (Procter & Gamble)
Eina Izabela Z. Concepcion earned her BS in business economics (magna cum laude and class salutatorian) from the University of the Philippines in 2016. She worked at the Philippine Competition Commission from 2016 to 2018 and, for a time, was seconded to the Australian Competition & Consumer Commission. She is currently working as a senior brand manager at Procter & Gamble in Singapore.

Emmanuel S. de Dios (University of the Philippines)
Emmanuel S. de Dios is a professor emeritus at the University of the Philippines (UP) School of Economics, where he also served as dean. He has published in the fields of institutions and governance, international economics, and the history of economic thought. He received the Outstanding Book Award as co-author in 2007, 2011 and 2014 from the National Academy of Science and Technology of the Philippines. In 2006, he was conferred the UP Chancellor's Award for Outstanding Teacher; he was chosen as one of the twelve centennial fellows of the university in 2007. He obtained his PhD in economics from the University of the Philippines in 1987.

Russel Matthew dela Cruz (Philippine Competition Commission)
Russel Matthew dela Cruz is a competition policy research officer at the Economics Office of the Philippine Competition Commission (PCC). His work includes market studies and competition impact assessments of various sector regulations and proposed legislations. He concurrently serves as technical assistant at PCC's Office of the Chairperson. Previously, he worked as an associate consultant for multinational firms across a wide range of industries. He earned his bachelor's degree (magna cum laude) in economics from the University of the Philippines Diliman in 2019.

Beulah Maria de la Peña (Bangko Sentral ng Pilipinas)
Beulah Maria de la Peña has worked extensively on Philippine agricultural policy, briefly in the Department of Agriculture, and as an independent consultant for many years. Her various engagements and papers focus on planning processes, value chains, trade policy and regulations.

Geoffrey M. Ducanes (Ateneo de Manila University)
Geoffrey M. Ducanes is an associate professor at the Ateneo de Manila University. He has worked for the International Labour Organization on a programme on labour migration and with the Asian Development Bank as a consultant in charge of the macro-econometric model of the Philippines. He has co-authored several papers on income poverty and inequality in the Philippines with Arsenio M. Balisacan. His research interests are poverty, inequality, education, migration, labour and applied econometrics. He received the Outstanding Young Scientist Award in 2014 from the National Academy of Science and Technology of the Philippines. He obtained his PhD in economics from the University of the Philippines in 2011.

Emmanuel F. Esguerra (University of the Philippines)
Emmanuel F. Esguerra had been a professor of economics at the School of Economics of the University of the Philippines until his retirement in 2019. He served as deputy director-general for policy and planning of the National Economic and Development Authority in 2012 and subsequently as director-general and secretary of socioeconomic planning until June 2016. He is a former editor of the *Philippine Review of Economics* and co-editor of *The Philippine Economy: No Longer the East Asian Exception?* (2018, Singapore: ISEAS – Yusof Ishak Institute).

Raul V. Fabella (University of the Philippines)
Raul V. Fabella is a professor emeritus of the University of the Philippines (UP), a member of the National Academy of Science and Technology (Philippines) and an honorary professor at the Asian Institute of Management. He was elevated to the status of National Scientist in 2011. He is highly respected for his outstanding contributions in the field of economics, particularly for extending the reach of the celebrated Nash bargaining solution to the more egalitarian Rawlsian grounds. His research covers diverse topics, including welfare effects of lobbying and rent-seeking, efficiency of teams and partnerships, and properties of contracts under weak governance. He served as dean of the UP School of Economics from 1998 to 2007. He obtained his PhD in economics from Yale University.

Nobuhiko Fuwa (University of Tokyo)
Nobuhiko Fuwa was a professor at the Graduate School of Public Policy of the University of Tokyo. After receiving his PhD in agricultural and resource economics from the University of California at Berkley in 1995, he worked at the World Bank, Chiba University, International Rice Research Institute and Waseda University. He conducted numerous household and community surveys in Asia and Africa on agricultural development, published extensively in peer-reviewed journals and edited several books, some jointly with Arsenio M. Balisacan.

Cielito F. Habito (Ateneo de Manila University)
Cielito F. Habito is a professor of economics at the Ateneo de Manila University and chairman of Brain Trust Inc. and Operation Compassion Philippines. He served as secretary of socio-economic planning and concurrent director-general of the National Economic and Development Authority. In 1998, he was elected as chairperson of the United Nations Commission on Sustainable Development in New York. He had worked

at the World Bank, Harvard University and Asian Development Bank Institute in Tokyo. He holds a PhD and MA in economics from Harvard University, master of economics from the University of New England (Australia) and BS in agriculture, major in agricultural economics, (summa cum laude) from the University of the Philippines.

Jikun Huang (Peking University)
Jikun Huang is a professor at the School of Advanced Agricultural Sciences and director of the China Center for Agricultural Policy, Peking University. He is a fellow of the World Academy of Sciences and Agricultural and Applied Economics Association, an honorary lifetime member of the International Association of Agricultural Economists, president of the Asian Society of Agricultural Economists, and vice president of the Chinese Association of Agro-Tech Economics. He received his PhD in agricultural economics from the University of the Philippines Los Baños in 1990. His research covers a wide range of issues on China's agricultural economics and rural development. He has published twenty-one books and more than 560 papers in *Science*, *Nature* and many leading journals in development economics. He is a recipient of various awards, including China's Outstanding Youth Scientist, Fudan Prize for Eminent Contributor to Management Science (2008) and Outstanding Alumni Award (2010) of the International Rice Research Institute.

Arlene B. Inocencio (De La Salle University)
Arlene B. Inocencio is a professor and dean of the School of Economics of De La Salle University (DLSU). Her research interests include water and irrigation, poverty, public finance, subnational economic accounts, and agricultural and environmental issues. Prior to DLSU, she was an economist at the International Water Management Institute (2002–8) and a research fellow at the Philippine Institute for Development Studies (1997–2001). She obtained her PhD in economics from the University of the Philippines in 1997.

Karl Robert L. Jandoc (University of the Philippines)
Karl Robert L. Jandoc is an associate professor at the School of Economics of the University of the Philippines. He obtained his PhD in economics from the University of Hawaii. He publishes in diverse fields covering theoretical and applied microeconomics, resource, environmental and energy economics.

Kei Kajisa (Aoyama Gakuin University)
Kei Kajisa is a professor of development economics at the School of International Politics, Economics and Communication of Aoyama Gakuin University. He was a senior scientist at the International Rice Research Institute in the Philippines (2006–12). He earned his PhD in agricultural economics at Michigan State University in 1999.

Cara T. Latinazo (Columbia University)
Cara T. Latinazo earned her bachelor's degree in economics (magna cum laude) from the University of the Philippines; she is currently pursuing her master's degree in quantitative methods in the social sciences at Columbia University. Previously, she served as head of policy research of the Office of Representative Stella Quimbo at the House of Representatives. She also worked at the Philippine Competition Commission from 2016 to 2019.

Gilberto M. Llanto (Philippine Institute for Development Studies)
Gilberto M. Llanto is former president of the Philippine Institute for Development Studies (PIDS), where he now serves as a trustee. He was the regional coordinator of the East Asian Development Network under the Global Development Network (GDN) and lead convenor of the Philippine APEC Study Center Network. He served as deputy director-general of the National Economic and Development Authority and executive director of the Agricultural Credit Policy Council. He has a PhD in economics from the University of the Philippines Diliman.

Eduardo Lucio (ASB Bank, Auckland)
Eduardo Lucio is a data scientist at ASB Bank Ltd. in Auckland, New Zealand, working on machine learning, big data and experimental design. He held various roles in financial sector supervision and policy research at the Bangko Sentral ng Pilipinas and in consumer lending and market risk management in a major commercial bank in the Philippines. He earned his PhD in applied statistics at the University of Queensland and his master's and bachelor's degrees at the University of Tokyo and the University of the Philippines, respectively.

Dennis S. Mapa (Philippine Statistics Authority and University of the Philippines)
Claire Dennis S. Mapa is the undersecretary, national statistician and civil-registrar general of the Philippine Statistics Authority (PSA). Prior to his appointment at PSA, he served as dean of the School of Statistics,

University of the Philippines (UP) Diliman. He was a research fellow at the USAID-funded Energy Policy and Development Program in 2014–18. He held the SEARCA Regional Professorial Chair in 2015 and was recognized as UP Scientist in 2018–20. In 2008, he received the Outstanding Young Scientist Award from the National Academy of Science and Technology of the Philippines. He obtained his PhD in economics and master's degrees in statistics and economics from the University of the Philippines.

Keijiro Otsuka (Kobe University)
Keijiro Otsuka is a professor of development economics at the Graduate School of Economics of Kobe University and chief senior researcher at the Institute of Developing Economies. He has been a member of the Japan Academy since 2018. He obtained his PhD in economics from the University of Chicago in 1979. He served as chairperson of the Board of Trustees of the International Rice Research Institute (2004–7) and president of the International Association of Agricultural Economists (2009–12). He has been serving as president of the Japanese Association for Development Economics since 2018. He received the Purple Ribbon Medal in 2010 and Orders of the Sacred Treasure, Gold and Silver Star in 2021 from the Japanese Emperor.

Nicostrato Perez (International Food Policy Research Institute)
Nicostrato D. Perez is a research fellow at the International Food Policy Research Institute (IFPRI) based in Washington, DC, USA. He obtained his PhD in agricultural and applied economics from Virginia Tech, USA, and MS and BS degrees from the University of the Philippines and Mindanao State University, respectively. He has worked in various capacities in the academe and in national and international agricultural research and development centres. His recent and current work includes global water and food security, adaptation to climate change, and economy-environment policy modelling of sustainable agriculture and food systems.

Ernesto M. Pernia (University of the Philippines)
Ernesto M. Pernia was the secretary of socio-economic planning of the National Economic and Development Authority of the Philippines in 2016– 20. He is a professor emeritus of economics at the University of the Philippines (UP). He was with the Asian Development Bank for more than 17 years, rising to lead economist. He was the chair of the board of trustees of the University of San Carlos (2011–14) and was a director

on the board of the Philippine-American Academy of Science and Engineering (PAASE, 2008–13). He received the first Outstanding Young Scientist (social sciences) award from the National Academy of Science and Technology. He was awarded the UP Centennial Professorial Chair in 2008, and was also chosen by the PAASE for the 2015 Koh Science Lectureship Award. He obtained his PhD degree from the University of California Berkeley.

Sharon Faye Piza (World Bank)
Sharon Faye Piza is an economist at the Equitable Growth, Finance and Institutions East Asia and the Pacific, Poverty and Equity Unit of the World Bank. She was a senior research associate at the Asia Pacific Policy Center and a research consultant for various organizations. Her research interests are regional development, poverty, migration and agriculture. She studied at the University of the Philippines.

Angga Pradesha (International Food Policy Research Institute)
Angga Pradesha is a senior research analyst at the International Food Policy Research Institute (IFPRI). His research interests are the application of partial and general equilibrium models to understand the complex interaction between economic growth, public finance, climate change, poverty and food security. He did his undergraduate study in agricultural and resource economics at Bogor Agricultural University in Indonesia and earned a master's degree in applied economics from the International Islamic University of Malaysia. He also obtained a master's degree in international development from the International University of Japan.

Jan Carlo B. Punongbayan (University of the Philippines)
Jan Carlo B. Punongbayan is an assistant professor at the School of Economics of the University of the Philippines. He served as head executive assistant to former Socio-economic Planning Secretary Arsenio Balisacan at the National Economic and Development Authority. He co-founded Usapang Econ, a group of Filipino economists popularizing economic concepts for the Filipino audience. He obtained his bachelor's in economics (summa cum laude and class valedictorian) from the University of the Philippines in 2009, and received the José Encarnación Jr. Award for Excellence in Economics and the Gerardo P. Sicat Award for Best Undergraduate Thesis. In 2013, he earned his M.A. degree from the UP School of Economics (UPSE), where he has since been teaching microeconomics, macroeconomics, development

economics and Philippine economic history as a teaching fellow and senior lecturer. He obtained his PhD from UPSE in October 2021.

Stella A. Quimbo (House of Representatives, Philippines)
Stella Luz A. Quimbo is the representative of the Second District of Marikina City and deputy minority leader of the 18th Congress. She previously served as commissioner of the Philippine Competition Commission. She was a professor and department chair of the School of Economics of the University of the Philippines, where she earned her bachelor's degree in business economics (summa cum laude) and master's and PhD degrees in economics. She spent a year at Brown University (Providence, Rhode Island, USA) as a post-doctoral fellow in 2002 at the Population Studies and Training Center. She obtained a master's degree in economics for competition law (with distinction) from King's College London.

Meg L. Regañon (Nathan Associates)
Meg L. Regañon holds a master's degree in applied economics from the National University of Singapore and a bachelor's degree in economics (summa cum laude) from the University of the Philippines. She worked at the Philippine Competition Commission from 2016 to 2018. She is currently with Nathan Associates, implementing the Better Access and Connectivity (BEACON) Project of the US Agency for International Development in the Philippines.

Agnes C. Rola (University of the Philippines)
Agnes C. Rola is a professor emerita at the University of the Philippines Los Baños (UPLB) and a member of the National Academy of Science and Technology of the Philippines. Her research interests are sustainable agriculture and natural resources management, water governance, agriculture and development, gender and development, and policy analysis of the convergence of water, food security and climate risk management. She is a member of the boards of trustees of international agricultural research centres and the editorial board of several journals. She obtained her PhD in agricultural economics from the University of Wisconsin-Madison, USA.

Mark W. Rosegrant (International Food Policy Research Institute)
Mark W. Rosegrant is a research fellow emeritus at the International Food Policy Research Institute. With a PhD in public policy from the University of Michigan, he has extensive experience in research and

policy analysis in agriculture and economic development and the future of world food security, with an emphasis on water resources and other critical natural resource and agricultural policy issues as they impact food security, rural livelihoods and environmental sustainability. He is the author/editor of twelve books and over a hundred refereed papers in agricultural economics, water resources and food policy analysis. He has won numerous awards, and is a fellow of the American Association for the Advancement of Science and of the Agricultural and Applied Economics Association.

Yasuyuki Sawada (University of Tokyo)
Yasuyuki Sawada is a professor at the Faculty of Economics, University of Tokyo. From March 2017 until August 2021, he was the chief economist of the Asian Development Bank and director general of its Economic Research and Regional Cooperation Department. Earlier, he served as an adjunct professor of economics at Korea University and a visiting professor at Stanford University. He obtained his PhD in economics from Stanford University.

Suthad Setboonsarng (International Rice Research Institute)
Suthad Setboonsarng is currently the chairperson of the board of trustees of the International Rice Research Institute. He was on the board of the Bank of Thailand in 2014–20. He was appointed as one of Thailand's trade representatives in 2009, following his career as a partner at PricewaterhouseCoopers from 2000 to 2008. Prior to this, he was the deputy secretary-general of the ASEAN Secretariat, where he pioneered the work on the ASEAN Free Trade Agreement and financial cooperation. He was an associate professor at the Asian Institute of Technology, research fellow at the Thailand Development Research Institute, and lecturer at Thammasat University. He did postdoctoral work at Yale University. He obtained his PhD in economics from the University of Hawaii.

Mercedita A. Sombilla (National Economic and Development Authority)
Mercedita A. Sombilla is currently the undersecretary of the Regional Development Office of the National Economic and Development Authority, Philippines. She served as assistant secretary of the same office and concurrent director of the Agriculture, Natural Resources and Environment Staff. She also served as research and development manager of the Southeast Asian Regional Center for Graduate Study and Research in Agriculture. She had worked with the International Food

Policy Research Institute and the International Rice Research Institute. She completed her PhD in agricultural and applied economics at the University of Minnesota. She holds an MA in economics and a BS in mathematics from the University of the Philippines Diliman.

Tetsushi Sonobe (Asian Development Bank Institute)
Tetsushi Sonobe is the dean and chief executive officer of the Asian Development Bank Institute, the Tokyo-based think tank of the Asian Development Bank. Previously, he was vice president of the National Graduate Institute for Policy Studies, Japan, and a professor at Tokyo Metropolitan University. His research interests span the roles of industrial clusters, human capital, social capital, management practices and market competition in inclusive, resilient and sustainable economic development. He holds a PhD in economics from Yale University and is the vice president of the Japanese Association for Development Economics.

Timothy Thomas (International Food Policy Research Institute)
Timothy S. Thomas has been a research fellow for the International Food Policy Research Institute since 2010. His research has focused on various aspects of climate change, agriculture, nutrition and the environment. Much of his research involves the use of crop models and bioeconomic models that embed direct climate effects in a wider model, reflecting global changes in the demand and supply of food. His recent work includes analysis of extreme events under climate change, effects of climate on aflatoxin frequency, and the effects of infrastructure, markets and climate on land-use change.

V. Bruce J. Tolentino (Bangko Sentral ng Pilipinas)
V. Bruce J. Tolentino serves as an independent member of the Monetary Board of the Bangko Sentral ng Pilipinas, tasked to focus on promoting financial inclusion for rural and agricultural development. He has over thirty-six years of senior-level experience working with international development agencies, government agencies and non-governmental organizations in development, governance, finance and socio-economic projects and organizations in Asia and Africa.

Philip Arnold P. Tuaño (Ateneo de Manila University)
Philip Arnold P. Tuaño is an associate professor and chair of the Department of Economics, School of Social Sciences, Ateneo de Manila University. He is also a project coordinator of the Human Development

Network, a network of academics and civil society leaders involved in advancing the cause of human development. His current research interests include welfare economic mobility, climate change and sustainable development, and the poverty and equity impacts of macroeconomic policies.

Marilou Uy (G-24 Secretariat)
Marilou Uy is the director of the Intergovernmental Group of Twenty-Four on International Monetary Affairs and Development (G-24). In this role, she manages the Group's work programme and is the focal point of its engagements with international forums, such as the G20, G77 and the United Nations. Previously, she was the senior adviser to the managing director at the World Bank. While at the World Bank, she held various management roles, among them as director, managing the Bank's financial and private sector programmes in the Africa and South Asia Regions and overseeing the Bank's financial sector operations and advisory work globally. She pursued her graduate studies in economics and finance at the University of the Philippines and the University of California, Los Angeles.

Peter Warr (Australian National University)
Peter Warr is the John Crawford Professor Emeritus of agricultural economics at the Australian National University. He studied at the University of Sydney, the London School of Economics and Stanford University, where he received his PhD in applied economics. His current research is on the relationship between economic policy and poverty incidence in Southeast Asia. He is a fellow of the Academy of Social Sciences in Australia and is a distinguished fellow and past president of the Australian Agricultural and Resource Economics Society.

Jeffrey G. Williamson (Harvard University)
Jeffrey G. Williamson, PhD, is the Laird Bell Professor of Economics (Emeritus) at Harvard University, where he twice received the Galbraith Prize for best teacher in the graduate economics programme. He is past-president of the Economic History Association (1994–95), from whom he received the Hughes Prize for outstanding teaching. He is also an affiliate and visiting professor at the School of Economics, University of the Philippines.

Acronyms

3SLS	three-stage least squares
4Ps	Pantawid Pamilyang Pilipino Program
ABS	Asian Barometer Survey
ADB	Asian Development Bank
AFMA	Agriculture and Fisheries Modernization Act
AFC	Asian financial crisis
AFTA-CEPT	ASEAN Free Trade Area-Common Effective Preferential Tariff
AI	artificial intelligence
AICO	ASEAN Industrial Corporation Scheme
AJAD	Asian Journal of Agricultural Development
ANOVA	analysis of variance
AO	Administrative Order
APCC	Asia-Pacific Policy Center
APTERR	ASEAN Plus Three Emergency Rice Reserve
AR4	Assessment Report 4
AR5	Assessment Report 5
ARMM	Autonomous Region in Muslim Mindanao
ASAE	Asian Society of Agricultural Economics
ASEAN	Association of Southeast Asian Nations
ASPBI	Annual Survey of Philippine Business and Industry
AT	agricultural transformation

ATI	Agricultural Training Institute
ATIGA	ASEAN Trade in Goods Agreement
ATM	automatic teller machine
BARMM	Bangsamoro Autonomous Region in Muslim Mindanao
BEPS	Base Erosion and Profit Shifting
BLU	branch lite unit
BMBE	Barangay Micro-business Enterprise
BOC	Bureau of Customs
BPI	Bureau of Plant Industry
BPO	business process outsourcing
BRICS	Brazil, Russia, India, China and South Africa
BSP	Bangko Sentral ng Pilipinas
CALABARZON	Cavite, Laguna, Batangas, Rizal and Quezon
CAR	Cordillera Administrative Region
CARL	Comprehensive Agrarian Reform Law
CARP	Comprehensive Agrarian Reform Program
CFS	Consumer Finance Survey
CGE	computable general equilibrium
CHED	Commission on Higher Education
CP	Charoen Pokphand
CPBI	Census of Philippine Business and Industry
CPIP	Credit Policy Improvement Project
CPR	contraceptive prevalence rate
CR4	four concentration ratio
CSE	consumer support estimate
CSIRO	Commonwealth Scientific and Industrial Research Organisation
CTE	consumer tax equivalent
DA	Department of Agriculture
DAR	Department of Agrarian Reform
DBM	Department of Budget and Management
DBP	Development Bank of the Philippines

DDA	Doha Development Agenda
DENR	Department of Environment and Natural Resources
DepEd	Department of Education
DFA	Department of Foreign Affairs
DILG	Department of Interior and Local Governments
DPWH	Department of Public Works and Highways
DOLE	Department of Labor and Employment
DOF	Department of Finance
DOF-BTr	Department of Finance-Bureau of Treasury
DOH	Department of Health
DOTr	Department of Transportation
DSSAT	Decision Support System for Agrotechnology Transfer
DSWD	Department of Social Welfare and Development
DTI	Department of Trade and Industry
EC	European Commission
EMI	electronic money issuer
EO	Executive Order
EPZ	export processing zone
EU	European Union
FAO	Food and Agriculture Organization
FDI	foreign direct investment
FFF	Federation of Free Farmers
FGP	farm-gate prices
FIES	Family Income and Expenditure Survey
FIES-LFS	Family Income Expenditures Survey and Labor Force Survey
FIML	full information maximum likelihood
FTA	free trade agreement
GATT-WTO	General Agreement on Tariffs and Trade-World Trade Organization
GCM	general circulation model
GDP	gross domestic product

GFC	global financial crisis
GFDL	General Fluid Dynamics Laboratory
GFI	government financial institution
GHG	greenhouse gas
GMVC	global manufacturing value chain
GNI	gross national income
GOCC	government-owned and controlled corporation
GPN	global production networks
GSDP	Grains Sector Development Program
GSIS	Government Service Insurance System
GVA	gross value added
GVC	global value chain
HadGEM	Hadley Centre Global Environmental Model
HCI	heavy and chemical industries
HDI	Human Development Index
HDD	hard disc drive
HHI	Herfindahl-Hirschman Index
ICT	information and communication technology
IDN	Indonesia
IMF	International Monetary Fund
IMPACT	International Model for Policy Analysis of Agricultural Commodities and Trade
IPCC	Intergovernmental Panel on Climate Change
IPSL	Institut Pierre-Simon Laplace
IR	inverse relationship
IRR	Implementing Rules and Regulations
IRRI	International Rice Research Institute
IT	information technology
IT-BPM	information technology-business processing management
IUSSP	International Union for the Scientific Study of Population
KFTC	Korean Fair Trade Commission
KHM	Cambodia

LA/AIDS	linear approximation of an almost ideal demand system
LFPR	labour force participation rate
LGU	local government units
LBP	Land Bank of the Philippines
MAV	minimum access volume
MBO	micro-banking office
MFA	Multi Fibre Arrangement
MFI	microfinance institution
MFN	most favoured nation
MIMAROPA	Mindoro, Marinduque, Romblon and Palawan
MIROC	Model for Interdisciplinary Research on Climate
MIX	Microfinance Information eXchange
MMSU	Mariano Marcos State University
MNE	multinational enterprises
MORB	Manual of Regulations for Banks
MSME	micro, small and medium enterprise
MRFTA	Monopoly Regulation and Fair Trade Act
MWL	minimum wage legislation
NBFI	non-bank financial institution
NCR	National Capital Region
NDA	National Dairy Administration
NDHS	National Demographic and Health Survey
NEDA	National Economic and Development Authority
NFA	National Food Authority
NGO	non-governmental organization
NHIS-PR	National Household Targeting System for Poverty Reduction
NIA	National Irrigation Administration
NIE	newly industrialized economy
NRA	nominal rate of assistance
NRP	nominal rate of protection
NSFI	National Strategy for Financial Inclusion

OECD	Organisation for Economic Co-operation and Development
OFW	overseas Filipino worker
OTCC	Office of the Trade Competition Commission
PAR	portfolio-at-risk
PCA	Philippine Coconut Authority
PCA	Philippine Competition Act
PCC	Philippine Competition Commission
PCIC	Philippine Crop Insurance Corporation
PCM	price cost margin
PD	Presidential Decree
PDP	Philippine Development Plan
PEZA	Philippine Export Zone Authority
PFC	Philippine Forest Corporation
PFDA	Philippine Fisheries Development Authority
Phil-DCGE	dynamic computable general equilibrium model of the Philippines
PhilMech	Philippine Center for Post-Harvest Development and Mechanization
PhilRice	Philippine Rice Research Institute
PHL	Philippines
PIDS	Philippine Institute for Development Studies
PISA	Programme for International Student Assessment
POUM	prospects for upward mobility
PLGU	provincial local government unit
PRiSM	Philippine Rice Information System
PSA	Philippine Statistics Authority
PSE	producer support estimate
PSIC	Philippines Standard Industry Classification
QR	quantitative restrictions
RBH2	Resolution of Both Houses No. 2
RCEF	Rice Competitiveness Enhancement Fund
RCEP	Regional Comprehensive Economic Partnership

RE	random effects
RER	real exchange rate
RMR	regular-milled rice
ROSCA	rotating savings and credit association
RPEP	Rice Productivity Enhancement Program
RSBSA	Registry System for Basic Sectors in Agriculture
RRA	relative rate of assistance
RRP	Rice Resiliency Program
RTL	Rice Tariffication Law
SCP	structure-conduct-performance
SDG	Sustainable Development Goals
SEARCA	Southeast Asian Regional Center for Graduate Study and Research in Agriculture
SEC	Securities and Exchange Commission
SEZ	special economic zone
SIJORI	Singapore-Johor-Riau Island
SLEX	South Luzon Expressway
SME	small and medium enterprise
Soccsksargen	South Cotabato, Cotabato, Sultan Kudarat, Sarangani and General Santos
SPS	sanitary and phytosanitary
SPSIC	safety-based sanitary and phytosanitary import clearance
SSS	Social Security System
ST	structural transformation
TCA	Trade Competition Act
TCC	Trade Competition Commission (Thailand)
TCE	transaction cost economics
TESDA	Technical Education and Skills Development Authority
TFP	total factor productivity
TFR	total fertility rate
TiVA	trade in value added
TRAIN	Tax Reform for Acceleration and Inclusion

TRI	trade reduction index
TRIPS	Trade Related Aspects of Intellectual Property Rights
U5MR	under-5 mortality rate
UNDP	United Nations Development Programme
UNFPA	United Nations Population Fund
UPLB	University of the Philippines Los Baños
UPSE	University of the Philippines School of Economics
USAID	US Agency for International Development
VMP	value of the marginal product
VNM	Vietnam
WaNuLCAS	Water, Nutrient and Light Capture in Agroforestry Systems model
WGI	World Governance Indicators
WIBI	weather index-based insurance
WMR	well-milled rice
WRI	welfare reduction index
WTO	World Trade Organization

PART 1

Introduction and Synthesis

1 From Agriculture to Competition: Overview and Lessons from the Philippines and Asia for Pro-poor Development

Hal Hill, Majah-Leah V. Ravago and James A. Roumasset

1 INTRODUCTION

The Philippines has a complex development history. Initially regarded as one of Asia's prospective stars, by 1980 it had clearly failed to live up to such a lofty expectation. It parted company with its dynamic East Asian neighbours during the 1980s, and experienced prolonged and deep twin crises, both economic and political. Popular commentary over this period labelled it "the sick man of Asia", "the East Asian exception", a "crony capitalist economy", "Asia's Latin American economy" and various other unflattering descriptors. It appeared at that time that poverty and inequality were deeply entrenched, that agriculture lacked the resilience of its neighbours, that the ethno-religious conflict in Mindanao was beyond resolution, and that macroeconomic adventurism was consigning the country to a bleak period of recurring debt crises. Many of its best and brightest citizens relocated abroad; the prospect was that the Philippines would become a "remittance economy".

However, just as the earlier optimistic prognostications proved to be mistaken, subsequent developments have been unkind to the 1980s doomsayers. The Philippines transitioned to a workable, decentralized democracy with governments that (mostly) enjoyed electoral legitimacy.

Economic reforms introduced in the wake of the 1980s' crises resulted in economic recovery and a return to growth, which, in turn, generated significant improvements in living standards. Prior to the COVID-19 pandemic, the country had enjoyed more than 70 quarters of continuously positive economic growth.[1] Moreover, from 2000 to 2019, its growth was not far short of those of Asia's most dynamic economies. Viewed from the crisis decade of the 1980s, both these outcomes would have been unimaginable.

Just as this renewed prosperity appeared to be durable, the COVID-19 pandemic struck with unexpected ferocity. The Philippines experienced one of the most severe economic downturns, with its 2020 decline in gross domestic product (GDP) almost three times the global average. It introduced one of the world's most severe lockdowns, partly in recognition of the weak capacity of the country's under-resourced public health system. Poverty and inequality have increased substantially as many of the poor and near-poor have been unable to sustain their livelihoods, and social protection measures have limited reach. While recovery is proceeding gradually in 2021, in some respects the country is once again back to being at the crossroads.

The Philippines therefore provides fertile material for many of the major issues and challenges in contemporary development economics. It also has a vibrant scholarly community, both within and outside the country, that has provided much illuminating research and policy materials, including comparative analyses that place the country's experience in broader Asian perspectives. This volume, comprising contributions by an eminent group of Filipino and international authors, showcases and builds on much of this research. The essays are written in honour of Arsenio M. Balisacan, an eminent Filipino scholar and public servant. They reflect his research and policy interests, which are central to understanding the Philippine development dynamics. The overarching theme is the challenge of overcoming the country's deep-seated poverty and inequality. As an analytical template, the volume focuses on agricultural, competition and other policies that are key to reducing poverty. These are also the issues that Arsenio Balisacan has focused on in his academic and policy careers. That is, agriculture, where many of the poor reside, remains an important sector. In the major emerging countries, particularly in Asia, successful

---

[1] In fact, prior to the pandemic, the last occasions of negative economic growth were the second and fourth quarters of 1998, during the worst of the Asian financial crisis.

poverty reduction had been achieved following productivity-driven economic growth and structural transformation away from the primacy of agriculture. Competition policy has long been recognized as a complementary pillar for socio-economic development in the Philippines, although it took nearly a quarter of a century for Congress to implement the 1987 constitutional provision against "combinations in restraint of trade or unfair competition".

This volume is divided into six themes. Theme I provides an interpretative essay on Philippine economic development in a comparative perspective. Theme II examines agricultural development and its relationship to economic development and poverty reduction. Theme III deals with poverty and economic policies for achieving targeted levels of living in the Philippines. Theme IV tackles inequality and economic development in the Philippines. Theme V covers competition law and policy, with a particular focus on the Philippines. The last theme touches on international dimensions.

This chapter provides a synthesis of each chapter and how each section relates to the academic and policy interests of Professor Balisacan. In the last part of this chapter, we sketch his interests, achievements and journey through life.

The volume commences with a scene-setting chapter 2 by Hill, Balisacan and dela Cruz, who reflect on and draw lessons for economic development and policy by examining the country's three main economic episodes over the post-independence era, namely: (a) the period of moderately strong growth from 1946 to the late 1970s, (b) the tumultuous crisis years from the late 1970s to the early 1990s, and (c) the period from the early 1990s to 2019 when the Philippines rejoined the dynamic East Asian mainstream.

2 AGRICULTURE AND ECONOMIC DEVELOPMENT

Balisacan's initial foray into academic publishing reflects his deep interest in agricultural development and political economy, a research theme he has maintained throughout his career.[2] This section establishes

---

[2] See, for example, Rosegrant, Roumasset, and Balisacan (1985), Balisacan and Roumasset (1987), Balisacan (1987), Balisacan and Nozawa (1993), David and Balisacan (1995), Balisacan and Ravago (2003), Balisacan and Fuwa (2007a), David, Intal, and Balisacan (2009), Ravago and Balisacan (2016), Ravago, Balisacan, and Sombilla (2018).

the importance of agricultural development and poverty reduction, describes the nature and consequences of price and non-price distortions, summarizes the policy implications (including for climate adaptation), and provides a case study of the political economy of policy reform. It provides some of the reasons why the Philippines has mostly been an outlier in the story of the East Asian miracle.

The unfinished agricultural policy reform agenda in East Asian countries is substantial. This is the subject of chapter 3 by Anderson's "Trade Distortions as Constraints to Agricultural Development in East Asia". Anderson traces the impacts of trade, farm and food policy developments since the 1950s, particularly in East Asia. The mid-1980s were characterized by anti-trade policies that added to the volatility of international food prices and to poverty and inequality in most developing countries. The subsequent two decades saw the gradual unwinding of those trade-distorting policies. The chapter details both the extent and consequences of trade and agricultural interventions. During the current century, international farm prices have increased, and the governments of many countries have reacted in ways that tended to insulate their domestic markets. Far from reducing the number of people who fell into poverty, the combined effect of those unilateral policy responses has exacerbated global poverty. The chapter concludes by noting alternatives to trade-related policies that can achieve the stated objectives far more efficiently and equitably than price-distorting policies.

In chapter 4, "Beyond Krugman: The Importance of Agriculture for East Asian Growth", Warr focuses on the role of agriculture in structural transformation to explain Asia's rapid economic growth over the two decades preceding Krugman's famous paper (1994), "The Myth of Asia's Miracle". In this paper, Krugman rightly discounts the "miracle" rhetoric that had been applied to Asia's rapid economic growth, but misses a key point. By focusing on the economic record of enclave, city-based economies like Singapore and Hong Kong, which lack traditional agriculture, Krugman overlooks the role of agriculture and the process of structural transformation. This is the mechanism through which workers gradually transition from low-productivity employment in agriculture to higher-productivity employment in the growing industry and services sectors. Using data for Thailand and Indonesia, Warr shows that the forces behind structural transformation, especially agricultural development, contributed 47 per cent of long-term growth in Thailand's labour productivity and 28 per cent in Indonesia.

Agriculture still employs a sizable share of the Philippine labour force, and the majority of the poor continue to work in this sector. Because of this and the sector's contributions to reducing the cost of living and industrialization, agricultural growth is important for poverty reduction. This is the focus of Huang's "The Role of Agricultural and Structural Transformations in Rural Poverty Reduction" in chapter 5. He begins with the observation that China and Southeast Asia have generally experienced rapid agricultural and structural transformation and that these events have been accompanied by declining rural poverty. Huang examines agricultural and structural transformation in China, Indonesia, Lao PDR, the Philippines and Vietnam. He finds that, while all five countries have undergone significant agricultural transformations, the stage and speed of these transformations have differed substantially. Rapid agricultural and structural transformation in particular are associated with rapid rural poverty reduction. The chapter also draws policy implications for more inclusive transformation.

The agricultural policy regime in the Philippines has contributed to its slow productivity growth. In chapter 6, "The Changing Relationship between Farm Size and Productivity: Asia and the Philippines", Otsuka highlights this slow growth compared with regional counterparts, and relates it to the controversy regarding the inverse relationship between farm size and productivity. More recently, the inverse relationship has waned in Asia and has been replaced by a U-shaped relationship. While family farms often exhibit something of an inverse relationship, larger and more commercial farms are able to take advantage of scale economies. The implication for the Philippines is that land policy reforms are needed to render the farmland market more robust in both rents and sales to allow the country to appropriate available scale economies, thereby increasing productivity and rural wages.

Market-oriented agricultural policy reform in the Philippines, as well as in many other countries, has been a slow process. Tolentino and de la Peña in chapter 7, "The Political Economy of Rice Policy in the Philippines", provide a hopeful perspective. They argue that the rice tariffication law (RTL), which became effective in March 2019, has dramatically changed the policy regime governing the Philippine rice industry. The reform promises enhanced and more sustainable food security for the nation, as well as increased economic efficiency and improved welfare for both rice consumers and producers. The authors note that the RTL passage was the result of more than thirty-five years of economic analysis, reform advocacy, political economy calculus and political leadership. Nevertheless, significant additional efforts are necessary to ensure that the reform's benefits are sustained and redound to both farmers and consumers. The authors review the experience of the Philippines in managing this reform and examine aspects of political governance that initially frustrated and later accelerated the reform efforts. They conclude that effective governance in facilitating policy change and delivering public-sector goods and services is crucial to sustainably boosting rice productivity and ensuring food security.

In the final chapter of Theme II, "Adapting Philippine Agriculture to Climate Change", Rosegrant, Sombilla and Associates examine climate and agriculture. After providing a global context, the authors discuss the threats that climate change poses to Philippine agriculture, including recent impacts. They estimate future impacts of climate change on agriculture, food security and the overall economy. They then examine the challenge of developing and modernizing the Philippine agriculture sector, including the process of structural transformation and patterns of agricultural growth and productivity. This includes a discussion of key government policies and programmes, their performance in climate adaptation, the promotion of productivity and sustainable consumption, and remaining gaps. Finally, the authors advance recommendations for policy and institutional changes needed to strengthen the agriculture sector and enhance its resilience.

3 ECONOMIC POLICIES FOR ACHIEVING TARGETED LEVELS OF LIVING IN THE PHILIPPINES

Theme III of this volume is a collection of papers reflecting Arsenio Balisacan's research and policy interest in poverty and Philippine economic growth and development.[3] During his stint as socio-economic planning secretary and concurrent director general of the National Economic and Development Authority (NEDA), he led efforts to create a positive long-term vision for the country (Balisacan 2018), known as *Ambisyon Natin 2040* (our ambition/vision for 2040). This section explores the channels by which structural transformation reduces

---

[3] See, for example, Balisacan (1990, 1995a, 1995b, 2001, 2007, 2009a, 2015), Balisacan and Bacawag (1995), Balisacan, Edillon, and Piza (2005), Balisacan and Fuwa (2007b), Balisacan, Chakravorty, and Ravago (2015).

poverty and how policy distortions have thwarted their effectiveness, including premature deindustrialization, limited participation in global value chains, and limitations to productivity growth in agriculture. It also explores why the Philippines has largely failed to appropriate the demographic dividend as well as promising avenues for expanding credit opportunities.

The slow poverty reduction in the Philippines in the post-Asian financial crisis period despite relatively rapid economic growth has long been a puzzle, especially in contrast to comparable East Asian neighbours. This is the focus of chapter 9, "Low Income Traps and Philippine Poverty Incidence" by Fabella and Ducanes. The authors argue that the relatively low growth elasticity of poverty is due to the premature deindustrialization of the Philippine economy until fairly recently. They show that the share of the formal sector in Philippine employment correlates positively and significantly with reduced poverty incidence among households. The share of agricultural employment has no effect on household poverty reduction, possibly because, as suggested elsewhere in this volume, agricultural productivity has been artificially constrained by misguided policies.

Continuing the focus on the manufacturing sector, Athukorala's chapter 10, "The Philippines in Global Manufacturing Value Chains: A Tale of Arrested Growth", examines how government policies and a country's investment climate condition the potential for export-oriented industrialization through global production sharing. He examines the experience of the Philippines from a Southeast Asian perspective. In the early 1970s, the Philippines had a promising start, participating in the Singapore-centred electronics assembly networks. However, the industrialization trajectory over the subsequent years has not lived up to the initial expectations. Manufacturing exports from the country have become increasingly characterized by low-end assembly processes undertaken within export processing zones (EPZs). The Philippines has also underperformed within the rapidly expanding global production networks instead of exploiting opportunities for backward integration. The lacklustre performance record is rooted in the dualistic, EPZ-centred investment climate: policies are liberal within EPZs and restrictive elsewhere.

Chapter 11, "The Limits of Trade Policy Liberalization in the Philippines" by Aldaba, Ang and Habito, further examines the Philippines' participation in the global value chain. It investigates how trade policies in the last thirty years have affected economic growth and poverty alleviation in the country. Trade policy liberalization has indeed increased trade, but the gains have been limited to a narrow segment of manufacturing, especially electronics. While this has helped stabilize the foreign exchange market, the benefits of increased trade have not been felt by the whole economy. The country continues to play only a minor role in global value chains, and one largely confined to electronics assembly. The agriculture sector meanwhile has also not benefited from trade liberalization due to agricultural policies that have constrained productivity growth. For many years, the services sector has carried the burden of the expanding economy, largely stimulated by the remittances of overseas workers.

Chapter 12 by Mapa, Pernia and Bersales investigates "Reaching for the Demographic Dividend to Achieve Inclusive Economic Growth". The *demographic transition* from high to low fertility and mortality potentially delivers a dividend to economic growth and development. This chapter looks at the population-age structure of the Philippines—using the population census, birth and fertility data, and projections of future population from the Philippine Statistics Authority—to estimate how these factors bear on the demographic transition. It presents the likely challenges to gaining the demographic dividend due to the COVID-19 pandemic's effect in terms of higher unemployment rates, particularly among younger workers. This, in turn, presents challenges to achieving the targets of *Ambisyon Natin 2040* for a strongly rooted, comfortable and secure life (*matatag, maginhawa at panatag na buhay*) for Filipinos.

A commonly observed constraint to the advancement of low-income farmers and consumers is the availability of credit at reasonable rates. In chapter 13,[4] "Collateralizing Wages: The Case of *Sangla* ATM", Fuwa, Kajisa, Lucio, Piza and Sawada examine an emerging credit arrangement called "*Sangla* ATM", the pawning of debit cards. In this informal loan arrangement, the borrower's debit card is the collateral. The lender uses the card to withdraw the repayment (principal and interest) from the

---

[4] Chapter 13 is dedicated to the memory of Nobuhiko Fuwa. Nobu was Arsi's long-time collaborator and dear friend. The two of them, together with associates at the Asia Pacific Policy Center, pioneered the innovative merging of data from the Philippines' Family Income and Expenditure Surveys with administrative data, including the development of a political dynasty index. This led to many publications, including Balisacan and Fuwa (2003) in *Economic Letters* and Balisacan and Fuwa (2004) in *World Development*.

linked account that receives regular salary deposits. Using their unique survey data of factory workers in an industrial estate near Metro Manila, the authors find that a large proportion of respondents had used *Sangla* ATM at least once, with the average loan amount approximating the average monthly salary. *Sangla* ATM can be regarded as an institutional innovation in the informal finance sector to relax credit constraints of borrowers without other collateralizable assets. However, such loan arrangements have both positive and negative aspects, and careful public policy actions are needed to minimize their adverse impacts.

4 INEQUALITY AND ECONOMIC DEVELOPMENT

Theme IV presents chapters on inequality and economic development, a topic that accounts for a big share in Arsenio Balisacan's research portfolio.[5] This section includes papers that review the history of inequality in the Philippines (both with and beyond Gini coefficients) and direct attention to policy implication and directions for further research.

Chapter 14, "An Essay on Markets, Distributive Justice and Social Safety Nets" by Canlas, characterizes the economic experience of the Philippines as growth with high and, for some periods, rising income inequality. As indicated by the Gini coefficient constructed from household income and expenditure data, income inequality continued to worsen through 2018. Canlas notes the adverse distribution effects of free markets that fall short of the neoclassical ideal due to imperfect and asymmetric information. He examines data on unemployment among heterogeneous workers in a labour market with job search and job matching, as well as with incomplete financial markets. Data on unemployment rates by age group and educational attainment, and credit starvation among low-income individuals and households are consistent with predictions of his analytical framework. Social safety nets that interfere with the workings of labour markets, such as minimum wage legislation and employment protection, are not helpful in easing the sorry plight of the unemployed and those employed at low wages. Financial-inclusion programmes aimed at addressing absent credit

---

[5] See, for example, Balisacan (1996a, 2003), Balisacan and Fuwa (2003, 2004, 2006), Balisacan and Pernia (2003), Ducanes and Balisacan (2019), Reardon et al. (2008).

markets for job search, higher education, entrepreneurship training and reforms of government financial institutions are more promising policy options.

Chapter 15, "Convergence of Philippine Spatial Inequality during the American Colonial Period" by Punongbayan, Williamson and Jandoc, explores spatial inequality in the Philippines during the American colonial period. The authors constructed a proxy Human Development Index (HDI) for regions of the Philippines for the American colonial period. They observe that the overall country index improved over the first four decades of American occupation. Finding convergence in the HDIs of outlying Philippine regions with Manila's, the authors explain how convergence relates to growth patterns of agriculture and industry as well as patterns of public expenditure on health and education. American colonial policies on health and education narrowed the disparity in literacy and infant mortality of the provinces relative to Manila. The growth patterns of agriculture and industry, however, may have had offsetting effects on spatial inequality. The terms-of-trade boom that benefited provinces producing commercial crops enabled these provinces to catch up. However, the terms-of-trade decline during the Depression era may have widened spatial inequality. These same forces also dampened real wages in large industries based in Manila, possibly narrowing spatial inequality. The authors call for further research to settle remaining ambiguities and to further explain patterns of spatial inequality up to the present.

In chapter 16, "Social Differentiation: The Middle Class and Its Discontents", de Dios and Tuaño review trends in social differentiation and social mobility, and outline the consequences for future directions and approaches in welfare provision and social protection. More than a decade of high growth before the pandemic-induced recession has placed the Philippines on the threshold of upper middle-income status. Internally, this has created a social differentiation in which the existentially poor are outnumbered by the vulnerable, the secure and the upper middle-income groups. Much of political rhetoric and social policy, however, continue to be guided by an outmoded dichotomy of rich and poor, leading to policy blind spots, inconsistencies and unintended social harm.

Chapter 17, "Redistributive Preferences and Prospects for Intergenerational Mobility in Southeast Asia" by Capuno, investigates whether the prospect for intergenerational mobility influences preferences for government redistribution. The "prospects of upward mobility" hypothesis holds that when people expect redistributive policies not to change for some time, those with income below the mean but who anticipate better fortunes may not support redistribution. The author examines this hypothesis in eight Southeast Asian countries, whose varied economic performances, redistributive programmes and governance regimes provide a rich setting. Using data from the fourth wave of the Asian Barometer Survey, Capuno finds that, after controlling for other factors, a greater preference for redistribution is expressed by those who consider themselves economically vulnerable and by those who expect their offspring in the future to surpass or match their own current socio-economic status. The second finding, which is inconsistent with the hypothesis, appears to hold more for those in the poorest two income quintiles, for whom the prospects are perhaps more aspirational than real. While the results for Malaysia, Vietnam and Myanmar are broadly consistent with the hypothesis, they are not for Cambodia, Indonesia, Philippines, Singapore and Thailand. The challenge facing the governments in these countries then is how to encourage their citizens to hope and aspire and to take responsibility for improving their lives, and to promote opportunities for doing so.

5   COMPETITION LAW AND POLICY

In February 2016, Arsenio Balisacan found himself in the arena of competition law and policy when he was appointed as the first chairperson of the newly formed Philippine Competition Commission. Theme V consists of chapters reflecting this stage of life in his research and policy work (Balisacan 2019; Balisacan and Papa 2020; Ravago, Roumasset, and Balisacan 2021), beginning with a chapter he co-authored with Ravago and Roumasset, two of this volume's editors. This section reviews the evolution of competition policy in Asia, estimates the effect of market competition on employment, and provides case studies on the shoe and microfinance industries. It also explains how agricultural subsidies can worsen market competition and how reforms aimed at increasing competition may turn out to be incomplete.

In chapter 18, "Adopting and Adapting Competition Policy: Asian Illustrations", Ravago, Roumasset and Balisacan investigate whether the needs of countries in different economic environments and at various stages of development warrant different policies. In the pursuit of economic development and consumer welfare, competition policy should curb rent-seeking and promote market efficiency. This requires the coordination of competition policy with other tools of development, especially trade, industrial, agricultural and infrastructure policies. The chapter examines the impact of the adoption of competition law on long-term economic growth using cross-country data for the period 1975–2015. Countries may choose to adopt—or not adopt—competition law depending on their circumstances, including level of economic development, institutions and geography. The authors employ an endogenous switching regression model to control for endogeneity and self-selection. The analysis shows that adoption of competition policy has increased growth in adopting countries but would have decreased growth in non-adopting countries. This suggests that countries should not be pressured into prematurely adopting competition law. Rather, more limited international or regional agreements can be pursued, aimed at harmonizing country treatment of multinational corporations. In addition to correcting the abuses of anticompetitive behaviour, competition policy should be designed to promote innovation and productivity growth. These arguments are reviewed focusing on the cases of Korea, Thailand and the Philippines, which capture the characteristics of the law and authorities at various stages of maturity.

Against the backdrop of a fairly new competition law in the Philippines, chapter 19, "Competition and Employment Growth in the Philippines: A Baseline Assessment" by Quimbo, Regañon, Concepcion and Latinazo, explains how increased competition tends to increase productivity via innovation and firm selection. They then estimate the relationship, finding that a 10 per cent decrease in the Herfindahl-Hirschman Index predicts a 1.8 per cent growth in employment and that employment effects are more pronounced in more labour-intensive industries and for more profitable firms. Effective enforcement of the competition law is needed to secure potential employment gains. Constitutional reform to promote the entry of foreign firms will also help to augment the employment effects from increased competition.

Investigating sector-specific competition policy issues, Sonobe's chapter 20, "Buyer Power and Late Payment Behaviour in the Shoe Capital of the Philippines", uses data collected on small and medium enterprises (SMEs) in the Philippine footwear industry circa 2000 to illustrate how widespread late payment practices are, why creditors allow debtors to delay payment for extended periods, and how late payment can stifle employment opportunities and hinder industrial development. Many payments in commercial transactions are made much later than the delivery of goods or the provision of services. Late payment affects the liquidity and financial stability of creditors, especially when the creditors are SMEs, and forces them to cancel or postpone planned investments and other activities. Late payment practices may also possibly inhibit the incentive and financial ability of industries to innovate, hence negatively impacting consumers' benefits and job creation. A major finding is that remarkably late payments are exploitative abuses of buyer power that large-scale retailers had vis-à-vis relatively large shoemakers in Marikina, the shoe capital of the country. They contributed to the stagnation of the Philippine shoe industry, instead of its adapting to competition from abroad.

In chapter 21, "Regulation, Market Evolution and Competition in the Philippine Microfinance Sector", Punongbayan, Llanto and Esguerra examine the status of competition in the microfinance sector of the Philippines in light of changes in the regulatory environment that opened up the sector to commercialization in the late 1990s. Specifically, they assessed the level of competition during the period 1999–2018 using three measures of concentration: the Herfindahl-Hirschman Index, the Panzar-Rosse method and the Boone indicator. The authors generally observe a weakening of competition after 2010, while the preceding years were characterized by steady to increasing competition. This development is less the result of regulation than industry dynamics. This chapter serves to break ground for further research on the microfinance industry, including the effect of competition on the performance of microfinance institutions (MFIs), MFI competition in product quality, the impact of the entry of new players on competition, e.g., fintech firms with innovative underwriting practices and loan screening techniques, and the effect of new technologies on competition and financial inclusion of the poor and the underbanked.

Chapters 22 and 23 deal with competition issues in the agriculture sector. Clarete's chapter 22, "Tariffication and Market Structure: The Case of the Philippine Rice Industry", explains the price effects of the 2019 Rice Tariffication Law, which replaced import control by the National Food Authority with a 35 per cent tariff on privately imported rice. Retail and farmer prices have thus far failed to meet expectations from the liberalization of rice importation. Tariffication has left behind a marketing system dominated by a few traders instead of the expected import competition. Nevertheless, instead of abolishing tariffication and returning to parastatal import controls, policymakers are urged to focus their efforts on facilitating competition in the rice market.

In chapter 23, "The Role of Government Subsidies in Philippine Agricultural Competition", Inocencio and Rola examine the impact of subsidies (e.g., income or price support) on competition in agriculture. Using the Philippine Statistics Authority's data on business and industry for 2010–15, the authors show that a few highly concentrated agriculture subsectors receive most of the subsidies. Moreover, the subsidies went largely to state-enabled monopolies, which may have dissipated potential rents via unnecessary costs and other inefficiencies. However, even if the subsidies do not lead to market-power abuse, the subsectors being subsidized are very highly concentrated, potentially blunting incentives for investment and growth. Performance assessments of selected government-owned and controlled corporations (GOCCs) indicate the need to study the coherence of the laws that created the GOCCs vis-à-vis the national competition policy. Given the resources poured into these subsectors, a review of the GOCCs' decision-making processes, governance structure, transparency and accountability, and consumer benefits are warranted.

6 INTERNATIONAL DIMENSIONS

When Arsenio Balisacan was first appointed as undersecretary for policy and planning at the Department of Agriculture from 2000 to 2001, he served as the country's chief negotiator in the World Trade Organization's Agriculture Negotiations and in various bilateral agriculture negotiations. He has also done research and policy work covering international dimensions and cooperation related to agriculture and development (e.g., Balisacan 1996b; Hill, Balisacan, and Piza 2007). This section underscores the importance of international cooperation for economic development, especially regarding agricultural policy, trade, tax havens and competition policy.

In chapter 24, "Modernization of the Global Rice Market," Suthad Setboonsarng discusses the destabilizing effect of government intervention during crises. Such beggar-thy-neighbour protectionism could be avoided by cooperation between countries. During the past decade, China has become the largest rice importer while India has become the largest exporter (although there is little trade between them). The Philippines, which was the largest importer during 2008–10, had dropped to the eighth position in 2018. With better packaging, information and connectivity (including e-commerce) since the turn of the millennium, both the international and domestic rice markets have become more competitive and better able to cater to diverse tastes and deliver improved quality.

In the last chapter, "International Cooperation for Development: Learning from Trade and Tax Policies", Uy explains how international cooperation on trade, corporate taxation and competition policies can help to promote an effective and fair competitive environment. Domestic policies are not always adequate nor sufficient to create the conditions for countries to achieve competitiveness, especially in the presence of multinational corporations. Developing countries have benefited from a rules-based multilateral trading system, which coordinated tariff reductions and trade practices that have levelled the playing field across firms and countries. As with liberty, eternal vigilance is the price of maintaining and extending the rules-based system, especially in light of the risks posed by the rise of populism in several large economies. International tax cooperation has been more elusive, and countries have continued to engage in wasteful corporate tax competition to attract investments to their shores. The recent international agreement on a minimum corporate tax is a promising step towards international cooperation. This chapter encourages policymakers from developing countries to improve their understanding of how the trade and tax policies of countries jointly affect firms' incentives, and advocates necessary international cooperation to optimize their development impacts. Competition policies could benefit from similar coordination across countries.

7 ARSENIO M. BALISACAN: HIS JOURNEY THROUGH LIFE, ACADEMIA AND PUBLIC POLICY

Finally, on the scholar and public servant in whose honour these essays are written: Arsenio Molina Balisacan, universally known as "Arsi" to his friends and colleagues. He was born on 8 November 1957 to a family of very modest means: his father was a tenant rice farmer, his mother also a farmer and a housewife. The family lived in the village of Solsona located at the foothills of the Sierra Madre Mountain Range in Ilocos Norte province, the traditionally poor, northernmost region of Luzon Island in the Philippines. The family relocated on several occasions during his childhood for various reasons, including an eviction from a squatter settlement. For a period, they lived in Laoag City, the provincial capital, where his father obtained work as a local school janitor. When some of the family followed his employed elder brother to Cebu in central Philippines, Arsi remained in Laoag City to continue his education at Divine Word College. He credits an aunt, a local mayor of modest means but a great heart, for support and inspiration. Under the influence of both his aunt and the Divine Word priests, he aspired to be a missionary priest. A priest he did not become, but he retained his missionary zeal, channelling it instead through the instruments of research, teaching and public service.

Arsi was a "scholarship student". As his family did not have the resources to support his continuing education, he knew his only path forward was securing high academic grades that would attract study support. This he did, first gaining entry to the local Mariano Marcos State University (MMSU), where he obtained his BS in agriculture *magna cum laude* in 1979. Starting as editor of MMSU's school paper, Arsi also had a career as a creative writer, even writing tragic love stories for the Ilocano counterpart of *Liwayway* magazine! He also published poems under the pen name Oinesra (Arsenio spelled backwards).

After college, Arsi got a job as research assistant at the Cotton Research and Development Institute. After a short while, he secured a scholarship from the Southeast Asian Regional Center for Graduate Study and Research in Agriculture (SEARCA) to enrol in the master's programme on agricultural economics of the University of the Philippines Los Baños (UPLB), the agricultural campus of the country's national university. This was to be his first exposure to the international world of scholarship, as UPLB hosted the famed International Rice Research Institute (IRRI). Arsi thrived in this environment, again achieving high academic grades. UPLB Professor Cristina David recruited him to work on fertilizer policy and to be part of a project on Philippine agricultural policy jointly with two professors of the University of Hawaii, John Power and James Roumasset. This led Roumasset to recruit Arsi to pursue his PhD in economics at the University of Hawaii and continue working on the *nature, causes, and consequences of agricultural policy*.

Adjusting quickly to graduate school in Hawaii, Arsi completed his course work and dissertation in just a little over three years, graduating in 1985.⁶ His dissertation (Balisacan 1985) reflects his continuing interest in agricultural development and political economy—why governments choose the policies they do. In particular, he sought to explain the strong correlation between a country's per capita income and its rate of agricultural protection. At the time, poorer countries tended to tax agriculture. His dissertation provides a theory of political influence by endogenous special interest groups and uses the theory to explain the stylized fact about increasing agricultural protection. In lower income countries, the forces of consumer provisionism and industrial profitability dominated those of agricultural protection. The balance of political influence gradually reversed with a country's economic development.

At this stage Arsi's personal characteristics were already evident: his well-developed work ethic, his pursuit of scientific knowledge, his choice of research topics (agricultural development, poverty) based on his personal experience and a sense of what was nationally important, and his interest in policymaking processes and outcomes. He saw economics as a means of understanding—and improving—the world, including the low agricultural productivity and deep-seated poverty in the Philippines. These interrelated topics occupied much of his research in the decades to come. In their pursuit, Arsi has epitomized Blinder's (1987) economist of *hard head and soft heart*.

After a stint as research fellow at Hawaii's East-West Center (1985–86), Arsi joined the World Bank's project on the political economy of agricultural pricing policies in developing countries, which, like Arsi's dissertation, documented and explained the bias against agriculture (e.g., Krueger 1992). A comfortable career as an international civil servant was in prospect. But this was a turbulent period in Philippine history, and he felt the need to go home. The People's Power movement toppled President Ferdinand Marcos in February 1986, but the economic crisis was deep and the political situation fluid. At the urging of Professor Gerry Sicat, also at the World Bank at the time, Arsi took up a teaching position as assistant professor at UPLB in 1987, transferring a year later to UP Diliman on the invitation of Dean Pepe Encarnacion of the UP School

---

⁶   While in Hawaii, Arsi fell in love with running, after observing joggers on Waikiki Beach. This has developed into a life-long interest. He has completed several full (42 km) marathons, including Hawaii in 2012, Chicago in 2017, Paris in 2019, and New York (virtually) in 2021. He is a regular sight at his favourite training ground, the leafy UP Diliman campus.

of Economics (UPSE). He rose rapidly through the ranks, becoming a full professor in 1995. The renowned UPSE became his home, on and off, for the next three decades.

From the late 1980s, Arsi began to establish an international reputation in the fields of agriculture and poverty. He had papers published in *Weltwirtschaftliches Archiv* (Balisacan and Roumasset 1987), *American Journal of Agricultural Economics* (Rosegrant, Roumasset, and Balisacan 1985), *Economic Development and Cultural Change* (Balisacan 1993, 1995a), *Journal of Agricultural Economics* (Reardon et al. 2008), *Economics Letters* (Balisacan and Fuwa 2003) and *World Development* (Balisacan and Fuwa 2004), in addition to many book chapters and articles in national and regional journals. He has carved out a niche as an economist who is analytically rigorous and takes data seriously. He built his academic consulting work by constructing, for the first time in the country's history, a rich panel data set based on the country's Family Income and Expenditure Surveys. Here his academic entrepreneurial skills came to the fore, as he employed well-trained young UP students as research assistants while they completed their doctoral dissertations. His work also displayed considerable conceptual originality—for example, he included a local "dynasty" variable to better understand subnational variations in poverty outcomes. It would be invidious to single out one paper over this period, but it is worth recording that his 1995 EDCC paper, "Anatomy of Poverty during Adjustment: The Case of the Philippines", was very widely cited in the international poverty debates at the time. He also began to develop collaborative international research projects, one of which resulted in a widely cited volume on the Philippine economy (Balisacan and Hill 2003).

Arsi's national profile resulted in his first call to government service at the turn of the century. During the Estrada administration, one of the country's most prominent figures, Edgardo J. Angara, was appointed secretary of the Department of Agriculture (DA). Arsi was, in turn, appointed undersecretary for policy, planning and research. Under their joint tenure, the DA spearheaded the implementation of the Agriculture and Fisheries Modernization Act, which boosted agricultural productivity, at least temporarily. This was Arsi's first immersion in public service and international affairs, particularly as head of the Philippine delegation to WTO agricultural trade negotiations. The work gave him a taste of the possibilities of promoting better policies.

In 2003, Arsi was appointed as director of SEARCA. SEARCA is a major regional treaty organization operating in 11 countries (the ASEAN

10 plus Timor Leste). The position involved managing a large agency with active research, training and policy advisory activities throughout the region. Arsi embraced the mission of reinvigorating SEARCA (almost four decades old then), engaging in rather courageous acts of reorganization and programme redirection. On completing his term, he wrote an influential roadmap charting the way forward for the agency (see Balisacan 2009b).

After six years of secondment to SEARCA, Arsi returned to UPSE, of which he was appointed dean in 2010. Over this period, he had numerous additional responsibilities, reflecting his role as an institution builder. He was president of the Philippine Economic Society in 2006 and of the Asian Society of Agricultural Economists in 2011–14. He founded the *Asian Journal of Agriculture and Development*, serving as its editor from 2004 to 2015. His work and achievements led to numerous awards, including his election to the country's pre-eminent academic body, the National Academy of Science and Technology.

One day in 2012, UPSE Dean Arsi received a call from Malacañang to meet with President Noynoy Aquino. Arsi assumed the President wanted advice on the replacement of UPSE colleague, Professor Cayetano Paderanga, who was retiring owing to poor health. Professor Paderanga was then serving as director general of NEDA and concurrent secretary of socio-economic planning. Traditionally, NEDA has been headed by a non-political technocrat. Starting with Professor Gerardo Sicat in the Marcos era, the occupant has often been an UPSE faculty member or graduate, including the five most recent appointees. In addition to its administrative responsibilities, NEDA serves as the national government's "think tank", with a remit to examine long-term development issues. Attached to NEDA are several important agencies, including the Philippine Statistics Authority and the Philippine Institute for Development Studies (PIDS), the region's premier policy research centre.

In fact, the purpose of Malacañang's summons was not to request presidential advice, but rather to invite Arsi to take up the position of NEDA head. Arsi accepted the cabinet-level position on the condition that he would not be involved in the political affairs of the administration. He helmed NEDA for nearly four years, until January 2016. While some of NEDA's responsibilities were familiar territory to Arsi (e.g., he was well acquainted with Philippine statistics and had worked as a consultant to PIDS), some were new, especially macroeconomic analysis and modelling. The job also entailed frequent international travel as

President Noynoy Aquino, an avid consumer of Arsi's expertise, would bring him to meetings with heads of state to give briefings on the Philippine economy as well as to answer the President's own questions. (When Arsi writes his memoirs, we may learn more about these meetings and his impressions of those heads of state.)

Arsi's NEDA directorship concurred with a run of good economic times, during which the country's economic growth was sustained at around 6.3 per cent. During this period, poverty was falling, living standards were rising, and the macroeconomy was sound. But Arsi was conscious that the country had been slipping behind its more dynamic neighbours for decades. His frustration peaked on reading the Asian Development Bank's landmark study, *Asia 2050: Realizing the Asian Century* (Kohli, Sharma, and Sood 2011). The study projected an optimistic future for developing Asia. However, it lumped the Philippines in the "slow-modest growth" group of countries, along with Afghanistan, North Korea, Nepal and the Pacific Island economies, among others. Arsi saw the report as an opportunity to remind the Philippine citizenry of the importance of maintaining the growth momentum. As he records in the foreword (Balisacan 2018) to a recent volume on the Philippine economy (Clarete, Esguerra, and Hill 2018):

> Both pride and necessity prodded me and my colleagues at NEDA ... to help change the narrative on the Philippine economy and society... We could not allow ourselves to be left behind, to remain a laggard in an otherwise highly dynamic, rapidly growing and prospering region.

Cognizant of the political realities of the fixed six-year term of the presidency and a new administration's predilection to abandon even good plans and programmes of its predecessor, Arsi and his staff prepared a long-term blueprint, *Ambisyon Natin 2040* (NEDA 2016), which articulates a common development vision for the Filipinos as a nation and for accelerated Philippine development. He was understandably pleased when the new Duterte administration adopted *Ambisyon Natin 2040* as a guiding policy document, issuing an Executive Order for all government offices and instrumentalities to develop and implement their plans consistent with this long-term vision.

Towards the end of his administration, President Noynoy Aquino had yet another assignment for Arsi. In 2015, Congress passed the Philippine Competition Act, which established the Philippine Competition Commission (PCC). The President appointed Arsi as the PCC's inaugural chairperson. This quasi-judicial body is an entirely new entity on the Philippine landscape; nothing like it hitherto existed.

While the PCC enjoys *de facto* independence, it can always suffer budget cuts if it loses support. Arsi's reputation as a non-partisan technocrat has helped the PCC maintain support across different administrations.

The PCC has arguably been Arsi's most challenging assignment as a public servant. It has involved establishing a new institution and administrative apparatus.[7] Undergirded by industrial organization and law and economics, competition policy has been a new endeavour for him. The Philippine economy is characterized by high levels of concentration in the modern sector, a complex, corruption-prone regulatory environment,[8] and the perception of a cosy relationship between the worlds of business and politics. After all, it is the country that popularized the phrase "crony capitalism". Thus, the challenge has been to establish an analytically rigorous and credible institution with "teeth", one that is faithful to its congressional mandate. At the same time, the Philippine business community has to be assured that the PCC will operate in a fair, transparent and non-political manner. It was important to quickly and publicly establish the Commission's credibility as an impartial enforcer of its mandate.[9]

This biographical sketch helps us understand why and how Arsi has achieved so much in his professional life. The prime factors are his work ethic and discipline. Born to an unprivileged life, he reaped scholastic achievements because of his ability, dedication, courage and hard work—habits he has maintained throughout his working life (his 4–5 a.m. starts have not only supported his running career). His experience reminds—nay, inspires—that, although the Philippines

---

[7] For a detailed discussion of the structure, conduct and scope of competition policy in the Philippines, see Balisacan (2019), Ravago, Roumasset, and Balisacan (2021), chapter 18 of this volume, and Arsi's forthcoming exit report when his term as chairperson of the PCC ends in January 2023.

[8] See, for example, the World Bank (2018), which argues that the Philippines is "one of the most restrictive economies in the world".

[9] The PCC's first abuse of dominance case was therefore crucial. The Commission responded to a case brought by residents of Urban Deca Homes Condominium in Tondo, Manila, who alleged that they were only allowed access to a single internet service provider that was slow, expensive and unreliable. Finding sufficient grounds of abuse of dominance, the PCC ordered the company to allow residents to contract with other internet service providers and to pay the fine of PHP27.11 million.

is a stratified and unequal society, children from poor families can progress.

Second, like all influential economists, he chose to work on important topics of national significance. His interest in agriculture reflects his experience as a young boy. It prompted him to seek answers for big questions: Why are the poor predominantly in this sector? Why has Philippine agricultural productivity lagged behind its neighbours? Why have aspects of the policy regime adversely affected the sector? Arsi's first degree was in agriculture, but he transferred to economics because he thought it would provide some answers to these pressing questions. Subsequently, his approach to economics has been in the conventional mainstream—what might be termed as pragmatic neoclassical economics. He believes in markets but also sees a role for government in direct poverty alleviation programmes (such as the country's *conditional cash transfers*) and in ensuring a competitive marketplace. His empirical work in poverty analysis is meticulous; unlike some commentators in the field, he takes data quality seriously and is inclined to "let the data tell their story".

Third, Arsi has shown a capacity to work effectively at many levels. Although not an overtly political person—and perhaps because of it—he has been trusted by the Philippine political class, as illustrated by cabinet-level appointments in four very different presidential administrations. He favours evidence-based policymaking advocacy, has generally eschewed going public on policy battles, and has learned to move on from the inevitable policy disappointments.[10]

Arsi's integrity and work ethic have been tested many times. When offered personal benefits in exchange for turning a blind eye towards agency irregularities, he resigned his position instead. When a relative was approached to influence him, the relative declined on the grounds that Arsi would not countenance even the appearance of corruption.

---

[10] While most of the policy battles have remained behind closed doors, occasionally they leaked to the press. One such example concerned the issue of rice production and importation in 2013, which resulted in accelerating inflation and the contrasting recommendations emanating from NEDA and the DA. On this occasion President Noynoy Aquino sided with the restrictive approach favoured by the DA, presumably because its Secretary Alcala was very close to the president. For press coverage of the case, see https://newsinfo.inquirer.net/504535.

He has successfully held senior positions in the academic world, sometimes taking tough decisions by developing a consensus for change, as well as building a wide array of international connections (as exemplified by the contributors to this volume). Like several of his UPSE colleagues, from Gerry Sicat onwards, he has moved easily and productively between the academic and policy worlds. He has also been a popular (and demanding) teacher, who has mentored many young academics. And in academic environments with scarce resources, he has well-developed entrepreneurial skills for securing research funds and using them productively.

REFERENCES

Balisacan, A. M. 1985. "A Positive Theory of Economic Protection: Agricultural Policies in Developed and Developing Countries". PhD dissertation, University of Hawaii.

———. 1987. "Political Investment in Economic Protection: A Note". *Philippine Review of Economics* 24, no. 1–2: 149–56.

———. 1990. "Why Do Governments Do What They Do? Agrarian Reform in the Philippines". In *Studies in Economic Policy and Institutions: The Philippines*, edited by Dante B. Canlas and Hideyoshi Sakai. Tokyo: Institute of Developing Economies.

———. 1993. "Agricultural Growth, Landlessness, Off-Farm Employment, and Rural Poverty in the Philippines". *Economic Development and Cultural Change* 41:533–62.

———. 1995a. "Anatomy of Poverty during Adjustment: The Case of the Philippines". *Economic Development and Cultural Change* 44:33–62.

———. 1995b. "Rural Poverty and Access to Land in the Philippines". Background Paper for Philippines: A Strategy to Fight Poverty. Country Department I, East Asia and Pacific Region. Washington, DC: World Bank.

———. 1996a. "Investing in Equity: Toward an Alternative Paradigm for Reforming Agricultural Land Relations". In *Financial Sector Issues in the Philippines*, edited by Raul V. Fabella and Kazuhisa Ito. Tokyo: Institute of Developing Economies.

———. 1996b. "Agricultural Trade in the Asia-Pacific Rim". In *Asia-Pacific Economic Cooperation: Theory and Policy*, edited by Richard Hooley, M. Jan Dutta, A. Nasution, and M. Pangestu, pp. 167–83. Greenwich, Connecticut: JAI Press.

———. 2001. "Poverty in the Philippines: An Update and Reexamination". *Philippine Review of Economics* 38, no. 1:15–52.

———. 2003. "Poverty and Inequality". In *The Philippine Economy: Development,*

Policies, and Challenges, edited by A. M. Balisacan and H. Hill. New York: Oxford University Press; Quezon City: Ateneo de Manila University Press.

———. 2007. "Local Growth and Poverty Reduction." In *The Dynamics of Regional Development: The Philippines in East Asia*, edited by A. M. Balisacan and H. Hill, pp. 398–421. Cheltenham, UK: Edward Elgar.

———. 2009a. "Poverty Reduction: Trends, Determinants, and Policies". In *Diagnosing the Philippine Economy: Toward Inclusive Growth*, edited by D. Canlas, M. E. Khan, and J. Zhuang, pp. 261–94. London: Asian Development Bank and Anthem Press.

———. 2009b. "Mainstreaming Agriculture in the Development Agenda". SEARCA Monograph. Los Baños, Philippines: SEARCA. https://www.searca.org/pubs/monographs?pid=289.

———. 2015. "The Growth-Poverty Nexus: Multidimensional Poverty in the Philippines". In *Sustainable Economic Development: Resources, Environment, and Institutions*, edited by A. M. Balisacan, U. Chakravorty, and M. V. Ravago, pp. 445–68. US and UK: Elsevier Inc.

———. 2018. "Foreword". *The Philippine Economy: No Longer the East Asian Exception?*, edited by R. L. Clarete, E. F. Esguerra, and H. Hill, pp. xix–xxvi. Singapore: ISEAS.

———. 2019. "Toward a Fairer Society: Inequality and Competition Policy in Developing Asia". *Philippine Review of Economics* 56, no. 1&2: 127–147.

Balisacan, A. M., and R. T. Bacawag. 1995. "Inequality, Poverty, and Urban-Rural Growth Linkages". In *Spatial Development, Land Use, and Urban-Rural Growth Linkages in the Philippines*, edited by Arsenio M. Balisacan and Ernesto Pernia. Pasig: National Economic and Development Authority.

Balisacan, A. M., U. Chakravorty, and M. V. Ravago, eds. 2015. *Sustainable Economic Development: Resources, Environment, and Institutions*. US and UK: Elsevier Inc.

Balisacan, A. M., R. G. Edillon, and S. F. Piza. 2005. "Rural Poverty in Southeast Asia: Issues, Policies, and Challenges". *Asian Journal of Agriculture and Development* 2, no. 1&2: 25–38.

Balisacan, A. M., and N. Fuwa. 2003. "Growth, Inequality, and Politics Revisited: A Developing-Country Case". *Economics Letters* 79: 53–58.

———. 2004. "Going Beyond Cross-Country Averages: Growth, Inequality and Poverty Reduction in the Philippines". *World Development* 32, no. 11: 1891–1907.

———. 2006. "Changes in Spatial Income Inequality in the Philippines: An Exploratory Analysis". In *Spatial Disparities in Human Development: Perspectives from Asia*, edited by Ravi Kanbur, Tony Venables, and Guanghua Wan, pp. 207–32. Tokyo: United Nations University Press.

———, eds. 2007a. *Reasserting the Rural Development Agenda: Lessons Learned and Emerging Challenges in Asia*. Singapore, Institute of Southeast Asian Studies; Los Baños, Philippines: SEARCA.

———. 2007b. "Poverty and Vulnerability". In *Reasserting the Rural Development Agenda: Lessons Learned and Emerging Challenges in Asia*, edited by A. M. Balisacan and N. Fuwa. Singapore, Institute of Southeast Asian Studies; Los Baños, Philippines: SEARCA.

Balisacan, A. M., and H. Hill, eds. 2003. *The Philippine Economy: Development, Policies, and Challenges*. New York: Oxford University Press. Philippine edition published by the Ateneo de Manila University Press.

Balisacan, A. M., and K. Nozawa, eds. 1993. *Structures and Reforms for Rural Development in the Philippines*. Tokyo: Institute of Developing Economies.

Balisacan, A. M., and L. Papa. 2020. "The Evolution of Competition Law and Policy in the Philippines". *Concurrences Review* 2: 52–57.

Balisacan, A. M., and E. M. Pernia. 2003. "Poverty, Inequality and Growth in the Philippines". In *Poverty, Growth and Institutions in Developing Asia*, edited by Ernesto M. Pernia and Anil B. Deolalikar. Hampshire, England: Palgrave Macmillan Publishers.

Balisacan, A. M., and M. V. Ravago. 2003. "The Rice Problem in the Philippines: Trends, Constraints, and Policy Imperatives". *Transactions of the National Academy of Science and Technology Philippines* 25: 221–36.

Balisacan, A. M., and J. A. Roumasset. 1987. "Public Choice of Economic Policy: The Growth of Agricultural Protection". *Weltwirtschaftliches Archiv* 123, no. 2: 232–48.

Blinder, A. 1987. *Hard Heads, Soft Hearts: Tough-Minded Economics for a Just Society*. Reading, MA: Addison-Wesley Publishing.

Clarete, R. L., E. F. Esguerra, and H. Hill, eds. 2018. *The Philippine Economy: No Longer the East Asian Exception?* Singapore: ISEAS.

David, C. C., and A. M. Balisacan. 1995. "Philippine Rice Supply and Demand: Prospects and Policy Implications". *Journal of Philippine Development* 22, no. 2: 233–63.

David, C. C., P. Intal, and A. M. Balisacan. 2009. "The Philippines." In *Distortions to Agricultural Incentives in Asia*, edited by Kym Anderson and Will Martin, pp. 223–54. Washington, DC: World Bank.

Ducanes, G. M., and A. M. Balisacan. 2019. "Reducing Inequality in the Philippines". In *Getting Even: Public Policies to Tackle Inequality in Asia*, edited by M. Talpur. Delhi: Bloomsbury.

Hill, H., A. M. Balisacan, and S. F. A. Piza. 2007. "The Philippines and Regional Development". In *The Dynamics of Regional Development: The Philippines in East Asia*, edited by A. M. Balisacan and H. Hill, pp. 1–47. Cheltenham, UK: Edward Elgar.

Kohli, H. S., A. Sharma, and A. Sood, eds. 2011. *Asia 2050: Realizing the Asian Century*. India: SAGE Publications. https://www.doi.org/10.4135/9781446270349.

Krueger, A. O. 1992. *The Political Economy of Agricultural Pricing Policy Volume 5. A Synthesis of the Economics in Developing Countries*. Baltimore and London: Johns Hopkins University Press for the World Bank.

Krugman, Paul. 1994. "The Myth of Asia's Miracle". *Foreign Affairs* 73, no. 6: 62–78.

NEDA (National Economic Development Authority). 2016. *Ambisyon Natin 2040*. Pasig: NEDA. https://2040.neda.gov.ph/.

Ravago, M. V., and A. M. Balisacan. 2016. "Agricultural Policy and Institutional Reforms in the Philippines: Experiences, Impacts, and Lessons". *Southeast Asian Agriculture and Development Primer Series*. Los Baños, Laguna: SEARCA. Second edition.

Ravago, M. V., A. M. Balisacan, and M. A. Sombilla. 2018. "Current Structure and Future Challenges of the Agricultural Sector". In *The Future of Philippine Agriculture: Scenarios, Policies, and Investments under Climate Change*, edited by M. Rosegrant and M. Sombilla. Singapore: ISEAS.

Ravago, M. V., J. Roumasset, and A. M. Balisacan. 2021. "What Influences Adoption of Competition Law? The Case of ASEAN Economies". *The Singapore Economic Review*. https://doi.org/10.1142/S0217590821430049

Reardon, T., J. E. Edwards, K. Stamoulis, P. Lanjouw, and A. M. Balisacan. 2008. "Effects of Non-farm Employment on Rural Income Inequality in Developing Countries: An Investment Perspective". *Journal of Agricultural Economics* 51, no. 2: 266–88.

Rosegrant, M. W., J. A. Roumasset, and A. M. Balisacan. 1985. "Biological Technology and Agricultural Policy: An Assessment of Azolla for Philippine Rice Production". *American Journal of Agricultural Economics* 67, no. 4: 726–48.

World Bank Group. 2018. *Fostering Competition in the Philippines: The Challenge of Restrictive Regulations*. Washington, DC: World Bank. https://openknowledge.worldbank.org/handle/10986/31353

2 Philippine Economic Development in Comparative Perspective: An Interpretative Essay[1]

Hal Hill, Arsenio M. Balisacan and Russel Matthew Dela Cruz

1 INTRODUCTION

The Philippine economy has often been characterized as a laggard, an "East Asian exception", and a "Latin American economy in East Asia". The forward-looking Asian Development Bank (ADB) publication, *Asia 2050*, (ADB 2011) classifies the country with the region's slower growing economies, including Afghanistan, Nepal, Myanmar and North Korea. But as the eminent Filipino economist Felipe Medalla has observed, the Philippines is an "average" economy, in the sense that its long-term economic performance is similar to the global average. Over the period 1960–2018, for example, the country's per capita gross

---

[1] This paper draws on the first two authors' collaborative research projects on the Philippine economy, in particular Balisacan and Hill (2003) and Clarete, Esguerra, and Hill (2018). In the case of the latter publication, Balisacan was the initiator of the project, and he also wrote the Foreword. The volume drew heavily on background papers prepared for the Philippine government's long-term development vision, *Ambisyon Natin 2040*, which was overseen by Balisacan in his capacity as socio-economic planning secretary.

domestic product (GDP) in real terms rose 2.9 times, exactly the same as that for the world as a whole. In other words, it is its deviation from the record of some very dynamic Asian economies that is distinctive; in global terms, its performance is not unusual.[2]

Importantly, these averages conceal a great deal of variation over time. Most countries have episodes of faster and slower growth, booms and busts. This is certainly the case for the post-independence Philippine economy. In fact, in this paper we argue that three more or less distinct periods are observable. Although the periods are not precise, they are approximately:

1. From independence (1946) to the late 1970s: high initial expectations, slowing growth
2. From the late 1970s to the early 1990s: growing into a deep and extended crisis
3. From the early 1990s to 2019: recovery, rejoining the East Asian economic mainstream

To these may now be added the current period, 2020–21, of the COVID-19 pandemic-induced health and economic crisis, which introduces a sharp discontinuity into our analysis.

There are therefore periods of both modest and quite strong economic growth, together with two major crisis episodes—the macroeconomic and political crisis of 1984–86 and its aftermath, and the COVID-19 pandemic of 2020–21. Note also that the three main economic episodes correspond loosely, but not exactly, to the country's political periods—that is, the democratic eras of 1946–72 and after 1986, and the authoritarian era of 1972–86, of Martial Law and its aftermath.[3]

---

[2] Over this period, the per capita GDP of developing Asia rose 14.9 times. Philippine GDP per capita actually rose more than the other major developing regions, Latin America and Caribbean (2.6 times) and Sub-Saharan Africa (1.5 times).

[3] According to the widely used Polity5 democracy scale, which ranges from 0 to 10 (least to most democratic), the Philippines scores 6 for the years 1950–68, 4 for 1969–71, 0 for 1972–85, and 8 from 1987 onwards. As comparators, Indonesia scores 0 during the Soeharto years (1966–98) and 8–9 from 2004 onwards. Over this period, the Malaysian score is in the 4–6 range.

It is instructive to examine these episodes and draw inferences from them. Economic development is rarely a smooth, continuous, linear process. Episodes help us understand a country's development dynamics and political economy. They also have implications for development economics in general. Of particular interest is the light they shed on the fundamental drivers of economic development, and how countries manage and respond to shocks, both internal and external. In addition, major crises are a special category deserving attention: their origins, the immediate domestic response, and the longer-term recovery trajectory.

We commence with a comparative survey of economic performance in section 2. We then provide an analytical summary of each of the three pre-COVID-19 episodes, briefly as it is well-traversed territory (sections 3–5). Section 6 extends the discussion of the stronger growth momentum by examining the drivers of growth, in particular the rising importance of service exports, in contrast to the sluggish performance of export-oriented manufacturing. Section 7 examines the current COVID-19 pandemic, its socio-economic impacts and the government's response to it. This most recent episode, which is still unfolding as we write, also provides an opportunity to assess the country's resilience in the face of the most serious shock to the peacetime global economy in 90 years. Section 8 outlines elements of the post-COVID-19 reform agenda, which, we argue, will need to be addressed if the strong development momentum of the past decade is to be regained. Section 9 sums up and draws out some broader implications for the country's growth dynamics and future trajectories. Wherever possible, we conduct the analysis in comparative context, using as the (high) benchmark the country's dynamic middle-income neighbours.

Although the Philippines' economic performance has lagged behind its neighbours for extended periods, our conclusions are nevertheless cautiously optimistic. We argue that policymakers— and the community at large—have learnt from earlier development missteps and reformed. To be sure, the reform process has been slow, incremental and partial. But at least until the COVID-19 crisis, we highlight several significant reform achievements. This crisis presents perhaps the biggest test yet of the ongoing validity of this proposition. Its impact has been very severe, and the authorities have struggled to develop a coherent and effective management strategy.

2 PHILIPPINE ECONOMIC GROWTH IN COMPARATIVE ASIAN PERSPECTIVE

Tables 2.1 and 2.2 provide comparative statistics on per capita incomes and growth rates over selected intervals during the independence era, and Figure 2.1 shows the Philippines' annual GDP growth and real per capita income since 1960.[4]

On the eve of the Pacific War and at the effective end of the colonial era, the Philippines had the third highest per capita income in Asia, behind only Japan (which was almost double the Philippine figure) and Singapore (Table 2.1). The Philippines' income was significantly higher than the five middle-income Asian comparators in the table. Apart from the brutal American takeover at the end of the nineteenth century, and unlike Indonesia and Vietnam, the Philippines did not experience a protracted struggle for independence. But it did suffer from extensive wartime destruction, especially in and around Manila. Thus, its estimated per capita income in 1950 had fallen to about two-thirds of the 1940 level, the sharpest decline among these six countries; by then, it had been overtaken by Malaysia.

The 1950s was a decade of strong growth, fuelled by reconstruction and import-substituting industrialization and building on earlier industrialization spurts (De Dios and Williamson 2015). By 1960, the Philippines was therefore well ahead of four of the comparators (and notably having more than double China's per capita income), and not far behind Malaysia. It maintained this relativity through the 1960s, although Thailand was then converging.

---

[4] We focus mainly on the period since 1960 because the national accounts are regarded as more reliable and because by then the country's immediate post-war rehabilitation had been completed and the institutions of an independent nation state were well established. The pioneering estimates of Hooley (1968) and others have extended the national accounts series back to 1902. The data in Table 2.1 are from the Maddison data set, which provides very long-term series. For the Philippines, there are point estimates for 1820 and 1870, and then a continuous series from 1902 onwards, except for the war years of 1941–45. The data in Table 2.2 and Figure 2.1 are from World Development Indicators. Both series are sourced from Philippine data. The methodological differences are explained in the Maddison website (https://www.rug.nl/ggdc/historicaldevelopment/maddison/releases/maddison-project-database-2013).

Table 2.1. Comparative Asian economic performance (1940–2010)

Country	GDP per capita (constant 2011$)							
	1940	1950	1960	1970	1980	1990	2000	2010
Philippines	2,402	1,706	2,353	2,812	3,787	3,502	4,034	5,694
Indonesia	1,766	1,280	1,613	1,882	2,981	4,007	5,384	8,386
Malaysia	2,037	2,485	2,439	3,314	5,829	8,179	13,475	18,574
Thailand	*1,317	1,302	1,718	2,700	4,071	7,385	9,627	13,344
Vietnam	n.a.	1,049	1,274	1,172	1,207	1,634	2,773	4,572
China	*1,003	799	1,057	1,398	1,930	2,982	4,730	9,658
India	1,093	987	1,200	1,384	1,495	2,087	2,753	4,526

Note: Data are for 1938.

Source: Maddison Project Database, University of Groningen (https://www.rug.nl/ggdc/historicaldevelopment/maddison/releases/maddison-project-database-2020?lang=en, accessed 1 September 2021).

Income continued to increase in the 1970s, but by 1980, Thailand had overtaken the Philippines and Malaysia had pulled further ahead (India meanwhile was still stuck in its "Hindu Equilibrium" growth rate). The major divergence occurred in the 1980s, when the Philippines was the only country in the group to experience an economic crisis, an outcome it shared with many indebted developing country commodity exporters in Africa and Latin America. By 1990, Indonesia had overtaken the Philippines, while the per capita incomes of Malaysia and Thailand were more than double that of the Philippines. Philippine growth resumed in the 1990s and, although the country navigated the Asian financial crisis (AFC) more successfully than the other three ASEAN countries in the table, over the decade, it continued to lag behind them and also China, which was then growing extraordinarily fast. These relativities have broadly persisted into the twenty-first century.

Table 2.2 tells a similar story of the ASEAN Five economies (and Vietnam for the most recent period), together with China and India. Over the long period, 1960–2019, China's growth record has been without peer. Within the ASEAN, Singapore leads by a significant margin. India and Indonesia are comparable. Over the medium term, 1980–2019, the rankings are similar, except that India and Thailand have joined Singapore as the most dynamic economies after China.

Table 2.2. Comparative Asian growth rates (1960–2019)

Country	Relative GDP per capita		
	2019/2000	2019/1980	2019/1960
Philippines	2.0	1.9	3.0
Indonesia	2.1	3.6	6.5
Malaysia	1.8	3.8	9.2
Thailand	1.9	4.6	11.4
Vietnam	2.7	n.a.	n.a
China	4.7	23.8	43.0
India	2.6	5.1	6.5

Source: World Development Indicators, World Bank (https://databank.worldbank.org/source/world-development-indicators, accessed 1 September 2021).

Figure 2.1. Philippine economic growth and per capita GDP (1960–2020)

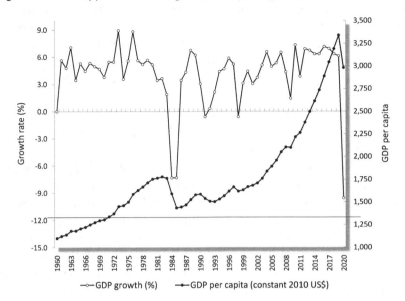

—○— GDP growth (%)   —●— GDP per capita (constant 2010 US$)

Source: World Development Indicators, World Bank (https://databank.worldbank.org/source/world-development-indicators, accessed 1 September 2021).

The most interesting (and reassuring) data from a Philippine perspective is for the twenty-first century: Philippine per capita income doubled from 2000 to 2019, an outcome that is slightly higher than Malaysia, Thailand and Singapore, but somewhat lower than Vietnam[5] — Southeast Asia's most dynamic economy over this period — and India. This is the essence of the proposition that the Philippines has rejoined the dynamic Asian mainstream in the twenty-first century.

3 THE FIRST THREE DECADES: HIGH EXPECTATIONS, SLOWING GROWTH

In the early post-colonial period, the Philippines was widely considered to have among the best prospects in Asia for rapid economic development

---

[5] The figures for Cambodia and Lao PDR are similar to that of Vietnam, confirming the mild convergence of per capita incomes that has been evident within the ASEAN for much of this century.

(Morawetz 1977; Golay 1961). It had relatively well-established political and legal institutions. It possessed a strong human capital base, including near universal adult literacy and widespread English-language fluency. It also had a special relationship with the dominant commercial power of that era, the United States, including preferential access to its market and, in the Cold War era, the security conferred by the presence of US military bases on its soil. As an indication of that confidence, in 1966 Manila was chosen as the headquarters of the region's premier development finance institution, the Asian Development Bank.

These expectations appeared to be validated initially. As noted, the country's economic growth compared quite favourably with neighbouring economies in the 1950s and 1960s. However, growth began to slow from around the late 1970s, at a time when Japan's very high growth was clearly established and the four newly industrialized economies (NIEs) were also following Japan's growth trajectory. The proximate explanations have been extensively analysed in the literature on Philippine economic development.[6] The country embarked on a comprehensive import substitution, accidentally in response to a balance of payments emergency. But the wide-ranging import controls quickly became embedded in the country's political economy. It led to a spurt in industrial growth, which slowed as soon as the limits to import substitution in a small domestic economy were reached. As Power and Sicat (1971, 33) observe:

> "The adoption of a strategy of encouraging manufacturing behind protection was more or less inadvertent ... and what began as an emergency tactic in balance of payments policy became the principal instrument for promoting industrialization over the decade of the 1950s."

Moreover, unlike other countries that pursued a similar strategy (e.g., Korea and earlier Japan), the underlying inefficiencies of the new industries and the vested interests that sprang up around them meant that the country was unable to engineer a smooth transition to export orientation.

---

[6] See, for example, ILO (1974), De Dios and Williamson (2015), Sicat (2014), the contributors to Balisacan and Hill (2003) and the decades of voluminous writings by members of the University of the Philippines School of Economics (UPSE).

This industrial strategy had the familiar effects of discriminating against the agriculture sector (except for some favoured irrigated rice areas) and poorer regions (where most of the population resided) and having a weak formal sector employment growth. There was therefore little progress in addressing the country's high level of interpersonal and interregional inequalities. The influential ILO (1974) study, also known as the "Ranis Report", referred to the country's "narrow and unbalanced" growth. In addition, there were recurring macroeconomic crises, mostly caused by the monetization of fiscal deficits (hence, the rising inflation) in the context of a fixed exchange rate regime, resulting in an appreciating real exchange rate. This led to periodic balance of payments crises, exchange rate realignments and partial liberalizations, before another episode of growing macroeconomic imbalance emerged (Baldwin 1975).

The fundamental reason for the slowing growth was that Philippine leadership did not possess the ruthless determination to elevate economic growth as the overriding development objective, unlike the leaders of Japan, South Korea, Taiwan, Singapore and (at least to some extent) some other ASEAN countries.[7]

4 DEEP CRISIS AND SLOW RECOVERY

The country's slide from slowing growth to deep crisis has also been extensively documented and analysed.[8] The 1970s was a decade of global economic turbulence dominated by OPEC-inspired rising oil prices. As an oil importer, the Philippines was adversely affected, but cushioned the negative terms of trade shock with aggressive international borrowings, a strategy sanctioned—in fact, encouraged—by international financial institutions concerned to recycle the Middle East's holdings of "petrodollars". In the eyes of these agencies, the Philippines appeared to be a good bet: its initial debt levels were modest, it was in a dynamic neighbourhood, the two Asian giants had effectively disengaged from the global economy, and President Marcos had appointed able technocrats to key portfolios in his administration.

---

[7] For a concise summary, see, e.g., De Dios and Hutchcroft (2003) and the references cited therein.
[8] See, e.g., Remolona, Mangahas, and Pante (1986), Dohner and Intal (1989), Sicat (1985) and several UPSE "white papers".

The country therefore recorded quite strong, albeit debt-driven, growth during most of the 1970s, averaging more than 6 per cent over the period 1975–80, further aided by some modest trade policy reforms.

By the early 1980s, however, its economic fortunes began to deteriorate quickly, as they did in many other developing countries, especially the indebted commodity exporters. A conjunction of four sets of factors generated a perfect storm that produced the country's biggest economic crisis in its four decades of independence. The first factor was US monetary policy. Global interest rates began to rise sharply as a result of the US Fed's determination to control inflation, the so-called "Volcker shock". Second, the prices of major Philippine commodity exports declined, especially coconut and sugar (although these negative effects were ameliorated by declining petroleum prices from around 1982). Third, a significant proportion of the international borrowings was invested in "prestige" projects, or on-lent to the politically well connected for projects of dubious commercial viability.[9] One infamous case, the mothballed Bataan Nuclear Power Plant, at one stage accounted for about 10 per cent of the total external debt. Fourth, the political legitimacy of the Marcos administration was eroding, accelerated by the blatant assassination of Benigno Aquino in August 1983, mounting political scandals, growing international opprobrium, and ultimately a fraudulent attempt to restore his electoral fortunes in early 1986.

The economy contracted by almost 15 per cent in the last two years of the Marcos administration (Figure 2.1).[10] The peaceful People's Power regime change of February 1986 signalled a change of political direction and the beginnings of a gradual economic revival. But the economy

---

[9] Hence, the widespread use of terms such as "booty capitalism" (Hutchcroft 1998) and "crony capitalism", the latter gaining international attention on the basis of the writings about the Philippines in the late Marcos era.

[10] In passing, there were similarities between the Philippine economic crisis of 1984–86 and the Indonesian crisis of 1997–99. Their economic contractions were of similar magnitudes; both crises resulted in the removal of long-established and by then unpopular authoritarian leaders, involved highly controversial IMF rescue programmes, and both led suddenly to the restoration of democracy and with a lag decentralization. The major differences were that the Indonesian crisis was unforeseen; it was growing considerably faster pre-crisis, and its economic recovery was faster (seven years to return to pre-crisis per capita income compared with almost 20 years for the Philippines).

grew slowly during the Corazon Aquino presidency (1986–92), such that by the end of the 1980s, real per capita income was still 7 per cent lower than that at the beginning of the decade. The slow growth resulted from protracted (and sometimes acrimonious) negotiations surrounding the unpopular rescue programme of the International Monetary Fund (IMF); several very serious natural disasters;[11] episodes of political agitation, mainly from dissident military ranks; and the complex, protracted public and commercial debt workouts. Rising fiscal deficits also triggered a near balance of payments crisis in 1991. Internationally, the Philippines missed out on the major East Asian economic restructuring that got underway in the wake of the September 1985 Plaza Accord, which resulted in the appreciation of the Japanese Yen and subsequently the currencies of the NIEs, and triggered the massive relocation of Japanese industry to Southeast Asia, especially Indonesia, Malaysia and Thailand.[12]

5   REJOINING THE EAST ASIAN MAINSTREAM

Whereas the Corazon Aquino presidency focused on democratic consolidation, resolution of the economic crisis and a halting economic recovery, the Fidel Ramos presidency (1992–98) was characterized by (unexpectedly) vigorous reform and a resultant dividend of stronger economic growth. The newly established, recapitalized and professionally managed Bangko Sentral ng Pilipinas (BSP) quickly restored monetary policy credibility. Combined with effective fiscal consolidation, the country was on the path to graduating from the controversial IMF programme. Together with a more effective fiscal policy, for the first time in decades, the ever-present risk of a macroeconomic crisis receded. Meanwhile, microeconomic reform injected greater competition in telecommunications, transport, trade and other key sectors. Neglected infrastructure investments resumed. The partial trade liberalization opened up new export opportunities as

---

[11]   Especially the Mt. Pinatubo volcanic eruption in June 1991, the largest of its kind in the twentieth century to have occurred in a densely populated region.

[12]   Recall that in the mid-1980s China was in the very early stages of its economic reforms, while India and the Mekong economies were essentially closed to FDI.

well as increasing competitive pressures in the tradable sectors. By 1996, the economy was again growing by 6 per cent.

The first major economic test over this period was the 1997–98 AFC. By this time, the Philippines shared some similarities with the other crisis-affected economies: the peso was appreciating, the current account deficits were widening to over 5 per cent of GDP, and short-term external debt was rising (and was then equivalent to the country's gross overseas reserves). The capital flight and collapse of the Thai Baht in July 1997 also triggered a capital exodus from the Philippines, and the peso was allowed to float later that month. However, the country was able to avoid the deep economic crisis experienced by its three ASEAN neighbours and South Korea. Its GDP in 1998 fell by just 0.5 per cent,[13] compared with Indonesia's decline of 13.4 per cent. The financial sector remained largely intact, again unlike its neighbours. By the first quarter of 1999, the economy had returned to positive growth.

Why was the Philippines less affected by the AFC than some of its neighbours? Several factors were at work.[14] First, painful lessons were learnt from the mid-1980s crisis and, as noted, these translated into improved economic policy, particularly monetary and fiscal policy. Policymakers had recent, first-hand experience of how to manage a sudden economic shock, and this knowledge was quickly applied from mid-1997. Second, policymakers and investors alike were still cautious in the wake of that crisis, unlike the ASEAN neighbours that had enjoyed three decades of fast, mostly uninterrupted growth. Arguably, overconfidence had permeated both the policy and business worlds of these countries. Third, and related to the second factor, there was not such a major build-up of debt, particularly unhedged foreign-currency borrowings. No boom (or at least a modest boom) meant no bust. Finally, unlike the mid-1980s and also Soeharto's Indonesia, there was no problem with regime legitimacy. The well-regarded Ramos administration was nearing the end of its (mandatory single) term; elections were held during the crisis year, and they proceeded smoothly.

---

[13] In fact, the severe drought of that year depressed agricultural output by 6 per cent and contributed significantly to the downturn.

[14] See, for example, Noland (2000), Sicat (1999), and Rodlauer et al (2000). The latter reflects the IMF assessment of economic management over this period.

Economic development proceeded apace during the twenty-first century. In spite of some unenthusiastic international perceptions,[15] the economy generally remained buoyant, notwithstanding various political and economic shocks. Among the former was the extra-parliamentary overthrow of President Joseph Estrada in 2001 and periods of congressional logjams (including the blocking of budgetary laws) during the Macapagal-Arroyo presidency of 2001–10. The major economic shock was the global financial crisis (GFC) of 2008–9, which the economy weathered with little difficulty. From 2010, the economy was regularly achieving annual growth rates of at least 6 per cent, coinciding with another smooth transfer of power to the Noynoy Aquino presidency (2010–16). Through to the COVID-19 crisis, the Philippines had achieved almost 80 quarters of continuously positive economic growth, a record for the country.

Stronger economic growth was clearly lifting living standards. As would be expected, the Philippine poverty trajectory has more or less tracked economic growth, declining during buoyant economic times and stagnating when the economy was in the doldrums. For most of the past half century, poverty has declined more slowly in the Philippines than in some of its dynamic neighbours because of slower economic growth and because historically poverty was less responsive to growth (Balisacan 2015; Clarete 2018). Both Indonesia and especially Vietnam now have lower headcount poverty incidence. But the decade of strong growth pre-COVID-19 resulted in an accelerated decline of poverty (Capuno 2020).

For comparability, Figure 2.2 tracks these trends for the Philippines and four middle-income ASEAN countries during the twenty-first century using the World Bank's internationally comparable Povcal data set and its US$3.20 "middle-income" poverty line. On this indicator, Philippine headcount poverty almost halved over the period 2000–2019, from 44 per cent to 23 per cent. The gloomy literature that asserts that the poor have not benefited from the stronger growth overlooks this significant achievement. Of course, the data also highlight that the record could have been much better. The key to poverty alleviation is a combination of growth and various "growth plus" factors, including social assistance, education, health and the labour market.

---

[15] Pritchett (2003) wonders whether the Philippines was a "democratic dud". The ADB typology that the country belongs to the slower growing economies has been referred to above.

Figure 2.2. Comparative headcount poverty estimates (2000–2019)

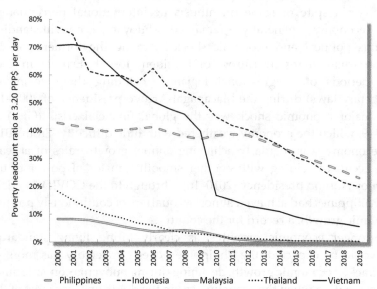

Note: Poverty estimates for Malaysia are based on income while the rest are based on consumption. Estimates for 2000–2019 are directly taken from PovCalNet with gaps filled using the same.

Source: PovCalNet, World Bank (http://iresearch.worldbank.org/PovcalNet/povOnDemand.aspx, accessed 1 September 2021).

That is, the provision of social safety nets, the system of public education and health, and access to employment opportunities.[16] We return to this issue below in the context of the COVID-19 pandemic.

6 DRIVERS OF GROWTH

Over this buoyant economic period, the Philippines' drivers of growth have differed from those of neighbouring economies and from the country's own growth path in earlier periods. The country has become a services-oriented economy while still in the lower middle-income group. Services now generate about 61 per cent of GDP, while agriculture's

---

[16] See, e.g., Clarete (2018) and Ravallion (2016). In addition, several other determining factors are relevant. These include changes in inequality (which has been relatively stable over this period), food prices, natural disasters and ease of access to relevant global labour markets.

share has shrunk to just 9 per cent. The share of manufacturing, currently about 18 per cent, has been stagnant or declining since the early 1970s, whereas in the late import-substitution era it peaked at 27 per cent.[17] Does this matter? In this section, we explore this issue with reference to two key dimensions of manufacturing and services.

First, manufacturing. The declining manufacturing share reflects the country's trade reforms, which lowered the incentives for the sector (and measured its value added at closer to international prices). It also tells us something about the competitiveness of tradable goods activities. A proxy indicator of international competitiveness in manufactures is the country's share of some key manufactures in global markets. To illustrate, we choose electronics parts and components, final electronic products, garments and footwear. These have been the backbone of the successful early-stage East Asian export-oriented industrialization drives, on the basis of a comparative advantage in the production of (unskilled and semi-skilled) labour-intensive activities. Table 2.3 reports these shares for the Philippines and four ASEAN comparators from 1990 to 2019.[18] Most countries have been losing their market share owing to the rise of China. However, the Philippines had performed quite strongly during the 1990s' decade of policy reform, with its share rising in electronics and garments. But in the twenty-first century, its shares have declined significantly, except for final electronics goods. By contrast, latecomer Vietnam has been the regional success story, with its shares rising dramatically in all three sectors. Indonesia's shares have also declined, while Malaysia and Thailand have remained competitive in electronics.

The declining electronics parts and components share of the Philippines is of some concern, as this is the dominant and fastest growing segment in the region's global production networks (GPNs), accounting for more than half of intra-ASEAN and intra-East Asian merchandise trade. The attraction of this sector is that its production activities span the factor intensity spectrum, from labour intensive to highly R&D and capital intensive. It is also open to newcomers

---

[17] In fact, the current share is even lower than that 60 years ago: in 1960 it was 25 per cent.
[18] We are grateful to Dr. Deasy Pane for kindly preparing these data.

Table 2.3. Comparative ASEAN manufactures export performance (1990–2019)

Global market shares (%)	1990	2000	2010	2019
Electronics parts and components				
Philippines	neg.	3.20	1.38	1.13
Indonesia	0.04	0.89	0.58	0.40
Malaysia	2.37	4.91	4.26	2.42
Thailand	1.24	2.06	2.78	1.93
Vietnam	neg.	0.13	0.48	3.87
Electronics final products				
Philippines	neg.	0.85	0.55	1.67
Indonesia	0.06	0.53	0.61	0.31
Malaysia	2.23	4.49	3.12	3.47
Thailand	0.78	1.74	1.77	1.24
Vietnam	neg.	0.01	0.33	3.01
Garments				
Philippines	0.67	1.40	0.33	0.22
Indonesia	1.65	2.60	2.04	1.93
Malaysia	1.30	1.22	1.15	1.26
Thailand	2.79	2.06	1.29	0.87
Vietnam	neg.	0.99	3.09	6.87
Footwear				
Philippines	0.29	0.22	0.01	0.09
Indonesia	2.08	4.60	3.08	3.34
Malaysia	neg.	neg.	neg.	neg.
Thailand	2.75	2.24	1.02	0.43
Vietnam	neg.	4.17	6.49	14.20

Note: "neg." denotes a non-zero but negligible share.
Source: UN Comtrade Database, United Nations (https://comtrade.un.org/, accessed 1 September 2021).

(like Vietnam and even Cambodia) including high-quality international logistics, open trade regime (at least in an export zone, if not economy wide), and liberal foreign investment and labour regimes.[19]
Does this indifferent industrial performance matter? It is beyond the scope of our paper to examine this intriguing question in any detail. Suffice it to note here that there are "yes", "no" and "maybe" answers to the question. According to one influential school (e.g., Lin 2017), rapid industrialization is an indispensable characteristic of successful economic development for almost all developing countries, as it provides mass employment opportunities for a semi-skilled workforce and creates opportunities for technological acquisition and other externalities. An alternative argument posits that the sectoral sources of economic growth are unimportant; what matters is the aggregate rate of growth. The Philippines' record of strong growth in recent decades lends at least some support to the latter proposition. Nevertheless, the failure to introduce the requisite (and relatively uncomplicated) reforms to facilitate a stronger manufactures export performance has meant that the country has been missing out on major investment and employment opportunities. Moreover, a plausible conjecture is that the comparatively low Philippine growth-poverty elasticity can be attributed in part to the stagnant manufacturing employment growth, at least prior to 2010.[20]

By contrast, the Philippines' service exports have performed strongly, mainly because of the vibrant business process outsourcing (BPO) operations. While traditional trade theory focuses on developing countries' comparative advantage in labour-intensive activities, in reality a more nuanced approach distinguishes between manufactures and services, in part because the latter requires more direct person-to-person contact. And it is in services where the Philippines' competitive strengths are clearly evident. Historically, this overwhelmingly took the form of overseas employment, seafarers, entertainment, nursing, domestic services and much else.[21]

---

[19] See Athukorala, this volume, chapter 10, who explains all these issues and includes some illustrative Philippine material. He characterizes the Philippine record as one of "arrested growth".
[20] See, e.g., Fabella (2018) and PHDR (2021).
[21] The one major exception is tourism, where the positive attraction of the legendary Philippine hospitality has been nullified by inadequate infrastructure and some lingering security concerns.

But an important, mainly twenty-first century, development has been the provision of international back-office services, in which the Philippines has become a major international player. The factors explaining this development, on both the supply and demand sides, are well-known. The digital economy revolution has enabled the rapid international off-shoring of many office accounting and customer-service activities. With its supply of well-educated, English-speaking college graduates, the Philippines was able to seize these opportunities, particularly in the US market, and is now the developing world's second largest supplier, behind India only.

A useful analytical framework for thinking about these internationally traded service exports is to view them in the context of the two mobile factors of production: capital and labour. When the Philippine economy was underperforming, there was little foreign investment; thus, workers were forced to seek employment abroad — that is, labour went in search of "capital". But thanks to the recent more conducive business environment, the country has been attracting capital, so the imperative to seek employment abroad has diminished. Figure 2.3 provides a simple illustration of this phenomenon by comparing remittances (i.e., the former flow) and BPO earnings, which is a proxy for capital entering the country in search of labour. The data clearly show that BPO earnings (which are almost entirely exports) have been closing the gap on remittances. In 2006, they were equivalent to 18 per cent of remittances; by 2018 they had increased to 73 per cent. Of course, the comparison is more complicated than this, in that the two activities tap into different labour market segments and international BPO flows have been rising faster than remittances. But the orders of magnitude are striking and indicative of the rising commercial attractiveness of the Philippines, in this sector at least.

The Philippines has frequently been the fourth largest developing country recipient of remittances. Therefore, it has sometimes been labelled as a "remittance economy", implying that it no longer has the capacity to generate the requisite domestic employment opportunities, and that it will suffer a permanent loss of talent. Such characterization has always been an exaggeration; international labour mobility is simply another manifestation of globalization (and rising labour shortages in the ageing rich economies). But for periods, the Philippine brain drain had been arguably of some concern. The BPO story constitutes a reassuring rebuttal of this issue.

Figure 2.3. Comparison of BPO revenues and OFW remittances (2006–18)

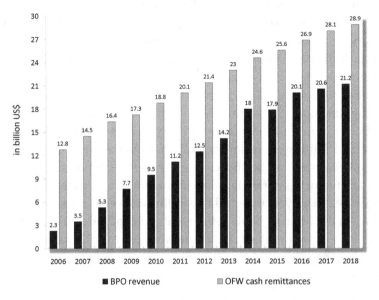

Source: External Accounts Statistics, Bangko Sentral ng Pilipinas (https://www.bsp.gov.ph/SitePages/Statistics/External.aspx?TabId=3, accessed 1 September 2021).

7 THE COVID-19 CRISIS

Had this paper been written in 2019 we would have ended on a cautiously optimistic note, concluding that there was every possibility that the strong economic momentum of the past decade would be maintained. However, the COVID-19 pandemic of 2020–21, and possibly beyond, has introduced a major discontinuity in our narrative. This is a perfect illustration of Kay and King's (2020) "radical uncertainty", an off-the-scale global event that was completely unforeseen (except perhaps in the realms of speculative epidemiology). It is the first major global pandemic in a century and the most serious setback to the peacetime global economy in 90 years. It has tested every aspect of government and society everywhere, from the frontline health system and macroeconomic management to the administrative apparatus and societal cohesion.

The Philippines has been particularly hit hard by the pandemic. By early September 2021, it has had an estimated 2.35 million COVID-19 cases and almost 37,000 fatalities. Both numbers are thought to be significant underestimates.[22] The economy has been plunged into a deep depression, with the GDP contracting by over 9 per cent in 2020. This is the most serious economic crisis in the country since independence, and first significant economic contraction in 34 years—itself an indicator of the country's stronger economic fundamentals in recent decades. It is also the country's largest growth collapse, from peak to trough of 15 per cent. Poverty and unemployment have risen significantly; there are major scarring effects in education and the labour market, and inequality is likely to have deteriorated. Large numbers of Philippine seafarers and other overseas Filipino workers (OFWs) have been left stranded, many experiencing dire conditions. The government has not undertaken the regular household expenditure surveys (i.e., Family Income and Expenditure Survey) at the time of this writing. In the interim, Table 2.4 presents a set of indicative estimates based on the growth rates for 2020 and forecast for 2021, assuming no change in inequality. Among the three countries, the poverty impacts are most severe in the Philippines, reflecting its larger GDP decline.

Table 2.4. *Comparative headcount poverty estimates (2019–21)*

Country	Poverty headcount ratio at 3.2 PPP$ per day (%)		
	2019	2020	2021
Philippines	23.06	29.96	27.86
Indonesia	19.95	23.89	22.44
Vietnam	5.69	5.53	4.64

Note: Poverty estimates for 2019 are directly taken from PovCalNet while those for 2020 and 2021 are computed using the same based on IMF July 2021 GDP forecasts and assuming that countries' Gini indices are unchanged.

Sources: Authors' estimates using PovCalNet and GDP projections from IMF; PovCalNet, World Bank (http://iresearch.worldbank.org/PovCalNet/povOnDemand.aspx, accessed 1 September 2021).

World Economic Outlook Update July 2021, International Monetary Fund (https://www.imf.org/-/media/Files/Publications/WEO/2021/Update/July/English/data/WEOJuly2021update.ashx, accessed 1 September 2021).

---

[22] See, for example, the methodology and estimates prepared by *The Economist* (www.economist.com/ExcessDeaths).

Moreover, the Philippines experienced the deepest economic recession among the seven middle-income Asian economies (Table 2.5), more severe even than the widely publicized Indian case. Its GDP decline was three times as large as the global figure. Its COVID-19 fatality rate has also been high, although not as high as India and Indonesia. The contrast with the highly successful Vietnam case is notable (successful with control measures at least in 2020). Vietnam closed its borders quickly, has had effective and consistent official messaging, and prompt quarantine and contact-tracing responses to localized flare-ups.[23] In all three respects, the Philippines has struggled, exacerbated by weaknesses in the decentralized, under-funded public health system. This has been the case despite its stringent lockdown measures, comparable in intensity to those of China and India. The stop-go relaxation of lockdown measures has also aggravated the problems.

In other respects, the impacts and outcomes of the COVID-19 pandemic have been more or less as expected. The government embarked on fiscal stimulus measures, financed in large part through unconventional monetary policy. As in most developing countries, these were relatively modest in scale (Figure 2.4). In any case, lax monetary policy is a necessary but not sufficient condition for addressing a health pandemic (Monsod and Gochoco-Bautista 2021). The sectoral impacts were highly uneven: employment fell sharply in "high-contact" sectors, such as accommodation, food services, tourism and transportation, but much less in low-contact activities, most notably agriculture and internet-based services (Figure 2.5). Remittances held up relatively well, as in previous crisis episodes. The BPO sector was only mildly affected, again reflecting its low-contact nature. Viewed in the regional context, Indonesia is arguably the most relevant comparator, given the similar geographies and political systems. Yet, in spite of the latter's muddle-through response to the pandemic (Hill 2021), its economic crisis in 2020 was much milder. Much therefore remains to be explained in the evolving Philippine situation.

---

[23] See, for example, https://asiafoundation.org/2021/05/26/covid-19-in-vietnam-holding-our-breath-in-wave-four.

Table 2.5. Comparative impacts of the COVID-19 pandemic

Country	COVID-19 cases per million	COVID-19 deaths per million	Share of population vaccinated (%)	Average lockdown stringency	2020 GDP growth estimate (%)	2021 GDP growth forecast (%)
Philippines	18,046.02	301.97	16.8	70.9	-9.6	5.4
Indonesia	14,836.13	483.70	22.8	64.9	-2.1	3.9
Malaysia	53,850.55	516.90	60.2	65.6	-5.6	4.7
Thailand	17,354.39	169.28	33.5	56.0	-6.1	2.1
Vietnam	4,823.63	120.89	17.7	64.8	2.9	6.5
China	65.77	3.21	74.3	72.6	2.3	8.1
India	23,547.17	315.07	35.7	71.9	-7.3	9.5
World	27,731.36	576.85	39.6	n.a.	-3.2	6.0

Note: (1) "COVID-19 cases per million" and "COVID-19 deaths per million" only include confirmed cases and deaths, respectively.
(2) "Share of population vaccinated" denotes share of population who have received at least one dose of a COVID-19 vaccine.
(3) "Average lockdown stringency index" denotes average lockdown stringency index, as computed by Oxford University, from the time of first imposition of a movement restriction to 1 September 2021.

Sources: Our World in Data, Global Change Data Lab (https://ourworldindata.org/coronavirus, accessed 1 September 2021). World Economic Outlook Update July 2021, International Monetary Fund (https://www.imf.org/-/media/Files/Publications/WEO/2021/Update/July/English/data/WEOJuly2021update.ashx, accessed 1 September 2021).

Figure 2.4. Comparative COVID-19 stimulus spending

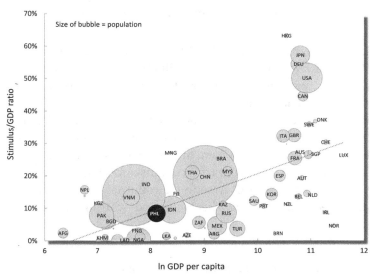

Note: "Stimulus-to-GDP ratio" denotes the total amount of liquidity support, credit creation, direct long-term lending, equity support, and health and income support provided by the government as of 15 June 2021 as a percentage of real GDP in 2019.

Sources: ADB COVID-19 Policy Database, Asian Development Bank (https://covid19policy.adb.org; accessed 15 June 2021); World Development Indicators, World Bank (https://databank.worldbank.org/source/world-development-indicators, accessed 15 June 2021).

Figure 2.5. Change in employment in high-contact sectors vs. low-contact sectors (January 2020 and January 2021)

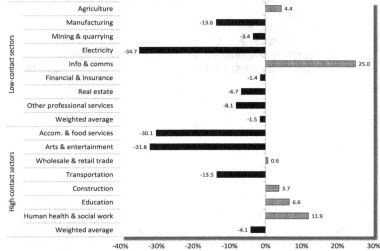

Source: Labor Force Surveys, Philippine Statistics Authority (https://psa.gov.ph/statistics/survey/labor-force/lfs-index, accessed 15 June 2021).

8 BEYOND COVID-19: ELEMENTS OF A REFORM AGENDA

As the world transitions from the COVID-19 pandemic emergency to a likely era of recurring endemic conditions, Philippine policymakers will be in a position to focus on the economic recovery agenda. This necessarily encompasses a broad mix of factors, including both a return to the pre-COVID-19 reform challenges and an additional set of underlying challenges that were accentuated by the pandemic. Figure 2.6 provides a useful indicative comparative schema that highlights not only the seriousness of the country's circumstances but also some major policy issues going forward. Among the countries, the Philippines has the largest economic decline, health-related scarring and economic-financial crisis legacies.[24]

Figure 2.6. Long-term COVID-19 vulnerability index

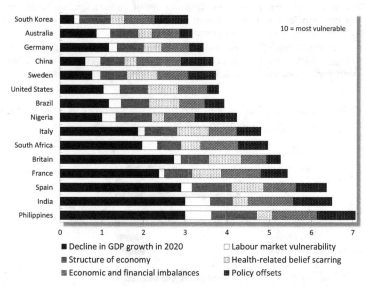

Source: Oxford Economics (2020, as cited in *The Economist* 2020).

---

[24] These estimates were prepared by Oxford Economics, as reported in *The Economist* (15 December 2020). For further explanation of the assumptions and methodologies, see https://www.economist.com/graphic-detail/2020/12/15/which-economies-are-most-vulnerable-to-covid-19s-long-term-effects. The Nikkei COVID-19 Recovery Index reaches a similar conclusion, ranking the Philippines 106 (lowest) out of 120 countries.

In this section, we identify and briefly discuss seven interrelated areas of major public policy focus. This list is neither original nor definitive. But we do believe that the items in it will be central to determining whether, and how quickly, the Philippines can return to its pre-COVID-19 economic dynamism.

8.1 Macroeconomic management

This has been a major policy success of the Philippines in the democratic era. A professional and independent central bank, the BSP, was established in 1991, enabling the country to navigate successive economic shocks, until the 2020 pandemic crisis. In contrast to the boom-and-bust growth patterns through to the mid-1980s, the country has not had a single balance of payments crisis for almost 30 years, despite two major external crises (the AFC and GFC), a decade of volatile global monetary conditions since the GFC, and periods of domestic political turbulence. It is no exaggeration to state that this is arguably the country's most important policy reform during the democratic era. The work of the BSP has also been supported by greater fiscal prudence for most of this period, and a better supervised financial system.

This greater macroeconomic prudence resulted in the Philippines having substantial economic buffers as the COVID-19 crisis hit.[25] It had more fiscal and monetary policy space than many developing economies, and it was able to embark on both a substantial fiscal stimulus (at least by developing country standards) and lax monetary policy settings without unduly alarming international financial markets. The government's two major fiscal packages in 2020 were the equivalent of almost 5 per cent of GDP, while the BSP lowered interest rates progressively by two percentage points, as well as eased bank reserve requirements and did other monetary loosening measures (IMF 2021). The BSP also effectively navigated through the period of financial market volatility in March 2020. It followed international practice by resorting to unconventional monetary policy measures that involved the purchase of government securities on the secondary market.

---

[25] For example, according to one widely referred to set of pre-crisis macroeconomic vulnerability indicators, the Philippines ranked sixth lowest (that is least vulnerable) among 66 developing countries. (See the set of indicators in *The Economist*, 2 May 2020.)

As the pandemic is brought under control and economic recovery sets in, there will need to be a return to fiscal and monetary policy orthodoxy. Large fiscal deficits during emergency periods with exceptionally low global interest rates make sense, but it is important that these deficits do not become embedded in the Philippine political economy. In 2020, the government ran a fiscal deficit of 7.6 per cent of GDP, which is likely to rise further in the near future. As a result, public debt rose from a comfortable 37 per cent of GDP immediately prior to the pandemic to 52 per cent at the end of 2020, with further increases inevitable. Though hardly alarming, these large deficits will need to have a cap, before they become politically irresistible. Moreover, global interest rates will eventually normalize, possibly suddenly as in the 2013 "taper tantrum" episode. The political appetite for extravagant spending inevitably invites waste and corruption. In recent memory, the country's senior policymakers have experienced the trauma of capital flight, sharply rising country risk premiums and IMF rescue packages. It would be a tragedy to undermine the country's hard-won reputation for fiscal probity and the BSP's independence and professionalism.

8.2 Economic openness

More open economic policies have been gradually introduced since the late 1980s, overturning the earlier and prolonged period of comprehensive import substitution. The merchandise trade regime, in particular, has become more open, driven by the intensive and prolonged analytical work undertaken by many of the country's leading economists, which gradually penetrated the policy and business worlds and found political champions.[26] Even reform in the highly politicized rice sector is finally underway as the process of tariffication of trade barriers proceeds (Tolentino and de la Peña, this volume, chapter 7).

Reform at the borders has been accompanied by reform behind borders. Major microeconomic reforms that dismantled long-established monopolies were introduced during the Ramos

---

[26] See Bautista and Tecson (2003) and Sicat (2014). Romeo Bautista and Gerardo Sicat have long been influential advocates of trade policy reform, both in their writings and being senior government officials.

presidency, and these have been maintained. Fortunately, the traditionally closed telecommunications sector was liberalized just in time for the country to exploit opportunities in internationally traded services in that sector. Without them, the BPO success story would not have been possible.

More recently, competition reforms were reinforced with the passage of the Philippine Competition Act (PCA) in 2015 and the consequent establishment of the Philippine Competition Commission (PCC) the following year. This development is significant considering that, while a comprehensive competition law and policy have been recognized as a key component of the country's economic reform agenda, it took Congress a quarter of a century to pass what would eventually become the PCA. The long delay reflects the political influence of the oligarchs and interest groups representing highly concentrated industries and markets with significant barriers to entry. Then President Benigno Aquino used his political capital to put in place this critical missing element of the reform agenda to promote a level playing field in the marketplace, thereby sustaining the economic momentum and making growth more inclusive.

Nevertheless, reform of the trade and investment regimes remains incomplete. As Table 2.6 illustrates, the Philippines is a less open economy than several of its neighbours. Pockets of resistance to trade liberalization persist, mainly in agriculture and services. The foreign investment regime remains one of the most restrictive in developing Asia, according to the OECD's FDI policy index—as Gerardo Sicat has frequently noted, in part owing to constitutional restrictions on foreign ownership. As a result, realized FDI is considerably lower than most of its neighbours. This factor explains why, since around 2000, the country has been missing out on extensive commercial opportunities in the dominant global production networks of East Asia, as is evident in Table 2.3 above and is explained in great detail by Athukorala, this volume, chapter 10.[27]

---

[27] There is some tangential evidence that Philippine start-ups lag some neighbouring economies. The hypothesis is that the restrictive FDI regime and the alleged entrenched power of conglomerates have been stifling factors. This interesting avenue for future research is the subject of frequent commentary in the financial press. See, for example, https://www.ft.com/content/aa5a3394-f775-490b-b4ff-d8f7573138e0?desktop=true&segmentId=7c8f09b9-9b61-4fbb-9430-9208a9e233c8#myft:notification:daily-email:content.

Table 2.6. Comparative economic openness (2019)

Country	Trade/GDP (%)	Weighted average tariff rate (%)		FDI stock/GDP (inward, %)	FDI restrictiveness index (1 = closed)
		All products	Primary products		
Philippines	68.84	1.68	4.00	24.10	0.37
Indonesia	37.45	2.00	2.57	20.50	0.35
Malaysia	123.00	4.02	3.52	46.07	0.25
Thailand	109.63	3.52	5.72	46.94	0.27
Vietnam	210.40	1.66	2.71	60.98	0.13
China	35.84	2.53	1.64	12.44	0.24
India	39.39	6.59	5.72	13.95	0.21

Note: Tariff rate data for Thailand and Malaysia are from 2015 and 2016, respectively.

Sources: World Development Indicators, World Bank (https://databank.worldbank.org/source/world-development-indicators, accessed 1 September 2021).

Organisation for Economic Co-operation and Development (https://data.oecd.org/fdi/fdi-restrictiveness.htm, accessed 1 September 2021).

8.3 Institutions and governance

Building stronger and more resilient institutions is a long-term process. Here, too, the Philippines has made some progress, albeit with a substantial ongoing reform agenda. The most important achievement has, of course, been the introduction of democratic reforms, resulting in the establishment of reasonably open and competitive political processes at both the national and local levels, since 1986 and 1992, respectively. All six presidents in the post-Marcos era have enjoyed democratic legitimacy, with the controversial exception of President Macapagal-Arroyo's assumption of power in 2001. Since around 1990, the military has returned to the barracks, with every prospect forever. Relatively independent professional agencies in key policy areas, such as the BSP and the PCC, have been established.

To be sure, this is an evolutionary process, as the extensive Philippine literature has emphasized.[28] Dynastic politics remains a powerful force at all levels of government. Political patronage and corruption remain

---

[28] See, for example, De Dios and Williamson (2015), Capuno (2020), Fabella (2018), Mendoza and Olfindo (2018), and Mendoza et al. (2015).

ever-present challenges. There has yet to be a sweeping reform of the civil service. Although the Philippines is in some respects a "weak state" (for example, as measured by its tax/GDP ratio), the power of popular presidents is such that they can introduce far-reaching policy decisions unilaterally, with limited checks and balances. For example, as Deinla and Reyes (2021) put it, judicial politics appear to have been driven as much by decisions taken by powerful political interests as by the Supreme Court itself. Furthermore, whilst geographically localized, peace in the decades-long conflict zones of Mindanao appears to be as elusive as ever (Hutchcroft 2016). And while the media is comparatively open, it has been the subject of frequent political assaults. Various international media monitors—for instance, the RSF's (Reporters Without Borders) World Press Freedom Index—have regularly ranked the Philippines as a comparatively unsafe country for journalists.

Writing two decades ago, primarily with reference to the reformist Ramos presidency, De Dios and Hutchcroft (2003, 57–59) identified four areas of reform (our summary of their arguments in parentheses): economic liberalization (substantial); stronger institutional foundations for development (difficult, some progress); redistributive measures and transfers (some progress, albeit slow and uneven); and reform of political and democratic structures (limited, and where the president "consistently had to rely on old-style pork barrel politics in order to promote new-style economics", p. 58). With the exception of the third area, where the reforms appear to be durable, their characterization of the country's institutional development is broadly applicable to current-day Philippines.

Measuring institutional quality is an inherently hazardous, subjective and controversial exercise. The relationship between institutional development and economic development is obviously an interactive one with bidirectional causality (contrary to the "institutions rule" school of thought). With these caveats, among the extensive menu of offerings, the World Governance Indicators (WGI) are the most widely used indicators. They are comparative, comprehensive, available over a reasonably long period and accessible to public scrutiny. They also attempt to "unpack" institutions into diverse components: voice and accountability, political stability, government effectiveness, regulatory quality, control of corruption and rule of law. Figure 2.7 presents the results for the Philippines and four ASEAN neighbours over the period 1996–2019.

Figure 2.7. Comparative ASEAN governance indicators (1996–2019)

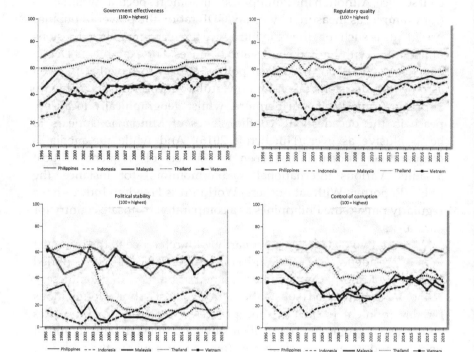

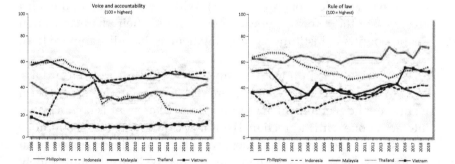

Source: World Development Indicators, World Bank (https://databank.worldbank.org/source/world-development-indicators, accessed 1 September 2021).

The indicators for the Philippines are fairly stable, generally as expected and mostly accord with priors. The rankings for economic governance indicators are typically similar to other countries in this income group. Along with Indonesia, the Philippines ranks highest for political governance (the voice and accountability indicator, in particular), apart from the period of political turbulence early in the twenty-first century and the recent decline. The country ranks rather low on government effectiveness and rule of law, but somewhat higher on regulatory quality and control of corruption. An obvious limitation of these indicators during the pandemic is that they miss key vulnerabilities related to a specific crisis. As argued above, for example, the Philippine record of macroeconomic management has been competent, but weaknesses in the public health system have been very evident.

For what the data are worth, therefore, the major conclusion is that democracy has been sustained, but it has yet to deliver a significant improvement in overall institutional quality, particularly in economic governance. Reassuringly, this is consistent with the literature referred to in footnote 28.

8.4 Accelerating the transition to the digital economy

The COVID-19 pandemic has highlighted the crucial importance of the digital economy; it also greatly accelerated its use. Internet usage has a dominant presence in the Philippines, from the BPO sector to various forms of social media that bring together the vast international Filipino diaspora. The country is reportedly one of the world's highest users of Facebook on a per capita basis. During the crisis, the internet became indispensable everywhere for remotely running offices and households and enabling communities to stay in touch with each other while in lockdown. People have been able to work, go to school and shop from home. While the face-to-face contact will resume after the pandemic, many of these trends are now entrenched and will define much of the future economic and societal intercourse.

The challenge for the Philippines is to ensure that the benefits of the digital economy are available to everybody, regardless of socio-economic status, occupation and geographical location. Currently, they are not. The pandemic has exposed and highlighted the country's large digital divide. Manila's middle-class households may have been able to work from home, have their children educated via the internet, avail of tele-health, and have food delivered to their doorstep, but poor households in Western Mindanao—and many other regions—have not been as fortunate. The adults have been forced to work outside the house, exposing them to heightened health risks, and the children have missed out on schooling, both because of weak or non-existent home internet (and electricity, in many cases) and because the public school they attend does not have the resources to quickly adapt to digital learning. In other words, the digital divide has exacerbated the country's pre-existing socio-economic and spatial inequalities.

The Philippine digital economy is unrecognizable from that of 30 years ago when Singapore Prime Minister Lee acerbically quipped that "98% of Filipinos are waiting for a telephone, and the other 2% are waiting for a dial tone." As noted, the country has been able to support one of the developing world's most vibrant and innovative BPO sectors. But it is underperforming on both efficiency and equity grounds. Table 2.7 provides some comparisons with other middle-income ASEAN countries. The Philippines has the lowest internet penetration, well below all but Indonesia. Its fixed broadband network has limited coverage, is costly and slow compared with all of its neighbours, except Indonesia. Its mobile network performs better, but still lags behind ASEAN middle-income best practice. Moreover, these figures do not draw out the inequality of internet provision, both between households and within the business sector and between the major corporates and small and medium-sized enterprises. For instance, the 2019 survey of the Philippine Statistics Authority found that internet access is 20 percentage points higher in urban than in rural areas. The difference is even larger—roughly 40 percentage points—between the National Capital Region (NCR) and the country's poorest region, the Bangsamoro Autonomous Region.

Central to the digital reform agenda is a policy framework that treats digital access analogously to universal public utilities and services. That is, the entire population should be entitled to quality internet services in the same way that it is entitled to at least basic literacy skills and access to a road and port network. The enabling technology is already available to meet such an objective. A first-best solution is arguably a competitive telecommunications service, overseen by a regulator that guards against anticompetitive behaviour. In this context, the entry of a third telecommunications supplier and the enactment of a "portability" law are a welcome start. This development needs to be complemented by a comprehensive open-access reform involving data transmission services, spectrum management, and rules on firms with substantial market power in the telecom industry.

Table 2.7. Comparative ASEAN internet statistics

Country	Total			Fixed broadband			Mobile broadband	
	Population with internet access (%)	Subscribers per 100 people	Cost per GB (PPP$)	Global speed rank	Subscribers per 100 people	Cost per GB (PPP$)	Global speed rank	
Philippines	43.00	5.48	12.96	62nd	*68.44	7.48	75th
Indonesia	47.70	3.80	19.93	116th	81.21	8.09	104th
Malaysia	84.20	9.28	9.96	47th	126.55	13.87	89th
Thailand	66.70	14.52	9.89	7th	86.68	11.77	48th
Vietnam	68.70	15.35	4.74	59th	72.46	4.19	58th

Note: (1) "Global speed rank" denotes global ranking in terms of internet download speed as of June 2021, as determined by the Speedtest Global Index.
(2) The rest of data used are from the International Telecommunication Union (ITU) database 2019 update, except for "Mobile broadband subscribers per 100 people" for the Philippines, which is from 2017.
(3) Data on fixed broadband cost at 5GB and mobile broadband cost at 1.5GB were rebased at 1GB ("cost per GB") for comparison.

Sources: ICT Statistics, International Telecommunication Union (https://www.itu.int/en/ITU-D/Statistics/Pages/stat/default.aspx, accessed 1 September 2021)
Speedtest Global Index, Ookla (https://www.speedtest.net/global-index, accessed 1 September 2021).

In addition, measures are needed to facilitate access for low-income and remote households, through direct subsidy, community service obligations or some other arrangements.

8.5 Transforming the health sector

The COVID-19 crisis has starkly illustrated the old adage that societies are "only as strong as their weakest link". Strong, inclusive public health systems and universal access to at least basic healthcare are therefore central to the management of the pandemic, and future pandemics.

The crisis has highlighted well-known vulnerabilities in the Philippine health system. The strength of the country's top-end medical education system is illustrated by the huge number of Philippine health professionals working abroad. The sizeable pockets of cost-effective, international-quality medical services have supported the country's growing "medical tourism" industry. However, the bottom third of the urban population and the majority of the rural areas rely on a weak, underfunded, decentralized public health system. Not surprisingly, the public health system was quickly overwhelmed at the onset of the pandemic, even as the country, like the rest of the world, imposed lockdowns to contain the spread of infections. Evidently, short-term measures cannot address decades of underinvestment in the health system and governance issues. More than a year and a half after the initial lockdowns, the country continues to struggle with comparatively high rates of infections and deaths. The indications are that the country's capacity to test, trace and treat infections remains a huge challenge. Limited supply and local-national government and public-private sector coordination issues have also hampered a quick implementation of an effective vaccination programme.

In their comprehensive pre-pandemic survey of the Philippine health sector, Banzon and Ho (2018) recognize the gradual improvements in the country's health indicators, but point to many challenges, some of which became evident during the pandemic. They argue that "what seems to be lacking is a clearly articulated, aspirational and unified vision for the system" (p. 204). They also document the spatial and socio-economic inequalities. For example, the top quintile of households and the wealthiest region (NCR) have infant mortality rates that are similar to those of much wealthier countries, while the lowest quintile and poorest regions have rates that resemble very low-income countries. Poor households also face out-of-pocket expenses that are frequently prohibitive.

Table 2.8 provides some comparative health indicators. The disability-adjusted life expectancy in the Philippines has been slowly improving for both males and females, while total health expenditure per capita and its share in total government expenditure are similar to comparable middle-income countries (but less than half that of Thailand). As a proportion of total health spending, the country's out-of-pocket health expenditures is one of the highest. This arises because PhilHealth is only able to cover a fraction of the cost of hospital care—about 35–40 per cent in government hospitals and lower in private hospitals—and poorer households have little or no top-up private health insurance.

The Philippine health system is therefore clearly in need of a major reform, recognizing also that there are no "quick fixes". As Banzon and Ho (2018) point out, it needs more resources, a clearer delineation of functions between the national and local governments and between the public and private sectors, and a special focus on high-burden diseases such as tuberculosis. Given the public-good nature of health conditions, there needs to be greater attention to equitable health outcomes to ensure universal access to essential health services. Health-service provision also needs to be more closely integrated with the national system of social protection.

Table 2.8. Comparative ASEAN health indicators

Country	Health-adjusted life expectancy		Total health spending per capita (PPP$)	Total health spending (% of GDP)	Out-of-pocket expenditure (% of total)
	Male	Female			
Philippines	60.1	63.9	393.9	4.4	53.85
Indonesia	61.9	63.8	375.2	2.9	34.85
Malaysia	64.5	66.9	1,193.9	3.8	35.12
Thailand	65.9	70.6	722.7	3.8	11.01
Vietnam	62.4	68.3	440.2	5.9	44.90

Note: (1) "Health-adjusted life expectancy" denotes the average number of years that a person can expect to live in "full health" by taking into account years lived in less than full health due to disease and/or injury.
(2) The reference year for "health-adjusted life expectancy" is 2019 while the remaining statistics are from 2018.

Sources: Global Health Observatory, World Health Organization (https://www.who.int/data, accessed 1 September 2021).
World Development Indicators, World Bank (https://databank.worldbank.org/source/world-development-indicators, accessed 1 September 2021).

8.6 Rebuilding the educational system and overcoming scarring

In a society with persistently high levels of wealth and income inequality, education has always been the key to social mobility in the Philippines. The country continues to have among the region's highest enrolment ratios at all levels. This educational strength, combined with widespread English-language proficiency, has underpinned the country's strength in internationally traded services, from BPOs to international employment. Compared with its middle-income neighbours, the Philippines continues to perform quite well on some education indicators, including expenditure levels and school completion rates (Table 2.9). However, it lags on quality indicators, in most cases by a significant margin. The OECD's Programme for International Student Assessment (PISA) test scores for maths, science and reading in Table 2.9[29] show that the Philippines ranks the lowest in all three areas; the gap between latecomer Vietnam is particularly pronounced.

Table 2.9.   Comparative ASEAN education indicators

Country	Basic education spending (% of GDP)	Basic education completion rate (%)	PISA mean performance		
			Mathematics	Science	Reading
Philippines	3.6	78.3	352.6	339.7	356.9
Indonesia	2.6	63.2	378.7	371.0	396.1
Malaysia	2.1	n.a.	440.2	415.0	437.6
Thailand	2.4	57.4	418.6	392.9	425.8
Vietnam	3.6	55.1	495.7	504.5	543.4

Note: (1) "Basic education spending" refers to the total amount spent on primary and secondary education as a percentage of total GDP.
(2) "Basic education completion rate" denotes the number of persons in the relevant age group who have completed the last grade of the given level of education and is expressed as a percentage of the total population (in the survey sample) of the same age group.
(3) Reference years for the basic education completion rate are as follows: Philippines (2018), Indonesia (2017), Thailand (2016) and Vietnam (2014), while all data points for basic education spending and PISA mean performance are from 2018.

Source: EdStats, World Bank (https://databank.worldbank.org/source/education-statistics-%5E-all-indicators, accessed 1 September 2021).

---

[29] The comparative rankings for TIMMS, the other major international testing programme, are broadly similar.

The key contemporary challenge is to maintain what remains of the educational advantage, as other countries aspire to catch up. The authoritative analysis by Villamil (2018) identifies several areas where the country's educational advantage is eroding, and where "greater effort" is required: broadening educational access, especially for the poor; raising educational quality at all levels; improved pedagogic techniques, making the system more relevant to a rapidly changing, globalized economy; and greater emphasis on innovation. With regard to the first of these challenges, schooling cohort survival rates vary sharply across socio-economic classes, while tertiary education is typically beyond the reach of poor families. The school system also needs to be fully integrated with the conditional cash transfer programme to address the problem of dropouts among poor families.

The pandemic has brought these underlying problems into sharp relief. As noted, unequal internet access has exacerbated pre-existing inequalities. Many children without effectively functioning home internet, or enrolled in a school that is unable to make provision for home schooling, have missed out on over a year's schooling. Given that only four of every ten Filipinos have access to the internet, the vast majority of children, especially in rural areas, have lost schooling opportunities. The loss is very likely to result in a permanent loss of lifetime human capital as these children will enter the labour market on a permanently lower skills trajectory. According to the ADB's estimates covering the period February 2020–April 2021, students from developing Asia stand to lose from the pandemic-induced school closure an average of US$180 per year, or about a 2.4 per cent decline in their future productivity and lifetime earnings.[30,31] As widely reported in the media,[32] given that the Philippines has had one of the most prolonged and severe school closures, and that the lockdowns are likely to extend throughout 2021, this is likely to be an underestimate.

---

[30] See ADB "Learning and Earning Losses from COVID-19 School Closures in Developing Asia", a Special Topic of ADB.

[31] In a similar vein, according to World Bank estimates for Latin America, the ten months of lost schooling will result in an average loss of lifetime earnings of US$24,000 in these countries. See "Latin America's silent tragedy", *The Economist* (19 June 2021).

[32] See, for example, "With Schools Closed, Covid-19 Deepens a Philippine Education Crisis", *The New York Times* (13 September 2021).

8.7 More effective social protection

The Philippine system of conditional cash transfers has been the country's major social policy innovation this century.[33] The *Pantawid Pamilyang Pilipino Program* (or 4Ps) is designed to overcome poverty by incentivizing poor households to keep their children in school and to avail of health services. As in its neighbours and most developing countries, these programmes are modest in scale and of relatively recent origin. Table 2.10 provides an approximate comparative picture. According to these estimates, the Philippines spends less than 1 per cent of GDP on social assistance programmes, as do its middle-income neighbours. However, the transfers are significant for the recipients, equivalent to more than one-tenth of their incomes. The country's targeting also appears to be among the most effective in the region.

These programmes were designed to achieve incremental social improvements in an era of steady economic growth and sound fiscal settings. They were never designed to be a crash welfare programme when many households beyond the bottom 40 per cent group fell on hard times. Hence, the emergency fiscal stimulus measures of 2020 and 2021 had to employ quick disbursements, without recourse to the targeting and conditionality that are cornerstones of the 4Ps. In the post-COVID-19 environment, the major policy priority will be to revert to the pre-existing objectives and modalities, to develop a more comprehensive national identification system, and to continue to focus on improved targeting. Given the modest scale, expanded funding would also be desirable, while recognizing that the government's fiscal parameters will be constrained.

9 SUMMING UP

The 75 years of Philippine independence have witnessed incremental progress on the basis of some hard-learnt lessons of economic development and policy. Indeed, one of us has summarized the Philippine development imperative as follows: "We could not allow ourselves to be left behind, to remain a laggard in an otherwise highly dynamic, rapidly growing and prospering region.

---

[33] See, for example, Orbeta and Paqueo (2016) and World Bank (2021), and references cited therein.

Table 2.10. Comparative social assistance—coverage, extent and targeting

Country	Total spending/GDP (%)	Coverage (%)	Extent of benefits (%)	Extent of benefits (1st quintile, %)	Beneficiary incidence (1st quintile, %)	Benefit incidence (1st quintile, %)
Philippines	0.6	27.4	11.6	20.9	41.9	45.2
Indonesia	0.7	53.9	n.a.	n.a.	30.3	n.a.
Malaysia	0.7	82.8	1.7	6.5	22.7	20.8
Thailand	0.5	70.4	3.7	2.5	24.3	7.4
Vietnam	0.5	20.9	16.5	20.5	41.5	13.8
Developing EA&P	0.6	45.5	5.5	7.8	32.4	12.5

Note: (1) "Coverage" denotes percentage of population participating in social assistance programmes (including direct and indirect beneficiaries).
(2) "Extent of benefits" denotes total transfer amount received, as a share of the total welfare of recipients.
(3) "Beneficiary incidence, poorest quintile" denotes percentage of programme beneficiaries belonging to the poorest quintile (of the post-transfer welfare distribution).
(4) "Benefit incidence, poorest quintile" denotes the percentage of total programme benefits received by the poorest quintile.

Source: ASPIRE Database, World Bank (https://databank.worldbank.org/source/1229, accessed 1 September 2021).

We needed to reshape our future ..." (Balisacan 2018) This is a positive story of the country's polity and officials learning from the past, selectively absorbing policy advice, and innovating when the political space facilitated policy reform.

Prior to the COVID-19 pandemic, the economy was reliably achieving annual GDP growth rates of 5–6 per cent, or approximately 3–4 per cent in per capita terms. This was putting the country on course to graduate to the ranks of the upper middle-income group of countries in the very near future, and for membership in the high-income group to no longer be a remote possibility. A simple numeric calculation illustrates these assertions. In the absence of the COVID-19 crisis and assuming plausible lower and upper bound per capita GDP growth rates of 2 per cent and 4 per cent, respectively, the Philippines would have joined the upper middle-income group sometime between 2021 and 2023, and the high-income group between 2049 and 2079. Consistently faster growth rates will obviously bring these estimates forward.[34]

Gazing into the future, the economics profession admittedly has a poor track record of forecasting beyond the very short-run. The early promises of the growth econometrics literature have not been realized (Pritchett 2018). Nevertheless, there is general agreement on growth-conducive factors: more open economies generally grow faster; economies with prudent macroeconomic management are less crisis-prone, thus, the growth process is less likely to be interrupted; inclusive growth is more likely to generate more stable polities; and stronger institutions are more likely to provide the basis for open, participatory governance and economic security for investors. These highly stylized propositions provide the basis for our concluding narrative. We have argued that the Philippines increasingly parted company from its high-growth neighbours from the late 1970s owing to a combination of inward-looking economic policies, adventurous macroeconomic management, blatant cronyism and corruption, and a failure to address deep-seated inequalities. The economic revival starting in the 1990s has been achieved mainly because these obstacles to development have been at least partly addressed, especially the first two.

---

[34] These calculations are based on gross national income (GNI) estimates using the World Bank Atlas method of computation. The 2019 (arbitrary) cut-off points for the upper middle- and high-income groups were US$4,125 and US$12,536, respectively.

If we had completed this paper in 2019, we would have concluded on a cautiously optimistic note. Across the country's three major episodes over three-quarters of a century, there have been both continuities and changes. Change is obviously the key message of this paper: not just in the highly variable development outcomes, but more importantly, in the major policy lessons absorbed and the reforms they triggered. "From Evidence to Policy" is how the authors who summarized the work of the country's leading development policy research institute characterized the process (Llanto, Paqueo, and Orbeta 2018). To be sure, some of the continuities remain: deeply entrenched poverty, conflict, a relatively narrow economic base, sluggish formal sector employment growth and the complexities of bureaucratic reform, to name just a few. But these are not insuperable barriers, as the record of twenty-first century progress attests.

The challenge now is to overcome the COVID-19 pandemic as quickly as possible and to return to the pre-existing development trajectory. The pandemic has set the country back at least four years. That is, a 9 per cent decline in GDP (about 11% in per capita terms) is equivalent to three or four years of strong growth. So, the country is back to around 2016 income levels. It is unclear at the time of this writing how quickly the economy will recover. The relatively slow vaccination rollout and the serious global inequities between rich and poor countries in vaccine availability suggest that the recovery may be slow. Certainly, the country will have to deal with further "unknown unknowns", whether in the form of really serious regional geo-strategic conflict or catastrophic climate events. But if a society can recover from the seemingly hopeless outlook that prevailed in the Philippines in the mid-1980s, these challenges could also be overcome.

REFERENCES

ADB (Asian Development Bank). 2011. *Asia 2050: Realizing the Asian Century*. Manila: ADB.

———. 2021. *Asian Development Outlook 2021*. Manila: ADB.

Baldwin, R. E. 1975. *Foreign Trade Regimes and Economic Development: The Philippines*. New York: Oxford University Press for the NBER.

Balisacan, A. M. 2015. "The Growth-Poverty Nexus: Multidimensional Poverty in the Philippines". In *Sustainable Economic Development: Resources, Environment and Institutions*, edited by A. M. Balisacan, U. Chakravorty, and M. V. Ravago, pp. 445–68. Amsterdam: Elsevier.

———. 2018. "Foreword." In *The Philippine Economy: No Longer the East Asian Exception?* edited by R. L. Clarete, E. F. Esguerra, and H. Hill. Singapore: Institute of Southeast Asian Studies.

Balisacan, A. M., and H. Hill, eds. 2003. *The Philippine Economy: Development, Policies, and Challenges*. New York: Oxford University Press.

Banzon, E., and B. L. Ho. 2018, "Universal Health Coverage, Health Security and Resilient Health Systems". In *The Philippine Economy: No Longer the East Asian Exception?*, edited by R. L. Clarete, E. F. Esguerra, and H. Hill, pp. 190-230. Singapore: Institute of Southeast Asian Studies.

Bautista, R., and G. Tecson. 2003. "International Dimensions". In *The Philippine Economy: Development, Policies, and Challenges*, edited by A. M. Balisacan and H. Hill, pp. 136–71. New York: Oxford University Press.

Capuno, J. J. 2020. "Dutertenomics: Populism, Progress, and Prospects". *Asian Economic Policy Review* 15, no. 2: 262–79.

Clarete, R. L. 2018. "Economic Growth and Poverty Reduction". In *The Philippine Economy: No Longer the East Asian Exception?*, edited by R. L. Clarete, E. F. Esguerra, and H. Hill, pp. 53–111. Singapore: Institute of Southeast Asian Studies.

Clarete, R. L., E. F. Esguerra, and H. Hill, eds. 2018. *The Philippine Economy: No Longer the East Asian Exception?* Singapore: Institute of Southeast Asian Studies.

De Dios, E. S., and P. D. Hutchcroft. 2003. "Political Economy". In *The Philippine Economy: Development, Policies, and Challenges*, edited by A. M. Balisacan and H. Hill, pp. 45–73. New York: Oxford University Press.

De Dios, E. S., and J. G. Williamson. 2015. "Deviant Behavior: A Century of Philippine Industrialization". In *Sustainable Economic Development: Resources, Environment and Institutions*, edited by A. M. Balisacan, U. Chakravorty, and M. V. Ravago, pp. 371–99. Amsterdam: Elsevier.

Deinla, I., and M. L. Reyes. 2021. "The Politics of Impeachment and Judicial Leadership in the Philippine Supreme Court". Unpublished paper.

Dohner, R. S., and P. Intal. 1989. "The Marcos Legacy: Economic Policy and Foreign Debt in the Philippines". In *Developing Country Debt and Economic Performance*, volume 3, edited by J. D. Sachs and S. M. Collins, pp. 371–614. Chicago: University of Chicago Press.

Fabella, R. V. 2018. *Capitalism and Inclusion under Weak Institutions*. Diliman, Quezon City: University of the Philippines Center for Integrative Studies.

Golay, F. H. 1961. *The Philippines: Public Policy and National Economic Development*. Ithaca, NY: Cornell University Press.

Hill, H. 2021. "Indonesia and the COVID-19 Crisis: A Light at the End of the Tunnel?". In *Economic Dimensions of COVID-19 in Indonesia. Responding to the Crisis*, edited by B. D. Lewis and F. Witoelar, pp. 5–23. Singapore: Institute of Southeast Asian Studies.

Hooley, R. 1968. "Long-Term Economic Growth of the Philippine Economy, 1902–1961". *Philippine Economic Journal* 7, no. 1.

Hutchcroft, P. 1998. *Booty Capitalism: The Politics of Banking in the Philippines*. Ithaca, NY: Cornell University Press.
Hutchcroft, P., ed. 2016. *Mindanao: The Long Journey to Peace and Prosperity*. Manila: Anvil.
ILO (International Labour Office). 1974. *Sharing in Development: A Program of Employment, Equity and Growth for the Philippines*. Geneva: ILO.
IMF (International Monetary Fund). 2021. "Philippines". Staff Report for the 2021 Article IV Consultation, IMF, Washington, DC.
Kay, J., and M. King. 2020. *Radical Uncertainty. Decision-making for an Unknowable Future*. London: Bridge Street Press.
Lin, J. Y. 2017. "Industrial Policies for Avoiding the Middle-Income Trap: A New Structural Economics Perspective". *Journal of Chinese Economic and Business Studies* 15, no. 1: 5–18.
Llanto, G. M., V. B. Paqueo, and A. C Orbeta, eds. 2018. *From Evidence to Policy: Celebrating 40 Years of Policy Research*. Quezon City: Philippine Institute for Development Studies.
Mendoza, R. U., E. L. Beja, J. C. Teehankee, A. G. M. La Vina, and M. F. Vallamejor-Mendoza, eds. 2015. *Building Inclusive Democracies in ASEAN*. Manila: Anvil.
Mendoza, R. U., and R. Olfindo. 2018. "Governance and Institutions". In *The Philippine Economy: No Longer the East Asian Exception?*, edited by R. L. Clarete, E. F. Esguerra, and H. Hill, pp. 375–417. Singapore: Institute of Southeast Asian Studies.
Monsod, T. C., and M. S. Gochoco-Bautista. 2021. "Rethinking 'Economic Fundamentals' in an Era of Global Physical Shocks: Insights from the Philippine Experience with COVID-19". *Asian Economic Papers* 20, no. 1: 109–40.
Morawetz, D. 1977. *Twenty-Five Years of Economic Development, 1950 to 1975*. Washington, DC: World Bank.
Noland, M. 2000. "The Philippines in the Asian Financial Crisis: How the Sick Man Avoided Pneumonia". *Asian Survey* 40, no. 3: 401–12.
Orbeta, A., and V. Paqueo. 2016. "Pantawid Pamilyang Pilipino Program: Boon or Bane?". *Discussion Paper Series No. 2016-56*. Makati: Philippine Institute for Development Studies.
PHDR (Philippine Human Development Report). 2021. *Philippine Human Development Report 2020-21*. Quezon City: Human Development Network. https://www.hdn.org.ph/2020-2021-philippine-human-development-report/.
Power, J. H., and G. P. Sicat. 1971. *The Philippines: Industrialization and Trade Policies*. Oxford: Oxford University Press.
Pritchett, L. 2003. "A Toy Collection, a Socialist Star, and a Democratic Dud? Growth Theory, Vietnam, and the Philippines". In *In Search of Prosperity: Analytical Narratives on Economic Growth*, edited by D. Rodrik, pp. 123–51. Princeton: Princeton University Press.

———. 2018. "Knowledge or Its Adoption?". *CGD Note*. Washington, DC: Center for Global Development.
Ravallion, M. 2016. *The Economics of Poverty: History, Measurement and Policy*. Oxford: Oxford University Press.
Remolona, E. M., M. Mangahas, and F. Pante. 1986. "Foreign Debt, Balance of Payments, and the Economic Crisis of the Philippines in 1983–84". *World Development* 14, no. 8: 993–1018.
Rodlauer, M., P. Loungani, V. Arora, C. Christofides, E. G. de la Piedra, P. Kongsamut, K. Kostial, V. Summers, and A. Vamvakidis. 2000. "The Philippines: Towards Sustainable and Rapid Growth". *IMF Occasional Paper 187*. Washington, DC: International Monetary Fund. https://www.imf.org/external/pubs/nft/op/187/.
Sicat, G. P. 1985. "A Historical and Current Perspective of Philippine Economic Problems". *Philippine Economic Journal* 24, no. 1: 24–63.
———. 1999. "The Philippine Economy in the Asian Crisis". In *Southeast Asia's Economic Crisis: Origins, Lessons, and the Way Forward*, edited by H. W. Arndt and H. Hill, pp. 41–50. Singapore: ISEAS.
———. 2014. *Cesar Virata. Life and Times through Four Decades of Philippine Economic History*. Quezon City: University of the Philippines Press.
The Economist. 2020. "Which Economies Are Most Vulnerable to COVID-19's Long-Term Effects?". *The Economist*, 15 December 2020. https://www.economist.com/graphic-detail/2020/12/15/which-economies-are-most-vulnerable-to-covid-19s-long-term-effects (accessed 1 September 2021).
Villamil, W. 2018. "Education and Training". In *The Philippine Economy: No Longer the East Asian Exception?*, edited by R. L. Clarete, E. F. Esguerra, and H. Hill, pp. 151–89. Singapore: Institute of Southeast Asian Studies.
World Bank. 2021. *Philippines Economic Update: Navigating a Challenging Recovery*. Manila: World Bank.

PART 2

Agricultural and Economic Development

3 Trade Distortions as Constraints to Agricultural Development in East Asia

Kym Anderson

1 INTRODUCTION

It has been understood, at least since Plato's *Republic*, that trade between two entities can be beneficial to both. The reason why that applies to countries was made very clear two centuries ago by Ricardo (1817) with his theory of comparative advantage. Yet most countries have restricted their international trade in products at various times. True, in the mid-19th century following the repeal of Britain's protective Corn Laws, the richest countries of Europe began opening their national markets, especially in farm goods, as they took more advantage of agricultural development opportunities in their colonies to secure food and fibre supplies. That globalization wave came to an end with World War I, and trade suffered further in the 1930s and early post-World War II. But during the lifetime of Arsenio M. Balisacan, empirical analyses of the effects of trade policies—including in the Philippines—have added to theoretical reasons for opening up to international trade. Arguably they have contributed to reforms of these policies since the 1980s, and thereby to the accompanying latest globalization wave.

This chapter surveys the findings of these empirical studies as they affect incentives in agricultural markets. A focus on policies affecting farm products is warranted because they adversely affect food security globally, and in particular the world's poorest households, which are mostly found in rural regions of developing countries.

More specifically, the chapter traces the impacts of these trade, farm and food policy developments since the 1950s, particularly in East Asia. It does so by subdividing the period into the years to the mid-1980s, which were characterized by anti-trade policies that added to the volatility of international food prices and to poverty and inequality in most developing countries, and the subsequent two decades, which saw the gradual undoing of these price- and trade-distorting policies. The chapter looks at both the extent of interventions insofar as they alter prices, and the market and welfare effects of these policies at home and abroad. During the most recent dozen years, international prices of farm products spiked and the government of the Philippines and of many other countries reacted in ways that aimed to insulate their domestic markets. Far from reducing the number of people who fell into poverty, the combined effects of these policy responses are shown to have exacerbated global poverty. The chapter concludes by noting alternatives to trade-related policies that can achieve society's stated objectives of trade and agricultural policies far more efficiently and equitably.

2   FROM THE 1950s TO THE MID-1980s

Following World War II, international trade in farm products, manufactures and services were highly restricted by a wide range of instruments, including import tariffs, import quotas and licensing, export taxes or prohibitions and multiple foreign exchange rates. Agricultural protectionism in industrial economies was the focus of an early study by the GATT Secretariat (Haberler 1958), followed up by FAO (1973, 1975) and then Anderson and Hayami (1986). Empirical studies of manufacturing protectionism took off in the 1960s, both in advanced industrial countries (Balassa 1965) and in numerous developing countries, including the Philippines (Little, Scitovsky, and Scott 1970; Balassa and Associates 1971).

Meanwhile, from the late 1950s, many newly independent developing countries taxed or quantitatively restricted their exports of farm and other primary products to keep down the domestic price of food in urban areas and to encourage industrialization.

These policy settings continued through to the early 1980s, which intrigued Professor Balisacan (see his PhD thesis: Balisacan 1985; Balisacan and Roumasset 1987). The nature, consequences and causes behind the policies of developing countries were also the focus of a World Bank study covering 18 developing economies (Krueger, Schiff and Valdés 1988, 1991).

3 POLICY REFORMS FROM THE MID-1980s

By the 1980s it had become evident that both advanced and developing countries were beginning to undertake major trade-related policy reforms. OECD (2020) has been monitoring annually the progress of agricultural support policies in advanced and large emerging economies since 1986. However, further monitoring of policies in poorer countries had been sporadic at best, until a follow-on World Bank research project to that by Krueger, Schiff, and Valdés analysed the period 1955–2007 (Anderson 2009a). The Philippines was a country case study in both World Bank undertakings (Intal and Power 1991; David, Intal, and Balisacan 2009).

In their study of the political economy of agricultural protection in Japan, South Korea and Taiwan relative to other industrial economies, Anderson and Hayami (1986) note that high-income countries tended to protect farmers more than producers of manufactures or other tradable goods, and that newly independent developing countries chose to protect their manufacturers and heavily tax (often in-kind) production or exports of agricultural goods. That evidence suggests that countries might gradually transform from taxing to increasingly assisting farmers relative to manufacturers in the course of national economic growth. Balisacan (1985, 1987) documents the same stylized fact and explains it in terms of public choice theory (relative strength of coalitions for and against protection). Anderson and Hayami (1986) find strong support for that hypothesis over the period 1955–80. They also note rising rates of protection to farmers in European and Northeast Asian industrial countries over that same period, which raised questions such as: Will these countries become more protectionist? Will agricultural protection growth spread to other emerging economies? If so, what determines how early in their growth process their policy will transition away from taxing to protecting farmers and how fast their rates of farm protection will rise? Are there countries that are exceptions to this "rule"? What are the international trade and welfare effects of such market interventions versus alternative policy interventions? What can be done to encourage these protectionist governments to move to more efficient means of achieving the stated objectives of these policies?

The rest of this chapter reveals the extent to which empirical studies have been able to gradually provide more answers to some of these questions, particularly for East Asia's rapidly expanding economies but in the context of policy developments in the rest of the world.[1]

4 INDICATORS OF THE EXTENT OF DISTORTIONS TO AGRICULTURAL INCENTIVES

The most common indicator of government interventions in agricultural markets historically has been to measure the extent to which domestic prices diverge from border prices in each country (the nominal rate of protection or NRP, see Corden 1971). This is the measure used by Anderson and Hayami (1986). Meanwhile, OECD (2020 and earlier), building on an indicator elaborated by FAO (1973, 1975), developed its agricultural producer and consumer support estimates (PSEs and CSEs). The PSE includes distortions to prices of not only outputs but also tradable farm inputs. It expresses the government's price supports in dollar terms as well as a percentage of the distorted value of domestic production. For the more recent World Bank study mentioned above, a similar measure—nominal rate of assistance (NRA)—was developed but was expressed as a percentage of the value of production at border price (Anderson et al. 2008).

A more novel contribution of Anderson et al. (2008) is the suggestion of also computing a production-weighted average NRA for non-agricultural tradables and comparing it with that for agricultural tradables by calculating a percentage relative rate of assistance (RRA). The latter is defined as $RRA = 100*[(100 + NRAag^t)/(100 + NRAnonagt) - 1]$, where $NRAag^t$ and $NRAnonag^t$ are the percentage NRAs for the tradables parts of the agricultural and non-agricultural sectors, respectively.[2]

---

[1] Space restrictions prevent focusing on the political economy question of why government policies evolve in this way, but see the survey of theoretical and empirical literature on that topic in Anderson, Rausser, and Swinnen (2013).

[2] Farmers are affected not just by prices of their own products but also by the incentives non-agricultural producers face. That is, it is relative prices and hence relative rates of government assistance that affect producer incentives. More than seventy years ago, Lerner (1936) provided his Symmetry Theorem that proves that in a two-sector economy, an import tax has the same effect

Since the NRA cannot be less than -100 per cent if producers are to earn anything, neither can the RRA. And if both of these sectors are equally assisted, the RRA is zero. This measure is useful in that if it is below (above) zero, it provides an internationally comparable indication of the extent to which a country's sectoral policy regime has an anti- (pro-)agricultural bias.

Both the OECD and World Bank studies consider also the extent to which consumers are taxed or subsidized. The latter's consumer tax equivalent (CTE) is defined as the percentage by which the price that consumers pay for their food domestically is above the international price of each food product at the nation's border.

Another novel contribution of Anderson et al. (2008) relates to currency exchange rates. In calculating the NRAs and CTEs for each sector of the economy, the methodology included the implicit trade tax distortions generated by dual or multiple exchange rates, drawing on the methodology of Dervis, de Melo, and Robinson (1981). This turned out to be especially important in the case of China prior to the mid-1990s. Such exchange rate systems implicitly tax both importers and exporters, reducing the openness of the economy and boosting the anti-trade bias of the government's interventions.

Sectoral aggregate estimates of NRAs and CTEs, even when weighted using production and consumption at undistorted prices as weights, are not always able to indicate very accurately the trade and welfare reductions caused by government interventions. This is especially so when some policies (such as import or export taxes) have negative effects on trade while other policies (such as export subsidies) have positive effects. Likewise, if the import-competing and exportables subsectors are each subject to trade taxes, sectoral average NRAs and CTEs may be close to zero even though both subsectors' policies are trade- and welfare-reducing. Furthermore, the welfare effect of a policy instrument is related to the square of the individual *ad valorem* distortion rate. This means that averages of the NRA (or CTE) fail to capture the fact that widely different rates of intervention across commodities within a policy instrument group have worse welfare effects than if all commodities had similar NRAs and CTEs.

---

as an export tax. This carries over to a model that also includes a third sector producing only non-tradables (Vousden 1990).

To help overcome these limitations, Anderson and Neary (2005) developed a family of indexes under the catch-all name of trade restrictiveness indexes. That innovation has been drawn on to generate indicators of price distortions imposed by each country's agricultural policies on its economic welfare and on its agricultural trade. With the help of a couple of assumptions about price elasticities, Lloyd, Croser, and Anderson (2010) define a welfare reduction index (WRI) and a trade reduction index (TRI) that can be calculated with no more than the same data needed to estimate the NRA and CTE. The TRI (or WRI) is the ad valorem trade tax rate which, if applied uniformly to all farm commodities in a country that year, would generate the same reduction in trade (or economic welfare) as the actual cross-commodity structure of agricultural NRAs and CTEs for that country, other things being equal.

5   ESTIMATES OF THE EXTENT OF PRICE DISTORTIONS IN ASIA

Anderson and Martin (2009) summarize estimates of distortions to Asian prices, updating the estimates in Anderson and Hayami (1986) and Krueger, Schiff, and Valdés (1991) and adding estimates for several other Asian countries. They find that while agricultural price and trade policies from the mid-1950s to the early 1980s reduced earnings of farmers in developing Asia on average by more than 20 per cent, effective taxation declined from the early 1980s. More than that, from the mid-1990s the NRA switched signs and became increasingly positive. That average hides considerable diversity within the region, however. Nominal assistance to farmers in South Korea and Taiwan was positive from the early 1960s (although very small initially when compared with more than 40% in Japan); Indonesia had some years in the 1970s and 1980s when its NRA was a little above zero, and India's and the Philippines' average NRAs became positive from the 1980s.

As is true for other regions of the world, assistance in Asia for the "rice pudding" products of sugar, milk and rice is among the highest (Anderson 2009b, Tables 5 and 6). But the NRAs even for these three products greatly vary across countries, with five-year averages ranging from almost zero to as much as 400 per cent for rice and 140 per cent for milk in South Korea. There is a great deal of NRA diversity also across commodities within each Asian economy's farm sector, and the extent (as measured by the standard deviation) has grown rather than diminished over the past five decades.

A striking feature of the distortion pattern within the farm sector is its strong anti-trade bias. This is evident in Figure 1 of Anderson (2009b), which depicts the average NRAs for agriculture's import-competing and export subsectors for the region: the former average is always positive and its trend is upward-sloping, whereas the NRA average for exportables is negative and did not diminish until the 1980s, after which it gradually approached zero. While the gap between the NRAs for these two subsectors has diminished little since the 1960s for the region as a whole, it hides the fact that in several countries (including Malaysia and Thailand) that gap has narrowed somewhat.

The anti-agricultural policy biases of the past in developing countries were due to not just agricultural policies. Also important to changes in incentives affecting intersectorally mobile resources have been the significant reductions in border protection to the manufacturing sector. That reduction in assistance to producers of non-farm tradables has been even more responsible for the improvement in farmer incentives than the reduction in direct taxation of agricultural industries. The NRA estimates for non-farm tradables before the 1990s are very sizeable. For Asia as a whole, the average NRA value has steadily declined throughout the past four or five decades as policy reforms have spread. This has therefore contributed to a decline in the estimated negative RRA for Asian farmers: the weighted average RRA was worse than -50 per cent up to the early 1970s but improved to an average of -32 per cent in the 1980s, -9 per cent in the 1990s and then became positive, averaging 7 per cent in 2000–2004 (Anderson 2009b, Figure 2).

The upward shift in agricultural NRAs and the RRAs towards zero and even the move to positive agricultural NRAs and RRAs recently are not unique to Asia. Similar trends, albeit less steep, have resulted from policy reforms in other developing country regions over the past four decades (Anderson 2009b, Figure 4). This suggests that similar political economy trends might be at work as economies develop.

This trend is reflected also in the trade and welfare reduction indexes. The TRIs for developing countries as a group were roughly constant or slightly rising until the early 1990s; thereafter they declined for all regions—Africa, Asia, Latin America and high-income countries. The aggregate results for developing countries were driven by the exportables subsector that was being taxed and the import-competing subsector that was being protected (albeit by less than in high-income countries, see Lloyd, Croser, and Anderson 2009, Tables 1 and 3). The WRI estimates reveal a constant or increasing tendency for policies to reduce welfare from the 1960s to the mid-1980s, but thereafter the opposite occurred with the gradual removal of agricultural taxation in developing countries. That is, the WRI correctly shows the adverse welfare consequences that result from both positive and negative agricultural assistance regimes.

The WRI and TRI for the world as a whole trace out a hill-shaped path and suggest that the global welfare cost of distortions to world agricultural markets was slightly less by the early 2000s than it was in the early 1960s (Lloyd, Croser, and Anderson 2009, Figure 2). The fall was due mostly to decreases in the welfare restrictiveness of policies in high-income countries (including Japan) and in developing Asia. High-income countries contributed over half of the change in the WRI, and Asia's developing countries more than one-third (Lloyd, Croser, and Anderson 2009, last column of Table 5). Among the Asian developing countries, China contributed most significantly to the reduction in the global WRI. Its RRA also had the most striking convergence to zero.

Updated estimates of NRAs and RRAs for China and a few other East Asian countries are summarized in Figures 3.1 and 3.2. The RRA for Chinese agriculture was just 1 per cent in 2000–2004, but it gradually rose over the next dozen years, averaging 14 per cent by 2015–16, while the average RRA for other developing countries remained just below zero.

Figure 3.1. Nominal and relative rates of government assistance to agriculture in China, Japan, Korea and Taiwan (1955–2016, %)

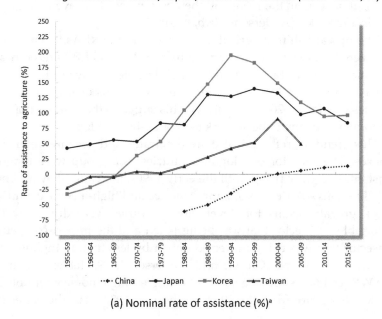

(a) Nominal rate of assistance (%)[a]

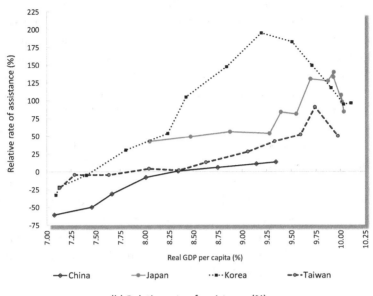

(b) Relative rate of assistance (%)

Note: ^a Final period shown for Taiwan is 2010–11.
Sources: Author's update from Anderson and Nelgen (2013) and OECD (2020).

Figure 3.2. *Nominal rates of government assistance to agriculture in China, Indonesia, Philippines and OECD countries (1980–2019, %)*

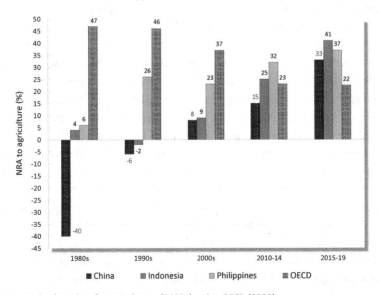

Source: Author's update from Anderson (2009a), using OECD (2020).

China taxed its farmers far more than either South Korea or Taiwan at similar real income levels in earlier decades. Its policy changes have had a major impact in terms of reducing the discouragement of its farm production (and the encouragement of food consumption), thus slowing the decline in agricultural self-sufficiency that otherwise would have occurred as industrialization proceeded in China (Anderson 2018). The reforms in the final two decades of the twentieth century also have added to national economic growth and welfare by reducing inter-sectoral resource misallocation; and they have reduced the extent to which growth in real incomes of urban households outpaced those of farm households. Of concern, though, is China's transition during the present century to subsidizing farmers relative to manufacturers. Indeed, the NRAs to Chinese, Indonesian and Philippine farmers are now higher than those to farmers in high-income countries on average, and are approaching the declining NRAs of their Northeast Asian neighbours (Figures 3.1 and 3.2).

6 MARKET AND WELFARE EFFECTS OF ASIA'S CHOSEN POLICY TRENDS

Prior to the 1990s, the global market and welfare effects of agricultural price distortions were generated by partial equilibrium multi-country models spanning the world, such as that of Tyers and Anderson (1992). But that type of modelling ignores the rest of the economy. Thus when a global economy-wide model with a similar level of farm commodity detail was developed in the early 1990s (the GTAP Model and database, see Hertel 1997), many new possibilities for analysis opened up.

An early application using the GTAP Model is Anderson et al. (1997). The study was undertaken following a dramatic rise in international grain prices and a drop in per capita world grain stocks to low levels in 1995/96. That, together with projections by the Worldwatch Institute of massive grain imports by China in the twenty-first century, called into question the long-term prospects for the world food situation. Meanwhile, other studies at that time suggested food would continue to be abundantly available in the foreseeable future so long as investments in agricultural research were maintained. Anderson et al. (1997) aimed to get a sense of which of these sets of projections were more likely, and what would happen if the global slowdown of agricultural research investments during the previous decade were to lower farm productivity growth. It also sought to understand what the projections implied about food production, consumption and self-sufficiency levels in rapidly industrializing East Asia and elsewhere, and to see who might supply the food-deficit countries and how the latter might pay for their food imports.

Contrary to earlier studies and the fears of many food-importing developing countries, the model results presented in Anderson et al. (1997) suggest that implementing the Uruguay Round was not going to have much impact on real international food prices. Those prices were projected to be only 2–4 per cent higher than they otherwise would be at the end of that implementation decade—a rise that would be imperceptible compared with the usual year-to-year fluctuations in food prices and foreign exchange rates. The rise is small partly because the agricultural commitments under the Uruguay Round by the most farm-protectionist countries were far more modest than was hoped for. Also, because many markets for non-farm products also were liberalized under the Uruguay Round, their prices rose in international markets as well. This moderates the increase in farm relative to non-farm prices—and it is *relative* prices that influence decisions of producers and consumers. That result was based on the assumption that farm productivity growth continued at the relatively high rates of the previous few decades. Sensitivity analysis shows that even a modest slowdown of about one-fifth (half a percentage point per year) in the growth rate of grain total factor productivity globally would have a sizeable impact on food prices. It also shows that the accession of China and Taiwan to the World Trade Organization (WTO) would provide a very significant boost to the gains from the Uruguay Round. With their accession, international grain price rises due to the Round would be twice as large, and livestock product prices would be 40 per cent greater. China, in that case, would import 4 per cent, instead of just 1 per cent, of its grain needs, and aggregate world trade would be 13 per cent instead of just 10 per cent greater, thanks to the Round. This was projected to boost the annual gain in global welfare from the Round by almost one-third as much, again with China becoming a WTO member.

Before implementation of the Uruguay Round was completed, and on the eve of China and Taiwan joining the WTO, the next round of multilateral trade negotiations was launched in Doha in late 2001.

Modellers soon began to provide ex ante analyses of various reform scenarios, with World Bank economists particularly focusing on how developing countries might be affected (Anderson and Martin 2006). Anderson, Martin, and van der Mensbrugghe (2006) summarize some of the findings. One is that, despite the Uruguay Round reforms, the global welfare cost of remaining trade distortions remains huge, and developing countries were bearing a disproportionate share of the costs of those distortions. Moreover, more than three-fifths of those costs were due to food and agricultural policies, even though agriculture accounted for less than 10 per cent of world trade and 4 per cent of global gross domestic product (GDP). While subsidies were partly responsible, most of the cost of farm policies was due to market access restrictions. Phasing out such trade-restrictive policies would "thicken" international food markets too, thereby lowering the volatility of prices in those markets. It would also ensure that the world's productive resources in the farm sector would be put to their best use, making agricultural production more sustainable globally.

Anderson, Martin, and van der Mensbrugghe (2006) compare these results from full global merchandise trade liberalization with a set of partial reforms proposed during the Doha Round negotiations. They show that even large cuts in bound agricultural tariffs and subsidies would accomplish little because legal bindings were set in the Uruguay Round at far above applied rates (hence, any agreed reduction in a bound rate that brings the legal binding only part-way down to the actual tariff being applied would not allow more imports).

A follow-on study at the World Bank sought to examine whether freeing up world merchandise trade would reduce poverty and inequality nationally and globally. A series of economy-wide models were enhanced with household survey data to address this question, all of which used the same protection database so as to be directly comparable. Anderson, Cockburn, and Martin (2011) provide a synopsis of the results for both own-country reform and rest-of-world reform. The study reveals that in most cases both types of trade reform would reduce both income inequality and poverty, with own-country reform typically being more important than reform by the rest of the world, except for the least-distorted economies. Again, agricultural distortions turn out to contribute most to this positive set of findings.

7 MARKET AND WELFARE EFFECTS OF VARYING TRADE RESTRICTIONS TO STABILIZE PRICES

The above studies mostly focus on long-run trends. As important, at least politically, is food price volatility because it can cause political unrest. That concern has led governments of many countries to insulate domestic food markets from gyrations in international food prices. This is especially the case for rice in Asia. Insulation is invoked most commonly in international price upswings to protect consumers: exporting countries temporarily restrict their exports, and importing countries temporarily lower or suspend their tariffs. Also, when international prices slump to low levels, some importing countries raise their import barriers to protect their farmers. Such policy actions may reduce the volatility of domestic prices in countries that insulate heavily, but the collective impact of such interventions by a large number of countries is to increase the volatility of international food prices, and thereby of domestic prices in more open countries. Moreover, if a similar proportion of the world's food-exporting countries insulate to the same degree as a group of food importers, each country group will fully offset the other's attempt to prevent their domestic price from moving as much as the international price. That is, these policy actions are as futile as everyone in a football stadium standing in an attempt to get a better view of the field (Martin and Anderson 2012).

Jensen and Anderson (2017) use a multi-product, multi-country model of the global economy that can take into account the interactions between markets for farm products that are closely related in production and/or consumption, and can estimate the impacts of those insulating policies on grain prices and on the grain trade and economic welfare of the world's various countries. They find that changes in national restrictions on global grain trade during 2006–8 were responsible for around one-third, one-ninth and one-fifteenth of the observed increases in the international prices of rice, coarse grains and wheat, respectively. Also, those altered trade restrictions caused domestic price increases to be only one-quarter less than what they otherwise would have been on average across all countries for rice and only one-eleventh less in the case of wheat and coarse grains. Moreover, the changes in trade restrictions enlarged the transfers in economic welfare from food-importing to food-exporting countries because of the respective changes in their international terms of trade. These results suggest that the actions of grain-exporting countries were being offset by those of import-competing countries, such that market-insulating interventions are rather ineffective in achieving their stated aim of avoiding large domestic price rises when international food prices spike.

Nor did the unilateral insulating policy actions prevent more people from falling below the poverty line. Anderson, Ivanic, and Martin (2014), using household income and expenditure survey data, find that, for a sample of thirty developing countries (including the biggest ones such as China, India, Indonesia, Nigeria and Pakistan), insulation behaviour by developing country governments would have prevented an extra eighty-two million people from temporarily falling below the US$1.25-a-day poverty line *if those government responses had had no impact on international food prices*. But because those actions exacerbated the international price spikes, the number of people saved from falling into poverty by that insulating policy action was estimated to be 7.5 million less than the number of those pushed into poverty. That is, developing countries as a group would probably see fewer of their people fall into poverty when international food prices spiked if they and all other countries agreed to abstain from altering trade restrictions in the hope of insulating their domestic markets from international price fluctuations.

8 FUTURE TRADE REFORM PROSPECTS

Looking to the future, the pace of economic growth in the East Asian region is expected to be slower than in the past, but structural changes will continue. The earlier industrializing Northeast Asian economies represent just 3 per cent of the world's population, so their rapid industrial growth was accommodated by the rest of the world without much difficulty, including in markets for primary products. China and India, by contrast, account for 36 per cent of humanity. Their rapid and persistent industrialization therefore has far greater significance for primary product markets and thus for food security than did earlier growth in far smaller economies of Northeast Asia.

Anderson and Strutt (2016) use the global economy-wide GTAP model to project such structural changes to national markets to 2030. How markets and governments respond to the associated food security concerns could have non-trivial effects in both the emerging economies of Asia and their trading partners. Projections in that study suggest that if relatively rapid economic growth in Asia and, to a lesser extent, in other developing countries continues to characterize world economic development, developing Asia's share of global agricultural GDP will almost double. But the increase would not be fast enough to keep pace with their growing consumption of farm products under current policies, in which case East Asia's imports of farm products would grow.

However, throughout the post-World War II era, many Asian governments, as elsewhere, have been reluctant to become very dependent on imports of staple foods. Were China and Indonesia to continue to follow Northeast Asian economies in raising their assistance to farmers as their per capita incomes grow, the contribution of farm policies to the global cost of goods trade barriers would rise. Clearly, such a policy development would be harmful to the farm trade interests of agriculture-exporting countries (Anderson et al. 2016).

One way agriculture-exporting countries have sought to maintain market access is through the GATT and its successor since 1995, the WTO. Reaching agreement on multilateral trade reform via the WTO's Doha Development Agenda (DDA) has proven to be even more difficult than in past rounds of negotiations, however, and not least because of differences over the extent of reform ambitions for farm policies.

Even if multilateral trade policy reform remains elusive and regional trade agreements such as Asia's proposed Regional Comprehensive Economic Partnership (RCEP) fail or prove to be unambitious, there is still the possibility of governments unilaterally reforming their food and agricultural policies. True, the projected continued decline in food self-sufficiency for densely populated Asian countries is likely to keep governments concerned, notwithstanding the fact that the region's access to food is projected to keep improving. But there are far more efficient ways to meet that social objective, and also to reduce poverty and rural-urban income inequality, than following an agricultural protection growth path.

In examining options for unilateral action, keep in mind that any market-distorting measure tends to reduce national income and hence the aggregate capacity to access food, in addition to having effects on income distribution. By contrast, investments in rural public goods can raise national income, boost economic growth and, in some cases, enhance the food security of both farm and non-farm households. Public agricultural research expenditure is one such high-payoff investment.

In addition to boosting national income growth, such investment could lower domestic consumer prices for some foods and so benefit not only farmers but also net buyers of those foods, thereby contributing to both the availability and access dimensions of food security. This contrasts with food import restrictions, which raise domestic prices, thus benefiting net food sellers but at the expense of net food buyers (and reduce overall availability if storage is managed poorly by parastatal agencies). The resulting increases in farm productivity also would improve agricultural self-sufficiency rates.

Poor infrastructure such as rural roads adds to the cost of farm inputs, and also to the gap between farm-gate and market prices of outputs. This reduces both farmer incentives and consumers' economic access to food. So too do poor-quality telecommunications in rural areas, through raising the costs of such things as price information in distant markets and e-banking and farm credit. Better rural infrastructure improves the opportunities for farm household members to earn part-time off-farm incomes by lowering commuting costs. Part-time off-farm earnings for farm household members can reduce rural poverty and the farm-non-farm income gap.

In short, it is possible to avoid the agricultural protection growth path that Japan and its neighbours chose and still be food secure and reduce poverty and the farm-non-farm income gap. Reversing protection has proven to be very painful politically for the governments of those high-income countries—which is all the more reason for emerging economies not to follow that policy path in the first place. Fortunately for emerging economies there are politically feasible alternative policy instruments that are more efficient and effective. Moreover, the information and communication technology (ICT) revolution is now making it far cheaper and easier than in the past for governments to provide direct income supplements to the poorest and hence most food-insecure households. Such payments were unaffordable in developing countries in the past because of the high cost of administering small handouts, especially in rural areas. However, the ICT revolution has brought financial inclusion to East Asia at an astonishingly fast pace (through both public and private innovations): the share of rural households with a bank or mobile-money account rose from 50 to 69 per cent in East Asia between 2011 and 2017. It is already above 20 per cent in the poorest of East Asia's countries (Figure 3.3)—and only one or two percentage points behind the access rate of urban households.

Figure 3.3. Share of rural households with a bank or mobile-money account or equivalent in Asian developing economies and high-income countries (2011 and 2017, %)

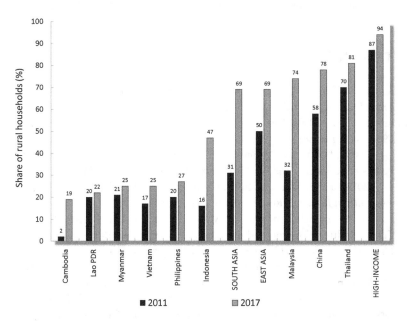

Note: Data are 2014 (not 2011) for Lao PDR and Myanmar.
Source: Demirgüç-Kunt et al. (2018).

9 CONCLUSION

The above findings provide some answers to questions raised early in this chapter. Specifically, most advanced economies do appear to have become more open to trade in farm products. However, there have been recent increases in domestic support to farmers (Anderson and Valenzuela 2021). So while traditional tariff-based growth in agricultural protection may not spread to emerging economies, other forms of support behind the border may emerge, as they have had in China. Ways to encourage governments to move to more efficient means of achieving the stated objectives of these policies have been suggested above. These can be encouraged during bilateral and regional trade negotiations. But the best hope for continuing with reform is if WTO members would return to the multilateral trade-negotiating table.

The transfer in the United States from the Trump administration to the Biden administration in 2021 provides the first chance in recent years to hope that a revival of that remarkable institution might be possible, notwithstanding President Biden's enormous domestic policy agenda.

REFERENCES

Anderson, J. E., and J. P. Neary. 2005. *Measuring the Restrictiveness of International Trade Policy*. Cambridge MA: MIT Press.

Anderson, K., ed. 2009a. *Distortions to Agricultural Incentives: A Global Perspective, 1955–2007*. London: Palgrave Macmillan.

———. 2009b. "Distorted Agricultural Incentives and Economic Development: Asia's Experience". *The World Economy* 32, no. 3 (March): 351–84.

———. 2018. "From Taxing to Subsidizing Farmers in China Post-1978". *China Agricultural Economic Review* 10, no. 1 (January): 36–47.

Anderson, K., J. Cockburn, and W. Martin. 2011. "Would Freeing Up World Trade Reduce Poverty and Inequality? The Vexed Role of Agricultural Distortions". *The World Economy* 34, no. 4 (April): 487–515.

Anderson, K., B. Dimaranan, T. Hertel, and W. Martin. 1997. "Asia-Pacific Food Markets and Trade in 2005: A Global, Economy-Wide Perspective". *Australian Journal of Agricultural and Resource Economics* 41, no. 1 (March): 19–44.

Anderson, K., and Y. Hayami. 1986. *The Political Economy of Agricultural Protection: East Asia in International Perspective*. London: Allen and Unwin. Re-published in World Scientific Reference on Asia-Pacific Trade Policies, Volume I, 2020, K. Anderson. London and Singapore: World Scientific.

Anderson, K., M. Ivanic, and W. Martin. 2014. "Food Price Spikes, Price Insulation, and Poverty". In *The Economics of Food Price Volatility*, edited by J.-P. Chavas, D. Hummels, and B.D. Wright, pp. 311–44. Chicago and London: University of Chicago Press for NBER.

Anderson, K., M. Kurzweil, W. Martin, D. Sandri, and E. Valenzuela. 2008. "Measuring Distortions to Agricultural Incentives, Revisited". *World Trade Review* 7, no. 4 (October): 675–704.

Anderson, K., and W. Martin, eds. 2006. *Agricultural Trade Reform and the Doha Development Agenda*. London: Palgrave Macmillan and Washington, DC: World Bank.

———. 2009. *Distortions to Agricultural Incentives in Asia*. Washington, DC: World Bank.

Anderson, K., W. Martin, and D. van der Mensbrugghe. 2006. "Doha Merchandise Trade Reform: What Is at Stake for Developing Countries?" *World Bank Economic Review* 20, no. 2 (July): 169–95.

Anderson, K., and S. Nelgen. 2013. *Updated National and Global Estimates of Distortions to Agricultural Incentives, 1955 to 2011*. World Bank. www.worldbank.org/agdistortions.

Anderson, K., G. Rausser, and J. F. M. Swinnen. 2013. "Political Economy of Public Policies: Insights from Distortions to Agricultural and Food Markets". *Journal of Economic Literature* 51, no. 2 (June): 423–77.

Anderson, K., and A. Strutt. 2016. "Impacts of Asia's Rise on African and Latin American Trade: Projections to 2030". *The World Economy* 39, no. 2 (February): 172–94.

Anderson, K., A. Strutt, S. Nelgen, and H. G. Jensen. 2016. "What Is the Appropriate Counterfactual When Estimating Effects of Multilateral Trade Policy Reform?" *Journal of Agricultural Economics* 67, no. 3 (September): 764–78.

Anderson, K., and E. Valenzuela. 2021. "What Impact Are Subsidies and Trade Barriers Abroad Having on Australasian and Brazilian Agriculture?" *Australian Journal of Agricultural and Resource Economics* 65, no. 2 (April): 265–90.

Balassa, B. 1965. "Tariff Protection in Industrial Countries: An Evaluation". *Journal of Political Economy* 73, no. 6 (December): 573–94.

Balassa, B., and Associates. 1971. *The Structure of Protection in Developing Countries*. Baltimore: Johns Hopkins University Press.

Balisacan, A. M. 1985. "A Positive Theory of Economic Protection: Agricultural Policies in Developed and Developing Countries". PhD dissertation, University of Hawaii.

———. 1987. "Political Investment in Economic Protection: A Note". *Philippine Review of Economics and Business* 24, no. 1&2: 149–57.

Balisacan, A. M., and J. A. Roumasset. 1987. "Public Choice of Economic Policy: The Growth of Agricultural Protection". *Weltwirtschaftliches Archiv* 123: 232–48.

Corden, W. M. 1971. *The Theory of Protection*. Oxford: Clarendon Press.

David, C., P. Intal, and A. M. Balisacan. 2009. "The Philippines". In *Distortions to Agricultural Incentives in Asia*, edited by K. Anderson and W. Martin, chapter 6. Washington, DC: World Bank.

Demirgüç-Kunt, A., L. Klapper, D. Singer, S. Ansar, and J. Hess. 2018. *The Global Findex Database 2017: Measuring Financial Inclusion and the Fintech Revolution*. Washington, DC: World Bank.

Dervis, K., J. de Melo, and S. Robinson. 1981. "A General Equilibrium Analysis of Foreign Exchange Shortages in a Developing Country". *Economic Journal* 91: 891–906.

FAO (Food and Agriculture Organization of the United Nations). 1973. *Agricultural Protection: Domestic Policy and International Trade*. Rome: UN Food and Agriculture Organization.

———. 1975. *Agricultural Protection and Stabilization Policies: A Framework for Measurement in the Context of Agricultural Adjustment*. Rome: UN Food and Agriculture Organization.

Haberler, G. 1958. *Trends in International Trade: A Report by a Panel of Experts*. Geneva: GATT Secretariat.

Hertel, T., ed. 1997. *Global Trade Analysis: Modeling and Applications.* Cambridge and New York: Cambridge University Press.

Intal, P., and J. H. Power. 1991. "The Philippines". In *The Political Economy of Agricultural Pricing Policy,* Volume 2: Asia, edited by A. O. Krueger, M. Schiff, and A. Valdés, chapter 5. Baltimore, MD: Johns Hopkins University Press for the World Bank.

Jensen, H. G., and K. Anderson. 2017. "Grain Price Spikes and Beggar-Thy-Neighbor Policy Responses: A Global CGE Analysis". *World Bank Economic Review* 31, no. 1: 158–75.

Krueger, A. O., M. Schiff, and A. Valdés. 1988. "Agricultural Incentives in Developing Countries: Measuring the Effect of Sectoral and Economy-wide Policies". *World Bank Economic Review* 2, no. 3 (September): 255–72.

———. 1991. *The Political Economy of Agricultural Pricing Policy, Volume 1: Latin America,* Volume 2: Asia, and Volume 3: Africa and the Mediterranean. Baltimore, MD: Johns Hopkins University Press for World Bank.

Lerner, A. 1936. "The Symmetry between Import and Export Taxes". *Economica* 3, no. 11: 306–13.

Little, I. M. D., T. Scitovsky, and M. Scott. 1970. *Industry and Trade in Some Developing Countries: A Comparative Study.* London: Oxford University Press.

Lloyd, P. J., J. L. Croser, and K. Anderson. 2010. "Global Distortions to Agricultural Markets: New Indicators of Trade and Welfare Impacts, 1960 to 2007". *Review of Development Economics* 14, no. 2 (May): 141–60.

Martin, W., and K. Anderson. 2012. "Export Restrictions and Price Insulation during Commodity Price Booms". *American Journal of Agricultural Economics* 94, no. 2: 422–27.

OECD (Organisation for Economic Co-operation and Development). 2020. "Producer and Consumer Support Estimates." Online database. www.oecd.org.

Ricardo, D. 1817. *On the Principles of Political Economy and Taxation.* Reprinted in *Works and Correspondence of David Ricardo,* Volume I, 1951, edited by P. Sraffa. Cambridge and New York: Cambridge University Press.

Tyers, R., and K. Anderson. 1992. *Disarray in World Food Markets: A Quantitative Assessment.* Cambridge and New York: Cambridge University Press.

Vousden, N. 1990. *The Economic Theory of Protection.* Cambridge and New York: Cambridge University Press.

4 Beyond Krugman: The Importance of Agriculture for East Asian Growth

Peter Warr

1 INTRODUCTION

Paul Krugman's 1994 *Foreign Affairs* article, "The Myth of Asia's Miracle", is one of the most widely read and debated essays ever written by an economist. In this justly famous polemic, Krugman debunks the notion that the rapid economic growth occurring in much of Asia over the two decades from the mid-1970s to the mid-1990s was attributable to forces that defy conventional economic logic. He contends instead that the source was boringly conventional, but also unsustainable. His conceptual target is summarized in the title of an influential World Bank report of the previous year, *The East Asian Miracle*. According to Krugman, there was no miracle. He was right about that, but wrong about the true sources of Asia's growth.

The analytical basis for Krugman's discussion is *growth accounting*, an approach to understanding the sources of economic growth that rests on the distinction between growth of output deriving from increases in the quantities of inputs employed and increases in the amount of output obtained per unit of these inputs—their productivity. The seminal contribution of Robert Solow (1957) relates the growth of output per worker in the United States to the growth of the capital stock per worker. Solow estimates that only 12.5 per cent of the long-term increase in the former was due to increases in the latter. The remaining 87.5 per cent was an unexplained residual, which Solow identifies as technical change.

According to Krugman, the empirical evidence assembled by earlier studies on East Asia reveals that, in contrast with Solow's findings for the United States, Asia's rapid per capita growth was due almost entirely to growth in the quantity of factor inputs employed per head of population, which he calls "perspiration". The "perspiration" had two components: increases in the size of the workforce per head of population—labour force participation—and increases in the quantities of capital inputs applied per worker. These capital inputs consisted of physical capital (in the form of machines, buildings and public infrastructure), and human capital (in the form of education and vocational training). When all these inputs were accounted for, the difference between the actual growth of output per worker and the growth attributable to increases in the quantity of inputs applied per worker—Solow's residual productivity growth, which Krugman calls "inspiration"—was negligible. It was nearly all "perspiration".

Krugman draws three implications from these propositions. First, at a conceptual level, there was nothing miraculous about Asia's economic growth, since it derived almost entirely from observable increases in the inputs employed. Second, Krugman dismisses claims that Asian productivity had increased through far-sighted industrial policies and selective protectionism; there was very little productivity growth available to be explained by these stories. Third, and even more controversially, Krugman argues that raising the share of investment within gross domestic product (GDP) and expansion of basic education were subject to diminishing returns. The growth they produced was not sustainable indefinitely. For example, literacy rates could be doubled from 40 to 80 per cent of the population but could not be doubled again, no matter how much was invested in education.[1] A long-term slowdown of growth based on these sources alone should therefore be expected.

Krugman's argument about the sources of Asia's growth rests on his own generalization from quantitative research conducted by

---

[1] This is Krugman's argument. It is of course true that educational investments can raise the quality of education, but Krugman would presumably respond that diminishing returns apply there as well.

earlier authors. He cites studies on economic growth in selected parts of East Asia, especially Singapore and Hong Kong and to a lesser extent Korea and Taiwan (Young 1992, 1994a, 1994b; Lau and Kim 1993, 1994). His own discussion of these empirical findings emphasizes especially what they reveal about economic growth in Singapore. In extrapolating from this to Asia's growth more broadly, Krugman's perspective was clearly influenced by his focus on these particular economies. But the city-based trading economies of Singapore and Hong Kong were then and still are highly atypical of Asia in one key structural feature. They lack the traditional, low-productivity agricultural sector that employs so much of Asia's population.

While Krugman's discussion of Asia's growth rightly stresses the process of industrialization, his account does not mention agriculture. It thereby ignores the process of structural transformation characterizing economic development in almost all of the rest of Asia, through which resources, especially labour, are gradually released from low-productivity agriculture and relocate to higher-productivity employment in industry and at least some services (Timmer 2014). In Singapore and Hong Kong, which are almost without agriculture and import nearly all their food, that sector might reasonably be disregarded, as Krugman does. But what about other rapidly growing Asian economies?

The present paper analyses the sources of growth in Thailand and Indonesia, two prominent Asian countries not mentioned by Krugman, although both were booming at the time he wrote his article. Both contain large, low-productivity agricultural sectors and higher-productivity industrial and services sectors.[2] In this respect, they are far more typical of developing Asia than Singapore or Hong Kong. We shall compare the economic experience of these two countries with Krugman's story.

Some analytical background is needed. It will be helpful to decompose the sources of productivity growth—expansion of aggregate output per worker—into three conceptual categories:

---

[2] The data for Thailand and Indonesia, presented in Figures 4.5 and 4.6, confirm higher average labour productivity in both industry and services overall than in agriculture in both countries. Despite this, there may be components of the services sector where labour productivity is no higher than in agriculture.

a. growth of factor inputs (physical and human capital) relative to raw unskilled labour, within each major sector (agriculture, industry and services);
b. growth of the productivity of these factors, through technical change, again within each sector; and
c. growth of aggregate output per worker due to the reallocation of labour from lower-productivity sectors (mainly agriculture) to higher-productivity sectors (mainly industry and some services).[3]

At the level of each sector, the distinction between (a) and (b) above is identical to the Solow-Krugman distinction between the quantity of inputs applied per worker and the productivity of these inputs. The distinction rests on an identity. But in the Solow-Krugman growth accounting framework, a similar mathematical identity that applies to individual sectors is also assumed to apply to the aggregate economy. The possibility that changes in the sectoral composition of the economy may disrupt this identity at the aggregate level is thereby overlooked.

Of course, if sources (a) and (b) together explained all empirically observed productivity growth at the level of the whole economy, that would leave no scope for (c). But is that true? The present paper attempts to ascertain the importance or otherwise of source (c). It is important that source (c) is distinct from both source (a) — increased application of factor inputs per unit of labour — and source (b) — technical change. In this paper, sources (a) and (b) combined are called *within-sector* productivity growth and source (c) is called *between-sector* productivity growth.

As an intuitive aid to understanding the role of structural change in contributing to aggregate productivity growth, a hypothetical illustration may be helpful. Consider the case where the initial levels of

---

[3] The analytical basis for the distinction between (a) + (b) and (c) is derived in the Appendix. In growth accounting terms, the aggregate contributions to overall growth attributable to sources (a) and (b) in each year are each given by the sum of that source across sectors, each weighted by the (time variant) share of that sector in GDP. The contribution of source (c) is calculated in each year as a residual: aggregate productivity growth minus the growth attributable to sources (a) + (b).

productivity per worker differ among sectors but where productivity growth (sources (a) + (b)) is zero in every sector. Does this mean that aggregate productivity growth is also zero? Not if labour moves from sectors with low *levels* of average productivity to sectors of higher productivity (source (c)). For this relocation to happen without reducing average productivity in the sectors to which the labour moves, the relocated labour must become more productive.[4]

How important is between-sector productivity growth? Does its recognition matter for our understanding of the sources of Asia's growth? Section 2 reviews the data on structural change in Thailand and Indonesia, noting the difference between structural change measured in terms of output, on one hand, and employment, on the other. Section 3 focuses on the productivity of labour in both countries and its relationship to structural change. Section 4 concludes.

In this study, the Thai and Indonesian economies are each disaggregated into three sectors—agriculture, industry and services. Productivity in each sector is measured as real value added per worker and productivity in aggregate is measured as the sum of real value added in each sector (real GDP) divided by the aggregate workforce. The data cover the period 1981–2017.

As background, over this 36-year period, real GDP grew at average annual rates of 5.14 and 4.87 per cent per year in Thailand and Indonesia, respectively. The population grew at 1.05 and 1.63 per cent per year, leading to GDP growth per capita of 4.09 and 3.24 per cent per year. Labour force participation grew in both countries, at annual rates of 0.54 per cent and 0.65 per cent per year, leading to real GDP growth per worker of 3.55 and 2.59 per cent per year.[5]

---

[4] The above calculations are *ex post* descriptions of the data, derived from an identity—the definition of GDP. Equation (3) is an identity that the data must necessarily satisfy. This should be distinguished from *ex ante* prescriptions of the requirements for structural change that will raise aggregate GDP per worker. For that, the focus must be on structural change that moves labour from sectors of lower marginal product to sectors of higher marginal product.

[5] For further background on the Thai and Indonesian economies, see Warr (2020) and Hill (2018).

2 STRUCTURAL TRANSFORMATION

Structural transformation will be defined simply as a reallocation of economic activity among sectors. It can be interpreted in terms of output or employment. When overall growth is positive, structural change will normally correspond to a reduction in agriculture's share of both output and employment, necessarily coinciding with an increase in the output and employment shares of industry and services combined. But the mix of industry and services in this structural change may vary greatly over time and may be quite different for output and employment. In addition, the pattern of structural transformation—both output and employment—may be very different during economic recessions (negative growth) and booms (unusually rapid growth) and from the pattern seen under normal, long-term rates of (positive) growth. In what follows, the long-term pattern of structural change will be reviewed for both Thailand and Indonesia.

2.1 Output shares

Figure 4.1 shows the composition of Thailand's sectoral output (value added) in agriculture, industry and services from 1981 to 2017. The first row of Table 4.1 summarizes the annual rates of change of these shares. Over this 36-year interval, agriculture's GDP share (agricultural value added/GDP) declined from 20 to 6 per cent, an annual rate of contraction of 0.39 percentage points. At the same time, the share of industry (including but not exclusively manufacturing) rose from 30 to 34 per cent, while that of services, from 49 to 60 per cent. That is, of the decline in agriculture's share of output (14% of GDP), one-third was taken up by an increase in the share of industry (column [2] of Table 4.1) and the remaining two-thirds by an increase in the share of services.

In the case of Indonesia (Figure 4.2 and second row of Table 4.1), agriculture's GDP share declined from 23 per cent in 1981 to 13 per cent in 2017, an annual rate of contraction of 0.28 percentage points. Industry's share remained unchanged at 43 per cent, while services' share rose from 33 to 45 per cent of GDP. That is, all of the contraction in agriculture's GDP share was absorbed by the increase in services' share and industry's share was unchanged.

Figure 4.1. GDP shares by sector (Thailand, 1981–2017)

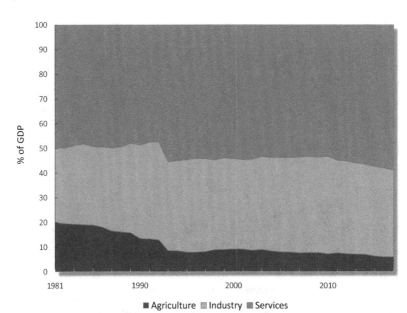

Source: Author's calculations, using data from World Bank, *World Development Indicators*, https://databank.worldbank.org/source/world-development-indicators.

Table 4.1. Agriculture's contraction and industrialization component (1981–2017)

Country	Output share		Employment share	
	Mean annual change of agriculture's % GDP share	Industry expansion as % of agriculture's contraction	Mean annual change of agriculture's % employment share	Industry expansion as % agriculture's contraction
	[1]	[2]	[3]	[4]
Thailand	−0.39	33	−1.02	34
Indonesia	−0.28	0	−0.71	32

Source: Author's calculations, using data from World Bank, *World Development Indicators*, https://databank.worldbank.org/source/world-development-indicators.

Figure 4.2 GDP shares by sector (Indonesia, 1981–2017)

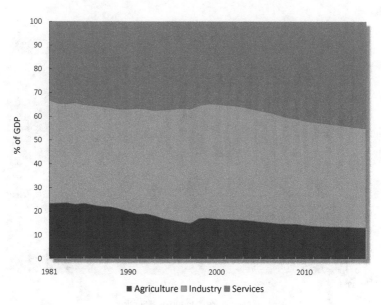

■ Agriculture ■ Industry ■ Services

Source: Author's calculations, using data from World Bank, *World Development Indicators*, https://databank.worldbank.org/source/world-development-indicators.

2.2 Employment Shares

These calculations yield more surprises when conducted in terms of employment shares. The data are shown in Figures 4.3 and 4.4 and summarized in columns [3] and [4] of Table 4.1. In Thailand, agriculture's employment share contracted by a dramatic 37 percentage points—from 68 to 31 per cent—from 1981 to 2017, an annual contraction rate of 1.02 per cent. At the same time, the employment share of industry and services rose by 12 and 24 percentage points, respectively. Abstracting from temporary unemployment, for every 100 workers leaving agriculture, 34 found jobs in industry and 66 in services.

Performing the same calculations for Indonesia, agriculture's employment share contracted by 25 percentage points, from 55 per cent to 30 per cent for the same period, an annual contraction rate of 0.71 per cent, while industry's share rose by 8 percentage points and services by 17 percentage points. Abstracting again from temporary unemployment, for every 100 workers leaving agriculture, 32 relocated to industry and 68 to services.

Figure 4.3. Employment shares by sector (Thailand, 1981–2017)

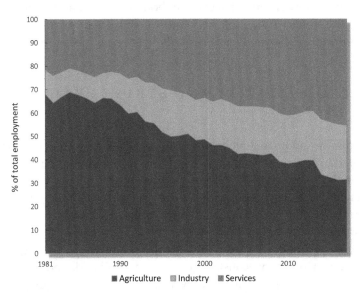

Source: Author's calculations, using data from World Bank, *World Development Indicators*, https://databank.worldbank.org/source/world-development-indicators.

Figure 4.4. Employment shares by sector (Indonesia, 1981–2017)

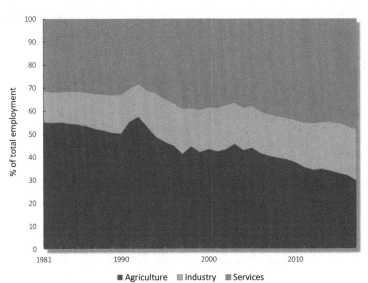

Source: Author's calculations, using data from World Bank, *World Development Indicators*, https://databank.worldbank.org/source/world-development-indicators.

The numbers for the two countries are remarkably similar. Structural transformation was a massive event in both. In output and employment terms, the relative size of agriculture contracted greatly, but the corresponding expansion was primarily in services, not industry.

3 PRODUCTIVITY AND STRUCTURAL CHANGE

Economic development involves more than just raising output per worker, but it certainly requires it. In another of his rightly famous contributions of 1994, Krugman (1994b) wrote memorably that in economic terms, "productivity isn't everything, but in the long run it is almost everything. A country's ability to improve its standard of living over time depends almost entirely on its ability to raise its output per worker."

Figures 4.5 and 4.6 summarize labour productivity (average value added per worker at constant prices) in Thailand and Indonesia, respectively, in agriculture, industry and services, and in aggregate.

Figure 4.5.   Labour productivity by sector (Thailand, 1981–2017)

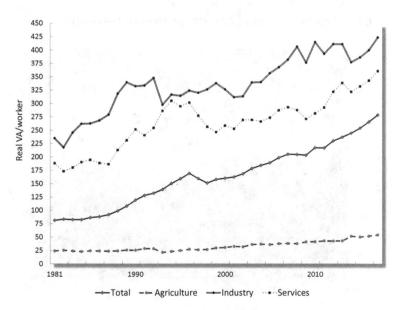

Source: Author's calculations, using data from World Bank, *World Development Indicators*, https://databank.worldbank.org/source/world-development-indicators.

Figure 4.6. Labour productivity by sector (Indonesia, 1981–2017)

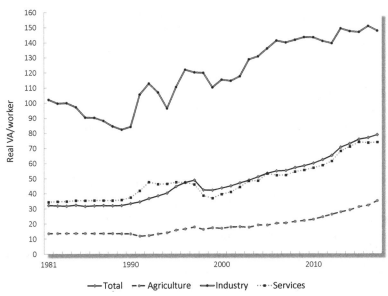

Source: Author's calculations, using data from World Bank, *World Development Indicators*, https://databank.worldbank.org/source/world-development-indicators.

As these charts show, in both countries the level of labour productivity in agriculture in 1981 was low, relative to other sectors. Over time, the gap between agricultural and non-agricultural labour productivity narrowed somewhat but remained large. Thailand's labour productivity level in agriculture in 1981 was only 10.3 per cent of the average level in industry and 12.7 per cent of the level in services. By 2017 these proportions were 12.6 and 25.4 per cent, respectively. Indonesia's story is qualitatively similar. In 1981 labour productivity in agriculture was 13.2 per cent of the average level in industry and 39.5 per cent of the level in services. By 2017 these proportions were 23.7 and 47.5 per cent, respectively.

Table 4.2 summarizes the key features of labour productivity growth in Thailand and Indonesia. In both countries, the average growth rate of labour productivity within agriculture (column [2]) exceeded that of industry and services. This finding contrasts with the fact that the average growth rate of total output from agriculture was lower than that from industry or services, as revealed by the decline in agriculture's share of GDP.

Table 4.2. Labour productivity growth by sector (1981–2017)

Country	Mean annual growth of real GDP per worker	Mean annual growth of sectoral real value added per worker		
		Agriculture	Industry	Services
	[1]	[2]	[3]	[4]
Thailand	3.55	2.57	1.82	1.98
Indonesia	2.59	2.78	1.22	2.29

Source: Author's calculations, using data from World Bank, *World Development Indicators*, https://databank.worldbank.org/source/world-development-indicators.

The difference occurs because in the calculation of sectoral labour productivity—sectoral output per worker employed—not just the numerator but also the denominator changed over time. Agriculture shed labour dramatically at the same time as its real output increased moderately. Output grew more rapidly in industry and services, but they absorbed additional labour in the process.

The mathematical relationship between productivity growth and structural change is derived in the Appendix, along with the residual method of calculation used to estimate this relationship using discrete (annual) data. Figures 4.7 and 4.8 present the annual decomposition implied by this analysis, using a three-year moving average to smooth annual fluctuations. Table 4.3 summarizes the decomposition for the full period, 1981–2017, including the Asian financial crisis period (1997–99) as well as for the pre-crisis (1981–96) and post-crisis (2000–2017) periods.[6]

Although in both countries productivity growth within agriculture was more rapid than in industry or services (columns [2], [3] and [4] of Table 4.2), agriculture's declining share of GDP meant that agriculture's within-sector productivity growth contributed (column [2] of Table 4.3) only a moderate proportion of economy-wide, within-sector productivity growth (column [5] of Table 4.3).

---

[6] The growth accounting framework implicitly assumes that output is supply constrained. When deficiency of aggregate demand constrains output, as in both Thailand and Indonesia during the 1997–99 Asian financial crisis, this assumption is invalid and supply-side growth accounting is potentially misleading. For this reason, Table 4.3 decomposes productivity growth for the full 1981–2017 period but also separately for the pre-crisis (1981–96) and post-crisis (2000–2017) periods.

Table 4.3. Contribution of structural change to aggregate productivity growth (1981–2017)

Country	Mean annual growth of real GDP per worker	Mean annual growth of GDP-share weighted sectoral real value added per worker			Contribution to productivity growth	
		Agriculture	Industry	Services	Within sector	Between sectors
	[1]	[2]	[3]	[4]	[5] = [2] + [3] + [4]	[6] = [1] − [5]
Thailand						
1981–2017: % per year	3.55	0.22	0.64	1.02	1.89	1.66
(1981–2017: % contribution)	(100)	(6)	(18)	(29)	(53)	(47)
1981–1996: % per year	4.39	0.11	0.72	1.31	2.14	2.25
(1981–1996: % contribution)	(100)	(3)	(16)	(30)	(49)	(51)
2000–2017: % per year	3.13	0.34	0.89	0.87	2.10	1.03
(2000–2017: % contribution)	(100)	(11)	(28)	(28)	(67)	(33)
Indonesia						
1981–2017: % per year	2.59	0.41	0.58	0.89	1.88	0.72
(1981–2017: % contribution)	(100)	(16)	(22)	(34)	(72)	(28)
1981–1996: % per year	2.70	0.29	0.65	0.71	1.65	1.05
(1981–1996: % contribution)	(100)	(11)	(24)	(26)	(61)	(39)
2000–2017: % per year	3.63	0.67	0.72	1.58	2.97	0.65
(2000–2017: % contribution)	(100)	(18)	(20)	(44)	(82)	(18)

Source: Author's calculations, using data from World Bank, *World Development Indicators*, https://databank.worldbank.org/source/world-development-indicators.

The reason is that the latter is weighted by agriculture's share of GDP, whereas the former is not. The proportion of economy-wide, within-sector productivity growth contributed by agriculture was 12 per cent in Thailand and 22 per cent in Indonesia. Relative to total growth of labour productivity (column [1] of Tables 4.2 and 4.3), productivity growth within agriculture itself (column [2] of Table 4.3) contributed only 6 per cent of total productivity growth in Thailand and 16 per cent in Indonesia. Productivity growth within industry and within services made larger contributions to overall productivity growth than productivity growth within agriculture in both countries, but services was the largest in both cases.

Table 4.3 reveals two key points about the percentage contribution of structural change to aggregate productivity growth. First, it was large: 47 per cent in Thailand and 28 per cent in Indonesia for the entire period (1981–2017). In both countries, structural transformation was a crucial component of the long-term increase in overall labour productivity. Second, this percentage contribution has declined, along with the declining economic importance of agriculture. Over the period following the Asian financial crisis (2000–2017), the estimated percentage contribution of structural change to aggregate productivity growth was substantially less than its pre-crisis (1981–1997) value in both countries.

Figures 4.7 and 4.8 reveal two further significant points. First, during the booming mid-1990s, structural change was an especially important contributor to aggregate productivity growth. Second, this contribution ceased during the Asian financial crisis (1997–99). Millions of workers who had relocated from agriculture to urban employment in manufacturing, construction and services during the boom lost their jobs during this period of contraction and were compelled to undertake low-productivity employment in farming and petty trading. This was reverse structural transformation. A similar phenomenon apparently occurred in 2020 in response to the COVID-19 pandemic.

The above observations suggest that faster overall labour productivity growth coincides with a higher percentage contribution from structural change. Figure 4.9 relates annual data on these variables for both countries, seemingly confirming a positive relationship for both countries. A simple linear regression was run separately for each country, with the annual percentage contribution of structural change to labour productivity growth as dependent variable and the annual rate of overall labour productivity growth as independent variable.

Figure 4.7. Productivity growth and structural change (Thailand, 1981–2017)

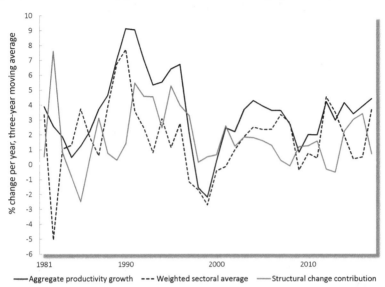

Source: Author's calculations, using data from World Bank, *World Development Indicators*, https://databank.worldbank.org/source/world-development-indicators.

Figure 4.8. Productivity growth and structural change (Indonesia, 1981–2017)

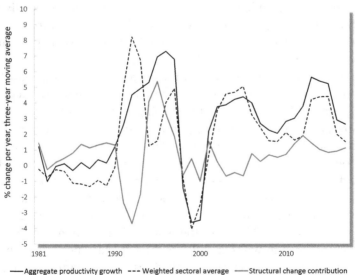

Source: Author's calculations, using data from World Bank, *World Development Indicators*, https://databank.worldbank.org/source/world-development-indicators.

Figure 4.9. Productivity growth and percentage contribution from structural change (Thailand and Indonesia, 1981–2017)

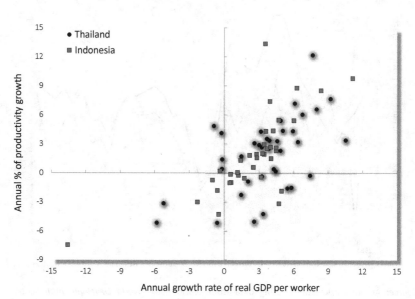

Source: Author's calculations, using data from World Bank, *World Development Indicators*, https://databank.worldbank.org/source/world-development-indicators.

The results (see Table 4.4) show that the relationship was positive and significant at the 99 per cent confidence level for each country. The data indicate that the proportional contribution of structural change is largest when overall productivity growth is most rapid.

Finally, it should be noted that the estimated share of productivity growth attributed to structural change will increase as the degree of disaggregation increases. Structural change occurs within agriculture, industry and services themselves, and it is distinct from factor growth or technical change. For example, if labour moves within agriculture from low-productivity rice production to higher-productivity vegetable production, or within services from low-productivity personal services to higher-productivity banking services, the measured contribution of structural change will increase in each case. If industries are disaggregated to, say, 20 sectors, the estimated proportional contribution of structural change will generally be higher than (not less than) that estimated with three sectors. If industries are disaggregated to, say, 40 sectors, the estimated proportional contribution will be higher again.

Table 4.4. Structural change and productivity growth rate: Regression results (Thailand and Indonesia, 1981–2017)

Parameter	Thailand		Indonesia	
Coefficient name	a	b	a	b
Coefficient value	−0.290	0.620	−0.190	0.790
Standard error	0.770	0.160	0.580	0.130
t-statistic	−0.380	4.010	−0.330	6.160
p-value	0.695	0.000	0.526	0.000
R^2	0.32		0.52	
$\overline{R}^2$	0.30		0.51	
F(0, 35)	16.10		39.94	
Years	1981–2017		1981–2014	
Observations	37		37	

Note: The above estimates relate to the regression equation $C_t^k = a^k + b^k \widehat{Z_t^k} + u_t^k$, where C_t^k is the percentage contribution of structural change to labour productivity growth in country k in year t, $\widehat{Z_t^k}$ is the growth rate of labour productivity in country k in year t and u_t^k is an error term. The coefficient a^k is an intercept term and b^k is the slope coefficient of interest.

Source: Author's calculations, using data from World Bank, *World Development Indicators*.

The above results show that in economies containing substantial traditional agricultural sectors, like most of Asia, the contribution of structural change is large, even within a framework that recognizes just three sectors.

4 CONCLUSIONS

Paul Krugman's celebrated essay of 1994 argues that the growth of labour productivity in Asia was due almost entirely to increasing labour force participation and adding capital to labour, as distinct from technical change. The article rightly discounts the miracle rhetoric that had been applied to Asia's rapid economic growth over the preceding two decades. Krugman's own account of Asia's growth rests on the distinction between "perspiration" and "inspiration". But his analysis misses a key point. By focusing on enclave, city-based economies like Singapore and Hong Kong, atypical of Asia because of the absence of traditional agriculture, Krugman overlooks the role of agriculture and the process of structural transformation.[7] This is the process through which workers relocate from agriculture to industry and, more especially, services, raising overall labour productivity. The process of labour relocation corresponds to neither of Krugman's categories of "perspiration" and "inspiration", but it contributed significantly to long-term growth of labour productivity in both Thailand and Indonesia. Between 1981 and 2017, that contribution was 47 per cent in Thailand and 28 per cent in Indonesia.

Leaving Krugman's analysis aside, overlooking the importance of agriculture in the development process is common, based on the view that this sector is static or backward. But this is a mistake. Understanding the key role of structural transformation changes the way we view the development process. It draws attention to the capacity of agriculture to contribute to overall output while *reducing* its claim on scarce productive resources, making them available for productive use elsewhere.

These issues matter. The policies that encourage (a) labour force participation and accumulation of capital relative to labour and (b) technical change in specific industries are not necessarily the same as those that facilitate (c) structural change. Recognition of the central developmental role of structural change directs attention to policies that can contribute to labour-saving technical change in agriculture and which facilitate the mobility of labour between sectors. These include not only productive investments in agriculture itself, but also in the public infrastructure required to improve the lives of people migrating from rural to urban areas, together with the education needed to aid their transition into non-agricultural employment.

---

[7] In the development economics literature, the role of the agricultural sector in the process of structural transformation and the importance of the latter in overall economic development have been well documented. Seminal examples are the classic presentation by Johnston and Mellor (1961), World Bank (2008) and Timmer (2014). In the context of the Philippines, these important issues are discussed in Ravago and Balisacan (2016, 5–9).

APPENDIX: LABOUR PRODUCTIVITY AND STRUCTURAL CHANGE

Continuous time derivation

By definition, real gross domestic product is given by $GDP = \sum_{j=1}^{J} V^j$, where V^j denotes real value added in sector j. Aggregate labour productivity can be written as

$$Z = GDP/L = \sum_{j=1}^{J} V^j / L = \sum_{j=1}^{J} S^{Lj} Z^j, \qquad (1)$$

where $L = \sum_{j=1}^{J} L^j$ is total employment, L^j is employment in sector j, is the $S^{Lj} = L^j/L$ is the share of sector j in total employment and $Z^j = V^j/L^j$ is the productivity of labour in sector j.

The change in total labour productivity—GDP per worker—is obtained by differentiating equation (1):

$$dZ = \sum_{j=1}^{J} S^{Lj} dZ^j + \sum_{j=1}^{J} Z^j dS^{Lj}. \qquad (2)$$

Equation (2) is intuitively helpful. It states that the total change in aggregate labour productivity is given by the sum of two terms: the sum across sectors of changes in labour productivity within individual sectors, each weighted by its share in total employment, and the sum across sectors of the changes in employment shares, each weighted by its level of labour productivity. The first of these terms becomes the basis for within-sector sources of productivity growth and the second becomes the basis for between-sector sources.

Using the notation $\hat{X} = dX/X$ for the proportional change of a variable X, it is readily confirmed from (2) that the proportional change in the aggregate productivity of labour is

$$\hat{Z} = \sum_{j=1}^{J} S^{Vj} \hat{Z}^j + \sum_{j=1}^{J} S^{Vj} \hat{S}^{Lj}, \qquad (3)$$

where $S^{Vj} = V^j/GDP$ is the GDP share of sector j.

Equation (3) states that the proportional change—growth rate—of aggregate labour productivity is equal to the sum across sectors of two terms: (i) the GDP-share-weighted proportional change in the sector's labour productivity ($\hat{Z}^j$) and (ii) the GDP-share-weighted proportional change in the employment share of that sector ($\hat{S}^{Lj}$). The contribution of structural change to aggregate productivity growth is therefore given by the difference between the proportional change of aggregate labour productivity ($\hat{Z}$) and the sectoral GDP-share-weighted sum of the proportional change of labour productivity in each sector:

$$\sum_{j=1}^{J} S^{Vj} \hat{S}^{Lj} = \hat{Z} - \sum_{j=1}^{J} S^{Vj} \hat{Z}^{j}. \qquad (4)$$

Discrete time application

For empirical application using discrete (annual) data, the method of calculation is as follows. Real GDP in year t is given by $GDP_t = \sum_j V_t^j$, where V_t^j is real value added in sector j at time t. Real GDP per worker = $GDP_t/L_t = Z_t$. Its annual growth rate, $\hat{Z}_t$, is calculated by

$$\hat{Z}_t = 100(Z_t - Z_{t-1})/Z_t. \qquad (5)$$

Sectoral real value added per worker in sector j is given by

$$Z_t^j = V_t^j / L_t^j, \qquad (6)$$

where L_t^j is employment in sector j at time t.

The growth rate of GDP can now be divided into two components. The first component corresponds to categories (a) and (b) combined, in the introductory section of the text, and the first right-hand term in equation (3). Using discrete period data, the GDP-share-weighted growth of real sectoral value added in all sectors at time t is approximated by

$$\sum_j [(S_t^j + S_{t-1}^j)/2] \hat{Z}_t^j, \qquad (7)$$

where $S_t^j = V_t^j/GDP_t$ is the share of sector j in GDP. Expression (7) makes allowance for the fact that when discrete (annual) data are being used, S_t^j and S_{t-1}^j will normally differ and equation (7) takes their linear mid-point.

The estimated contribution of structural change corresponds to category (c) in the text. It takes account of the movement of resources between sectors and is calculated as a residual from

$$\hat{Z} - \sum_j [(S_t^j + S_{t-1}^j)/2] \hat{Z}_t^j. \qquad (8)$$

ACKNOWLEDGEMENT

The research assistance of Huong Lien Do and the helpful comments of Prema-chandra Athukorala, Hal Hill and Majah-Leah V. Ravago are gratefully acknowledged. The author is responsible for all views and any errors.

REFERENCES

Hill, Hal. 2018. "Asia's Third Giant: A Survey of the Indonesian Economy". *The Economic Record* 94, no. 307: 469–99.

Johnston, Bruce F., and Mellor, John W. 1961. "The Role of Agriculture in Economic Development". *American Economic Review* 51, no. 4: 566–93.

Krugman, Paul. 1994a. "The Myth of Asia's Miracle". *Foreign Affairs* 73, no. 6: 62–78.

———. 1994b. *The Age of Diminished Expectations*. Cambridge, MA: MIT Press.

Lau, Lawrence J., and Kim, Jong-Il. 1993. "The Role of Human Capital in the Economic Growth of the East Asian Newly Industrialized Countries". mimeo, Stanford University.

———. 1994. "The Sources of Growth of the East Asian Newly Industrialized Countries". *Journal of the Japanese and International Economies* 8: 235–271.

Ravago, Majah-Leah V., and Arsenio M. Balisacan, eds. 2016. *Agricultural Policy and Institutional Reforms in the Philippines: Experiences, Impacts, and Lessons*. Los Baños, Philippines: SEARCA.

Solow, Robert. 1957. "Technical Change and the Aggregate Production Function". *Review of Economics and Statistics* 39, no. 3: 312–20.

Timmer, C. Peter. 2014. "Managing Structural Transformation: A Political Economy Approach". *WIDER Annual Lecture* 18. Helsinki: United Nations University.

Warr, Peter. 2020. "Economic Development of Post-War Thailand". In *Handbook of Contemporary Thailand*, edited by Pavin Chachavalpongpun, pp. 36–51. London: Routledge.

World Bank. 2008. *World Development Report 2008: Agriculture for Development*. London: Oxford University Press for the World Bank.

Young, Alvin. 1992. "A Tale of Two Cities: Factor Accumulation and Technical Change in Hong Kong and Singapore". *NBER Macroeconomics Annual* 7: 13–54.

———. 1994a. "Lessons from the East Asian NICs: A Contrarian View". *European Economic Review* 38: 964–73.

———. 1994b. "The Tyranny of Numbers: Confronting the Statistical Realities of the East Asian Growth Experience". *NBER Working Paper* No. 4680 (March). Cambridge, MA: National Bureau of Economic Research.

5 The Role of Agricultural and Structural Transformations in Rural Poverty Reduction

Jikun Huang

1　INTRODUCTION

It is my great honour to participate in this Festschrift to recognize the contribution of Professor Arsenio M. Balisacan in development economics, especially in agricultural and rural development. I took his course on macroeconomics at the University of the Philippines Los Baños in the late 1980s; we have closely kept in touch through various academic activities and conferences since the early 1990s. Professor Balisacan has contributed significantly to our understanding of rural development and poverty reduction in Asia, in general, and the Philippines, in particular. Because of this, I decided to write this paper on facilitating a more inclusive agricultural transformation, focusing on China, the Philippines and three other Southeast Asian countries for which I have data.

China and Southeast Asia are interesting cases because they have experienced rapid economic growth. Average annual growth of gross domestic product (GDP) in China and Southeast Asia recorded 9.5 per cent and 5.0 per cent, respectively, in 1990–2019, which were much higher than the 3.3 per cent global GDP annual growth rate over the same period. China and Southeast Asia have also experienced rapid urbanization. The share of urban population increased from 19 per cent in 1980 to 61 per cent in 2019 in China; it was from 26 per cent to nearly 50 per cent in Southeast Asia for the same period.[1]

The rising income and urbanization have resulted in significant changes in the food demand and rural transformation in China and Southeast Asia. In general, as income increased and urban areas expanded, so has consumer demand for more food and diversified diets (Reardon and Timmer 2014). In responding to the food demand changes, agricultural production has also been gradually shifting from cereal to non-cereal commodities, including high-value crops, livestock and fishery.[2] Urbanization and structural transformation have been accompanied also by rapid growth of off-farm employment in China and many countries in Asia (Haggblade, Hazell, and Reardon 2010; Hoang, Cong, and Ulubasoglu 2014; Huang and Shi 2021).

In Asia, rural transformation within agriculture is often associated with the fall in rural poverty (IFAD 2016). From 1981 to 2011, the share of population under poverty in developing countries in Asia had declined from 71 per cent to 15 per cent (based on the PPP US$1/day poverty yardstick), and from 91 per cent to 40 per cent (based on the PPP $2/day poverty yardstick) (World Bank 2020). However, poverty reduction rates vary largely among these countries.

This paper provides an overview of the paths and inclusiveness of rural transformation within agriculture (or agricultural transformation) in China and Southeast Asia, particularly Cambodia (KHM), Indonesia (IDN), the Philippines (PHL) and Vietnam (VNM). Rural transformation is defined as "a process that involves rising agricultural productivity, increasing commercialization and marketable surpluses, and diversification of production patterns and livelihoods. It also involves expanded decent off-farm employment and entrepreneurial opportunities, better rural coverage and access to services and infrastructure, and greater access to, and capacity to influence, relevant policy processes" (IFAD 2016).

Given that off-farm employment data over time are not available and recognizing that rural transformation is interconnected with structural transformation, this paper focuses on rural transformation within agriculture, addressing three questions: What are the paths, levels and speeds of agricultural transformation and structural transformation

---

[1] Estimated based on the data from World Development Indicators, World Bank (2020).
[2] Based on FAOSTAT (FAO 2020).

in China and the selected Southeast Asia countries in the past three to four decades? How inclusive are the agricultural and structural transformations in these countries? What policy implications are likely to facilitate inclusive agricultural transformation? Because inclusiveness in development covers many dimensions (e.g., poverty, income distribution, gender, youth, indigenous people, left behind regions), this study limits its scope by focusing the analysis on rural poverty. The analysis is based on graphical analysis using secondary data at the national level.

The paper is organized as follows: Section 2 introduces the overall trends of structural transformation and agricultural transformation in the studied countries. Section 3 examines the inclusiveness of agricultural transformations, focusing on rural poverty reduction and typology of inclusive agricultural transformation. The last section concludes with policy implications.

2 STRUCTURAL AND AGRICULTURAL TRANSFORMATIONS

Structural transformation (ST) and agricultural transformation (AT) are interconnected. A successful AT can stimulate economic growth and ST, and ST can enhance AT and provide rural labour more off-farm employment, which raises agricultural labour productivity (IFAD 2016).

2.1 Structural transformation

Generally, all five countries studied have experienced smooth structural transformation since the 1980s. Figure 5.1 shows the ST trends in these countries. Across countries, higher income is generally associated with lower share of agriculture in overall GDP; within a country, rising income is accompanied with a fall in agricultural GDP share. Moreover, the gap between agricultural GDP share and agricultural employment share tends to converge with the ST process. The trends observed in Figure 5.1 confirm the findings on ST advanced by Timmer (2009 and 2014).

The convergence of agricultural GDP and employment shares in the economies suggests that agricultural productivity growth and the ability of the non-agriculture sector to generate employment for rural labour are essential for rapid structural transformation.

The Role of Agricultural and Structural Transformations in Rural Poverty Reduction   119

Figure 5.1.   Convergence of agricultural shares in GDP and employment in China and selected Southeast Asian countries (1980s, 2000 and 2019)

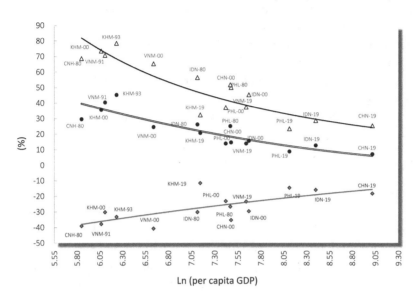

● Agricultural GDP (%)   △ Agricultural employmnet (%)   ◆ Agricultrural GDP (%) - agricultural employment (%)

Note: (1) Per capita GDP is in real terms at a constant US$ of 2010 and take Ln form (X-axis).
(2) The triangle, circle and square dots represent agricultural employment (%), agricultural GDP (%) and the difference between agricultural GDP (%) and agricultural employment (%), respectively. The countries are Cambodia (KHM), China (CHN), Indonesia (IDN), the Philippines (PHL) and Vietnam (VNM).
(3) The starting year is 1980, except for VNM (1991) and KHM (1993) due to data availability.

Figure 5.1 also shows that the stage and speed of ST differ largely among countries. A more rapid structural transformation occurred in China than the other countries. China reached the Lewis Turning Point in the middle 2000s. After reaching this point, agricultural employment as a percentage of total employment tends to fall faster than agricultural GDP share, which ultimately closes the gap between the two ratios. The Philippines had the highest ST level in 1980 among the five countries studied, however, its ST speed had been the lowest in the past four decades.

While not shown in Figure 5.1, the countries with higher agricultural growth often also had higher overall economic growth and faster ST, reflecting the well-documented linkage effects of agriculture on industry and services (Johnston and Mellor 1961; Schultz 1964; Johnston 1970; Timmer 2009). These effects include the following: (1) release of surplus rural labour for industry and service sectors; (2) lowering of food prices, which helps keep down wages for workers in the urban economy; (3) lowering of the prices of fibre and other agricultural commodities used as inputs in industrial production; (4) supply of exportable commodities that can help finance imports of needed technology, capital equipment and others; and (5) raising of farmers' incomes, which can increase demand for industrial products.

2.2 Agricultural transformation

Within Asia's agriculture sector, the transformation normally starts with staple food (e.g., cereal) production. Rising agricultural productivity facilitates agricultural production, which moves from cereal production to the production of more diversified and high-value commodities (e.g., cash crops, meats and fishes) to meet the growing demand for diversified foods. In this study, we use two indicators to measure agricultural transformation: output value share of non-cereal products in agriculture and agricultural labour productivity measured in agricultural value added per agricultural labour. The latter is also used by IFAD (2016) as an important indicator for rural transformation.

Figure 5.2 shows that agricultural transformation has been occurring in all countries but through different pathways. In response to food demand changes, agriculture has gradually moved from largely cereal production to higher-value crops and livestock in three of the five countries studied. China (in the past four decades) and Vietnam (in the past three decades) have gradually diversified their agriculture from cereal-based to a more high-value one (e.g., vegetables, fruits, edible oils and livestock). Indonesia has also smoothly diversified from being dominantly rice to a more high-value agriculture (e.g., vegetable, fruits, palm oil and other oil crops, poultry, cattle and sheep) in the past four decades. Cambodia and the Philippines are exceptions—they have tended to move towards a more cereal-based or less diversified agriculture in the past several decades (Figure 5.2). The high rice price protection may largely explain the path of agricultural transformation in the Philippines.

Figure 5.2. Output value share of non-cereal products in agriculture (crop and livestock) in China and selected Southeast Asian countries (1981–2018)

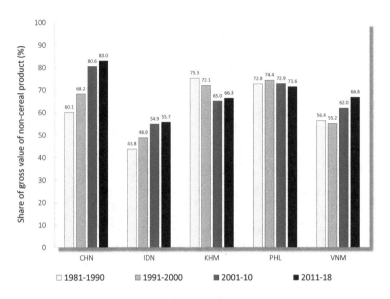

Note: Agriculture here includes only crops and livestock, excluding fishery.
Sources: The raw data are from FAO (2020) for Cambodia, Indonesia, the Philippines and Vietnam and from NBSC (various years) for China

Agricultural transformation measured by agricultural labour productivity has taken a similar path in all countries, but its level and speed differ significantly among the five countries (Figure 5.3). Agricultural labour productivity has increased in all countries in the past three decades. It was much higher in China and Indonesia than the other three countries in recent years. Because China started with a much lower level than Indonesia, it has increased faster than the latter. The Philippines and Indonesia started with a similarly high level of agricultural labour productivity in the 1990s, but the former has ended up at a much lower level in the past decade. The speed of structural transformation (creating more non-farm employment) and agricultural transformation (moving to high-value agriculture) as well as annual population growth (1.90% in the Philippines and 1.37% in Indonesia in 1991–2019) may explain the speed of agricultural labour productivity growth in these two countries. On the other hand, Cambodia and

Figure 5.3.   Agricultural labour productivity in China and selected Southeast Asian countries (1991–2019)

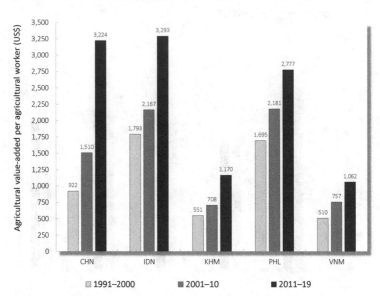

Note: (1)   Agricultural labour productivity is in real terms at a constant US$ of 2010.
(2)   KHM data for agricultural value added per agricultural labour are for the period 1994–2019.
Source: The raw data are from FAO (2020) for all countries.

Vietnam have remained at a low level and have experienced moderate agricultural transformation in terms of agricultural labour productivity in the past three decades (Figure 5.3).

3   INCLUSIVENESS OF STRUCTURAL AND AGRICULTURAL TRANSFORMATIONS

Although all the five countries have experienced large reductions in rural poverty in the recent decades, the extent differs from country to country. China and Indonesia have the most significant decline in rural poverty incidence in the entire period studied. The reduction is significant also in Vietnam, Cambodia and the Philippines in the later stages (Figure 5.4).[3]

---

[3]   Rural poverty data are not available for recent years in WDI database.

Figure 5.4. Share of rural population under poverty in China and selected Southeast Asian countries (1987–2012)

(a) Rural poverty headcount ratio at US$1.25 a day (PPP) (% of population)

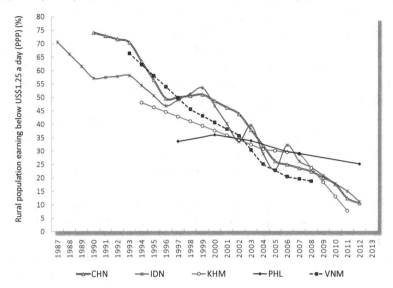

(b) Rural poverty headcount ratio at US$2 a day (PPP) (% of population)

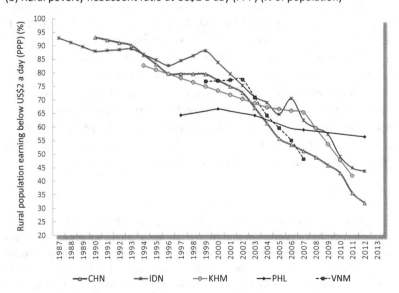

Source: Based on World Development Indicators (World Bank 2015).

3.1 Structural transformation and rural poverty reduction

Previous studies have demonstrated that economic growth is essential for poverty reduction, but its impact on rural poverty reduction differs among countries due to the nature or inclusiveness of growth (Balisacan and Fuwa 2003; Huang, Zhang, and Rozelle 2008; Timmer 2009; World Bank 2008). Because economic growth is also an outcome of structural and rural transformations, here we address the roles of structural transformation on rural poverty reduction. On the relationship between structural transformation and rural poverty reduction, we calculate average annual change in the share of non-agricultural GDP (or non-agricultural employment) as the speed of structural change and average annual change in rural poverty rate as the speed of rural poverty reduction in the studied periods. The results are presented in Figure 5.5.

The results show a general negative relationship between the speed of structural transformation and the speed of rural poverty reduction. In Figure 5.5, the coordinate point is the mean for each of the five countries. The Philippines, located in the second quadrant (upper left quadrant), had both slow ST and slow rural poverty reduction; while Cambodia, China and Vietnam, located in the fourth quadrant (lower right quadrant), experienced fast ST and fast rural poverty reduction. A higher annual increase in the share of non-agricultural GDP (or share of non-agricultural employment) is associated with more rapid rural poverty reduction, which can be explained by the fact that industrialization has provided more employment for rural labour and, therefore, raised the income of rural households and reduced rural poverty.[4] Indonesia is an exception: despite having a relatively slower ST than other countries, its rate of rural poverty reduction was slightly above average. Timmer (2004) argues that Indonesia's long-run pro-poor growth record is among the best in Southeast Asia due to the country's efforts to balance growth and distribution during its structural transformation.

---

[4] The positive relationship between the speed of structural transformation and rural poverty reduction should be stronger than the results presented in Figure 5.5 if we consider that rural poverty incidence (%) is always higher than urban poverty incidence in the five countries studied and that the poverty incidence of urban migrants from rural areas and their families is often lower than the poverty incidence of all households who are in rural areas.

Figure 5.5. Average annual change in share of agricultural GDP (or employment) and average annual reduction in rural poverty incidence in the period indicated in China and selected Southeast Asian countries

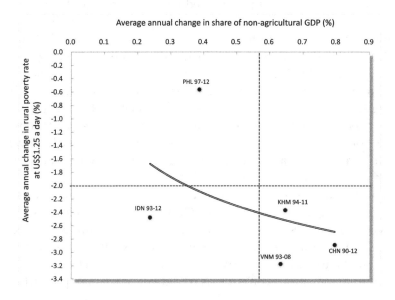

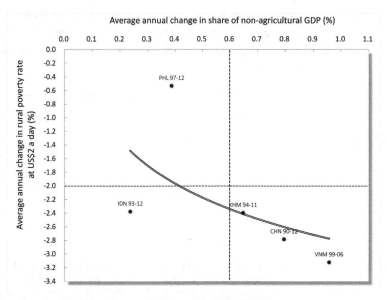

Source: Based on World Development Indicators (World Bank 2015).

3.2 Agricultural transformation and rural poverty reduction

Following the same approach as that in structural transformation, we examine the relationship between the speed of agricultural transformation and rural poverty reduction. For speed of agricultural transformation, we use average annual change in the share of non-cereal output value in agriculture and average annual growth rate of agricultural labour productivity. The results are presented in Figures 5.6 and 5.7. Generally, there is a negative relationship between the speed of rural transformation and annual change in rural poverty incidence. That is, the faster the speed of agricultural transformation, the faster the rate of rural poverty reduction. Interestingly, the above general relationship holds for agricultural transformation measured either in high-value agriculture share or agricultural labour productivity and rural poverty based on either at US$1.25/day or US$2/day.

The relationships presented in Figures 5.6 and 5.7 are consistent with the findings of a study by IFAD (2016) that includes more countries in Asia. As agriculture shifts faster to high-value commodities, rural households or farmers can achieve higher income growth, thus increasing their ability to escape poverty. The other common characteristic of agricultural transformation is the rise of agricultural labour productivity.

Figure 5.6. Average annual change of non-cereal output value share in agriculture and average annual reduction in rural poverty incidence in the period indicated in China and selected Southeast Asian countries

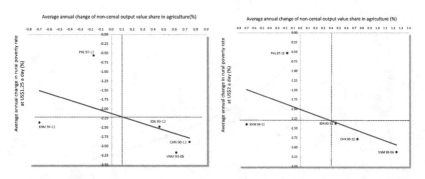

Sources: The raw data for non-cereal output value share are from FAO (2020) for Cambodia, Indonesia, the Philippines and Vietnam and from NBSC (various years) for China. The raw data for rural poverty incidence are from World Development Indicators (World Bank 2015).

Figure 5.7. Average annual growth of agricultural labour productivity and average annual reduction in rural poverty incidence in the period indicated in China and selected Southeast Asian countries

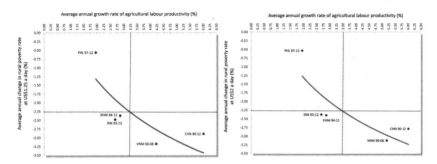

Sources: The raw data are from FAO (2020) for agricultural labour productivity and from World Development Indicators (World Bank 2015) for rural poverty incidence.

Overall, the five countries studied have experienced high growth in agricultural labour productivity, although the growth rates vary across countries. As most of the poor in these countries live in rural areas and are heavily dependent on agriculture for their livelihoods, agricultural labour productivity is important for rural poverty reduction.

3.3 Typology of agricultural transformation

Based on the speed of rural poverty reduction and the speeds of ST and AT, we classify the five countries into different categories of inclusiveness of agricultural and structural transformations. First, we use the average annual change in AT of the five countries in the studied periods and then classify these countries into two groups: fast AT and slow AT. Second, we follow a similar approach and classify each country as either fast ST or slow ST. Third, the five countries are grouped into fast, moderate and slow rural poverty reduction, based on their speed of rural poverty reduction during the studied periods. Following the above rules, Table 5.1 presents the categories of inclusive agricultural transformation in the five countries. The left-side column of Table 5.1 presents the AT typology as measured using output value share of non-cereal products in agriculture (AT1); the right side presents the AT typology as measured using agricultural labour productivity (AT2). Interestingly, the resulting categories of inclusive AT based on the two measurements are consistent for all five countries.

Table 5.1. Categories of inclusive agricultural transformation (AT) based on the speeds of structural transformation (ST) and AT

		Speed of rural poverty reduction					
		AT based on AT1			AT based on AT2		
		Fast	Moderate	Slow	Fast	Moderate	Slow
Fast AT	Fast ST	China	Indonesia		China	Indonesia	
	Slow ST						
Slow AT	Fast ST	Vietnam	Cambodia		Vietnam	Cambodia	
	Slow ST			Philippines			Philippines

Table 5.1 reveals the following important observations:
1. No country has experienced fast rural poverty reduction in the absence of both fast ST and fast AT (the bottom left corner of Table 5.1 is empty).
2. No country has experienced slow rural poverty reduction in the presence of both fast ST and fast AT (the top right corner of Table 5.1 is empty).
3. The country that has gone through both fast ST and fast AT experiences fast rural poverty reduction (i.e., China).
4. The country that has gone through both slow ST and slow AT experiences slow rural poverty reduction (i.e., the Philippines).
5. The country that has gone through either a fast ST or a fast AT experiences moderate rural poverty reduction (i.e., Cambodia and Indonesia).

Based on these results, we further divide these five countries into three categories:

Category I: fast ST, AT and rural poverty reduction country (e.g., China). This category is classic but characterized by a much more rapid ST and AT than the "classic" transformation experienced by developed countries in the twentieth century. A successful AT facilitates ST and vice versa, as AT and ST are strongly linked and interact with each other. Combined, they also significantly reduce rural poverty.

Category II: fast (or slow) in either ST or AT and moderate poverty reduction (e.g., Cambodia and Indonesia) or fast poverty reduction (e.g., Vietnam). Vietnam is an interesting case as the country achieved fast poverty reduction even if AT was not very fast.

Category III: slow ST, AT and poverty reduction (e.g., the Philippines). A slow ST and AT contribute to slow rural poverty reduction.

4 CONCLUSIONS AND POLICY IMPLICATIONS

China, Cambodian, Indonesia, the Philippines and Vietnam have experienced structural transformation similar to many other developing countries, but with differing speeds. Such structural transformation is characterized by the fall of agricultural share in total GDP and employment and the convergence of the shares of agricultural GDP and employment in the economy. However, the extent of convergence of the transformation varies among the countries studied.

At the same time, all five countries have also undergone agricultural or rural transformation. Such transformation often started with the adoption of modern varieties of rice and wheat and increasing access to water and modern inputs (or the Green Revolution). Increases in grain production due to agricultural productivity growth have enabled farmers to expand production to higher-value cash crops, livestock and fishery products. As the agricultural production structure shifts to high-value products, agricultural labour productivity increases also. This rural transformation within agriculture strongly correlates with rural poverty reduction.

Structural transformation and agricultural transformation are interlinked and affect each other. Successful agricultural transformation can stimulate economic growth and urbanization, and therefore overall structural transformation; vice versa, structural transformation, particularly through labour-intensive industrialization, can enhance agricultural and rural transformations by creating more jobs for rural labour.

The path and speed of ST and AT affect the inclusiveness of the transformations. Our typological analysis for the five countries shows that the country with both fast ST and AT experiences fast rural poverty reduction; the country with both slow ST and AT experiences slow rural poverty reduction; and the country with either fast (or slow) ST and AT experiences moderate or fast rural poverty reduction.

Differences in the speed of ST and AT lie mainly in agricultural productivity growth and the extent of employment generation in the farm and non-farm sectors in both rural and urban areas. While many factors may affect the path and speed of ST and AT, this paper focuses on the major factors and how they affect the transformations. More investigations are needed to understand how institutions (e.g., land), policies (e.g., various incentive policies) and investments (e.g., technology, irrigation and roads) affect the path, speed and inclusiveness of agricultural transformation.

The results of this study have several policy implications for inclusive agricultural transformation. Strategies to facilitate inclusive agricultural transformation need strategic focus, as follows:

- Use both structural transformation and agricultural transformation as major national strategies to enhance inclusive rural transformation. Growth and inclusiveness are outcomes of ST and AT. Without significant ST and AT, it is hard to achieve rapid growth and more inclusive outcomes.

- Identify the country's stage of rural transformation and seek the most appropriate institution, policy and investment that can help the country shift or graduate faster from the current to the next stage of rural transformation.
- For category I countries (fast in ST, AT and poverty reduction), enhance the current institutions, policies and investments that have facilitated the rapid ST and AT and inclusiveness (e.g., rural poverty reduction).
- For category II countries (fast or slow in either ST and AT and moderate or fast rural poverty reduction), bring the country back on the track of both fast ST and AT, and overcome major institutional, policy and investment failures that have prevented the country from having a successful ST and AT.
- For category III countries (slow ST, AT and rural poverty reduction), facilitate the country's faster ST and AT. Major institutions, policies and investment programmes governing ST and AT in the country should be carefully reviewed and evaluated. Compared with countries in the other categories, those in category III have much more room for changes in their national development strategies and policies.

ACKNOWLEDGEMENT

The author acknowledges the financial support from the International Fund for Agricultural Development (IFAD: 2000000866) and Australian Centre for International Agricultural Research (ADP/2017/024). He thanks the research assistance provided by Pengfei Shi, Huayong Zhi and Qiu Chen.

REFERENCES

Balisacan, A. M., and N. Fuwa. 2003. "Growth, Inequality and Politics Revisited: A Developing-Country Case". *Economics Letters* 79: 53–58.

FAO (Food and Agriculture Organization). 2020. FAO STAT. http://faostat3.fao.org/home/E.

Haggblade, S., P. Hazell, and T. Reardon. 2010. "The Rural Non-farm Economy: Prospects for Growth and Poverty Reduction". *World Development* 38, no. 10: 1429–42.

Hoang, T. X., S. P. Cong, and M.A. Ulubasoglu. 2014. "Non-farm Activity, Household Expenditure and Poverty Reduction in Rural Vietnam: 2002–2008". *World Development* 64: 554–68.

Huang, J. K., and P. F. Shi. 2021. "Regional Rural and Structural Transformation and Farmer's Income in the Past Four Decades in China". *China Agricultural Economic Review*. https://doi.org/10.1108/CAER-11-2020-0262.

Huang, J. K., Q. Zhang, and S. Rozelle. 2008. "Economic Growth, the Nature of Growth and Poverty Reduction in Rural China". *China Economic Journal* 1, no. 1: 107–22.

IFAD (International Fund for Agricultural Development). 2016. *Rural Development Report 2016: Fostering Inclusive Rural Transformation*. Rome: IFAD.

Johnston, B. F. 1970. "Agriculture and Structural Transformation in Developing Countries: A Survey of Research". *Journal of Economic Literature* 8: 101–45.

Johnston, B. F., and J. W. Mellor. 1961. "The Role of Agriculture in Economic Development". *American Economic Review* 51, no. 4: 566–93.

NBSC (National Bureau of Statistics of China). 1981–2020. *Statistical Yearbook of China*. Beijing: China Statistical Press.

Reardon, T., and C. P. Timmer. 2014. "Five Interlinked Transformations in the Asian Agri-food Economy: Food Security Implications". *Global Food Security* 3, no. 2: 108–17.

Schultz, T. W. 1964. *Transforming Traditional Agriculture*. New Haven: Yale University Press.

Timmer, C. P. 2004. "The Road to Pro-Poor Growth: The Indonesian Experience in Regional Perspective". *Bulletin of Indonesian Economic Studies* 40, no. 2: 177–207.

———. 2009. *A World without Agriculture: The Structural Transformation in Historical Perspective*. Washington, DC: AEI Press.

———. 2014. "Managing Structural Transformation: A Political Economy Approach". *WIDER Annual Lecture* 18. Helsinki, UNU: World Institute for Development Economics Research.

World Bank. 2008. *World Development Report 2008: Agriculture for Development*. Washington, DC: World Bank.

———. 2015. *World Development Indicators*. Washington, DC: World Bank.

———. 2020. *World Development Indicators Database*. https://data.worldbank.org/.

6 The Changing Relationship between Farm Size and Productivity: Asia and the Philippines

Keijiro Otsuka

1 INTRODUCTION

No controversy in the history of agricultural economics has been more perennial than the relationship between farm size and productivity. From the days of Chayanov (1926) to the present, the dominant view has been the inverse relationship (IR) between farm size and productivity, particularly when productivity is measured by physical yield or gross value of production per hectare (e.g., Barrett, Bellemare, and Hou 2010; Larson et al. 2014; Delvaux, Riesgo, and Paloma 2020). Feder (1985) theoretically demonstrates that large farms tend to be less productive than small farms because they tend to use hired labour more intensively than small farms, and because hired workers do not work as hard as family workers. Based on this IR, Lipton (2012) advocates redistributive land reform as it is supposed to be conducive to both efficiency and equity.

However, Otsuka (2007) argues that the IR is partly a consequence of land reform programmes that suppress land rental transactions between less productive large farmers and more productive small farmers. He points out that the IR is found primarily in South Asia, where land reform programmes were widely implemented, but not in Southeast Asia, where they were not implemented rigorously, except in the Philippines.[1] Otsuka (2013), Estudillo and Otsuka (2016) and Otsuka, Liu, and Yamauchi (2016a) also maintain that by nature, small farms in Asia employ labour-intensive production methods. Since the wage rate has been rising sharply in many high-performing Asian countries, the production cost of small-scale farming has been increasing also. This has resulted in agriculture's loss of comparative advantage in this region. This argument suggests that the IR has been weakened in Asia because small farms' labour-intensive production is no longer advantageous. Using cross-country data from 1980 to 2010, Otsuka, Liu, and Yamauchi (2013) confirm the decline in the efficiency of smallholder agriculture. Thus, Asia as a whole may become a major importer of food grains unless farm-size expansion and large-scale mechanization take place (Yamauchi, Huang, and Otsuka, 2021).

A recent meta-regression analysis of roughly 1,000 cases by Delvaux, Riesgo, and Paloma (2020) shows the following results: (1) a strong IR tends to be found when gross value of output per hectare or physical yield is used to measure productivity; (2) a weak IR is generally found when net value of output (i.e., gross value of output minus cost of purchased inputs) is used; and (3) the farm size-productivity relationship becomes unclear when profit (i.e., net value of output minus imputed value of owned resources, including family labour) or total factor productivity is used.[2] Furthermore, several studies found a U-shaped relationship between farm size and productivity in Pakistan (Heltberg 1998), Brazil (Rada and Fuglie 2019) and China (Sheng, Ding, and Huang 2019). As will be discussed later, a positive relationship between farm size and productivity has been reported also in high-wage economies.

If factor markets work efficiently, no difference in productivity should be found across farms of different sizes because resources are transferred from less productive to more productive farms through land renting or labour employment (Kevane 1996). Therefore, the existence of an IR, positive or U-shaped relationship implies

---

[1] A possible exception is a study by Benjamin (1995), which found the IR in Indonesia when farm size was used as an explanatory variable, but found no relation between farm size and productivity when instruments were used to determine farm size.

[2] I presume that since both profit per hectare and total factor productivity take into account the contribution of whole inputs to production, they are highly correlated.

inefficiency of production due to market failures, which must be eradicated—ideally by means of policy.[3] To do so, we must clearly understand the causes of these different types of relationship between farm size and productivity.

First, this article aims to identify causes of the different and changing relationships between farm size and productivity based on a literature review. I have observed that an IR tends to be found in low-wage economies where farms are small and use labour-intensive methods. In contrast, a positive relationship tends to be found in high-wage economies where farms are large and adopt large-scale mechanization. The U-shaped relationship is found in economies where small-scale and large-scale farming systems coexist.

Second, this article reviews changes in farm size and the food self-sufficiency ratio over time in selected Asian countries in order to examine how farm size relates to the comparative advantage of agriculture. I would like to show that food self-sufficiency declines with economic development, which accompanies wage growth, unless significant farm-size expansion occurs (Otsuka 2013).

Third and last, this article aims to draw policy implications of the changing relationship between farm size and productivity for the future of Philippine agriculture, based on a review of rice farming systems in Central Luzon from 1966 to 2015. I assert that unless land reform policies are redirected towards farm-size expansion, the efficiency of Philippine agriculture is bound to decline with economic development in the future.

This article is organized as follows: Section 2 examines the theoretical causes of the inverse, positive and U-shaped relationships between farm size and productivity. Section 3 reviews the empirical evidence. Section 4 considers the future of small farms in East Asia (i.e., Northeast and Southeast Asia), reviews the long-term changes in rice farming systems in Central Luzon, and re-examines the impact of land reform programmes in the Philippines. The last section considers appropriate land policies for efficient land use in the course of successful economic development.

---

[3] I assume that soil quality is not different among farms of different sizes. See section 2 for a discussion on the possible impacts of soil quality difference on the farm size-productivity relationship.

2 ECONOMICS OF FARM SIZE-PRODUCTIVITY RELATIONSHIP

2.1 Conceptual framework

In order to grasp why differential productivity is observed across farms of different sizes, let us consider the following production function:

$$Q = F(A, L_f, L_h, X, K) \qquad (1)$$

where Q is output, A is the land area or farm size, L_f is family labour, L_h is hired labour, X is purchased inputs (including fertilizer and pesticides) and K is capital service. Family labour and hired labour are not perfect substitutes and thus are treated as separate inputs. The former is primarily engaged in care-intensive tasks, such as land preparation, crop care and supervision of hired workers, whereas the latter is engaged in simple tasks, such as transplanting, harvesting and threshing (Otsuka, Chuma, and Hayami 1992; Hayami and Otsuka 1993). Otsuka, Chuma, and Hayami (1993) demonstrate that tenancy contracts are chosen over labour contracts wherever tenancy contracts are allowed. This implies that the labour market does not work efficiently in spatially dispersed and ecologically diverse agricultural environments.[4] It is also noteworthy that roughly 90 per cent of farms in the world are family farms relying on family labour (Lowder, Skoet, and Raney 2016). This underscores the importance of family labour in the management of farms. Note that labour inputs are assumed to be measured in terms of labour time in equation (1). Since family workers are motived to work harder than hired workers, the marginal product of family labour is higher than that of hired labour (i.e., $\partial Q/\partial L_f > \partial Q/\partial L_h > 0$) in the observable range of labour inputs.

For simplicity, assume that the production function is subject to constant returns to scale. Then, equation (1) can be rewritten as:

$$q = f(l_f, l_h, x, k) \qquad (2)$$

where lower-case letters show output or input per hectare, corresponding to capital letters in equation (1). Farmer's profit maximization is assumed to lead to the optimum input use functions, in which input (or input per hectare) is a function of real wage, real rental price and farm size. Farm size can change in the long run through market transactions, but

---

[4] Supporting evidence is provided in the analysis of labour use data in Central Luzon in section 4.

is assumed to be fixed in the short-run or due to suppression of the land market.

Let us also assume that there are two types of technologies: labour-intensive and capital-intensive technologies. While it is optimal to choose labour-intensive technology in low-wage economies, it is optimum to choose capital-intensive technology in high-wage economies. First, let us consider the case of low-wage economies. Since the use of capital is negligible, let us assume that k is low and fixed or $k = 0$. The question is how optimum l_f, l_h and x change when A changes. Since it is reasonable to assume that the endowment of family labour is largely fixed, L_f cannot increase proportionally with an increase in A, which implies that $\partial l_f/\partial A < 0$. Large farms must employ large numbers of hired workers, which implies that $\partial l_h/\partial A > 0$. Whether x increases with an increase in A is uncertain (i.e., $\partial x/\partial A \lessgtr 0$) because x tends to decrease with an increase in A if family labour and purchased inputs are complements, but increases if larger farmers have better access to credit.

In this framework, the IR is explained primarily by lower productivity of hired labour than family labour and the more extensive employment of hired labour per unit of land on larger farms. If the amount of purchased inputs per unit of land decreases with an increase in farm size (i.e., $\partial x/\partial A < 0$), the tendency towards IR is strengthened. If the land market (whether land rental or land sales market) works efficiently, however, the IR will be eradicated by the transfer of land from less to more efficient farmers. Therefore, the IR can be explained by multiple market failures, or at least by failures in both labour and land markets (Kevane 1996).

Next, let us consider the case of high-wage economies, where the intensive use of capital service or mechanization is advantageous. The important point is that since the tractor is a substitute for family labour for land preparation, it reduces the demand for family labour. On the other hand, hired workers can be employed to drive tractors.[5] In other words, the use of tractors reduces the productivity of family labour and increases that of hired labour so that the marginal product of family labour can be either higher or lower than hired labour (i.e., $\partial q/\partial l_f \lessgtr \partial q/\partial l_h$). According to Deininger et al. (2018, 239), "family labor use was more efficient than hired labor in 1982 and 1999 but not in 2008" in India when farms became highly mechanized.

---

[5] If a farmer rents the tractor, the tractor's owner usually sends a driver along with the tractor.

Furthermore, the use of combine harvesters reduces both the demand for hired labour in harvesting and threshing and for family labour in supervision. Thus, we expect that $\partial l_f/\partial A < 0$ and $\partial l_h/\partial A < 0$, so that the use of both family and hired labour is lower on larger farms. Since labour inputs are no longer critically important, it is likely that x is determined primarily by credit access, which confers an advantage to large farms. Thus, we expect that $\partial x/\partial A > 0$. Finally, considering that capital input is an indivisible factor of production,[6] its use is more effective on larger farms, which means that $\partial k/\partial A > 0$.

Consequently, we expect to observe a positive relationship between farm size and yield due to the efficient use of capital and the application of larger amounts of purchased inputs. Similar to the IR, such a positive relationship will disappear if the land or labour market works efficiently.

2.2 Methodological issues

Soil quality is implicitly assumed as the same between small and large farms in the conceptual framework. It tends to be higher on small farms, however, which may result in an IR. According to Barrett, Bellemare, and Hou (2010), the difference in soil quality explains only a small part of the IR. The meta-analysis of Delvaux, Riesgo, and Paloma (2020) also points out that the inclusion of soil quality reduces the IR but does not eradicate it.

Another possible issue is measurement error. Smallholders may overestimate output and underestimate farm size. According to Carletto, Savastano, and Zezza (2013), farm size that is actually measured instead of just being estimated by farmers strengthens the IR. That is, farmers seem to consistently overestimate the size of small plots and underestimate large ones.[7] On the other hand, Desiere and Jolliffe (2018) report that the IR is strong when self-reported production data are used, but it disappears when crop-cut estimates are used. As the generalizability of this finding is not clear, it seems safe to assume that the measurement errors of output do not entirely cause the IR, until further supporting evidence provided by additional studies indicates otherwise.

---

[6] If the machine rental market is developed, machine service can be a divisible input. Yet, larger machines can be used more efficiently on larger farms.
[7] I do not know the theory that explains why the size of small plots is overestimated and that of large ones is underestimated.

Some authors argue that since yield or gross value of output per hectare does not show production efficiency, profit per hectare or total factor productivity (TFP) should be used to discuss the issue of production efficiency associated with farm size (Muyanga and Jayne 2019; Rada and Fuglie 2019; Delvaux, Riesgo, and Paloma 2020).[8] While I agree that gross value of output per hectare or yield is not an appropriate measure of production efficiency at the farm level, I strongly disagree that only the profit per hectare or TFP should be examined. Figure 6.1 illustrates this point. Acknowledging the meta-analysis findings of Delvaux, Riesgo, and Paloma (2020), Figure 6.1 shows a strong IR for the gross value of production per hectare; a less strong yet significant IR is drawn for the net value of production and a less clear relationship is shown between farm size and profit per hectare.[9] The source of the problem is that labour cost includes the imputed cost of family labour, which is unpaid. Imputation usually uses the prevailing market wage rate, but it can be questioned whether it is really an appropriate shadow price of family labour. In other words, the estimated profit, which is obtained by deducting estimated family labour cost as well as imputed costs of using other family-owned resources from the net value of production, is subject to errors. If TFP is used, the estimations of factor shares and amount of labour input (which is usually simply the sum of family and hired labour time) are subject to errors because family labour and hired labour are not perfect substitutes. Therefore, it is risky to rely only on estimated profit or TFP when analysing the relationship between farm size and productivity.

It must be well understood that it is more relevant to analyse simultaneously the gross value of production, net value of production and profit per hectare. Indeed, the fact that the gross value of output and the net value of output (which can be measured accurately, at least in theory) differ between small and large farms clearly indicates that resources are misallocated between farms, even though the extent of misallocation cannot be immediately ascertained. It is also desirable to examine the robustness of estimated profit and TFP by changing the assumed shadow wages of family labour.

---

[8] The estimated profit is supposed to show return to land and management efficiency, aside from errors of imputing family labour cost.
[9] Although statistical evidence is weak, I suspect that the IR is stronger in farming systems that are complicated (e.g., mixed cropping system) than in simple ones (e.g., monoculture often adopted by plantations).

Figure 6.1. Illustration of the inverse relationships between farm size and productivity measured by gross value of production, net value of production and profit per unit of land

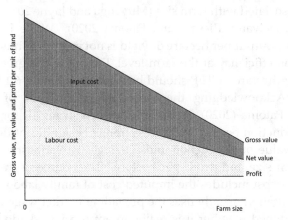

3 REVIEW OF EMPIRICAL EVIDENCE

Numerous empirical studies have found a stable IR of yield or gross value of output per hectare (see Lipton 2012 for a survey of earlier studies). Selected recent studies include Barrett, Bellemare, and Hou (2010) on Madagascar; Li et al. (2013) on China around the turn of the century; Carletto, Savastano, and Zezza (2013) on Uganda; Larson et al. (2014) on Malawi, Tanzania, Kenya and Uganda; Wang et al. (2015) on India; and Rada and Fuglie (2019) on Malawi, Tanzania, Uganda and Bangladesh. Consistent with the conceptual framework, the IR was found in low-wage economies, such as those in Sub-Saharan Africa, South Asia and China during the early years.[10] Li et al. (2013) did not find any relationship when TFP was used. Larson et al. (2014) observed the IR for family labour per hectare and a positive relationship for hired labour per hectare.

More recent studies found the weakening tendency of the IR in several Asian countries, many of which experienced high economic growth and rising wage rates. Wang et al. (2016) discovered declining IR in China; Deininger et al. (2018) report similar tendencies in India. Furthermore,

---

[10] The IR is found in Sub-Saharan Africa even though land rental transactions have gradually become active (Holden, Otsuka, and Deininger 2013; Holden, Otsuka, and Place 2009).

Gautum and Ahmed (2019) and Liu et al. (2020) found similar phenomena in Bangladesh and Vietnam, respectively. These studies commonly report on farm-size expansion and progress of mechanization, particularly through renting of machinery services,[11] which lead to the lessened advantage of intensive family labour use on small farms. This is consistent with Otsuka, Liu, and Yamauchi's (2013) finding from the cross-country regression that labour-saving mechanization has taken place significantly in countries where farm sizes are large. Earlier, Hayami and Kawagoe (1986) found the emergence of scale economies in rice farming in Japan when riding tractors were introduced in the mid-1960s. This suggests the emergence of a positive relationship between farm size and productivity in this country. Later, Kawasaki (2010) confirmed that the cost of rice production increases less than proportionally with an increase in output, implying the emergence of the positive relationship in Japan. Rada and Fuglie (2019) report the positive relationship between farm size and TFP in Australia and the USA. The same was found in emerging economies such as China (Wang et al. 2015) and Indonesia (Yamauchi 2016), as well as some areas in Vietnam where farm sizes are relatively large or expanding through land renting, and mechanization is taking place through machine renting (Liu et al. 2020). The upward sloping curve in Figure 6.2 portrays the positive relationship between farm size and productivity.

Figure 6.2   Conceptual relationships between farm size and productivity under labour- and capital-intensive farming systems

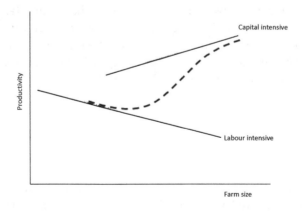

---

[11] In Vietnam, land consolidation has also taken place, which facilitates mechanization (Nguyen and Warr 2020).

On the other hand, several studies found a U-shaped relationship between farm size and productivity. Heltberg (1998) was the first to report the U-shaped relationship between farm size and net output per hectare in Pakistan, where smallholders and significantly large farmers coexist.[12] Later, such relationships were reported in Brazil (Rada and Fuglie 2019) and China (Sheng, Ding, and Huang 2019), where small farms adopting labour-intensive production methods and large farms using large machinery coexist.

The dotted curve (Figure 6.2) illustrates such a relationship. Somewhat surprisingly, a U-shaped relationship between cultivated area and profit per hectare or TFP was reported in Kenya by Muyanga and Jayne (2019), where the bottom of the U-shape was around 5 ha. According to them, large farms have newly emerged and use highly mechanized farming systems, in contrast to small farms, which rely on labour-intensive production methods.[13]

To sum up, the traditional labour-intensive farming system tends to be subject to the IR, whereas capital-intensive mechanized farming systems are subject to a positive farm size-productivity relationship. When both farming systems coexist, a U-shaped relationship between farm size and productivity is likely to be observed.

4   FUTURE OF SMALL FARMS IN EAST ASIA

As shown, small farms in East Asia have been losing the advantage of using family labour as wage rates rise and mechanization takes place. As such, farm size should be increased to prevent agriculture's loss of comparative advantage; otherwise, food self-sufficiency will decline in the region. The issues relating to changes in farm size and grain self-sufficiency are examined in this section.

---

[12] As far as profit per hectare is concerned, he found a positive relationship.
[13] I have some reservations on their findings because half of the land owned by large farms was unused; their study excluded such land and focused only on the cultivated area. I believe the entire land should be considered in the analysis of production efficiency. It is also unclear how the cost of using owned large machinery was reckoned.

4.1 Changing farm size in East Asia

Figure 6.3 shows the changing operational farm size in six East Asian countries: Japan, Republic of Korea, China, Indonesia, the Philippines and Thailand. In the early 1960s, the average farm size was small, ranging from 1 ha in Japan and Indonesia, 2 ha in the Republic of Korea, to 3.5 ha in the Philippines and Thailand. It has subsequently declined in all these countries, except Japan, because of rapid population growth and limited area for expansion in rural areas (FAO 2010). This is consistent with the generally declining farm size in developing countries (Lowder, Skoet, and Raney 2016). The decrease in farm size is particularly pronounced in the Philippines, which can be explained by the implementation of land reform in the 1970s, continued population growth in rural areas, and the failure of growth of non-farm sectors, which can absorb rural labour. If this downward trend in farm size continues and the economy sustains a fairly high growth rate, the agriculture sector's inefficiency can become a major constraint to further economic growth. In Japan, although farm sizes have increased, reaching 3 ha in recent years, they are far below the average farm size in Europe and North America, where farms larger than 100 ha are common. Considering the high wage rate in this country, it is obvious that Japanese agriculture is losing its comparative advantage.

Figure 6.3 *Changes in average farm sizes (ha) in selected East Asian countries*

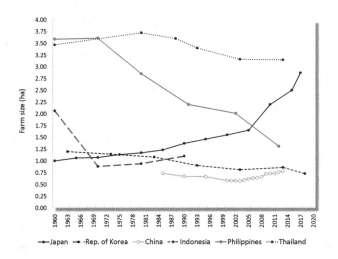

Sources: FAO (2010); Huang and Ding (2016); Japan Ministry of Agriculture, Forestry, and Fisheries (various years).

The average farm size in China is tiny. However, it increased from 0.57 ha in 2003 to 0.79 ha in 2013 (Huang and Ding 2016), or a 0.22 ha increase in a span of a decade. With wage rates rising sharply in the last few decades and a positive relationship between farm size and productivity emerging in this country, retaining small farms could result in increased cost of domestic production and massive food importation. In fact, China is already a major importer of soybean. There is a possibility that China will import massive amounts of other grains unless farm-size expansion and large-scale mechanization take place.

The declining farm size in the Philippines, Thailand and Indonesia; the gradually increasing farm size in China; and the increasing but still small farm size in Japan cannot be compatible with rising wage rates and the actual or possible emergence of a positive relationship between farm size and productivity. This suggests that agriculture in these countries is losing or will lose its comparative advantage (Otsuka, Liu, and Yamauchi 2016a, 2016b).

4.2 Changing levels of grain self-sufficiency in East Asia

Figure 6.4 shows changes in grain self-sufficiency ratio, which is calculated by dividing domestic production of rice, wheat, maize and soybean by the sum of domestic production and net imports of the above four crops. Since production, consumption and trade are evaluated simply by weight, the self-sufficiency ratio is a rough measure of agriculture's comparative advantage. It is also affected by the distortionary agricultural policies of various governments. Thus, it should be interpreted with caution, even though large ratio changes over time and large differences across countries could indeed indicate underlying changes and differences in comparative advantage.

The estimated grain self-sufficiency ratio in Japan has declined rapidly since 1961, attesting to the sharply declining comparative advantage of agriculture in this country. Such ratio has similarly declined in the Republic of Korea, almost in parallel with that of Japan. While farm sizes in the Republic of Korea are slightly smaller than in Japan, the wage rates in both countries have increased continuously. There seems to be little doubt that a fundamental cause of the loss of agriculture's comparative advantage in these two Northeast Asian countries has been the preservation of labour-intensive small-scale agriculture amid high and rising wages. This is consistent with the findings of cross-country regression analysis by Otsuka, Liu, and Yamauchi (2013) that grain

Figure 6.4 Changes in grain self-sufficiency ratios in selected East Asian countries

Note: Domestic production of rice, wheat, maize and soybean divided by domestic production plus net imports of the above four crops in terms of weight

Source: FAOSTAT (2020).

self-sufficiency ratio in Asia decreases when gross domestic product (GDP) per capita exceeds a threshold level.

Thailand has been a net exporter of grains—its self-sufficiency ratio exceeds unity. However, the ratio has been declining, falling to just slightly above the self-sufficient level in the 2010s. Although the average farm size in Thailand is fairly large by Asian standards (see Figure 6.3), it seems not large enough to maintain agriculture's comparative advantage.

Self-sufficiency ratios in the Philippines, Indonesia and China were close to unity in the 1960s to the mid-1980s, and then slightly declining thereafter. The declining trend since the mid-1980s in the Philippines is consistent with the sharply declining farm size in this country. The slightly declining self-sufficiency ratios in Indonesia and China are worrisome, as these are large, populous countries. Moreover, the average farm sizes in these two countries are even lower than those in Japan and the Republic of Korea. If these countries become gigantic importers of grains, world grain prices will significantly shoot up, adversely affecting the well-being of consumers throughout the world, particularly the poor ones.[14] These possibilities cannot be denied, unless farm size increases significantly and large-scale mechanization takes place (Yamauchi, Huang, and Otsuka, forthcoming).

4.3 Changes in rice farming in Central Luzon

In this section, we examine the long-term changes in farm size, labour use and mechanization using rice farming data collected by the Central Luzon Survey, carried out more or less every four years from 1966 to 2015 (Moya et al. 2015). This data set is valuable because it reports not only significant changes in paddy yield but also dramatic changes in family and hired labour and machine use. Estudillo and Otsuka (1999), using the same survey data, observed a mild IR in this region from 1966 to 1994.[15] However, the case of Central Luzon, being an advanced rice-growing region in the Philippines, should not be taken as representative of the country, although similar changes seem to have taken place gradually in other rice-growing areas in this country (Mataia et al. 2020).

Table 6.1 shows that farm size in Central Luzon has been largely unchanged at around 2 ha from 1966 to 2015, except for a brief period in 1970 and 1974. Paddy yield increased from 2.3 t/ha in 1966 to 4.1 t/ha in 1982, owing to the Green Revolution. Yield had been largely unchanged from 1982 to 2015, although there were some fluctuations due mainly to climate variations. High-yielding hybrid varieties were introduced around 2010, but their adoption rates have remained very low in Central Luzon. It is interesting to observe the substantial changes in total labour use per hectare: it increased from 1966–70 to 1974–82, gradually decreased until 1999, and drastically declined towards 2015 after some increases in 2008–11. The following subsections explore what happened to the use of family and hired labour and mechanization in rice farming in Central Luzon during the past five decades.

---

[14] Since comparative advantage is an elusive concept, it is not possible to prove in this study that agriculture's declining comparative advantage is a major cause for declining grain self-sufficiency in these two countries. It is clear, however, that increasingly protectionist policy for rice farming in Indonesia is detrimental to the competitiveness of rice production in this country (Otsuka 2021).

[15] Part of the reason could be the provision of credit with relatively low interest rates by traders to small farmers.

Table 6.1. Average farm size (ha), paddy yield (t/ha) and labour use (person-days/ha) during the wet season in Central Luzon (1966–2015)

Year	No. of sample farms	Farm size (ha)	Paddy yield (t/ha)	Labour use (person-days/ha)
1966	95	2.1	2.3	69
1970	62	2.5	2.5	68
1974	59	2.6	2.0	85
1979	148	1.9	3.6	82
1982	135	1.8	4.1	83
1986	120	1.8	3.5	71
1990	108	1.8	3.5	74
1994	100	1.7	4.1	71
1999	85	1.6	3.5	60
2003	116	1.9	4.3	61
2008	107	1.8	4.5	66
2011	95	1.9	3.9	71
2015	89	1.8	3.8	46

Sources: Moya et al. (2015); IRRI (2016).

4.4 Changing family labour and hired labour use

Figure 6.5 shows changes in family and hired labour use in care-intensive activities (i.e., land preparation and crop care) and other activities (e.g., crop establishment, harvesting and threshing). Several important observations can be made. First, traditionally in the 1960s and 1970s, family labour was used for care-intensive activities significantly more than hired labour. As pointed out by Otsuka, Chuma, and Hayami (1992) and Hayami and Otsuka (1993), the hired labour market does not seem to work for care-intensive tasks, which require proper care and judgement. Clearly, family labour and hired labour are not perfect substitutes. Second, the use of hired labour has been dominant in other activities (simple tasks that do not require much care and judgement) and remained relatively stable from 1966 to 2010. Thus, it is clear that the hired labour market works for these activities. Family labour is used primarily for supervision, which accounts for a small portion of these activities. It must be pointed out that the dominant use of family labour for care-intensive activities and that of hired labour for other activities are observed throughout rice farming areas in Asia (David and Otsuka 1994). Third, family labour use in care-intensive activities began decreasing in the late 1970s: from 24.1 days/ha in 1966 to a mere 7.5 days/ha in 2015. Thus, the advantage of small farms arising from the intensive use of family labour, if any, must have eroded over time. This finding is consistent with the weakening IR in Asia discussed in the previous section. Fourth, all of a sudden, hired labour use dropped from 2011 to 2015. This is likely due to the introduction of hired labour-saving technologies.

I would like to postulate the hypothesis that drastic changes in family and hired labour use can be explained mainly by mechanization, some of which save on family labour and others save on hired labour. The validity of this hypothesis is examined in the next subsection.

Figure 6.5.   Changes in family and hired labour use (person-days/ha) for care-intensive and other activities during the wet season in Central Luzon (1966–2015)

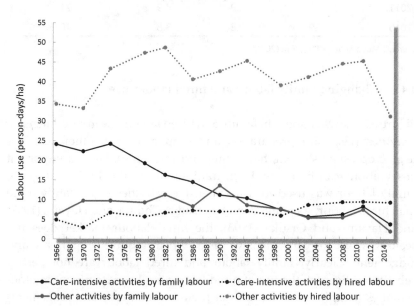

Sources: Moya et al. (2015); IRRI (2016).

4.5 Mechanization in Central Luzon

Threshing was traditionally carried out by large threshing machines called *tilyadora*, which were used to measure the quantity of paddy produced by share tenants (Hayami and Kikuchi 1982). The adoption rate of *tilyadora* was 87 per cent in 1966 and 74 per cent in 1970. As share tenancy declined due to the implementation of land reform (Otsuka 1991), the adoption rate dropped to 44 per cent in 1974 and 31 per cent in 1979. Such changes are consistent with low hired labour use in 1966 and 1970 and its increase in 1974 and 1979 (see Figure 6.5) because the *tilyadora* can replace hired labour. Small threshers were almost completely adopted by 1986; thereafter hired labour use had been fairly stable until 2011.

The decreasing family labour use for care-intensive activities since 1974 can be explained primarily by the increasing adoption of power tillers, as well as the gradually increasing adoption of riding tractors and rotavators (Figure 6.6). In fact, family labour use in land preparation significantly decreased over time. The use of animals or water buffalos decreased but did not become negligible because they were used to plow the edges of paddy fields. In contrast, hired labour use in land preparation increased from about 2 days/ha in 1966 and 1970 to 7.6 days/ha in 2011 and 2015. This can be explained by the fact that most farmers rent power

Figure 6.6. Tractorization in land preparation and use of combine harvesters during the wet season in Central Luzon (1966–2015)

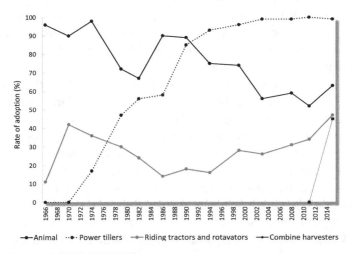

Sources: Moya et al. (2015); IRRI (2016).

tillers and tractors along with their drivers, who are also hired workers. Thus, family labour has been substituted by tractors and hired labour. It is no wonder that the advantage of small farms arising from intensive family labour use no longer existed once tractors were introduced. This is similar to the case of postwar Japan as reported earlier.

The adoption of combine harvesters is another major mechanization. No farmer in Central Luzon was using this machine before 2011. But thereafter, when the combine harvester was introduced, its adoption rate jumped to 45 per cent in 2015. As a result, hired labour use in other activities (i.e., harvesting and threshing) precipitously declined from 2011 to 2015 (see Figure 6.5). It is likely that as the adoption rate of combine harvesters increased, hired labour use declined further. There seems to be no question that combine harvesters save on hired labour. This suggests that the disadvantage of large farms associated with the supervision of hired labour decreases with the adoption of combine harvesters.

In sum, it is reasonable to conclude that while tractorization has reduced the advantages of small farms, the introduction of combine harvesters has reduced the disadvantage of large farms. This implies that the optimum farm size increases with increased adoption of agricultural machinery.

4.6 Need for redesigning land reform in the Philippines

If the IR is observed and small farms are more efficient than large farms, the redistributive land reform programme, known as the land-to-the-tiller programme widely implemented in India and the Philippines, can contribute—at least in theory—to both production efficiency and social equity. The fundamental problem is that the land reform programme suppresses land tenancy transactions, which prevents efficient transfer of cultivation rights from inefficient to efficient farmers (Fabella 2014; Jandoc and Roumasset 2019). Another problem is that the land-to-the-tiller programme applied to tenant-cultivated land, exempting owner-cultivated land using hired labour (Otsuka 2007). This motivated landlords to evict tenants and undertake owner cultivation using hired labour. As a consequence, the land (rental) market cannot allocate land from inefficient farms to efficient farms. Such a policy, which suppresses the land rental market's function, is responsible for both inefficient land allocation and inequitable income distribution.

Setting a ceiling over which land is transferred to tenants also distorts land allocation (Adamopoulos and Restuccia 2014; Fabella 2014;

Jandoc and Roumasset 2019). The Comprehensive Agrarian Reform Program (CARP) of the Philippines set the ceiling of 5 ha for non-rice and non-maize land and 7 ha for rice and maize land (Adriano 1991). This is detrimental to the efficiency of land allocation, particularly when a positive relationship emerges between farm size and productivity. Thus, in all likelihood, a positive relationship will be observed in the Philippines in view of the large-scale mechanization of land preparation, harvesting and threshing. Because of the failure of the CARP to generate an effective land rental market, the land is inefficiently allocated even at present (Michler and Shively 2015).

In the face of the changing relationship between farm size and productivity, it is critical to recognize the role of land rental markets in reallocating land from the less productive to the more productive farms. It should not be government law but the market that ought to determine the desirable allocation of land. The Philippines is no exception, and if the land market continues to be distorted, increasingly large and serious inefficiencies will arise because of inefficient land resource allocation in this country.

To the best of my knowledge, no government in Asia clearly recognizes the positive role of land markets and the negative social impact of land ceiling in achieving efficient land allocation among farmers. In all likelihood, the best land policy is the implementation of no detrimental policy in Thailand.

5 CONCLUDING REMARKS

The world has been changing rapidly, and so has agriculture throughout the globe. Otsuka and Fan (2021) observed rapid growth in labour productivity in agriculture in all major regions of the world due to rapid mechanization. According to this study, such changes would have increased the advantage of large farms and decreased the advantage of small farms. Nonetheless, if the small farms are preserved, as in Japan and the Republic of Korea, the comparative advantage of agriculture will be lost. Consequently, food self-sufficiency will decline.

I do not simply advocate the dominance of large farms, like Collier and Dercon (2014) and Adamopoulos and Restuccia (2014). When wage rates are low and land is scarce, efficient farms are likely to be small family farms. Thus, Larson, Muraoka, and Otsuka (2016) advocate the promotion of agricultural development based on small farms in Sub-Saharan Africa. Such small farm-based development can potentially lead to a full-fledged Green Revolution in Sub-Saharan Africa, judging from the Green Revolution experience in Asia (Otsuka and Larson 2013, 2016). It is critically important to recognize that such development is both efficient and equitable.

As an economy develops, wage rates increase, which tends to induce mechanization. For mechanization to be effective, farm sizes must expand. In the adjustment process of farm-size expansion, a positive relationship between farm size and productivity tends to emerge. If the government wants to maintain or even strengthen the comparative advantage of agriculture, it must promote land transfer from less productive small farms to more productive large farms. At the least, the government should not discourage farm-size expansion by suppressing land tenancy transactions and setting land ceilings. This policy is diametrically opposite to the conventional land reform policy, which was desirable when the economy was poor. This policy shift is a significant challenge for policymakers who are interested in sustainable economic development.

How can the government implement an efficient land policy in the course of economic development? The critical point is that the efficient allocation of land should be achieved by the land market, particularly by the land rental market. A ceiling in the transfer of land from land-rich to land-poor farmers may be set, but it must be lifted once land redistribution has been completed. Similarly, the exemption of owner-cultivation from the implementation of land reform must be abolished to facilitate land renting. It must be clearly understood that the land market ought to play the vital role of transferring land rights from less productive to more productive farmers. Its suppression leads to potentially devastating consequences on the efficiency of agriculture, as has happened in Japan and the Republic of Korea. This recommendation is particularly important for the Philippines and India, where historically the redistributive land reform programmes had been extensively implemented in favour of small farms.

REFERENCES

Adamopoulos, T., and D. Restuccia. 2014. "The Size Distribution of Farms and International Productivity Differences". *American Economic Review* 104, no. 6: 1667–97.

Adriano, L. S. 1991. "A General Assessment of the Comprehensive Agrarian Reform Program". *Philippine Institute for Development Studies Working Paper* No. 91–13.

Barrett, C. B., M. F. Bellemare, and J. Y. Hou. 2010. "Reconsidering Conventional Explanations of the Inverse Productivity-Size Relationship". *World Development* 38, no. 1: 88–97.

Benjamin, D. 1995. "Can Observed Land Quality Explain the Inverse Productivity Relationship?" *Journal of Development Economics* 46, no. 1: 51–84.

Carletto, C., S. Savastano, and A. Zezza. 2013. "Fact or Artifact: The Impact of Measurement Errors on the Farm Size-Productivity Relationship". *Journal of Development Economics* 103: 254–61.

Chayanov, A. V. 1926. *The Theory of Peasant Economy*. Madison, WI: University of Wisconsin Press.

Collier, P., and S. Dercon. 2014. "African Agriculture in 50 Years: Smallholders in a Rapidly Changing World". *World Development* 63: 92–101.

David, C. C., and K. Otsuka, eds. 1994. *Modern Rice Technology and Income Distribution in Asia*. Boulder, CO: Lynne Rienner.

Deininger, K., S. Jin, Y. Liu, and S. K. Singh. 2018. "Can Labor-Market Imperfections Explain Changes in the Inverse Farm Size-Productivity Relationship? Longitudinal Evidence from Rural India". *Land Economics* 94, no. 2: 239–58.

Delvaux, P. A. G, L. Riesgo, and S.G. Paloma. 2020. "Are Small Farms More Performant than Larger Ones in Developing Countries?". *Science Advances* 6, no. 41. https:doi.org/10.1126/sciadv.abb8235.

Desiere, S., and D. Jolliffe. 2018. "Land Productivity and Plot Size: Is Measurement Error Driving the Inverse Relationship?" *Journal of Development Economics* 130: 84–98.

Estudillo, J. P., and K. Otsuka. 1999. "Green Revolution, Human Capital, and Off-Farm Employment: Changing Sources of Income among Farm Households in Central Luzon, 1966–94". *Economic Development and Cultural Change* 47, no. 3: 497–523.

———. 2016. *Moving out of Poverty: An Inquiry into Inclusive Growth in Asia*. London, UK: Routledge.

Fabella, R. V. 2014. "Comprehensive Agrarian Reform Program (CARP): Time to Let Go". *Philippine Review of Economics* 50, no. 1: 1–18.

Feder, G. 1985. "The Relations between Farm Size and Farm Productivity: The Role of Family Labor, Supervision, and Credit Constraints". *Journal of Development Economics* 18, no. 2&3: 297–313.

FAO. 2010. *World Census of Agriculture*. Rome, Italy.

———. 2020. FAOSTAT. http://www.fao.org/faostat/en/.

Gautum, M., and M. Ahmed. 2019. "Too Small to Be Beautiful? The Farm Size and Productivity Relationship in Bangladesh". *Food Policy* 84: 165–75.

Hayami, Y., and T. Kawagoe. 1986. "Farm Mechanization, Scale Economies, and Polarization: The Japanese Experience". *Journal of Development Economics* 31, no. 2: 221–39.

Hayami, Y., and M. Kikuchi. 1982. *Asian Village Economy at the Crossroads*. Baltimore, MD: Johns Hopkins University Press.

Hayami, Y., and K. Otsuka. 1993. *The Economics of Contract Choice: An Agrarian Perspective*. Oxford: Clarendon Press.

Heltberg, R. 1998. "Rural Market Imperfections and the Farm Size-Productivity Relationship: Evidence from Pakistan". *World Development* 26, no. 10: 1807–26.

Holden, S., K. Otsuka, and K. Deininger. 2013. *Land Tenure Reforms in Asia and Africa: Assessing Impacts on Poverty and Natural Resource Management*. Hampshire, UK: Palgrave Macmillan.

Holden, S., K. Otsuka, and F. Place. 2009. *The Emergence of Land Markets in Africa: Assessing the Impacts on Poverty, Equity, and Efficiency*. Baltimore, MD: Resources for the Future.

Huang, J., and J. Ding. 2016. "Institutional Innovation and Policy Support to Facilitate Small-Scale Framing Transformation". *Agricultural Economics* 47 (S1): 227.

IRRI (International Rice Research Institute). 2016. *Central Luzon Loop Survey 2015–16*. Los Baños, Laguna, Philippines: International Rice Research Institute.

Jandoc, K. L., and J. A. Roumasset. 2019. "The Case against the Case for Land Reform: Transaction Costs and Misplaced Exogeneity". *Philippine Review of Economics* 56, no. 1&2: 80–126.

Japan Ministry of Agriculture, Forestry, and Fisheries. Various years. "The Statistical Yearbook of MAFF". http://www.maff.go.jp/e/data/stat/index.html.

Kawasaki, K. 2010. "The Costs and Benefits of Land Fragmentation of Rice Farms in Japan". *Australian Journal of Agricultural and Resource Economics* 54, no. 4: 509–26.

Kevane, M. 1996. "Agrarian Structure and Agricultural Practice: Typology and Application to Western Sudan". *American Journal of Agricultural Economics* 78, no. 1: 236–45.

Larson, D. F., R. Muraoka, and K. Otsuka. 2016. "Why African Rural Development Strategies Must Depend on Small Farms". *Global Food Security* 10: 39–51.

Larson, D. F., K. Otsuka, T. Matsumoto, and T. Killic. 2014. "Should African Rural Development Strategy Depend on Smallholder Farmers? An Exploration of the Inverse-Productivity Hypothesis". *Agricultural Economics* 45, no. 3: 355–67.

Li, G., Z. Feng, L. You, and L. Fan. 2013. "Re-examining the Inverse Relationship between Farm Size and Efficiency: The Empirical Evidence in China". *China Agricultural Economic Review* 5, no. 4: 473–88.

Lipton, M. 2012. *Land Reform in Developing Countries: Property Rights and Property Wrongs*. London, UK: Routledge.

Liu, Y., C. Barrett, T. Pham, and W. Violette. 2020. "The Intertemporal Evolution of Agriculture and Labor over a Rapid Structural Transformation: Lessons from Vietnam". *Food Policy* 94. https://doi.org/10.1016/j.foodpol.2020.101913.

Lowder, S. K., J. Skoet, and T. Raney. 2016. "The Number, Size, and Distribution of Farms, Smallholder Farms, and Family Farms Worldwide". *World Development* 87: 16–29.

Mataia, A. B., J. C. Beltran, R. G. Manalili, B. M. Catudan, N. M. Francisco, and A. C. Flores. 2020. "Rice Value Chain Analysis in the Philippines: Value Addition, Constraints, and Upgrading Strategies". *Asian Journal of Agriculture and Development* 17, no. 2: 19–41.

Michler, J. D., and G. E. Shively. 2015. "Land Tenure, Tenure Security, and Farm Efficiency: Panel Evidence from the Philippines". *Journal of Agricultural Economics* 66, no. 1: 155–69.

Moya, P., K. Kajisa, R. Barker, S. Mohanty, F. Gascon, and M. R. S. Valentin. 2015. *Changes in Rice Farming in the Philippines: Insights from Five Decades of a Household Survey*. Los Baños, Laguna, Philippines: International Rice Research Institute.

Muyanga, M., and T. S. Jayne. 2019. "Revisiting the Farm Size-Productivity Relationship Based on a Relatively Wide Range of Farm Sizes: Evidence from Kenya". *American Journal of Agricultural Economics* 101, no. 4: 1140–63.

Nguyen, H. Q., and Peter Warr. 2020. "Land Consolidation as a Technical Change: Economic Impacts in Rural Vietnam". *World Development* 127. https://doi.org/10.1016/j.worlddev.2019.104750.

Otsuka, K. 1991. "Determinants and Consequences of Land Reform Implementation in the Philippines". *Journal of Development Economics* 35, no. 2: 339–55.

———. 2007. "Efficiency and Equity Effects of Land Markets". In *Handbook of Agricultural Economics*, Volume 3, edited by R. Evenson and P. Pingali, pp. 2672–703. Amsterdam: North-Holland.

———. 2013. "Food Insecurity, Income Inequality, and the Changing Comparative Advantage in World Agriculture". *Agricultural Economics* 44 (S1): 7–11.

———. 2021. "Strategy for Tranforming Indonesian Agriculture". *Bulletin of Indonesian Economic Studies* 57(3): 321–41.

Otsuka, K., and S. Fan, eds. 2021. *Agricultural Development: New Perspectives in a Changing World*. Washington, DC: International Food Policy Research Institute.

Otsuka, K., and D. Larson, eds. 2013. *An African Green Revolution: Finding Ways to Boost Productivity on Small Farms*. Dordrecht, Netherlands: Springer.

———. 2016. *In Pursuit of an African Green Revolution: Views from Rice and Maize Farmers' Fields*. Dordrecht, Netherlands: Springer.

Otsuka, K., H. Chuma, and Y. Hayami. 1992. "Land and Labor Contracts in Agrarian Economies: Theories and Facts". *Journal of Economic Literature* 30, no. 4:1965–2018.

———. 1993. "Permanent Labor and Land Tenancy Contracts in Agrarian Economies: An Integrated Analysis". *Economica* 60, no. 237: 57–77.

Otsuka, K., Y. Liu, and F. Yamauchi. 2013. "Factor Endowments, Wage Growth, Changing Food Self-Sufficiency: Evidence from Country-Level Panel Data". *American Journal of Agricultural Economics* 95, no. 5: 1252–58.

———. 2016a. "The Future of Small Farms in Asia". *Development Policy Review* 34, no. 3: 441–61.

———. 2016b. "Growing Advantage of Large Farms in Asia and Its Implications for Global Food Security". *Global Food Security* 11: 5–10.

Rada, N. E., and K. O. Fuglie. 2019. "New Perspectives on Farm Size and Productivity". *Food Policy* 84: 147–52.

Sheng, Y., J. Ding, and J. Huang. 2019. "The Relationship between Farm Size and Productivity in Agriculture: Evidence from Maize Production in Northern China". *American Journal of Agricultural Economics* 101, no. 3: 790–806.

Wang, J., K. Z. Chen, S. D. Gupta, and Z. Huang. 2015. "Is Small Still Beautiful? A Comparative Study of Rice Farm Size and Productivity in China and India". *China Agricultural Economics Review* 7, no. 3: 484–509.

Wang, X., F. Yamauchi, K. Otsuka, and J. Huang. 2016. "Wage Growth, Landholding, and Mechanization in Chinese Agriculture". *World Development* 86, no. 10: 30–45.

Yamauchi, F. 2016. "Rising Real Wages, Mechanization, and Growing Advantage of Larger Farms: Evidence from Indonesia". *Food Policy* 58: 62–69.

Yamauchi, F., J. Huang, and K. Otsuka. 2021. "Changing Farm Size and Agricultural Development in East Asia". In *Agricultural Development: New Perspectives in a Changing World*, edited by K. Otsuka and S. Fan, pp. 79–110. Washington, DC: International Food Policy Research Institute.

7 The Political Economy of Rice Policy in the Philippines

V. Bruce J. Tolentino and Beulah Maria de la Peña

The Philippines has a long history of efforts to improve its performance in agricultural productivity and food security. Its record has been always described as poor, with little progress in reducing hunger incidence and increasing productivity and competitiveness. A long-standing strategy of pursuing self-sufficiency in rice production, coupled with trade protection, not only failed to foster sustainable food security but also hindered the growth of agriculture competitiveness even as world trade has become much more globalized.

The pressure to reform had been a continuing challenge, demanded by economic efficiency but sensitive to evolving political contexts. Reforming the rice sector also increasingly became an international concern, especially among rice-trading countries, as the country's failed strategy resulted in ever-growing imports of rice. Trade disciplines that the country subscribed to under agreements with the World Trade Organization (WTO) and Association of South East Asian Nations (ASEAN) provided added reform pressures and complications.

On 14 February 2019, the Philippines finally drastically changed its strategy for food security when it enacted Republic Act 11203, "An Act Liberalizing the Importation, Exportation and Trading of Rice, Lifting for the Purpose the Quantitative Import Restriction on Rice, and for Other Purposes". The Act deregulates rice, liberalizing importation and scrapping quantitative restrictions (QRs) on imports in favour of tariffs. It also eliminates the regulatory functions of the National Food Authority (NFA), constraining the agency to focus on buffer stocking only.

The passage of RA 11203 came about after more than 35 years of economic analysis, reform advocacy and political-economy calculus. Earlier efforts were met with challenges, not the least of which was the fluidity of governance, exacerbated by the lack of organized constituency for and the resistance of strong interests against reform. It took a rare confluence of events, circumstances and unusual alliances to finally see the reform through—a food security "crisis" that could not be addressed by the existing regulatory and institutional framework, the influence of reform-oriented technocrats backed up by good analysis, and a strong president who listened to his economic team.

This paper reviews the experience of the Philippines in reforming the rice industry and examines aspects of political governance that have frustrated and may continue to hinder rapid progress in the reform efforts. It is organized into three parts. Part 1 summarizes the performance of the Philippine rice sector over the past two to three decades. Part 2 describes past efforts at food security reform and how the country's institutional structure of governance for food security had not been conducive to reform. Part 3 discusses the reform environment and its outlook, and offers ideas on how the reform can be sustained to finally achieve improved food security and agricultural productivity.

1 THE PHILIPPINES' PERFORMANCE IN THE RICE SECTOR

Food security is an important objective of the Philippine development agenda. The major strategy towards this end had been rice production at levels considered sufficient for domestic requirements. Thus, rice self-sufficiency became an overriding objective of the Philippine programme for the agriculture sector. This was legislated in Republic Act 8435, the Agriculture and Fisheries Modernization Act of 1997, wherein Section 4 (Definition of Terms) says:

> "Food Security" refers to the policy objective, plan and strategy of meeting the food requirements of the present and future generations of Filipinos in substantial quantity, ensuring the availability and affordability of food to all, either through local production or importation, or both,

based on the country's existing and potential resource endowment and related production advantages, and consistent with the overall national development objectives and policies. However, sufficiency in rice and white corn should be pursued.

1.1 Food and agricultural policy

Philippine food and agricultural policies are circumscribed by a myriad laws, key of which are the Comprehensive Agarian Reform Law (CARL) of 1988 and the Agriculture and Fisheries Modernization Act (AFMA) of 1997. CARL sought to address farmer landlessness and rural unrest by mandating the implementation of the Comprehensive Agarian Reform Program (CARP). CARP targeted to distribute some eight million hectares to tenants and landless farmers over ten years, with beneficiaries to be provided with comprehensive support services. AFMA provides the blueprint for agricultural modernization and rural development. It lays out five broad core objectives of the agricultural policy: poverty alleviation and social equity; food security, including self-sufficiency in staples; rational use of resources; global competitiveness; sustainable development; empowerment of people; and protection from unfair competition.

Other significant laws are the Magna Carta for Small Farmers of 1991, the Seed Act of 1992, the High-Value Crops Development Act of 1995, the Agricultural Tariffication Act of 1996 and the Fisheries Code of 1998.

The above laws have been largely carried forward into development plans such as the National Economic and Development Authority's Medium Term Philippine Development Plan and the Department of Agriculture's Agriculture and Fisheries Modernization Plan. The implementation of these laws have been fraught with issues, however. CARP, originally programmed for ten years, had been slow, prompting several extensions and affecting investment flow as landowners yet to be covered scaled back investments (Habito et al. 2003; Briones 2002). Irrigation investments, despite picking up starting in 1995, focused largely on rice and had not been enough to increase irrigated areas. Much of the resources have gone to repair large systems, with some 20 per cent of areas remaining inoperative (Inocencio and Briones 2020). Research and development has remained underfunded, barely reaching 0.4 per cent of agriculture gross value added (GVA), and also inordinately focused on rice (Habito and Briones 2005).

Extension services, decentralized when the function was devolved to the local government units (LGUs), remain unresponsive to farmers' needs. Despite progress in trade liberalization with the removal of import QRs in favour of safety-based regulations, tariff levels and rules administration are still skewed towards protecting local production. Production and marketing support in the form of input subsidies, price support, postharvest facilities and credit subsidies takes up most of budget allocations (Habito and Briones 2005).

Shortcomings in the policy and institutional environment of the agriculture sector mainly account for poor sector performance (Habito and Briones 2005; David 2003). Too many policy objectives have been confusing and contradictory when translated to strategies. Public expenditures in the sector have been both inadequate and poorly allocated, with rice as a sector given undue importance and production and income subsidies the preferred intervention.

1.2 Imports, productivity and prices

For years, efforts aimed at self-sufficiency took precedence over other programmes in the distribution of resources. Despite this, imports in relation to domestic supply grew over time. In the 1970s the country imported less than 2 per cent of its requirements. In the past decade, imports as a proportion of total supply had climbed to a high of 18 per cent (Table 7.1). Production increases, on average, began to outpace population growth from 2004 as the latter declined from 2.6 per cent yearly in the 1990s to about 2.2 per cent after 2000. Annual population growth further declined to about 1.6 per cent after 2010 but rice self-sufficiency was never achieved as the growth of rice production plateaued around 2014 (Figure 7.1).

Table 7.1. Rice imports (% of domestic supply, 1970–2019)

Period	Average imports share
1970–79	4.0
1980–89	1.8
1990–99	7.3
2000–2009	12.4
2010–19	9.9

Source of basic data: BAS, PSA (accessed 7 December 2020).

Figure 7.1. Rice production, estimated food use and population (production and use in thousand mt rice terms, population in 10,000)

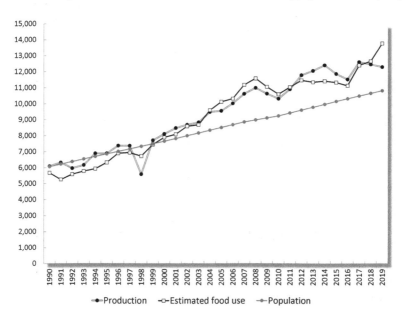

Source: Population estimates for 1990, 1995, 2000, 2007, 2010 and 2015–20 from PSA (accessed 7 December 2020).

More importantly, productivity growth of the Philippines has been slower than that of other rice-producing countries in the ASEAN region. From 1990, rice yields in Vietnam and Thailand spurted upwards, a trend that continued for Vietnam while Thailand slowed down a bit around 2007. In volume terms, the Philippines' average yield barely reached 4 mt/ha in 2017 and in 2019, while Vietnam already achieved more than 5 mt/ha in 2007, ten years earlier (Figure 7.2).

The growth of Philippine rice production has been slower also than its neighbours'. Again, while the country fared better than Indonesia sometime starting 2000, it failed to catch up with the gains of Vietnam and Thailand, at least up to 2014 when Thailand seemed to have suffered a major setback. Also, the Philippines started 1990 with a total production level of 9.8 million mt, which is about half of Thailand's 17.1 million mt and Vietnam's 19.2 million mt and less than a quarter of Indonesia's 45 million mt. Reckoning from this lower base level makes the Philippines' production growth rates even more unimpressive (Figure 7.3).

Figure 7.2.   Comparative paddy yields (1990 = 100)

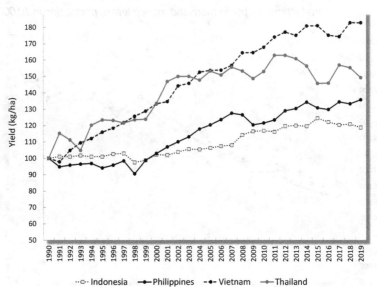

Source: FAO (accessed 7 December 2020).

Figure 7.3.   Comparative paddy production (1990 = 100)

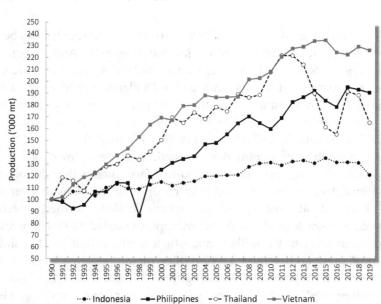

Source: FAO (accessed 7 December 2020).

The uncompetitive state of the Philippine rice sector is most obvious when one considers prices. Wholesale prices in Vietnam and Thailand are about a third to half of Philippine prices. The exception was sometime in 2008–09 when the Philippines, acting somewhat in a panic in the midst of a global food price crisis that accompanied the global financial crisis, sought huge import volumes in the face of steeply rising domestic consumer prices—in turn pulling prices up in the exporting countries, especially Thailand and Vietnam (Figure 7.4).

1.3   Governance institutions in the rice sector

Knowledge of the complex structure of officials, offices, departments and agencies with roles in the rice sector is necessary to appreciate the obstacles to rice sector reform. By law, the Philippines has three key agencies responsible for rural and agricultural development: the Department of Agriculture (DA), the Department of Environment and Natural Resources (DENR) and the Department of Agrarian Reform (DAR). Prior to 1972, the roles and functions now split among these three departments were placed in only one agency—the Department of Agriculture and Natural Resources.

Figure 7.4.   Comparative rice prices (Jan 2000–Oct 2020)

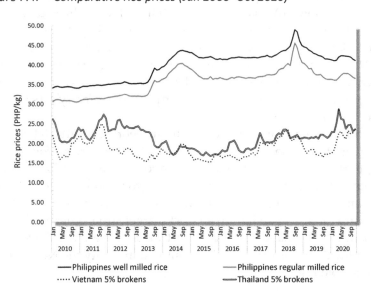

Source: FAO (accessed 7 December 2020).

The DA, DENR and DAR are each headed by a department secretary. The Office of the Secretary usually includes three undersecretaries and three assistant secretaries. The rest of the Departmental organization is made up of bureaus, regional and other local offices, and attached agencies and corporations. The bureaus—the core units of the departments—are generally tasked to undertake or provide specialist and technical functions and services. As of end of 2019, the DA was composed of 15 regional offices, 8 bureaus, 7 attached agencies and 13 attached corporations.

As overseer of the agriculture sector, it crafts and implements the rice productivity programme guided by policies espoused in AFMA and the Philippine Development Plan—the six-year blueprint for the country's development. Three DA agencies and one bureau are directly involved in rice—the NFA, the Philippine Rice Research Institute (PhilRice) and the Philippine Center for Post-Harvest Development and Mechanization (PhilMech), which are focused on rice technology research, and the Bureau of Plant Industry (BPI), which regulates private sector seed production.

A big chunk of the rice budget goes to market support and irrigation maintenance. These interventions are made through the NFA and the National Irrigation Administration (NIA), respectively. Supervision of these agencies has moved back and forth between the DA and the Office of the President in the past 30 years. As of end of 2019, the NFA was under DA while NIA has remained with the Office of the President.

The NFA is the key agency regulating the Philippine rice market. Its mandate and functions are defined in Presidential Decree (PD) 4 (1972) as amended by Executive Order (EO) 1028 (1985). It is basically tasked to stabilize the supply and price of rice, seeking to protect both producers and consumers. The agriculture secretary acts as NFA Council Chairperson.

Before the enactment of RA 11203 in February 2019, NFA's key tools were to maintain a rice buffer stock, buy from rice producers at a support price (buy high) and sell rice to consumers at lower prices (sell low). The NFA also had sole authority to import rice or authorize other entities to do so. It bought only a small percentage of its stocks from farm sales, instead it sourced stocks largely from other countries— Vietnam and Thailand—whose export prices were much lower than Philippine domestic prices. This meant that in reality the NFA bought low and sold high.

2 AGRICULTURE SECTOR REFORMS

Over the past 40 years, the Philippines has struggled to substantially implement a broad range of policy and institutional reforms necessary for long-term sustainable growth and development. A reform programme focused on deregulation and privatization was defined in the early 1980s when the Philippine economy needed rescue by the International Monetary Fund and the World Bank during the waning years of the Marcos dictatorship. Major economic restructuring reforms were started after 1986 during the revolutionary government of President Corazon C. Aquino and continued through the 1990s under President Fidel V. Ramos.

The international trade of a number of agricultural products controlled by government was privatized, most export taxes were eliminated, and many import QRs on non-sensitive products were eliminated quite easily as soon as President Aquino took over. The next wave of agricultural reforms was enacted when the Philippines joined the WTO in 1995; agriculture trade was to be liberalized over a ten-year schedule, except the constraints on rice.

2.1 NFA reform

Given the importance of rice to the economy, numerous attempts were made to reform the rice sector and the NFA. Since the post-World War II years, the NFA has exercised a monopoly of power over the international trade of rice in the Philippines, even after the country's accession to the WTO. Rice was exempted from tariffication or the removal of import QRs, a requirement for agricultural commodities under the WTO Agreement on Agriculture. NFA's monopoly of power and its tight implementation of the QRs have kept high the country's farm-gate prices of rice and thereby the consumer rice prices as well. This has contributed to an over reliance of policymakers on price intervention instruments rather than productivity increases to support farmers' incomes and ensure domestic food security.

2.2 Grains Sector Development Program and GSDP loans

Many of the attempts to reform the NFA were supported with technical assistance and loans from development partners. One major effort was the Grains Sector Development Program (GSDP) supported by the Asian Development Bank (ADB).

The formulation of the GSDP and the associated GSDP Loans began in 1990 under the administration of President Aquino. These were reformulated and developed through the term of President Ramos from 1992 to 1998. The government and ADB finally reached an agreement on the terms in 2000, and the ADB loan became effective in August 2000 under President Joseph E. Estrada and Agriculture Secretary Edgardo J. Angara.

The GSDP was an integrated package of policy and institutional reforms, sector investments and advisory technical assistance projects aimed at making the grains sector more productive and internationally competitive, while helping the country meet its food security objectives. The loans totalled US$175 million, to be disbursed from 2000 to 2005.

The first loan, the GSDP investment project loan of US$75 million, was to finance investments in irrigation, advanced rice and maize production technology, and improved capacity in policy and planning. Thus it was allocated to irrigation, hybrid rice development, rice biotechnology, maize substitutes to rice, integrated crop management technology, soils laboratories, agricultural statistics and regional training centres.

The second loan, the GSDP policy loan of US$100 million, was provided as general budget support. It was to be released in three tranches, contingent on the implementation of policy and institutional reforms. The Philippine government and ADB agreed on a policy matrix that focused on the following: (a) liberalized, more cost-effective grains pricing and import policies, (b) improved grains buffer stock administration, (c) restructuring of the NFA such that it focuses on grains trading (regulation of procurement levels is to be assigned to a separate government line agency), and (d) design and implementation of a targeted food subsidy safety net for the poor.

2.3 GSDP-linked policy reforms, end of 2003

The Philippine government and the ADB agreed that the attainment of the policy goals set in the GSDP policy matrix would serve as triggers for the release of financing under the GSDP Loan. The first tranche was to be released upon loan effectivity and compliance with the first tranche release conditions. The terms linked to the first tranche were completed in August 2000. The second tranche conditions were programmed for completion by May 2001. Finally, the terms linked to the third tranche were programmed for completion within 24 months from loan effectivity, or by August 2002.

The GSDP loans were cancelled in late 2003, however, by mutual agreement of the Philippine government and ADB, due to non-implementation of the agreements. The key reason for this was the changes in the incumbent officials accountable for the grains sector reforms. These changes took place after Gloria Macapagal-Arroyo replaced Joseph Estrada as president of the Philippines in January 2001. A change in the country's top leadership is usually accompanied by changes in key government officials (Table 7.2).

The resolution of the items in the GSDP policy matrix languished because the new officials needed to know and understand the complex reforms envisioned. Since 1986, the secretaries of agriculture have tended towards populist and short-term positions, having come into office on the back of "people-powered" agendas that promised much to the population. Moreover, the political coalitions that banded together in support of these officials' entry into government were fragile, held together by expectations of immediate reward due to regime changes.

It was clear that the reforms would take much more time to implement, if ever. To begin with, the government felt no urgency for it at that time. Furthermore, there was visible resistance to the reforms by (a) representatives of the few farmers who do benefit from NFA procurement,

Table 7.2. *Officials in key posts relative to the Grain Sector Development Program (pre- and post-January 2001)*

Post	Pre-January 2001	Post-January 2001
Secretary of agriculture	Edgardo J. Angara (May 1999–Dec 2000)	Leonardo Q. Montemayor (15 Feb 2001–Nov 2002)
	Domingo F. Panganiban (Jan 2001–15 Feb 2001)	Luis P. Lorenzo Jr. (Dec 2002–Jul 2004)
Secretary of finance	Jose T. Pardo (Jan 2000–Jan 2001)	Alberto G. Romulo (Jan 2001–June 2001)
		Jose Isidro N. Camacho (June 2001–Dec 2003)
Administrator of the National Food Authority	Domingo F. Panganiban (Acting Administrator up to Jan 2001)	Antonio A. Abad (Feb 2001–Dec 2002)
		Arthur C. Yap (Jan 2003–Aug 2004)

(b) the NFA Employees Association and (c) grains businessmen who have developed their enterprises around NFA operations, especially imports. Indeed, the interests represented by these groups proved far more focused than the interests of all consumers and taxpayers who pay for the cost of rice price distortions. Moreover, public debate on the issues only appreciated through the selective lens of the media, but these issues became political and prone to short-sighted assessments.

2.4 Frequent changes in rice sector bureaucrats

Over the past three decades until 2004, the DA had undergone several reorganizations and devolutions: 1983–84 under Secretaries Arturo Tanco and Salvador Escudero, 1986–87 under Secretaries Ramon Mitra and Carlos Dominguez, 1992–94 under Secretaries Senen Bacani and Roberto Sebastian, and 1998–2001 under Secretaries Edgardo Angara, Domingo Panganiban and Leonardo Montemayor.

Political appointments. Virtually all senior-level officials of the departments of the Philippine government, from assistant director up to the secretary, are political appointees and appointed directly by the President of the Philippines (assistant directors are at the fifth level of the Philippine bureaucracy, with cabinet secretaries occupying the first level below the president.) For example, the DA has about 180 posts to be filled by presidential appointment. Thus when presidents change, the appointees to the top levels of government also change. The country has had six presidents since the departure of Ferdinand Marcos in 1986, and there have been at least six sets of changes of all political appointees since then.

Six presidents in thirty-six years. President Ferdinand E. Marcos was in office for 20 years, from December 1965 to February 1986. In the next 36 years (February 1986–2019), six presidents have occupied the office. Presidents Aquino and Ramos each served the full six years in office. (The Philippine constitution limits the chief executive's term of office to six years without reelection.) President Estrada's tenure was foreshortened, while President Macapagal-Arroyo served for nine years—three years of President Estrada's unserved period plus a full term of six years. President Benigno Simeon C. Aquino III also completed his six-year term. President Rodrigo R. Duterte was elected in 2016 and is expected to serve for six years also.

Thirteen agriculture secretaries in thirty-six years. There have been thirteen secretaries of agriculture since the EDSA revolution of 1986;

three of them served twice in separate periods. The average period of service is about 24 months, although there is great variability in their lengths of service (Table 7.3).

The top leadership of the DA was quite stable prior to 1986, with the secretary and his team being in place for at least five and a half years. Arturo M. Tanco was secretary from 1971 to 1984. After him came Salvador H. Escudero (1984–86). Both Tanco and Escudero were no strangers to DA. Tanco was assistant secretary for several years prior to being appointed secretary. Escudero was director of the Bureau of Animal Industry for several years before being promoted to the Agriculture portfolio in 1984.

Table 7.3. Department of Agriculture leadership (1971–2003)

Years in office	Secretary of agriculture	Months of service
Jan 1971–Jun 1984	Arturo M. Tanco*	162
Jul 1984–Feb1986	Salvador H. Escudero	20
Mar 1986–Feb 1987	Ramon V. Mitra	12
Mar 1987–Dec 1989	Carlos G. Dominguez	34
Jan 1990–Jun 1992	Senen C. Bacani	30
Mar 1996–Jun 1998	Salvador H. Escudero	25
Jul 1998–Apr 1999	William D. Dar**	9
May 1999–Dec 2000	Edgardo J. Angara	19
Jan 2001–15 Feb 2001	Domingo F. Panganiban	1
Feb 2001–Nov 2002	Leonardo Q. Montemayor	22
Dec 2002–Jul 2004	Luis P. Lorenzo Jr.	20
Aug 2004–Jun 2005	Arthur C. Yap	11
Jul 2005–Oct 2006	Domingo F. Panganiban	16
Nov 2006–Feb 2010	Arthur C. Yap	40
Mar 2010–May 2010	Bernie Fondevilla**	3
Jun 2010–Jun 2016	Proceso J. Alcala	72
Jul 2016–Jul 2019	Emmanuel F. Piñol	36
Aug 2019–	William D. Dar	

Note: *Including Environment, Natural Resources and Agrarian Reform
  **Acting secretary

In contrast, there has been a quick succession of agriculture secretaries from February 1986 to the present. Of the thirteen people appointed to the post, only one served the full-term of six years; two served for at least three years (half a president's term). Excluding the current term of the incumbent, the other ten served an average of 16 months only.

Reckoning by administration, President Benigno S. C. Aquino III had only one agriculture secretary; President Corazon Aquino had three; President Ramos, two; President Estrada, two; President Arroyo, five (but two served twice, i.e., seven turnovers in all); and President Duterte has had two so far.

2.5 Changing leaders, changing styles, changing programmes

With each changing of the guard in the departments came changes in sectoral and departmental goals, objectives, strategies, timetables, programmes, projects and activities. Such changes were unavoidable, first because there were new people in the department's top positions, which at the very least meant different leadership styles and work arrangements. The combination of new initiatives and people new to government service meant that some time was needed to "learn the job". It required a very steep learning curve over a short period—and consequently not a few birthing pains and mistakes. The task of learning the job was complicated by the need for visibility and impact soonest after taking office, pushed by the urge to "erase" the programmes of the previous appointee and announce programmes labeled as one's own— no matter if the difference is only the label.

The landmark programme *Masagana 99* (Productive 99), implemented during the tenure of President Marcos and Agriculture Secretaries Tanco and Escudero, was touted to have helped bring the country from the brink of starvation in the early 1970s to self-sufficiency and some exports by 1979. The programme ran for 15 years, relying heavily on the promotion of new varieties through extension, irrigation and credit subsidies. In the end, it resulted in massive indebtedness among farmers and a weakened rural banking system.

All rice and food security programmes since 1986 have been short-lived, at least in name. In 1986, the DA abandoned the key features of *Masagana 99*; it limited new investments in irrigation infrastructure and phased out subsidized credit in favour of seed and fertilizer distribution and farm procurement. The revised programme was named *Rice Productivity Enhancement Program* (RPEP) under the administration of Secretary Carlos Dominguez. Since 1989, RPEP has been revived and relabeled at least five times under five agriculture secretaries.

2.6 Politicization of food security in the Philippines

By any measure, the management of the agriculture and rural sector of any country for sustainable growth is complex and difficult. In the Philippines, the task of managing this sector has become even more onerous due to the intensely political atmosphere that has come to envelop the bureaucracy. The politicization of food security has been driven partly by the instability of the bureaucracy over the past two decades.

An earlier section already provided some details of the very brief stints—averaging about 24 months only—of agriculture sector leadership in the Philippines since the mid-1980s. As presidents came and went, along with the frequent replacement of cabinet secretaries, the premium on political connections as currency for bureaucratic survival grew in value. Therefore, it is no surprise that particularly in the past three decades, most of the men and women appointed as secretaries and senior officials of the DA, DAR and DENR exhibit more the qualities of politicians rather than sector experts.

As in other grains-producing nations, the grains sector in the Philippines comprises a very large number of stakeholders, both on the supply side and the multi-layered demand side, as well as on the processing and distribution chains for various related products in between. These stakeholders' interests diverge and change, depending on the economic conditions and opportunities. However, to a degree more intensive than in many other countries, decision-making in modern Philippine society is heavily influenced by an unfettered press, a largely undisciplined and interventionist legislature, and a citizenry that often exercises its rights to freely speak, assemble and act. These features of openness and participatory action make media and mass action very important tools and participants in the decision-making process. In turn, the decision-making hierarchy has become particularly sensitive to media, since media helps shape the political implications of policy decisions.

Grains sector management is therefore a very complex challenge. Given the combination of a free press and an open society, policy reform initiatives and processes must be very carefully managed and executed— with deliberate consideration of any adverse political consequences, especially for the ruling political administration.

3 RICE TRADE LIBERALIZATION AND IMPLEMENTATION OUTLOOK

After numerous attempts to reform the rice policy over more than 30 years, the country finally realized trade liberalization on 14 February 2019, when Congress passed and the president signed into law Republic Act 11203, "An Act Liberalizing the Importation, Exportation and Trading of Rice, Lifting for the Purpose the Quantitative Import Restriction on Rice, and for Other Purposes" or the Rice Tariffication Law (RTL). The law liberalizes rice importation with the removal of NFA's sole power to import and with the tariffication of the import QRs. Through the RTL, the country moved away from pursuing rice self-sufficiency and curtailing imports to allowing a competitive rice market and encouraging production efficiency.

A confluence of factors enabled the reform to be put in place (Tolentino and dela Peña 2019). For one, rice prices rose sharply, inflation peaked and government efforts could not dampen the price increases. Moreover, the rice sector policy reform analysis was available, and reform advocates had access to reform-oriented technocrats. Last but not least, there was bold political leadership.

3.1 Rice sector reform

When Rodrigo R. Duterte was elected president in 2016, he filled his economic cabinet with reform-minded technocrats. They included Carlos Dominguez for finance, Ernesto Pernia for economic planning, Benjamin Diokno for budget management and Ramon Lopez for trade and industry. Rice sector reform was an unfinished business for Secretary Dominguez, who was agriculture secretary under President Corazon Aquino. With support from Secretary Pernia, rice deregulation became part of the economic agenda defined in the Philippine Development Plan 2016–2022.

It was opportune time since the waiver on rice tariffication obtained by the country from the WTO was to lapse in July 2017. This waiver, first negotiated for a ten-year period in 1995 and extended twice for five-year periods, allowed the Philippines to keep its rice import QRs. To grant the second waiver extension, trading partners extracted deep commitments from the Philippines—bigger minimum access volumes (MAVs) on rice, which remained under NFA control, and lower tariffs on livestock, poultry, meat, peas, potatoes and oilseeds. A third waiver extension would certainly mean even deeper and broader trade liberalization commitments. Having MAVs is a compromise made in the WTO, allowing countries to retain QRs or replace them with high tariffs but requiring some volume (the MAV) to be imported at a lower tariff. This allows trading partners to have market access while the QR or high tariffs are in place. Tariffication of QR and commitments to lower tariffs would have eventually made the MAV redundant. Also, a really large MAV would work like QR elimination.

In February 2017, the National Economic and Development Authority (NEDA) Board, chaired by President Duterte, decided that the Philippines would no longer seek a further extension of special treatment for rice. Because Congress had to be convinced, it was also decided that the country would first request the WTO for time to put in place a rice tariffication legislation. The president then issued EO 23 in April 2017, which extended, until the rice QR was tariffied, the annual rice MAV and the "most favoured nation" (MFN) tariff rates on various agricultural products as committed by the Philippines when it got the 2012–17 WTO waiver on rice. The annual rice MAV was 805,200 mt while the committed tariffs ranged from 1 to 5 per cent on selected livestock, poultry, vegetable, dairy and oilseed products—economically insignificant to the country's producers.

The NFA was under the Office of the President when Duterte assumed office. In early 2017, an open disagreement emerged between Cabinet Secretary Leoncio Evasco Jr., assigned as NFA Council Chairperson, and NFA Administrator Jason Aquino (also a Duterte appointee) on rice import timing, rules, procedures and pricing. They also accused each other of corruption. As the intra-office conflict worsened, the NFA Council, charged by law to govern NFA operations, was rendered inutile. NFA's decisions about rice imports were seriously delayed and, when finally made, were poorly considered or hurriedly executed. Consequently, NFA's participation in the domestic rice market fell, NFA-held stocks were drawn down to negligible levels by early 2018, and rice prices rose sharply. The president transferred supervision of the NFA back to DA in June 2018.

The rest of government got involved in various efforts to stem the rice price increase. The Department of Trade and Industry (DTI) imposed suggested retail prices in October 2018. Around the same time, the president announced that rice imports will be allowed unimpeded. DTI offered to facilitate NFA's import clearances for the big traders/supermarkets it oversees. The DA secretary suggested to legalize "smuggling" in the Zamboanga area, where inflation had broken 9 per cent and rice prices were highest.

Other inflationary pressures came to the fore. Increasing global oil prices, exacerbated by higher taxes imposed on fuel in 2018 with the implementation of the Tax Reform for Acceleration and Inclusion (TRAIN),[1] exerted upward pressure on prices of domestic goods, including rice. The country's headline inflation rate exceeded 4 per cent by March 2018, breaking the Bangko Sentral ng Pilipinas' (BSP) policy rate range of 2–4 per cent, and peaked at 6.7 per cent in September 2018. With rice being a major contributor to inflation, the Monetary Board, chaired then by BSP Governor Nestor Espenilla Jr. came out in support of rice import liberalization.

Congress had started hearings, as early as 2016, on the implications of the lapsed rice special treatment under the WTO. Support for tariffication began to slowly build up in 2017. In December 2017, the Senate Economic Planning Office released a Policy Brief (PB-17-02) on the necessity of rice tariffication. Then in 2018, the Congressional Policy and Budget Research Department of the House of Representatives released a paper on the impacts of shifting the rice trade policy regime (PB 2018-04). Legislative interest in the NFA and tariffication intensified as the agency bungled rice supply management and prices soared.

The DA was initially opposed to tariffication,[2] having held nationwide consultations with farmers in 2016 on the lapse of the WTO waiver and concluding that the rice sector needed two more years of protection. But a heated discussion in the cabinet economic cluster saw a stronger position for reform. As inflation worsened from March to September 2018 and with the open support of the president for tariffication, the positions of the executive and legislative branches coalesced. The Rice Tariffication Law was enacted and signed by the president on 14 February 2019.

3.2 Implementing the Rice Tariffication Law (RTL)

The key RTL provisions on eliminating the rice QR in favour of tariffs were implemented on 5 March 2019, or 15 days after the law's publication

---

[1] The first tranche of TRAIN was passed into law in December 2017. It reduces taxes for individual taxpayers but imposes higher taxes on some items including cars, tobacco, sweetened drinks and fuel.
[2] Agriculture departments/ministries worldwide have traditionally been protectionist towards the agriculture sector.

in the Official Gazette. These provisions were viewed as self-executing — that is, its implementation is not contingent on the Implementing Rules and Regulations (IRR) mandated to be issued within 45 days of a law's enactment. Following DA's conduct of a series of consultations with stakeholders in Northern Luzon, Southern Luzon, Mindanao and Visayas and separate online consultations led by NEDA, the IRR was issued on 5 April 2019 via a joint memorandum circular of the DA, NEDA and the Department of Budget and Management (DBM).

3.2.1 Sanitary and phytosanitary import clearance

The NFA lost its authority to issue QR-based rice import permits with RTL's enactment. Instead, importers are required to get the safety-based sanitary and phytosanitary import clearance (SPSIC) from the BPI. A Rice Traders Forum on 29 April 2019 was conducted to familiarize traders on the new rice trading rules. It became apparent then that the government needed a streamlined and consolidated process for rice importing to guide not only traders but also government agencies involved in processing the imports, namely, the BPI and the Bureau of Customs (BOC). This consolidated process was agreed upon in a series of inter-agency meetings and disseminated to the public shortly thereafter.

3.2.2 Tariff rates

The shift to tariffs as protection was not without confusion. While the RTL says that the maximum bound rates to the ASEAN Trade in Goods Agreement (ATIGA) and the WTO shall apply — and NEDA and the DA accordingly informed the public that these rates as listed in the Tariff and Customs Code were 35 per cent for imports from ASEAN countries, 40 per cent for imports within the MAV and 50 per cent for other imports — the law also provides that the tariff rate on rice imported from non-ASEAN, WTO-member countries shall be 180 per cent or the tariff equivalent of the QR, whichever is higher.

3.2.3 Leadership change

When the implementation of the RTL began, Agriculture Secretary Emmanuel Piñol, who somewhat only reluctantly supported the reform, was asked by President Duterte to take up another post. The president then appointed William Dar as DA acting secretary in August 2019.

Secretary Dar's fresh mandate allowed him to implement the RTL without the burden of any previous contrary statements and move the DA closer to the rice reform policy stance of the rest of the economic cabinet cluster.

3.2.4 Rice competitiveness enhancement fund

The RTL, which supports rice sector productivity, mandates an appropriation of PHP10 billion every year over a six-year period to a rice competitiveness enhancement fund (RCEF). The RCEF is to provide PHP5 billion worth of farm machinery through PhilMech; PHP3 billion for inbred certified palay seeds through PhilRice; PHP1 billion for credit through government banks (Development Bank of the Philippines and Land Bank of the Philippines); and PHP1 billion for training and extension through the Technical Education and Skills Development Authority (TESDA) and the Agricultural Training Institute (ATI). The law provides that the RCEF recipients be farmers, farmworkers and their family registered under the Registry System for Basic Sectors in Agriculture (RSBSA).[3]

Despite a slow start, the DA reported towards the end of 2019 that 36 per cent of RCEF's PHP10 billion allocation for the year had been obligated. Total RCEF disbursements as of February 2020, a year after the RTL was passed, was PHP1.6 billion.

The COVID-19 pandemic came during RTL's second year of implementation, challenging the conduct of business and putting greater urgency in efforts to sustain and increase rice productivity. By 27 October 2020, the government managed to obligate some PHP5.6 billion and disburse PHP1.4 billion of the RCEF allocation for the year. Accomplishment was high in the seed and credit components, while the mechanization component, which had an additional PHP5 billon allotment carried from the previous year, continued to have slow progress (Table 7.4).

---

[3] The RSBSA was started in 2012 as a joint effort of various government agencies led by the DBM to generate a list of potential beneficiaries of various government farm programmes. By 2017, some 9.8 million farmers, farmworkers and fisherfolk were registered in the system, of which 3.8 million were rice farmers (Reyes and Gloria 2017). The Registry was transferred to the DA in the same year, noting that it had to be updated and cleaned as it did not match the numbers and names in the lists of the DA, DAR and the Philippine Crop Insurance Corporation (PCIC).

Table 7.4. Financial status of 2020 RCEF (as of 27 Oct 2020)

Component	Allotment (PHP)	Obligation Thousand Pesos	% obligated	Disbursement Thousand Pesos	% disbursed
Mechanization	10 B	1,638,628.65	2	7,077.18	0.43
Seeds	3 B	2,798,007.60	95	1,160,947.55	41.00
Extension	1 B	372,219.72	37	98,897.81	27.00
ATI	100 M	61,140.35	61	52,771.04	86.00
PhilRice	100 M	55,649.00	56	35,125.00	63.00
PhilMech	100 M	9,719.37	10	4,371.77	45.00
TESDA	700 M	245,711.00	35	6,630.00	3.00
Credit	1 B	877,450.00	88	133,950.00	14.00
LBP	500 M	484,050.00	97	132,510.00	15.00
DBP	500 M	393,400.00	79	1,440.00	27.00
TOTAL	15 B*	5,686,305.97	38	1,400,872.54	25.00

Note: * Inclusive of 2019 PHP5 billion allocation for mechanization

Source: RCEF PSC Meeting Presentation (27 October 2020).

3.3 Imports and prices

An immediate impact expected of the RTL was lower rice prices for consumers. The country imported some 2.7 million mt of rice in 2019, of which 1.8 million mt arrived starting March that year. The imports brought down rice prices and inflation. Inflation declined from a peak of 6.7 per cent in October 2018 to only 0.8 per cent in October 2019. The contribution of rice to inflation dropped from 10.7 per cent to −9.7 per cent in the same time frame (Figure 7.5).

Retail prices of well-milled and regular-milled rice averaged PHP42.25/kg and PHP37.35/kg, respectively, during the third quarter of 2019, the rice lean season—down from PHP46.81/kg and PHP42.82/kg in the same period in 2018. Rice prices stabilized the rest of 2019 through 2020.

The impact on palay prices of the RTL and the attention this garnered in the press became a concern. Palay prices normally dip during the harvest season, with the lowest prices observed in the last quarter of the year. Palay prices in the fourth quarter of 2019 averaged PHP14.77/kg, compared with PHP19.67/kg in the same period in 2018.

Figure 7.5. Monthly headline and rice inflation (2016–20)

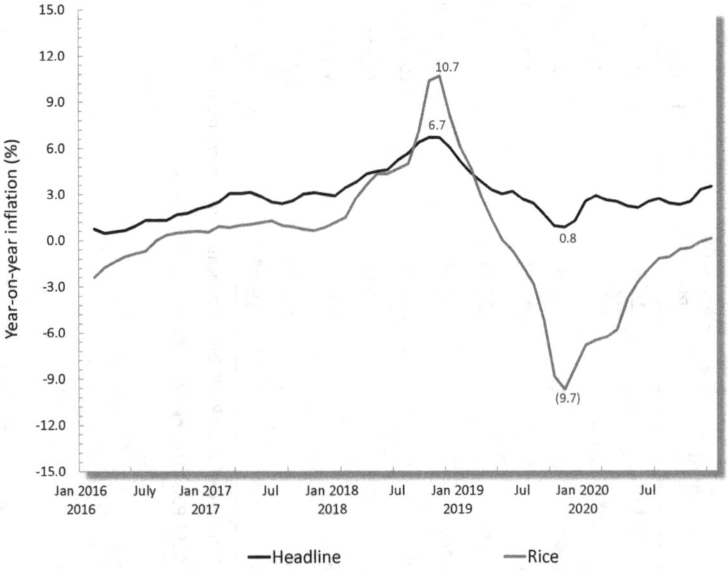

Source: BSP (accessed 12 January 2021).

It appears that the drop in palay prices was steeper than the decline in rice retail prices. Average growth from year-ago level for prices of regular-milled rice in 2019 was −3.9 per cent, −12.5 per cent and −14.0 per cent for the second, third and fourth quarter, respectively. The respective changes in palay prices were −17.3 per cent, −26.4 per cent and −24.9 per cent. The year 2020 saw smaller average year-on-year changes in retail and farm-gate prices (Table 7.5).

The discrepancy in the movement of rice and palay prices in 2019 seems to indicate the presence of rice stocks not entering the market. There were varied reports of imported stocks without corresponding import papers being held in warehouses and warehouses being leased in anticipation of import arrivals. Responding to possible manipulation of stocks and warehouses to suppress palay buying as well as to ensure that the palay and rice markets remain competitive, the DA and the Philippine Competition Commission (PCC, headed by Arsenio M. Balisacan) signed an agreement in October 2019 to coordinate and collaborate against illegal trade practices and anticompetitive practices. Moreover, the DA (with support of the Department of Finance) asked the BOC to strengthen its efforts to collect proper duties on rice imports. Further government action to make the domestic market more competitive is important, including improving rice price and supply information and addressing distribution infrastructure bottlenecks.

3.4 Income and price support

Clearly, farmers affected by the RTL need support, not only to increase productivity but also to offset income losses due to palay price changes, especially felt during the peak harvest season in the last quarter of the year. As early as 2019, some farmer groups clamoured for a tightening of BOC's processes for determining prices on which to base tariff computations and the imposition of special safeguard duties. Similarly, during the last quarter of 2020, there were again proposals and pressure, this time coming from legislators, to slow down imports by tightening the SPSIC issuance requirements.

So far the government has been successful in avoiding measures that could undo the consumer price and inflation gains from the RTL, especially in light of the adverse impacts of the pandemic on the general population. Instead, it has put in place a number of income and price support programmes for farmers.

Table 7.5. Prices of rice and palay (PHP/kg, % change from year ago)

Period FGP/WMR/RMR		3-month average price (PHP/kg)			3-month average year-on-year growth (%)		
		FGP	WMR	RMR	FGP	WMR	RMR
2017	Q1	41.86	36.73	17.92	0.95	0.49	4.23
	Q2	41.88	36.87	18.26	0.67	0.85	6.46
	Q3	42.23	37.25	18.61	0.77	1.12	0.83
	Q4	42.14	37.49	18.05	0.67	2.05	6.99
2018	Q1	42.98	38.52	19.77	2.68	4.88	10.28
	Q2	43.84	39.78	20.24	4.68	7.90	10.82
	Q3	46.81	42.82	21.92	10.82	14.95	17.85
	Q4	46.51	42.41	19.67	10.39	13.11	9.07
2019	Q1	44.24	39.74	18.27	2.95	3.19	(7.35)
	Q2	43.07	38.21	16.75	(1.75)	(3.92)	(17.25)
	Q3	42.25	37.35	16.09	(9.61)	(12.48)	(26.44)
	Q4	41.49	36.42	14.77	(10.72)	(14.02)	(24.92)

Table 7.5 (continued)

Table 7.5 (continued)

Period FGP/WMR/RMR		3-month average price (PHP/kg)			3-month average year-on-year growth (%)		
		FGP	WMR	RMR	FGP	WMR	RMR
2020	Q1	41.18	36.22	16.13	(6.92)	(8.84)	(11.53)
	Q2	42.23	37.32	18.46	(1.95)	(2.29)	10.23
	Q3	42.14	37.68	16.55	(0.26)	0.87	2.79
	Q4	41.21	36.55	15.76	(0.67)	0.37	6.75

Note: (1) Farm-gate prices of palay reported by PSA refer to the price received by farmers for the sale of dry palay (14% moisture content) at the first point of sale, net of freight costs.
(2) The conversion of palay to milled rice typically follows a milling recovery rate of 65 per cent. Meanwhile, retail rice prices from PSA refer to the prices at which retailers sell the milled rice to consumers in the marketplace.
(3) Data from PSA OpenStat are only until Sep 2020 for farm-gate prices (FGP) and up to Nov 2020 for well-milled rice (WMR) and regular-milled rice (RMR) prices. The series was continued using updates from the weekly report on rice prices from PSA which is based on a different survey methodology. Data for Oct-Dec 2020 are subject to change.

Sources: PSA Retail Price Survey of Selected Agricultural Commodities and the Farm Prices Survey accessed from the PSA OpenStat; BSP for forex rate.

3.5 Rice programme

The RTL provides that the RCEF shall only supplement and complement the regular rice programme of the government. The DA has continued to provide seed and fertilizer support to rice farmers under the Rice Resiliency Program (RRP) specifically to mitigate the impacts of the pandemic on farm production. Realizing that the services of the RCEF and the RRP overlap in some rice areas such that some farmers received seed assistance from both, the operating guidelines of these programmes were recently revised, assigning each of them exclusive provinces of operation. RCEF's seed support will focus on 42 provinces while the RRP will be active in 15 provinces. This is expeced to result in clearer accountability and better operational efficiency of both programmes. A less-popular consequence, however, is that farmers in the 42 RCEF seed provinces will no longer receive fertilizer support from the RRP. Early programme outcomes indicate yield increases, especially among seed subsidy beneficiaries. It is not clear, however, if such increase in productivity is sustainable without the subsidies. Of course, continuously investing in research and development to develop new rice varieties and technologies is key to sustaining productivity increases.

3.6 Monitoring losses and benefits

There is continuing effort to monitor RTL's impact on farmers and consumers. Farmer groups and the government have come to differing conclusions so far. The former finds that the losses sustained by farmers are larger than consumer gains, mainly because of the faster decline of farm-gate prices relative to rice prices. On the other hand, the government's analyses show that farmers may be losing due to lower farm-gate prices but these losses are offset by benefits received from the government's support programmes. Consumers benefit from lower-priced rice and the availability of a greater variety of rice in terms of quality and price. Farmers and consumers also benefit from lower inflation (Table 7.6).

3.7 Sustaining the reform

Policy reform is a complex, dynamic, long-term process. It is hard to sustain because situations change. It requires institutional capacity and buy-in from key stakeholders. Most of all, it requires political commitment (Abonyi 2007).

Table 7.6. Estimated losses and benefits from Rice Tariffication Law (Apr 2019–Mar 2020, in billion PHP)

	Parameter	A Joint NEDA and DOF (unpublished, Oct 2020)	E FFF 2 (Montemayor article Sep 2020)	F Roehlando Briones (unpublished, Mar 2020)	G FFF 1 (press release Feb 2020)	H IBON (press release Feb 2020)
A.	**Net farmer income loss from lower palay price**	**−28.3**	**−31.1**	**−24.6**	**−51.9**	**−56.8**
1	Farmer income loss	–	−48.6	−38.4	−81.0	−88.6
2	Add: Unsold palay produce (17%)	–	17.5	13.8	29.1	31.8
B.	**Obligated production support for rice farmers**	**51.2**	**6.0**	**43.8**	**43.8**	**43.8**
B1.	**Production support from the Rice Competitiveness Enhancement Fund (RCEF)**	**3.3**	**3.0**	**1.5**	**1.5**	**1.5**
3	Add: RCEF	3.3	3.0	1.5	1.5	1.5
4	Add: RCEF excess tariff collection	–	–	–	–	–
4A	Expanded crop insurance programme on rice	–	–	–	–	–
4B	Crop diversifiaction programme	–	–	–	–	–
B2.	**Production support interventions in response to RTL**	**8.3**	**3.0**	**20.0**	**20.0**	**20.0**
5	Add: Financial subsidy to rice farmers	–	–	–	–	–
6	Add: Rice resiliency programme	–	–	–	–	–

Table 7.6 (continued)

Table 7.6 (continued)

	Parameters	A Joint NEDA and DOF (unpublished, Oct 2020)	E FFF 2 (Montemayor article Sep 2020)	F Roehlando Briones (unpublished, Mar 2020)	G FFF 1 (press release Feb 2020)	H IBON (press release Feb 2020)
7 Add:	Farmer cash transfer	3.0	3.0	0.6	0.6	0.6
8 Add:	SURE aid loan programme	2.5	–	2.5	2.5	2.5
9 Add:	Palay ng lalawigan programme	–	–	0.0	0.0	0.0
10 Add:	BuyANIhan programme	0.2	–	0.2	0.2	0.2
11 Add:	PLGU commitments	0.1	–	0.1	0.1	0.1
12 Add:	Palay procurement (NFA)	2.5	–	16.7	16.7	16.7
B3.	**Regular rice programmes**	**39.7**	–	**22.2**	**22.2**	**22.2**
13 Add:	National rice programme	7.3	–	7.3	7.3	7.3
14 Add:	NIA	32.4	–	14.9	14.9	14.9
C.	**Net benefit for palay production**	**22.9**	**−25.1**	**19.2**	**−8.1**	**−13.0**
D.	**Gains from lower rice prices**	**21.6**	**0.2**	**21.6**	**21.6**	**21.6**
15 Add:	Consumer gain of rice farmers from lower retail rice price	1.0	–	1.0	1.0	1.0
16 Add:	Consumer gain of all non-rice farmers from lower retail rice price	20.6	–	20.6	20.6	20.6
E.	**Gains from lower inflation**	**49.9**	**0.0**	**49.9**	**49.9**	**49.9**

Table 7.6 (continued)

Table 7.6 (continued)

	Parameters	A Joint NEDA and DOF (unpublished, Oct 2020)	E FFF 2 (Montemayor article Sep 2020)	F Roehlando Briones (unpublished, Mar 2020)	G FFF 1 (press release Feb 2020)	H IBON (press release Feb 2020)
17 Add:	Consumer gain of rice farmers from lower inflation in general	1.8	0.0	1.8	1.8	1.8
18 Add:	Consumer gain of all non-rice farmers from lower inflation in general	48.1	0.0	48.1	48.1	48.1
F.	**Rice farmer gains from lower prices and lower inflation**	**2.8**	**–**	**2.8**	**2.8**	**2.8**
G.	**Non-rice farmer consumer gains from lower prices and lower inflation**	**68.6**	**–**	**68.6**	**68.6**	**68.6**
H.	Net benefit to rice farmers	25.7	-25.1	22.0	-5.3	-10.2
I.	Total net benefit to the people	94.3	-24.9	90.6	63.3	58.4

Note: (1) SURE - Expanded Survival and Recovery Assistance Programme for Rice Farmers of DA extends a one-time, zero-interest financial aid of PHP15,000 to rice farmers with farm area of 1 ha or less, payable in eight years.
(2) BuyANIhan provides working capital loans for farmers' cooperatives or associations to buy palay directly from farmers, and processes and markets the rice to institutional buyers.
(4) Provincial local government units (PLGUs) pledge to buy palay to help prop up prices.
(5) NFA has continued to procure palay.
(6) NIA has continued its irrigation development programme.

Source: DOF and NEDA (October 2020).

First, DA's outlook and strategy on grains sector reforms can change, and may keep changing, as political and populist pressures wax and wane. Second, resistance to the reforms mounted by selected stakeholder groups that benefited from the old system will be intense. Third, the time and resources required for the advocacy and completion of the envisioned reforms in the face of the sheer size and diversity of the stakeholders cannot be underestimated. It is crucial that advocacy is intensive and continuing.

Moving the grains sector reforms forward is a challenge for the political administration. Rice being a political commodity must be fully accepted and its operational implications recognized and factored into the strategy of sustaining the reforms. Therefore, the operational goal of the political administration should be the building and deployment of political coalitions in support of the reforms. It should continuously remind the public and policymakers of RTL's positive contributions towards food security and sustainable development.

3.8 Fostering stability in sector governance

It is crucial also that stability and long-term vision are institutionalized in sector management. Quite clearly, the level of the president and even cabinet secretaries will remain political, thus subject to political tides. At the very least, however, a professional, technical core group of managers, administrators and technical experts must be installed in each of the departments for the long term. These key posts must not become spoils to be distributed as rewards in the aftermath of political contests.

As a starting point, the majority of undersecretaries, assistant secretaries and agency heads should not be subject to political appointment. This can be achieved quickly by a presidential order that may later be confirmed by legislation. Another measure to induce more stability in the service is to accelerate the conferment of Career Executive Service Officer status on qualified officials. This is easily accomplished as part of the management powers of the president and the Civil Service Commission. Another easily accomplished step is to subject all senior officials to a fixed term of office, say at least three or four years, with the possibility of renewal (perhaps limited) given some minimum acceptable level of performance.

The experience of the past three decades indicates that any period of service beyond two years is already a major achievement. A minimum of one year is required to thoroughly "learn the job". Thus a term of three to four years will enable appointees to focus the rest of their time on accomplishing results.

5 CONCLUSION

Poor growth in agriculture, weak rural development and fragile food security worsen poverty and hunger. Add to these domestic challenges the imperative of managing the country's unavoidable participation in international relations and trade. Given these, RA 11203 was a decisive step in putting the country's rice sector and agriculture on a sustainable growth path. It has allowed market forces greater influence in shaping the sector, cognizant of the realities of limited domestic resources, increasing domestic demands and globalization. But more and significant efforts are necessary to ensure that the benefits of the reform are made durable and long lasting.

International literature offers a stylized fact on the success or failure of policy reforms. In general, public policy reforms are successful in the context of a crises, often times associated with macroeconomic issues. The crisis presents a window of opportunity as it can embolden political leadership to adopt difficult changes. The bureaucracy may support changes when it realizes that the system being administered has become increasingly dysfunctional. Ultimately, reform is driven by "a mixture of factors, including necessity, the triumph of ideas, and the conjunction of reform-oriented political leadership aided by technocratic advisers" (Hill 2013).

Moving the grains sector reforms forward will be a continuing challenge in governance. It is important to keep on reminding the many stakeholders of the reforms' positive contributions towards food security and sustainable development and to sustain the political coalitions supporting the reforms. More fundamentally, the basics of stability and competence in sector governance have to be promoted and sustained into the long term, given that reform is a long-term task. Strong measures must be initiated to stabilize sector leadership and shield it from excessive politicking that characterized previous policy dialogues and programme decision-making.

REFERENCES

Abonyi, G. 2007. "Public Policy Reform Process: Political Economy Perspective". Slide presentation for an Introductory Course on Economic Analysis of Policy-Based Lending Operations, 8 June 2007, ADB, Manila, Philippines.

Briones, R. 2002. "Agricultural Investments and the Pace of Land Reform". *Loyola Schools Review* (Social Sciences Edition) 2: 29–42.

Buzan, B., O. Waever, and J. de Wilde. 1998. *Security: A New Framework for Analysis*. Boulder, CO: Lynne Rienner.

DA (Department of Agriculture). 1998. "Implementing Rules and Regulations of RA 8435—the Agriculture and Fisheries Modernization Act of 1997". Administrative Order 6 (July 1998), Department of Agriculture, Quezon City, Philippines.

DA, and ADB (Asian Development Bank). 2002. "Final Report of TA 3429-PHI: Grains Policy and Institutional Reforms Advisory Technical Assistance Project". ADB, Manila, Philippines.

DA, DF (Department of Finance), and ADB. 2001. "TA 3429: Enhancing the Effectivity and Efficiency of the NFA in Food Security". ADB, Manila, Philippines.

David, C. 2003. "Agriculture". In *The Philippine Economy: Development, Policies, and Challenges*, edited by A. Balisacan and H. Hill. Quezon City, Philippines: Ateneo de Manila University Press.

Habito, C., and R. Briones. 2005. "Philippine Agriculture over the Years: Performance, Policies and Pitfalls". Paper presented in a conference on Policies to Strengthen Productivity in the Philippines, held by the Asia-Europe Meeting (ASEM) Trust Fund, Asian Institute of Management Policy Center, Foreign Investment Advisory Service, Philippines Institute of Development Studies and the World Bank in Makati City, Philippines.

Habito, C., R. Briones, and E. Paterno. 2003. "Investments, Productivity, and Land Market Impacts of the Comprehensive Agrarian Reform Program (CARP)." *CARP Impact Assessment Studies* vol. 4. Quezon City: Department of Agrarian Reform.

Hill, H. 2013. "The Political Economy of Policy Reform: Insights from Southeast Asia". *Asian Development Review* 30, no. 1: 108–30.

Inocencio, A., and R. Briones. 2020. "Irrigation Investments: Some Recurrent and Emerging Issues". *PIDS Policy Notes* No. 2020-05. Manila, Philippines: Philippine Institute of Development Studies.

Reyes C., and R. Gloria. 2017. "Evaluation of the Registry System for Basic Sectors in Agriculture". *PIDS Discussion Paper Series* No. 2017-03. Manila, Philippines: Philippine Institute of Development Studies.

Tolentino, V. B. J., E. Noveno, B. de la Peña, I. Villapando, and B. Rayco. 2001. *101 Facts About Rice in the Philippines*. Manila, Philippines: Department of Agriculture and Asian Development Bank.

Tolentino, V. B. J. 2001. "Organizing for Food Security and Poverty Alleviation: An Initial Action Program for the Department of Agriculture". Paper presented at the Department of Agriculture, Quezon City, Philippines, March 2001.

Tolentino, V. B. J. 1999. "Monopoly and Regulatory Constraints to Rapid Agricultural Growth and Sustainable Food Security in the Philippines". Working paper for the Foundation for Economic Freedom and the Trade and Investment Policy Analysis and Advocacy Support Project, Manila.

Tolentino, V.B.J., and B. de la Peña. 2020. *Deregulation and Tariffication At Last: The Saga of Rice Sector Reform in the Philippines*. Mandaluyong, Philippines: The Asia Foundation.

Waever, Ole. 1995. "Securitization and Desecuritization". In *On Security*, edited by Ronnie Lipschutz. New York: University Press.

8 Adapting Philippine Agriculture to Climate Change

Mark W. Rosegrant and Mercedita A. Sombilla with Nicostrato Perez, Angga Pradesha and Timothy Thomas

1 INTRODUCTION

Agriculture is an important part of the Philippine economy. Almost a third of the country's total land area of 30 million hectares was devoted to agriculture in 2015 (PSA 2017). As in other Asian countries, the share of agriculture in the gross domestic product (GDP) has declined with economic development—from 17.3 per cent of GDP in 1980 to 10.2 per cent in 2020. Employment in agriculture has fallen from 51.9 per cent in 1987 to a still high 24.5 per cent in 2020. This underscores agriculture's continued importance as a source of income for households, especially in the rural areas (World Bank 2018). However, the sector's annual agricultural productivity growth of 2.87 per cent from 1961 to 2012 has lagged compared with the 3.73 per cent of Indonesia, 4.10 per cent of Malaysia, 3.21 per cent of Thailand, 3.67 per cent of Myanmar and 4.16 per cent of Vietnam (AGRIMAG 2018). The challenges faced by the sector continue to be amplified by the increasing domestic and foreign demand for food due to continued economic growth, rising population and increasing involvement in international trade—amid losses of arable land because of extensive structural changes and urbanization and agriculture's vulnerability to natural disasters, including climate change. Food insecurity, malnutrition and rural poverty have thus remained issues to be addressed.

Climate change is defined here as medium- and long-term changes in average climate, including temperature and rainfall, as projected by general circulation models. The stress caused by these longer-term changes will further increase the country's already high vulnerability to climate and weather, including higher frequency and intensity of heatwaves, floods, droughts and typhoons that contribute to land degradation, reduced water availability and increased incidence of climate-sensitive infectious diseases. Climate change can disrupt crop productivity, which, in turn, affects domestic agricultural production, consumption and food security. Such consequences are triggered by both the direct impacts on agricultural production and changes in international prices because of climate change, considering the global nature of the phenomenon, which would then stimulate changes in domestic prices that could adversely affect Philippine agriculture and the country's overall economy. The poor are particularly at risk from these challenges because many of them live in hazard-prone areas and are dependent on natural resources for their livelihoods (Garcia-Rincon and Virtucio 2008).

This chapter examines the impact of climate change on the Philippines' agriculture sector, food security and the broader economy, particularly GDP and employment. Policy interventions for climate change adaptation are assessed and modifications are recommended to sustain domestic agricultural production and raise agricultural productivity. These are key to accelerating broader structural transformation for a more inclusive economic growth and poverty reduction, the dynamics of which have been limited by policy and governance constraints (Ravago and Balisacan 2018). We therefore also explore policies that would help accelerate this process in the context of climate change.

2 MODELLING FRAMEWORK

Based on a linked modelling approach, we assess the effects of alternative macroeconomic and agricultural policies and climate adaptation interventions under a range of simulated climate and socio-economic "futures" to evaluate their effectiveness in responding to climate change impacts in the Philippines. The analytical framework integrates a range of macro- and microeconomic modelling components, which include:

(1) general circulation models (GCMs) that generate climate change scenarios; (2) regional biophysical crop modelling using the Decision Support System for Agrotechnology Transfer (DSSAT) for field crops and the Water, Nutrient and Light Capture in Agroforestry Systems model (WaNuLCAS) for coconuts and bananas; (3) partial equilibrium economic modelling of the agriculture sector using the International Model for Policy Analysis of Agricultural Commodities and Trade (IMPACT); and (4) economy-wide analyses using a dynamic computable general equilibrium model of the Philippines (Phil-DCGE).[1] A more detailed description of the models is provided in Appendix A. Figure 8.1 shows how the models are linked such that the results of one serve as inputs to another.

Figure 8.1. *Interlinked modelling system used to assess the agricultural impacts of climate change on the Philippine economy*

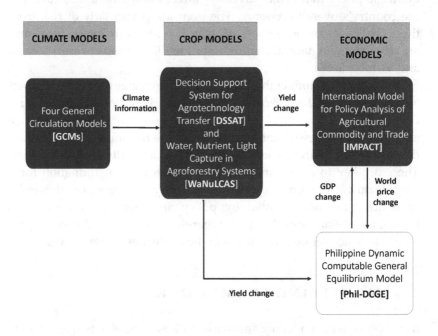

---

[1] See Thomas, Nazareth, and Folledo (2018), Perez and Rosegrant (2018) and Pradesha and Robinson (2018) for a detailed description of these models. This chapter draws on these sources and Rosegrant et al. (2016).

3   IMPACT OF CLIMATE CHANGE ON COMMODITY PRODUCTION, PRICES AND ECONOMIC WELFARE

GCMs provide monthly rainfall and temperature data under alternative climate change scenarios, the results of which are downscaled to the pixel level for input into the crop models. The biophysical impacts from the crop models, particularly changes in crop yields, are fed into the IMPACT agricultural economic model to project the broader economic effects of climate change.

The crop model results analysed by regions are summarized in Table 8.1. They show that the impact of climate change on crop yields varies across regions. The negative impact is highest for maize, followed by bananas, sugarcane and rainfed rice. Coconuts are projected to have small gains. Regions in Luzon are projected to be the hardest hit, followed by those in the Visayas and Mindanao.

Changes in crop yields across countries affect the global supply of crop and livestock commodities. Lower crop yields mean lower global supply of commodities, which could result in higher world prices and lower food consumption. At the same time, however, higher world commodity prices induce higher levels of farm production, partially offsetting the negative impact of climate change on yields. To determine the eventual impact of climate change in the Philippines, these positive and negative effects are taken into account in the IMPACT model, assuming the full transmission of higher world prices to domestic markets in the long run.

The average results across the four GCMs project a 1.7 per cent contraction of total crop production in 2050 compared with baseline levels (i.e., without climate change). Cereal production is projected to fall by 6.1 per cent in 2050 compared with baseline levels. The negative impact of climate change on maize production (a decline of 13.0%) is projected to be significantly higher than for rice production (a decline of only 3.2%). This is because the projected temperature increases are higher in maize-growing regions. While average rainfall is projected to increase in these areas, so are periods of drought. On the other hand, much of rice production is irrigated, providing protection against droughts. Due to links with cereals used as feed, meat production is also projected to decline by about 0.9 per cent.

The resulting effects of reduced productivity and production on the accessibility of agricultural commodities for consumption are substantial. Agricultural food commodity prices are projected to increase in 2030

Table 8.1. Summary of crop model results in major crop yields due to climate change (2000–2050)

	Rice					Maize		Sugarcane		Bananas	Coconuts
	Rainfed		Irrigated			Rainfed		Rainfed	Irrigated	Rainfed	Rainfed
Region	Low	High	Low	High		Low	High				
					Per cent (%)						
1. Luzon	-7.4	-7.7	-0.2	-0.1		-18.9	-20.6	-8.6	-3.6	-11.2	1.4
1.1. Luzon	-7.5	-7.8	-0.2	-0.2		-19.1	-20.7	-8.7	-3.6	-11.1	1.4
1.2. CAR	-6.7	-6.7	0.2	2.0		-16.6	-18.6	-6.6	-2.2	-12.3	-1.7
2. Visayas	-4.1	-3.9	-1.1	-0.6		-22.8	-25.0	-5.8	-5.6	-4.8	0.9
3. Mindanao	-0.5	-0.6	-0.8	0.7		-18.7	-21.2	-0.5	-1.2	-1.4	2.5
3.1. Mindanao	-0.4	-0.5	-0.8	1.0		-18.1	-20.6	-0.4	-1.2	-1.6	2.4
3.2. ARMM	-0.8	-1.0	-0.9	-1.5		-21.3	-24.1	-3.9	-0.4	-0.1	2.8
Total	**-4.5**	**-4.5**	**-0.4**	**0.0**		**-19.3**	**-21.6**	**-4.7**	**-4.3**	**-3.7**	**1.7**

Note: (1) Grid cell values were tabulated using weights from SPAM 2005.
(2) "Low" and "High" refer to levels of fertilizer, which for the analyses done mean 30 kg/ha and 90 kg/ha of nitrogen, respectively.
(3) The sugarcane model did not respond to changing nitrogen levels, so it was run without.

Sources: Thomas, Pradesha, and Perez (2016); Thomas, Nazareth, and Folledo (2018).

and 2050 due to climate change compared with the baseline, making food less accessible generally, but especially to poor people. Averaged across the results from the four GCMs, consumer prices are projected to increase substantially by 2050 for cereals (24%), fruits and vegetables (13%) and pulses (12%) compared with baseline values. Meat prices are projected to increase by 4 per cent. Among cereals, prices of rice are projected to increase by 17 per cent, maize by 44 per cent and wheat by 11 per cent. Greater reliance on imports happens, however, filling the supply gap and tempering the domestic price increases of commodities affected by climate change.

Income is also reduced relative to the baseline, as shown by the total surplus analysis below, thus further reducing the ability to purchase food. The decline in average per capita consumption in 2050 relative to the baseline without climate change is projected to be 3.1 per cent for cereals, 2.3 per cent for fruits and vegetables, 2.4 per cent for sugar, 0.9 per cent for roots and tubers, 0.4 per cent for pulses and 0.3 per cent for meat. Among cereals, per capita consumption of maize is projected to decline in 2050 by an average of 5.6 per cent (mainly for direct human consumption, with smaller reductions for animal feed use), wheat by 3.4 per cent and rice by 2.9 per cent (Perez and Rosegrant 2018).

4 IMPACT OF CLIMATE CHANGE ON FOOD SECURITY, CHILDHOOD MALNUTRITION AND HUNGER

With climate change causing higher prices and lower production, further improvement of food security is endangered. In this analysis, food security is measured as the prevalence of childhood malnutrition and the number of people experiencing hunger or at risk of hunger. Three million Filipino children were classified as malnourished in 2010. Under a baseline scenario (without climate change), this number is projected to decline by 2.7 million in 2030 and 2.15 million in 2050. Based on average results from the four GCMs, it is projected that with climate change the number of malnourished children will increase by 40,000 (2%) in 2030 and 50,000 (3%) in 2050 compared with the baseline. The impact of climate change on the number of people at risk of hunger is estimated to be even more severe. Averaging the results across the GCMs, increases in the number of people at risk of hunger are projected at 1.3 million in 2030 (8%) and 2.0 million in 2050 (13%) compared with the "no climate change" baseline (Perez and Rosegrant 2018).

The higher levels of childhood malnutrition and hunger are driven by the higher prices and lower incomes under climate change relative to the baseline scenario, which reduces calorie consumption, especially for the poor. The improved policies and widespread adoption of production technologies that boost productivity and income (analysed below) would result in reduction of hunger and malnourishment under climate change. These technology and policy changes are projected to increase food availability (2.9%), reduce prices and increase incomes. Subsequently, these would reduce the number of malnourished children (by 3.4%) and hungry people (by 14.3%) in 2050 compared with the climate change scenario without these changes (Perez and Rosegrant 2018).

Reyes et al. (2014), using household-level data, also find that climate change can adversely affect food security. They find that changes in climate variables, through their negative effects on farming income, can result in increased food insecurity. Households' vulnerability to being more food insecure is further influenced by their characteristics, particularly level of educational attainment, demographic features and access to infrastructure and housing. Nonetheless, climate change effects on farming income can be dampened by government expenditure on agriculture, farm inputs and infrastructure.

5   IMPACT OF CLIMATE CHANGE ON ECONOMIC WELFARE IN AGRICULTURE

The estimates of the impact of climate change on the supply and demand of agricultural commodities presented above can be used to measure shifts in the economic welfare of the Philippine population, based on changes in "economic surplus" to producers and consumers. Figure 8.2 shows the average results of the four GCMs as to the overall welfare effect in 2050 compared with the baseline scenario (without climate change) and assuming full transmission of world prices to the Philippines. This assumption oversimplifies the situation in the case of commodities like white maize, which have low levels of international trade. However, increases in yellow maize prices are likely to also induce increases in white maize prices in the medium and longer term. Results project a total welfare loss to the Philippines of US$16.72 billion over the 40-year period or US$418 million per year (in net present value). The net welfare loss to the agriculture sector due to climate change is thus equivalent to PHP18.81 billion per year. These costs are borne by consumers, with welfare losses of US$71.69 billion or US$1.79 billion per year, while producers gain US$54.98 billion or US$1.37 billion per year. Even though producers incur costs due to declines in production under climate change, they also benefit from the global impact of climate change on world food prices, which gets transmitted to domestic markets. Nevertheless, a large share of Filipino farmers—especially smallholders—are net food consumers, purchasing food from the market. So, farmers gain as producers, but also experience losses as consumers (Perez and Rosegrant 2018).

Figure 8.2. Impact of climate change on indicators of economic welfare (2050)

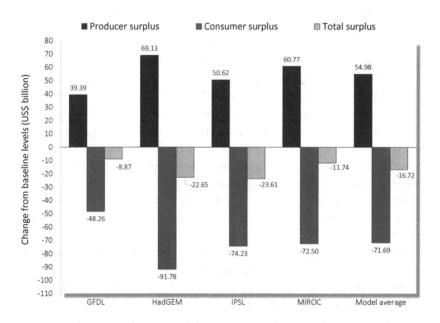

Note: (1) Data indicate changes from baseline levels (i.e., without climate change) from each of the four climate models and averages of the results of all four models.
(2) GFDL = General Fluid Dynamics Laboratory
HadGEM = Hadley Centre Global Environmental Model
IPSL = Institut Pierre-Simon Laplace
MIROC = Model for Interdisciplinary Research on Climate

Source: Rosegrant et al. (2016).

6 AGRICULTURAL TECHNOLOGIES FOR ADAPTATION AND PRODUCTIVITY GROWTH

The agriculture-sector modelling also assesses the potential of several technologies to compensate for the adverse effects of climate change on crop production and yields and to boost agricultural productivity growth. We examined existing and currently available agricultural technologies (e.g., adding fertilizer in the case of low fertilizer input farms, changing planting dates and changing seed varieties), as well as emerging and new technologies, whether under development, being field tested or in limited release (e.g., technologies focusing on varietal traits such as drought and heat tolerance and nitrogen-use efficiency, farm-management technologies like precision and no-till agriculture and integrated soil fertility management, and improved crop protection).

Results show the strong potential of these technologies to deliver productivity gains. The combination of optimizing fertilizer use, crop variety and planting date under climate change is projected to increase rice yields by up to 6 per cent and maize yields by 4 per cent. More advanced technologies have the potential to deliver considerably higher crop yields if successfully adopted. This is indicated in Tables 8.2–8.4, which show results of an additional crop modelling exercise using the Commonwealth Scientific and Industrial Research Organisation (CSIRO) and the Model for Interdisciplinary Research on Climate (MIROC) General Circulation Models (GCMs) from Assessment Report 4 of the International Panel on Climate Change and under a high emission scenario.

These technologies and others that can enhance productivity growth and provide protection against climate change (e.g., precision farming, conservation tillage, integrated soil and water management, and innovative fertilizer formulations and practices) have been adopted relatively slowly in the Philippines. Constraints include the perceived risks of adopting new technologies, poor access to inputs and output markets and timely information services due to weak hard and soft infrastructure, and lack of access to financing and risk-reducing instruments. Some of these technologies may take years to come to fruition, posing an additional barrier to adoption. However, improved policies and services can overcome these constraints and facilitate adoption of new technologies. These are discussed in section 8.

Table 8.2. Projected improvements in rainfed maize yields from various technologies (2050)

Region	Drought-tolerant varieties	Heat-tolerant varieties	Nitrogen-efficient varieties	No-till agriculture	Crop-disease protection	Pest protection	Weed protection	Integrated soil fertility management	Water harvesting
					Per cent (%)				
1. Luzon	5.1	13.2	11.9	25.4	11.3	16.3	12.5	34.7	0.5
1.1. Luzon	5.3	16.2	10.8	26.4	11.4	16.4	12.8	32.6	0.7
1.2. CAR	4.6	2.9	15.7	21.9	11.2	15.7	11.3	42.1	0.1
2. Visayas	4.1	11.3	12.7	24.7	10.0	13.1	10.7	32.1	0.0
3. Mindanao	2.6	8.2	14.2	23.7	12.4	17.1	14.4	31.8	0.9
3.1. Mindanao	2.9	8.2	14.2	24.6	12.2	17.1	14.1	31.4	1.1
3.2. ARMM	1.1	8.2	13.9	19.1	13.5	17.3	16.3	34.2	0.2
Total	**3.2**	**9.4**	**13.7**	**24.1**	**12.0**	**16.7**	**13.9**	**32.4**	**0.8**

Source: Rosegrant et al. (2014).

Table 8.3. Projected improvements in irrigated rice yields from various technologies (2050)

Region	Heat-tolerant varieties	Nitrogen-efficient varieties	Precision agriculture	Crop-disease protection	Pest protection	Weed protection	Integrated soil fertility management
				Per cent (%)			
1. Luzon	1.8	52.1	22.6	10.2	8.1	5.1	24.4
1.1. Luzon	1.7	51.3	21.5	10.2	8.1	5.1	22.8
1.2. CAR	2.7	61.1	35.0	10.3	7.2	4.7	40.5
2. Visayas	1.7	49.1	31.9	8.9	10.4	7.3	33.7
3. Mindanao	1.5	56.7	32.8	11.7	9.6	7.6	34.4
3.1. Mindanao	1.7	56.4	32.0	11.6	9.5	7.5	33.6
3.2. ARMM	0.1	59.0	39.1	11.9	10.2	8.4	40.6
Total	**1.7**	**53.1**	**25.6**	**10.6**	**8.6**	**5.8**	**27.4**

Source: Rosegrant et al. (2014).

Table 8.4. Projected improvements in rainfed rice yields from various technologies (2050)

Region	Drought-tolerant varieties	Heat-tolerant varieties	Nitrogen-efficient varieties	Precision agriculture	Crop disease protection	Pest protection	Weed protection	Integrated soil fertility management
				Per cent (%)				
1. Luzon	1.8	1.9	11.2	3.0	9.8	8.1	5.4	8.0
1.1. Luzon	1.9	2.0	11.0	3.2	9.9	8.2	5.5	8.1
1.2. CAR	1.5	1.2	11.9	2.4	9.3	7.9	5.0	7.8
2. Visayas	1.2	0.4	13.3	2.2	9.8	9.5	5.9	6.8
3. Mindanao	1.3	0.4	11.6	0.6	11.6	9.7	7.8	4.9
3.1. Mindanao	1.4	0.3	11.2	0.5	11.3	9.5	7.4	3.9
3.2. ARMM	0.6	1.0	13.4	0.8	12.8	10.5	9.5	9.0
Total	**1.4**	**0.9**	**12.0**	**1.9**	**10.4**	**9.1**	**6.4**	**6.6**

Source: Rosegrant et al. (2014), as cited in Thomas, Nazareth, and Folledo (2018).

7 ECONOMY-WIDE IMPACT OF CLIMATE CHANGE ON AGRICULTURE[2]

This section presents the economy-wide impact of climate change on the agriculture sector by focusing on movements in the labour markets and their long-term effect on economic growth and income distribution in the Philippines (Pradesha and Robinson 2018). The analysis employed the Phil-DCGE model, linked with DSSAT and IMPACT to capture both the local and global effects of climate change. The first shock on yield changes is derived from the DSSAT model to show the local climate effect on Philippine agriculture. The world price shocks for agriculture, derived from IMPACT, are used to model international commodity price changes in the Phil-DCGE model as part of the global climate shock.

7.1 Climate impacts

Climate change is projected to reduce GDP growth in the Philippines by 0.9 per cent in 2050 (Figure 8.3). At the sectoral level, its global impact on trade—which results in higher prices—creates an incentive for farmers to increase production of agricultural export commodities. The local productivity effect, however, decreases the production of agricultural commodities due to reductions in yield of most crops, including rice.

Given interlinkages among the different sectors of the economy, the net productivity gains of the agriculture sector due to increased demand for and prices of agricultural exports under climate change are insufficient to compensate for the negative impacts on the productivity of the non-agriculture sectors. The change in demand for all agricultural commodities due to climate change causes shifts in input markets that eventually drive a reallocation of resources. Key among these shifts is the movement of labour (especially unskilled labour) from agriculture to non-agriculture sectors. Climate change effects that are mainly driven by global trade adjustment have created incentives to keep more labour working in the agriculture sector. This is reflected by higher demand for labour in the agriculture sector, which directly affects the labour market in the non-agriculture sectors (Figure 8.5).

---

[2] This section draws primarily from Pradesha and Robinson (2018) and Rosegrant et al. (2016).

Figure 8.3. Impact of climate change on Philippine GDP by sector (2050)

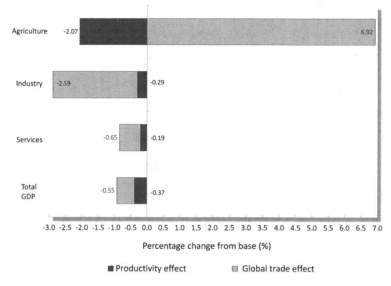

Sources: Pradesha and Robinson (2018); Rosegrant et al. (2016).

Climate change is projected to increase the demand for unskilled labour in the agriculture sector by 4 per cent, consequently reducing the absorption level for labour by the non-agriculture sectors by 6.5 per cent on average in 2050. As a result, value added in both industry and services sectors declines in response to the contraction of available workforce to support production (Figure 8.3).

Bigger changes in demand for skilled labour in agriculture do not have much impact, as the employment share of this type of worker in the sector is minimal; it only slightly affects the labour demand in the non-agriculture sectors (Figure 8.4).

On the other hand, the movement of labour induced by climate change directly impacts the structural transformation process, a key indicator of which is the movement of labour out of the agriculture sector (Figure 8.5). The upward sloping trend line indicates how labour is held back from moving out of the agriculture sector due to higher demand for unskilled labour in response to climate change. In contrast, the downward sloping trend line indicates the resulting decline in GDP levels due to less labour being employed in the non-agriculture sectors.

Figure 8.4. Impact of climate change on demand for labour by sector and type of labour (2050)

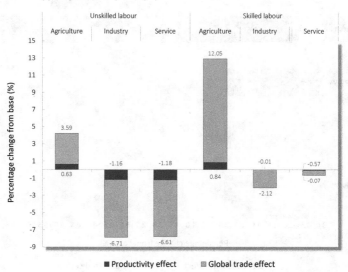

Note: Results indicate the per centage change from baseline levels (without climate change).
Source: Rosegrant et al. (2016).

Figure 8.5. Impact of climate change on GDP through demand for agricultural labour (2011–50)

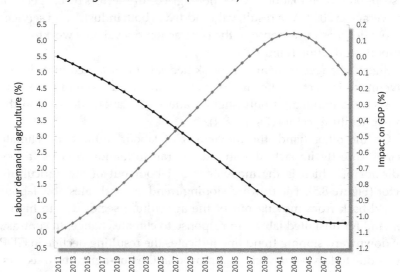

Note: Results indicate the per centage change from baseline levels (without climate change).
Source: Pradesha and Robinson (2018).

This negative relationship reflects a reality in the Philippines, that, based on the average value of real wages, labour is five times less productive in agriculture than in industry or services. In this way, climate change creates the wrong incentives for resource allocation (especially unskilled labour), thus deterring the structural transformation process and impeding long-term economic growth.

The economic cost of climate change can be calculated based on "real absorption value", which reflects consumption and investment levels in the Philippines. On this basis, climate change is projected to cost about PHP145 billion per year, mainly due to reduced levels of private consumption and total investment. The impact of global trade dominates this result, indicating the importance of international agricultural prices as drivers of resource allocation. The adverse impacts of climate change that drive labour to stay in agriculture mainly explain the decrease in the national income and ultimately the reduction in consumption and investment levels.

7.2 Adaptation strategies

The study also explores opportunities for the Philippine government to mitigate the adverse impacts of climate change through policy interventions designed to promote higher economic growth and better income distribution. Three adaptation strategies have the potential to promote higher domestic rice production. The first strategy focuses on rice productivity by increasing investments in research and development; the second targets investment to expand the irrigation infrastructure; and the third involves reducing agricultural tariffs and gearing towards more trade liberalization in rice.

Each of these three options is analysed under climate change, with and without the country's rice self-sufficiency policy that was in place until 2019 via the mandate of the National Food Authority (NFA) to buy palay high from farmers and sell rice low to consumers and to restrict imports at the same time. This work was undertaken during the time when final considerations for the Rice Tariffication Law were underway (the law was enacted in February 2019). Nevertheless, the results remain instructive, as they show the potential cost of returning to the previous rice policies. The analysis also illustrates the potential costs of maintaining rice tariffs at the tariff equivalent to the previous quotas, which was around 51 per cent. Including the with and without NFA's rice subsidies scenarios helps shed light on how the policy affects the impact of the three adaptation strategies, and the potential long-term benefits of the ongoing rice policy reform. By reducing the adverse impacts of climate change, all three adaptation strategies are projected to have significant net welfare benefits (Figure 8.6). No single strategy is projected to mitigate the full financial cost of climate change (estimated to be about PHP145 billion per year), but gains of PHP128 billion per year are projected for rice productivity investments, PHP118 billion for irrigation investments, and PHP81 billion for elimination of rice tariffs.

Figure 8.6. Impact of three adaptation strategies on net welfare (with and without NFA rice subsidy, 2011–50)

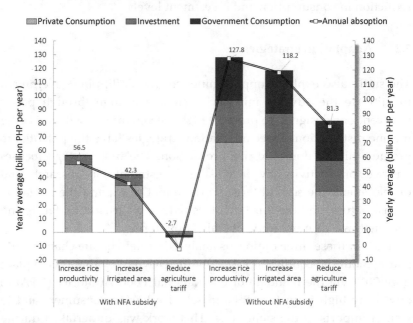

Note: NFA = National Food Authority.
Source: Pradesha and Robinson (2018).

Comparing the results of the with and without price subsidy scenarios shows that increasing rice productivity, for example, is projected to mitigate welfare losses by PHP57 billion per year with price subsidy in place, but by PHP128 billion per year without subsidy. Eliminating the subsidy policy alone could potentially reduce the negative impact of climate change by PHP71 billion per year. The highest gains of eliminating this policy occur when it is combined with the strategy of reducing agricultural/implicit tariffs, where welfare is increased from PHP–3 billion to PHP81 billion, an annual gain of PHP84 billion. In the analysis, the tariff equivalent of the rice quota was used for rice tariff; tariffs on other commodities were based on official tariff data from the Philippine Tariff Finder (DOF 2014). The key reason for the results is that the incentive that the subsidy creates for farmers to grow more rice induces more unskilled labour to remain in the agriculture sector. As previously discussed, the lack of available labour for use in the more productive non-agriculture sectors impedes the structural transformation process and, hence, the long-term economic growth. The lack of productivity growth in the agriculture sector slows the process of structural transformation.

Modelling results show that all three adaptation strategies have a positive effect on the economy, as reflected in higher GDP levels compared with projections under climate change without the adaptation strategies (Figure 8.6). Increasing rice productivity has the largest impact, followed by expanding irrigation area and reducing agricultural tariffs. Rice productivity has such a high impact mainly because it constitutes the highest share of agricultural value added.

7.3 Implications of rice subsidy removal on welfare

The success of the adaptation strategies in mitigating the adverse impacts of climate change when the NFA subsidy is removed is not only due to changes in the labour markets, but also reallocation of huge government budget to activities that enhance the competitive stance of sectors, especially agriculture. Given the significant resources provided to fund rice subsidy policies, including the NFA's operations and infrastructure, government consumption and investment are lower with this policy in place. Official data indicate that, on average, 70 per cent of funds used to finance the NFA's operations are derived from the private sector (SEPO 2010). This reality is reflected in the analysis through reduced investment, which has a negative flow-on effect on the rest of the economy.

When the NFA subsidies are eliminated, government consumption is projected to increase by PHP32 billion per year and private consumption by PHP66 billion, due to improved economic conditions from higher rice productivity and more efficient resource allocation that stimulates the market (Figure 8.6). This analysis clearly illustrates that the pursuit of rice self-sufficiency through the NFA subsidy is both costly and ineffective in addressing the adverse impacts of climate change.

On average, even with slight decreases in the rice self-sufficiency rate, adaptation strategies are projected to provide welfare gains in the range of PHP81 billion–PHP128 billion per year when the NFA rice subsidy is abandoned (Table 8.5). Looking at how these potential gains are distributed across household types, results confirm that abolishing the policy may negatively affect some vulnerable households. However, compensating these lower-income households to maintain their welfare status would cost less than PHP4 billion per year, on average—much less than the total welfare gain observed in all the three adaptation strategies. This demonstrates the feasibility of removing the subsidy and reallocating the increase in government consumption to compensation of vulnerable households via direct transfer or a special assistance programme.

Table 8.5. *Average net yearly impact of adaptation strategies on household welfare by income group (with and without NFA subsidy, 2011–50)*

Indicator	With NFA subsidy			Without NFA subsidy		
	Adaptation strategy					
	1	2	3	1	2	3
Rice self-sufficiency rate	0.2	0.1	0.0	−1.4	−1.6	−3.3
Total welfare gain	56.5	42.3	−2.7	127.8	118.2	81.3
Household welfare gain	45.8	34.1	1.9	65.2	56.6	32.2
Rural	4.3	6.3	−2.1	−0.5	1.6	−6.7
Lower income	3.0	2.6	−0.2	0.1	−0.3	−2.6
Upper income	1.2	3.7	−1.9	−0.5	1.9	−4.0
Urban	41.5	27.8	4.0	65.7	55.0	38.8
Lower income	2.1	1.8	0.1	0.9	0.6	−0.7
Upper income	39.4	26.0	3.9	64.8	54.3	39.6

Note: (1) 1 = increase rice productivity; 2 = expand irrigation; 3 = reduce agricultural tariffs.
(2) Total welfare and household welfare are measured in billion PHP per year.

Sources: Pradesha and Robinson (2018); Rosegrant et al. (2016).

8 POLICIES, INSTITUTIONS, TECHNOLOGIES AND INVESTMENTS FOR CLIMATE CHANGE ADAPTATION

The modelling assessments above provide a broad brush of adaptation polices to respond to climate change. Here we do a deeper dive on how the Philippines can respond to climate change.

8.1 Application of modern climate-smart agricultural technologies and crop management

Farmers can improve their climate resiliency by adopting climate-smart technologies and practices while reducing production risks. Dikitanan et al. (2017) note that site-specific nutrient management and integrated pest management can reduce incidence of pests and diseases—and thus economic losses due to pests and diseases—and increase productivity and food availability. Appropriate sourcing, timing, amount and placement of fertilizers, as can be done by precision agriculture, can lessen the negative effects of excessive fertilization and reduce soil salinity and nutrient leaching, while lowering emissions of methane and other greenhouse gases (GHG) related to rice production and excessive use of pesticides. Conservation tillage and integrated soil and water management can enhance crop yield due to improved soil fertility, as well as maintain or improve soil, above- and below-ground carbon stocks and organic matter content.

Crop modelling assessments presented above show that each of these technologies have the biophysical potential to substantially increase the yields of rice and maize in the Philippines (Thomas, Nazareth, and Folledo 2018). Realizing the potential benefits of these technologies will require widespread adoption by farmers. Adoption rates are influenced by many factors, including profitability, initial costs, risk, farmer's income and knowledge, and complexity of the technology. In addition, there is the need to retool/upskill small farmers and fisherfolk on appropriate cropping systems and technologies.

8.2 Higher investment in agricultural research and development

Greater investment in agricultural R&D, with increased emphasis on traits that respond to stresses due to climate shocks and variability (e.g., drought and heat tolerance), can produce substantial benefits. In taking steps to achieve food security under climate change, efficiency-enhancing technologies need to be increasingly included in agricultural R&D programmes. To help improve farmers' preparedness and response efficiency to calamities and disasters, existing decision-support tools like multi-hazard forecasting and early warning systems and information systems like the Philippine Rice Information System (PRiSM) should be enhanced to generate and provide timely and site-specific weather and climate advisories. Increased investment in agricultural R&D will be a key driver of technology development. Real-time weather information can assist farmers in making decisions on planting date and farm management. The provision of effective agricultural extension by the government, private sector and non-governmental organizations—employing innovative methods such as information and communication technologies—can educate farmers as regards the adoption of more complex technologies. A strong seed industry that is accessible to farmers would facilitate the adoption of variety-related technologies. With additional investment and policy reform, the adoption of technologies for adaptation and productivity can be further enhanced.

8.3 Improvement of extension services

The rapid dissemination of climate-smart technologies described above and their proper adoption and use are critical steps beyond intensified agricultural R&D. Extension systems should seek to improve farmers' knowledge and increase their capacity. Moreover, there should be wider use of innovative extension channels, including radio, mobile phone and other advanced information and communication technologies (ICT). For greater coherence in extension, the national government should provide more direction to improve coordination of public extension with the private sector and non-governmental organizations that provide similar services. Stronger organizational, information and extension strategies will give smallholders access to both domestic and international trade.

Establishing close linkages between farmers' organizations and research institutions (e.g., Philippine Rice Research Institute, International Rice Research Institute and universities) would help farmers' adoption of integrated management practices, such as integrated soil fertility management, site-specific nutrient management and integrated pest management. In addition, strengthening institutional linkages through joint ventures with private stakeholders/business community will help strengthen and facilitate R&D and extension.

To further improve targeting of adaptation and mitigation investments at the local level, there should be more efforts to establish integrated decision-support structures and extension systems that compile and analyse weather, agronomic and market information and deliver timely results to a range of stakeholders and decision-makers (Dikitanan et al. 2017). Capacity development of local government units (LGUs) in dealing with climate change is important. LGUs depend on the national government for solutions and resources. Since many services have been devolved to LGUs, there is a need to better involve and strengthen coordination among the LGUs.

8.4 Investment in rural infrastructure: Irrigation and roads

The findings from both the agriculture-sector modelling and CGE modelling show the benefits of expanding investments in irrigation. Selective new investment in cost-effective irrigation expansion as well as rehabilitation and modernization of existing systems would be beneficial in protecting against climate change and climate shocks, as well as increasing crop yields. Greater adoption of small-scale irrigation, such as drip and sprinkler irrigation, can also increase yields and reduce on-farm water use. Developing the rural transportation network is another priority to improve farmers' access to input and output markets and reduce marketing margins and post-harvest crop losses; it also enables more remote villages to have access to services and assistance. In addition, especially with increasing climate variability due to climate change, appropriate identification of the location of irrigation and transportation facilities is essential, including ensuring that their structural and engineering design is suitably resilient to the adverse impacts of climate. Existing structures may have to be retrofitted to be disaster and climate resilient.

8.5 International trade policy

Managing fluctuations in food and agricultural prices is a major policy concern as climate change increases variability in weather and food production. Even small changes in domestic or global production levels can lead to large changes in food prices, with severe adverse effects on household well-being. Improved farm technologies and management cannot completely mitigate production losses, so trade (and trade policy) becomes an important mechanism for smoothing price fluctuations and offsetting food shortfalls. The analysis of rice-trade restrictions above shows the high cost of inappropriate trade policies. The increased variability in production over time due to climate change can increase the benefits from removal of agricultural trade and macroeconomic distortions. Open trade becomes even more important because climate change will increase the reliance of many developing countries, possibly including the Philippines, on food imports.

8.6 Strengthening climate risk management and risk-sharing mechanisms

The government should explore the potential for developing and offering more effective agricultural insurance products to farmers. An example is weather index-based insurance (WIBI), which has been piloted with some success in several areas of the Philippines, including Tuguegarao and Penablanca in Cagayan, Dumangas in Iloilo and a number of rural communities in Mindanao. Index-based insurance relies on publicly available information, is standardized and more transparent, and cannot be easily manipulated by the insured. Thus, it is less costly to administer than general agricultural insurance, making it a more viable option. Nevertheless, given that WIBI coverage is based on a predetermined index of damages, it involves "basis risk", whereby a household's insurance coverage has the potential to be either higher or lower than the losses incurred by the household. As a result, to be sustainable, index-based insurance requires subsidies. The implementation of WIBI in the Philippines has been beset with operational issues and challenges. These include the development of necessary location- and crop-specific, weather-based indexes, the availability of climate-based risk profiles for specific locations and the need to minimize subsidies. These issues should be resolved through collaborative R&D activities involving the Philippine Crop Insurance Corporation, academic institutions and relevant development agencies (Sombilla and Rosegrant 2018). Other risk-management mechanisms should also be explored, including risk-contingent credit for farmers and disaster risk-financing mechanisms.

8.7 Further development of social safety nets

Even if the policy reforms and investments described here boost agricultural and economic growth in the Philippines, still some of the poor will be reached slowly, if at all, and many of them will remain vulnerable to economic reversals. These groups can be helped through income transfers or safety nets that will alleviate their nutritional needs and socio-economic conditions during short-term shocks. Bowen (2015, 2016) notes that emergency cash transfer programmes provided to communities in a timely, coordinated and transparent manner could be a highly effective response to future climate shocks. The Philippine government has implemented, via various agencies, a wide range of social safety nets, including subsidies, insurance, emergency cash transfer programmes, cash-for-work and other programmes. These should be evaluated, targeted and expanded as needed.

9 SUMMARY AND CONCLUSIONS

The impact of climate change on agriculture is projected to cost the Philippine economy about PHP145 billion per year through 2050. The three adaptation strategies analysed in this study have shown potential to significantly mitigate the high costs of climate change. Their impact is projected to be much higher if the Philippines abandons its rice subsidy policy, which introduces economic incentives that impede structural transformation. Fortunately, the country has reformed its rice policy with the passage of the Rice Tariffication Law in February 2019, which removes said subsidies. Box 1 presents the early gains of the law amid the pandemic and the series of typhoons that affected the country in 2020.

The results of the cost-benefit analyses indicate that investments in increasing rice productivity and expanding irrigation infrastructure have the highest impact in mitigating the impacts of climate change. Estimates of the return on investments in irrigation infrastructure indicate a cost-benefit ratio of 1.38, but only if the government acts quickly. While delaying investment reduces the overall cost of this adaptation strategy, it also reduces its benefits even more (Perez and Rosegrant 2018).

Box 8.1. Early gains of the Rice Tariffication Law: Softening the impacts of typhoons and the COVID-19 pandemic

With the passage of the Rice Tariffication Law (RTL) in February 2019, the Philippines is now slowly reaping the benefits that the law promises, particularly through ensuring low and stable rice prices for consumers amid typhoons and the COVID-19 pandemic. The average retail price of regular-milled rice (RMR) from March 2019 through 2020 was PHP37.19/kg. This is about PHP8.50/kg lower than the highest RMR retail price in September 2018. While the average price in 2020 was only slightly lower by 0.42 per cent than that in 2017 and 2.63 per cent than that in 2019, rice prices have been on a downward trend.

More importantly, the RTL has kept rice prices more stable, thus preventing consumers from sliding deeper into poverty, especially in 2020 when the Philippines, like the rest of the world, was enduring the impact of the pandemic on top of several typhoons that have become more frequent and damaging. The low general price inflation rates resulting from the low and stable rice prices have likewise helped keep food security and malnutrition from getting worse.

Farm gate prices of dry palay have also settled from the average level of PHP20.40/kg in 2018 to PHP16.72/kg in 2020, while rice producers are continually being supported through various programmes and assistance to make them more competitive. Rice production was at 19.3 million mt in 2020, the highest achieved in years, despite the typhoons and the pandemic. The first quarter palay harvest of 4.627 million mt in 2021 was also a record, surpassing the first quarter harvest of 2018 of 4.623 million mt.

As seen in the projections presented in this chapter, the continued implementation of RTL can accelerate these initial gains to spur agricultural growth and facilitate the long-delayed structural transformation of the economy.

Source: NEDA (2021).

An updated National Irrigation Master Plan 2020–2030 (NIMP 2020–2030) has just been completed, with physical targets based on the National Irrigation Administration's Geodatabase that includes estimates of potential irrigable areas at various slope limits, water resources information, soils, slope, and other vital information for irrigation system planning. The NIMP's physical targets and desired results include food security options, food production targets, new irrigated areas, rehabilitation and restoration targets, crop diversification, enhanced farmers' competitiveness and climate resiliency. These national-level targets and desired results guide the local level irrigation development plans and projects.

In the Philippine Nationally Determined Contribution submitted to the United Nations Framework Convention on Climate Change in April 2021, the country has committed to implement a number of climate-smart agricultural technologies and crop management practices to reduce the carbon footprint of the agriculture sector, thus contributing to the goal of reducing the country's GHG emissions by 75 per cent in 2040. These technologies and practices include alternate wetting and drying and use of renewable energy for water management and flood control system; nature-based solutions like the use of biochar and organic fertilizer to enhance soil fertility; greater application of precision agriculture like laser land-levelling technique and other digital-based technologies to improve land-use preparation and management; and optimizing the use of science-based decision tools like Rice Crop Manager to improve soil and pest management, including the greater use of climate information systems.

Additional strategies to further mitigate the impacts of climate change include developing real-time weather information systems to support farmers' decision-making; improving the provision of agricultural extension services through innovative methods, such as information and communication technologies; and supporting a stronger seed industry to facilitate the adoption of new varieties.

In taking steps to achieve food security under climate change, the focus of policy needs to shift from productivity-enhancing measures to efficiency-enhancing ones, guided by *a holistic, rational and comprehensive land-use and physical-planning mechanism to appropriately identify land-use and allocation patterns*. Finally, food security policy needs to be oriented towards facilitating—rather than inhibiting—trade, competition, crop diversification and other reforms to achieve inclusive access to food, while generating long-term productivity and income growth to bring about economic transformation.

APPENDIX

A. Modelling Framework

General circulation models (GCMs) are developed by scientists to determine how the climate might change in response to greenhouse gas (GHG) accumulation in the upper atmosphere. The Intergovernmental Panel on Climate Change (IPCC) has a process by which teams submit models for use in IPCC assessment reports. Assessment Report 4 (AR4) incorporated 24 models, whereas Assessment Report 5 (AR5) included 61 models. The analyses presented in this chapter are based on the following four AR5 models:
1. GFDL-ESM2M, which was developed by the National Oceanographic and Atmosphere Administration's General Fluid Dynamics Laboratory (GFDL) (Dunne et al. 2012, 2013)
2. HadGEM2-ES, the Hadley Centre Global Environmental Model (HadGEM), from the Met Office Hadley Centre (Collins et al. 2011; Martin et al. 2011)
3. IPSL-CM5A-LR, generated by Institut Pierre-Simon Laplace (IPSL) (Dufresne et al. 2013)
4. MIROC-ESM-CHEM (MIROC) from the Japan Agency for Marine-Earth Science and Technology, Atmosphere and Ocean Research Institute (University of Tokyo) and National Institute for Environmental Studies (Sakamoto et al. 2012)

DSSAT, developed by Jones et al. (2003), integrates crop, soil and weather databases into standard formats for use in crop models and other applications. Weather statistics from climate models are incorporated in to estimate crop yields under existing and various future climate scenarios. Similarly, WaNuLCAS (van Noordwijk, Lusiana, and Khasanah 2004) models daily plant growth, accounting for water, nutrients, light and soil properties. These biophysical models are used to estimate the impacts of climate change and crop management and technology on crop yields, the results of which constitute inputs into IMPACT and the Phil-DCGE model under alternative scenarios.

IMPACT was originally developed by IFPRI to project food supply, demand, prices, trade and security to 2020 and beyond (Rosegrant and IMPACT Development Team 2012). It has been expanded to include the impact of water resources and climate change. It analyses 62 crop and livestock commodities in 151 countries and regions of the world that together cover the earth's land surface (except Antarctica). The model also links national production and demand relationships through international trade flows and prices. Results from IMPACT are then fed into the Phil-DCGE model to assess economy-wide impacts of the agriculture sector outcomes.

The Phil-DCGE model was developed for this study to assess the economy-wide impacts of climate change on the agriculture sector and to explore policy alternatives to offset these effects. The model includes 14 agriculture subsectors, 2 mining subsectors, 14 food-industry subsectors, 7 other manufacturing subsectors and 2 service sectors; 5 factors of production (labour, land, agricultural capital, livestock capital and non-agricultural capital); and 30 types of households, subdivided into the three regions (Luzon, Visayas and Mindanao), two locations (urban and rural) and by income quintile.

REFERENCES

AGRIMAG. 2018. "The Philippines Way Behind Other ASEAN Countries in Agricultural Performance". 7 December 2018. https://www.agriculture.com.ph/2018/12/07/philippines-way-behind-other-asean-countries-in-agri-performance/.

Bowen, T. 2015. "Social Protection and Disaster Risk Management in the Philippines: The Case of Typhoon Yolanda (Haiyan)". *Policy Research Working Paper* No. 7482. Washington, DC: World Bank. https://openknowledge.worldbank.org/handle/10986/23448.

———. 2016. "Typhoon Yolanda (Haiyan) and the Case for Building an Emergency Cash Transfer Program in the Philippines (English)". *Philippine Social Protection Note* no. 10. Washington, DC: World Bank Group. http://documents.worldbank.org/curated/en/967551504637043989/Typhoon-Yolanda-Haiyan-and-the-case-for-building-an-emergency-cash-transfer-program-in-the-Philippines

Collins, W., N. Bellouin, M. Doutriaux-Boucher, N. Gedney, P. Halloran, T. Hinton, J. Hughes, et al. 2011. "Development and Evaluation of an Earth–System Model—HadGEM2," *Geoscience Model Development* 4(4): 1051–75.

Dikitanan, R., G. Grosjean, A. Nowak, and J. Leyte. 2017. "Climate-Resilient Agriculture in the Philippines". *CSA Country Profiles for Asia Series*. Manila, Philippines: International Center for Tropical Agriculture (CIAT) and Department of Agriculture-Adaptation and Mitigation Initiative in Agriculture, Government of the Philippines. 24 p.

DOF (Department of Finance). 2014. "Philippine Tariff Finder". www.tariffcommission.gov.ph/ (accessed 7 July 2014).
Dufresne, J.-L., M.-A. Foujols, S. Denvil, A. Caubel, O. Marti, O. Aumont, Y. Balkanski, et al. 2013. "Climate Change Projections Using the IPSL–CM5 Earth System Model: From CMIP3 to CMIP5". *Climate Dynamics* 40, no. 9/10: 2123–65.
Dunne, J., J. John, A. Adcroft, S. Griffies, R. Hallberg, E. Shevliakova, R. Stouffer, et al. 2012. "GFDL's ESM2 Global Coupled Climate–Carbon Earth System Models Part I: Physical Formulation and Baseline Simulation Characteristics," *Journal of Climate* 25 (19): 6646–65.
Dunne, J., J. John, E. Shevliakova, R. Stouffer, J. Krasting, S. Malyshev, P. Milly, et al. 2013. "GFDL's ESM2 Global Coupled Climate–Carbon Earth System Models. Part II: Carbon System Formation and Baseline Simulation Characteristics", *Journal of Climate* 26 (7): 2247–67.
Garcia-Rincon, M. F., and F. Virtucio. 2008. "Climate Change in the Philippines". In *World Bank Country Environmental Analysis (CEA) for the Philippines*. Washington, DC: World Bank.
Jones, J., G. Hoogenboom, C. Porter, K. Boote, W. Batchelor, L. Hunt, P. Wilkens, et al. 2003. "The DSSAT Cropping System Model". *European Journal of Agronomy* 18 (3/4): 235–65.
Martin, G., N. Bellouin, W. Collins, I. Culverwell, P. Halloran, S. Hardiman, T. Hinton, et al. 2011. "The HadGEM2 Family of Met Office Unified Model Climate Configurations". *Geophysical Model Development* 4: 723–57.
NEDA (National Economic Development Authority). 2021. "Early Assessment of the Rice Tariffication Law." (unpublished report)
Perez, N. D., and M. W. Rosegrant. 2018. "A Partial Equilibrium Approach to Modelling Alternative Agricultural Futures under Climate Change". In *The Future of Philippine Agriculture under a Changing Climate: Policies, Investments and Scenarios*, edited by M. W. Rosegrant and M. A. Sombilla. Singapore: ISEAS-Yusof Ishak Institute; CGIAR Research Program on Policies, Institutions, and Markets (PIM); and CGIAR Research Program on Climate Change, Agriculture and Food Security (CCAFS).
Pradesha, A., and S. Robinson. 2018. "A General Equilibrium Approach to Modeling Alternative Agricultural Futures under Climate Change". In *The Future of Philippine Agriculture under a Changing Climate: Policies, Investments and Scenarios*, edited by M. W. Rosegrant and M. A. Sombilla. Singapore: ISEAS-Yusof Ishak Institute; CGIAR Research Program on Policies, Institutions, and Markets (PIM); and CGIAR Research Program on Climate Change, Agriculture and Food Security (CCAFS).
PSA (Philippine Statistics Authority). CountryStat 2017. http://countrystat.psa.gov.ph/.

Ravago, M. L., and A. M. Balisacan. 2018. "Current Structure and Future Challenges of the Agricultural Sector". In *The Future of Philippine Agriculture under a Changing Climate: Policies, Investments and Scenarios*, edited by M. W. Rosegrant and M. A. Sombilla. Singapore: ISEAS-Yusof Ishak Institute; CGIAR Research Program on Policies, Institutions, and Markets (PIM); and CGIAR Research Program on Climate Change, Agriculture and Food Security (CCAFS).

Reyes, C., J. Bancolita, N. L. Leyso, and S. J. Calubayan. 2014. *Impacts of Climate Change on Household Food Security in the Philippines*. Rome: Food and Agriculture Organization.

Rosegrant, M., and IMPACT Development Team. 2012. *International Model for Policy Analysis of Agricultural Commodities and Trade (IMPACT) Model Description*. Washington, DC: International Food Policy Research Institute.

Rosegrant, M., J. Koo, N. Cenacchi, C. Ringler, R. Robertson, M. Fisher, C. Cox, et al. 2014. *Food Security in a World of Natural Resource Scarcity: The Role of Agricultural Technologies*. Washington, DC: International Food Policy Research Institute.

Rosegrant, M. W., N. Perez, A. Pradesha, and T. S. Thomas. 2016. "The Agricultural and Economywide Impacts of Climate Change on Philippine Agriculture". *Project Policy Note* 2. Washington, DC: International Food Policy Research Institute.

Rosegrant, M. W., and M. A. Sombilla, eds. 2018. *The Future of Philippine Agriculture under a Changing Climate: Policies, Investments, and Scenarios*. Singapore: ISEAS-Yusof Ishak Institute; CGIAR Research Program on Policies, Institutions, and Markets (PIM); and CGIAR Research Program on Climate Change, Agriculture and Food Security (CCAFS).

Rosegrant, M. W., N. Perez, A. Pradesha, and T. S. Thomas. 2016. *The Agricultural and Economywide Impacts of Climate Change on Philippine Agriculture*. Project Policy Note 2, International Food Policy Research Institute.

Rosegrant, M., and the IMPACT Development Team. 2012. *International Model for Policy Analysis of Agricultural Commodities and Trade (IMPACT) Model Description*. Washington, DC: International Food Policy Research Institute.

Rosegrant, M., J. Koo, N. Cenacchi, C. Ringler, R. Robertson, M. Fisher, C. Cox, et al. 2014. *Food Security in a World of Natural Resource Scarcity: The Role of Agricultural Technologies*. Washington, DC: International Food Policy Research Institute.

Sakamoto, T., Y. Komuro, T. Nishimura, M. Ishii, H. Tatebe, H. Shiogama, A. Hasegawa, et al. 2012. "MIROC4h: A New High-Resolution Atmosphere–Ocean Coupled General Circulation Model". *Journal of Meteorology Society of Japan* 90 (3): 325–59.

SEPO (Senate of the Philippines). 2010. "Subsidizing National Food Authority: Is It a Good Policy?". *Policy Brief* PB-10-04. Manila: Senate of the Philippines.

Sombilla, M. A., and M. W. Rosegrant. 2018. "Summary and Policy Recommendations". In *The Future of Philippine Agriculture under a Changing Climate: Policies, Investments, and Scenarios*, edited by M. W. Rosegrant and M. A. Sombilla. Singapore: ISEAS-Yusof Ishak Institute; CGIAR Research Program on Policies, Institutions, and Markets (PIM); and CGIAR Research Program on Climate Change, Agriculture and Food Security (CCAFS).

Thomas, T., V. Nazareth, and R. Folledo. 2018. "A Biophysical Approach to Modeling Alternative Agricultural Futures under Climate Change". In *The future of Philippine Agriculture under a Changing Climate: Policies, Investments and Scenarios*, edited by M. W. Rosegrant and M. A. Sombilla. Singapore: ISEAS-Yusof Ishak Institute; CGIAR Research Program on Policies, Institutions, and Markets (PIM); and CGIAR Research Program on Climate Change, Agriculture and Food Security (CCAFS).

Thomas, T. S., A. Pradesha, and N. Perez. 2016. "Agricultural Growth, Climate Resilience and Food Security in the Philippines: Sub-national Impacts of Selected Investment Strategies and Policies". *Project Policy Note* 2. Washington, DC: International Food Policy Research Institute.

Van Noordwijk, M., B. Lusiana, and N. Khasanah. 2004. WaNuLCAS *Version 3.1: Background on a Model of Water Nutrient and Light Capture in Agroforestry Systems*. International Center for Research in Agroforestry (ICRAF). Bogor, Indonesia.

World Bank-World Development Indicators (WB-WDI) database 2018. http://data.worldbank.org/data-catalog/world-development-indicators

PART 3

Economic Policies for Achieving Targeted Levels of Living in the Philippines

9 Low Income Traps and Philippine Poverty Incidence

Raul V. Fabella and Geoffrey M. Ducanes

1 INTRODUCTION

A notable feature of the Philippine economy post-Asian financial crisis and until fairly recently had been the slow response of income poverty to fairly robust economic growth (Balisacan 2011; Balisacan 2010; Balisacan 2009; Ducanes and Balisacan 2019; World Bank 2011; ADB 2009). This contrasts with the experience of China and Vietnam (Balisacan, Pernia, and Estrada 2003), where poverty markedly declined as their economies grew in the decade following the Asian financial crisis, as well as with other countries in the region whose economies grew even earlier, such as Thailand and Malaysia. The income elasticity of headcount poverty was estimated to be only −1.3 in the Philippines, compared with −2.3 for East Asia as a whole (World Bank 2011).[1]

---

[1] A confounding issue is that, during the same period, international remittances to Philippine households have been found to be severely underestimated in the Family Income Expenditures Survey, whose data are used for official poverty computations (Ducanes 2010). However, because remittances go mainly to higher income households, this is likely to impact inequality measures more than poverty measures (Ducanes 2015).

We argue in this paper and show empirically using regional-level data that the reason for the slow response of income poverty to economic growth in the Philippines is the erstwhile pattern of economic growth, which had been dominated by higher-end services. From 2012 to 2015, as the pattern of economic growth began to favour industry, a strong poverty response has been observed.

The transformation of rural employment from a largely informal to a largely formal sector activity as the root cause of modernization and development follows the Ranis-Fei model (Ranis and Fei 1964). The Ranis-Fei model of growth envisions a dual economy with, on one hand, a backward economy serving as a sink for surplus labour and with a low fixed wage level and, on the other, a modern sector with rising productivity and high wages, courtesy of modern technology, large capital complement and scale economies. The transfer of labour from the backward sector to the modern sector underpins economic growth and the rise in income. As the process unfolds, average incomes of households in the backward economy are pulled up and poverty drops. A clear case is Taiwan's development in the 1960s, where rural incomes rose and rural poverty incidence fell with the increasing availability of rural non-farm employment (Anderson and Leiserson 1980).

Another development paradigm apropos the relationship between industrial structure and poverty reduction is development progeria, which applies to low-income countries. Development progeria (Fabella 2013; see also Daway-Ducanes and Fabella 2015) refers to the phenomenon where the share of manufacturing value added in total gross domestic product (GDP) drops while that of the services sector rises over time in low-income countries (<US$10,000 per capita). This industry shares dynamics of lagging manufacturing is normal for high-income mature economies where labour is scarce and capital is abundant, but is pathological for low-income countries. Erstwhile low-income countries that closed the gap between themselves and the rich countries (i.e., joined the club of developed economies) experienced decades of convergent growth, where the share of manufacturing in total GDP grew faster than the share of the services sector. Daway-Ducanes and Fabella (2015), using cross-country panel data, show that the share of manufacturing value added in GDP in low-income countries associates strongly with lower poverty incidence, while the share of the services sector associates strongly with higher poverty incidence.

The cross-country data seem to show that the services sector works in opposite direction to the manufacturing sector in poverty reduction. One question we explore here is whether this conflicting effect on poverty reduction is replicated or not in the case of the Philippines, where labour surplus exists in the rural areas.

The backwardness of the Philippine rural sector comes from extreme fragmentation resulting from progressive parcelization of land through inheritance, but largely from the government's Comprehensive Land Reform Program (CARP), which killed the formal land market and reduced farm sizes to areas so small as to be uneconomical. Adamopoulos and Restuccia (2020) show that CARP reduced average farm size by 34 per cent and agricultural productivity by 17 per cent. It also resulted in the flight of private capital from the rural sector due to mandated restrictions such as the five-hectare ownership ceiling of farmlands and the prohibition on alienation of awarded lands (see, e.g., Fabella 2014). Together, these have led to the demise of the collateral-based formal market for finance in the rural areas. With formal sector capital unavailable, the farm sector is in a permanent credit squeeze, with the only credit flow being the underground market where interest rates are sky high. The farm sector has become a permanent ward of the state. Poverty in the Philippines is concentrated in agriculture.

The more people employed in manufacturing activities, the more rural labour move from informal low-wage activities to formal higher-wage activities. The relationship between manufacturing and poverty reduction while intuitively plausible still needs more parsing. For example, why privilege manufacturing jobs and not services jobs as lynchpin? Why not agricultural jobs? Operationally, we reduce these questions into one query: how do different industrial employments in the formal sector contribute to the reduction of household poverty in the rural sector. Alternatively, the question is: Are jobs opened in different economic sectors equal in their contribution to rural poverty reduction?

We test the following hypotheses:
1. Ranis-Fei dualistic model hypothesis: Household poverty incidence associates negatively and significantly with the share in total employment of all modern/formal sectors (industry, manufacturing, other industry and services) in total employment.

2. The association between household poverty and each of formal sector employment shares has the same sign and magnitude.
3. Ranis-Fei labour surplus hypothesis: Household poverty incidence is unaffected by the share of agriculture in total employment.
4. Manufacturing vs. services sector null hypothesis: There is no difference in the size and direction of the estimated relationship between the respective shares of manufacturing and services in total employment and household poverty.
5. Human capital in services sector hypothesis: The association between the services sector's share in total employment is not robust against the addition of human capital among the regressors, showing that it is the human capital-intensive services jobs (formal-sector services such as bank tellers, teachers, police, nurses requiring college education) that drive household poverty reduction effect.

2   STYLIZED FACTS

The 2000s, which includes the years under study, was a period of economic growth for the Philippines (Table 9.1). From 2001 to 2015, the country's GDP growth averaged 5.1 per cent annually; it did stumble during the height of the global financial crisis, but still managed to grow.[2] The services sector drove much of the growth in the first decade of the new millennium, but from 2010 to 2015 the industry sector surpassed services, even as the latter continued to grow robustly.[3] Manufacturing, in particular, experienced a resurgence, but so did construction, due to a strong demand for residential condominiums (in part from overseas Filipinos) and office spaces from the burgeoning business process outsourcing sector. The agriculture sector had the weakest growth in the period, growing from 2001 to 2015 at an annual average rate of 2.5 per cent only.

---

[2] From 2016 to 2019, the economy grew at an average annual rate of 6.6 per cent. In 2020, due to the economic fallout from the COVID-19 pandemic, the country's GDP growth declined by 9.5 per cent.

[3] From 2016 to 2019, the services sector again outpaced the industry sector, having an annual average growth of 7.5 per cent compared with the latter's 6.8 per cent.

Table 9.1. Sectoral gross value-added growth (2001–15, in %)

Sector	Average annual GVA growth (%)				
	2001–6	2007–9	2010–12	2013–15	2001–15
Agriculture, hunting, forestry and fishing	4.4	2.4	1.7	1.0	2.5
Industry sector	4.7	2.8	6.8	7.8	4.9
Manufacturing	4.6	0.9	7.1	8.1	4.8
Other industry	4.9	7.4	6.3	7.3	5.4
Services sector	6.9	5.0	6.4	6.6	5.9
GDP	5.8	3.9	6.0	6.4	5.1

Source of basic data: Philippine Statistics Authority.

However, even as the economy achieved a more than respectable economic growth from 2001 to 2012, poverty barely budged. A change in the methodology for computing official poverty starting from 2006 somewhat complicates poverty comparisons pre-2006 and post-2006. Using the old methodology, poverty incidence was estimated to have dropped from 2000 to 2003, only to rise again to its 2000 level in 2006. Using the revised methodology, poverty incidence among households was estimated at 21 per cent in 2006, 20.5 per cent in 2009 and 19.7 per cent in 2012, showing very little movement in the period.

Table 9.2 shows estimates of poverty incidence among employed workers only for 2015.[4] Poverty incidence among workers in agriculture (32.8%) is about three times that of industry and more than four times that of services. Workers in agriculture make up 61 per cent of all poor workers, services sector workers 27.1 per cent, and industry sector workers 12.3 per cent. In comparison, agriculture workers make up only 27.3 per cent of all workers, services sector workers 56.1 per cent, and industry workers 16.6 per cent.

---

[4] It should be noted that an individual's classification as poor or non-poor depends on the per capita income of his or her household.

Table 9.2. Poverty incidence among the employed by sector of employment (2015)

Sector	Poverty incidence (%)	Contribution to poverty incidence (%)	Total no. of poor among employed (in thousands)
Agriculture, hunting, forestry & fishing	32.8	60.6	3,614
Industry sector	10.9	12.3	737
Manufacturing	9.6	5.4	319
Other industry	12.2	7.0	417
Services sector	7.1	27.1	1,614
All employed	14.7	100.0	5,964

Source of basic data: Philippine Statistics Authority, merged FIES-LFS 2015.

The three sectors differ in their workers' educational profile: agriculture sector workers have the lowest educational attainment, on average, followed by industry sector workers and then services sector workers (Table 9.3). Almost three-fourths of the agriculture sector workers had at most incomplete high school education and only 6.4 per cent had at least some college education. For the industry sector, while a substantial 41.8 per cent of the workers did not complete high school, more than half completed secondary schooling and 17.3 per cent had at least some college education. For those in the services sector, only a little over a fourth had at most incomplete high school education, 36.6 per cent had at least some college education and 25.2 per cent were college graduates. The services sector covers a wide range of occupations, ranging from workers doing elementary tasks to professionals. Working members of low-income households typically have less education, so this means that agriculture sector jobs are most accessible to them, followed by industry sector jobs; services sector jobs are the least accessible, particularly higher-end ones.

Table 9.4 shows the reported basic pay per day of the workers in the different sectors. The average pay per day is lowest in agriculture at only PHP201. Based on the means, the pay rates in the industry sector (about PHP361) and services sector (about PHP441) are 80 per cent and 120 per cent higher, respectively, than in the agriculture sector.

Table 9.3. Educational attainment of employed workers by sector (2015, in %)

Sector	High school incomplete and below (%)	High school graduate (%)	Post-secondary incomplete (%)	Post-secondary graduate (%)	College incomplete (%)	College graduate (%)	Total (%)
Agriculture, hunting, forestry & fishing	73.0	19.0	0.3	1.3	3.9	2.5	100.0
Industry sector	41.8	36.0	0.9	3.9	8.0	9.3	100.0
Manufacturing	32.2	39.7	1.0	5.4	10.1	11.7	100.0
Other industry	51.2	32.4	0.7	2.6	6.0	7.0	100.0
Services sector	27.5	29.7	0.9	5.1	11.6	25.2	100.0
All employed	42.2	27.9	0.7	3.9	8.9	16.3	100.0

Source of basic data: Philippine Statistics Authority, merged FIES-LFS 2015.

Table 9.4. Average basic pay per day among the employed by sector of employment (2015, in PHP)

Sector	Mean basic pay per day (PHP)	Median basic pay per day (PHP)
Agriculture, hunting, forestry & fishing	201	200
Industry sector	361	330
Manufacturing	359	340
Other industry	363	300
Services sector	441	340
All employed	384	300

Source of basic data: Philippine Statistics Authority, merged FIES-LFS 2015.

Additionally, the spread of basic pay by sector is indicated by the difference between the mean and median values. The large gap between the mean and median values of basic pay per day in services, with the mean being much higher than the median, indicates there are observations with relatively very high values of basic pay per day relative to the rest. The smaller differences between mean and median basic pay per day for agriculture and industry indicate less extreme values.

Taken together, the data provide insights on why the growth in the modern sector, especially industry, has been associated with notable poverty reduction in the period under study. The rapid growth of the modern sector had resulted in increased employment in the sector. Low-income workers were able to avail themselves of these employment opportunities, especially in industry where they could meet the educational requirement and the pay is relatively higher than in agriculture—at least high enough to put them above the poverty line. We show this more formally in the next sections.

3 DATA AND METHODOLOGY

3.1 Data

In our analysis, we use the Philippine Statistics Authority's (PSA) merged Family Income Expenditures Survey and Labor Force Survey (merged FIES-LFS) for years 2009, 2012 and 2015.[5] The FIES is a nationally representative household survey conducted by the PSA every three years, with the household as unit of analysis, to collect information on the income and expenditure patterns of Philippine households. It is the main data used for computations of income or expenditure-based poverty and inequality measures in the country. The LFS is a nationally representative household survey conducted quarterly by the PSA also, with the individual as unit of analysis, to collect information on employment-related information from household members, including industry of employment. It is the primary source of unemployment, underemployment, and labour force participation statistics in the country. It also contains the demographic characteristics of all household members. The FIES uses (more or less) the same sample of households as the LFS conducted in the same period, which is why they can be merged.

Using the various merged FIES-LFS, we construct a four-period panel data at the level of region-area type (area type is either urban or rural) of the variables used in our estimations, namely, poverty incidence and employment in the different sectors as share of the working-age population, as well as additional control variables, specifically the share of those who finished at least high school and those who finished college in the working-age population. In computing poverty incidence by region-area type, we use the regional-level poverty thresholds published by the PSA in its website, which is reproduced in Appendix Table 9A (PSA 2016). The rest of the Appendix tables show the main data used in our estimations. Appendix Table 9B shows poverty incidence by region-area type from 2009 to 2015. Appendix Tables 9C and 9D show the share in the working-age population of those employed in the three major sectors, as well as in manufacturing.

3.2 Methodology

Let

$$P_{it} = \alpha + \lambda_t + \rho_1 Ag\_shr_{it} + \rho_2 In\_shr_{it} + \rho_3 Se\_shr_{it} + A'_i \gamma \\ + C'_i \pi + X'_{it} \beta + \epsilon_{it}, \quad (1)$$

---

[5] More specifically, it is the 2009 FIES merged with the January 2010 LFS, the 2012 FIES merged with the January 2013 LFS, and the 2015 FIES merged with the January 2016 LFS.

where P_{it} denotes the level of poverty in region-area type i at time t; Ag_shr_{it} denotes the share of the working-age population employed in agriculture; In_shr_{it} denotes the share of the working-age population employed in industry; Se_shr_{it} denotes the share of the working-age population employed in services; A_i is a vector of unobserved but time-invariant factors (e.g., geography); C_i a vector of observed time-invariant factors; X_{it} is a vector of observed time-varying factors; λ_t denotes the time period effect; and ϵ_{it} is an idiosyncratic error.

Equation (1) may be simplified to

$$P_{it} = \alpha_i + \lambda_t + \rho_1 Ag\_shr_{it} + \rho_2 In\_shr_{it} + \rho_3 Se\_shr_{it} + X'_{it}\beta + \epsilon_{it}, \quad (2)$$

where $\alpha_i = \alpha + A'_i\gamma + C'_i\pi$. This is a fixed effects model. In practice, the equation is not estimated in this form. Given panel data, the key parameters of interest for us ($\rho_1, \rho_2,$ and ρ_3) can be estimated using the transformation shown below.

The average of (2) for each region-area type is given by

$$\bar{P}_i = \alpha_i + \bar{\lambda} + \rho_1 \overline{Ag\_shr}_i + \rho_2 \overline{In\_shr}_i + \rho_3 \overline{Se\_shr}_i + \bar{X}'_i\beta + \bar{\epsilon}_i. \quad (3)$$

Taking the difference between (2) and (3) yields

$$P_{it} - \bar{P}_i = \lambda_t - \bar{\lambda} + \rho_1 (Ag_{shr_{it}} - \overline{Ag_{shr_i}}) + \rho_2(In_{shr_{it}} - \overline{In_{shr_i}}) \\ + \rho_3(Se_{shr_{it}} - \overline{Se_{shr_i}}) + (X'_{it} - \bar{X}'_i)\beta + (\epsilon_{it} - \bar{\epsilon}_i), \quad (4)$$

which allows the estimation of the parameters $\rho_1, \rho_2,$ and ρ_3 of the key variables of interest Ag_shr, In_shr and Se_shr, respectively, without having to generate individual estimates of the fixed effects.

We use panel fixed effects regression to generate a robust estimate of the relationship between poverty incidence and employment in the different economic sectors (measured as a share in the working-age population). The main advantage of panel fixed effects regression is that it leads to a consistent estimate of the key parameters of interest even if the key variables are correlated with unobserved but time-invariant factors, or correlated with unobserved time-varying variables that affect all region-area types uniformly (Angrist and Pischke 2009; Wooldridge 2002). Without panel data, and short of a randomized experiment, it is extremely difficult to control for these confounding factors.[6]

---

[6] The weakness of panel fixed effects regression is that it is not able to control for unobserved and time-varying factors.

4 RESULTS

Table 9.5 shows the estimation results. Six estimation models are presented. Model 1 relates poverty incidence only to employment in the three major economic sectors. Model 2 is similar to the first but breaks down the industry sector into two parts, manufacturing and other industry, where the latter encompasses construction, mining and utilities. Because we employ panel fixed effects regression, Models 1 and 2 are in effect controlling only for factors that are time-invariant (for the period of the study) that may be operating at the region-area type level, which would include geography, culture, etc. Model 3 is similar to Model 1 and Model 4 is similar to Model 2, but with year dummy variables included. This means that apart from time-invariant factors, Models 3 and 4 are also controlling for unobserved time-varying variables that uniformly affect all region-area types. Models 5 and 6 are similar to Models 3 and 4, respectively, but with the addition of two time-varying human capital variables as control variables, namely, share of the working-age population who are at least high school graduate and share of the working-age population who are at least college graduate.

All the models are statistically significant with the *within* coefficient of variation (R-squared) ranging from 37 to 47 per cent. The different models consistently show a strong negative association between poverty incidence and employment in the modern sector (industry, manufacturing, other industry, services). In Models 1, 3 and 5, a 1 percentage point increase in the share of the working-age population employed in the industry sector is associated with a decline in poverty incidence by 1.8–2.1 percentage points. Models 2, 4 and 6 show that a 1 percentage point increase in the share of the working-age population employed in the manufacturing sector is associated with a decline in poverty incidence by 1.2–1.3 percentage points, and that a 1 percentage point increase in the share of the working-age population employed in other industry is associated with a decline in poverty incidence by 2.1–2.4 percentage points.

Models 1 to 4 show a negative association between the share of the working-age population in the services sector and poverty incidence, but at about only a third of the magnitude for industry. The relationship between services employment and poverty incidence becomes statistically insignificant in Models 5 and 6, when human capital variables are introduced.

Table 9.5. *Fixed effects model: Household poverty incidence as a function of employment in different economic sectors (region-urban/rural level data, 2009–15)*

Explanatory variable	Model 1	Model 2	Model 3	Model 4	Model 5	Model 6
Sector employment						
Agriculture workers as a share of working-age population (%)	-0.090 (0.303)	-0.100 (0.292)	-0.070 (0.285)	-0.060 (0.274)	-0.030 (0.282)	-0.030 (0.279)
Industry workers as a share of working-age population (%)	-2.070*** (0.627)		-1.770** (0.687)		-1.760** (0.664)	
Manufacturing workers as a share of working-age population (%)		-1.320* (0.697)		-1.270* (0.681)		-1.210+ (0.732)
Other industry workers as a share of working-age population (%)		-2.420*** (0.696)		-2.120** (0.841)		-2.130*** (0.791)
Service workers as a share of working-age population (%)	-0.600** (0.295)	-0.560* (0.289)	-0.560* (0.299)	-0.540* (0.289)	-0.130 (0.462)	-0.090 (0.461)
Human capital						
High school graduates and up share in working age population (%)					0.040 (0.297)	0.000 (0.313)
College graduates and up share in working age population (%)					-1.020 (0.812)	-1.010 (0.814)

Table 9.5 *(continued)*

Table 9.5 (continued)

Explanatory variable	Model 1	Model 2	Model 3	Model 4	Model 5	Model 6
Time period effect						
Year 2012 dummy			1.440	1.600*	1.340	1.560
			(0.932)	(0.936)	(1.110)	(1.150)
Year 2015 dummy			−0.710	−0.260	−0.180	0.360
			(1.330)	(1.470)	(1.590)	(1.810)
Constant	59.700***	57.200***	55.400***	53.700***	51.900**	51.600**
	(18.500)	(17.600)	(18.100)	(17.100)	(25.100)	(25.100)
No. of observations	99	99	99	99	99	99
No. of groups	33	33	33	33	33	33
F-stat	7.140***	5.610***	19.280***	16.420***	18.070***	19.920***
R^2 within	0.367	0.379	0.415	0.421	0.457	0.465
R^2 between	0.605	0.626	0.615	0.637	0.698	0.699
R^2 overall	0.584	0.602	0.597	0.615	0.676	0.677

Note: (1) Data used were derived from the merged LFS-FIES surveys for 2009–10, 2012–13 and 2015–16.
(2) The unit of analysis was the region subdivided into urban and rural areas, so the panel data was composed of 33 cross-section units (17 rural areas and 16 urban areas, since Metro Manila has no rural area) and three time periods.
(3) Official regional poverty lines were used in computing household poverty incidence.
(4) *** significant at 1% level; ** 5% level; * 10% level; + 11% level.
(5) Figures in parentheses are standard errors.

In particular, the effect of services employment appears to be taken up by the human capital variable *college graduates and up share in the working-age population*, which has a relatively large (–1) though statistically insignificant coefficient in Models 5 and 6.[7] This suggests that it is high-end services employment, which require college education, that is associated with some poverty reduction.

All the models consistently show a lack of relationship between agricultural employment and poverty incidence, with coefficients very close to zero, suggesting that Philippine agriculture is the low productivity sink of surplus labour. In the time period studied, poverty reduction ensued when workers moved into the relatively more productive services and industry sectors, but especially the latter.

5 SUMMARY AND CONCLUSION

To summarize our results:
- Hypothesis 1: There is no reason to believe that the association between household poverty and the share of modern sector employment, whether industry, manufacturing, other industry or services, in total employment is false.
- Hypothesis 2: There is no reason to believe that different non-farm industry employment shares have the same effect on household poverty.
- Hypothesis 3: There is no reason to believe that the share of agriculture in total employment affects household poverty incidence.
- Hypothesis 4: The direction of the association with household poverty does not differ between manufacturing share and services share but the size of the coefficient of manufacturing is more than twice the coefficient of services.
- Hypothesis 5: The positive association between services employment share and household poverty vanishes with the addition of human capital among the regressors, while that of manufacturing share persists.

---

[7] The variable *college graduates share in the working-age population* is statistically significant when regressed against poverty incidence by itself using the fixed effects model.

At the start of the administration of President Rodrigo Duterte, the revival of manufacturing—especially manufacturing in the regions (meaning outside Metro Manila and nearby regions)—was a prominent part of the strategy to reduce poverty. The Department of Trade and Industry spearheaded the Manufacturing Resurgence Program intended to "rebuild the existing capacity of industries, strengthen new ones and maintain the competitiveness of industries with comparative advantage". Some of the steps identified were to "build up agriculture-based manufacturing that generates employment" and to integrate farm production with the value chain of large commercial enterprises "for marketing and financing purposes". Though the general vision still needs fleshing out, these initiatives, if successfully implemented, will increasingly transform the rural sector from largely informal and low-productivity activities to high-wage and high-productivity formal sector activities, transforming rural labour employment into increasingly formal and high-wage employment. The economic fallout from the COVID-19 pandemic has put a damper on the programme, however.

Such emphasis on manufacturing job creation, rather than job creation in services or agriculture, for household poverty reduction is supported by evidence, as our results demonstrate. The strategy to target farm produce-based processing manufacturing and to hitch farms to the value chain of large commercial corporations is correct. The latter is especially promising, and large commercial companies are keenly interested but they are unable to get the stable volumes and stable quality of produce they require—features that imports from China and elsewhere deliver. Farm produce manufacturing enterprises require sizeable capital investment, which small farmers cannot finance. Large farms, especially associated those with large private businesses, can deliver such stable volumes with consistent quality.

The dearth of formal private capital in farm production is a fundamental problem that must be solved for rural manufacturing to happen. State capital does not have the smarts nor the motivation to substitute for private capital. Private capital flight from farm production must be reversed. The reasons for the private capital flight are well known (see, e.g., Fabella 2014): private capital cannot own more than five hectares of farm land and consolidation to attain scale economies through long-term rent is politically risky. Currently, there is a bill in Congress purporting to raise the farm-ownership limit for households and for corporations—this deserves support. Larger farms and tradable property rights will restore the formal market for land assets and allow farmers to reconnect with private formal financial institutions. Beyond that, the government itself must get actively involved in farmland consolidation, perhaps through separate enactments to reduce the risk associated with the land reform law and attract large private capital to the farm sector. Large private capital is not interested in owning farmlands; rather, it is interested in cultivating commercial-sized farms accessed through long-term contracts with a single-entity, government or otherwise, as counterparty. The return of private capital to the farm sector will not only create more employment in the agriculture sector, more importantly it will make farms more productive, reduce surplus labour and raise wages from farm employment.

On the macroeconomic front, since farm products are tradable, a strong domestic currency makes competition by imports a very important hurdle for farm production. Illicit importation could become a permanent scourge to the farm sector. Having a weaker peso to discourage illicit importation would provide a reprieve for farm products and will certainly make farm production more attractive to investors.

APPENDIX

Table 9A.   Regional poverty thresholds used in the analysis

Region	Annual per capita poverty threshold		
	2009	2012	2015
NCR	19,227	20,344	25,007
CAR	17,243	19,483	21,770
Region I	17,595	18,373	20,488
Region II	17,330	19,125	21,860
Region III	18,188	20,071	23,200
Region IV-A	17,033	19,137	22,121
Region IV-B	15,613	17,292	20,224
Region V	16,888	18,257	21,476
Region VI	15,971	18,029	21,070

Table 9A *(continued)*

Table 9A *(continued)*

Region	Annual per capita poverty threshold		
	2009	2012	2015
Region VIII	16,278	18,076	21,304
Region IX	16,260	18,054	20,925
Region X	16,878	19,335	22,345
Region XI	17,120	19,967	22,754
Region XII	16,405	18,737	21,025
Caraga	18,309	19,629	22,570
ARMM	16,683	20,517	21,563

Note: NCR – National Capital Region
CAR – Cordillera Administrative Region
Region I – Ilocos
Region II – Cagayan Valley
Region III – Central Luzon
Region IV-A – Cavite, Laguna, Batangas, Rizal and Quezon (CALABARZON)
Region IV-B – Mindoro, Marinduque, Romblon and Palawan (MIMAROPA)
Region V – Bicol
Region VI – Western Visayas
Region VII – Central Visayas
Region VIII – Eastern Visayas
Region IX – Zamboanga Peninsula
Region X – Northern Mindanao
Region XI – Davao
Region XII – S. Cotabato, Cotabato, Sultan Kudarat, Sarangani and Gen. Santos (Soccsksargen)
Caraga – Caraga Administrative Region
ARMM – Autonomous Region in Muslim Mindanao
Source: Philippine Statistics Authority.

Table 9B.   Poverty incidence by region-area type (2009–15, in %)

Region	Poverty Incidence (%)		
	2009	2012	2015
URBAN			
NCR	2.6	2.6	2.7
CAR	2.7	3.1	2.9
Region I	12.4	8.8	5.4
Region II	6.3	16.0	4.6
Region III	8.4	6.2	3.7
Region IV-A	5.4	3.1	3.8

Table 9B *(continued)*

Table 9B *(continued)*

Region	Poverty Incidence (%)		
	2009	2012	2015
Region V	20.2	17.8	11.1
Region VI	9.9	21.4	18.3
Region VII	14.1	11.4	14.3
Region VIII	20.6	19.0	16.5
Region IX	14.3	11.5	6.5
Region X	17.7	18.1	14.9
Region XI	11.9	13.5	7.6
Region XII	15.2	26.3	17.1
Caraga	24.3	38.1	34.7
ARMM	29.5	21.1	20.5
RURAL			
CAR	26.0	23.3	19.0
Region I	20.3	15.0	9.8
Region II	17.5	17.1	12.2
Region III	17.4	14.7	13.5
Region IV-A	19.7	14.8	11.2
Region IV-B	30.9	26.4	19.5
Region V	42.7	34.1	29.3
Region VI	29.9	22.9	15.9
Region VII	44.8	35.2	29.8
Region VIII	36.4	40.1	31.7
Region IX	44.0	46.0	35.8
Region X	43.3	42.2	40.1
Region XI	35.0	42.0	32.6
Region XII	34.9	47.1	40.9
Caraga	40.8	53.9	53.8
ARMM	44.8	36.3	34.6

Source: Authors' computations based on PSA data.

Table 9C. Share of working-age population employed in agriculture and services

Region	Share of working-age population employed in agriculture (%)			Share of working-age population employed in services (%)		
	2009	2012	2015	2009	2012	2015
URBAN						
NCR	0.3	0.3	0.3	45.2	46.2	48.0
CAR	8.6	8.4	7.8	35.8	37.0	36.5
Region I	9.7	7.9	5.1	34.2	37.3	40.9
Region II	20.5	10.2	6.7	34.8	38.7	48.3
Region III	5.7	3.2	2.3	35.8	38.1	42.5
Region IV-A	3.0	2.0	1.8	36.6	39.3	39.6
Region IV-B	24.4	18.5	14.2	31.0	35.8	42.6
Region V	7.8	6.3	5.8	42.2	45.2	38.0
Region VI	7.5	17.5	14.7	45.8	37.7	37.7
Region VII	4.5	3.9	5.6	39.2	41.5	40.1
Region VIII	11.3	5.1	6.7	39.5	46.6	41.7
Region IX	9.9	11.0	8.3	41.6	37.5	39.5
Region X	10.8	9.2	7.8	40.1	40.6	41.8
Region XI	10.9	12.9	11.0	37.3	36.7	39.9
Region XII	14.8	16.0	10.8	37.8	37.1	39.8
Caraga	19.3	11.2	5.1	24.8	32.3	31.7
ARMM	13.8	7.8	9.3	35.1	35.2	38.9
RURAL						
CAR	50.5	37.0	34.8	15.3	21.3	24.6
Region I	26.5	20.2	18.6	24.2	29.8	30.6
Region II	43.9	37.9	35.5	18.8	21.2	23.2
Region III	22.3	19.5	15.5	28.0	29.5	32.5
Region IV-A	23.7	15.2	13.5	27.8	31.3	33.5
Region IV-B	36.7	34.7	31.1	24.1	24.2	23.3

Table 9C *(continued)*

Table 9C *(continued)*

Region	Share of working-age population employed in agriculture (%)			Share of working-age population employed in services (%)		
	2009	2012	2015	2009	2012	2015
Region V	32.9	24.7	22.5	22.7	26.1	28.0
Region VI	33.2	24.5	24.2	24.1	29.3	28.9
Region VII	32.1	25.5	23.1	22.2	25.6	28.7
Region VIII	31.9	27.4	22.2	24.5	26.9	27.6
Region IX	39.1	41.2	32.7	22.0	20.2	23.7
Region X	41.2	35.5	29.4	24.2	25.7	25.3
Region XI	33.6	39.3	33.4	22.7	18.1	21.8
Region XII	40.4	44.0	38.5	20.2	17.4	19.4
Caraga	46.0	41.8	37.1	12.0	11.8	12.6
ARMM	28.6	26.7	23.5	23.1	26.0	24.5

Source: Authors' computations based on PSA data.

Table 9D.   Share of working-age population employed in industry and manufacturing

Region	Share of working-age population employed in industry (%)			Share of working-age population employed in manufacturing (%)		
	2009	2012	2015	2009	2012	2015
URBAN						
NCR	10.5	11.3	11.0	6.2	6.4	5.8
CAR	10.4	11.5	11.1	2.5	2.1	2.2
Region I	8.6	8.9	9.7	3.7	2.6	4.5
Region II	5.5	6.0	6.7	2.7	3.7	1.9
Region III	12.3	13.3	13.1	7.5	8.0	7.7
Region IV-A	15.1	15.6	17.1	10.6	11.1	11.3
Region IV-B	7.4	9.3	7.4	3.0	4.0	3.1
Region V	7.6	8.4	12.3	2.8	3.2	5.1

Table 9D *(continued)*

Table 9D *(continued)*

Region	Share of working-age population employed in industry (%)			Share of working-age population employed in manufacturing (%)		
	2009	2012	2015	2009	2012	2015
Region VI	6.8	6.4	7.2	3.0	2.9	2.9
Region VII	12.7	13.0	12.4	8.4	8.8	7.6
Region VIII	7.1	6.4	8.1	3.8	3.1	1.8
Region IX	8.8	10.2	9.8	4.0	4.3	4.7
Region X	9.5	10.6	9.1	4.3	4.8	3.9
Region XI	10.0	9.4	9.3	5.6	4.0	4.3
Region XII	8.6	7.1	9.7	5.1	4.2	5.3
Caraga	1.4	3.4	4.0	0.7	1.1	0.6
ARMM	8.8	11.3	11.3	4.9	5.9	4.9
RURAL						
CAR	5.1	7.3	7.4	1.0	0.8	1.2
Region I	7.5	7.8	8.7	3.6	3.4	2.7
Region II	4.0	4.4	5.3	1.7	1.7	1.4
Region III	8.7	9.2	10.6	4.7	4.5	5.2
Region IV-A	11.8	13.6	15.4	7.8	8.5	9.8
Region IV-B	6.5	6.4	8.1	3.3	3.4	2.9
Region V	7.4	8.3	8.9	3.8	3.9	3.0
Region VI	6.2	6.8	8.1	3.2	3.4	2.9
Region VII	9.1	10.1	11.6	4.5	5.1	5.5
Region VIII	5.0	6.5	7.9	2.9	3.4	3.2
Region IX	5.8	4.7	6.1	2.8	2.1	2.8
Region X	5.4	5.8	7.5	2.3	2.3	2.7
Region XI	6.7	5.2	6.4	2.8	2.5	1.7
Region XII	5.2	3.7	4.1	2.9	2.1	2.6
Caraga	1.1	1.7	1.7	0.6	1.0	0.9
ARMM	9.1	8.7	10.4	3.7	2.2	3.3

Source: Authors' computations based on PSA data

REFERENCES

Adamopoulos, Tasso, and Diego Restuccia. 2020. "Land Reform and Productivity: A Quantitative Analysis with Micro-Data". *American Economic Journal: Macroeconomics* 12, no. 3: 1–39.

Anderson, Dennis, and Mark Leiserson. 1980. "Rural Nonfarm Employment in Developing Countries". *Economic Development and Cultural Change* 28: 227–48.

Angrist Joshua, and Jurn Steffen Pischke. 2009. *Mostly Harmless Econometrics: An Empiricist's Companion*. New Jersey: Princeton University Press. First edition.

ADB (Asian Development Bank). 2009. *Poverty in the Philippines: Causes, Constraints, and Opportunities*. Manila: Asian Development Bank. https:// www.adb.org/publications/poverty-philippines-causes-constraints-and-opportunities.

Balisacan, Arsenio. 2009. "Poverty Reduction: Trends, Determinants, and Policies". In *Diagnosing the Philippine Economy: Toward Inclusive Growth*, edited by D. Canlas, M. E. Khan and J. Zhuang. London: Anthem Press and Manila: Asian Development Bank.

———. 2010. "MDGs in the Philippines: Setting the Poverty Scores Right and Achieving the Targets". *Philippine Review of Economics* 47, no. 2: 1–20.

———. 2011. "What Has Really Happened to Poverty in the Philippines? New Measures, Evidence, and Policy Implications". *UPSE Discussion Paper 2011–14*. Quezon City: School of Economics, University of the Philippines.

Balisacan, Arsenio, Ernesto Pernia, and Gemma Estrada. 2003. "Economic Growth and Poverty Reduction in Vietnam". In *Poverty, Growth, and Institution in Developing Asia*, edited by E. Pernia and A. Deolalikar. London: Palgrave Macmillan.

Daway-Ducanes, Sarah Lynne, and Raul Fabella. 2015. "Development Progeria: The Role of Institutions and the Exchange Rate". *Philippine Review of Economics* 52, no. 2: 84–99.

Ducanes, Geoffrey. 2010. "The Case of the Missing Remittances in the FIES: Could It Be Causing Us to Mismeasure Welfare Changes?". *UPSE Discussion Paper 2010–04*. Quezon City: School of Economics, University of the Philippines.

———. 2015. "The Welfare Impact of Overseas Migration on Philippine Households: Analysis Using Panel Data". *Asian and Pacific Migration Journal* 24, no. 1: 79–106.

Ducanes, Geoffrey, and Arsenio Balisacan. 2019. "Reducing Inequality in the Philippines". In *Getting Even: Public Policies to Tackle Inequality in Asia*, edited by Mustafa Talpur. New Delhi, India: Bloomsbury.

Fabella, Raul. 2013. "Development Progeria: Malady and Remedy". *Transactions of the National Academy of Science and Technology (Philippines)* 35. 191–92.

———. 2014. "Comprehensive Agrarian Reform Program (CARP): Time to Let Go". *Philippine Review of Economics* 51, no. 1: 1–18.

PSA (Philippine Statistics Authority). 2016. "Poverty Incidence among Filipinos Registered at 21.6% in 2015 – PSA". *2015 Full Year Poverty Statistics.* https://psa.gov.ph/content/poverty-incidence-among-filipinos-registered-216-2015-psa

Ranis Gustav, and John C. H. Fei. 1964. *The Development of Labor Surplus Economy: Theory and Policy.* Homewood, III: R.D. Irwin.

Wooldridge, Jeffrey. 2002. *Econometric Analysis of Cross Section and Panel Data.* Cambridge: MIT Press.

World Bank. 2011. *Philippines: Fostering More Inclusive Growth.* Washington, DC: World Bank. http://hdl.handle.net/10986/27384.

10 The Philippines in Global Manufacturing Value Chains: A Tale of Arrested Growth

Prema-chandra Athukorala

1 INTRODUCTION

Cross-border dispersion of the different stages/slices of production processes within vertically integrated global industries has been a key structural feature of economic globalization in recent decades. This international division of labour, which we label "global production sharing" in this chapter, opens opportunities for countries to specialize in different slices (tasks) of a production process within a global manufacturing value chain (GMVC). Trade based on global production sharing—that is, trade of parts and components and final assembly within GMVC[1]—has primarily driven the dramatic shift in the

---

[1] The term "global manufacturing value chain" (GMVC), rather than the widely used term "global value chain" (GVC), is used in this chapter to reflect its specific focus on *global production sharing in manufacturing*. The term GVC was popularized by economic sociologists working on the "structure of governance" (interaction among different actors) involved in the value chain of *both* primary products and manufactured goods. It is important to distinguish GMVC from the broader concept of GVC because, unlike in the case of primary commodity trade, a specific focus on trade and investment policy regimes of individual countries and developments in the ongoing process of global production sharing is needed to broaden understanding of the industrialization process in this era of global economic integration.

geographical profile of world manufacturing exports from developed to developing countries. High-performing developing countries in East and Southeast Asia have been the main beneficiaries of this structural shift in world trade. In the early 1970s, the Philippines had a promising start in export-oriented industrialization by engaging in GMVCs. But subsequently, its growth trajectory has not lived up to the initial expectations.

This chapter aims to document and analyse the Philippines' engagement in GMVCs from a comparative Southeast Asian perspective. This has been motivated by two related objectives: (a) to inform the policy debate in the Philippines on the feasibility and desirability of export-oriented industrialization by joining GMVCs and (b) to contribute to the wider literature on GMVC participation as a vehicle for global economic integration of developing countries and the related policy issues. The importance of this phenomenon in designing national industrialization strategies is now widely acknowledged in both academic and policy circles. However, there is a dearth of time-profile studies of individual countries, which are needed to broaden our understanding of how government policies and the overall investment climate condition a country's potential for export-oriented industrialization by joining GMVCs. The Philippines provides a valuable laboratory for a case study of this subject, given the country's engagement in global production sharing since the early years of the GMVCs' arrival in the region and its mixed achievements in the ensuing years compared with other Asian countries.

The next section presents a brief typology of GMVCs to provide the analytical context for the ensuing analytical narrative. This is followed by an overview of the Philippines' engagement in global production sharing, focusing on the interplay of the unfolding development of global production sharing and the country's political and policy setting. The next two sections examine trends and patterns of Philippine exports within GMVCs ("GMVC trade") and the implications of global production sharing on the growth and structural changes in domestic manufacturing. We then briefly discuss policy options for effective participation in GMVCs. The concluding section summarizes the key findings and draws some policy inferences.

2   TYPOLOGY OF GLOBAL MANUFACTURING VALUE CHAINS

In terms of the organizational structure of production sharing, GMVCs take two major forms: buyer-driven production networks and producer-driven production networks (Gereffi 1994, 1999; Khan, Mann, and Peterson 2021). This distinction is important to understand the policy options for effective participation in GMVCs and to assess the resulting implications for the economic development process.

Buyer-driven GMVCs are common in diffused technology-based consumer goods industries, such as clothing, footwear, travel goods, toys and sport goods. The "lead firms" in such production networks are the international buyers: large retailers (e.g., Walmart, Marks & Spencer and H&M) and brand manufacturers (e.g., Victoria's Secret, Gap, Zara and Nike). Production sharing within takes place predominantly through arm's length relationships, with global sourcing companies (value-chain intermediaries) playing a key role in linking producers and lead firms. Therefore, there is room for local firms to directly engage in export through links established with foreign buyers, without direct involvement of foreign direct investment (FDI). If foreign investors are involved, usually it is through joint ventures with local entrepreneurs (not by forming fully owned subsidiaries). Input procurement is monitored by the lead firm, but there is room to use domestic inputs that meet the quality standards. As the East Asian experience indicates, joining buyer-driven production networks is a promising start for export-oriented industrialization.

Producer-centred production networks are common in vertically integrated global industries such as electronics, electrical goods, automobiles, and scientific and medical devices. In these networks, the "lead firms" are multinational enterprises (MNEs), such as Intel, Motorola, Apple, Toyota and Samsung. Global production sharing takes place predominantly through the lead firms' global branch networks and/or their close operational links with established contract manufacturers (e.g., Foxconn, Flextronics) that undertake assembly for these global corporations.

In these high-tech industries, production technology is specific to the lead firm and is closely protected to limit imitations. Also, the production of final goods requires highly customized and specialized parts and components, whose quality cannot be verified or assured by a third party. Therefore, the bulk of global production sharing takes place through intra-firm linkages rather than in an arm's-length manner.

This is particularly the case when it comes to setting up production units in countries that are newcomers to global production networks. As the production unit becomes well established in the country and forges business links with private- and public-sector agents, arm's-length subcontracting arrangements for components procurement could develop, but this greatly depends on the domestic business climate.

Export-oriented industrialization in the high-performing East Asian economies (South Korea and Taiwan) began with engagement in buyer-driven production networks. From about the early 1960s, international buyers, first from Japan and then from the other mature industrialized countries, had played a pivotal role in the expansion of labour-intensive standard consumer goods (garments, toys and sport goods) from these countries. Until about the late 1970s, activities in producer-driven production networks in these countries were basically limited to subcontracting arrangements between Japanese electronic and electrical goods-producing companies and fledgling local firms (Hone 1974; Feenstra and Hamilton 2006; Hobday 1998). By contrast, export-led industrialization in Southeast Asia began with engagements in producer-driven GMVCs (Athukorala and Kohpaiboon 2014). Buyer-driven production networks began to spread in some low-wage Southeast Asian countries from the East Asian countries starting around the late 1970s only (Wells 1983; Gereffi 1999). This was propelled by the rapid increase in wages in the East Asian countries combined with the tightening by developed countries of quotas imposed on apparel imports from these countries under the Multi Fibre Arrangement (MFA).

3 THE PHILIPPINES IN GMVCs: A BRIEF HISTORY

Singapore's embrace of the "MNE-led development strategy" (à la Hobday 2013) after the country separated from the Malaysian Federation in 1965 set the stage for the Southeast Asian economies' participation in global production networks. The process started in 1968 when two US companies—National Semiconductors and Texas Instruments—set up factories in Singapore to assemble semiconductor devices. By the early 1970s, Singapore had become the main offshore assembly base for semiconductor manufacturers in the United States and Europe. The next five years witnessed a notable change in the composition of Singapore's electronics industry, with computer peripherals (especially hard disc drives) becoming relatively more important than semiconductor assembly. By the late 1980s, Singapore accounted for almost half of the world production of hard disc drives (Athukorala and Kohpaiboon 2014; McKendrick et al. 2000).

As early as 1972, some MNEs with production facilities in Singapore began to relocate some low-end assembly activities to neighbouring countries, in response to Singapore's rapidly rising wages and rental costs. The emergence of a Singapore-centred regional production network was aided by the embrace of the MNE-led development strategy by other Southeast Asia countries following the Singaporean experience. Subsequently, many new MNEs also set up production bases in these countries, bypassing Singapore.

The Philippines had promising preconditions for benefiting from the regional spread of production networks. The strong presence of US MNEs—part of the country's colonial inheritance—was a significant force in the Philippine economy, with manufacturing as the major recipient (Lindsay and Valencia 1982; Golay 1966). In spite of a restrictive approach to FDI during the first two decades of the Philippines' post-independence era, the colonial ties of MNEs continued to remain much stronger in the country compared with the other Southeast Asian countries. Under the Laurel-Langley Agreement of 1955, US investors enjoyed the unique privilege of investing in the Philippines on equal terms with Filipino citizens (Suhrke 1975). Moreover, the country had the following advantages: a favourable geographical location, a large relatively better educated labour pool with widespread English language proficiency, and a relatively strong education system with potentials for generating technical manpower[2] (Abrenica and Tecson 2003: Phan and Coxhead 2015).

In the early 1970s, towards the end of the second term of the Marcos regime (labelled the "new society" regime), there were some prospects for transitioning to an export-oriented industrialization (Bautista 1988; Shepherd and Alburo 1991). The policy regime had become relatively more favourable to FDI. Professional economists, the so-called "technocrats", occupied key economic portfolios in the president's cabinet, giving the business community a sense of "right" policy directions in the country. Setting up of export processing zones (EPZs) with attractive government incentives was the main agenda

---

[2] Until the 1990s, the Philippines was the regional leader in tertiary education (Phan and Coxhead 2015).

of the Board of Investment, which was formed in 1971 (Warr 1989). The Bataan EPZ, established in 1969, started operating in 1973. With the imposition of Martial Law in September 1972, the government was able to achieve some political tranquillity by reducing violent urban crime and supressing the communist insurgency in most areas, and by silencing nationalist critics of foreign aid and investment. Therefore, the international investment community initially responded favourably to the Martial Law regime.

The first wave of semiconductors assembly in the Philippines began with the arrival of Intel Corporation in 1974. It set up its second offshore assembly and testing factory in Makati City (later moved to a larger factory in the Cavite EPZ), after two years of successful operation in Penang, Malaysia. Intel's arrival was a symbolic vote of confidence, paving the way for some other electronic companies to come to the Philippines: Motorola (1979), Texas Instruments (1979), Temic Telefunken (1974) and Philips Semiconductors (1981), to name some. Following the arrival of lead electronics firms, a network of ancillary industries began to emerge to meet their requirements: stamped metal components, automation equipment, gigs and fixtures, machine tools and moulded rubber products. In the beginning, these supporting industries were dominated by small and medium-sized enterprises from Japan, Singapore and Taiwan. Subsequently, local subcontracting firms began to spring up. On 2 November 1979, *The Philippine Daily Express* carried an article headlined "Electronics Fervor Hits Philippines Zones".[3]

The "electronic fervour" did not last long, however. From the early 1980s through the early 1990s, the domestic investment climate became inhospitable to FDI. Preferential treatment accorded to US investors ended with the termination of the Laurel-Langley Agreement on 4 July 1974, and divestment of US equity and landholdings led to some legal disputes and alleged political interference in Supreme Court rulings (Lindsay and Valencia 1982). Under the Martial Law regime, there was unprecedented concentration of power around the president, with rampant allegations of "cronyism" (Hill 1982). Trade protection increased markedly across industries, often penalizing labour-intensive activities in which the country was expected to have comparative advantage (Bautista 1988). Following the end of Martial Law in 1981, the Philippines became mired in political uncertainty: student demonstrations and violent urban guerrilla activities

---

[3] As cited in Grunwald and Flamm (1985, 77).

increased. With the deteriorating overall business climate in the country, the growth spurt created by the entry of electronics MNEs remained arrested within the EPZs, which were cushioned against the distorted overall business environment by EPZ-specific liberal trade regime and attractive incentives. Thus, the EPZs, which were initially conceived as an integral part of economic liberalization reforms, became "enclaves" within the economy (Kleibert 2018; Bautista, Power, and Associates 1979; Warr 1989).

The People's Power movement that toppled the Marcos regime in February 1986 ushered in an unstable era of democratic governance. Political uncertainly extended well into the Aquino administration (1986–92), which faced considerable internal dissension and repeated coup attempts, as well as charges of corruption and human rights abuses. The well-publicized kidnapping of Japanese executives in December 1989 shattered the investment climate.

Overall, the 1980s was a lost decade of foreign direct investment and engagement in global production networks for the Philippines. The Philippines missed the opportunity to benefit from three important developments in the regional GMVCs during this period. First, there was the first wave of hard disc drive (HDD) investment in the region. Starting in the late 1980s, most major players in the HDD industry (e.g., Seagate, Maxtor, Hitachi Metals, Control Data, Applied Magnetic and Conner Peripherals) first came to Singapore and then spread their operations to Malaysia and Thailand (McKendrick et al. 2000). Second, after the Plaza Accord in 1985 there was a new wave of investment by Japanese MNEs in the manufacturing sector in Southeast Asian countries in response to the appreciation of the yen (Batalla 2011). Third, with the targeting of import quota restrictions by the major importing countries under the MFA, apparel exporting firms in Taiwan, Hong Kong and South Korea started shifting production bases to other low-wage countries in the region. Foreign investors and international buyers involved in these three waves of production relocation bypassed the Philippines (Wells 1994).

The business environment in the Philippines improved significantly during the Ramos administration (1992–98). Political stability was restored after successful negotiations with military rebels and Muslim separatist movements. The trade and foreign investment regimes were significantly liberalized. EPZ operations were streamlined by passing a new Foreign Investment Act in 1991. With industrial peace prevailing in the country on the whole, employment and working conditions became much more conducive and firms continued to enjoy free-trade status within EPZs (Hill 2003; Remedio 1996; Bernardo and Tang 2008).

The regime shift paved the way for a wave of HDD investments in the Philippines' EPZs, with Japanese firms dominating (Mody, Dasgupta, and Sinha 1999; Batalla 2011).[4] The HDD boom began with the arrival of Hitachi in 1994, followed by Fujitsu, Toshiba and NEC. Japanese firms selected the Philippines because of its proximity to Japan, the relatively abundant supply of engineers of technical grades, and the pool of relatively cheap English speaking, semi-skilled, trainable labour (Amano 2010). On the other hand, US firms ignored the Philippines, except Seagate, which started producing HDD heads through subcontracting arrangements. By this time, US HDD firms had already consolidated their presence in Singapore, Thailand and Malaysia, following initial operations in Singapore in the early 1980s (McKendrik et al. 2000, 110).

The financial and budgetary reforms initiated during the Ramos era continued during the ensuing years under a professional economic management, despite political regime shifts (Bernardo and Tang 2008; Batalla 2018). However, there was a notable backsliding from policy reforms relating to trade and industry amid an atmosphere of political divisiveness. Industrial peace continued to prevail in the four EPZs, which had more conducive working conditions than the rest of the country. The investment and trade policy regime in the rest of the country suffered from the tension between the traditional aversion to foreign investment and the recognition of its role in economic development in this era of economic globalization. The policy regime restricted FDI to minority participation, except in relation to activities defined as "pioneer" under legislation, and to EPZs. Thus, the EPZ and non-EPZ divide in the overall incentive structure of the economy was exacerbated over the years. The Philippine economy grew at an average annual rate of 6.4 per cent during 2010–19, up from 4.8 per cent

---

[4] In the 1990s until the onset of the East Asian financial crisis in mid-1997, the real exchange rate (RER) of the Philippine pesos markedly appreciated, eroding the relative profitability of tradable production (Bautista and Tecson 2003). The advent of the HDD boom against the backdrop of RER appreciation is consistent with available evidence that global production sharing has weakened the link between trade flows and relative prices: site-selection decisions of MNEs are fundamentally based on long-term considerations that govern their global operations (Athukorala and Khan 2016).

during the previous decade.[5] The growth has been increasingly services oriented, fuelled by migrant-worker remittances and the expansion of business process outsourcing (BPO), which are not directly affected by the distorted domestic incentive structure (Batalla 2018).

From about the mid-1990s, the special economic zones (SEZs) run by the private sector have experienced a significant boom. However, unlike in the four state-run EPZs, activities within SEZs have been heavily concentrated in the services sector, predominantly BPO (mostly call centre) operations (Dumayas 2008). There is no evidence of significant new manufacturing investors arriving in the state-run EPZs. Export performance within GMVCs has been predominantly driven by incumbent firms (that is, the "intensive" rather than "extensive" margin). Rates of new firm entry have fallen sharply since 1999, and most new entrants are small firms, with average revenue amounting only to a third of that of the average revenue of all firms covered in the study (Balaoing-Pelkmans 2017).[6]

On 2 April 2008, Intel Corporation, the largest exporting firm in the country during the previous two decades, announced its decision to close operations in the Philippines and move to Ho Chi Minh City, Vietnam. Relatively higher wages and cost of electricity, and frequent supply interruption of electricity were conjectured by media as main reasons for Intel's departure. Presumably, the attractive investment incentive package offered by the Vietnamese government (particularly land rent exemption) would have played a role too (UNCTAD 2008). At the time of its departure, Intel subsidiary in the Philippines was employing 3,000 workers and had an accumulated total investment of US$1.5 billion. Its annual turnover the previous year was over US$100 million (Calimag 2008). Intel's new Vietnam plant involved an initial investment of US$605 million in 2006 and additional investment of US$475 million in the next four years. It is now the largest of Intel's assembly and test sites in the world (Turicum Investments Management 2021).

---

[5] Data compiled from ADB (2021).
[6] The study stopped short of examining whether the lack of new entrants was partly due to market power of incumbent firms and the dualistic incentive structure. However, it is unlikely that market power of incumbent firms would have been a significant influence because most, if not all, of these firms are involved in "relationship specific" assembly task within GMVCs, rather than in producing final products in a competitive market setting.

Some early signs of integration of the domestic auto industry (which had remained domestic-market oriented until recently) within the emerging ASEAN auto production networks have been observed in recent years (Ofreneo 2016; Doner, Noble, and Ravenhill 2021). With the Philippines accounting for 20 per cent of total wiring harnesses used in Toyota's global production networks (Ofreneo 2016), it has been dubbed by the media as the "transmission capital" of Toyota. Some carmakers have begun to assemble certain models specially catered to the Philippine market but also sold in other countries in the region (and beyond). For instance, Ford assembles Ford Focus, and Mazda assembles Mazda Tribute and Mazda 3 in the Philippines.

How can we understand this export story in the Philippine auto industry given the overall incentive bias in the economy against manufacturing and the absence of new firms entering other industries within global production networks (i.e., the absence of "extensive margin" in export performance)? It seems to be a unique development associated with the internationalization of the automobile industry over the past few decades: a restructuring of the global operations of automakers to cater to rapidly increasing vehicle sales in emerging markets. The ASEAN region, which has 660 million people and an increasing middle class, has been a key focus of this corporate strategy of global carmakers. Carmakers have begun to locate different segments of the auto value chain in individual countries in the region, depending on their relative cost advantage to produce for the entire region and beyond. In this inter-regional division of labour within auto production networks, the Philippines has become a producer of selected car parts such as wire harness and transmissions and brake systems, which are exported both regionally and globally.

This inter-regional division of labour in auto production has been aided by the ASEAN Industrial Corporation Scheme (AICO), which grants preferential tariff of 0–5 per cent on imports of parts and components and assembled cars for companies with subsidiaries in two or more ASEAN countries (subject to 40% ASEAN content of the products) (Yoshimatsu 2002). The abolition of long-standing local content requirements for auto-part production and auto assembly by the Philippine government in the late 1990s as part of its WTO commitments has also facilitated the process. Following the abolition of the local content requirement, auto-part producers and auto assemblers now have the flexibility to determine their input mix to meet the quality/standard requirements specified by buyers.

4 EXPORT PERFORMANCE

This section examines the Philippines' export performance within GMVCs using data compiled from the standard Customs records, based on data compiled from the UN Comtrade database.[7] By the time the electronic boom started in the mid-1970s, manufactured goods accounted for about 10 per cent of total merchandise exports of the Philippines. This increased to 44 per cent by the early 1980s following the "electronic fervour" in the second half of the 1970s (Table 10.1). GMVC exports dominated by electronics accounted for nearly two-thirds of total manufacturing exports during 1980–84. The second GMVC boom dominated by HDD exports is clearly reflected in the export growth figures in the 1990s and early 2000s. During the interim years between the two booms and the years after, total manufacturing exports grew much slower owing to slower growth of GMVC exports. Interestingly, the share of GMVC products in total manufacturing exports increased continuously. By 2015–19, GMVC products accounted for almost 90 per cent of total manufacturing exports, up from about 72 per cent in the early 1980s.

This pattern of continued GMVC dominance in manufacturing exports throughout the period studied seems to reflect a combination of the site-selection process of MNEs and the increasingly dualistic nature of the overall investment climate of the country. Setting up a production base in a given country and training workers involve a sizeable sunk cost. Moreover, workers who gain experience through on-the-job training become part of the valuable intangible assets of the MNE subsidiaries. Because of these reasons, MNE affiliates tend to become deeply rooted in a given host country based on their initial success. As regards the overall investment climate in the Philippines, as already noted, the environment in EPZs, where almost all MNE affiliates are located, has continued to remain much more conducive for export-oriented production compared with the rest of the country.

---

[7] The data classification system used for delineating parts and components and final assembly traded within GMVCs ("GMVC exports") from the standard trade data is discussed in the Appendix of Athukorala (2018).

Table 10.1. The Philippines: Key indicators of global production sharing and export performance

Year	Export value (US$ million)		Export growth (%)		Manufacturing as % of total exports share (%)	GMVC products as % of mfg	Producer-driven GMVC as % of total GMVC products	Parts and component in GMVC products (%)
	Mfg, exports	GMVC products	Mfg, products	GMVC products				
1970–74	210	68	34.2	32.1	11.8	32.6		
1975–79	922	529	37.7	56.3	25.0	53.7	28.4	80.1
1980–84	2,562	1,850	13.7	17.9	41.6	71.8	63.5	87.3
1985–89	3,864	2,605	11.3	4.3	54.7	68.9	63.4	82.3
1990–94	8,052	6,661	17.4	28.8	67.8	82.0	62.4	86.1
1995–99	23,972	22,012	23.8	25.9	83.0	91.3	84.5	88.9
2000–2004	43,554	40,955	10.2	10.4	88.8	94.0	91.9	88.8
2005–09	54,940	51,101	-2.8	-3.4	83.5	92.9	94.2	90.7
2010–14	59,954	53,955	9.3	9.2	78.2	90.0	95.1	88.2
2015–19	65,075	58,350	3.4	3.2	80.0	89.7	94.7	84.5
1970–2019	26,311	23,808	15.4	18.2	61.4	76.7	75.4	86.3

Source: Data compiled from UN *Comtrade* database.

At the same time, the MNEs' dominance in export production seems to have been compounded by the incentive bias against manufacturing in the rest of the country, which has deterred the emergence of export-oriented local enterprises, and the generous fiscal incentives offered to firms operating under the Philippine Export Zone Authority (PEZA).

As depicted in Figure 10.1, the profitability of manufacturing production (compared with non-tradable production) in the economy has declined continuously from the mid-2000s. Reflecting this incentive bias, the share of manufacturing in the economy contracted from over 25 per cent in the early 2000s to about 17 per cent in 2019. The remarkable stability of the nominal exchange rate of the Philippine peso[8] and growth of domestic demand, both underpinned by migrant-worker remittances and the BPO boom, seem to have contributed to the incentive bias against manufacturing.

Figure 10.1. Real exchange rate (RER)[1] and manufacturing share in GDP (%) in the Philippines (2000–2020)

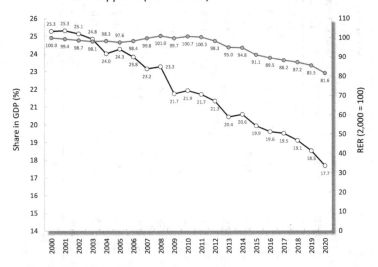

Note: (1) Manufacturing price relative to price of non-tradable (services, construction and utilities).
Source: Price indices are derived as implicit deflators from current and constant-price sectoral GDP data extracted from ADB (2021).

---

[8] The average annual PHP-US$ exchange rate varied in the narrow range of PHP42–52 per US$1 since 2000; the average rate of appreciation was about 3 per cent during 2010–19.

Until about the mid-1980s, the Philippines had the third highest share in total world exports of GMVC products among the six main countries in Southeast Asia, after Singapore and Malaysia (Figure 10.2). Thailand accounted for a much smaller share compared with the Philippines. From the mid-1980s, Thailand's market share has increased steadily, whereas that of the Philippines has lagged, reflecting its adverse domestic investment environment. The HDD boom in the late 1990s brought the market shares of the two countries closer, but the gap has widened since then. By the mid-2010s, Thailand's export market share was 1.9 per cent, while that of the Philippines was only 0.8 per cent.

The meteoric rise of late-starter Vietnam within the GMVCs is particularly important in understanding the emerging opportunities for export-oriented industrialization through global production sharing. Vietnam's world market share, which was much smaller than that of the Philippines, had increased to over 3.0 per cent by 2019. Indonesia is the only country among the six Southeast Asian countries whose export share has continuously lagged behind that of the Philippines.

Figure 10.2. Share in world exports of GMVC products of the Philippines and other ASEAN countries (1976–2019, %)

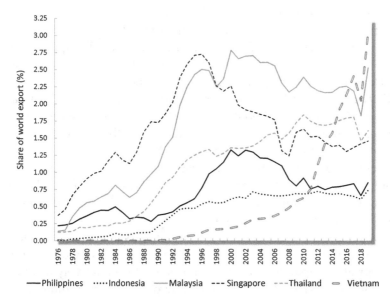

Source: Data compiled from UN *Comtrade* database.

In the early 1970s, when labour and rental costs in Singapore started to increase rapidly, neighbouring Indonesia was an obvious alternative site considered by MNEs for relocating low-wage segments of the production processes. Two of the major electronics MNEs operating in Singapore set up assembly plants there (Fairchild and National Semiconductor in 1973 and 1974, respectively), but both plants closed down in 1986 because of unresolved labour market issues. Since then, major MNEs have shunned Indonesia as a potential host country. Indonesia's engagement in producer-driven global production networks has so far been limited mostly to low-end electronic assembly activities undertaken mostly by Singaporean subcontracting companies in the Batam economic zone and Singapore-Johor-Riau Island (SIJORI) growth triangle, and some export spillover from predominantly domestic market-oriented automobile assembly plants (Athukorala and Kohpaiboon 2014).

Products exported within producer-driven GMVC continued to dominate the commodity composition of GMVC exports from the Philippines (Table 10.2). Exports within buyer-driven GMVCs (predominantly apparel and other standard consumer goods), which generally involved greater local enterprise involvement, continued to account for a small and shrinking share in the export composition. In 2015–19, producer-driven GMVC products accounted for 94 per cent of total GMVC exports, up from 82 per cent in the early 1980s. Producer-driven GMVC exports from the Philippines had been heavily concentrated in semiconductors and electronics and electrical components (SITC 75 and 76). The commodity structure initially determined by the semiconductor boom in the early 1970s and reinforced by the HDD boom in the 1990s had basically endured over the past two decades. Semiconductor devices (SITC 776) continued to account for over 40 per cent of the total GMVC exports.

Compared with the other Southeast Asian countries, the commodity composition of GMVC exports from the Philippines is much more similar to that of Singapore and Malaysia than Thailand and Vietnam (Table 10.3). This similarity contrasts with what one would have expected based on the stages of economic advancement and labour market conditions: Thailand and Vietnam are obviously more appropriate comparators for the Philippines. As a relatively low-wage country with a sizeable domestic labour pool, the Philippines would have become an attractive production base for buyer-driven GMVCs under a business environment conducive for international buyers to forge links with domestic entrepreneurs.

Table 10.2. Composition of GMVC exports from the Philippines (1979–2019,[1] %, US$ million)

Products (SITC[2] code in bracket)	1979–80	1989–90	1999–2000	2009–10	2018–19
Producer-driven	82.1	66.1	90.6	95.3	94.6
Chemical and related products (SITC 5)	–	–	0.1	0.2	0.1
Manufactured goods classified chiefly by material (SITC 6)	–	0.4	0.4	0.4	0.3
Power-generating machinery and equipment (71)	0.2	0.5	0.5	1.4	1.9
Machinery specialized for particular industries (72)	0.4	0.3	0.1	0.2	0.2
General industrial machinery and equipment and parts (74)	0.1	0.2	0.3	0.8	0.8
Office machines and automatic data-processing machines (75)	2.2	7.7	29.1	15.0	16.4
Telecommunications and sound-recording equipment (76)	2.5	8.5	4.6	6.3	6.4
Electrical machinery, apparatus and appliances (77 other than 776)[3]	3.1	8.2	7.8	11.8	17.5
Thermionic, cold cathode or photo-cathode valves and tubes (776)[4]	53.9	34.1	43.8	52.7	43.3
Road vehicles (78)	3.9	0.9	0.9	1.9	1.5
Other transport equipment (79)	0.7	0.4	0.1	0.7	1.2
Professional, scientific and controlling instruments and apparatus (87)	0.3	0.6	1.2	2.7	3.2
Photographic apparatus, optical goods, and watches and clocks (88)	11.8	3.2	1.4	1.1	1.7
Miscellaneous	2.9	0.9	0.2	0.2	0.3

Table 10.2 (continued)

Table 10.2 (continued)

Products (SITC[2] code in bracket)	1979–80	1989–90	1999–2000	2009–10	2018–19
Buyer-driven	17.9	33.9	9.4	4.7	5.4
Textile and textile products (other than apparel) (656 & 657)	2.2	2.8	0.0	0.2	0.1
Travel goods, handbags and similar containers (83)	0.7	1.1	0.9	0.2	1.3
Articles of apparel and clothing accessories (84)	0.3	24.3	7.4	3.5	2.9
Footwear (85)	11.8	3.2	0.3	–	0.5
Toys, games and sporting goods (894)	2.9	2.5	0.7	0.9	0.7
Total GMVC	100.0	100.0	100.0	100.0	100.0
US$ million	856.0	3,436.0	34,960.0	46,689.0	58,340.0

Note: [1] Two-year averages
[2] Standard International Trade Classification
[3] Mostly semiconductors
[4] Include auto parts, mostly wire harnesses; —zero or less than 0.045 per cent

Source: Data compiled from UN Comtrade database.

Table 10.3. Composition of GMVC exports from the Philippines and other ASEAN (2018–19,[1] %, US$ million)

Export commodity	Philippines	Indonesia	Malaysia	Singapore	Thailand	Vietnam
Producer-driven	94.6	60.9	95.8	99.4	93.7	67.5
Chemical and related products (SITC 5)	0.1	1.5	1.0	1.3	1.2	0.4
Manufactured goods classified chiefly by material (SITC 6)	0.3	2.4	0.6	0.3	1.8	1.2
Power-generating machinery and equipment (71)	1.9	2.5	0.5	5.3	3.5	1.0
Machinery specialized for particular industries (72)	0.2	1.1	1.1	2.5	0.6	0.2
Metalworking machinery (73)	0.0	0.2	0.0	0.1	0.1	0.0
General industrial machinery and equipment and parts (74)	0.8	2.2	1.3	1.9	5.6	0.8
Office machines and automatic data-processing machines (75)	16.4	5.0	7.9	10.3	11.5	4.5
Telecommunications and sound-recording equipment (76)	6.4	7.1	10.8	4.9	13.5	38.2
Electrical machinery and appliances, (77 other than 776)	17.5	15.4	10.3	8.1	11.8	6.4
Thermionic, cold cathode valves and tubes (776)	43.3	2.0	53.6	47.2	13.1	10.1
Road vehicles (including air-cushion vehicles) (78)	1.5	14.3	1.2	0.8	24.1	1.4
Other transport equipment (79)	1.2	2.6	1.0	5.6	0.3	0.3
Professional, scientific and controlling apparatus (87)	3.2	1.7	5.2	9.7	3.5	1.8
Photographic and optical goods, and watches and clocks (88)	1.7	0.8	0.8	1.5	2.6	0.4
Miscellaneous	0.3	2.2	0.4	0.1	0.6	0.7

Table 10.3 (continued)

Table 10.3 *(continued)*

Export commodity	Philippines	Indonesia	Malaysia	Singapore	Thailand	Vietnam
Buyer-driven						
Textile and textile products (other than apparel) (656 & 657)	5.4	39.1	4.2	0.6	6.3	32.5
Travel goods, handbags and similar containers (83)	0.1	1.5	0.2	0.1	0.7	0.6
Articles of apparel and clothing accessories (84)	1.3	1.6	0.0	0.1	0.3	2.1
Footwear (85)	2.9	20.1	3.6	0.2	3.8	16.5
Toys, games and sporting goods (894)	0.5	14.0	0.1	0.1	0.6	12.0
	0.7	1.9	0.3	0.1	0.9	1.2
Total GMVC	100.0	100.0	100.0	100.0	100.0	100.0
US$ billion	58.3	52.0	167.5	111.0	118.2	196.2

Note: [1] Two-year averages
Source: Data compiled from UN *Comtrade* database.

It is important to note that the data reported in Table 10.3 at the two-digit level hide notable variations among countries in the degree of industrial upgrading within the global manufacturing value chain. For instance, semiconductor production has three segments: design, manufacturing (fabrication), and assembly, testing and packaging. Of these, the assembly and testing segment is much more labour intensive and has the lowest barrier to entry, whereas the other two segments are capital and technology intensive and of high value. In HDD production, head-stack assembly is semi-skilled and labour intensive compared with the other stages of the production process. Firm-level data required to study product upgrading in the Philippines are not readily available, compared with the other Southeast Asian countries. However, a comparison of available case-study based evidence suggests that the Philippines has lagged in "industrial upgrading" (moving from simple assembly at the bottom of the value chain to high-value segments of the production process) compared with Singapore and Penang (Malaysia) (Tecson 1999; Balaoing-Pelkmans 2017; Mathews and Cho 2000; Athukorala 2014; Wong 2007; Diez and Kiese 2006).[9]

5 GMVC PARTICIPATION AND MANUFACTURING PERFORMANCE

Data compiled from the Manufacturing Census of 2012 on the role of global production shares in the Philippines manufacturing are summarized in Table 10.4. It is not possible to directly link the production-side data available from this source with export data. The second-best approach followed here is to delineate industries where global production sharing is heavily concentrated, as revealed by the analysis of trade patterns in the previous section. We focus on four products identified at the three-digit level of the Philippines Standard Industry Classification (PSIC): manufacture of electronic components (PSIC 261), computers and peripheral equipment and accessories (PSIC 262), communication equipment (PSIC 263), and parts and accessories for motor vehicles (PSIC 293). These products roughly accounted for over 90 per cent of total GMVC exports from the Philippines.

---

[9] Some early studies, which used conventional factor intensity classifications of export composition that failed to capture peculiarities of specialization patterns within GMVCs, have come up with the puzzling inference that the Philippine had the most "R&D-intensive" export structure in Asia (Lall 2000; Abrenica and Tecson 2003).

Table 10.4. Key indicators of GMVC participation in manufacturing in the Philippines (2012)

Commodity	Employment (%)	Gross output (%)	Value added (%)	Value added/ gross output (%)	Labour productivity (PHP)	Female share of total employment (%)	Wage per worker[1] (US$)
Manufacture of electronic components (C261)	12.0	17.0	27.8	42.9	53,409	83.4	5,213
Computers and peripheral eqpt and accessories (C262)	4.8	5.6	9.9	46.4	47,660	76.6	5,553
Consumer electronics (C264)	1.0	1.0	0.8	21.0	18,802	81.6	3,584
Parts and accessories for motor vehicles (C293)	5.0	3.6	3.1	22.9	14,329	61.5	4,529
GMVC products	23.0	27.3	41.7	40.1	41,925	76.9	5,046
Other manufacturing	77.0	72.7	58.3	21.1	17,529	36.6	3,339
Total manufacturing	100	100	100	26.3	23,137	45.9	3,731

Note: [1] Annual direct compensation per worker; compensation to direct labour

Source: Compiled from PSA (2015).

The four industries taken together accounted for about 23 per cent of total manufacturing employment, 27 per cent of gross output and 47 per cent of manufacturing value added. The strikingly large difference between gross output and value-added shares perhaps reflects the much greater profitability of GMVC operations within EPZs in the country.[10] Electronics (mostly semiconductor assembly and testing) was by far the largest GMVC industry in the Philippines, accounting for about half of the GMVC work force and over two-thirds of GMVC manufacturing value added. According to the disaggregated census data (not reported here), electronics was also the single largest industry in the country, measured at the three-digit level of PSIC.

Female workers accounted for 76 per cent of the work force in GMVC production compared with 37 per cent in non-GMVC production. Labour productivity in GMVC production (US$41,000 per worker) is 160 per cent higher than that of non-GMVC manufacturing (US$18,000); the average wage differential is about 60 per cent (US$5,000 versus US$3,400 per annum).

Data on the geographical location of the four GMVC industries are summarized in Table 10.5. These industries are concentrated in just

Table 10.5. Geographical profile of GMVC manufacturing in the Philippines: Employment and gross output[1] (%)

Region	Employment	Gross output
National Capital region	3.0	202
Cordillera	1.4	12.8
Central Luzon	10.3	5.3
Calabarzon	72.8	76.2
Central Visayas	11.7	2.1
Other 18 provinces	0.9	1.5
Philippines	100.0	100.0
	272,228.0	28,477.0

Note: [1] Data relate to the four three-digit industries listed in Table 10.4.
Source: Compiled from the *2012 Census of Philippine Business and Industry: Manufacturing*, Philippines Statistics Authority.

---

[10] The standard national account definition used in the Manufacturing Census captures wages and profits. The share of intermediate inputs in production operations within GMVC is naturally higher than the other manufacturing, and the MNE affiliates seem to pay higher wages on average.

four of the 18 regions in the country; Calabarzon accounts for over 72 per cent of total GMVC employment and over 76 per cent of GMVC gross output. At first glance, the geographical pattern is consistent with the popular perception that global production sharing in the Philippines is an enclave operation in the country. The underlying reasons for the heavy geographic concentration, however, are the vast differences between the EPZs and the rest of the country in terms of the nature of the incentive structure and the vast disparities among regions in terms of infrastructure provision.

A popular criticism in the Philippine policy circles (and elsewhere) of specialization within GMVC is that the resultant pattern of industrialization is "shallow", with limited linkages with the rest of the economy. The standard performance indicator used in this critique is the value-added ratio, which is defined as the percentage of domestic retained value (domestic content) in gross output.[11] However, the application of this conventional value-added criterion in assessing national gains from GMVC specialization is questionable. Global production sharing essentially means geographical dispersion of total value added in a vertically integrated production process. Naturally, the percentage of value added of a given product in a particular location within the value chain is going to be low compared with that under horizontal specialization (i.e., when the product is entirely made in one country). Moreover, the input structure of component and final assembly in a given country within the global value chain is determined as part of the overall international production process. It is virtually impossible to adapt it to suit the policy priorities of a given country. National gains for a given country in terms of contribution to national income resulting from engagement in global sharing in a given country, therefore, depend largely (if not solely) on the "volume factor", the expansion of sales turnover (hence, gross output) through access to a vast global market.

To illustrate this counter argument, we tabulate data on the value-added ratio and total value added of the "computer, electronics and electrical equipment industries" from the OECD trade in value added (TiVA) database. This is the "industry" where GMVC trade is heavily concentrated among the 22 two-digit industries for which

---

[11] Domestic retained value is the sum of domestically procured intermediate inputs, wage bill (worker remuneration) and profit. So, it is different from the national account concept of value added, which includes only the latter two components.

disaggregated data are available in the database. The estimates cover both direct and indirect value added, delineated using the standard input-output methodology. The data are plotted in Figures 10.3 and 10.4.

Interestingly, contrary to popular perception, value-added shares in gross output are higher in the Philippines than in the other five countries (Figure 10.3). This presumably reflects the fact that, at this level of data analysis, both exported and domestically sold products are lumped together. Such product aggregation is likely to have overestimated the domestic value-added ratio because there is much more scope to use locally sourced inputs in the production process of industries predominantly oriented to the domestic market.[12]

Figure 10.3. *Value-added share in gross output in computer, electronics and electrical equipment industries in Southeast Asian countries (%)*

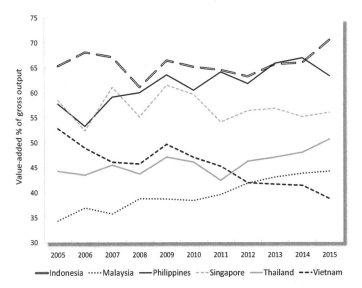

Source: OECD TiVA database (https://www.oecd.org/industry/ind/measuring-trade-in-value-added.htm).

---

[12] Estimates of value added in the TiVA are based on the assumption that the import content of export production in each industry is identical with that of production for the domestic market. But the usual pattern is that even when industries are finely classified, import content in an industry's production for export is higher than in its production for the domestic market. The estimation bias would naturally be greater at the two-digit level of industry classification used in the TiVA database (Athukorala and Patunru 2021).

A contrasting pattern emerges when the countries are ranked in terms of total domestic value added (contribution to GDP) (Figure 10.4) and in terms of value added to gross output ratio (Figure 10.3). Singapore and Malaysia, which have much lower value-added ratios than the Philippines, top the rank in terms of total value added (total retained value). Thailand occupies the third position, even though its value-added ratio is much smaller than that of the Philippines. Even when the data are taken at face value (ignoring the possibility of overestimating the value-added ratio), the Philippines is at the bottom of the rank.

The other countries with relatively poor GMVC records also rank poorly in total value added in contrast to their high ranking in terms of value-added ratio. All in all, it seems that in an era of global production sharing, forging domestic industrial linkages (increasing domestic value-added ratio) and achieving rapid growth through engaging in international production are not mutually consistent policy objectives.

Figure 10.4. Total domestic value added of exports in computer, electronics and electrical equipment industries

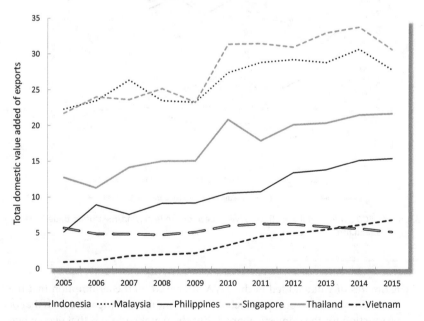

Source: OECD TiVA database (https://www.oecd.org/industry/ind/measuring-trade-in-value-added.htm).

6 DETERMINANTS OF PARTICIPATION IN GLOBAL PRODUCTION NETWORKS

Given that capital, managerial know-how and technology are mobile within production networks, the relative wages of "trainable" production workers are a key determinant of a country's participation in production sharing (Jones and Kierzkowski 2004). The term "trainable" is important because, under global production sharing, developed countries normally shift low skill-intensive parts of the value chain to developing countries. But, the least skill-intensive activities in developed countries can be more skill-intensive than the most skill-intensive activities in developing countries.

The availability of trainable labour at competitive wages per se does not ensure a country's successful participation in global production sharing, however. There are two other prerequisites: political stability and policy certainty, and country-specific "service link cost" associated with production sharing (Golub, Jones, and Kierzkowsk 2007; Jones and Kierzkowski 2004). Here, "service link cost" refers to costs involved in arrangements to connect and coordinate activities in a given country with those in other countries within the production network. Service link cost is determined by the overall investment climate of a given country, encompassing foreign trade and investment regimes and the quality of trade-related infrastructure and logistics, property rights protection and enforcement of contracts.

How does the Philippines meet these preconditions required for successful participation in global production sharing within global production networks? The Philippines is a relatively low-wage country in the region, even though its average manufacturing wage is slightly higher than that of Vietnam (Table 10.6). The sharply rising labour costs in the high-performing countries in the region, including China, is an opportunity for the Philippines to make inroads into global production networks, provided it meets the other preconditions. The country's large labour pool is an advantage, particularly for final goods assembly within global production networks, which require production in factories employing many workers. Assembly processes within production networks, particularly in producer-driven ones, require much more middle-level (supervisory) workforce (in addition to the availability of trainable low-cost unskilled labour) than traditional labour-intensive manufacturing activities. The Philippines seems to have the capacity to meet this requirement (Phan and Coxhead 2015).

Table 10.6. Nominal average monthly earnings[1] in the manufacturing sector (US$)

Country	Year	Ave. monthly earning (US$)
China	2016	746
South Korea	2019	3,405
Taiwan	2018	1,756
Indonesia[2]	2016	169
Malaysia	2018	636
Philippines	2019	261
Thailand	2019	470
Vietnam	2019	287
Cambodia	2016	184
Lao PDR	2017	260
Myanmar	2017	127
India	2016	147
Bangladesh	2017	142
Sri Lanka	2018	167

Note: [1] Gross remuneration in cash and kind
[2] The figure for Indonesia is the average monthly earnings of workers in both organized and informal manufacturing.
Source: International Labour Organisation: ILOstat, ilo.org/topics/wages/ (updated 2 May 2021).

Unlike those involved in light consumer goods industries, foreign firms engaged in vertically integrated assembly industries are particularly sensitive, as they view investment risk from a long-term perspective. They are particularly sensitive to political stability because disruptions in a production base in the value chain disturb the entire value chain. As we have observed, political instability and policy discontinuity in the Philippines have been a major deterrent to FDI during most years since the country's independence. The electronics boom in the early 1970s and the HDD boom in the 1990s were times of relative political stability and perceived policy continuity. Figures 10.5 and 10.6 respectively show the political stability and rule of law subindices extracted from the World Bank Government Effectiveness database. Over the past two decades, there has not been any notable change in the Philippines' position on these indicators among the countries in the region.

Figure 10.5. Political stability: Selected Southeast Asian countries

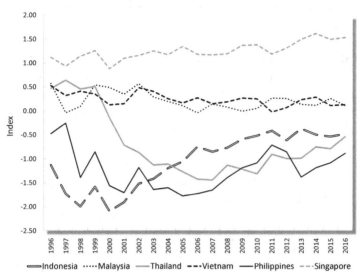

Note: Political stability and/or absence of politically motivated violence, including terrorism. The index ranges from −2.5 (weak) to 2.5 (strong).

Source: World Governance Indicator, World Bank (https://info.worldbank.org/governance/wgi/).

Figure 10.6. Rule of law: Selected Southeast Asian countries

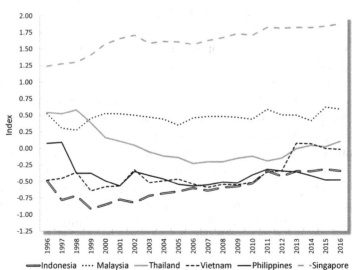

Note: Rule of law refers to the extent to which agents have confidence in and abide by the rules of the society, particularly the quality of contract enforcement, and property rights. The index ranges from −2.5 (weak) to 2.5 (strong).

Source: World Governance Indicators, World Bank (https://info.worldbank.org/governance/wgi/).

It is not possible to come up with a single indicator of service link cost associated with global production sharing. However, in terms of the World Bank's Doing Business database,[13] which ranks countries from 1 (best performing country), the Philippines ranks 95, well below the other Southeast Asian countries: Singapore, 2; Malaysia, 12; Thailand, 21; Vietnam, 70; and Indonesia, 73. On the subindices of starting a business, trading across borders and enforcement of contracts, the Philippines ranks below 100 among 190 countries covered. Regarding electricity, the Philippines ranks 23 on the "getting electricity" subindex, but this does not accurately capture the relative cost of electricity in the country. In terms of price of electricity measured in US cents per kWh (DB16-20 methodology), the Philippines (18.10) is the second highest in Asia after Japan (23.70).[14] The figures for the other five major ASEAN countries are: Singapore, 5.5; Indonesia, 10.7; Malaysia, 12.0; Vietnam 12.5; and Thailand, 13.7. The World Bank's logistic performance index,[15] which covers 160 countries, ranks the Philippines at 60, while Singapore is 7, Thailand 32, Vietnam 39 and Malaysia 41. The Philippines' cumbersome customs procedures and poor logistic services figure prominently in the country's list of obstacles to business.

7 CONCLUDING REMARKS

In the early 1970s, the Philippines had a promising start in export-oriented industrialization by engaging in GMVCs. In terms of initial prerequisites, the country was relatively better placed than most other countries in Southeast Asia to gain from opportunities opened up by the ongoing process of production sharing. However, its subsequent growth trajectory had not lived up to the initial expectations, reflecting the country's failure to combine its favourable initial conditions with a deep-seated commitment to international orientation. The lacklustre performance record is rooted in the dualistic incentive structure of the economy, which had "arrested" the country's participation in global production networks within the EPZs. The EPZs, initially conceived

---

[13] World Bank, Doing Business: https://www.doingbusiness.org/en/doingbusiness
[14] World Bank, GovData360 (https://govdata360.worldbank.org/)
[15] https://lpi.worldbank.org/international

as harbingers of global integration of domestic manufacturing, have eventually become "enclaves" within the economy.

The trajectory of the country's industrialization over the past decades has been characterized by an increased reliance of export performance on global production sharing against the backdrop of its lacklustre overall performance within global production networks. The share of GMVC-based products in total manufacturing exports has increased from about 80 per cent in the 1970s to over 90 per cent in recent years, even though the country's share in total exports within production networks has varied in the range of 0.5–0.7 per cent only. The country's role within production networks is heavily concentrated in low-end tasks in semiconductor and disc drive production undertaken by MNE subsidiaries located within the EPZs, which are protected from the constraints holding back export-oriented production in the rest of the economy. Critics of the EPZ-centred engagement in global production sharing have failed to understand that this lopsided (enclave) nature of export-oriented industrialization has been rooted in the very nature of the overall investment climate of the country, rather than a reflection of fundamental structural flaws of the ongoing process of global production sharing.

How can the Philippines reverse its performance record and set the stage for achieving industrial dynamism based on the country's unexploited potential? Critics of economic globalization advocate building local firms' capabilities through horizontal specialization while keeping MNEs at arm's length. However, opportunities for industrialization have dramatically changed in view of the ongoing process of global production sharing; "lumpy industries" located within national boundaries are now a vanishing breed. In this era of global production sharing, the policy challenge is to pursue industrialization by building domestic entrepreneurial capabilities while remaining open to trade and MNE participation. This, in turn, requires economy-wide reforms to improve the overall business climate, with a focus on redressing the incentive bias against tradable production and extending the EPZ incentives to the rest of the economy.

ACKNOWLEDGEMENT

I am grateful to Hal Hill, Arianto Patunru and Jim Roumasset for their excellent comments and suggestions.

REFERENCES

Abrenica, Joy V., and Gwendolyn R. Tecson. 2003. "Can the Philippines Ever Catch-up?". In *Competitiveness, FDI and Technological Activity in East Asia*, edited by Sanjaya Lall and Shujiro Urata, pp. 268–305. Cheltenham: Edward Elgar.

Amano, Tomofumi. 2010. "Competitive Strategy of Japanese and US Multinationls in Global Production Networks and Clusters: The Case of the Hard Disk Drive Industry". In *The Rise of Asia: Trade and Investment in Global Perspective*, edited by Prema-chandra Athukorala, pp. 109–26. London: Routledge.

ADB (Asian Development Bank). 2021. *Key Indicators for Asia and the Pacific*. https://www.adb.org/publications/key-indicators-asia-and-pacific-2021.

Athukorala, Prema-chandra. 2018. "Joining Global Production Networks: Experience and Prospects of India". *Trade and Development Working Paper No. 08/2018*. Australia: Arndt-Corden Department of Economics, Crawford School of Public Policy, Australian National University. https://acde.crawford.anu.edu.au/acde-research/working-papers-trade-and-development (accessed 8 July 2018).

Athukorala, Prema-chandra, and Fahad Khan. 2016. "Global Production Sharing and the Measurement of Price Elasticity in International Trade". *Economics Letters* 139: 27–30.

Athukorala, Prema-chandra, and Archanun Kohpaiboon. 2014. "Global Production Sharing, Trade Patterns, and Industrialization in Southeast Asia". In *Routledge Handbook of Southeast Asian Economics*, edited by I. Coxhead, pp. 161–83. London: Routledge.

Athukorala, Prema-chandra, and Arianto Patunru. 2021. "Measuring Trade in Value Added: How Valid is the Proportionality Assumption?". *Economic Systems Research*. https://www.tandfonline.com/doi/full/10.1080/09535314.2021.1965549.

Balaoing-Pelkmans, Annette O. 2017. "A New Look at Philippine Export Performance: A Firm-Level View". *Philippine Review of Economics* 54, no. 1:1–31.

Batalla, Eric V. C. 2011. "Japan and the Philippine's Lost Decade: Foreign Direct Investment and International Relations". *VRF Series, No 464*. Tokyo: Institute of Developing Economies.

———. 2018. "Bypassing Industrial Development". In *Routledge Handbook of the Contemporary Philippines*, edited by Mark R. Thompson and Eric V. C. Batalla, pp. 211–24. London: Routledge.

Bautista, Romeo M. 1988. *Impediments to Trade Liberalization in the Philippines*. London: Gower Publishing Company.

Bautista, Romeo M., John H. Power, and Associates. 1979. *Industrial Promotion Policies in the Philippines*. Manila: Philippine Institute for Development Studies.

Bernardo, Romeo M., and Marie-Christine G. Tang. 2008. "The Political Economy of Reform during the Ramos Administration (1992-98)". *Commission on Growth and Development Working Paper 39*. Washington, DC: World Bank.

Bautista, Romeo M., and Gwendolyn Tecson. 2003. "International Dimensions". In *The Philippine Economy: Development, Policies and Challenges*, edited by Arsenio M. Balisacan and Hal Hill, pp. 136–71. New York: Oxford University Press.

Calimag, Melvin G. 2008. "Intel Prepares to Close Philippines Plant". *Bloomberg*, 8 April 2008. https://www.zdnet.com/article/intel-prepares-to-close-philippine-plant/.

Diez, Javier R., and Matthias Kiese. 2006. "Scaling Innovation in South East Asia: Empirical Evidence from Singapore, Penang (Malaysia) and Bangkok". *Regional Studies* 40, no. 9: 1005–23.

Doner, Richard F., Gregory W. Noble, and John Ravenhill. 2021. "The Philippines and Indonesia: Extensive Development Arrested and Delayed". In *The Political Economy of Automotive Industrialisation in East Asia*, edited by Richard Doner, Gregory W. Noble, and John Ravenhill, pp. 127–54. New York: Oxford University Press.

Dumayas, Arianne Dela Rosa. 2008. "The Evolution of Economic Zones in the Philippines". In *Locational Analysis of Firms' Activities from a Strategic Perspective*, edited by Teshiharu Ishikawa, pp. 151–74. New York: Springer.

Feenstra, Robert C., and Gary G. Hamilton. 2006. *Emergent Economies, Divergent Paths: Economic Organization and International Trade in South Korea and Taiwan*. Cambridge: Cambridge University Press.

Golay, Frank H. 1966. "Economic Collaboration: The Role of American Investment". In *The United States and the Philippines*, edited by Frank H. Golay, pp. 95–124. Englewood, NJ: Prentice Hall.

Golub S. S., R. W. Jones, and H. Kierzkowsk. 2007. "Globalization and Country – Specific Service Links". *Journal of Economic Policy Reform* 10, no. 2: 63–88.

Grunwald, Joseph, and Kenneth Flamm. 1985. *The Global Factory: Foreign Assembly in International Trade*. Washington, DC: Brookings Institution.

Hill, Hal. 1982. "The Philippine Economy under Marcos: A Balance Sheet". *Australian Journal of International Affairs* 36, no. 3: 32–39.

———. 2003. "Industry". In *The Philippine Economy: Development, Politics and Challenges*, edited by Arsenio M. Balisacan and Hal Hill, pp. 219–53. New York: Oxford University Press.

Hobday, Mike. 1998. "Latecomer Catch-up Strategies in Econtronics: Samsung of Korea and ACER of Japan". In *Korean Business: Internal and External Industrialisation*, edited by Chris Rowley and Jongseok Bae, pp. 49–83. London: Frank Cass.

———. 2013. "Learning from Asia's Success: Beyond Simplistic 'Lesson-Making'". In *Pathways to Industrialisation in the Twenty-First Century: New Challenges and Emerging Paradigms*, edited by Adman Szirmai, Wim Naude, and Ludovico Alcorta, pp. 131–54. Oxford: Oxford University Press.

Hone, Angus. 1974. "Multinational Corporations and Multinational Buying Groups: Their Impact on the Growth of Asia's Exports of Manufactures – Myths and Realities". *World Development* 2, no. 2: 145–49.

Gereffi, Gerry. 1994. "The Organization of Buyer-Driven Global Commodity Chains: How US Retailers Shape Overseas Production Networks". In *Commodity Chains and Global Capitalism*, edited by Gerry Gereffi and Miguel Korzeniewicz, pp. 95–122. Westport, CT: Praeger.

———. 1999. "International Trade and Industrial Upgrading in the Apparel Commodity Chain". *Journal of International Economics* 48, no. 1: 37–70.

Jones, Ronald W., and Henrik Kierzkowski. 2004. "Globalization and the Consequences of International Fragmentation". In *Money, Factor Mobility and Trade: Essays in Honor of Robert A. Mundell*, edited by Dornbusch Rudiger Galimore Calvo and Maurice Obstfeld, pp. 365–81. Cambridge, MA: MIT Press.

Khan, Saif M., Alexander Mann, and Dahlia Peterson. 2021. *The Semiconductor Supply Chain: Assessing National Competitiveness*. Washington, DC: Center for Security and Emerging Technology, Georgetown University. https://cset.georgetown.edu/wp-content/uploads/The-Semiconductor-Supply-Chain-Issue-Brief.pdf.

Kleibert, Jana M. 2018. "Exclusive Development(s): Special Economic Zones and Enclave Urbanism in the Philippines". *Critical Sociology* 44, no. 3: 471–85.

Lall, Sanjaya. 2000. "The Technological Structure and Performance of Developing Country Manufactured Exports". *Oxford Development Studies* 28, no. 3: 337–69.

Lindsay, Charles, and Ernesto M. Valencia. 1982. "Foreign Direct Investment in the Philippines: A Review of Literature". In *Survey of Philippines Development Research 11*. Manila: Philippine Institute for Development Studies.

Mathews, John A., and Dong-Sung Cho. 2000. *Tiger Technology: The Creation of a Semiconductor Industry in East Asia*. Cambridge: Cambridge University Press.

McKendrick, David G., Richard F. Doner, and Stephan Haggard. 2000. *From Silicon Valley to Singapore*. New York: Stanford University Press.

Mody, Ashoka, Susmita Dasgupta, and Sarbajit Sinha. 1999. "Japanese Multinationals in Asia: Drivers and Attractors". *Oxford Development Studies* 27, no. 2: 149–64.

Ofreneo, Rene E. 2016. "Auto and Car Parts Production: Can the Philippines Catch Up with Asia?". *Asia Pacific Business Review* 22, no. 1: 48–64.

Phan, Diep, and Ian Coxhead. 2015. "Education in Southeast Asia: Investment, Achievements, and Returns". In *Routledge Handbook of Southeast Asian Economics*, edited by Ian Coxhead, pp. 245–69. London: Routledge.

PSA (Philippine Statistics Authority). 2015. *Census of Philippines Business and Industry: Manufacturing 2012*. Manila: PSA. https://psa.gov.ph/content/census-philippine-business-and-industry-cpbi (accessed 12 May 2021).

Remedio, Elizabeth M. 1996. "Export Processing Zones in the Philippines: A Review of Employment, Working Conditions and Labour Relations". *ILO Working Papers 993146103402676*. Geneva: International Labour Organization.

Shepherd, Geoffrey, and Florian Alburo. 1991. "The Philippines". In *Liberalising Foreign Trade: Korea, the Philippine and Singapore*, edited by Demetris Papageorgiou, Michael Michaely, and Armene M. Choksi, pp. 132–308. Oxford: Basil Blackwell.

Suhrke, Astri. 1975. "US-Philippines: The End of a Special Relationship". *The World Today* 31, no. 2: 80–88.

Tecson, Gwendolyn R. 1999. "The Hard Disk Drive Industry in the Philippines and Japanese Direct Investments". *Philippine Review of Economics and Business* 36, no. 2: 205–56.

Turicum Investment Management. 2021. "Intel Increases Vietnam Chip Investment by Nearly 50%". 27 January 2021. https://timvest.ch/intel-increases-vietnam-chip-investment-by-nearly-50/.

UNCTAD (United Nations Conference on Trade and Development). 2008. *Investment Policy Review*. Vietnam. Geneva: UNCTAD.

Yoshimatsu, Hidetaka. 2002. "Preferences, Interests, and Regional Integration: The Development of the ASEAN Industrial Cooperation Arrangement". *Review of International Political Economy* 9, no. 1: 123–49.

Warr, Peter G. 1989. "Export Processing Zones: The Economics of Enclave Manufacturing". *World Bank Research Observer* 4, no. 1: 65–87.

Wells, Louis T. 1983. *Third World Multinationals: The Rise of Foreign Investments from Developing Countries*. Cambridge, MA: MIT Press.

———. 1994. "Mobile Exporters: New Foreign Direct Investment in East Asia". In *Foreign Direct Investment*, edited by Kenneth A. Foot, pp. 173–91. Chicago: Chicago University Press.

Wong, Poh Kam. 2007. "The Remaking of Singapore's High-Tech Enterprise System". In *Making IT: The Rise of Asian in High Tech*, edited by Henry S. Rowen, Marguerite G. Hancock, and Lilliam F. Miller, pp. 123–74. Stanford, CA: Stanford University Press.

11 The Limits of Trade Policy Liberalization in the Philippines

Fernando T. Aldaba, Alvin Ang and Cielito F. Habito

1 INTRODUCTION

The Philippines struggled in the 1980s and 1990s to lower poverty levels amid an inward-oriented economic policy. Poverty levels hovered around 30–40 per cent until the year 2000. The situation can be traced largely to slow economic growth, which averaged only 1.3 per cent annually, and high unemployment, which averaged 9.3 per cent during those decades. In terms of economic structure, the average share of agriculture had fallen from more than 20 per cent in the 1980s to 16 per cent in 2000. Meanwhile, the share of services increased from about 40 per cent to 52 per cent, while that of industry remained largely unchanged. This effectively transitioned the country into a services-led economy without going through an industrialization phase typical in the evolution of similar economies.

As regards international trade, the country's total trade was equivalent to one-third of the gross domestic product (GDP) in the 1980s, increasing to nearly 100 per cent of GDP in 1998 prior to the Asian financial crisis. Expanding trade was the natural outcome as the country embarked on a trade and financial liberalization policy, coupled with privatization, during this period. This strategy was aimed at increasing investment and export capacities. It included unilateral tariff reduction from the 1980s from up to 100 per cent to a range of 10–50 per cent. The country also participated actively in trade agreements, particularly the ASEAN Free Trade Area-Common Effective Preferential Tariff (AFTA-CEPT) in 1993, the General Agreement on Tariffs and Trade-World Trade Organization (GATT-WTO) in 1995, and the ASEAN Trade in Goods Agreement (ATIGA) in 2009. In addition, the country was party to free trade agreements entered into by the ASEAN bilaterally with China, Japan, Korea, and Australia and New Zealand during the 2000s.

Beyond the opening of trade and relaxing of tariffs, the economy also implemented liberalization of industries to attract foreign investments. Annual foreign investment inflows had remained below US$1 billion from the 1980s to the 1990s. Liberalization and privatization reforms in the mid-1990s helped raise investments above US$2 billion, as investments were attracted in telecommunications, water utilities and banks, among others.

More than two decades hence, the impact of globalization policies has helped open the economy and achieve some improvement: poverty incidence fell from 33 per cent of the population in 2000 to 16.5 per cent in 2018; economic growth averaged 5.5 per cent from 2000 to 2019; and unemployment rates declined from 11.2 per cent in 2000 to 5.1 per cent in 2019. Foreign investment inflows also peaked at US$10 billion in 2017 and has hovered around US$8 billion, nearly quadruple of the levels seen in the 1990s. The country was seen to be well on its way to becoming an upper middle-income country prior to the onset of the pandemic in early 2020. Broadly, globalization policies are seen to have resulted in better economic performance. However, unlike its ASEAN neighbours, the observed improvements in the Philippine economy came not so much through increasing the contribution of tradables, but through the expansion in services. This shift has turned the country into a predominantly services-driven economy, skipping the industrialization path taken by developed countries and the neighbouring newly industrializing economies such as Singapore, Thailand, Malaysia and Hong Kong. While not necessarily bad in itself, this services-dominated structure has led to an economy dependent on international production, including for food and basic industrial outputs, and relying on services incomes to compensate for these purchases.

Against such background and context, this paper examines the role that outward-oriented policies in the form of trade liberalization and increased global participation have played towards shaping the current state of the Philippine economy. It attempts to analyse in detail which among the external openings contributed to the dominance of the services sector, and why trade liberalization has failed to boost trade to the same degree experienced by the country's more dynamic neighbours. The paper is organized as follows: Section 2 reviews other studies that have examined the role of international trade and investments in the current economic structure of the Philippines. Section 3 gives a detailed assessment of poverty and employment and relates how trade and investments impact these indicators. Section 4 undertakes a focused analysis of the agriculture sector, examining its failure to improve output, productivity and rural poverty, thereby contributing to the further expansion of services. Section 5 concludes with some thoughts on how the country might ensure the sustainability of improvements in poverty and employment, particularly through adjustment of trade and investment policies in agriculture, industry and services.

2 IMPACT OF TRADE AND GLOBALIZATION IN THE PHILIPPINES

Theories and relevant studies have anticipated that the implementation of globalization policies would lead to winners and losers in the economy. An important consideration is whether the losers were compensated from the gains made in the course of liberalization. This section reviews various studies that sought to explain the impact of trade and globalization on various aspects of the Philippine economy, particularly employment, poverty and inequality, foreign aid, and winners and losers of trade liberalization.

2.1 Economic growth, trade liberalization and employment

Various studies suggest that globalization or a more open world economy typically yields a positive impact on a country's economic growth and employment. This has been evidenced by the rapid expansion of East and Southeast Asian economies from the 1980s to 2000s as they increased their exports under a more open trade and investment environment. Guinigundo (2018) notes that trade openness and foreign portfolio flows have contributed to higher per capita GDP growth in the Philippines, following liberalization reforms in trade and foreign exchange.

Moreover, the continued mobility of Filipino workers in the past three to four decades has brought significant annual increases in remittances, raising consumption, investment, labour productivity and economic growth (Ang, Sugiyarto, and Jha 2009). Capital flows mainly through foreign direct investments (FDI) increased overall economic growth and, consequently, employment in the benefited sectors (Aldaba and Aldaba 2013) The sustained growth in employment and wages obtained over the years from the global offshore information technology (IT)-enabled services industry has also greatly increased household spending and investments (Remulla and Medina 2012).

Habito and Cororaton (2000) show that while the tariff reforms from 1995 to 2000 would result in a modest decline in the number of jobs in agriculture and services, the new jobs created in manufacturing would more than compensate for such job loss. Real GDP would increase and income distribution would improve, with the "poorest quintile income group receiving the largest share of the GDP growth". However, Clarete (2005) notes that it was the services sector that led in job creation. Ex-post assessment shows findings contrary to results obtained from ex-ante general equilibrium simulations looking at the effects of trade reforms, where industry should have increased employment generation to offset job reductions in agriculture and services.

In general terms, Ang, Cruz, and Custodio (2019) find that the employment situation in the Philippines in the past two decades had remained relatively unchanged in favour of the services sector, despite the liberalization efforts and some gains and improvements in the overall economy. The expectations that trade liberalization and the adoption of an open economy would lead to expanded FDIs and creation of more jobs failed to fully materialize. Several factors led to this outcome, including: (a) the lack of necessary manpower required for the expansion of manufacturing, despite the country having one of the largest private education sectors in the region, and (b) the lack of export diversification, which has constrained greater job generation in the other export sectors of the economy.

2.2   Growth, poverty alleviation and inequality

Has economic growth contributed to poverty reduction and lowered income inequality? Dollar, Kleinberg, and Kraay (2013) show evidence that higher rates of economic expansion can reduce poverty. However, GDP growth that is accompanied by rising inequality could exacerbate poverty. Bourguignon (2004) also argues that both changes in growth and inequality affect poverty dynamics. This means that adjustments in income distribution can widely affect changes in poverty and these changes may mitigate the positive effects of economic growth.

Balisacan and Pernia (2002) show that while economic growth highly influences poverty reduction, other factors also play a role. These include infrastructure, human capital, and location-specific characteristics and institutions (e.g., political economy and agrarian reform). They assert that "while growth is indeed good for the poor, it is not good enough." Balisacan (2011) highlights the huge diversity of both deprivation intensity and magnitude of poverty across geographic areas and sectors of Philippine society, implying that much more is needed beyond economic growth to make development more inclusive.

Similarly, Reyes and Tabuga (2011) find that while growth rate matters greatly in poverty reduction, so does income redistribution. This implies that the nature of economic growth matters. While globalization has no direct impact on poverty, globalization can indirectly affect poverty through its impact on economic growth and income inequality.

Bayangos' (2012) empirical study shows that an increase in trade openness contributes to reduction in income inequality in the Philippines. However, overseas workers' remittances contribute to higher income inequality. The study's estimates also show that trade openness has no significant impact on poverty, but worker remittances can help decrease poverty.

Sawada and Estudillo (2006), employing a computable general equilibrium (CGE) model, find that both non-transfer and transfer incomes decreased poverty in the Philippines. At the provincial level of aggregation, the growth of non-transfer income was the more important driving force behind poverty reduction. At the household level, however, transfer income was more important. The study also notes that while external openness had reduced poverty significantly in 1988 and 1994, it had a reverse impact in 2000, mainly due to the effects of the Asian financial crisis.

Simulations by Cororaton and Cockburn (2005) show that the impact of external openness (through the Doha trade agreements) in the Philippines is very small, but biased against the inward-oriented agriculture sector and favourable to the unskilled labour-intensive export industries. That is, pursuing domestic trade reforms by eliminating all tariffs and rice quotas would magnify the anti-agricultural bias and increase poverty. Rural households would be hit in terms of increased poverty, whereas urban households would see poverty rates decline.

Similarly, the simulation done by Cororaton and Corong (2006) shows the price of agricultural imports falling the most, resulting in the contraction of the agriculture sector as this substantial decline in prices induces consumers to substitute towards it. Meanwhile, the reduced price of imported inputs decreases the domestic cost of production, benefiting the outward-oriented, import-dependent industry sector. A more open trade regime also appears to benefit the services sector as the wholesale and trading subsector expands.

Hasan and Jandoc (2010) examine the role of trade liberalization in accounting for increased wage inequality in the Philippines from 1994 to 2000—a period wherein trade protection declined and inequality increased dramatically. They find that trade-induced effects on industry wage premiums and industry-specific skill premiums account for an insignificant increase in wage inequality. The reduced protection led to a shift in employment to the more protected sectors, especially in services where wage inequality tends to be high to begin with. However, other key drivers like changes in economy-wide returns to education and changes in industry membership over time have a much stronger effect on wage inequality.

2.3 Winners and losers of globalization

Globalization has brought about winners and losers in the economy. Guinigundo (2018) notes that industries that are less able to compete and workers whose skills have become less relevant may be adversely affected and will have difficulty in adjusting to changes due to globalization. Sibal (2005, as cited by Guinigundo 2018) shows that among the losers in the globalization process in the Philippines are firms mostly in the small and medium categories in the agriculture sector (e.g., producers of vegetables, palay, maize and poultry), sunset industries and labour-intensive firms (e.g., garments and apparel). These firms need to upgrade their technologies and improve production efficiency and productivity to be able to compete.

A micro-level study of firm entry and exits by Aldaba (2012) shows that firms in garments, leather and non-metallic products, furniture and other manufactured products registered the highest exit rates in 1997–2006. These firms were relatively younger and smaller in terms of average size of employment, had lower productivity and were less capital intensive than survivors. They also seemed to be more oriented towards the domestic market and had slightly higher tariff and effective protection rates. Entrants were also relatively younger but larger in terms of number of workers, were more capital intensive, and had higher productivity and higher export intensity than exitors. In terms of protection, entrants had higher tariff and effective protection rates than exitors and survivors.

Meanwhile, Malaluan (2011) asserts that the CGE simulations of Clarete (2011) and Cororaton and Cockburn (2005) indicate that agriculture and industry were losers during trade liberalization. According to him, instead of industry taking off due to improved resource allocation, resources (both capital and labour) shifted to the non-tradable services sector. Between 1985 and 2010, services became the overall winner in terms of share in output, while those of agriculture and industry fell.

2.4 Trade openness, development aid and poverty

Brun and Gnangnon (2017) explore whether trade openness could be an important driver of financing for development flows, notably development aid (ODA), FDI inflows and government public revenue. Their empirical analysis using an unbalanced panel data set of 125 countries finds two important pieces of evidence: (a) international trade openness is a significant strategy for driving financial flows for development, including public revenues, development assistance and FDI; and (b) these provide substantial financial resources needed for development, including the implementation of the Sustainable Development Goals (SDGs).

Mahembe and Odhiambo (2019), in their review of literature, find that foreign aid has a positive impact on poverty, as reported by the majority of studies of both non-monetary and monetary measures of poverty. Vathis (2013) notes that over the years, aid has demonstrated some spectacular successes, such as the eradication of diseases and the increase of life expectancy in the developing world, but poverty, while reduced worldwide, has remained a serious problem. The studies cited in Mahembe and Odhiambo (2019) show that development aid was generally effective in reducing poverty, with certain factors at play: (a) democratic institutions enhance effectiveness; (b) aid that targets pro-poor public expenditures (e.g., agriculture, education, health and other social services) was effective; and (c) aid disbursed in production sectors, infrastructure and economic development was even more effective.

However, some of the studies cited by Mahembe and Odhiambo (2019) are highly critical of foreign aid, such as Friedman (1958) and Easterly (2003, 2006, 2008). Meanwhile, other studies conclude that aid can be effective only under certain conditions (Burnside and Dollar 2000, 2004; Collier and Dollar 2002; Collier 2007) or will depend on the donors' aid allocation method and the recipient country's characteristics, such as governance and institutional capacity (Riddell 2008).

On the other hand, there is a dearth of current and recent studies on the impact of development aid on the Philippine economy, except for evaluation reports on specific bilateral or multilateral aid agencies, such as "Assessment of Development Results: Evaluation of UNDP Contribution to the Philippines" (UNDP 2010) and "Evaluation of Japan's ODA to the Philippines" (Ministry of Foreign Affairs of Japan 2019).

Kang (2010) finds that the Philippines' absorptive performance for foreign aid had declined during the period 2003–08 compared with 1986–88. Mitra and Hossain (2013), in examining the role of foreign aid in per capita economic growth in the Philippines, performed a quantitative analysis for the period 1970–2010. Their results indicate a significantly negative relationship between foreign aid and per capita economic growth. That is, a 1 per cent rise in the share of aid in GDP decreases per capita real income by 0.51 per cent.

Llanto, Navarro and Ortiz (2015) note that the Philippines was in a "sweet" spot at that time in terms of development finance and aid because of its access to higher volumes of ODA, which was not the case previously. They cite the following reasons for the situation: (a) an improved fiscal position through reforms and better governance, (b) credit rating upgrades, (c) strong commitment made by the international donor community to keep ODA flowing, (d) an improving private financial market in a regime of low inflation and financial stability, (e) continuing stream of huge amounts of remittances from overseas workers, and (f) strong economic performance, which started to attract more foreign direct investments.

3 TRADE AND INVESTMENTS IN INDUSTRY AND SERVICES

The previous section shows the Philippine experience in globalization, providing various perspectives on how outward-oriented policies have affected the economy. Among the main findings of the cited studies are as follows: (a) trade openness and workers' remittances have contributed to growth; however, it is the latter that helped reduce poverty more; (b) the expected job losses in agriculture and services were to be compensated by jobs generated in manufacturing; however, jobs were generated in the services sector instead; (c) growth was not enough to reduce poverty due to sectoral and geographical differences;

(d) trade openness also led to falling prices of agricultural imports, creating a substitution effect that further weakened the agriculture sector; and (e) job growth went mostly to services, which is a protected sector.

This section synthesizes these points into three factors that have led to the country's economic structure of today. These are lack of diversity in industry, the "protected" services sector and the overseas Filipino worker (OFW) phenomenon.

3.1 Lack of diversity in industry

Unlike the rest of Southeast Asia, the Philippines' foray in opening its economy did not begin to bear fruit until the 2000s. The Japanese FDI wave in the late 1980s substantially bypassed the Philippines, resulting in a gap in the supporting investments that could have pushed exports at the level of its ASEAN neighbours. After the 1986 EDSA People Power Revolution, the country refocused on strengthening its weakened institutions. Outward-oriented policies were gradually implemented as the economy recovered from deep recessions in 1984 and 1985. Foreign direct investments remained largely below US$2 billion and the country was limited by its debt burden, which exceeded 60 per cent of GDP. The liberalization policies were not enough to push export growth as gross domestic capital formation was capped at below 20 per cent of GDP for most of the 1980s. Exports' share in GDP remained below 20 per cent throughout the 1980s and the mid-1990s, while those of peer economies in the ASEAN were more than 25 per cent (see Figure 11.1).

The outward-looking policies started to bear fruit in the mid-1990s when the country's main export products started to shift from traditional goods to intra-industry goods in the ASEAN, especially those related to electronics and electrical and transport machineries. The Philippines had the biggest tariff reduction in the ASEAN from the 1970s to the mid-1990s (Paderon 2017). Moreover, the average effective rate of protection declined from about 50 per cent in 1985 to about 10 per cent in the mid-2000s (Aldaba et al. 2015). However, it should be noted that the fall in protection rates was unevenly implemented across sectors, leaving agriculture and related food processing with rates much higher than manufacturing. This partly explains the significant increase of non-traditional manufacturing exports from 1995 as the traditional exports started to become uncompetitive in the regional and global markets. Figure 11.2 shows that electrical and electronics-related exports dominated the share of export goods and eased out the traditional agriculture and garments exports.

289

Figure 11.1 Selected indicators as per cent of GDP (1983–2000)

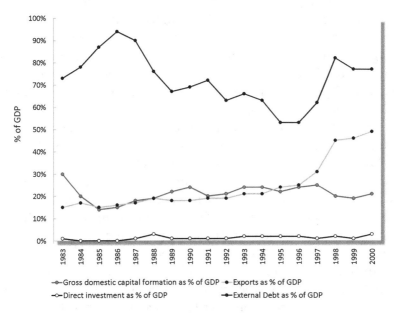

Figure 11.2. Composition of export goods (1990–2000)

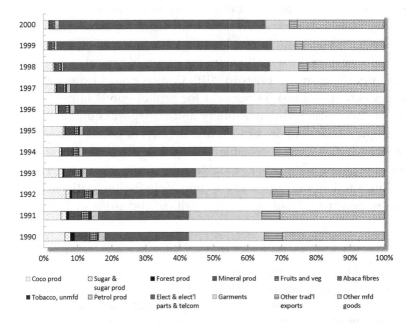

Thus, trade liberalization essentially skewed its benefits towards the manufacturing sector, which required higher skills and did not contribute the most to output. This limited opportunities to create more jobs, particularly in the countryside where most activities of the agriculture sector are located. For the period 1990–2000, the share of agriculture in GDP averaged 21 per cent; for employment, it was double at 42 per cent. On the other hand, the share of manufacturing in GDP averaged 25 per cent, but only 10 per cent in employment. The share of the services sector, especially the wholesale and retail trade and transportation subsectors, was 55 per cent both in GDP and in employment. The outward-oriented policies also did not lead to export diversification, with the continued increase in the share of electronics and electrical machinery in the last two decades, approximating 70 per cent of total goods exports. The Philippine Economic Zone Authority (PEZA), created in the late 1990s, established and dispersed economic zones around the country. It has helped bring in foreign direct investments across different locations. However, these zones have catered mostly to the production of electronics-related industries, limiting job opportunities in their locations due to their higher skill requirements.[1] In addition, most of the outputs of these manufacturing facilities require importation of intermediate or raw materials from other countries as part of the regional intra-industry value chain. Hence, the actual net export value added brought by trade liberalization has been the skills and higher learning capacities of Filipino workers. This observation is exemplified by the shares of capital goods exports and imports from the 1990s to 2010. Capital goods export averaged 66 per cent as against 53 per cent for capital goods imports during the period. Specifically, machinery and transport equipment logged the highest share in both exports and imports of goods. The outward-oriented policies were not able to improve productivity nor create job opportunities in other tradable manufacturing and agriculture products as they were not ready to compete in the international market. As the productivity of agriculture fell, so did primary agricultural

---

[1] The Philippine education system has consistently produced more business and education graduates (representing roughly 50% of all graduates) than graduates of engineering, the sciences and technical skill courses needed by the manufacturing sector.

outputs. Table 11.1 shows the share of specific products for exports and imports, comparing 1995 and 2015. It can be observed that the country has become a net food importer as exemplified by the reversal of export and import shares in food products, animals and vegetables. Also, the share of textile exports—a major export product in prior decades—significantly declined by more than 10 per cent, signifying also a loss in competitiveness.

Table 11.1. Shares of specific goods in total export and total import (1995 vs. 2015)

Commodity	1995		2015	
	Export	Import	Export	Import
Animal	1.47	1.94	0.99	2.84
Chemicals	1.41	5.93	2.05	7.30
Food products	3.53	2.72	3.24	5.02
Footwear	1.22	0.21	0.24	0.40
Fuels	1.86	9.20	1.32	11.87
Hides and skins	1.29	0.34	0.91	0.34
Machinery & electronics	54.85	43.46	58.27	39.95
Metals	3.09	7.15	3.52	5.72
Minerals	1.16	2.23	2.83	0.85
Miscellaneous	5.29	2.70	5.64	2.72
Plastic or rubber	1.00	3.98	1.51	3.87
Stone and glass	1.69	0.71	1.23	1.53
Textiles and clothing	12.74	4.63	2.83	1.93
Transportation	1.75	8.41	6.04	8.98
Vegetable	5.64	3.61	3.98	4.39
Wood	2.02	2.80	5.39	2.29

Source: Ang, Cruz, and Custodio (2019).

3.2 The rise of the protected sector

The higher quality skills requirement of the manufacturing sector has limited job switching from the low-productivity agriculture sector. Nevertheless, agriculture continued to employ at least 40 per cent of the workforce in the early 1990s. With income relatively lower and stagnant, workers started to leave the agriculture sector to look for jobs in the urban centres. From 40 per cent in 1995, the share of services in employment breached 50 per cent in 2010, while that of agriculture fell from 42 per cent to about 33 per cent. Notably, there was no significant change in the share of industry workers during the same period. In fact, the share of manufacturing value added in GDP had remained unchanged at about 25 per cent since the 1960s, despite trade liberalization reforms. Indonesia, Malaysia and Thailand outpaced the Philippines in the mid-1980s; by the mid-2000s Thailand was at 35 per cent, Malaysia at 30 per cent and Indonesia at 27 per cent (World Bank 2018).

The country's value-added per capita in agriculture was also the lowest among these ASEAN countries during the same period. This weak agricultural productivity depressed income and explains largely why poverty had remained stubbornly high during the implementation of the outward-oriented policies. Poverty rates stayed above 25 per cent until the mid-2000s, as the poor were unable to move to higher productivity sectors. This is validated by the 2006 Family Income and Expenditure Survey (FIES), which reports that more than 50 per cent of the poor live in rural areas, 35 per cent work in agriculture, and 44 per cent are informal sector workers (World Bank 2018).

These observations point to the reality that outward-oriented economic policies are necessary but not sufficient to increase economic activities and lower poverty rates. There are other constraints that need to be addressed to foster domestic competition in all sectors.[2] With the industry and manufacturing sector remaining relatively stagnant, the services sector became the easier and shorter route to urban jobs

---

[2] The 2018 World Bank Report on Fostering Competition in the Philippines points out that Philippine markets are relatively concentrated compared with peers in the ASEAN. This is due to barriers to entrepreneurship, trade and investments.

and stable income sources. In addition, most domestic investments had gone to services, particularly real estate, finance, retail trade, transport and accommodations, where the investment required are not as large as in manufacturing and not as challenging as in agriculture. Not surprisingly, these sectors have remained relatively closed to foreign investments, including ownership of land. Figure 11.3 shows the comparative average shares of the economic sectors in employment, growth and export for 2010–20. Much of jobs outside the tradable sectors are in construction, wholesale and retail, accommodations and transport. These largely reflect lower-quality jobs than those in finance and information, and therefore either have lower pay or are informal in nature. These are where most agricultural workers who shifted to urban centres can be found.

The information and communication sector ranks a close second among contributors to total exports across sectors. As the country searched for alternative export winners, the rise of the business process outsourcing (BPO) industry became an opportunity from 2005 onwards. The rising labour costs in Western economies have resulted in standard and predictable business activities being repackaged for outsourcing in countries with cheaper labour. The improving efficiency of the internet and the prevalent use of the English language in the Philippines enabled this industry to flourish. Foreign investments flowed into this industry as it has no significant barriers, unlike other sectors such as those in public utilities and other services. Thus, the BPO industry has become an important source of foreign exchange for the country. It has created jobs, especially for tertiary-education graduates who are unable to find employment due to skills mismatch. The industry has also located in many urban centres, thus helping increase the demand for office spaces and residential condominiums. As of 2019, the BPO industry had contributed 7 per cent to total GDP and employed about 1.3 million of the total 40 million workers in the labour force (Magellan Solutions 2020). Nonetheless, its contribution to poverty alleviation and employment generation may still be considered small. Like manufacturing, it requires higher-level skills, employing mostly tertiary-education graduates. This is a formidable barrier to entry for most workers in the agriculture sector.

Figure 11.3. Comparative shares in exports, GDP and employment (2010–20)

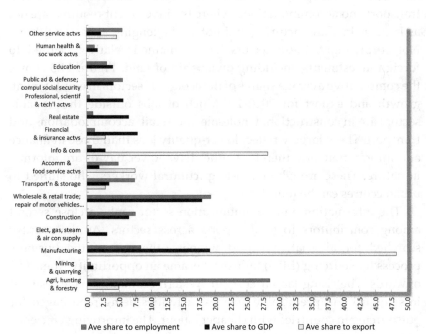

3.3 The OFW phenomenon

The opening up of the economy has also led to Filipino skills and labour flowing out of the country. What was a temporary policy to address the unemployment problems in the 1970s became a well-organized economic response to job creation. With many educated professionals unable to find quality jobs, the world job market has become an opportunity for a large number of Filipinos. Initially, the country deployed professionals such as medical doctors, nurses, engineers and administrators in the 1970s to the early 1980s. Starting in the 1990s and up to the present, however, the job opportunities have shifted to middle- and lower-skilled workers. Attracted by the huge wage differentials, agricultural landowners would sell their assets to pay for placement fees and work abroad as domestic helpers, construction workers and farmers. The OFW phenomenon has made the Philippines the fourth largest remittance receiving country in the world after China, India and Mexico. The annual remittances of about US$30 billion, roughly 10 per cent of GDP, have helped create a sustainable consumption base for the economy. Remittances have also contributed to the development of urban centres beyond the national capital, with the establishment of clusters of education, retail and basic services, and real estate development. Unlike in manufacturing and BPOs, which require higher-level skills and education, those in the agriculture sector do not face similar barriers as long as placement fees are paid. Bayangos (2012) asserts that a generation of overseas work helped lower poverty across the country more than trade openness. Figures 11.4 and 11.5 present data from two periods of overseas work and poverty, indicating that poverty rates in regions with more OFWs significantly declined in a decade.

Figure 11.4. Number of OFWs and poverty rates (2009)

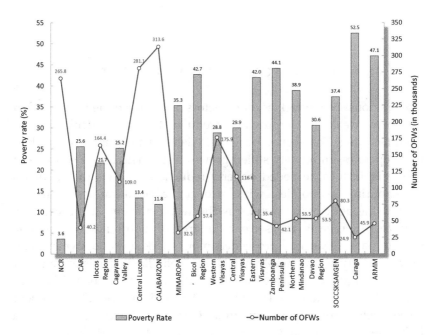

Figure 11.5. Number of OFWs and poverty rates (2018)

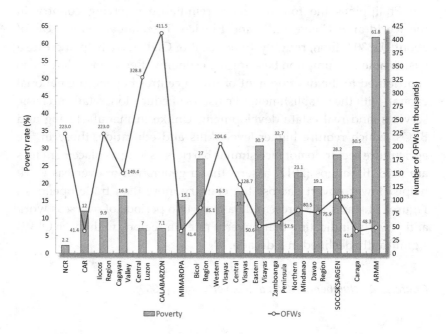

4 TRADE, AGRICULTURE AND POVERTY

The previous section tackles other factors that made trade liberalization relatively weak in improving productivities in agriculture and manufacturing. This section provides a detailed analysis of how lack of trade openness ultimately stifled growth in the agriculture sector, and how this, in turn, impeded poverty reduction vis-à-vis the country's neighbouring economies with stronger agricultural performance. In fact, the agriculture sector has the worst poverty in the country. This clearly reflects the sector's failure to contribute to economic transformation that has proceeded more markedly and dynamically in the country's comparable neighbours. The lagging performance of Philippine agriculture is highlighted by the fact that Vietnam, Thailand and Malaysia earned US$41 billion, US$39.5 billion and US$25 billion, respectively, from their agricultural exports in 2019, while the Philippines only managed US$6.7 billion. This marked disparity has prevailed for many years (see Table 11.2 for data spanning 2000–2012). There may be various reasons for such underperformance in agricultural exports, including lack of trade openness (as discussed below), declining

Table 11.2. Agriculture and fisheries export values and shares in total exports

Country	Value of A&F exports (US$ millions)				Share of A&F exports to total exports (%)			
	2000	2005	2010	2012	2000	2005	2010	2012
Brunei				6				0.0
Cambodia	13	29	92	229	1.0	1.0	1.6	2.9
Indonesia	5,725	10,284	26,281	34,599	9.2	12.0	16.7	18.2
Malaysia	5,789	10,318	24,413	29,548	5.9	7.3	12.3	13.0
Myanmar			1,506				19.7	
Philippines	1,929	2,625	3,964	4,879	5.1	6.4	7.7	9.4
Singapore	3,221	3,955	7,095	9,084	2.3	1.7	2.0	2.2
Thailand	10,208	13,247	26,127	32,369	14.8	12.0	13.4	14.1
Vietnam	3,745	6,696	14,351	18,695	25.9	20.6	19.9	19.3
China	14,852	26,467	47,682	61,143	6.0	3.5	3.0	3.0
European Union	189,966	317,889	459,929	501,262	8.0	8.0	9.1	9.7
Japan	2,359	3,153	5,097	4,963	0.5	0.5	0.7	0.6
United States	54,439	61,884	112,656	139,198	7.6	7.7	10.0	10.3

Source: Clarete and Villamil (2015).

comparative advantage in agriculture, high population density and conflict in important agricultural regions, particularly in Mindanao. The sad irony is that many leading agricultural scientists in those same neighbours with dynamic farm sectors studied at the University of the Philippines Los Baños, especially in the 1960s to 1980s.

Trade openness in the agriculture and fisheries sectors (measured by the ratio of the sectors' exports and imports to total exports and imports) has been on the uptrend in the ASEAN region, particularly Malaysia, Thailand and Vietnam, but had actually declined in the Philippines (Table 11.3). In fact, trade openness in agricultural products has served as a major impetus for growth, especially among the low-income ASEAN members. Shares of agricultural exports in total exports rose for most ASEAN member states between 2000 and 2012, with the Philippines being a notable exception. On the other hand, the 2015 ASEAN Investment Report shows that intra-ASEAN foreign direct investments in agriculture (together with those in finance) nearly doubled between 2013 and 2014 (ASEAN Secretariat 2015). Large agribusiness companies from within the ASEAN—such as Thailand's Charoen Pokphand and Betagro Groups, Malaysia's Leong Hup and QL Group and the Philippines' Universal Robina Corporation—have leveraged on complementarities in the food and agriculture industries across the region.

Table 11.3. Trade-openness index (1990–2012)

Country	1990	1990	2000	2005	2010	2012
Brunei						3%
Cambodia			4%	3%	4%	5%
Indonesia	4%	4%	6%	5%	5%	6%
Malaysia	13%	12%	10%	11%	15%	15%
Myanmar						
Philippines			6%	6%	5%	5%
Singapore	19%	13%	8%	8%	8%	8%
Thailand	10%	8%	11%	10%	11%	12%
Vietnam			15%	17%	21%	23%
China		3%	2%	2%	2%	2%
European Union	1%	5%	5%	5%	6%	6%
Japan	1%	1%	1%	1%	1%	1%
United States		1%	1%	1%	1%	2%

Source: Clarete and Villamil (2015).

4.1 Wider agribusiness linkages

Even before the establishment of the ASEAN Economic Community and, independently, of the intergovernmental efforts to establish it, various forms and scales of private-sector linkages leading to closer regional integration in the context of agribusiness had already been working. These private-sector platforms provide promising venues in ensuring more sustainable agriculture and rural development and achieving food security and inclusive growth (Habito 2016). Some examples of such cross-border business linkages include investments in poultry by the Charoen Pokphand (CP) Group of Thailand into Malaysia, Myanmar and Indonesia; the Leong Hup, QL Group and Wilmar from Malaysia into Indonesia, Vietnam and the Philippines; and in pork by Betagro of Thailand into Cambodia and Lao PDR. In some investments, finished products are exported back to the investors' home country, such as rice.

Regional integration of rice value chains has already been happening, with significant cross-border investments in mills and processing plants that play a pivotal role in transforming the upstream and downstream segments of rice value chains. Investments cover supply of inputs, contract farming in various forms, and provision of agricultural support services, apart from modern distributive trade (e.g., via supermarkets), to enhance productivity and international trade. Such initiatives have further enriched border trade as well, which has become a growing and legitimate part of the formal trade and investment relationships between bordering countries, and no longer confined to informal and often illegal transactions across the border (Wong and Adriano 2016). The private sector appears to have moved faster than governments in terms of treating the ASEAN as a common production base and market via such strategic cross-border investments, through the establishment of national and regional networks, often leveraged on global agri-food value chains (Habito 2016). This has extended the perspective of regional integration well beyond the traditional regional trade concerns.

This value-chain phenomenon dispels earlier scepticism on the usefulness of the ASEAN regional integration to the farm sector. The scepticism was based on the premise that Southeast Asian countries would more likely compete than complement, especially in agriculture. And yet cross-border value-chain relationships have actually spurred trade in agricultural and agri-based products, similar to the way they have expanded trade in manufactured products. This is remarkable because prior to closer ASEAN integration in the 1990s, it was widely thought that little was to be gained from freer trade and investment policies with one another because the member economies were seen to be producing largely the same agricultural products. Trade outcomes after the establishment of the ASEAN Free Trade Agreement (AFTA) suggest that more complementation has occurred than earlier expected.

Headway has also been achieved on trade facilitation, which, coupled with the virtual elimination of tariffs, has reduced trade costs by about 15 per cent within the region and around 8 per cent in the rest of the world (World Bank 2015). Still, much scope remains for improvement in harmonizing and simplifying border customs procedures. The greater challenge now is in the area of non-tariff measures, which are generally perceived to be on the rise. Agriculture has in fact registered the most number of such trade-distorting and highly protective measures (Nathan Associates Inc. 2013).

4.2 Integration into the wider global economy

The bilateral free trade agreements (FTAs) that the ASEAN as a block has forged with its six dialogue partners—India, Japan, China, Korea, Australia and New Zealand—have given its member economies liberal access to a wider market comprising half the world's population. Of significant importance, especially for less developed latecomers like Cambodia, Lao PDR and Myanmar, is the access given by these agreements to advanced agri-based science and technology resources from China and Japan. These bilateral FTAs have recently been consolidated with the formation and formal establishment of the Regional Comprehensive Economic Partnership (RCEP), comprising the ASEAN member states and five of the six dialogue partners (India opted out of the grouping late in the process).

At the same time, China's ambitious Belt and Road Initiative—which seeks to strengthen land and maritime links between Asia, on one hand, and Europe and Africa, on the other—could further benefit the region's agricultural and rural economies. All these could bolster global value chains, in which six ASEAN member states (Singapore, Malaysia, the Philippines, Malaysia, Thailand, Vietnam and Indonesia) are already well connected. Crucial in these trade agreements and initiatives are provisions that address pertinent trade facilitation measures (rules of origin, simplified customs procedures across borders, etc.) and non-tariff measures (including sanitary and phytosanitary standards and general standards and conformance issues). With proper management and enforcement, these could redound to positive gains to the agriculture sector and rural economies of the ASEAN member states, which the agreements identify as strategic areas for strengthened economic cooperation (ASEAN 2015).

4.3 Progress in poverty reduction

Farmers and fishers have consistently ranked the poorest among the Filipino poor. As of the latest official poverty data in 2018, nearly one in three farmers (31.6%) and about one in four fishers (26.2%) are poor. These occupations likewise registered the highest poverty incidences in 2015 at 40.8 per cent and 36.9 per cent, respectively (PSA 2020).

Apart from the Philippines exceeding overall poverty incidence in most ASEAN member states, its pace of poverty reduction since 2001 has been markedly slower than comparable neighbours, except Thailand, which already had a low poverty incidence rate to begin with (Table 11.4).

Table 11.4. Poverty, under-5 stunting and mortality across the ASEAN

Country	Population in poverty %			Ave. annual reduction (%)	Under-5 stunting (%)	Under-5 mortality (per 1,000 live births)		
	2001	2009	2018		2017–18	2000	2009	2018
Brunei	–	–	–	–	–	–	7	12
Cambodia	35.9	30.1	12.9	9.9	32.4	135	88	28
Indonesia	23.4	13.3	9.4	8.3	30.5	48	39	25
Lao PDR	38.6	27.6	23.2	3.7	33.1	105	59	47
Malaysia	8.1	3.8	0.4	106.9	20.7	9	6	8
Myanmar	–	–	24.8	–	29.4	110	71	46
Philippines	40.0	26.5	16.6	7.8	30.3	40	33	28
Singapore	–	–	–	–	–	4	3	3
Thailand	12.9	8.1	9.9	1.7	10.5	29	14	9
Vietnam	37.0	13.4	5.8	29.9	23.8	39	24	21

Source of data: Asian Development Bank.

Closely related to poverty are health and nutrition indicators, particularly stunting due to severe malnutrition and mortality in children below 5 years old. In particular, Thailand, Malaysia and Vietnam's under-5 stunting incidence (10.5%, 20.7% and 23.8%, respectively) is well below that of the Philippines (30.3%). Stunting is of particular concern because medical research has long established that a child stunted at five years of age will never achieve full brain and physical development potential. Long-term consequences include poor cognition and educational performance, low adult wages, lost productivity and increased risk of nutrition-related chronic diseases in adult life when accompanied by excessive weight gain later in childhood (WHO 2015). In other words, a stunted five-year old is "damaged for life".

Similarly, under-5 child mortality in the Philippines exceeds that in Indonesia, Malaysia, Thailand and Vietnam. Furthermore, the Philippines' progress in bringing down under-5 child mortality since 2001 has been significantly slower (a reduction of 12 children out of 1,000 live births) than in Thailand (reduced by 20), Vietnam (by 18) and Indonesia (by 23). The slower pace in Malaysia and Singapore simply reflects the fact that these countries already had single-digit figures in 2001, hence have little room to improve. Quite clearly, the Philippines has lagged behind its comparable neighbours in poverty reduction, both in the income poverty sense and in terms of human welfare conditions as exemplified by health and nutrition.

Numerous factors contribute to poverty incidence in any country, but the relative underperformance of Philippine agriculture relative to neighbouring countries appears to correlate closely with the country's poor poverty performance. In turn, the correlation between trade openness and agricultural performance observed in the previous section suggests that trade openness is also associated with and likely has been instrumental in the significant gains in reducing poverty in the Asian region.

4.4 Food security and trade

Food security in the Philippines presents a similar story. The country lags behind its comparable neighbours in the ASEAN-5, falling even below Vietnam and Myanmar (Table 11.5). Among the four food security indicators of food affordability, food availability, food quality and safety, and natural resources and resilience, the Philippines ranks worst in food affordability, implying that the poor are the most food insecure

Table 11.5. Food security index (2020, ASEAN member countries)

Country	Overall rank	Overall index	Affordability	Availability	Quality & safety	Nat res & resilience
Singapore	19	75.7	87.3	75.8	82.3	47.4
Malaysia	43	67.9	85.5	58.8	72.5	47.5
Thailand	51	64.0	82.8	55.3	59.5	50.0
Vietnam	63	60.3	66.7	61.3	61.4	45.9
Indonesia	65	59.5	73.5	64.7	49.6	34.1
Myanmar	70	56.6	58.1	53.9	59.3	56.3
Philippines	73	55.7	66.5	57.6	52.0	35.8
Cambodia	81	51.5	57.5	57.4	40.1	41.2
Lao PDR	90	46.4	45.8	47.8	46.2	45.1

Source: 2020 Global Food Security Index, Economist Intelligence Unit.

in the country as they are the least able to afford food. The country also ranks lowest among its five ASEAN peers, including Vietnam, in food affordability. Across the nine ASEAN countries (excluding Brunei, for which EIU does not provide data), the Philippines is outranked in overall food security by all but two (Cambodia and Lao PDR) of its neighbours—even Myanmar is more food secure.

In the nine-year period from 2012 to 2020, the Philippines had among the slowest rates of improvement in food security; it chalked up only 0.7 points, while Myanmar scored 9.1 points (Figure 11.1). While the country showed better improvement than Vietnam (+0.5) and Malaysia (−0.2), both these countries have already well exceeded the Philippines in food security starting in 2012, hence are significantly more food secure to the present.

Recalling the data on trade openness (see Table 11.3), it can be inferred that the Philippines' trade restrictiveness relative to its neighbours has been associated with lower food security. Conversely, its more trade-open ASEAN neighbours have not only achieved higher levels of food security, but have also made faster progress in improving it. Singapore, in particular, relies on imports for the bulk of its food requirements, yet is the most food secure in the ASEAN and ranks high worldwide (19th of 133 countries) (Figure 11.6).

Figure 11.6 Changes in food security index in the ASEAN countries (2012–20)

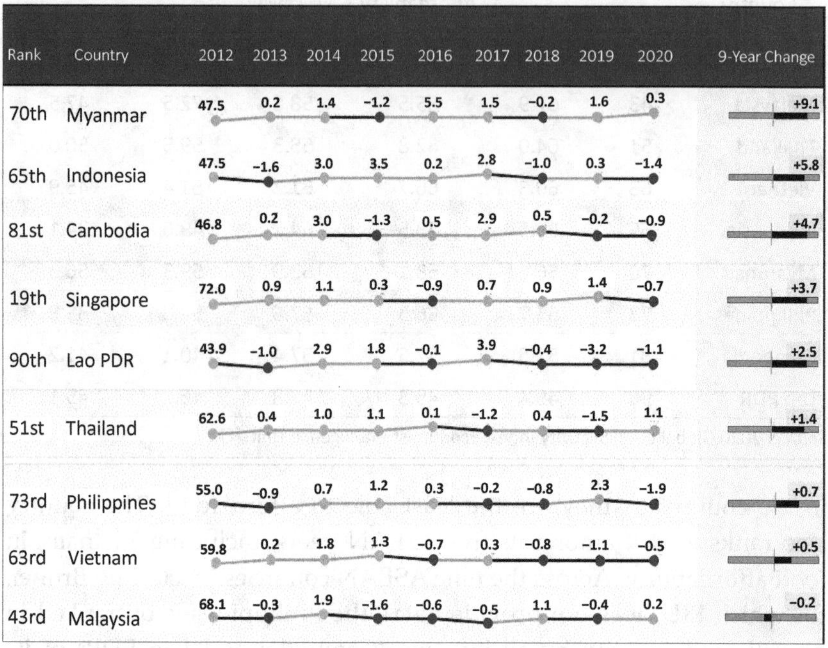

Rank	Country	2012	2013	2014	2015	2016	2017	2018	2019	2020	9-Year Change
70th	Myanmar	47.5	0.2	1.4	-1.2	5.5	1.5	-0.2	1.6	0.3	+9.1
65th	Indonesia	47.5	-1.6	3.0	3.5	0.2	2.8	-1.0	0.3	-1.4	+5.8
81st	Cambodia	46.8	0.2	3.0	-1.3	0.5	2.9	0.5	-0.2	-0.9	+4.7
19th	Singapore	72.0	0.9	1.1	0.3	-0.9	0.7	0.9	1.4	-0.7	+3.7
90th	Lao PDR	43.9	-1.0	2.9	1.8	-0.1	3.9	-0.4	-3.2	-1.1	+2.5
51st	Thailand	62.6	0.4	1.0	1.1	0.1	-1.2	0.4	-1.5	1.1	+1.4
73rd	Philippines	55.0	-0.9	0.7	1.2	0.3	-0.2	-0.8	2.3	-1.9	+0.7
63rd	Vietnam	59.8	0.2	1.8	1.3	-0.7	0.3	-0.8	-1.1	-0.5	+0.5
43rd	Malaysia	68.1	-0.3	1.9	-1.6	-0.6	-0.5	1.1	-0.4	0.2	-0.2

Source: 2020 Global Food Security Index, Economist Intelligence Unit.

These observations lend support to the argument that food security cannot be equated to food self-sufficiency, especially when restrictive trade policies lead to higher domestic food prices, thereby impacting food affordability. It stands to reason that the Philippines' high rates of severe malnutrition and stunting in young children, which would have long-term adverse consequences on labour productivity, could ultimately be traced to restrictive trade policies, especially for agricultural products, most prominently rice. For this reason, the elimination of quantitative restrictions on rice importation by law in 2019 after decades of postponing this commitment made to the World Trade Organization, is widely expected to be the game changer. It will not only improve food accessibility and affordability especially for the poor, but will ultimately impel improvement in productivity and competitiveness in the Philippine rice industry and the overall agriculture sector.

5   CONCLUSIONS AND RECOMMENDATIONS

The preceding sections traced how trade openness has impacted the current state of the Philippine economy. Reeling from the impact of a severe recession in the mid-1980s, the Philippines embarked on opening the economy through phased trade liberalization throughout the 1990s. Expecting net welfare improvement through job creation, a wider export base and sustained poverty reduction, the country underwent an economic transformation that skipped improving the productivity of the tradable sectors and instead became a services-dominated economy.

The resulting outcome was a manufacturing sector that is low value adding, a relatively protected agriculture sector that stifled productivity improvement and remained largely uncompetitive relative to the ASEAN neighbours, and a large services sector that became the main engine of growth. Consequently, poverty reduction and job creation slowed until the 2000s. Gross domestic capital formation was lured into the more protected services sector, skewing away from the tradable sectors as they were opened to international competition. With mismatched products of the education sector and (new) land owners of low-productivity agricultural lands finding overseas work more lucrative, remittances from overseas work and business process outsourcing have become the primary drivers of economic growth until the present. Meanwhile, limited trade openness in the agriculture sector has stifled improvement in exports and stunted productivity in the sector.

The current situation, nonetheless, cannot be an argument against trade openness. As discussed in the previous sections, trade openness alone cannot and did not lead to better trade performance and stronger exports, poverty reduction and improved productivity in the tradable sectors, without accompanying improvements elsewhere. It needs to be complemented with a strong domestic support mechanism involving public and private partnerships in the following: education and skills development, harmonized incentive mechanisms, facilitated and standardized ease of doing business, and public finance focused on safety nets to offset transition losses and improve productivity, among others. Hopefully, these will result in greater financial flows to the country — that is, development assistance and foreign direct investments.

Moving forward, the country has already put in place various industry roadmaps, which need to be implemented and updated considering the impact of the COVID-19 pandemic. These roadmaps need to clearly identify the implications of trade openness in terms of benefits and costs to firms, job creation, poverty alleviation and environmental sustainability, and the role that digitalization can play to convert gains for wider welfare improvement. They also need to identify imperatives associated with trade openness, if it is to have its desired results of expanded trade and employment, increased incomes, and reduced poverty and inequality. This has particular importance to agriculture, since the improvement of food security greatly hinges on significantly boosting the productivity of the whole agriculture sector, an outcome made elusive by persistent protection and historical lack of trade openness.

REFERENCES

Aldaba, Rafaelita M. 2012. "Surviving Trade Liberalization in Philippine Manufacturing". *PIDS Discussion Paper Series*, no. 2012–10. Manila: Philippine Institute for Development Studies.

Aldaba, Rafaelita M., and F. T. Aldaba. 2013. "Do FDI Inflows Have Positive Spillover Effects? The Case of the Philippine Manufacturing Industry". *Philippine Journal of Development* 37, no. 2b.

Aldaba, R. M., E. Medalla, J. Yap, M. Rosellon, F. del Prado, M. Mantaring, and V. Ledda. 2015. "How Are Firms Responding to Philippine Free Trade Agreements?". *PIDS Discussion Paper Series*, no. 2015–022. Makati City: Philippine Institute for Development Studies.

Ang, Alvin P., G. Sugiyarto, and S. Jha. 2009. "Remittances and Household Behavior in the Philippines". *ADB Economics Working Paper Series*, no. 188, December. Manila: Asian Development Bank.

Ang, A. P., J. Cruz, and N. Custodio. 2019. *The Impact of Trade on Employment in the Philippines: Country Report*. Manila: ILO Philippines Country Office.

ASEAN (Association of South East Asian Nations). 2015. *Vision and Strategic Plan for ASEAN Cooperation in Food, Agriculture and Forestry*. Jakarta, Indonesia: ASEAN Secretariat.

ASEAN Secretariat. 2015. *ASEAN Investment Report: Infrastructure Investment and Connectivity*. Jakarta, Indonesia: ASEAN Secretariat.

Asian Development Bank. 2019. *Key Indicators for Asia and the Pacific 2019*. 50th edition. Manila: Asian Development Bank.

Balisacan, Arsenio M. 2011. "What Has Really Happened to Poverty in the Philippines? New Measures, Evidence, and Policy Implications". *UPSE Discussion Paper Series*, no. 2011–14. Diliman, Quezon City: School of Economics (UPSE), University of the Philippines.

Balisacan, Arsenio M., and Ernesto M. Pernia. 2002. "Probing Beneath Cross-National Averages: Poverty, Inequality, and Growth in the Philippines". *ERD Working Paper Series*, no. 7. Manila: Asian Development Bank.

Bayangos, V. 2012. "Going with Remittances: The Case of the Philippines". *BSP Working Paper Series*, no. 2012–01, July. Manila: Bangko Sentral ng Pilipinas.

Bourguignon, F. 2004. *The Poverty-Growth-Inequality Triangle*. Washington, DC: World Bank.

Brun, Jean Francois, and Sena Kimm Gnangnon, 2017. "Does Trade Openness Contribute to Driving Financing Flows for Development". *WTO Working Paper ERSD-2017-06*. Geneva, Switzerland: World Trade Organization.

Burnside, C., and D. Dollar. 2000. "Aid, Policies and Growth". *American Economic Review 90*, no. 4: 847–68. https://doi.org/10.1257/aer.90.4.847.

———. 2004. "Aid, Policies, and Growth: Revisiting the Evidence". *Working Paper Series*, no. 3251.Washington, DC: World Bank.

Clarete, Ramon. 2005. "Ex-post Effects of Trade Liberalization in the Philippines". *UPSE Discussion Paper*, no. 2005-04. Diliman, Quezon City: School of Economics, University of the Philippines.

———. 2005. "Philippines: Ex-Post Effects of Trade Liberalization". Paper presented at the Conference on Adjusting to Trade Reforms: Major Challenges for Developing Countries, organized by the Trade Analysis Branch, United Nations Conference on Trade and Development, Geneva, Switzerland, 18–19 January 2005.

Clarete, R., and I. Villamil. 2015. "Readiness of the Philippine Agriculture and Fisheries Sectors for the 2015 ASEAN Economic Community: A Rapid Appraisal". *PIDS Discussion Paper Series*, no. 2015–43. Manila: Philippine Institute for Development Studies.

Collier, Paul. 2007. *The Bottom Billion: Why the Poorest Countries Are Failing and What Can Be Done about It*. New York: Oxford University Press.

Collier, Paul, and David Dollar. 2002. "Aid Allocation and Poverty Reduction". *European Economic Review 46*, no. 8: 1475–1500.

Cororaton, Caesar B., and J. Cockburn. 2005. "Trade Reform and Poverty in the Philippines: A Computable General Equilibrium Microsimulation Analysis". *CIRPEE Working Paper Series*, no. 05–13. Quebec, Canada: Laval University.

Cororaton, Caesar B., and E. Corong. 2006. "Agriculture-Sector Policies and Poverty in the Philippines: A Computable General Equilibrium (CGE) Analysis". *PEP Working Paper Series*, no. 2006–09. Manila.

Dollar, David, T. Kleinberg, and A. Kraay. 2013. "Growth Still Is Good for the Poor". *Policy Research Working Paper Series*, no. 6568. Washington, DC: World Bank.

Easterly, W. 2003. "Can Foreign Aid Buy Growth?". *The Journal of Economic Perspectives 17*, no. 3: 23–48. https://doi.org/10.1257/089533003769204344.

———. 2006. *The White Man's Burden: Why the West's Efforts to Aid the Rest have Done So Much Ill and So Little Good*. New York: Penguin Books.

———. 2008. "Introduction: Can't Take It Anymore?". In *Reinventing Foreign Aid*, edited by W. Easterly, pp. 1–45. London: MIT Press.

Economist Intelligence Unit. 2020. "Global Food Security Index." https://foodsecurityindex.eiu.com/Index.

Guinigundo, D.C. 2018. "The Globalisation Experience and Its Challenges for the Philippine Economy". Paper prepared for the Bank for International Settlements (BIS) Emerging Markets Deputy Governors Meeting, Basel, Switzerland, 8–9 February 2018.

Habito, Cielito F. 2016. "A Holistic Perspective on Agricultural and Rural Development". In *Farms, Food and Futures: Toward Inclusive and Sustainable Agricultural and Rural Development in South East Asia*, edited by C. F. Habito, D. Capistrano, and G. C. Saguiguit Jr., pp. 1–29. Los Baños, Philippines: Southeast Asian Regional Center for Graduate Study and Research in Agriculture.

Habito, Cielito F., Doris Capistrano, and Gil C. Saguiguit Jr., eds. 2016. *Farms, Food and Futures: Toward Inclusive and Sustainable Agricultural and Rural Development in South East Asia*. Los Baños, Philippines: Southeast Asian Regional Center for Graduate Study and Research in Agriculture.

Habito, Cielito F., and C. Cororaton. 2000. "WTO and the Philippine Economy: An Empirical and Analytical Assessment of Post-WTO Trade Reforms in the Philippines". Study Report for USAID/Philippines' AGILE Program. Manila, Philippines.

Hasan, Rana, and K. Jandoc. 2010. "Trade Liberalisation and Wage Inequality in the Philippines". *Economics Working Papers*. Manila, Philippines: Asian Development Bank.

Kang, Hyewon. 2010. "The Philippines' Absorptive Capacity for Foreign Aid". *Development Economics Working Paper Series*, no. 23097. East Asian Bureau of Economic Research. Canberra, Australia: Australian National University.

Llanto, Gilberto M., Adoracion M. Navarro, and Ma. Kristina P. Ortiz. 2015. "Development Finance and Aid in the Philippines: Policy, Institutional Arrangements and Flows". *PIDS Discussion Paper Series*, no. 2015–10. Manila: Philippine Institute for Development Studies.

Magellan Solutions. 2020. "2020 Latest Report: BPO Industry in the Philippines Statistics". https://www.magellan-solutions.com/blog/whats-the-number-analysis-of-the-latest-statistics-of-the-bpo-industry/ (accessed February 2021).

Malaluan, Nepomuceno. 2011. "Philippine Trade Liberalization: Faith Damns, Losers Can Only Weep". *Development Round Table Series (DRTS) Integrative Papers*. Quezon City, Philippines: Focus on the Global South-Philippines.

Mahembe, Edmore, and N. M. Odhiambo. 2019. "Foreign Aid and Poverty Reduction: A Review of International Literature." *Cogent Social Science* 5, no. 1:1–15.

Ministry of Foreign Affairs of Japan. 2019. *Evaluation of Japan's ODA to the Philippines*. Tokyo, Japan.

Mitra, Rajarshi, and Md. Sharif Hossain, 2013. "Foreign Aid and Economic Growth in the Philippines". Economics Bulletin, *AccessEcon* 33, no. 3: 1706–14.

Nathan Associates Inc. 2013. "Non-tariff Barriers to Trade: A Regional Agricultural Trade Environment (RATE) Summary Report". Paper prepared for the USAID project on Maximizing Agricultural Revenue through Knowledge, Enterprise Development and Trade (MARKET). USAID Regional Development Mission for Asia.

Paderon, M. M. 2017. "An Economic Evaluation of the ASEAN Free Trade Agreement (AFTA): The Case of the Philippines". *MBC Research Report*. Makati, Philippines: Makati Business Club.

PSA (Philippine Statistics Authority). 2020. "Farmers, Fisherfolks, Individuals Residing in Rural Areas and Children Posted the Highest Poverty Incidences among the Basic Sectors in 2018". https://psa.gov.ph/content/farmers-fisherfolks-individuals-residing-rural-areas-and-children-posted-highest-poverty.

Ravago, M. V., A. M. Balisacan, and M. A. Sombilla. 2018. "Current Structure and Future Challenges of the Agricultural Sector". In *The Future of Philippine Agriculture: Scenarios, Policies, and Investments under Climate Change*, edited by M. Rosegrant and M. Sombilla. Singapore: Institute of Southeast Asian Studies.

Remulla, Marriel M., and G.M. Medina. 2012. "Measuring the Contribution to the Philippine Economy of Information Technology Business Process Outsourcing (IT-BPO) Services". *Bangko Sentral Review* 14 no. 1: 1–16.

Reyes, C., and A. Tabuga. 2011. "A Note on Economic Growth, Inequality, and Poverty in the Philippines". *Discussion Paper Series*, no. 2011-30. Manila: Philippine Institute for Development Studies.

Riddell, Roger C. 2008. *Does Foreign Aid Really Work?* New York: Oxford University Press.

Sawada, Yasuyuki, and J. P. Estudillo. 2006. "Trade, Migration, and Poverty Reduction in the Globalizing Economy: The Case of the Philippines". *Research Paper 2006/058*. Helsinki: UNU-WIDER.

Sibal, Jorge. 2005. "The Effects of Globalization and Economic Restructuring on Philippine Labor Policies and the Responses of the Actors of the Philippine Industrial Relations System". Paper presented at International Society of Labour and Social Security Law (ISLSSL), Eighth Asian Regional Congress, Taiwan, 31 October–3 November 2005.

UNDP. 2010. "Assessment of Development Results: Evaluation of UNDP Contribution to the Philippines". Evaluation Office. New York: United Nations Development Programme.

Vathis, Oresthis. 2013. "Aide Effectiveness: A Literature Review". *The Jean Monet Papers on Political Economy*. University of the Peloponnese. https://www.uop.gr/jean-monnet-papers.

Wong, Larry C. Y., and Lourdes S. Adriano. 2016. "Regional Integration as Anchor of Sustainable Agricultural and Rural Development". In *Farms, Food and Futures: Toward Inclusive and Sustainable Agricultural and Rural Development in South East Asia*, edited by C. F. Habito, D. Capistrano, and G. C. Saguiguit Jr., pp. 31–88. Los Baños, Philippines: Southeast Asian Regional Center for Graduate Study and Research in Agriculture.

World Bank. 2015. *World Development Report 2015: Mind, Society and Behavior*. Washington, DC: World Bank.

———. 2018. *Making Growth Work for the Poor: A Poverty Assessment for the Philippines*. Washington, DC: World Bank.

World Health Organization. 2015. "Stunting in a Nutshell". https://www.who.int/news/item/19-11-2015-stunting-in-a-nutshell.

12 Reaching for the Demographic Dividend to Achieve Inclusive Economic Growth

Dennis S. Mapa, Ernesto M. Pernia and Lisa Grace S. Bersales

I BACKGROUND AND INTRODUCTION

The past seven decades, starting in the 1950s, have seen rapid changes in the population age structure of most countries across the world, notably in the Asia-Pacific region. This phenomenon, known as the demographic transition, had opened a window of opportunity for countries to experience rapid economic growth over a fairly long period, accompanied by poverty reduction. Backed by right policies on human capital, labour market, public health, infrastructure and governance, the demographic transition had accounted for a substantial portion of the economic growth—known as the demographic dividend—experienced by the "Asian tigers" (mainly South Korea, Taiwan and Singapore) from the early 1960s to the 1990s.

Demographic transition is the link between population dynamics (or changing age structure) and economic development. It denotes a change from a situation of high fertility and high mortality to one of low fertility and low mortality (Figure 12.1). A country that undergoes demographic transition experiences sizable changes in the age distribution of the population, which, in turn, positively influence economic growth, given the right socio-economic policies.

Figure 12.1. Declining mortality, declining fertility and the demographic transition

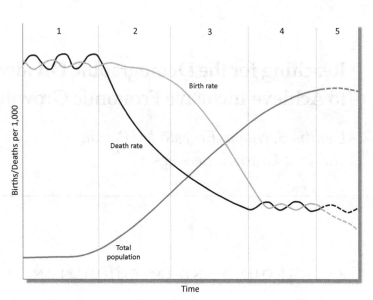

Sources: International Union for the Scientific Study of Population (IUSSP) and United Nations Population Fund (UNFPA).

The demographic transition has three phases, each having a different impact on a country's economic growth and development. The first phase is an initial decline in infant mortality (death rate), with fertility rate (birth rate) remaining high. This leads to an expansion in the number of children, resulting in increased demand for basic education, primary health care, nutrition, and other services. This was the situation in the Philippines in 2000 (Figure 12.2). The country had an increasing youth dependency ratio (population aged 0–14 years to total population), posing a challenge to the economy as scarce resources had to be channelled to consumption spending instead of investment from savings for economic growth (Mapa and Bersales 2008).

In the second phase, the proportion of working-age population (persons aged 15–64 years) is larger relative to the young dependents (aged 0–14 years) and the older population (65 years and above). This was the situation in Thailand in 2000 (Figure 12.3). The policy challenge in the second phase is how the labour market can absorb the increased working-age group, particularly those aged 15–24 years. If employment opportunities are made available, the country's economic growth accelerates during this phase.

Figure 12.2. Phase 1 of demographic transition (Philippines, 2000)

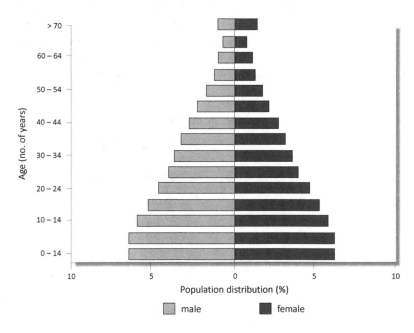

Figure 12.3. Phase 2 of demographic transition (Thailand, 2000)

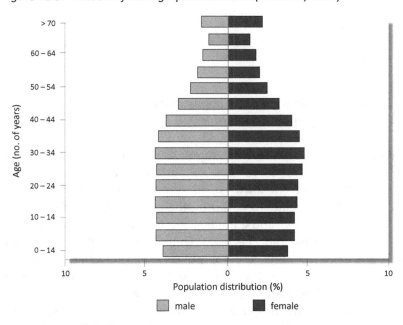

In the third and final phase of the transition, the share of the older population (those aged 65 years and above) expands relative to the total population. This was the situation in Japan in 2000 (Figure 12.4). The challenge to a country's economy in this phase is that the consumption of the older people (especially for healthcare services) grows faster than the output of the working population, while their income declines.

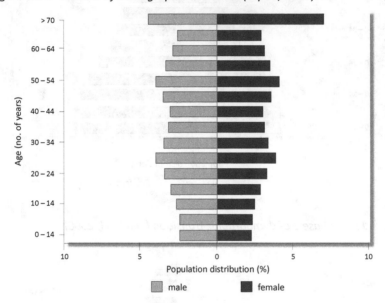

Figure 12.4. Phase 3 of demographic transition (Japan, 2000)

1.1 Demographic window of opportunity and demographic dividend

Studies on the impact of the demographic transition on economic growth show that it accounts for a sizeable portion—estimated by various authors to be about one-third—of the economic growth experienced by East Asia's economic tigers during the period 1965–95 (Bloom and Williamson 1997; Bloom and Canning 2001; Bloom, Canning, and Sevilla 2001; Radelet, Sachs, and Lee 1997). Unlike most Southeast and East Asian countries, however, the Philippines failed to achieve a similar demographic transition in the same period. The mortality rates in these countries (including the Philippines) declined at broadly similar rates. However, fertility rates dropped slowly in the Philippines, resulting in a persistently high population growth rate compared with its neighbours.

Accordingly, the country's demographic transition has been extremely slow and its demographic dividend correspondingly negligible. The sluggish fertility decline in the Philippines can be attributed in no small measure to the adamant opposition of the Catholic Church hierarchy, backed by conservative "pro-life" groups, to the government's family planning programme, which, initiated in 1969, was effectively scuttled in the late 1970s (Pernia 2011).

1.1.1 First demographic dividend

The effect of the demographic transition on income growth is referred to as the first demographic dividend. During the demographic transition, countries experience an increasing share of the working-age population relative to the total population, resulting in higher per capita income. To measure the impact of the demographic transition on income growth in the Philippines, Mapa and Balisacan (2004) use cross-country data from 80 countries over the period 1975–2000. They show that differences in the population age structure of Thailand (in the second phase of the demographic transition) and the Philippines (in first phase of the demographic transition) account for about 0.77 percentage points of forgone average annual growth (missed first dividend) for the Philippines from 1975 to 2000, other things being equal (including economic policies). This forgone growth cumulates to about 22 per cent of the average income per person by year 2000. The loss becomes even more remarkable when translated to monetary values: instead of a per capita gross domestic product (GDP) of merely US$993 in 2000, Filipinos could have had US$1,210. Moreover, poverty would have been reduced by about 3.6 million persons, resulting in a palpably lower poverty incidence in 2000.

A follow-up study by Mapa, Balisacan, and Briones (2006) to measure the missing first dividend, this time using Philippine provincial data from 1985 to 2003, shows that a 1.0 percentage point increase in the proportion of young dependents in 1985 (proxy for the demographic transition variable) results in an estimated 9.0 basis points decrease in the average growth of income per person in the provinces, ceteris paribus (controlling for other factors). This shows that had the provincial average proportion of young dependents in 1985 been lower at 36 per cent (the average for the lowest 10 provinces) instead of a high of 42 per cent (the actual value), the average per capita income growth could have risen by 0.63 percentage points per year, representing an increase of 7.12 per cent in the average per capita income in 2003.

1.1.2 Second demographic dividend

In addition to the commonly identified first dividend, Mason (2007) discusses another form of dividend from the demographic transition, referring to it as the second demographic dividend. This second dividend is realized from society's response to the prospect of an ageing population as the nation's age structure enters the third phase of the demographic transition. The challenge facing societies (and governments) when a substantial proportion of the population becomes older is how to support their consumption, given their reduced income. The common approaches to this problem include: (a) relying on public (or familial) transfer systems, (b) increasing saving rates and (c) accumulating greater physical wealth or capital. Individuals accumulate savings in their working years, which serve as a buffer during retirement years. While capital accumulation can be used to deal with the life-cycle deficit in the older ages, it also influences economic growth. Increased savings rate in a society results in a more rapid economic growth, creating the second demographic dividend. Mason (2007) estimates that the first and second demographic dividends accounted for about one-third of the yearly average per capita growth rate of Japan from 1950 to 1980.

It should be emphasized, though, that demographic dividends are not automatic. The demographic transition simply creates a window of opportunity that, when coupled with the right kind of policy environment, ushers in a sustained period of economic growth. The growing number of adults (particularly those aged 15–24 years) during the second phase of the transition will be productive only when the labour market is flexible, allowing for expansion. Government policies play a critical role in guaranteeing the generation of the demographic dividend.

This paper looks into the population age structure of the Philippines, using the population census, birth and fertility data, and projections of future population from the Philippine Statistics Authority (PSA), to estimate how these factors impact the demographic transition of the country. It aims to show the challenges to reaping the demographic dividend, given the impact of the COVID-19 pandemic in terms of higher unemployment rates and business losses or closures. It shows as well the challenges to achieving the objectives of *Ambisyon Natin* 2040 for a strongly rooted, comfortable and secure life (*matatag, maginhawa at panatag na buhay*) for Filipinos (Balisacan 2018). (*Ambisyon Natin 2040* is a long-term visioning exercise, based on a nationwide survey of about 10,000 respondents and over 300 citizen participants in focus group discussions.)

2 ACCELERATING THE DEMOGRAPHIC TRANSITION: LOW FERTILITY IS KEY

The links between rapid population growth—or high total fertility rate (TFR)—of a country and its economic growth and poverty incidence have been amply studied and documented across the world. The common conclusion is that rapid population growth in poor and developing countries constrains economic development, pushing the next generation of citizens into a poverty trap. In response, many countries have initiated or expanded voluntary programmes to reduce fertility rates among households. In the Philippines, after years of advocacy by civil society organizations, the government enacted the Responsible Parenthood and Reproductive Health Act of 2012 (Republic Act 10354), widely known as the RH Law, in December 2012. The RH Law guarantees free access to practically all modern contraceptive methods for all citizens, especially impoverished communities, at government health centres.

How can the demographic transition be accelerated so that it opens the window of opportunity for the demographic dividend? The necessary condition for a country to speed up the demographic transition is to lower its fertility rate. Sachs (2008) points out that demographic transitions, where they have occurred, have typically been accelerated and even triggered by proactive government policies related to voluntary reduction in fertility rates, particularly among poor households.

2.1 The Goldilocks period: Replacement fertility rate

As countries move from large families (high fertility rate) and high poverty into small families (low fertility), high living standards and ageing, they pass through what is called a Goldilocks period, wherein for a generation or two the fertility rate is neither too high nor too low (*The Economist* 2009). Such fertility rate, consistent with a stable population, is around 2.1 (average total number of children per woman during her reproductive years), which is also known as the replacement fertility rate. Achieving the replacement fertility rate is a unique and valuable opportunity for a country's higher economic growth and inclusivity (Pernia and Pernia 2015).

Table 12.1 shows the total fertility rates for selected countries in East Asia from 1960 to 2017. The rich countries that have gone through the demographic transition, as well as the poor countries racing through it, and achieved the replacement fertility rate of 2.1 are as follows: Singapore in the mid-1970s, South Korea in the mid-1980s, Thailand in 1990, Vietnam in 2006 and Brunei Darussalam and Malaysia in 2013. On the other hand, five countries have TFRs above 2.1 in 2017: the Philippines (2.7), Lao PDR (2.7), Cambodia (2.5), Indonesia (2.3) and Myanmar (2.2).

Table 12.1. Total fertility rate (TFR) in the ASEAN and South Korea (1960–2017)

Country	Year							
	1960	1970	1980	1990	2000	2006	2013	2017
South Korea	5.7	4.5	2.8	1.6	1.5	1.1	1.2	1.1
ASEAN 5								
Singapore	5.5	3.1	1.7	1.9	1.4	1.3	1.2	1.2
Thailand	6.4	5.3	3.2	2.1	1.9	1.9	1.4	1.5
Indonesia	5.5	5.4	4.4	3.1	2.4	2.2	2.3	2.3
Malaysia	6.8	5.5	4.2	3.7	3.0	2.7	2.0	2.0
Philippines	7.0	6.2	5.2	4.3	3.6	3.3	3.0	2.7
Rest of Southeast Asia								
Vietnam	6.1	5.9	5.0	3.6	1.9	2.1	1.7	2.0
Myanmar	6.1	6.0	4.5	3.4	2.4	2.1	1.9	2.2
Brunei Darussalam	6.8	5.6	4.0	3.2	2.6	2.3	2.0	1.9
Cambodia	6.3	5.8	5.8	5.7	4.0	3.3	2.9	2.5
Lao PDR	6.4	6.4	6.4	6.1	4.0	3.3	3.0	2.7

Note: TFR is the average number of children a woman would bear during her lifetime given current age-specific fertility rates.

Source: World Development Indicators, World Bank.

The slow pace of TFR reduction in the Philippines, from about 7.0 in 1960 to 2.7 in 2017 or a measly 1.7 per cent per year, can be attributed to the lack of a clear and sustained government policy, induced by the Catholic Church hierarchy and conservative groups, on population management (including family planning), resulting in a persistently low contraceptive prevalence rate. Comparing the Philippines and Vietnam, a study conducted by the National Transfer Accounts (2012) concludes that the Philippines is experiencing a slower demographic transition due to its continued high fertility rate; it will be in 2050 when the country is expected to have a favourable demographic condition like Vietnam's, but without the important opportunities to save and invest (results of the first and second demographic dividends) that Vietnam has been experiencing since 2010.

The country's average TFR in 2017 was 2.7, and the picture worsens when TFRs across the different wealth quintiles are compared (Table 12.2). While the TFR of the poorest 20 per cent of households in the country decreased slowly from 2008 to 2017, it still registered a high of 4.3 in 2017, similar to the country's average TFR in 1990. Given the close relationship between number of children and poverty incidence, it is not surprising that these households were caught in the vicious cycle of high fertility and high poverty.

Table 12.2. Total fertility rate (TFR) by wealth quintile (2008, 2013 and 2017)

Wealth quintile	Total fertility rate		
	NDHS 2008	NDHS 2013	NDHS 2017
Bottom (poorest)	5.2	5.2	4.3
Second	4.2	3.7	3.2
Third	3.3	3.1	2.6
Fourth	2.7	2.4	2.1
Highest (richest)	1.9	1.7	1.7
Overall	3.3	3.0	2.7

Note: The TFR has a three-year reference period.

Sources: National Demographic and Health Survey (NHDS) 2008 and 2013, Philippine Statistics Authority (PSA).

Table 12.3 shows the regional TFRs for the survey periods 1998, 2003, 2008, 2013 and 2017. Of the 17 regions, only the National Capital Region (NCR) has a TFR (1.9) below the replacement rate of 2.1 in 2017. The rest have average TFRs above this replacement rate; seven regions have at least 3.0. The regions with the highest TFRs in 2017—Autonomous Region in Muslim Mindanao/Bangsamoro Autonomous Region in Muslim Mindanao (ARMM/BARMM) and Bicol Region—are also among those with the highest poverty incidence among families (ARMM/BARMM with 54.2% and Bicol with 20.0%), as officially reported by the PSA in 2018.

Table 12.3.   Total fertility rate (TFR) by region (1998, 2003, 2008, 2013 and 2017)

Region	Total fertility rate				
	1998	2003	2008	2013	2017
NCR	2.5	2.8	2.3	2.3	1.9
CAR	4.8	3.8	3.3	2.9	2.5
Ilocos Region	3.4	3.8	3.4	2.8	2.6
Cagayan Valley	3.6	3.4	4.1	3.2	3.1
Central Luzon	3.5	3.1	3.0	2.8	2.4
CALABARZON	3.7	3.2	3.0	2.7	2.6
MIMAROPA	–	5.0	4.3	3.7	2.9
Bicol Region	5.5	4.3	4.1	4.1	3.2
Western Visayas	4.0	4.0	3.3	3.8	3.0
Central Visayas	3.7	3.6	3.2	3.2	2.5
Eastern Visayas	5.9	4.6	4.3	3.5	3.1
Zamboanga Peninsula	3.9	4.2	3.8	3.5	3.6
Northern Mindanao	4.8	3.8	3.3	3.5	3.1
Davao Region	3.7	3.1	3.3	2.9	2.7
SOCCSKSARGEN	4.2	4.2	3.6	3.2	3.4
Caraga	4.7	4.1	4.3	3.6	3.0
ARMM/BARMM	4.6	4.2	4.3	4.2	3.1

Note: NCR = National Capital Region
CAR = Cordillera Administrative Region
CALABARZON = Cavite, Laguna, Batangas, Rizal and Quezon
MIMAROPA = Mindoro, Marinduque, Romblon and Palawan
SOCCSKSARGEN = South Cotabato, Cotabato, Sultan Kudarat, Sarangani and General Santos
ARMM/BARMM = Autonomous Region in Muslim Mindanao/Bangsamoro Autonomous Region in Muslim Mindanao

Source: National Demographic and Health Survey (NDHS), Philippine Statistics Authority.

3   POLICY LEVERS IN REDUCING FERTILITY RATES

The critical factor in taking advantage of the demographic window of opportunity is to reduce fertility rate to a degree conducive to higher economic growth. Government policy intervention that also strengthens private efforts to lower fertility rate, thereby benefiting not only families but society as a whole, is a public good initiative (Pernia 2007). Herrin and Costello (1996) identify three possible sources of future population growth (estimated at an average of 1.9% per year during the period 2000–2010): (a) unwanted fertility, (b) wanted fertility and (c) population momentum. Our estimates show that unwanted fertility contributes about 16 per cent to future population growth, wanted fertility adds another 19 per cent, and population momentum contributes the remaining bulk of 65 per cent.[1] Government intervention through the RH Law can significantly lower the country's overall fertility rate, particularly among the poorest 20 per cent of the population where TFR is highest (Pernia et al. 2011).

Simulations by Mapa, Balisacan, and Corpuz (2010), using the 2008 TFR of 3.3 as base value, show that the Goldilocks period (TFR of 2.1) will be reached by 2030 under the business-as-usual scenario. In another (second) scenario where government intervention (i.e., sustained implementation of the RH Law) targets only households with unwanted fertility and has a 90 per cent success rate, the Goldilocks period will be achieved 10 years sooner or by 2020. The TFR of the poorest 20 per cent will be at a more manageable level of 2.3 by 2040. Without government intervention, however, the TFR of the poorest 20 per cent of the households will still be at a high of 3.5 by 2040.

---

[1] Births are considered unwanted if they occur after a woman has reached the point at which she does not wish to continue childbearing. All other births, including those that are mistimed are considered wanted. Population momentum refers to the tendency of population growth to continue beyond the time that replacement-level fertility has been achieved because of a relatively high concentration of people in the childbearing years. This phenomenon is due to past high fertility rates, which result in a large number of young people. As these young people grow older and move through the reproductive ages, the greater number of births will exceed the number of deaths in the older populations. Population momentum is relevant to the Philippines because its population is composed mostly of young individuals (median age is 23–25 years).

Indeed, there is a pressing need to identify policies that will reduce, or better yet eliminate, unwanted fertility to speed up the demographic transition. On the other hand, it is also important to identify other policy options that will help lower the fertility rate by targeting the effects of wanted fertility (e.g., encouraging households to reduce family size) and the population momentum. It should be noted that wanted fertility and population momentum contribute an estimated 84 per cent to future population growth. Efforts to lower fertility through direct government policy (e.g., RH Law) can complement the other policy options aimed at lowering wanted fertility and lessening the impact of population momentum. The challenge is to identify the drivers of income growth, which have been shown to be a major determinant of fertility rate. A second-best solution to the problem is to identify which of these drivers have the most impact on fertility rate for a given amount of investment.

McNicoll (2006) identifies some key policy lessons from the demographic transition that played a crucial role in the "East Asian economic miracle" (countries studied were China, Indonesia, Malaysia, South Korea, Taiwan, Thailand and Vietnam). Primarily, government policies in three relevant areas significantly influence the acceleration of the demographic transition: health services, family planning and education.

Three main fertility-reducing variables have merited the attention of researchers in demography and economics: education of women, female labour force participation and health of children. These determinants have also been the mainstream policy variables that influence income growth or economic well-being. Studies have shown these three variables to be significant in reducing fertility rate; hence, many have considered them as feasible solutions to the problems brought about by rapid population growth. It is also worth noting that these solutions could be viewed as second-best policy options in lowering fertility rate; that is, these are different from addressing biological and behavioural factors through which socio-economic, cultural and environmental variables affect fertility (Bongaarts 1978). The latter set of variables are called the intermediate fertility determinants and include exposure factors (proportion married), deliberate marital fertility control factors (contraception) and natural marital fertility factors (sterility, spontaneous intrauterine mortality and duration of the fertile period).[2]

---

[2] See Davis and Blake (1956) for a more detailed discussion.

3.1 Education of women

Education is a key determinant of fertility; it is commonly deemed to be negatively correlated with fertility. This idea is supported by an economic theory of fertility, whereby women value the sum quality of all their offspring and optimize fertility and child investment choices accordingly (Becker 1960). There are several channels through which women's education can affect fertility.[3] First, a higher permanent income due to better education will induce a woman to tilt her optimal fertility choices towards fewer offspring of higher quality (Mincer 1963; Becker and Lewis 1973). Second, a highly educated woman will more likely pair herself with a highly educated man via what is called positive assortative mating, which can further increase household permanent income and alter optimal fertility choices (Behrman and Rosenzweig 2002). Third, a woman's education may directly improve her knowledge of fertility options and healthy pregnancy, as well as her ability to process the information, thereby resulting in lower fertility rate (Grossman 1972).

Education affects fertility at the aggregate and individual levels. At the aggregate level,[4] proxy variables include the number of schools in the nearby village where the household is located (Casterline 1985), average length of education on cumulated fertility (Tienda, Diaz, and Smith 1985), measures of cumulated fertility and proximate determinants (Lesthaeghe et al. 1985), proportion of women with post-primary education (Hirschman and Guest 1990), mean educational level in the community (Thomas 1999) and proportion of literate women (Steele, Diamond, and Wang 1996). The results of these different studies show that the aggregate level of education has negative effects on the first- and higher-order births. Moreover, women living in areas with a higher percentage of literate women and high average level of education have weaker fertility desires than women with the same educational level but living in other areas (Kravdal 2001). This result, however, is only significant in models with an urban or rural area as part of the control variables. By facilitating the diffusion of new ideas and information on the advantages of smaller families and by presenting a new set of opportunities to women that make childbearing and rearing more costly, households in more highly educated communities promote lower fertility (Tienda, Diaz, and Smith 1985).

---

[3] These are drawn from McCrary and Royer (2011).
[4] See Kravdal (2001) for a more detailed discussion.

At the individual level, education creates a substantial and significant difference in fertility between an educated and an uneducated woman. The former normally displays lower fertility than the latter. Kravdal (2001) summarizes the reasons why this is so: (1) high opportunity costs of childbearing involved in some types of work that may be offered to the better educated woman, (2) cash expenses and children's reduced contribution to domestic and agricultural work as a result of children's schooling, which tends to be encouraged by educated mothers, (3) reduced need for children as an old-age security, (4) higher prevalence of nucleated families, which may reduce fertility partly because childbearing costs must be covered to a larger extent by parents, (5) stronger desire to spend more time caring for the child and to invest more in each child, (6) stronger preferences for consumer goods or other sources of satisfaction, (7) lower infant and child mortality (due to better maternal knowledge), (8) possible stimulating impact of higher purchasing power resulting from the educated woman's own work or marriage into a relatively rich family, (9) relatively higher age before entering married life among better educated women, and (10) knowledge and acceptance of modern contraception and ability to use it sufficiently, as well as more efficient use of traditional methods because of better knowledge of their own bodies. Further, these studies have shown that women's schooling is negatively correlated with fertility and positively correlated with contraception use.

Significantly, it is argued that while investment in primary education is necessary, it is better to invest in higher levels of education as fertility and contraception models show that the impact increases with education level (Tuman, Ayoub, and Roth-Johnson 2007). Some econometric models show a positive relationship between some primary schooling and fertility, suggesting that schooling does not negatively affect fertility until the secondary level (Ainsworth, Beegle, and Nyamete 1996). Additionally, research suggests that higher levels of education have a strong negative effect on fertility in rural areas, a finding that is associated with women's labour market potential.

3.2 Labour force participation of women

The relationship between fertility and female labour force participation is supported by empirical studies, such as Easterlin's (1973, 1980) relative income hypothesis, Becker's (1981) new home economics, and

Cigno's (1992) and Cigno and Rosati's (1996) asset theory of children.[5] The relative income hypothesis emphasizes the role of male incomes relative to economic aspirations as the driving force behind fertility and female labour force participation. The new home economics theory stresses the role of female wages, representing the opportunity costs of childbearing, as determinant of fertility. Finally, the asset theory of children focuses on children as investment goods in a model of intergenerational transfers.

Like women's education, labour force participation is also important in explaining women's fertility behaviour, including childbearing and child-rearing. Childbearing is time-consuming, often restricting the parents, particularly the mother, from participating in the labour market (Weller 1977). Similarly, childcaring and rearing have a negative relationship with female labour force participation and fertility. Brewster and Rindfuss (2000) show that the mother's time spent on childcare has a significant negative effect on the likelihood of having another birth and reduces the mother's labour supply (Hotz and Miller 1988)—a relationship observed mostly in developing countries. Women in developing countries are less likely to participate in the labour market when they have multiple births (Porter and King 2009). Using sex of the first child as instrument for fertility decisions in Korea, Chun and Oh (2002) find that, on average, having an additional child reduces labour force participation by almost 40 per cent. Adsera (2003) finds that, on the one hand, when unemployment is low and institutions easily accommodate the entry into or exit from the labour market, fertility rates are around replacement rate. On the other hand, whenever the costs of childbearing in terms of loss of present or future income are higher due to high unemployment and rigid labour markets, fertility rates are very low. Government employment can have positive effects on fertility as it provides more stable opportunities for women's employment during economic downturns as well as more liberal leave programmes. In developed countries, women in general have found ways to combine work and child-rearing (Brewster and Rindfuss 2000).

---

[5] See McNown and Rajbhandary (2003) for more information on these theories.

3.3 Child mortality

The negative relationship between mortality[6] and fertility is explained by two hypotheses. The child survival hypothesis refers to the parents' perceptions of the child mortality conditions in their social setting, while the child replacement hypothesis refers to the parents' response to mortality incidence in their own household. Scrimshaw (1978) believes that the assumption that high fertility is a necessary biological and behavioural response to high mortality is manifested in different theories or hypotheses: the demographic transition theory states that mortality declines are eventually followed by fertility declines; child replacement hypothesis says that parents try to replace children who die; and child survival hypothesis states that couples target a specific number of children who can survive to adulthood. Ben-Porath (1976) discusses two types of fertility response to child mortality: (a) hoarding or the parents' response to expected mortality, and (b) replacement or the parents' response to an experienced death of a child in the household. Using micro data of retrospectively reported births of Israeli women, he shows that experienced mortality reduces the probability of stopping at a given birth and reduces the intervals between births. Hondroyiannis and Papapetrou (2002) show that, in the long run, a decrease in infant mortality rates reduces fertility rates, controlling for economic performance and the labour market policies.

However, some researchers remain sceptical about the fertility-inflating effects of child mortality. For instance, Sah (1991) argues that a single-stage choice model can only give ambiguous explanation of the mortality-fertility relationship. Presenting a more complex fertility model, he shows the contrary: fertility increases as mortality rate declines. Dyson and Murphy (1985) also show that, in some cases, a decline in mortality rate can be accompanied by a brief increase in fertility rate due to the contemporaneous changes in other factors such as a decrease in widowhood and disease-related sterility. Using data from Pakistan and Bangladesh where moderately high levels of fertility and mortality are observed, Chowdhury, Khan, and Chen (1976) find no significant evidence of increased desire to replace a child in households that experienced a death of a child. In summary, the research studies have varying results on whether reducing child mortality will reduce fertility rate, controlling for other factors.

---

[6] In the literature, mortality can refer to either infant or child mortality.

4 INTRA-COUNTRY ECONOMETRIC MODELS

An econometric model using an intra-country provincial panel data[7] is constructed to quantify the impact of women's education (average number of years of schooling), health services (proxied by under-5 mortality rate), family planning (using contraceptives, both modern and natural methods) and employment rate of women (aged 15–49 years) on total fertility rate (average number of births a woman would have during her entire reproductive age: 15–49 years old). The TFR model of the ith province in year t, with independent variables as defined in Table 12.4, is:

$$TFRit = \alpha + \beta_1 Ypc_{it} + \beta_2 Educ_{it} + \beta_3 LFPR_{it} + \beta_4 U5MR_{it} + \beta_5 CPR_{it} + \varepsilon_{it}, \quad \varepsilon_{it} \sim (0,\sigma^2).$$

The panel data set covers the period 1993, 1998, 2003, 2008 and 2013. These years coincide with the National Demographic and Health Survey (NDHS) that PSA conducts every five years. The data are supplemented by provincial averages on other variables using the PSA's Labor Force Survey (LFS) and Family Income and Expenditure Survey (FIES).

Table 12.4 shows the results of the econometric model employed to determine the factors that influence the average number of children a woman aged 15–49 years (TFR) would have. Interestingly, controlling for other factors such as per capita income, education of the woman has the largest impact on TFR. The result shows that increasing the number of years of schooling of a married woman by one more year will decrease TFR by about 0.25 children (using the fixed effects model). This result supports the findings of McNicoll (2006) that education, particularly of women, plays a significant role in accelerating the demographic transition in East Asian economies. Moreover, education has a positive and significant effect on the average per capita income growth rate of the country. In an earlier study based on Philippine data from 1985 to 2003, Mapa, Balisacan, and Briones (2006) show that education of the household head (the variable used in their econometric model) has a significant and positive impact on the average per capita income growth.

---

[7] The provincial database of the former Asia-Pacific Policy Center (APPC) was updated and used in the econometric models. The resulting provincial panel data set has 73 cross sectional units (provinces) and 5 time periods (1993, 1998, 2003, 2008 and 2013), for a total of 365 observations.

Table 12.4. Econometric models for total children ever born (TFR) (provincial panel data, 1993–2013)

Variable	Model 1 Least squares	Model 2 Panel fixed effects
Log of per capita income (Ypc)	−0.290**	−0.160
Average years of education of women (Educ)	−0.270	−0.250***
Labour force participation rate of women (LFPR)	0.001	−0.020***
Under-5 mortality rate (U5MR)	0.008***	0.003*
Contraceptive prevalence rate (CPR)	−1.410***	−1.520**
Constant	8.623***	6.347***
N	362	362
R-Squared	0.361	0.215
F-Stat	33.420	18.760
p-value	0.000	0.000

Note: (1) Panel fixed effects model is better compared with least squares based on unobserved effects F-test.
(2) Significance: * 10% level one-sided test, ** 5% level, *** 1% level of significance

That is, increasing the household head's education by one more year will increase the average yearly per capita income growth rate by about 0.16 to 0.27 percentage points, all things being the same. This shows that education is a significant factor in decreasing total fertility rate and in increasing average income growth rate.

As regards contraceptive prevalence rate (CPR, proxy for family planning), the empirical results show that it is negatively and significantly related to TFR, holding other factors constant. In model 2, increasing modern CPR by 10 percentage points will decrease current TFR by about 0.15, controlling for other factors. The results suggest that the government should increase CPR, particularly modern family planning methods, to significantly reduce the country's total fertility rate. Currently, the CPR in the Philippines is quite low, estimated at only 48.9 per cent in 2011, lower than the CPR of 50.6 per cent in 2006.[8]

---

[8] Data from the 2011 Family Health Survey (FHS) show that overall CPR decreased to 48.9 per cent from 50.6 per cent in 2006. Modern methods constitute 36.9 percentage points of the 48.9 per cent CPR in 2011, with traditional method at 12 percentage points. The 2010 target of the Commission on Population and Development was to increase CPR to 60 per cent, which obviously was not realized.

Another relevant variable that significantly reduces fertility rate is under-5 mortality rate (U5MR), the proxy for quality of health services. The result from the econometric model shows that decreasing U5MR by 1 per 1,000 children will decrease the TFR by about 0.003, holding the other factors constant. As in the education variable, this empirical result is consistent with the findings of McNicoll (2006) that preventive measures for health outcomes offer a relatively high pay-off in terms of reducing fertility rates, as experienced by the East Asian economies.

Women's employment rate is also negatively and significantly related to fertility rate. Table 12.4 shows that if women's employment rate increases by 10 percentage points, TFR will decrease by about 0.20, holding all other factors constant.

5 Twin Challenges to Obtaining the Demographic Dividend: High Fertility and High Youth Unemployment Rates

Changes in the age structure of the population affect the growth of the economy because people earn and consume at different levels over their lifetime. For example, working adults in the aggregate produce more than they consume, while young children and the older group consume more than they produce. Understanding what happens during the economic life cycle, which varies depending on the population structure of the economy, is essential to understanding the strength of the potential demographic opportunity for the country. Lowering the country's total fertility rate is key to earning the demographic dividend. It is the necessary condition for speeding up the demographic transition. As Sachs (2008) points out, in countries that have undergone the demographic transition (e.g., Japan, South Korea, China, Singapore, Thailand and Vietnam), the changes in the population structure had typically been triggered and accelerated by proactive government policies related to voluntary fertility reduction, particularly among poor households.

While the TFR of the Philippines in 2017 was relatively high at 2.7, the silver lining is that it has been trending down in recent years, albeit slowly. As Figure 12.5 shows, annual crude birth rates (number of births per 1000 population) have been declining from 19.14 in 2010 to 15.60 in 2019 to 13.94 in 2020.[9]

---

[9] The number for 2020 is preliminary because of a substantial number of late reporting of births due to the lockdown caused by the COVID-19 pandemic.

Figure 12.5. Crude birth rates in the Philippines (2010–20)

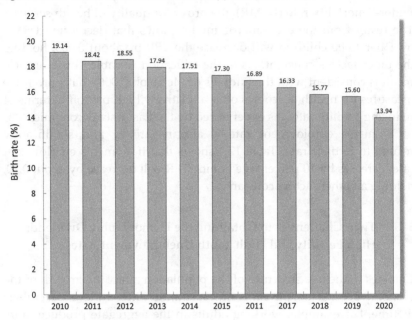

Note: The value in 2020 is preliminary.
Source: Philippine Statistics Authority.

The more active implementation of the family planning policy by the Duterte administration seems to be bearing fruit, resulting in reduced number of children of couples; it has the potential to gain momentum in the coming years, thereby surpassing the first challenge of the demographic dividend—high fertility. A threat to this gain, however, is the possible uptick in fertility rates due to the lockdown during the pandemic. More couples staying at home for long periods of time may result in a spike in the number of births.

Figure 12.6 shows the labour force participation rates (LFPR) of males and females in the country from the second quarter of 2005 to the fourth quarter of 2020. A downward trend is observed in the LFPR of women beginning 2016, reaching a trough during the second quarter of 2020 at 41.5 per cent (when the strictest lockdown was imposed). The LFPR of women in 2020 is recorded at only 45.9 per cent, nearly 2 percentage points lower than the previous year's 47.9 per cent. The shock in the LFPR of women resulting from the impact of the COVID-19 pandemic is a potential threat to the gains in reducing the overall fertility rate of the

Figure 12.6. Labour force participation rate (LFPR) in the Philippines (male and female, 2nd quarter 2005 to 4th quarter 2020)

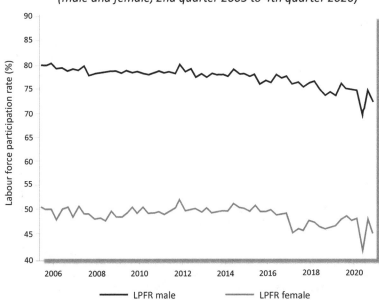

Source: Philippine Statistics Authority.

country. As previously shown in the intra-country econometric model, increasing the labour force participation of women significantly reduces the overall TFR.

The bigger challenge for the country as regards the demographic dividend is the high unemployment rate, which has been exacerbated by the pandemic. As previously noted, the demographic dividend does not automatically occur. While lowering the country's fertility rate will trigger the demographic transition, this simply creates a window of opportunity that, when coupled with the right kind of policy environment, results in a sustained period of economic growth — the demographic dividend. To reiterate, the growing number of adults (particularly those aged 15–24 years, the first to enter the labour force) will be productive only when the labour market is flexible, allowing for expansion. Government policies play the vital role in guaranteeing the generation of this demographic dividend.

Figure 12.7 shows the unemployment rates of male and female workers in the country from 2005 to 2020, using the PSA's quarterly survey data. The downward trend in the unemployment rates from 2005 to 2019 was

Figure 12.7. Unemployment rate of male and female workers in the Philippines (2nd quarter 2005 to 4th quarter 2020)

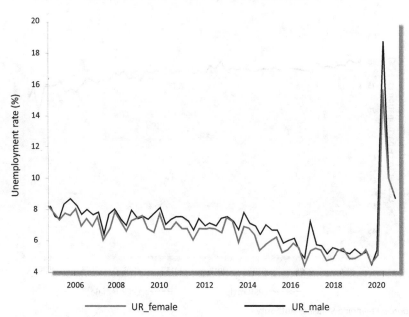

Source: Philippine Statistics Authority.

reversed during the pandemic. Unemployment rates peaked during the second quarter of 2020 at 18.8 per cent and 15.6 per cent for male and female workers, respectively. While the numbers decreased with the opening of the economy thereafter, the average unemployment rates for male and female workers in 2020 are about twice the rates in 2019 (9.9% vs. 4.9% for female workers and 10.7% vs. 5.1% for male workers).

In addition, youth unemployment rate also increased rapidly during the pandemic, peaking at 31.5 per cent during the second quarter of 2020 (Figure 12.8). The full-year average youth unemployment rate for 2020 of 21.7 per cent is 8 percentage points higher than 2019's 13.7 per cent. This high rate creates a roadblock to achieving the demographic dividend for the country. As the young adults transition to the labour market from school, facing the challenges associated with high unemployment and possibly low-paying jobs could create in them a high level of discontentment.

Figure 12.8. Youth unemployment rate in the Philippines (2nd quarter 2005 to 4th quarter 2020)

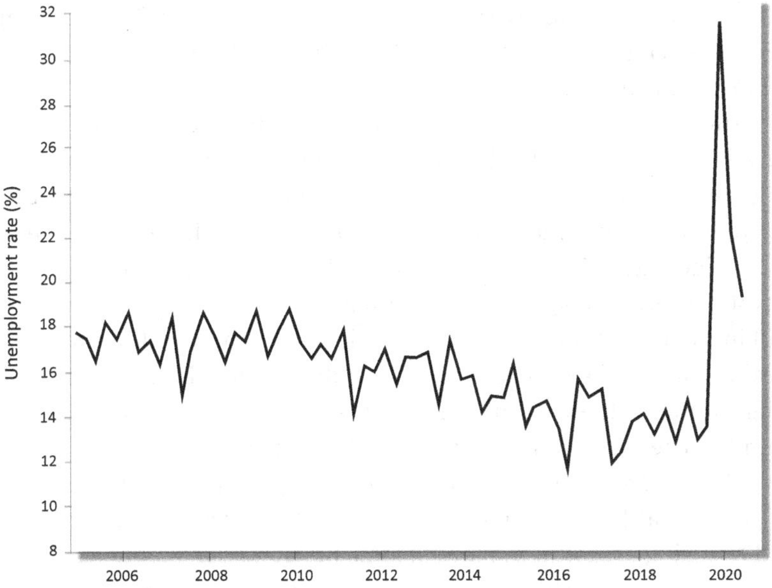

Source: Philippine Statistics Authority.

6 CONCLUSION AND POLICY RECOMMENDATIONS

In the context of East and Southeast Asia, the demographic transition of the Philippines started late and has been progressing very slowly. Under a business-as-usual scenario, the country can expect to reap the demographic dividend by 2030 yet, or perhaps 10 years sooner if its total fertility rate is reduced faster to the replacement fertility rate of 2.1 with appropriate public policy measures. By comparison, Thailand achieved replacement fertility in 1990 and Vietnam in 2006. The difference represents huge missed opportunities for the Philippines to achieve inclusive socio-economic development.

However, the country still has a rare demographic window of opportunity, a fleeting chance for it to benefit from a relatively young population. This window of opportunity can result in a demographic dividend that can usher the country to a self-sustaining, inclusive economic growth. Nevertheless, two major challenges confront the country: the slow fertility reduction, particularly among the poorest households, and the high unemployment and underemployment rates among young workers, particularly the 20–24 years old. These challenges are likely to constrain the country's ability to reap the demographic bonus.

Crucial work must be carried out if the country is to take advantage of the benefits brought about by its changing age structure. Lowering the fertility rate is the necessary policy objective to bring about the demographic window of opportunity. To this end, the country must vigorously implement public policy measures and strengthen private efforts to speed up voluntary reduction in fertility rates. Full implementation of the Responsible Parenthood and Reproductive Health Law is key to lowering fertility—which is in fact a major programme in the current administration's ten-point socio-economic agenda. The government must aim to ratchet up the contraceptive prevalence rate from the current level of just under 50 per cent to 70 per cent at least in the next five years, favouring modern methods and ensuring access of the low-income households.

To be sure, fertility rate reduction is the country's principal objective for the demographic transition to happen. But to reap the demographic dividend requires implementing the right government policies, particularly on education, healthcare and the labour market. The transition from school to the work force has important consequences for human well-being and inclusive economic growth. As shown by the data, the young adults—the first to join the work force—experience challenges associated with high unemployment and underemployment rates and low wages. The highest possible demographic dividend can be achieved only when employment opportunities for young adults improve from the current situation.

Without government's vigorous and sustained efforts, coupled with society's cooperation, to reduce the country's total fertility rate and implement policies geared towards generating more jobs, the window of opportunity made possible by the demographic transition could close quickly. That would be a considerable setback for the country— which by all means must be forestalled.

ACKNOWLEDGEMENT

This paper is a result of decades of research by the authors in the areas of population and development, benefitting in the process from the insights of various research collaborators.

REFERENCES

Adsera, A. 2003. "Changing Fertility Rates in Developed Countries: The Impact of Labor Market Institutions". *Journal of Population Economics* 17: 17–43.
Ainsworth, M., K. Beegle, and A. Nyamete. 1996. "The Impact of Women's Schooling on Fertility and Contraceptive Use: A Study of Fourteen Sub-Saharan African Countries". *The World Bank Economic Review* 10, no. 1: 85–122.
Balisacan, A. M. 2018. Foreword. In *The Philippine Economy*, edited by R. L. Clarete, E. F. Esguerra, and H. Hill. Singapore: ISEAS.
Becker, G. S. 1960. "An Economic Analysis of Fertility". In *Demographic and Economic Change in Developed Countries* (Universities–National Bureau Conference Series 11), pp. 209–40. Princeton: Princeton University Press.
———. 1981. *A Treatise on the Family*. Cambridge: Harvard University Press. First edition.
Becker, G. S., and G. Lewis. 1973. "On the Interaction between the Quantity and Quality of Children". *Journal of Political Economy, Part 2: New Economic Approaches to Fertility* 81, no. 2: S279–88.
Behrman, J. R., and M. R. Rosenzweig. 2002. "Does Increasing Women's Schooling Raise the Schooling of the Next Generation?". *American Economic Review* 92, no. 1: 323–34.
Ben-Porath, Y. 1976. "Fertility Response to Child Mortality: Micro Data from Israel". *Journal of Political Economy* 84, no. 4: S163–78.
Bongaarts, J. 1978. "A Framework for Analyzing the Proximate Determinants of Fertility". *Population and Development Review* 4, no. 1: 105–32.
Brewster, K. L., and R. R. Rindfuss. 2000. "Fertility and Women's Employment in Industrialized Nations. *Annual Review of Sociology* 26: 271–96.
Bloom, D., and D. Canning. 2001. "Cumulative Causality, Economic Growth, and the Demographic Transition". In *Population Matters, Demographic Change, Economic Growth and Poverty in the Developing World*, edited by N. Birdsall, A. C. Kelly, and S.W. Sinding. UK: Oxford University Press.
Bloom, D. E., D. Canning, and J. Sevilla. 2001. "Economic Growth and Demographic Transition". *NBER Working Paper No. w8685*. Washington, DC: National Bureau of Economic Research.
Bloom, D. E., and J. G. Williamson. 1997. "Demographic Transitions and Economic Miracles in Emerging Asia". *NBER Working Paper No. 6268*. Washington, DC: National Bureau of Economic Research.

Casterline, J. B. 1985. "Community Effects on Fertility". In *The Collection and Analysis of Community Data*, edited by J. B. Casterline. Voorburg: International Statistical Institute.

Chowdhury, A. K. M, A. R. Khan, and L. C. Chen. 1976. "The Effect of Child Mortality Experience on Subsequent Fertility: In Pakistan and Bangladesh". *Population Studies* 30, no. 2: 249–62.

Chun, H., and J. Oh. 2002. "An Instrumental Variable Estimate of the Effect of Fertility on the Labor Force Participation of Married Women". *Applied Economic Letters* 9: 631–34.

Cigno, A. 1992. "Children and Pensions". *Journal of Population Economics* 5: 175–83.

Cigno, A., and F. C. Rosati. 1996. "Jointly Determined Saving and Fertility Behavior: Theory, and Estimates for Germany, Italy, UK, and USA". *European Economic Review* 40: 1561–89.

Collado, R. V. 2010. "Regional Divides in the Correlates of Fertility: An Analysis of the 2008 NDHS". Paper presented at the 11th National Convention on Statistics (NCS), EDSA Shangri-La Hotel, Mandaluyong City, Philippines, October 2010.

Dyson, T., and M. Murphy. 1985. "The Onset of Fertility Transition". *Population and Development Review* 11: 399–440.

Easterlin, R. A. 1973. "Does Money Buy Happiness?" *The Public Interest* 30 (Winter): 3–10.

———. 1980. "American Population Since 1940". In *The American Economy in Transition*, edited by M. Feldstein, pp. 275–321. Chicago: University of Chicago Press.

Grossman, M. 1972. "On the Concept of Health Capital and the Demand for Health". *Journal of Political Economy* 80, no. 2: 233–55.

Herrin, A. N., and M. P. Costello. 1996. *Sources of Future Population Growth in the Philippines and Implications for Public Policy*. New York: The Population Council.

Hirschman, C., and P. Guest. 1990. "Multilevel Models of Fertility Determination in Four Southeast Asian Countries: 1970 and 1980". *Demography* 27: 369–96.

Hondroyiannis, G., and E. Papapetrou. 2002. "Demographic Transition and Economic Growth: Empirical Evidence from Greece". *Journal of Population Economics* 15, no. 2: 221–42.

Hotz, J., and R. A. Miller. 1988. "An Empirical Analysis of Life Cycle Fertility and Female Labor Supply". *Journal of the Econometric Society* 56, no. 1: 91–118.

Kravdal, O. 2001. "Main and Interaction Effects of Women's Education and Status on Fertility: The Case of Tanzania". *European Journal of Population* 17: 107–36.

Lesthaeghe, R., C. Vanderhoeft, S. Gaise, and G. Delaine. 1985. "Regional Variation in Components of Child-Spacing: The Role of Women's Education". In *Reproduction and Social Organization in Sub-Saharan Africa*, edited by R. Lesthaeghe. Berkeley: University of California Press.

Mapa, D. S., M. L. Albis, L. G. Bersales, and J. Daquis. 2011. "Determinants of Poverty in the Elderly-Headed Household". *Working Paper No. 2011–04*. Quezon City: School of Statistics, University of the Philippines Diliman.

Mapa, D. S., and A. M. Balisacan. 2004. "Quantifying the Impact of Population on Economic Growth and Poverty: The Philippines in an East Asian Context". In *Population and Development in the Philippines: The Ties That Bind*, edited by L. A. Sevilla. Makati City: AIM Policy Center.

Mapa, D. S., A. M. Balisacan, and K. J. Briones. 2006. "Robust Determinants of Income Growth in the Philippines". *Philippine Journal of Development* 33, no. 1–2: 1–32.

Mapa, D. S., A. M. Balisacan, and J. R. Corpuz. 2010. "Population Management Should Be Mainstreamed in the Philippine Development Agenda". *PCPD Policy Brief No. 2010–01*. Makati City: Philippine Center for Population and Development.

Mapa, D. S., and L. G. Bersales. 2008. "Population Dynamics and Household Saving: Evidence from the Philippines". *Philippine Statistician* 57, no. 1–4: 1–27.

Mason, A. 2007. "Demographic Dividends: The Past, the Present and the Future". In *Population Change, Labor Markets and Sustainable Growth: Towards a New Economic Paradigm*, edited by A. Mason and Mitoshi Yamaguchi. Amsterdam: Elsevier.

McCrary, J., and H. Royer. 2011. "The Effect of Female Education on Fertility and Infant Health: Evidence from School Entry Policies Using Exact Date of Birth". *American Economic Review* 101, no. 1: 158–95. https://www.doi.org/10.1257/aer.101.1.158.

McNicoll, G. 2006. "Policy Lessons of the East Asian Demographic Transition". *Population and Development Review* 32, no. 1: 1–25.

McNown, R., and S. Rajbhandary. 2003. "Time Series Analysis of Fertility and Female Labor Market Behavior". *Journal of Population Economics* 16, no. 3: 501–23.

Mincer, J. 1963. "Market Prices, Opportunity Costs, and Income Effects". In *Measurement in Economics: Studies in Mathematical Economics and Econometrics in Memory of Yehuda Grunfeld*, edited by C. Christ. Stanford: Stanford University Press.

Pernia, E. M. 2007. "Population as Public Interest". *UPSE Discussion Paper No. 2007–08*. Quezon City: School of Economics, University of the Philippines Diliman.

———. 2011. "Arguments Contra and Pro RH Bill". *The Philippine Star*, 22 September 2011.

Pernia, E. M., S. Alabastro-Quimbo, M. J. V. Abrenica, Ruperto P. Alonzo, Agustin L. Arcenas, Arsenio M. Balisacan, Dante B. Canlas et al. 2011. "Population, Poverty, Politics and the Reproductive Health Bill". *UPSE Discussion Paper* No. 2011–01. Quezon City: School of Economics, University of the Philippines Diliman.

Pernia, E. M., and E. E. Pernia. 2015. "Population, Economic Growth, and Inclusivity". *International Journal of Philippine Science and Technology* 1, no. 1: 12–16.

Porter, M., and E. M. King. 2009. "Fertility and Women's Labor Force Participation in Developing Countries". *Discussion Paper*. Washington, DC: World Bank.

Radelet, S., J. Sachs, and J. Lee. 1997. "Emerging Asia: Changes and Challenges". *Economic Growth in Asia*. Manila: Asian Development Bank.

Sachs, J. D. 2008. *Common Wealth: Economics for a Crowded Planet*. London: Penguin Books.

Sah, R. K. 1991. "The Effects of Child Mortality Changes on Fertility Choice and Parental Welfare". *Journal of Political Economy* 99, no. 3: 582–606.

Scrimchaw, S. C. M. 1978. "Infant Mortality and Behavior in the Regulation of Family Size". *Population and Development Review* 4, no. 3: 383–403.

Steele, F., I. Diamond, and D. L. Wang. 1996. "The Determinants of Contraceptive Use in China: A Multilevel Multinomial Discrete Hazards Modelling Approach". *Demography*, no. 33: 12–24.

Tienda, M., V. G. Diaz, and S. A. Smith. 1985. "Community Education and Differential Fertility in Peru". *Canadian Studies in Population* 12, no. 2: 137–58.

The Economist. 2009. "Falling Fertility: How the Population Problem Is Solving Itself". October 2009.

Thomas, D. 1999. "Fertility, Education and Resources in South Africa". In *Critical Perspectives on Schooling and Fertility in the Developing World*, edited by C. H. Bledsoe, J. B. Casterline, J. A. Johnson-Kuhn, and J. G. Haaga, pp. 138–80. Washington: National Academy Press.

Tuman, J. P., A. S. Ayoub, and D. Roth-Johnson. 2007. "The Effects of Education on Fertility in Colombia and Peru: Implications for Health and Family Planning Policies". *Global Health Governance* 1, no. 2.

Weller, R. H. 1977. "Wife's Employment and Cumulative Family Size in the United States, 1970 and 1960". *Demography* 14, no. 1: 46–65.

13 Collateralizing Wages: The Case of *Sangla* ATM

Nobuhiko Fuwa, Kei Kajisa, Eduardo Lucio, Sharon Faye Piza and Yasuyuki Sawada

1 INTRODUCTION

Informal lending is one of the more common sources of household financing in many developing countries, including the Philippines. Informal finance arrangements through business counterparts and extended family members, pawnshops, rotating savings and credit associations (ROSCAs), and informal money lenders often prove more efficient than their formal counterparts around the globe (Adams and Hunter 2019). Despite the wide acceptance and integration into society of these informal financing institutions, studies on them are few, especially in the context of developing countries (see, e.g., Agabin et al. 1989; Agabin 1993; Nagarajan, David, and Meyer 1992; Floro and Ray 1997; Adams and Hunter 2019).

Surveys by the Bangko Sentral ng Pilipinas (BSP, Central Bank of the Philippines) point to a growing share of informal money lenders among households' funding sources in recent years, despite the regulators' push to encourage a more inclusive financial sector, such as utilizing microfinance institutions and digital banks and easing regulatory requirements to entice households to join the formal financial system (Karlan and Morduch 2010; Kritz 2013; BSP 2018, 2020). The 2019 Financial Inclusion Survey of the BSP shows that informal money lenders held a significant role in various financing decisions of households (BSP 2020).

The expansion of the informal financing channel does not refer only to the increased client base, but also to product innovations that money lenders introduce. For instance, collaterals accepted by money lenders have evolved from goods, jewelries, land titles and household appliances to, recently, automatic teller machine (ATM) or debit cards.

This study takes a close look at a newly emerged credit arrangement called *Sangla* ATM[1] or debit card pawning. *Sangla* ATM is an informal loan arrangement where a borrower uses as collateral an ATM card linked to an account that receives a regular salary or other forms of income. The borrower surrenders the ATM card and its personal identification number to the lender, who then uses the card to withdraw the loan repayment (principal and interest) on a regular frequency (typically twice a month) until the entire amount is fully repaid.[2]

The popularity of debit card pawning in the Philippines has reached a broad range of borrowers who have access to an ATM-linked bank account—from conditional cash transfer recipients of the government to private-sector employees and even government personnel (ABS-CBN 2018, 2020). The 2014 Consumer Finance Survey (CFS) of the BSP reveals that ATM cards were the most popular collateral for personal, salary, multipurpose, business and educational loans, accounting for 40 per cent for the country and even higher at 64 per cent for Metro Manila (BSP 2017). It was followed by land at 23 per cent for the country and 14 per cent for Metro Manila.

---

[1] *"Sangla"* is Filipino for "pawn".

[2] Lenders face two types of risks under the *Sangla* ATM arrangement. First is the risk of borrowers having unpaid leave of absence or being terminated. However, since this informal arrangement typically has a short loan term, ranging from several weeks to a couple of months, the risk is minimal. The other risk is the possibility of borrowers withdrawing their money through ways other than using the ATM card (e.g., over-the-counter bank transaction). To avoid this risk, the lenders usually withdraw the repayment money on the payday itself. Recent developments in internet banking have made transactions through non-ATM means easier, rendering ATM cards less suitable as collateral. Therefore, it has become more common for lenders either to additionally request ordinary cashable collaterals or to limit transactions to trustworthy borrowers. When we conducted our survey in 2013, internet banking was not as popular as now (2021).

While the popularity of *Sangla* ATM has been increasing, its nature is yet to be well understood. The canonical imperfect information paradigm on informal credit markets by Hoff and Stiglitz (1993) emphasizes underlying factors such as adverse selection, moral hazard and enforcement problems; under such perverse conditions, informal lending can serve as an important vehicle for access to credit. Increased access would also contribute to consumption smoothing because credit is regarded as an important insurance device (see Balisacan and Fuwa 2007 for a comprehensive review). Recent literature, which has incorporated time-inconsistent behavioural assumptions, notes concerns on seemingly irrational borrowing behaviour, such as over borrowing by present-biased or hyperbolic discounters (e.g., Ashraf, Karlan, and Yin 2006 in the Philippines; Bauer, Chytilová, and Morduch 2012 in India; Meier and Sprenger 2010 in the United States). There are pros and cons in the emerging informal arrangements. Given this background, this study aims to gain a better understanding of *Sangla* ATM by determining the features of this credit arrangement and characterizing its users.

The rest of this paper is organized as follows: Section 2 explains the *Sangla* ATM phenomenon vis-à-vis the overall picture of informal finance in the Philippines. Section 3 describes our data set, summarizing the main characteristics of *Sangla* ATM transactions as observed. Section 4 concludes and presents possible policy implications.

2 INFORMAL FINANCIAL SECTOR IN THE PHILIPPINES AND *SANGLA* ATM

Informal finance has been widely used in the Philippines. The results of the first CFS in the Philippines conducted in 2009 by the BSP reveal that informal money lenders were important sources of financing for households (Table 13.1) (BSP 2012). Almost a decade later, the 2019 Financial Inclusion Survey obtains a similar finding: the informal financial sector has continued to have a strong foothold in the Filipino households. It shows that the number of unbanked Filipino adults stood at 51.2 million in 2019, or 71 per cent of the total adult population. This does not mean that credit transaction was limited, however. Indeed, the incidence of borrowing was high, but mostly sourced from informal sources such as family and friends (44%) and informal lenders (10%). Meanwhile, among formal lenders, microfinance non-governmental organizations (NGOs) remained the top choice (31%), followed by government institutions (11%).

Table 13.1. Rank of informal money lender as source of financing

Type of loan	Rank	All regions (% share)	Metro Manila (% share)	Outside Metro Manila (% share)
Housing loan	4th out of 16	9.6	6.8	15.8
Other real property loan (aside from residence)	1st out of 12	36.5	28.3	47.2
Vehicle loan	5th out of 10	4.0	4.8	3.4
Appliances/Equipment loan	4th out of 9	8.0	14.0	5.3

Source: 2009 Consumer Finance Survey, BSP (2012).

The survey report also shows that formal borrowing increased only by 4 percentage points from 2017 to 2019, while informal borrowing grew significantly by 10 percentage points.

The report also reveals that 48 per cent of the survey respondents perceived that access to the formal financial sector is difficult. Their reasons include strict documentary requirements (58%), not having collateral (42%), not having enough identification cards (37%) and not having enough salary (30%). It is clear from these reasons that the lack of formal collateral generates a credit constraint, a situation that *Sangla* ATM could resolve because it allows borrowers without assets to collateralize future income flows. Hence, theoretically speaking, it can be considered as an institutional innovation in response to market demand and facilitated by the emergence of new technology. With the increasing availability of ATMs, many firms have opted to pay employees' salaries through direct bank deposits—a safer and cheaper alternative to cash delivery. As such, the use of ATM cards as collateral for loans extended to the regular employees of these companies (or government) could provide an effective mechanism to mitigate traditional problems arising from information asymmetry in credit markets such as adverse selection, moral hazard and imperfect enforcement problems (Armendariz and Morduch 2010).

On the negative side, increased credit opportunities may provide easy money to borrowers, resulting in overborrowing and unnecessary debt burden, thus eventually decreasing the welfare of borrowers.[3]

---

[3] A Philippines Congress Resolution (P.S. Res. No. 632) was made in 2014 to prevent the occurrence of more fraudulent activities in *Sangla* ATM. In 2018, the BSP said the practice is legal because there is no law that states otherwise, but is highly discouraged.

These happen especially when the borrowers have biased decision-making behaviour and are not fully rational economically. *Sangla* ATM could provide a means to give in to temptations for luxury consumption and potentially to overborrow. These possibilities have been pointed out in recent literature on overborrowing in the context of credit card debt or payday loans in developed countries (Meier and Sprenger 2010; Agarwal, Skiba, and Tobacman 2009; Stegman 2007).

3 SURVEY DATA AND ANALYSIS

Our empirical analysis is based on a 2013 survey of factory workers conducted in three medium-scale factories manufacturing automobile parts located in an industrial estate in Laguna, an adjacent province south of Metro Manila. Laguna is the third biggest province in the Philippines, with more than three million residents. Industrial parks have emerged in the area since the opening of the South Luzon Expressway (SLEX) in the late 1970s, which connects Metro Manila and the western part of Laguna.

The survey was conducted by Asia Research Organization, with supervision by the authors. With the cooperation of the factories' management, personal interviews were conducted at the factories' premises, with all the employees at work at the time of our survey participating. A total of 320 workers—195 (61%) men and 125 (39%) women—were interviewed: 107, 78 and 135 from firms A, B and C, respectively (Table 13.2).

3.1 Respondent profile

The respondents were 30 years old and had 7 years of work experience, on average; 53 per cent of them were married and 49 per cent had children. A great majority (72%) were regular employees, 23 per cent were contractual workers and 5 per cent were on probation. One-third of the respondents were college graduates, 45 per cent had either vocational or some college education and 21 per cent were high school graduates or had lower educational attainment (Table 13.2).

Except for those recently employed (4%), the workers were paid their salaries through direct bank deposits (Table 13.3). In all three companies, the workers were paid twice a month; the average monthly salary was PHP15,000 (US$345 at US$/PHP exchange rate of 0.023). For most workers, their salary accounts (the bank accounts where their salaries were deposited) were their only bank account; only 20 per cent of them had another bank account (mostly ordinary deposit account).

Table 13.2. Characteristics of the respondents (factory workers, Sangla *ATM Survey*)

Category	Response
Total no. of respondents	320 respondents
Company A	107 respondents
Company B	78 respondents
Company C	135 respondents
Sex of respondents	
Male	195 respondents (61%)
Female	125 respondents (39%)
Average age	30 years
Proportion of married respondents	168 respondents (53%)
Those with children	157 respondents (49%)
Average number of children	1.96 children
Living with parent(s)	81 respondents (25%)
Type of employment	
Regular	229 respondents (72%)
Probational	16 respondents (5%)
Contractual	75 respondents (23%)
Average no. of years employed	6.9 years
Level of schooling	
High school graduate or lower	67 respondents (21%)
Vocational schooling (undergrad or grad)	97 respondents (30%)
College undergraduate	49 respondents (15%)
College graduate or higher	107 respondents (33%)

Table 13.3. Mode of salary payment and access to bank accounts (Sangla ATM Survey)

Category	Response
Mode of salary payment	
Bank deposit	316 respondents (99%)
Cash	4 respondents (1%)
Frequency of salary payment	Twice a month: 320 respondents (100%)
Average salary level (per half month)	PHP7,543: 317 respondents (3 no answer)
Amount withdrawn on or the day after payday (per half month)	PHP5,583
Average share of amount withdrawn in total salary	65% of total salary
Average amount of own allowance	PHP3,061
Average share of own allowance in total salary	48%
Own a bank account other than salary account	
Salary account (no interest) only	234 respondents (73.0%)
Own savings account	82 respondents (26.0%)
Own term-deposit account	1 respondent (0.4%)
Own trust account	1 respondent (0.4%)
Own current (checking) account	2 respondents (0.6%)
Average amount left in salary account	PHP52,821 (84 respondents)
Type of outstanding loans (counts, possible multiple loans per respondent)	
Sangla ATM	42 respondents (11.0%)
Microfinance institutions, banks and financial institutions	28 respondents (7.3%)
SSS/Pag-IBIG	239 respondents (62.4%)
Private money lenders, relatives, friends, etc.	74 respondents (19.3%)
Microfinance institutions, banks and financial institutions	28 respondents (7.3%)

3.2 *Sangla* ATM transactions

Table 13.4 shows that almost all (93%) of the respondents were aware of *Sangla* ATM, and slightly less than half (134 of 320 or 42%) had used it at least once. Of the 134 respondents, 37 per cent had borrowed via *Sangla* ATM within the past six months; but for almost half (46%) of them, the last *Sangla* ATM transaction took place more than one year earlier. At the time of our interviews, 42 respondents (31% of those who had borrowed via *Sangla* ATM) had outstanding balances in their *Sangla* ATM loans. This suggests that borrowing via *Sangla* ATM is not necessarily a regular or continuous transaction, unlike microfinance loans. Indeed, according to the last row of Table 13.3, which shows types of currently outstanding loans, the largest sources of loans are publicly granted salary loans (i.e., Social Security System) and loans from the government-owned Home Development Mutual Fund (also known as Pag-IBIG Fund) (62.4%), followed by credit from private money lenders, relatives, friends, etc. (19.3%) and *Sangla* ATM (11%).[4] In contrast, borrowings from microfinance institutions, banks and other financial institutions account for 7.3 per cent only.

Among the 134 respondents who had borrowed via *Sangla* ATM, the average loan amount (principal) was PHP15,220, with an average duration of 5.2 months (Table 13.4). This amount is equivalent to 1.3 times their average monthly salary. During the repayment phase, *Sangla* ATM lenders withdrew an average of PHP2,702 from the borrowers' salary accounts, which was equivalent to 34 per cent of their salaries. The monthly interest rate ranged between 0 and 20 per cent, averaging 3 per cent per month (equivalent to an annual compounded rate of 40%).

The loan proceeds were used mainly for medical expenses (21%), daily consumption (19%), children's education (16%), house repair/renovation (9%) and religious and social events (8%). In terms of the amount of expenses that benefited from ATM loans, medical expenses were also the largest (roughly PHP20,000), followed by religious and social events (PHP18,000), education (PHP16,500) and house repair/renovation (PHP15,000). This is another difference between *Sangla* ATM loans and microfinance loans, which are confined to investment purposes.

---

[4] If we exclude loans from Pag-IBIG Fund, the proportion of *Sangla* ATM borrowings becomes 32 per cent of the total outstanding debt. Since the 2014 CFS reveals that the most popular collateral for the non-housing loans was *Sangla* ATM (40% for the country and 64% for Metro Manila), we believe that our data are comparable with the 2014 CFS data.

Table 13.4 Utilization of Sangla *ATM*

Category	Response
Do you know *Sangla* ATM?	Yes: 297 respondents (93%)
Have you borrowed via *Sangla* ATM?	Yes: 134 (42%)
Male	41 respondents (33% of total male)
Female	93 respondents (48% of total female)
When did you last borrow via *Sangla* ATM?	
Within the last 6 months	50 respondents (37%)
Between 6 months and 1 year ago	23 respondents (17%)
More than a year ago	61 respondents (46%)
Outstanding *Sangla* ATM debt balance (as of interview date)	
With outstanding balance	42 respondents
Average balance	PHP14,578.88 (42 respondents)
Range of outstanding balance	PHP1,500~PHP47,600
Sources of *Sangla* ATM borrowing (n = 134)	
Individual money lenders	72 respondents (54%)
Colleagues	28 respondents (21%)
Friends	21 respondents (16%)
Neighbours	8 respondents (6%)
Relatives	5 respondents (4%)
Amount borrowed via *Sangla* ATM	PHP15,220~134 respondents: range = PHP1,000~100,000) = equivalent to 1.3 month average salary (133 responses: range = 0.07~5.00 months)
Term of *Sangla* ATM borrowing (n = 134)	
Average term	5.2 months
Range of term	1 week~2 years
Monthly repayment amount on payday (n = 133)	
Average monthly repayment	PHP2,702
Range of monthly repayment	PHP350~20,000
Share of repayment in total salary (n = 124)	
Average share of repayment	34.4%
Range of share of repayment	0.05%~100.0%

Table 13.4 *(continued)*

Table 13.4 *(continued)*

Category	Response
Use/purpose of most recent *Sangla* ATM borrowing (n = 134)	
Medical expenditure	28 respondents (21%)
Living expenses/consumption	26 respondents (19%)
Educational expenses	21 respondents (16%)
House repair	12 respondents (9%)
Social, religious expenses	11 respondents (8%)
Motorcycle purchase	5 respondents (4%)
Debt repayment:	4 respondents (3%)
Other purposes: Appliances, personal emergencies, leisure, etc.	27 respondents (20%)
Average amount borrowed by use/purpose (n = 134)	
Medical	PHP19,393 (28 respondents)
Living expenses	PHP9,038 (26 respondents)
Education	PHP16,476 (21 respondents)
House repair	PHP15,250 (12 respondents)
Social, religious	PHP17,727 (11 respondents)
Average interest rate (n = 134)	3.02% per month
Only for those who have never borrowed via *Sangla* ATM: Why have you not borrowed via *Sangla* ATM? (n = 186)	
No need	141 respondents (76%)
Don't want to be in debt	23 respondents (12%)
High interest rate	16 respondents (9%)
Can borrow from relatives with no interest	4 respondents (2%)
Others: Likely to be denied of loan, don't know a lender, etc.	2 respondents (1%)
Only for those who have never borrowed via *Sangla* ATM: Do you have any intention to borrow via *Sangla* ATM in the future? (n = 186)	
Yes	65 respondents (35%)
No	121 respondents (65%)
How much is the maximum amount that you think you can borrow? (n = 316)	Average = PHP32,954 Range = PHP500~100,000

The survey also shows that private money lenders were the most common provider (54%) of *Sangla* ATM loans, followed by colleagues (21%), friends (16%), neighbours (6%) and relatives (4%). That is, the majority of *Sangla* ATM loans were informal transactions with professional money lenders who were mostly individuals, rather than firms.

3.3 Comparison of *Sangla* ATM and the Philippine Consumer Finance Survey

We put our (admittedly small) sample of respondents into perspective by comparing its profile and borrowing characteristics with a comparable group from the 2009 CFS (BSP 2012).

Among the 9,402 responding households in the CFS, Metro Manila's 1,141 respondents with regular employment form a relatively comparable subgroup with our 320 *Sangla* ATM respondents. These responding households, whose incomes were dependent on employment (i.e., at least one of the household head and the spouse is fully employed and wage-income receiver), availed themselves of multipurpose cash loans in 2008.

In terms of demographic characteristics, the average age of the CFS Metro Manila subsample (42 years old) is higher than that of the *Sangla* ATM respondents (30 years old) (Table 13.5). As to educational attainment level, it is significantly lower for the CFS subsample, where 62 per cent had at most high school education (compared with 21% in our sample) and the remaining 38 per cent had at least started college (compared with 48% in our sample). Among the CFS subsample respondents who were fully employed, 54 per cent were regular employees (compared with 72% in our survey). On the other hand, the mean salary of the CFS subsample (PHP19,000 after adjusting for inflation) is higher than that of our survey respondents (PHP15,000) (Table 13.6).

Comparing the multipurpose cash loan borrowing characteristics of the two groups of respondents, the average amount borrowed by the CFS group (PHP44,900, adjusted for inflation) is about three times higher than that of the *Sangla* ATM group (Table 13.7). This may be because the loan uses of the CFS subsample included business start-up and expansion and purchase of high-value assets (e.g., properties and cars). However, on the aggregate, the loan uses of both surveys are similar. The majority of the CFS group's multipurpose cash loans were used for living expenses and consumption (31%), medical expenses and other emergencies (12%) and educational expenses (9%). Similar to observations on the *Sangla* ATM data, the CFS sample obtained the majority of these multipurpose loans from individual money lenders (36%).

Table 13.5. Characteristics of households with multipurpose cash loans (2009 Consumer Finance Survey)

Characteristic	All regions	Metro Manila
Total number of households	1,141 households	329 households
Sex of respondents		
Male:	453 (40%)	116 (35%)
Female:	688 (60%)	213 (65%)
Average age of respondents	42.35 years old	41.89 years old
Proportion of married respondents	969 (85%)	256 (78%)
Average household size	5.30 people	5.14 people
Employment type of respondent		
Employed	612 (54%)	176 (54%)
Self-employed	176 (15%)	47 (14%)
Homemaker	218 (19%)	66 (20%)
Unemployed	116 (10%)	33 (10%)
Others	19 (2%)	7 (2%)
Contract type of employed respondent		
Permanent	305 (50%)	100 (57%)
Temporary/Fixed-term	73 (12%)	28 (16%)
No formal contract	196 (32%)	41 (23%)
Other employment	38 (6%)	7 (4%)
Level of schooling of respondent		
No formal education	7 (1%)	1 (1%)
At most elementary	449 (39%)	89 (27%)
At most high school	352 (31%)	112 (34%)
At least college	333 (29%)	127 (38%)

Note: Based on households with existing multipurpose cash loan and dependent on employment income, 2009 Consumer Finance Survey

Source: BSP (2012).

Table 13.6. Access to bank account (2009 Consumer Finance Survey)

Characteristic	All regions	Metro Manila
Owns at least one financial asset		
Yes	313 (27%)	119 (36%)
No	828 (73%)	210 (64%)
Owns a deposit account (if with financial asset)		
Yes	311 (99%)	119 (100%)
No	2 (1%)	
Average salary level (per half month of both respondent and spouse)		
2008 level	PHP5,732.21	PHP8,200.95
Adj. 2013 level	PHP6,895.12[+]	PHP9,501.38[++]

Note: (1) Based on households with existing multipurpose cash loan and dependent on employment income, 2009 Consumer Finance Survey
(2) [+]Adjusted using CPI deflator for whole Philippines
[++] Adjusted using CPI deflator for Metro Manila

Source: BSP (2012).

Table 13.7. Sources and uses of multipurpose cash loan (2009 Consumer Finance Survey)

Characteristic	All regions	Metro Manila
Average amount of cash borrowed		
2008 level	PHP31,160.51	PHP38,772.36
Adj. 2013 level	PHP37,482.12[+]	PHP44,920.50[++]
Source of multipurpose cash loan		
Individual money lenders	474 (42%)	120 (36%)
Government financial agencies	227 (20%)	97 (29%)
Cooperatives	146 (13%)	35 (11%)
Non-bank financial institutions	139 (12%)	36 (11%)
Banks	106 (9%)	14 (4%)
Friends, relatives, etc.	49 (4%)	27 (8%)

Table 13.7 (continued)

Table 13.7 *(continued)*

Characteristic	All regions	Metro Manila
Use of multipurpose cash loan		
Living expenses/consumption	328 (29%)	101 (31%)
Debt repayment	126 (11%)	30 (9%)
Medical expenses /emergency	126 (11%)	40 (12%)
Educational expenses	122 (11%)	29 (9%)
Business start-up	114 (10%)	25 (8%)
House improvement	114 (10%)	32 (10%)
Business expansion	100 (9%)	27 (8%)
Purchase home appliance	32 (3%)	16 (5%)
Purchase car	27 (2%)	6 (2%)
Leisure/vacation/celebration	19 (2%)	10 (3%)
Purchase property	18 (2%)	7 (2%)
Foreign job application	15 (1%)	6 (2%)

Note: (1) Based on households with existing multipurpose cash loan and dependent on employment income, 2009 Consumer Finance Survey
(2) ⁺Adjusted using CPI deflator for whole Philippines
⁺⁺ Adjusted using CPI deflator for Metro Manila

Source: BSP (2012).

3.4 Characteristics of *Sangla* ATM users

Since we analysed observed data, not data from a controlled experiment, it is difficult to identify causal effects on the uses of *Sangla* ATM by nature. Yet, in order to figure out, at least partly, the determinants of borrowing via *Sangla* ATM, we postulate a regression model for a binary dependent variable of Sangla ATM use:

$$S^* = Z\gamma + v, \qquad (1)$$

where we assume a linear model for the propensity to use *Sangla* ATM, S^*, which is a latent variable with a set of the following independent variables, Z (i.e., each borrower's characteristics as independent variables): we include age and age squared, sex, marital status, number of children, co-residence with parents, mode of employment, education level, income level and ownership of deposit account, except the deposit account for the regular salary deposits, together with company fixed effects.

In equation (1), S^* is a latent variable for which a binary discrete variable is observed, which takes 1 if the respondent has borrowed from *Sangla* ATM and 0 otherwise. The probabilities of using and not using *Sangla* ATM for an individual i are described as $Prob(S^* > 0) = Prob(v < Z\gamma)$ and $Prob(S^* < 0) = 1 - Prob(v < Z\gamma)$, respectively, if the error term, v, follows a symmetric distribution. We assume that v follows the logistic distribution so that our model becomes a logit model.

Estimation results of coefficients, γ, of equation (1) are reported in Table 13.8. Note that each of the estimated coefficients corresponds to a marginal effect evaluated at the mean for continuous variables or the change from 0 to 1 for dummy variables. We find that age, sex, number of children, co-residence with parents, employment modality, salary level and one of the company fixed effects are statistically significant. First, there is a non-linear age effect. The peak of *Sangla* ATM use is around age of 35, below (above) which there is a positive (negative) correlation

Table 13.8. Logit regression results on the determinants of borrowing via Sangla ATM (marginal effects)

Independent variable	Coefficient	Standard. error
Age	0.141***	0.049
Age squared	−0.002***	0.001
Female (dummy)	−0.196***	0.068
Married (dummy)	0.063	0.088
Number of children	0.067*	0.040
Living with parent(s) (dummy)	−0.170***	0.065
Regular employee (dummy)	0.314***	0.070
Vocational school (dummy)	−0.059	0.099
With higher education (dummy)	−0.023	0.095
Amount of salary (/PHP1,000)	−0.035***	0.012
Owns bank account other than salary account (dummy)	−0.175***	0.067
Company A (dummy)	−0.148**	0.074
Company B (dummy)	0.074	0.097
N−	317	
Pseudo-R^2	0.2715	

Note: (1) The dependent variable takes 1 if the respondent has borrowed from *Sangla* ATM; 0 otherwise.
(2) Marginal effect is the value evaluated at the means for continuous variables or the discrete change from 0 to 1 for dummy variables.
(3) *** significant at 1%, ** significant at 5%, * significant at 10%

between age and borrowing. This pattern seems to be consistent with the presumption of the life-cycle permanent income hypothesis, since there would be a higher demand for credit at the earlier stages of one's life.

Second, demand factors seem to play a key role. While number of children is positively related to use of *Sangla* ATM, salary level and additional deposit account ownership have positive correlation with it. These are reasonable results since a larger family would need more resources to finance daily expenses; higher income means less necessity to borrow money to support a certain consumption level; and an additional deposit account can potentially provide an alternative financing device for *Sangla* ATM.

Third, the use of *Sangla* ATM is also affected by supply-side factors. The negative coefficient on co-residence can be driven by larger availability of informal credit rather than *Sangla* ATM. The positive coefficient on regular employee status suggests that it is relatively easy for these employees to borrow via *Sangla* ATM because of stable future income. The negative coefficient on the company A dummy may be driven by another credit supply programme through the company's internal loan scheme by collateralizing a retirement allowance.

Finally, we find that men borrowed more via *Sangla* ATM than women. This may be a reflection of gender differences in self-control as regards luxury expenses and financial management of own resources (Ashraf 2009).

4 CONCLUDING REMARKS

This study investigates the emerging informal credit arrangement in the Philippines, called *Sangla* ATM. Our unique survey data uncovered unexpectedly high prevalence of such credit arrangement among factory workers. As the classic work on rural credit markets by Hoff and Stiglitz (1993) points out, generally three imperfect information problems prevent poor individuals without assets from borrowing money: screening or adverse selection problem, moral hazard problem and enforcement problem. Theoretically, *Sangla* ATM can be regarded as an institutional innovation to mitigate these problems using financial technologies, thus relaxing credit constraints of borrowers without collateralizable assets. Yet, we should also note that there are negative sides to such loan arrangement, potentially leading to a debt overhang problem. Careful public policy actions are needed to minimize the adverse impacts of such credit arrangement. To identify proper policy instruments, further investigations of the arrangements must be done to understand better the mechanisms behind the use of *Sangla* ATM.

On this respect, recent behavioural economics literature suggests that debit card pawning may have a range of possible implications for borrowers whose behaviour is not time consistent (Kremer, Rao, and Schilbach 2019). In particular, potential impacts of this new credit arrangement may differ, depending on whether such time-inconsistent borrowers are "naïve" or "sophisticated". Fuwa et al. (2016) find that, among the respondents of the *Sangla* ATM survey, roughly one-third were hyperbolic discounters, tending to hold higher loan balances with *Sangla* ATM transactions than those whose preferences were time consistent. This shows that the hyperbolic discounters are naïve, suggesting that the emergence of *Sangla* ATM may have encouraged them to overborrow to finance luxury expenses. The results imply the possibility that expanding credit access through *Sangla* ATM in the Philippines may not necessarily be desirable, especially for hyperbolic discounters who are largely naïve. It is necessary to provide commitment devices for *Sangla* ATM to minimize its potential negative impacts, which include not only overborrowing and debt overhang but also obesity, overeating, gambling, smoking, drinking and other procrastination behaviour.

ACKNOWLEDGEMENT

This paper is dedicated to the memory of the late Professor Nobuhiko Fuwa of the University of Tokyo. Professor Fuwa, who initiated this study in 2013, passed away in February 2018 before completing this research. The paper draws heavily on his original draft. The financial assistance for data collection provided by Sumitomo Mitsui Banking Corporation Foundation for International Cooperation is gratefully acknowledged.

REFERENCES

ABS-CBN. 2020. "DepEd Warns Teachers: Pawning ATM Payroll Account 'Illegal'". 16 October 2020. https://news.abs-cbn.com/news/10/16/20/deped-warns-teachers-pawning-atm-payroll-account-illegal.

———. 2018. "Bangko Sentral Warns Borrowers, Lenders against 'Sangla ATM' Scheme". 3 August 2018. https://news.abs-cbn.com/business/08/03/18/bangko-sentral-warns-borrowers-lenders-against-sangla-atm-scheme.

Adams, Dale W., and Robert E. Hunter, eds. 2019. *Informal Finance in Low-Income Countries*. New York, USA: Routledge.

Agabin, M. 1993. "The Informal Credit Markets in the Philippines". *Asian Economic Journal* 7, no. 2: 209–47.

Agabin, M., M. Lamberte, M. K. Mangahas, and M. Mangahas. 1989. "Integrative Report on Informal Credit Markets in the Philippines". *PIDS Working Paper Series No. 89–10*. Manila, Philippines: Philippine Institute for Development Studies.

Agarwal, Sumit, Paige Marta Skiba, and Jeremy Tobacman. 2009. "Payday Loans and Credit Cards: New Liquidity and Credit Scoring Puzzles?" *American Economic Review* 99, no. 2: 412–17.

Armendáriz, Beatriz, and Jonathan Morduch. 2010. *The Economics of Microfinance*. Cambridge, MA: MIT Press. Second edition.

Ashraf, Nava. 2009. "Spousal Control and Intra-household Decision Making: An Experimental Study in the Philippines". *American Economic Review* 99, no. 4: 1245–77.

Ashraf, Nava, Dean Karlan, and Wesley Yin. 2006. "Tying Odysseus to the Mast: Evidence from a Commitment Savings Product in the Philippines". *Quarterly Journal of Economics* 121, no. 2: 635–72.

Balisacan, Arsenio M., and Nobuhiko Fuwa. 2007. "Poverty and Vulnerability". In *Reasserting the Rural Development Agenda: Lessons Learned and Emerging Challenges in Asia*, edited by Arsenio M. Balisacan and Nobuhiko Fuwa. Singapore: Institute of Southeast Asian Studies and Los Baños, Philippines: Southeast Asian Regional Center for Graduate Study and Research in Agriculture.

BSP (Bangko Sentral ng Pilipinas). 2012. *2009 Consumer Finance Survey*. Department of Economic Statistics. Bangko Sentral ng Pilipinas. Manila, Philippines.

———. 2017. *2014 Consumer Finance Survey*. Department of Economic Statistics, Bangko Sentral ng Pilipinas. Manila, Philippines.

———. 2018. *2017 Financial Inclusion Survey - Moving towards Digital Financial Inclusion*. Center for Learning and Inclusion Advocacy, Bangko Sentral ng Pilipinas. Manila, Philippines.

———. 2020. *2019 Financial Inclusion Survey*. Center for Learning and Inclusion Advocacy, Bangko Sentral ng Pilipinas. Manila, Philippines.

Bauer, Michal, Julie Chytilova, and Jonathan Morduch. 2012. "Behavioral Foundations of Microcredit: Experimental and Survey Evidence from Rural India". *American Economic Review* 102, no. 2: 1118–39.

Floro, Maria Sagrario, and Debraj Ray. 1997. "Vertical Links between Formal and Informal Financial Institutions". *Review of Development Economics* 1, no. 1: 34–56.

Fuwa, Nobuhiko, Kei Kajisa, Eduardo Lucio, Sharon Faye Piza, and Yasuyuki Sawada. 2016. "Hyperbolic Discounting and an Induced Informal Credit Institution by a New Technology: A Case of Debit Card Pawning in the Philippines". Paper presented at the 2016 North American Winter Meetings of the Econometric Society, San Francisco, California, USA, 3–5 January 2016.

Hoff, Karla, and Joseph Stiglitz. 1993. "Imperfect Information and Rural Credit Markets: Puzzles and Policy Perspectives." In *The Economics of Rural Organization: Theory, Practice and Policy*, edited by Karla Hoff, Avishay Braverman, and Joseph Stiglitz. New York, NY: Oxford University Press.

Karlan, Dean, and Jonathan Morduch. 2010. "Access to Finance". In *Handbook of Development Economics Volume 5*, edited by Dani Rodrik and Mark Rosenzweig, pp. 4703–84. North Holland: Elsevier.

Kremer, Michael, Gautam Rao, and Frank Schilbach. 2019. "Behavioral Development Economics". In *Handbook of Behavioral Economics: Foundations and Applications 2, Volume 2*, edited by Douglas Bernheim, Stefano DellaVigna, and David Laibson. Amsterdam: North-Holland.

Kritz, Ben. 2013. "The Informal Lending Trap". *The Manila Times*. http://www.manilatimes.net/the-informal-lending-trap/26457/ (accessed 8 September 2014).

Meier, Stephan, and Charles Sprenger. 2010. "Present-Biased Preferences and Credit Card Borrowing". *American Economic Journal: Applied Economics* 2, no. 1: 193–210.

Nagarajan, G., C. David, and R. Meyer. 1992. "Informal Finance through Land Pawning Contracts: Evidence from the Philippines". *The Journal of Development Studies* 29, no. 1: 93–107.

Stegman, Michael, A. 2007. "Payday Lending". *Journal of Economic Perspectives* 21, no. 1: 169–90.

PART 4

Inequality and Economic Development

14 An Essay on Markets, Distributive Justice and Social Safety Nets

Dante B. Canlas

---

1 INTRODUCTION AND OVERVIEW

I am delighted to contribute to this Festschrift in honour of Dr. Arsenio M. Balisacan, a professor of economics and colleague at the UP School of Economics, who has reached the mandatory retirement age in government. He was appointed on special detail in 2012 and served up to 2016 as director-general of the National Economic and Development Authority (NEDA) and concurrent secretary of socio-economic planning in the President's Cabinet. As a professor, Dr. Balisacan has made important contributions to understanding poverty and income inequality in the Philippines. During his tenure at NEDA, he coordinated the preparation of the medium-term Philippine Development Plan (PDP), which has inclusive growth as theme—essentially, sustained and broad-based economic growth. This is a timely opportunity for me to visit and explore the current challenge of growth with high income inequality and some rising episodes of such inequality in the country.

The post-World War II economic history of the Philippines shows that the real gross domestic product (GDP, adjusted for inflation) expanded about 34.4 times between 1946 and 2016—an annual real GDP growth rate of about 5.4 per cent. The GDP expansion was accompanied by high and, in some years, increasing income inequality, however. For instance, the Gini index was 0.44 in 2015 and worsened to nearly 0.48 in 2018.

The basic data come from the Family Income and Expenditure Survey (FIES), which the Philippine Statistics Authority (PSA) collects and releases every three years.[1]

Growth with high income inequality has long been a concern of the Philippine government under a succession of administrations since 1986. The inequality problem persists amid a variety of policy interventions geared towards inclusive growth. By no means has the problem been solved at this point. Is there something the Philippines can do to arrest growth with high income inequality, often decried as lack of distributive justice?

Several economists view lack of distributive justice as the result mainly of unequal distribution of initial endowments, which a market system tends to replicate across time. And so instead of interfering with the workings of markets, many economists counsel collective actions designed to correct the inequitable distribution of initial endowments. In this regard, an example of a collective action biased towards equality is land reform in economies that at the early stage of their industrial development were predominantly agricultural. However, despite land reform and fiscal measures deemed equitable, the problem of income inequality has remained a formidable challenge up to now, highlighting the need to further investigate market forces underpinning income inequality in the Philippines. Political choices through elections, not necessarily underpinned by sound economics, dictate to a great extent intervening public policy measures, which may be termed social safety nets, aimed at narrowing income inequality and reducing poverty incidence.[2]

---

[1] The Gini index is a statistical construct reflective of the Lorenz curve, a means of measuring income inequality (see Atkinson 1970); its estimation starts with the size distribution of family income taken from the FIES. The figures reported here are estimates of the World Bank and reported in the *Philippine Statistical Yearbook* that PSA publishes. The Gini ranges between 0 and 1, with 1 indicating perfect inequality and 0, perfect equality.

[2] Each of the Philippine Development Plans (PDPs) associated with the elected Philippine President since 1986, the year martial-law rule ended and democratic political institutions were restored, focused on poverty alleviation. The current PDP's theme is inclusive growth.

1.1 What markets do: An overview of theory

Modern economies with democratic institutions generally rely on a market system guided by a decentralized price system to coordinate a variety of economic and business activities. Prices are seen as capable of directing resources to their most valued uses. The allocation outcomes tend to exhibit balance and are widely considered efficient. Prices that clear all markets exist for various commodities, consisting of goods and services that are produced and sold. The price of a particular commodity represents the marginal value people attach to it.

Both buyers (assumed to be utility maximizers) and sellers (profit maximizers) can achieve their respective goals with the commodity allocation that each market agent gets. In other words, mutually beneficial trades are realized. Markets facilitate mutually beneficial exchanges; meanwhile, a missing market means some needs are not being met, thereby diminishing human welfare. An important part of competitive equilibrium analysis relates to explaining why some markets are missing or incomplete.

The most developed formal description of this market process is a competitive equilibrium system, popularly known in the microeconomics literature as the Arrow-Debreu (A–D) model (see Arrow and Debreu 1954). Under well-defined assumptions about buyers' preferences and sellers' production technologies, a competitive equilibrium exists and is Pareto optimal—the *first fundamental theorem of welfare economics*. The *second welfare theorem* asserts that any Pareto optimal allocation is attainable as a competitive equilibrium after suitable (lump-sum) income transfers.

The A–D model is an abstract model and has been extended in many ways, including presence of externalities that account for market failures, to bring the model closer to a representation of reality. Collective actions are indicated and, frequently, the government with power to tax and disburse tax collection has an advantage in delivering the collective actions to correct shortcomings of competitive markets. It is widely understood, however, that the government has no monopoly over collective actions; organizations outside the government may do just as well.

Another important extension of the A–D model pertains to allocation in the presence of risk and uncertainty, which stem from limited information. Aside from being limited, information is often not equally distributed among market agents, commonly described as asymmetric information. Radner (1968, 1970) points out the limitations of competitive equilibrium analysis and the applications of its two welfare theorems in dealing with limited and asymmetric information. Limited computational abilities of people, for instance, preclude the completeness of markets (whether spot or forward) proposed by the A–D model under uncertainty.[3] In addition, the presence of transaction costs that cannot be offset by the expected returns on investment in a financial asset makes some markets inactive (see, e.g., Hahn 1971). They may be activated at a later time, however, resulting in a sequence economy (see Radner 1972; Arrow and Hahn 1999.) Given incomplete markets, departures from the welfare theorems are proposed.[4]

1.2 Growth and income inequality in the Philippines

This essay attempts to shed some light on the experience of the Philippines on growth with high income inequality, a problem illustrative of weak distributive justice. The phenomenon is not unique to the Philippines. It has been noticed by a long line of eminent economists in other settings (see, e.g., Kuznets 1955; Jorgenson 1988 for the US economy). Income inequality in the competitive equilibrium model is examined based on the functional distribution of production. In a competitive equilibrium model, the production factors, mainly labour and capital, are paid the value of their respective marginal products.[5] The model explains income

---

[3] Under uncertainty, the A-D competitive equilibrium model proposes an expansion of the commodity space (see Arrow 1963). Commodities are distinguished not only by their physical attributes, but also by the date and state of nature in which they are delivered. An expanded commodity space permits a complete set of spot and forward markets, thereby resulting in the forging of buy-and-sell contracts contingent on the occurrence of a specific state of nature. Limited information and computational ability, however, result in missing markets, such as incomplete insurance markets.

[4] Modifications have been many. In financial markets, see Grossman and Stiglitz (1976), Geanakoplos (1990) and Cass (2006). In the context of labour markets, see Spence (1974), Lippman and McCall (1976), Diamond (1982, 1984) and Mortensen and Pissarides (1994). Concerning trade with missing insurance markets, see Newbery and Stiglitz (1984).

[5] This is the starting point in discussing functional distribution in microeconomics (see, e.g., Varian 1987), which informs aggregate growth

differences without being judgemental about desirability of such differences. But it opens up the need to investigate the operations of labour and capital markets—specifically, the forces that yield differences in the mean returns to the factors and their dispersions.

In this connection, this essay pursues the roles that incomplete labour and financial markets play and looks at how far such market limitations contribute to explaining observed income differences and inequality. At one level, this paper may be viewed as a selective survey of extensions to standard models of labour and financial markets that clear. Specifically, we focus on constraints posed by limited and asymmetric information, resulting in incomplete markets. On another level, the paper hopes to trigger interest not only in the descriptive aspects of competitive market analysis with limited labour and financial markets, but also in prescriptive elements, which might contribute to building a reliable social safety net structure in the Philippines. We revisit common interventions, say minimum wage legislation, and discuss alternative perspectives stemming from incomplete markets, without judging whether they are desirable policies. This approach may be regarded as lending a descriptive approach to prescriptive economics.

Quite often, studies about income inequality inexorably go beyond being descriptive. The effects on human welfare of income inequality are so significant that they often invite prescriptions. Scholars belonging to the radical economics school, for example, cite market incentives to behave in a way that runs counter to public interest.[6] Outside the radical school, Arrow (1974) points out in his 1972 Nobel lecture that competitive equilibrium analysis is silent on distributive justice. Some individuals and groups are favoured with abundant allocations, while others tend to be impoverished. Though the lack or absence of distributive justice is not necessarily an offshoot of market failures, it still generates calls for collective actions intended to redress income inequality. One major reason stems from the destructive effects on social cohesiveness that lopsided commodity allocations induce.[7]

---

decomposition analysis (see Solow 1957). In a growth context, Barro and Sala-i-Martin ([1995] 2021) is an excellent reference that uses as point of departure the Solow model (1957).

[6] Bowles (2008), for instance, argues that self-interestedness creates incentives to behave against the good of many in organized societies.

[7] Persson and Tabellini (1994) inquire into whether inequality is harmful to growth. Using a model of endogenous growth and endogenous choice of public policy, the answer is "yes" in a society with distributional conflict.

1.3 Role of limited labour markets

Being employed for pay or profit gives individuals and households command over goods and services traded in commodity markets. A first step is to understand how income inequality is generated in limited labour markets. The study focuses on how the workings of labour markets with heterogeneous workers affect employment and unemployment status and the constraints labour-market frictions pose to individual productivity and human-capital accumulation. The latter influences wages and earnings that ultimately affect the size distribution of household income. Increasing productivity is the primary source of income growth. Factors that constrain productivity improvements generate income inequality among individuals and households. As the paper examines the constraints to productivity in labour markets, it tries to identify, based on some theories about the workings of limited labour markets, factors vital to understanding the persistence of high income inequality in the Philippines.

1.4 Role of incomplete financial markets

One critical constraint to productivity stems from limited financial markets. If complete, financial markets allow people to shift resources across time. At the most fundamental level, expenditures and income receipts need not coincide at a given point in time if there are, for example, complete credit markets. People can satisfy some of their commodity demands in the current period, even if at present they do not earn enough or have no savings to pay for the desired commodity. If they have access to a credit market, they can acquire the commodity bundle they want using their claims to future income to pay for it in the present period. Financial markets are largely incomplete, however, on account of limited and asymmetric information (see footnote 4). For instance, there are no loan markets for higher education, which to a great extent is internally financed by households. Able but poor students cannot enter college unless their families have some savings. Given the high return from higher education, income inequality thus gets transmitted across generations. Similarly, there are no loans to finance job search, which may also be viewed as a form of accumulating human capital with effects on wage profiles over time. Moreover, interest rates do not typically adjust to clear excess demand for loans. Probability of default exists, inducing banks and other financial intermediaries to ration credit (see, e.g., Jaffee and Russell 1976; Stiglitz and Weiss 1981).

The evidence suggests that there are disadvantaged individuals and families, namely, the low income and those who fall below official poverty income thresholds. In many settings, a consensus normally emerges in the political process of well-organized societies that government ought to have programmes that assist these disadvantaged members of society to be assured of a minimum standard of living wherever they may be residing, whether in the rural or urban areas. The existing conditional cash transfer programme to poor families is illustrative of such a Philippine government programme.[8]

1.5 Some social safety nets

In response to persistent income inequality, the government intervenes and designs some social safety nets to assist workers who go through long spells of unemployment, or if employed, are generally trapped in low-wage jobs.[9] Minimum wage legislation (MWL) is an example of such government policy intervention. In analysing the effects of MWL, we do not rely solely on the notion of other analysts who maintain that eliminating MWL can be trusted to raise employment levels because it leads to a clearing of the labour market.[10] A labour market that clears is generally used as a starting point for understanding wage and employment determination, but the robustness of its results is questionable in situations where labour mobility and flows in and out of employment and unemployment are crucial in understanding the labour-force status of heterogeneous workers and employers.

---

[8] This is a public programme implemented by the Department of Social Work and Development, which gives monthly cash transfers to low-income families on condition that parents bring their children below 5 years old to health clinics for wellness visits and children of elementary schooling age are enrolled.

[9] Labour force statisticians call them underemployed: though employed full time, they express a desire for extra work, an offshoot of being employed at low wages.

[10] In the United States, Acemoglu (2021) argues the case for raising the minimum wage, saying earlier studies based on the standard labour market-clearing model tended to overstate the disemployment effects of a minimum wage hike. As evidence, Acemoglu cites the empirical works of Card (1992) and Card and Krueger (1996), which find that increasing the minimum wage has no adverse effects on employment.

Instead, we adopt a job-search and job-matching framework. We depart from the thinking that, in the presence of high unemployment rates, eliminating MWL serves to clear the labour market for low-wage workers covered by such legislation. By focusing on labour market flows, we show that differing unemployment rates for different age groups can materialize, not necessarily due to the failure of wage rates to adjust and clear labour markets. We adopt some implications of the search theoretic and job-matching models of, for example, Diamond (1982), Mortensen (1986) and Mortensen and Pissarides (1994) to shed light on the duration of unemployment spells and wage paths of various types of workers.

Meanwhile, in financial markets, the government intervenes amid credit rationing by establishing publicly owned banks and encouraging the formation of small private development banks that lend to small businesses.[11] In addition, it accords special tax incentives to microfinance institutions to induce them to lend to micro, small and medium enterprises (MSMEs).

We note, however, that social safety nets are social choices. They evolve in representative democracies from voting, thereby ushering in a role for politicians. Assuming politicians are driven by personal interests, one cannot expect social choices to be optimal in this context.

The paper is organized as follows: Section 2 revisits allocation under a competitive equilibrium system. Section 3 presents some facts on the size distribution of income in the Philippines, illustrating the lack of distributive justice. Section 4 discusses a labour market framework with job search and job matching, along with the unemployment spells it yields and corresponding forgone human capital. Section 5 presents unemployment rates by age group and educational attainment. Section 6 discusses incomplete financial markets and the latter's distributional consequences. Section 7 describes some social safety nets and points out how many of them fail as such. Section 8 presents concluding remarks.

---

[11] There are at present two government financial institutions: Land Bank of the Philippines, originally set up to lend to small landless farmers, the main beneficiaries of the government's land reform programme, and Development Bank of the Philippines, a wholesale lender mainly to firms in the industry sector.

2 ALLOCATION IN COMPETITIVE MARKETS

In this section, we sketch an economic environment where numerous consumers have stable preferences, and each one maximizes utility subject to a budget constraint. A demand function for each commodity emerges. Meanwhile, given several atomistic firms with access to a production technology, whereby each one is profit maximizing subject to a budget constraint for the inputs used in production, a supply function for each commodity exists. In equilibrium, prices that clear all markets are determined. Mutually beneficial exchanges take place in competitive equilibrium markets. Under well-defined conditions, beginning with complete markets, equilibrium allocations are Pareto optimal in the sense that they cannot be improved upon.

At a formal level, the analysis dwells on the existence and uniqueness of the equilibrium allocations and commodity prices that clear all markets. A fixed-point theorem is invoked to show existence. The existence and Pareto optimality of equilibrium allocations are established in the two fundamental theorems of welfare (see Arrow 1951a). For optimality to hold, complete market and convexity conditions are essential.

2.1 Externalities

The competitive equilibrium model is extended in a number of ways. One extension dwells on externalities, either positive or negative, that block commodity pricing, resulting in either market failures or incomplete markets. Pollution illustrates a negative externality. If polluters are not made to pay for the harm their actions inflict on other people, then pollution persists. Meanwhile, in the case of positive externalities, such as clean air, if people are not compensated for the benefits that third parties capture, then clean air tends to be underproduced. To curb individual behaviour biased towards pollution, polluters are taxed commensurate to the costs they impose on others.

Market failures can occur in the presence of externalities or spillover effects on third parties. Markets may not fail completely but may be rendered incomplete, precluding some mutually beneficial trades and resulting in loss of human welfare. Collective actions are called for to correct market failures or address the inadequacy of market allocations. Though the government does not have a monopoly over collective actions that compensate for failed or incomplete markets, in several instances it is the one relied on for collective actions; its tax-and-spending powers give the government comparative advantage therein. This is seen, for instance, in the delivery of public goods, including national defence, peace and order, and provision of a legal and judicial framework for contractual performance and adjudication of contractual disputes.

Competitive equilibrium analysis also tackles the far-reaching implications of a legal framework for economic growth and development. An exchange economy guided by a decentralized price system operates smoothly to the extent contracts, whether explicit or implicit, are enforceable. Contract enforcement is a public good in the following sense: no single individual is willing to quote the price he or she is willing to pay to have such a contractual setting since everybody benefits. Since pricing is not possible without truthful revelation of preferences, the government steps in to provide a legal and judicial system conducive to contractual enforcement. And if contractual disputes emerge, the judicial system adjudicates. Once the highest court rules on a dispute, then constitutional rules and jurisprudence dictate outcomes in future similar cases.

2.2 Risk and uncertainty

Limited and asymmetric information results in market transactions under risk and uncertainty. Trade is not deterred by uncertainty, however. In an uncertain environment, market agents make contracts contingent on the occurrence of a particular state of nature. Arrow (1963) proposes to deal with uncertainty based on the A–D model by expanding the commodity space. Goods are distinguished not only by their physical attributes, but also by the date and state of nature they are delivered. For example, an ice cream in summer is different from an ice cream in winter.

Contracts in insurance markets are illustrative; they shift resources across states of nature. An insurance contract stipulates payments to be made once an unfavourable state of nature occurs against which insurance was procured. An example is the burning down of an insured property. The insurer pays, provided the fire is established to be a genuine accident, not a case of arson.

Information in many cases is not only limited; frequently, it is unequally distributed among agents—a case of asymmetric information. Markets with asymmetric information may yield inefficient outcomes or fail completely. Moral hazard and adverse selection are two forms of asymmetric information problems that in insurance, labour and financial markets produce sup-Pareto outcomes. Hence, some collective actions to improve welfare may be indicated.

Adverse selection arises if, for instance, a potential insurer is confronted with buyers of insurance who are heterogeneous in terms of their degree of aversion towards risk. Some buyers are more risk averse than others. Ideally, the insurer wants to distinguish its potential clients by risk type so that a higher risk premium can be levied on the riskier than on the less risky. If this differentiation is not possible, the insurer charges a uniform premium to all buyers. In this situation, the less risky buyers end up subsidizing the riskier, since the latter tend to claim more insurance payments than the former. In cases where only the riskier types buy insurance, then insurance firms can potentially be out of business.

Moral hazard is an ex-post issue. If an unfavourable state of nature occurs, the insurer asks whether the event is a true accident or an offshoot of deliberate action. For instance, a house burns down for which an insurance policy has been procured. The insurer, before making any payment, investigates whether it was arson or a real accident. Payment is made once it is established that the accident is genuine.

Asymmetric information, whether in the form of adverse selection or moral hazard, does not impede market transactions. Contingent claim contracts with explicit conditions can be written. In the case of buyers of car insurance, for instance, teenagers driving sports cars are levied a higher insurance premium than adult buyers who drive conventional sedans; the former are perceived riskier than the latter. This is an attempt to address adverse selection. In addition, co-payments are written as conditions to mitigate moral hazard. This minimizes carelessness once insurance is purchased.

Another anomaly that may emerge from pure market allocation is the lack or absence of distributive justice. Some individuals, households and groups get abundant allocations, but others are impoverished. The inequality in commodity allocations is traceable to income inequality. The presence and persistence of inequality can generate some social problems.

The poor, for instance, may be mired in unhealthy and hazardous environments, vulnerable to contracting communicable diseases that can spread to society's healthy members. The government can use its tax-and-spending powers to generate revenues, assist the poor and minimize the spread of infectious diseases.

Similarly, the poor lack access to education even at the most basic level. This creates a socio-political problem, since a literate population is critical to making democratic political institutions like elections work. Government intervention through the provision of basic education sans out-of-pocket costs to parents helps build a responsible citizenry. In exercising the right to vote, for instance, the poor may be instructed not to sell their vote.

It thus helps society to usher in distributive justice where none exists or where society regards the unequal income distribution as intolerable. We begin by examining imperfections in labour markets that pose barriers to productivity, the source of income growth. An understanding of labour-market processes and existing limitations, if any, can shed light on how income inequality is generated, thereby providing guides to policymakers in formulating labour-market reforms.

Labour markets reward individuals who bring more human capital to the workplace. Human capital is widely viewed as the amount of efficiency units, obtained from investments in education and health, that people bring to the workplace. Assuming the price of every efficiency unit is constant, workers who are endowed with a larger set of efficiency units have higher earnings. Workers are heterogeneous, however. They may have the same observable attributes like schooling and work experience, but differ in some latent attributes like drive and motivation that enhance their efficiency units in the workplace.[12] This has resulted in extensions of the standard labour-market clearing model to internal labour markets with hierarchically organized firms.

Income inequality may warrant some collective actions. Traditionally, however, most economists trace such inequality to unequal distribution of initial endowments. Land reform, for instance, is prescribed to an economy that is predominantly agricultural in its stage of development. Land is a major factor of production; ownership of land assets can

---

[12] Latent attributes are often revealed on the job to supervisors, resulting in observationally identical workers exhibiting wage differentials. The more motivated workers are not only endowed with more efficiency units, but each of their efficiency units is also priced higher than the less driven. Theoretically, this has not gone unnoticed (see Stiglitz 1974). Empirically, Heckman and Borjas (1980) examine the role of heterogeneity among workers, who may be observationally identical.

dictate income distribution in the long run. The policy advice is thus to correct inequality in initial endowments, rather than interfering with the workings of a market system.

It is important to note that social choices emerging in democratic societies from individual values are done primarily by voting (see Arrow 1951b). Elected politicians determine the quantity of public goods to be provided through the government budget. For example, land-to-the-landless programmes may entail procuring private lands at market prices using public funds and selling them at subsidized prices to small landless farmer-tenants.

3 INCOME INEQUALITY

This section lends some empirical favour to the paper by describing income inequality in the Philippines based on the size distribution of household income and looking at commonly used measures of income inequality. All data unless otherwise indicated are from FIES. Most figures also appear in the *Philippine Statistical Yearbook* of the PSA (various years). Household income is arrayed hierarchically by income decile from lowest to highest, with the corresponding frequency distribution of households. The Gini index or coefficient, based on the cumulative income share by decile, is commonly used as a measure of income inequality, estimates of which are made by the World Bank. The PSA issues the Gini every three years.

Table 14.1 shows the Gini coefficient for the years 2000, 2003, 2006, 2009, 2012, 2015 and 2018. Between 2000 and 2003, the Gini improved from 0.48 to 0.46, which means declining income inequality. It remained at 0.46 from 2003 to 2012, then declined to 0.44 in 2015, suggesting further improvement in income distribution. However, the Gini worsened to nearly 0.48 again in 2018.

Table 14.1. Gini coefficient (2000–2018)

Year	2000	2003	2006	2009	2012	2015	2018
Gini	0.48	0.46	0.46	0.46	0.46	0.44	0.48

Note: Gini estimates are from the World Bank.
Source of basic data: PSA (various years), *Family Income and Expenditure Survey*.

Even if the Gini coefficient declined between 2000 and 2015, one disturbing development stems from the inability of families in low income deciles to catch up with those in the high income deciles. Table 14.2 shows the mean income by decile for 2012 and 2015.

Table 14.3 shows the difference in mean income between the top and bottom 10 per cent in panel A. For 2012 the difference in mean income is PHP778,141. This increased to PHP852,075 in 2015. The lowest income decile has fallen further behind in absolute terms.

Panel B shows the difference in mean income between the top and bottom 20 per cent. The widening of the income difference between 2012 and 2015 also holds. Panels C, D and E exhibit the same trend in mean income difference between the top and bottom 30 per cent, between the top and bottom 40 per cent, and between the top and bottom 50 per cent. In all cases, the bottom income deciles increasingly fall behind the top deciles between 2012 and 2015.

It is reasonable to conclude that the worsening of the Gini in 2018 further widened the mean income differences estimated in the forgoing.

Table 14.2. Mean income by decile (2012 and 2015, in PHP)

Decile	Mean income, 2012	Mean income, 2015
1	47,659	58,580
2	72,012	88,094
3	92,425	111,867
4	113,940	135,782
5	138,622	163,623
6	169,932	199,153
7	214,513	248,868
8	281,384	319,205
9	393,383	440,385
10	825,800	910,655

Source of basic data: PSA (various years), Family Income and Expenditure Survey.

Table 14.3. Difference in mean income between top- and low-income decile (2012 and 2015, in PHP)

Year	2012	2015
Panel A		
Top 10%	825,800	910,655
Bottom 10%	47,659	58,580
Difference	778,141	852,075
Panel B		
Top 20%	1,219,183	1,350,960
Bottom 20%	119,671	146,674
Difference	1,099,512	1,204,286
Panel C		
Top 30%	1,500,567	1,670,165
Bottom 30%	212,096	258,541
Difference	1,288,471	1,416,624
Panel D		
Top 40%	1,715,080	1,919,033
Bottom 40%	326,036	394,323
Difference	1,389,044	1,524,710
Panel E		
Top 50%	1,885,012	2,118,186
Bottom 50%	464,658	557,946
Difference	1,420,354	1,560,240

Sources: Basic data are from PSA (various years), *Family Income and Expenditure Survey*. Figures are the author's estimates.

The data pertain to household income, much of which consists of wages and salaries for the employed. For self-employed household heads, the income partially represents returns to entrepreneurship. To understand the income inequality documented in this section, it helps to analyse the constraints that labour markets pose to the productivity of working members in the household. We focus here on labour market flows that are an offshoot of search, whether by workers or by firms. Job search entails cost. Workers without savings and access to credit markets are unable to generate enough job offers if they cannot finance their job search. Their income pales in comparison with workers capable of doing a more active and intensive job search. We also examine extensions to the basic labour-market clearing model, focusing on new perspectives they offer in looking at traditional safety nets for low-wage workers, such as MWL. We want to find out how robust are the disemployment effects predicted by the basic labour-market clearing model.

4 LABOUR MARKETS WITH JOB SEARCH AND MATCHING

We extend the standard labour-market clearing model and adopt a perspective shaped by labour markets with job search and matching to account for the contribution of labour-market processes to observed unemployment and income inequality in the Philippines.

Both workers and employers engage in job search (see, e.g., Lippman and McCall 1976; Mortensen 1986; Mortensen and Pissarides 1994). A firm screens job applicants using a variety of means, such as testing for skills, to identify applicants whose expected productivities on the job exceed the firm's reservation marginal productivities in various job positions and tasks. It makes a job offer, which, if accepted by the worker, results in a job-worker match, thereby ending the worker's spell of search unemployment.

4.1 Job search and matching by workers and employers

There are many aspects to job searching by workers. One is the decision to enter the labour force and the ensuing search activities that bring them to a particular classification: employed, unemployed or remaining out of the labour force. Those who belong to the working-age population, 15–19 and 20–24 years old, are frequently the seekers of entry-level jobs. Applicants have a reservation wage; they terminate their search once they get an offer that meets their reservation wage. Another aspect of job search involves movement from employment to unemployment, wherein employed workers quit current jobs to search. There are other flows in the labour market. For example, a young, educated, married woman in the early stage of forming a family may opt out of the labour force to raise a preschooler; however, she may re-enter the labour force once her child is in school. She may have to retrain to learn and master new production techniques that emerged while she was out of the labour force. She may be unemployed while retraining. On the other hand, an unemployed worker in search of a job may become impatient and discouraged, and decide to drop out of the labour force. This tends to happen when a recession is taking longer than expected.

Summing up, various labour-market flows and movements result in unemployment rates that differ for workers by age group, gender and educational attainment. A disturbing thought is that being unemployed means loss of human capital, which influences people's time paths of employment, wages and earnings. For instance, those who go through many intermittent spells of search unemployment forgo more human capital and tend to end up in the bottom deciles of the income distribution.

Employers also engage in search. Firms have a reservation marginal-worker productivity and choose applicants who meet it. Once a worker accepts a firm's job offer, a job-worker match is forged. Workers are aware of firms' search process and, in this context, invest in skills-enhancing training and education to signal to firms that they are high-productivity workers (see Spence 1974).

As firms search and maintain vacancies even amid high unemployment, workers experience spells of unemployment, the duration of which depends on when the two parties forge a match. In any event, a spell of unemployment means forgone human capital from reduced experience on the job. Workers who are heterogeneous by skills and other observable attributes, say, education and work experience, go through different spells of unemployment; the spells tend to be longer for the unskilled and semi-skilled. Unskilled or semi-skilled applicants have a higher probability of being rejected by employers since they are likely to have marginal products that fall below the latter's reservation productivities. The model predicts higher unemployment rates for the less skilled than the skilled.

More complicated possibilities emerge in the course of technological advances and other real shocks. Some jobs are destroyed, never to be filled up, and replaced by new jobs and tasks. Job destruction and job creation coexist, with differing effects on the duration of unemployment. This theme has been formally explored by Mortensen and Pissarides (1994).

5 PHILIPPINE UNEMPLOYMENT RATES BY AGE GROUP

The labour force concepts that the PSA has adopted for its surveys start with the working age population of 15–64 years old. The unemployed consist of those actively seeking work, but failing to get a job match. The labour force (LF) is thus the sum of the employed (N) and unemployed (U). That is $LF = N + U$. Dividing both sides by LF yields the unemployment rate (u), as $u = 1 - n$, where $u = U/LF$ and $n = N/LF$.

Table 14.4 shows aggregate labour force size (LF), employed (N), unemployed (U) and their corresponding rates in 2016 denoted in lower case letters for employment rate (n) and unemployment rate (u). The labour force participation rate was 63.5 per cent in 2016. The unemployment rate was 5.4 per cent, putting the employment rate at 94.6 per cent.

The study now turns to unemployment rate by age group—an initial attempt to empirically consider heterogeneity among workers. Table 14.5 shows the unemployed by age group and the corresponding unemployment rates in 2012 and 2016. To get the unemployment rate by age group, we divide the number of unemployed in each age group by the labour force, LF.

Table 14.4. Labour force, employed and unemployed (2016, in '000 and %)

Year	LF ('000)	N ('000)	U ('000)	LFPR (%)	N (%)	U (%)
2016	43,631	40,998	3,364	63.5	94.6	5.4

Note: (1) LF - labour force, N - employed, U - unemployed, LFPR - labour force participation rate.
(2) LFPR is obtained by dividing LF by the size of the working-age population.
Source of basic data: PSA (various years), *Labor Force Survey*.

Table 14.5. Unemployment by age group (2016, in %)

Age group (in years)	u_{2012}	u_{2016}
15–24	3.49	2.62
25–34	2.09	1.59
35–44	0.70	0.59
45–54	0.46	0.39
55–64	0.23	0.20
65 and above	0.05	0.05
TOTAL	6.96	5.42

Note: $u_i = U_i/LF$, where u_i refers to unemployment rate in the ith age group.
Source: PSA (various years, 2017), *Philippine Statistical Yearbook*.

The youngest age cohort (15–24 years old) had the highest unemployment rate: 3.49 per cent in 2012 or about half of the total unemployment rate and 2.62 per cent in 2016 or 48 per cent of the total. The unemployment rate declines as the age group goes higher. It is clear from these figures that the unemployment rate in the Philippines is largely a youth unemployment problem. In the context of job search and job matching, young workers, usually less skilled, go through a longer period of search than their older counterparts who have longer work experience.

Education is one attribute of workers that matters a lot in job search and job matching. Workers with high school and college education are likely to search in the same job market, where signalling by job applicants and screening by firms are practiced. All things held equal, college graduates signal to firms a higher productivity level and are likely to receive job offers in a shorter time than high school graduates. The latter go through longer spells of search unemployment than college graduates.

Table 14.6 shows unemployment rates by educational attainment. Both in 2012 and 2016, workers with high school education had the highest unemployment rate at 3.15 per cent and 2.33 per cent, respectively.

We note that the lowest unemployment rates in 2012 and 2016 are workers with no grade completed and those with post-secondary and elementary education. The job search and matching framework hardly applies to those with no grade completed and those with elementary education. The job market where they apply is largely characterized by free entry and exit, involving low skills and low wages. Labour markets in rural agricultural areas and the informal urban sector are illustrative.

Table 14.6. Unemployment rate by educational attainment (2012 and 2016, in '000 and %)

Educational attainment	U_{2012} (in '000)	u_{2012} (in %)	U_{2016} (in '000)	u_{2016} (in %)
No grade completed	14	0.03	16	0.03
Elementary	373	0.92	305	0.70
High school	1,275	3.15	1,011	2.33
Post-secondary	66	0.16	200	0.46
College	931	2.30	831	1.91

Note: (1) Upper case U is number of unemployed in thousands; lower case u is unemployment rate in %.
(2) Labour force size is 40,426,000 for 2012 and 43,361,000 for 2016.

Source of basic data: PSA (various years), Labor Force Survey.

As for those with post-secondary education, their training is largely vocational and technical. They have skills that are valued in the labour market, but possibly they do not go through a long job search in the sector where they are likely to be hired. Construction is an example of such a sector.

At the other extreme are college graduates who face a labour market wherein job search and matching are prevalent. They show high unemployment rates, next to high school graduates. College graduates, however, are likely to have a higher reservation wage than high school graduates, thus, they tend to engage in more search, resulting in spells of unemployment.

One of the fastest growing sectors for job creation is business process outsourcing, commonly referred to as call centres. High school graduates qualify for these jobs. However, all things being equal, companies tend to prefer college graduates to high school graduates, which might explain the latter's higher unemployment rates.

Labour markets with job search and job matching are consistent with observed unemployment rates of heterogeneous workers that differ in education, work, experience, gender and other observable attributes. However, it must be noted that workers also differ in some latent characteristics, say, drive and motivation, that affect their wage and employment profiles across time (see footnote 12).

6 INCOMPLETE FINANCIAL MARKETS AS CONSTRAINTS TO PRODUCTIVITY

The principal role of financial markets, which include debt, securities and equity markets, is to match (1) borrowers who are short on funds but with projects that are expected to be profitable and (2) savers who are without projects but are willing to lend their surplus funds to agents with projects that stand to earn profits in the future. Borrowers and lenders do not have to meet personally; institutions emerge and act as financial intermediaries. Examples are banks and stock exchanges. Financial transactions are conducted generally under limited and asymmetric information, giving rise to risk and uncertainty.

Financial intermediaries build up expertise in assessing default risk of borrowers, but always confront limits to the available information. Hence, financial markets tend to be incomplete; there are missing financial markets, with adverse consequences on human welfare and income distribution.[13] Similar to insurance markets, when credit markets are incomplete, some needs are not met, posing obstacles to productivity.

One prominent example is the absence of a loan market to finance investments in human capital, such as higher education and job search. The job searcher finances college education and job search; he or she must accumulate savings first to be able to support both activities. Alternatively, the family must be sufficiently wealthy so it can support the college education or job search of a family member. Both higher education and job search are remunerative investments. In the absence of loans for these human capital investments, income inequality tends to be transmitted across generations.

Furthermore, there are no credit institutions that support shifts from employment to self-employment or entrepreneurship. Only individuals and households with initial savings can engage in these occupational shifts. An absent credit market is inefficient to the extent laid-off employees during a business downturn may want to start their own business ventures, for example, but have no access to funds.

Some estimates of returns to higher education range from 15 to 20 per cent, making higher education a worthy investment for many. College graduates can capture the returns on their investments in the form of future earnings, which are higher than what they will earn if they do not invest in college education. Low-income students qualified to tackle college education but without sufficient funds benefit if they can access loans for college education.

There are no known estimates of returns to job search in the Philippines. It is reasonable to expect, however, that job search is remunerative too. Job searchers coming from a state of inactivity in the labour force, such as graduates who attended college on a full-time basis, can expect a higher entry-level wage offer than those who do not engage in job search. Moreover, doing a job search while already employed can be an efficient move insofar as it usually results in a higher wage in the new firm. The wage path across time of workers who actively engage in job search tends to outperform the wage path of those who do not search.

Job search is not costless, however. For example, some firms may charge applicants with skill-testing fees. The fees are usually intended to induce self-selection among applicants. Those who are likely to fail

---

[13] The theory of incomplete financial markets is a large and growing body of knowledge; it extends the risk and uncertainty aspects of the A–D model (see, e.g., Magill and Quinzii 2002).

the tests are dissuaded from applying and taking the tests, thereby minimizing depreciation of testing equipment. If the job searcher intends to generate several wage offers before deciding on any offer, the transaction costs involved are typically large. Without loans for job search, applicants from poor and low-income households are placed at a disadvantage.

Job search is a productive investment. If collective actions, whether public or private, can be marshalled to address absent markets in support of job search and higher education, low-income individuals and families may benefit.

7   SOCIAL SAFETY NETS

This section examines some social safety nets that are prominently observed in the Philippines to see how they can deliver beneficial effects to individuals and households. Social safety nets are societal choices. Voting determines how they emerge from individual values. The process opens up a role for politicians who allocate public funds in a representative democracy where the executive and legislative branches possess independent powers.

Unemployment and underemployment, which is employment at low wages, have induced a variety of policy interventions that may be regarded as attempts to provide social safety nets to disadvantaged workers.[14]

Furthermore, credit rationing is prevalent. Banks do not lower interest rates to clear excess demand for credit. Instead, banks resort to credit rationing. As a result, financial inclusion programmes targeted at low-income firms and consumers may be beneficial.[15]

We start with an analysis of the MWL, incorporating some aspects of job search and job matching.

---

[14] After the Great Depression of the 1930s, the US Congress enacted the Employment Act of 1946, aimed at creating employment opportunities for all American workers.

[15] In 2015, the Philippine government, under the leadership of the Bangko Sentral ng Pilipinas and the Department of Finance, launched the National Strategy for Financial Inclusion, aimed at expanding access of Filipinos to a wide variety of financial products and services.

7.1 Minimum wage legislation

Suppose the government raises the legal minimum wage from an equilibrium position, where the value of the marginal product (VMP) of identical workers is equal to the wage rate (W). An increase in MWL disturbs equilibrium in a competitive labour market; that is, W is greater than VMP. To restore equilibrium, firms will intensify search for workers whose VMP exceeds W.

Using the standard labour-market clearing model, the firm terminates employees whose VMP is less than W, thereby raising unemployment. But this prediction does not hold in an extended model where a sector of the economy is not covered by MWL. If it is difficult to generate wage offers in the covered labour market, laid-off workers may be induced to search in labour markets not covered by MWL. Assume there is freedom of entry and exit in the uncovered sector, say, in the informal urban sector and in subsistence agriculture. The unemployment triggered in raising the minimum wage vanishes. However, the wage rate in the uncovered sector goes down with the increase in the supply of workers. Consequently, income inequality worsens. The unemployment spells last until laid-off workers give up job search in the covered sector and enter the uncovered sector. These are the inefficiencies arising from raising the minimum wage. But the higher unemployment is overstated by the basic labour-market clearing model. These predictions are consistent with the empirics of Card (1992) and Card and Krueger (1996) that "disemployment" from MWL is overstated.

Complications arise if firms are big and hierarchical, and able to exercise monopsonistic powers. Wages may stagnate. Meanwhile, given internal labour markets, it is widely observed that executive compensation that includes bonuses and stock options far outpaces wages, resulting in a large earnings gap. Acemoglu (2021) points out this inequality and advocates higher minimum wages.

7.2 Employment protection

The other social safety net, frequently proposed by labour unions, is employment protection. Specifically, unions petition government to declare illegal the end-of-employment contract (so-called "endo") that Philippine firms practice. Here, firms lay off workers after six months of employment to avoid making them regular employees, then rehire them after the lapse of a short period of time under another six-month contract.

The effect of such employment protection policy is like raising the MWL. The duration of the search process of firms is lengthened. Some of the laid-off workers may no longer be rehired; workers with higher VMPs may replace them. On the part of the workers, they need to invest in market signals, such as training, to convince firms that their VMPs are high and they deserve to be rehired. This means longer spells of unemployment.

It is useful to note that both MWL and employment protection are not effective social protection measures. They interfere in the workings of labour markets. Both labour demand and supply are at work, and measures that interfere with privately reached employment and wage contracts are not likely to produce salutary results.

Meanwhile, the perspective from a labour market that incorporates job search and job matching underscores the importance of an expanded labour market database that improves the operations of labour markets. A labour market information system focused on flows like turnovers, vacancies and applications is helpful in addressing the problems of uninformed workers experiencing hardships in the labour market.

7.3 Financial inclusion

The National Strategy for Financial Inclusion (NSFI) seeks to assist individuals, families and firms that are traditionally underserved by the financial system, specifically by the commercial banking system (see footnote 15). These include members of poor families and MSMEs. The financial institutions include savings and loans associations, thrift banks, small development banks, rural banks and cooperative banks.

This is a step in the right direction, particularly if the policies and programmes succeed in solving the missing credit markets for financing job search and higher education. Banks catering to financial inclusion can write loan contracts supportive of job search and higher education, which they can apply for rediscounting with the Bangko Sentral ng Pilipinas (BSP). The BSP should also aim to improve the tradability of loan assets of banks engaged in financial inclusion. In case banks encounter a surge in liquidity demand, they can sell their loan assets. The two major government financial institutions (GFIs)—Development Bank of the Philippines (DBP) and Land Bank of the Philippines (LBP)—can be enlisted to solve missing financial markets.

Currently, the LBP and DBP have commercial banking functions that do not go far in easing the problems of credit-starved clients, such as land-reform beneficiaries and local government units. Large business enterprises are adequately served by private commercial banks. It is useful to review the mandate of these two GFIs. One option is to merge them into an independent development bank wholly owned by the government that would cater to credit-starved agents, be adequately capitalized and be authorized to issue its own securities. Their commercial banking functions can be privatized.

8 CONCLUDING REMARKS

The economic experience of the Philippines since World War II has been one of growth with high income inequality. The period 2015–18 had been an episode of rising income inequality, going by the Gini coefficients. To address this disturbing trend, the government has intervened in various ways, anchored on heavy reliance on competitive markets guided by a decentralized price system. Such an approach has delivered efficient results but has failed the equity test. Markets guided by a decentralized price system are hardly concerned with distributive justice.

This paper draws attention to operations of labour and financial markets, and how they replicate the existing income inequality unless government takes corrective actions. Drawing from the perspective of a labour market with job search and matching, the study generated information on how heterogeneous workers come to a state of unemployment and the duration of their unemployment spells, with implications on their wage and earnings profiles over time. Using this labour market framework, policymakers are well advised to go beyond mere counting of the employed and the unemployed, which is of little use in determining who among workers are encountering hardships in the labour market. It is preferable for government to develop a labour market information system that focuses on labour market flows, such as turnovers, quits, vacancies and applications. Social safety nets that try to invalidate privately reached employment and wage contracts, such as MWL and employment protection, are hardly helpful in improving the welfare of workers employed at low wages. MWL helps when big firms dominate and can exercise labour market powers.

The paper also draws attention to incomplete financial markets, bringing out the plight of credit-starved and credit-rationed agents. Many of the imperfections in financial markets stem from limited and asymmetric information, which must be addressed to improve outcomes. Because the credit-starved agents are unable to shift resources across time with limited or zero access to credit in support of productive activities, their income suffers across time. An important initiative is to initiate in-depth reviews of the LBP and DBP, with a view towards privatizing their commercial banking functions and merging them into one independent development bank of the government that would lend to credit-starved agents.

The upshot: as a starting point, policymakers must look at the operations and processes of labour and financial markets to stand a chance of containing growth with high income inequality in the Philippines. It is well understood that income inequality is rooted in several factors, many of them institutional and should be considered in a second wave of reforms. For instance, political processes that favour powerful vested interest groups and pork-barrel allocations in national government budget deliberations mangle redistribution policies through the budget, thereby worsening income inequality. They must be eliminated.

Social safety nets are collective choices underpinned by individual preferences. In representative democracies, these societal choices are arrived at by voting. The allocation of taxpayers' money among competing public goods are thus largely determined by the political process (see Persson and Tabellini 2000; Lizzeri and Persico 2001).

Lastly, from an institutional standpoint, the question is whether policy reforms in labour and financial markets and instituting social safety nets work under decentralization. The challenge is defining the proper division of labour between the national government and local government units that delivers efficient and equitable results from labour and financial market reforms, as well as from instituting social safety net programmes, which are attempts at redistribution. The local government units are in a good position to respond in a timely manner to concerns confronting their constituents in the labour and financial markets.

ACKNOWLEDGEMENT

I gratefully acknowledge a research grant from the University of the Philippines in Diliman. This essay is a revised version of my working paper entitled, "Markets, Distributive Justice, and Social Safety Nets," which came out in 2018. At that time, only the Gini index for 2015 was available. I thank the editors for their helpful comments, which led me to introduce some expositional and content changes, and add some articles looking at political incentives in the provision of public goods.

REFERENCES

Acemoglu, Daron. 2021. "The Case for a Higher Minimum Wage". https://www.project-syndicate.org (accessed 27 February 2021).
Atkinson, A. B. 1970. "On the Measurement of Inequality". *Journal of Economic Theory* 2, no. 3: 244–63.
Arrow, Kenneth. 1951a. "An Extension of the Basic Theorems of Classical Welfare Economics". In *Proceedings of the Second Berkeley Symposium on Mathematical Statistics and Probability*, edited by Jerzy Neyman, pp. 507–32. Berkeley: University of California Press.
———. 1951b. *Social Choice and Individual Values*. New York: John Wiley and Sons.
———. 1963. "The Role of Securities in the Optimal Allocation of Risk Bearing". *Review of Economic Studies* 31:91–96. First published 1953 (in French).
———. 1974. "General Economic Equilibrium: Purpose, Analytic Techniques, Collective Choice". *American Economic Review* 64, no. 2: 253–72.
Arrow, Kenneth, and Gerard Debreu. 1954. "Existence of an Equilibrium for a Competitive Economy". *Econometrica* 22 (July): 265–90.
Arrow, Kenneth, and Frank Hahn. 1999. "Notes on Sequence Economies, Transaction Costs, and Uncertainty". *Journal of Economic Theory* 86, no. 2: 203–18.
Diamond, Peter. 1982. "Wage Determination and Efficiency in Search Equilibrium". *Review of Economic Studies* 49, no. 2: 217–27.
———. 1984. *A Search Equilibrium Approach to the Micro Foundations of Macroeconomics*. Cambridge, Massachusetts: MIT Press.
Barro, Robert, and Xavier Sala-i-Martin. (1995) 2021. *Economic Growth*. Cambridge, Massachusetts: MIT Press.
Bowles, Samuel. 2008. "Policies Designed for Self-Interested Citizens May Undermine the Moral Sentiments: Evidence from Economic Experiments". *Science* 520: 1605–9.

Canlas, Dante. 2018. "Markets, Distributive Justice, and Social Safety Nets". Working Paper, School of Economics, University of the Philippines. Quezon City, Philippines.

Card, David. 1992. "Do Minimum Wages Reduce Employment: A Case Study of California, 1987–1989". *Industrial and Labor Relations Review* 46, no. 1: 38–54.

Card, David, and Alan Krueger. 1996. "Myth and Measurement: The New Economics of the Minimum Wage Law". *Economic Journal* 106, no. 434: 228–49.

Cass, David. 2006. "Competitive Equilibrium with Incomplete Financial Markets". *Journal of Mathematical Economics* 42: 384–405.

Geanokoplos, John. 1990. "An Introduction to General Equilibrium with Incomplete Asset Markets". *Journal of Mathematical Economics* 19: 1–38.

Grossman, Sanford, and Joseph Stiglitz. 1976. "Information and Competitive Price Systems". *American Economic Review* 66: 246–53.

Hahn, Frank. 1971. "Competitive Equilibrium with Transaction Costs". *Econometrica* 39, no. 3: 418–39.

Heckman, James, and George Borjas. 1980. "Does Unemployment Cause Future Unemployment? Questions and Answers from a Continuous Time Model of Heterogeneity and State Dependence". *Economica* 47: 247–83.

Jaffee, Dwight, and Thomas Russell. 1976. "Imperfect Information, Uncertainty, and Credit Rationing". *Quarterly Journal of Economics* 90: 651–66.

Jorgenson, Dale. 1988. "Productivity and Postwar Economic Growth". *Journal of Economic Perspectives* 2, no. 4: 23–41.

Kuznets, Simon. 1955. "Economic Growth and Income Inequality". *American Economic Growth* 45, no. 1: 1–28.

Lippman, Steven, and John McCall. 1976. "Job Search in a Dynamic Economy". *Journal of Economic Theory* 12, no. 3: 365 –90.

Lizzeri, Alessandro, and Nicola Persico. 2001. "The Provision of Public Goods under Alternative Electoral Incentives". *American Economic Review* 91: 225–39.

Magill, Michael, and Martine Quinzii. 2002. *Theory of Incomplete Markets*. Cambridge, Massachusetts: MIT Press.

Mortensen, Dale. 1986. "Job Search and Labor Market Analysis," In *Handbook of Labor Economics*, vol. 2, edited by O. Ashenfelter and R. Layard. USA: Elsevier Science Publishers, BV.

Mortensen, Dale, and Christopher Pissarides. 1994. "Job Creation and Job Destruction in the Theory of Unemployment". *Review of Economic Studies* 61, no. 3: 397–415.

Newbery, David, and Joseph Stiglitz. 1984. "Pareto Inferior Trade". *Review of Economic Studies* 51, no. 1: 1–12.

Persson, Torsten, and Guido Tabellini. 1994 "Is Inequality Harmful for Growth". *American Economic Review* 84: 600–621.

———. 2000. "Comparative Politics and Public Finance". *Journal of Political Economy* 108: 1121–61.
PSA (Philippine Statistics Authority). various years. *Philippine Statistical Yearbook*. Manila: PSA.
———. various years. *Family Income and Expenditure Survey*. Manila: PSA.
———. various years. *Labor Force Survey*. Manila: PSA.
Radner, Roy. 1968. "Competitive Equilibrium under Uncertainty". *Econometrica* 36, no. 1: 31–58.
———. 1970. "Problems in the Theory of Markets under Uncertainty". *AER Papers and Proceedings* 60, no. 2: 454–60.
———. 1972. "Existence of Equilibrium of Plans, Prices, and Price Expectations in a Sequence of Markets". *Econometrica* 40, no. 2: 289–303.
Solow, Robert. 1957. "Technical Change and the Aggregate Production Function". *Review of Economics and Statistics* 39: 312–20.
Spence, Michael. 1974. *Market Signaling*. Cambridge, Massachusetts: Harvard University Press.
Stiglitz, Joseph. 1974. "Alternative Theories of Wage Determination and Unemployment in LDCs: The Labor Turnover Model". *Quarterly Journal of Economics* 88, no. 2: 194–227.
Stiglitz, Joseph, and Andrew Weiss. 1981 "Credit Rationing in Markets with Imperfect Information". *American Economic Review* 71, no. 3: 393–411.
Varian, Hall. 1987. *Microeconomic Analysis*. New York: W.W. Norton and Co. First published 1978.

15 Convergence of Philippine Spatial Inequality during the American Colonial Period

Jan Carlo B. Punongbayan, Jeffrey G. Williamson and Karl Robert L. Jandoc

1 INTRODUCTION

This paper explores spatial inequality in the Philippines during the American colonial period. Although there is sizable literature on regional development and dynamics in the Philippines in the late twentieth century (see Balisacan and Hill 2007; Estudillo 1997), comparatively little has been said about the economic and development disparities across regions in the *early* twentieth century, and how these disparities may have been shaped during the American colonial rule.

The Philippines was a country in shambles at the beginning of the twentieth century. Engaged in sporadic battles since the Revolution of 1896 and eventually declaring independence from Spain in 1898, the country found itself confronting yet another emerging empire, the United States. In 1898, just months after Spain ceded the Philippines to America via the Treaty of Paris, the nascent Philippine Republic waged war against its new colonial master. The atrocities inflicted on the population were staggering: the US army corralled men, women and children in Laguna and Batangas—about 300,000 of them—in concentration camps and razed houses, farms and livestock. The economic dislocation proved to be so widespread, it would take several decades for the country to recover

(Corpuz 1997). The conflict also exacted a tremendous toll on human development, from which the Philippines took decades to recover. For instance, Bassino, Dovis, and Komlos (2018) find that Filipinos' heights in the 1930s (a proxy for nutrition adequacy) took 60 years to recover from levels recorded back in the 1870s.

After quelling the armed resistance as well as co-opting Filipino elites by its "policy of attraction", America embarked on an ambitious project to prepare Filipinos towards independence and self-government. This entailed building institutions such as the civil service, public infrastructure and economic policies for the "prosperity and contentment to the country of the Philippines" (Corpuz 1997). The thinking was that a dynamic Philippine economy, serving as "a ready and attractive field of enterprise", will not be a burden to the American people (Booth 2012; Corpuz 1997).

As a result of this deliberate policy, and partly because the economy was coming from a low base, the country's gross domestic product (GDP) grew by an average annual rate of 5.2 per cent from 1902 to 1910 and 5.79 per cent from 1910 to 1920. Figure 15.1 shows that the latter was the country's fastest growth rate, except during the post-war reconstruction from 1950 to 1960 (average of 6.21%) and in 2010–19, right before the pandemic (average of 6.11%).

Figure 15.1 GDP and per capita GDP growth of the Philippines (by decade)

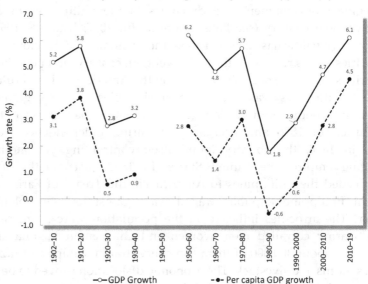

Sources: Hooley (2005) for 1902–1940 (base year 1985)
Philippine Statistics Authority for 1950–2019 (base year 2018).

In addition, per capita GDP rose the fastest historically in 1910–20, except during the 2010s. The Philippines also enjoyed higher living standards compared with the rest of Southeast Asia during this period (Booth 2012).

Despite the newfound and remarkable growth during this era, little is known (and no systematic investigation has yet been done) on how such growth was distributed among the Philippine regions (especially outside the capital, Manila), how it could have affected development outcomes across regions, and how it could have contributed to overall inequality. For example, how much more prosperous, educated and healthy were people in Manila vis-à-vis those in the rest of Luzon, Visayas and Mindanao?

In what follows, we focus on spatial inequality and attempt to document the changes in measures of well-being and human development, not just in the aggregate but more importantly across the main island groups of Luzon, Visayas and Mindanao. We use census data from the different waves of American colonial period to construct a human development index (HDI) that captures elements of health, education and income. We look at how the HDI had changed in Luzon, Visayas and Mindanao from the turn of the century until 1939.[1] Finally, we hypothesize which factors primarily drove the HDI movements, as well as the individual indicators of well-being.

2 DATA AND METHODS

2.1 Census data

We use historical census data throughout the analysis. For 1903, 1918 and 1939, we use the Census of the Philippine Islands compiled and published by the US Bureau of the Census.[2] The 1903 census, collected under the auspices of the Philippine Commission in 1903, contains a

---

[1] As far as we know, Metzer (1998) is the only attempt to construct an HDI for the Philippines during the American colonial period. However, the calculation was made only for 1939, missing out on the high-growth period of the earlier decades of American occupation. Moreover, Metzer's measure is for the whole country and not disaggregated spatially.

[2] We would have used the 1948 census as well, but it does not contain data on health indicators.

wealth of data on population, mortality, education, housing, agricultural, industrial and social statistics. The 1918 and 1939 censuses were taken under the direction of the Philippine legislature and compiled by the Census Office of the Philippine Islands. Changes in geographic divisions were inevitable over the nearly forty-year period of our data set (e.g., provinces were merged or split), but in our analysis we focus on the development measures for Metro Manila vis-á-vis the major island groupings of Luzon, Visayas and Mindanao, and the Philippines as a whole.

2.2 Regional human development index

We construct a regional HDI using indicators available across historical censuses:
   a. Health: infant mortality rate per 1,000 live births (deaths under 1 year of age)
   b. Education: literacy rate (per cent among those aged 10 and above)
   c. Prosperity: population density (people per square kilometre)

Since income data are unavailable in the historical censuses, we instead use population density as a proxy for growth and economic development (Yegorov 2015).

The formula for each indicator's corresponding sub-index is given in equation (1):

$$dimension\ index = I_i = \frac{Actual\ value - minimum\ goalpost}{Maximum\ goalpost - minimum\ goalpost} \quad (1)$$

where i denotes the three dimensions of health, education and prosperity. We use maximum and minimum "goalposts", by which the indicators are converted into subindices ranging from 0 to 1. When working with indicators that can take on dispersed values (e.g., life expectancy versus population density), this goalpost method is particularly useful in standardizing and bringing them together.

Table 15.1 below shows the goalposts we used in the analysis, based on the minimum and maximum values found throughout the censuses. For population density, the goalposts are 1 and 20,000, the latter being an arbitrary maximum that exceeds the maximum observed in each census. For literacy rate, the goalposts are 0 per cent and 100 per cent. For infant mortality, we use the inverse of the raw data so that a higher value is more desirable; accordingly, we use 0 and 1 as the minimum and maximum goalposts, respectively.

Table 15.1. Goalposts used in the analysis

Indicator	Min	Max.
Population density	1	20,000
Literacy rate	0	100
Infant mortality (inverse)	0	1

We then combine these subindices using the geometric average:

$$HDI = \sqrt[3]{I_{health} * I_{education} * I_{prosperity}}. \qquad (2)$$

Compared with the simple mean, the geometric mean is preferred because it "penalizes" inequality across indicators (i.e., the HDI is lower if there is greater inequality across the indicators) and requires a greater improvement in any one indicator to increase the HDI.

The method described above follows the HDI computation of the United Nations Development Programme (UNDP). Since the UNDP began reporting on HDIs across countries in 1990, the HDI has always captured three important aspects of development: health and longevity, education and income. Aggregating such indicators to come up with an overall index has its challenges. UNDP (2015) documents various methodologies in calculating the HDI over the years. It eventually came up with the goalpost method, which is adopted in our study. In the current HDI, actual life expectancy in a country (which proxies for health) is compared against a fixed minimum goalpost of 20 years and a maximum goalpost of 85 years. For education, which is indicated by mean years and expected years of schooling, the goalposts are 0 (minimum) for both and 15 and 18 (maximum), respectively. Finally, the minimum and minimum goalposts for gross national income (GNI) per capita (in 2011 international dollars, PPP) are $100 and $75,000, respectively. Although these goalposts may seem arbitrary, they largely depend on reasonable minimum and maximum values based on cross-country data. These subindices are then aggregated in a number of possible ways. Initially, the HDI was just the simple average of these sub-indices, but since 2010 the geometric average has been used.

Obviously, the sparseness of income and schooling data prevents us from faithfully adopting the HDI in our historical analysis. But we see the HDI methodology as a suitable way to summarize development outcomes across regions of the Philippines and make meaningful spatial comparisons to the extent that historical data allow. The resulting values can also show if development outcomes across regions have tended to improve, deteriorate, diverge or converge over time.

3 RESULTS

This section presents results of our HDI analysis. Figure 15.2 shows the absolute and relative HDI values across the major island groups and the Philippines as a whole.[3] In panel A, development as measured by our HDI steadily rose from 1901 to 1939, with Visayas consistently having higher values than Luzon (excluding Manila) and Mindanao.[4] There was an initial spurt in the HDI values for Luzon and Visayas from 1901 to 1918, but afterwards their growth slowed down relative to the national average (panel B). All in all, after an initial divergence between 1903 and 1918, some convergence in the development outcomes of the major island groups is seen from 1918 to 1939.

We move on to parse what happened to the specific indicators over time. Figure 15.3 shows a steady increase in population density in the regions, with the values for Manila (panel A) being significantly higher.

Figure 15.2. Development index (absolute vs. relative levels, 1903–39)

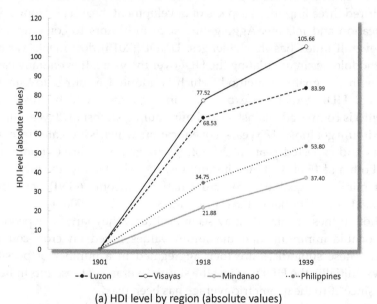

(a) HDI level by region (absolute values)

Figure 15.2 *(continued)*

---

[3] We excluded Metro Manila, which has extreme values for population density.
[4] We extended the series to 2010; the values for Visayas went below the national average in recent decades.

Figure 15.2 *(continued)*

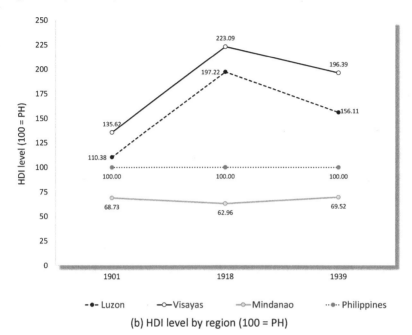

(b) HDI level by region (100 = PH)

Note: Data normalized to Philippine level (=100)
Source: Authors' computation using the 1903, 1918 and 1939 census.

Manila's population density tremendously increased as shown by the 1903 and 1939 censuses. However, after subsequent government proclamations to incorporate neighbouring towns and cities to form Greater Manila, the land area of Manila increased from 37 km² in 1948 to 636 km² in 1960. The changes in the official land area of Manila over time account for the significant reduction in population density between 1939 and 1960.

Figure 15.4 shows a steady rise in literacy rates across the regions. Manila initially had a huge advantage over the other regions; Luzon was slightly above the national average; and Visayas and Mindanao were both below the national average. But some degree of convergence is observed, as evidenced by the narrowing gaps between Manila, on one hand, and Visayas and Mindanao, on the other.

Figure 15.3. Population density across regions

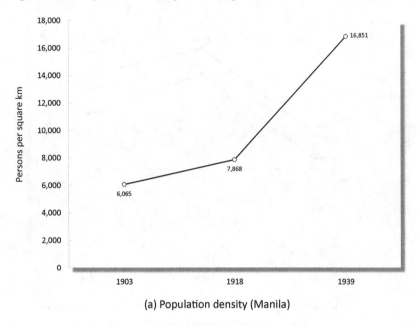

(a) Population density (Manila)

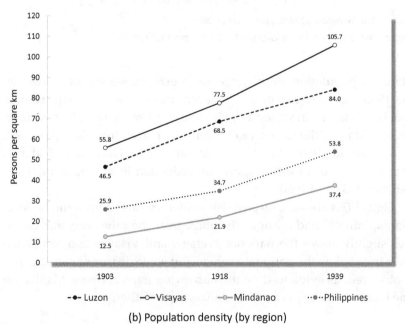

(b) Population density (by region)

Note: Data normalized to Philippine level (= 100)
Source: Authors' computation using the 1903, 1918 and 1939 census.

Figure 15.4. Literacy rates across regions

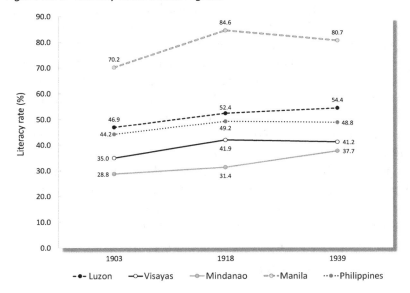

(a) Literacy rate by region (absolute levels)

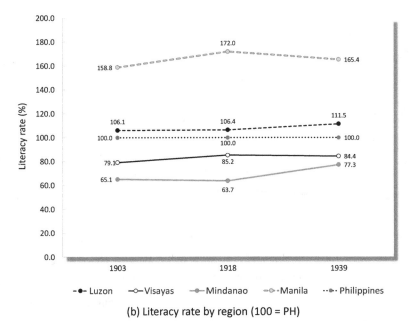

(b) Literacy rate by region (100 = PH)

Note: Data normalized to Philippine level (= 100)
Source: Authors' computation using the 1903, 1918 and 1939 census.

Figure 15.5 shows the trends in infant mortality. At the beginning of the twentieth century, infant mortality was especially high in Manila. The 1903 Census says, "It is evident that the environment of Manila is deadly to young children," with no less than 1,515 children under 1 dying per 1,000 population. At that time, Manila accounted for about a third of the children between ages 5 and 9 who died. Among the causes of mortality were convulsion and cholera, the latter affecting Manila more than any other region. The 1903 figure for Manila seems anomalous, since it is measured per 1,000 children under age 1. However, Concepcion and Smith (1977) note that severe under-registration of deaths may have compromised the accuracy of demographic data in the early twentieth century, among other data issues. The data issues notwithstanding, a steady decline in infant mortality is clearly observed from 1903 to 1939, especially in Manila vis-à-vis the rest of the nation.

Figure 15.5. Infant mortality rate across regions

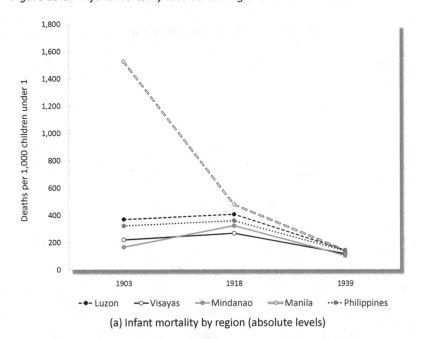

(a) Infant mortality by region (absolute levels)

Figure 15.5 *(continued)*

Figure 15.5 *(continued)*

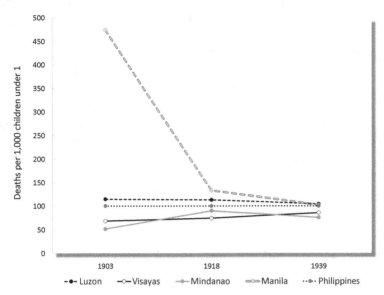

(b) Infant mortality by region (absolute levels)

Note: Data normalized to Philippine level (= 100)
Source: Authors' computation using the 1903, 1918 and 1939 census.

4 DISCUSSION

What could have driven these changes in the HDI, which indicate not only improvement of well-being for the whole country but also convergence among the different regions? While no definite answer is attempted here due to a paucity of disaggregated data, we nevertheless enumerate some factors that may have directed (or at least influenced) the patterns shown in the previous section. In particular, we focus on the pattern of agricultural and industrial growth and the pattern of public expenditures on education and health.

4.1 Pattern of agricultural and industrial growth

Agriculture and industry were the most dynamic sectors of the economy during the American colonial period. Agriculture's share in the GDP averaged almost 40 per cent; this high share was maintained over the four decades of pre-war twentieth century (Figure 15.6). Agricultural growth was highest during the first two decades of American rule, but slowly decelerated thereafter (Figure 15.7). Philippine agriculture during this period was characterized by its dualistic nature. On one hand, a segment of agriculture—mostly cash crops for exports—hinged on the "economy of special relations" with the United States. On the other hand, there was the traditional agricultural production (rice and maize) dominated by subsistence small farmers (Corpuz 1997). Figure 15.8 shows that all land areas planted to the main crops, especially rice, increased from 1903 to 1939. The strong growth of the rice sector was due to the early big-ticket irrigation projects in the provinces of Bulacan, Pampanga and Tarlac. Agricultural growth, which resulted in increased productivity and incomes in areas outside Manila, may have contributed to a salutary effect on spatial inequality during this period.

Figure 15.6. Shares of agriculture, industry and services in GDP

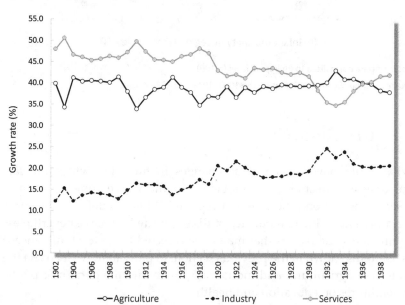

Source: Authors' computation from Hooley (2005).

Figure 15.7. Growth in agriculture and its components

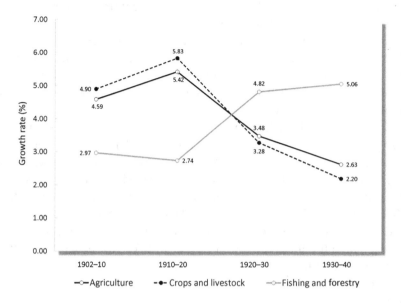

Source: Hooley (2005).

Figure 15.8. Land area planted to leading crops

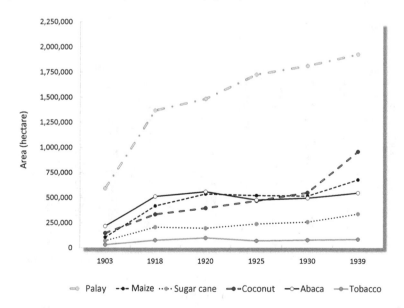

Source: Corpuz (1997).

To see if there is any evidence of this effect on spatial inequality, we examine the regional heterogeneity of agricultural performance in regions outside Manila. Figure 15.9 shows a shift away from commercial crops (coconut, sugar cane, abaca, maguey, cotton, tobacco) in Bicol, Mindanao, Ilocos and Cagayan Valley, and an increase in cereal (rice and maize) production in the 1918–39 period. The land area planted to other crops (legumes, vegetables, fruits, etc.) increased for almost all regions in the country in the same period.

Specific regions benefited immensely from the expansion of commercial crop production, especially Eastern Visayas, Western Visayas, Southern Tagalog and Central Luzon (Table 15.9 panel B). Sugar production played a key role in these regions, as encouraged by the United States through the preferential treatment for the country's sugar export to the US market (with the enactment of the Underwood-Simmons Tariff Act in 1913), along with a rise in world sugar prices especially during the second half of the 1920s (Corpuz 1997). In addition, the enactment of the Smoot-Hawley Tariff Act in the 1930s further increased Philippine sugar production, as the United States curtailed its sugar imports from Cuba (Merleaux 2012).

Figure 15.9. Per cent regional share of agricultural produce (in ha)

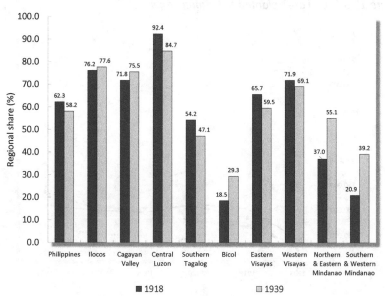

(a) Cereals

Figure 15.9 *(continued)*

Figure 15.9 *(continued)*

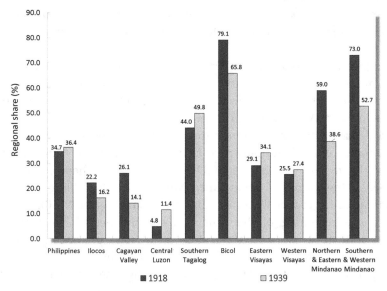

(b) Commercial crops

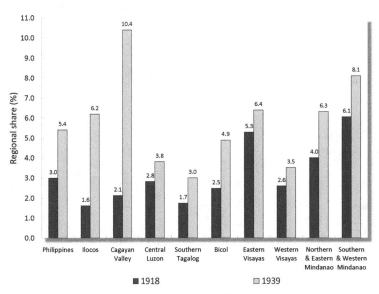

(c) Other food crops

Note: Cereals = rice and maize
Other food crops = legumes, tubers and root crops, vegetables, pineapple
Commercial crops = coconut, sugar cane, abaca, maguey, cotton, tobacco

Source: Various census years, Palacios (1973).

In Mindanao, there was a major shift away from commercial crops towards cereals. Palacios (1973) posits this had something to do with the migration of peasant farmers into the region (actively promoted by government) and the technological difficulties of commercial crop planting.

Figure 15.6 also shows that industry's share in GDP experienced a secular increase during the American colonial period. This was a break from decades of weak industrial performance in the nineteenth century (de Dios and Williamson 2014). Mining grew the fastest during this period, driven by American investments and the export boost from the devaluation of the Philippine peso in 1934 (Hooley 2005). While mining grew the fastest, its share in GDP was miniscule; hence, the true leader of the industrial renaissance was small-scale, labour-intensive manufacturing, especially commodity processing (Figure 15.10).

At the beginning of the American colonial period, most of the large industries were concentrated in a few provinces, mainly in Manila (Table 15.2). Evidence is scant, however, regarding the performance of these industries during the pre-war period.

Figure 15.10. Contribution to industrial growth of various sectors

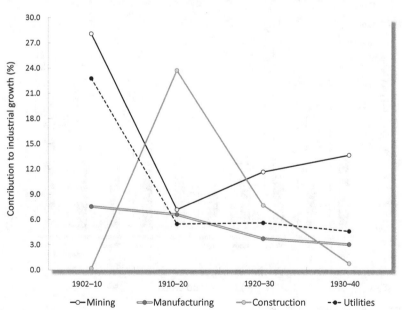

Source: Authors' estimates from Hooley (2005).

Table 15.2. Industrial establishments (ranked by value of production, 1902)

Industry description	No. of establishments	Value of production (PHP)	No. provinces of operation
Cigars and cigarettes	108	8,698,634	10
Boat building	26	4,449,170	10
Spirituous liquors, beer	287	4,388,319	21
Sawn lumber	78	2,736,754	11
Bread and bakery products	326	2,084,106	31
Gas and electricity	3	1,461,143	2
Presses and printers	73	1,024,338	10
Rice mills	28	1,010,965	3
Machine shops	29	968,225	5
Men's clothing, tailors	119	559,788	7
Soap	90	551,585	16

Source: Corpuz (1997, 172–173).

For instance, the cigar manufacturing industry, a high-value industry located mainly in Manila, initially grew fast in the early 1900s but stagnated in the next two decades. It is reported that real wages in the sector plummeted during this period due to stagnant international demand (Chiba 2005). Other industries, such as liquors, had more presence in provinces outside Manila. For instance, *lambanog* (coconut wine) production thrived in Laguna when prices of copra fell during the crisis of the 1930s (Fujii 2005).

Further studies need to be conducted on how these patterns of agricultural and industrial growth affected the convergence of development outcomes of Manila and the other regions of the Philippines. On the one hand, the boom in trade in the first two decades of the 1900s enabled some provinces in Luzon and Visayas to catch up with Manila, but the subsequent plunge in trade in the early 1920s up to the Great Depression set them back. On the other hand, since most large industries were located in Manila, the decline in demand during the Great Depression took a toll on these industries. These forces may have offset the relative contribution of agricultural and industrial growth to spatial inequality. This is an area for more study.

4.2 Pattern of public expenditure on education and health

The improvement and convergence of infant mortality rates and literacy rates across the Philippine regions show the commitment of the colonial American government towards improving the health and education systems in the country. This is reflected in the higher per capita government expenditures on health and education, compared with those of the other Southeast Asian countries (Table 15.3).

Warwick (1992) notes that the Americans adopted a much more scientific approach to public health than the Spaniards. Early in the American occupation, the Board of Health was decentralized to reach out and provide public health services to the provinces. This had been helpful, for instance, in the large-scale compulsory smallpox vaccination drives across the country. In addition, the Board of Health instituted programmes against infectious diseases, such as anthrax, chicken pox, cholera, typhus and typhoid fever (Planta 2008). These programmes had a palpable effect on the health of the population—for example, infant mortality rates plunged across all regions in the country.

The early twentieth century also saw a significant expansion of the public school system, especially in the elementary level. The number of elementary schools grew from 6,900 in 1899 to more than 1.14 million by 1932 (Figure 15.11). Consequently, there was also tremendous growth in the number of enrollees in primary schools from 1900 to 1940, which was the highest in Southeast Asia up to the 1930s (Table 15.4). These indicators validate the increasing literacy rates of Philippine children across the country, as shown in section 3.

Education had been the bedrock of American colonial rule. As early as 1901, the Philippine Commission passed Act 74 or the Organic School Law. This mandated, among other things, the establishment of local school boards in different municipalities.

Table 15.3. *Total government expenditure per capita in Southeast Asia (in US$)*

Country	1910	1920	1929	1934	1938
Vietnam	1	3	3	3	2
Indonesia	2	7	5	5	4
Philippines	3	6	6	4	5
Thailand	3	4	4	3	4

Source: Booth (2007).

Figure 15.11. Number of enrolled students in the primary and secondary levels

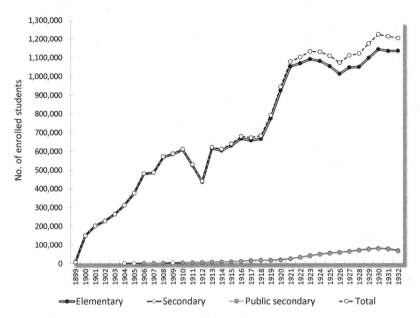

Source: Annual Report of the Governor General (various years).

Table 15.4. Primary school enrolment rates in Southeast Asia (% of school-aged children)

Country/ Region	1900	1910	1920	1930	1935–40
Burma	11.5	11.8	10.3	13.4	13.3
Indochina	0.5	1.0	2.8	6.9	10.8
Indonesia	2.5	7.0	7.0	12.2	13.3
Malaysia	7.5	8.9	19.4	24.6	69.2
Philippines	19.3	28.4	35.8	32.4	44.8

Source: Bassino and Williamson (2017).

In 1918, the Thirty Million Peso Act[5] substantially expanded the number of primary schools, the enrolment of pupils, the hiring of primary school teachers and the construction of school buildings outside Manila (Acierto 1980). Because of these measures, most provinces were able to increase per pupil expenditures by an average of 80 per cent from 1913 to 1923, whereas Manila's per pupil expenditure increased by 4.5 per cent only (Table 15.5). Thus, the provinces were able to catch up with Manila in terms of literacy.

Both health and education policies during the studied period point to a narrowing of inequality between Manila and the outlying provinces. This is reflected in the convergence of the HDI measures in section 3, where health (infant mortality) and education (literacy rate) outcomes improved in areas outside Manila.

Table 15.5. Per pupil educational expenditures for current expenses (in PHP)

Province	1913	1918	1923	% increase (1913–23)
Abra	–	–	22.89	–
Agusan	22.70	–	18.72	–17.53
Albay	12.18	13.05	19.18	57.47
Antique	10.23	8.17	20.60	101.37
Bataan	–	14.81	14.86	–
Batanes	–	8.47	24.57	–
Batangas	11.02	11.16	21.19	92.29
Bohol	5.10	8.52	16.04	214.51
Bukidnon	–	–	20.26	–
Bulacan	10.57	10.92	16.64	57.43
Cagayan	10.39	11.21	15.13	45.62
Camarines	10.19	12.24	21.49	110.89
Capiz	9.12	10.20	18.42	101.97
Cavite	9.91	9.72	18.05	82.14
Cebu	9.26	11.47	17.10	84.67
Cotabato	–	–	22.56	–
Davao	–	–	32.56	–

Table 15.5 (continued)

[5] Act No. 2782 entitled "An Act Appropriating the Sum of Thirty Million Seven Hundred and Five Thousand Eight Hundred and Twenty-Four Pesos for the Extension of Free Elemental Instruction to All Children of School Age"

Table 15.5 *(continued)*

Province	1913	1918	1923	% increase (1913–23)
Ilocos Norte	7.39	12.29	12.71	71.99
Ilocos Sur	9.80	7.70	16.29	66.22
Iloilo	7.98	10.62	17.71	121.93
Isabela		13.05	16.69	
La Union	8.35	7.94	17.60	110.78
Laguna	9.99	9.94	17.18	71.97
Lanao	–	–	20.48	–
Leyte	8.59	8.74	15.16	76.48
Manila	**36.29**	**32.52**	**37.94**	**4.55**
Marinduque	–	–	15.01	–
Masbate	–	–	17.44	–
Mindoro	13.23	11.30	24.57	85.71
Misamis	10.06	11.37	13.72	36.38
Mountain Province	43.67	45.57	35.53	-18.64
Nueva Ecija	10.30	8.50	16.80	63.11
Nueva Vizcaya	18.80	46.69	19.08	1.49
Occidental Negros	9.22	12.10	16.52	79.18
Oriental Negros	7.62	10.90	20.87	173.88
Palawan	20.79	17.14	21.51	3.46
Pampanga	9.95	12.44	21.91	120.20
Pangasinan	7.21	9.59	13.25	83.77
Rizal	10.01	12.06	18.18	81.62
Romblon	–	–	17.80	–
Samar	8.36	8.42	20.18	141.39
Sorsogon	8.75	11.78	16.38	87.20
Sulu	–	1.74	25.22	–
Surigao	–	11.41	20.26	–
Tarlac	9.00	11.47	18.98	110.89
Tayabas	9.82	10.14	17.55	78.72
Zambales	8.85	8.79	13.02	47.12
Zamboanga	–	–	25.17	–

Source: Monroe (1925).

5 CONCLUSION

This paper attempts to construct a human development index (HDI) for the Philippines during the American colonial period. Our analysis shows that the country's HDI improved over the first four decades of American occupation. Moreover, the HDI of outlying regions converged with that of the centre, Manila. This convergence is related to the patterns of agricultural and industrial growth and development, as well as the patterns of public expenditure on health and education. Clearly, American colonial policies on health and education had narrowed the disparity in literacy and infant mortality between the provinces and Manila. On the other hand, the patterns of agricultural and industrial growth may have had offsetting forces on spatial inequality. The trade boom benefited provinces producing commercial crops, enabling them to catch up with Manila. However, the trade bust in the Great Depression era may have widened spatial inequality, although it could have also dampened real wages in large industries based in Manila, possibly narrowing spatial inequality. Further research is needed to shed more light on this ambiguity.

Examining economic trends during the American colonial period is made difficult by the paucity of data. This "dark age" in Philippine statistics, as Richard Hooley puts it, is not due to the lack of data collection efforts. Rather, the problem lies in the absence of a systematic database that would allow the identification of stylized facts, statistical analyses and econometric exercises. This is a low-hanging fruit that future researchers should invest in. Studies in inequality using indicators such as skill premiums, urban-rural wage gaps and non-farm income distributions could be estimated with the availability of such a systematic American colonial statistical database (Williamson 2017).

While there is substantial literature on Philippine post-war and post-independence overall income inequality (Balisacan and Fuwa 2004; Balisacan and Pernia 2003), future research should conduct a similar census data analysis to construct the HDI on the years after the country's independence to see whether spatial inequality has improved or worsened in the post-war years.[6] This would need information on trade and global prices, domestic policies on agriculture and industry, and patterns of migration, both domestic and international.

---

[6] Balisacan and Fuwa (2006) is an important attempt to examine regional income inequality.

REFERENCES

Acierto, M. 1980. "American Influence in Shaping Philippine Secondary Education: An Historical Perspective, 1898–1978". PhD dissertation, Loyola University of Chicago.

Balisacan, A. M., and N. Fuwa. 2004. "Going Beyond Cross-Country Averages: Growth, Inequality and Poverty Reduction in the Philippines". *World Development* 32, no. 11: 1891–1907.

———. 2006. "Changes in Spatial Income Inequality in the Philippines: An Exploratory Analysis". In *Spatial Disparities in Human Development: Perspectives from Asia*, edited by Ravi Kanbur, Tony Venables, and Guanghua Wan, pp. 207–32. Tokyo: United Nations University Press.

Balisacan, A. M., and H. Hill, eds. 2007. *The Dynamics of Regional Development: The Philippines in East Asia*. Quezon City: Ateneo de Manila University Press.

Balisacan, A. M., and E. M. Pernia. 2003. "Poverty, Inequality and Growth in the Philippines". In *Poverty, Growth and Institutions in Developing Asia*, edited by Ernesto M. Pernia and Anil B. Deolalikar. Hampshire, England: Palgrave Macmillan.

Bassino, J., M. Dovis, and J. Komlos. 2018. "Biological Well-being in Late Nineteenth-Century Philippines". *Cliometrica* 12, no. 1: 33–60.

Bassino, J., and J. Williamson. 2017. "From Commodity Booms to Economic Miracles: Why Southeast Asian Industry Lagged Behind". In *The Spread of Modern Industry to the Periphery Since 1871*, edited by K. O'Rourke and J.G. Williamson, pp. 56–286. Oxford, England: Oxford University Press.

Booth, A. 2007. *Colonial Legacies: Economic and Social Development in East and Southeast Asia*. Honolulu: University of Hawai'i Press.

———. 2012. "Measuring Living Standards in Different Colonial Systems: Some Evidence from South East Asia, 1900–1942". *Modern Asian Studies* 46, no. 5: 1145–81.

Chiba, Y. 2005. "Cigar-Makers in American Colonial Manila: Survival during Structural Depression in the 1920s". *Journal of Southeast Asian Studies* 36, no. 3: 373–97.

Concepcion, M., and P. Smith. 1977. "The Demographic Situation in the Philippines: An Assessment in 1977". *Paper No. 44*. Honolulu: East-West Population Institute.

Corpuz, O. D. 1997. *An Economic History of the Philippines*. Quezon City: University of the Philippines Press.

De Dios, E., and J. Williamson. 2014. "Deviant Behavior: A Century of Philippine Industrialization". In *Sustainable Economic Development: Resources, Environment, and Institutions*, pp. 372–99. San Diego, CA: Academic Press–Elsevier.

Estudillo, J. P. 1997. "Income Inequality in the Philippines, 1961–1991". *Developing Economies* 35, no. 1: 68–95.

Fujii, M. 2005. "Livelihood Change in a Philippine Coconut Farming Village: A Case Study in Laguna Province". *African Study Monographs* 29 (suppl): 115–24.

Hooley, R. 2005. "American Economic Policy in the Philippines, 1902–1940: Exploring a Dark Age in Colonial Statistics". *Journal of Asian Economics* 16: 464–88.

Merleaux, A. 2012. "The Political Culture of Sugar Tariffs: Immigration, Race, and Empire, 1898–1930". *International Labor and Working-Class History* 81: 28–48.

Metzer, J. 1998. *The Divided Economy of Mandatory Palestine*. Cambridge: Cambridge University Press.

Monroe, P. 1925. *A Survey of the Educational System of the Philippine Islands by the Board of Educational Survey Created under Acts 3162 and 3196 of the Philippine Legislature*. Philippines: Bureau of Printing.

Palacios, V. 1973. "An Analysis of the Allocation of Farm Area Planted to Cereals, Other Food Crops, and Commercial Crops: 1918, 1939, 1948, 1955 and 1960". Undergraduate thesis, School of Economics, University of the Philippines.

Planta, M. 2008. "Prerequisites to a Civilized Life: The American Colonial Public Health System in the Philippines, 1901 to 1927". PhD dissertation, National University of Singapore.

UNDP (United Nations Development Programme). 2015. "Training Material for Producing National Human Development Reports". *Occasional Paper*. UNDP Human Development Report Office. http://hdr.undp.org/sites/default/files/hdi_training.pdf.

Warwick, A. 1992. "Colonial Pathologies: American Medicine in the Philippines, 1898–1921". PhD dissertation, University of Pennsylvania.

Williamson, J. 2017. "Philippine Inequality across the Twentieth Century: Slim Evidence, but Fat Questions". *Philippine Review of Economics* 54, no. 2: 37–60.

Yegorov, Y. 2015. "Economic Role of Population Density". Paper presented at the ERSA Congress, Lisbon, Portugal, 25–28 August 2015.

16 Social Differentiation: The Middle Class and Its Discontents

*Emmanuel S. de Dios
and Philip Arnold P. Tuaño*

1 INTRODUCTION

Like all other countries, the Philippines has been severely affected by the COVID-19 pandemic that has engulfed the world since early 2020. As of this writing, growth performance for 2020 had been the worst since the country's debt crisis in the 1980s (NEDA 2020; World Bank 2020). Most analysts expect the country to recover fully in late 2022 at the earliest. Conservative estimates place the number of Filipinos put out of work at one million due to government-mandated lockdowns; early in the lockdown, approximately more than 11 million out of the 18 million casual and temporary workers on the main island of Luzon have been affected by the crisis (Muyrong 2020). Close to four million of these workers were employed in the micro- and small-enterprise sector, as well as the retail and transportation sectors, which have been significantly affected by the crisis. Of these two sectors, only the food retail business was allowed to operate during the Luzon shutdown from April to May 2020 (Macaraeg 2020). There can be no doubt of the pandemic's severe and lasting toll on the country's efforts to reduce poverty and increase human development opportunities.

This turn of events becomes even more striking since the Philippines has performed well over the past decade relative to its historical record of growth and poverty reduction. Growth accelerated significantly and steadily since the mid-2000s; employment growth improved, decreasing the share of individuals and families below the poverty line. The country's economic performance since 2012 has been regarded as among the best in the region (World Bank 2018a), amid cautious hopes that the country had finally shed its traditional label of being "an East Asian exception" (Clarete, Esguerra, and Hill 2018).

Among the immediate effects of these changes in welfare over the past years has been an increasing differentiation among Filipino households. The proportion of households belonging to categories between the richest and lowest income classes has increased—there has been an expansion in what may be called the "middle classes" of society. This is visible in the explosion in the number of retail-trade establishments, including large shopping malls; the expansion of demand for residential developments; and the rise in spending on consumer durables, including mobile devices, motor vehicles and household appliances. Even the growth of domestic transportation and tourism can be traced to the growth in disposable income of many Filipinos now able to spend more on leisure and entertainment activities. Underpinning this middle-class growth have been overseas workers' remittances and the rise of a globally oriented information technology-business processing management (IT-BPM) industry[1]—both activities themselves providing opportunities to the more educated and the middle class. The strong external balances made possible by these two sources[2] effectively ended the foreign exchange-constrained boom-bust cycle that historically characterized Philippine economic performance. They also fuelled a growth oriented towards domestic services and local consumption, laying the basis for new domestically oriented service industries that created further opportunities for middle-class employment.

However, the pandemic has pushed to precariousness many middle-class households whose situation has improved in the past. Many families that used to rely on overseas remittances have seen their incomes fall as thousands of overseas Filipino workers (OFWs) have

---

[1] Colloquially known as the BPO (business-process outsourcing) sector.
[2] The outsize importance of the remittances and the IT-BPM sectors is evident in that they account for an equivalent of all foreign-exchange earnings from all merchandise exports (Clarete, Esguerra, and Hill 2018, 6).

been forced to return home. The export-oriented IT-BPM industry, on the other hand, was disrupted as recession gripped the major markets it served and work arrangements had to be adjusted. On the whole, though, these two important drivers of middle-class growth were only moderately affected, at worst experiencing a break in their growth momentum. The drop in overseas remittances in particular was not as precipitous as originally feared: remittances fell by 0.8 per cent in 2020, as compared with its average annual growth of 5.8 per cent since 2010.[3] The IT-BPM sector also managed to post small increases in both employment and revenue, despite the recession.[4]

The wider devastation in middle-class incomes and employment has occurred instead in that part of the services sector that serves the home market—particularly retail trade, hospitality, transport and tourism, which have been hardest hit by the restrictions on movement and the forced shutdown of businesses for public health reasons. With the country having implemented one of the longest lockdowns in 2020 yet still currently struggling with high rates of infection and delayed vaccination, the final shape of the Philippine economy—as and when it finally emerges from the pandemic-cum-recession—remains uncertain. Economic scarring will be greater the longer the country takes to gain control over the disease and fully but safely reopen the economy. At the same time, however, there is every prospect that the long-term socio-economic trends that preceded the pandemic will resume. This follows from the fact, already mentioned, that the major drivers of middle-class growth—overseas remittances and the IT-BPM sector—remain largely intact. Even as pandemic restrictions at home impose major income and employment losses and cause dissaving among households, well-established social differentials in human, financial and social capital will mean the ability to adapt and ultimately recover will vary significantly across social classes and result in a post-pandemic economy that largely reproduces previously prevailing social differences. In particular, barring a deep and prolonged

---

[3] Original estimates by the World Bank projected a decline of as much as 20 per cent. Nonetheless 2020 was the first year personal remittances had fallen since 2001.

[4] Full-time employment in the sector increased by 1.8 per cent to 1.32 million in 2020, while revenues rose marginally from US$26.3 to US$26.7 billion (Nishimori 2021).

recession, the social differentiation that saw the emergence of a middle-class plurality is likely to be restored. It is this changed socio-economic structure that the Philippine government has been slow to recognize and reflect in both policy and programmes (which partly explains its inadequate response to the pandemic, as discussed below).

This paper argues the case for government and civil society to reassess their manner of analysing socio-economic needs and undertaking social programmes in view of the differing trajectories for improved economic outcomes among various social classes and the greater heterogeneity of contemporary Philippine society. A complex picture of welfare and human development has emerged over the past decade, with middle-class households growing in the millions. This is so even if it is equally true that many others have not quite managed to make the transition and long-term trends have been disrupted by the effects of the pandemic. Despite episodic fits and stops in these developments, the consequences of a growing Filipino middle class on the economy and politics have become too important to be ignored.

The Philippines has undergone a socio-economic transition over the past roughly two decades that has attracted insufficient attention: a change into a minority-poor society. Using data from the Family Income and Expenditure Surveys (FIES), Table 16.1 shows how shares of households in different socio-economic classes have changed from 1997 to 2018. Households are classified into five socio-economic categories based on daily per capita expenditure:[5] the very poor, the poor, the vulnerable, the economically secure, the upper middle class and the topmost class.[6]

---

[5] Expenditure is preferred to income as a welfare measure, since it is less variable and captures a household's ability to mobilize financial resources other than income, including savings, borrowing, remittances and support from relatives. In short, it is more reflective of wealth broadly defined, which is arguably a better measure of material welfare. This well-known point is incidentally one that Arsenio Balisacan was among the first to insist on and advocate in the production of the Philippines' poverty statistics. See, for example, Balisacan (2001) for a full discussion of the methodology for calculating poverty indices that respects the "principle of consistency" for spatial and intertemporal comparisons of absolute poverty.

[6] Thresholds used to define expenditure classes correspond with those used by the World Bank in its 2018 East Asia and the Pacific Report, adjusted for inflation. See World Bank (2018b) for details.

The relative importance of these various classes or groups, whether in absolute or relative terms, has undergone marked changes throughout the 21-year period covered. The share in all households of the "very poor" first increased in 1997–2000, due in part to the Asian financial crisis in the late 1990s. This share began to decline from about 2000 onwards, with significant reductions in 2006–9 and again in 2012–18. By 2018, the relative size of this class had shrunk to less than 4 per cent. The trend of movements of the different groups is shown in Figure 16.1.

Table 16.1. *Share of families by socio-economic (expenditure) category (1997–2018), in per cent of total*

Social class by expenditure	1997	2000	2003	2006	2009	2012	2015	2018
Extremely poor	12.63	14.67	13.31	12.79	8.84	9.70	6.36	3.60
Poor	22.81	23.77	22.15	23.06	22.63	22.98	20.67	17.25
Vulnerable	28.62	27.74	28.28	27.75	30.16	29.81	31.15	32.91
Economically secure	29.44	27.73	29.85	29.72	31.22	30.74	34.62	38.97
Upper middle class	6.03	5.68	6.14	6.44	6.87	6.51	6.93	7.01
Top	0.47	0.42	0.27	0.25	0.28	0.26	0.27	0.26

Note: (1) Figures may not add up to 100 per cent due to rounding.
(2) Daily per capita expenditure of (a) extremely poor: US$1.9 or less
(b) poor: between US$1.9 and US$3.1
(c) vulnerable: between US$3.1 and US$5.5
(d) economically secure: between US$5.5 and US$15
(e) upper middle: between US$15 and US$50
(f) top: US$50 or more
(3) These figures differ from the poverty incidence data provided by the Philippine Statistics Authority owing to differences in thresholds.

Source of data: Computed from Family Income and Expenditure Survey (various years), PSA.

Figure 16.1. Shares of poor, vulnerable and middle-class households (in %, 1997–2018)

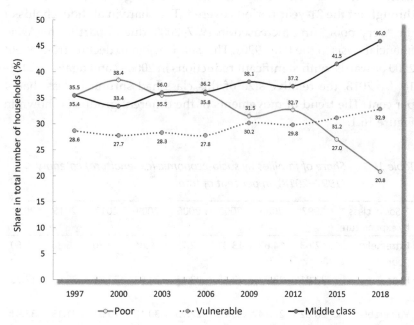

Source of basic data: Family Income and Expenditure Survey (various years), PSA.

On the other hand, the share of the vulnerable and economically secure categories increased beginning about 2012, as did the upper middle class. The proportion of the vulnerable increased from 28 per cent in 1997 to 30 per cent in 2012, 31 per cent in 2015 and then 33 per cent by 2018. Similarly, the percentages of those in the economically secure increased from 29 per cent in 1997 to 39 per cent in 2018, and the upper middle class, from 6 to 7 per cent. In contrast, the proportion of households in the top expenditure category was halved from 0.40 per cent in 1997 to 0.21 per cent in 2015.

These trends become more distinct if the two lowest expenditure groups are combined into a broad "poor" category and the economically secure and upper middle categories are grouped into a broad "middle class". Then the decline in the former and increase in the latter over the two-decade period becomes clearer, whether measured in terms of share or total number of families. The share of the poor as broadly defined fell from 35.4 per cent of families in 1997 to 20.9 per cent in 2018, with a significant decline occurring from 2012. This reflects the same trends, if not exactly the magnitudes, seen in official poverty measures.[7]

Meanwhile, the broadly defined middle class increased from 35.5 per cent to 46.0 per cent in the same period. It is also significant, however, that the proportion of the vulnerable remained high and even increased from 28.6 to 32.9 per cent (Figure 16.1). This is an expected consequence of progress in poverty reduction, but also indicates that the foothold on economic security remains precarious for many.

Nonetheless, by 2018, a notable milestone was passed: the middle class, broadly defined, constituted more than twice all families classified as poor. In this sense—and if such trends resume beyond the pandemic recession—the Philippines should be on its way to becoming a predominantly middle-class society. The middle class more than doubled from 5 million to some 11.4 million families between 1997 and 2018. On the other hand, the number of vulnerable families rose from 3.9 million to 7 million (Figure 16.2). These trends mean the middle class may have constituted half of all families—that is, until the pandemic-induced recession hit the county.

While not typically mentioned in social and development literature in the country, several studies have shown that the vulnerable and the broad middle class have grown significantly in both share and number in the country's population. Though defining the "middle class" in slightly different terms, Virola et al. (2013) and Albert, Gaspar, and Raymundo (2015), using FIES data, find a moderate increase in the share of families belonging to the middle-income category in the late 2000s and early 2010s.

---

[7] According to the latest official poverty incidence measures, poverty incidence (by families) was 18.0 per cent in 2015 and 12.1 per cent in 2018, using the latest methodology reflecting changes in rural-urban classifications and in the average family size. In the previous methodology, incidence by families was 21.0 per cent in 2006, 20.5 per cent in 2009, 19.7 per cent in 2012 and 16.5 per cent in 2015 (PSA, various years). While the official figures and the figures presented here are not the same, they broadly reflect similar movements in the incidence across time.

Figure 16.2. Number of poor, vulnerable and middle-class households (1997–2018)

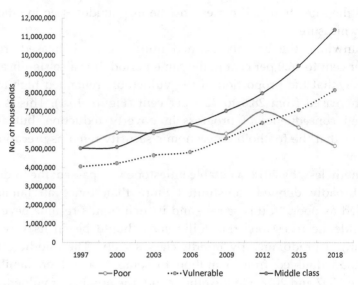

Source of basic data: Family Income and Expenditure Survey (various years), PSA.

The World Bank (2018b) similarly observes a slow growth of the middle class, although it finds that the proportion of the country's "upper middle class" remains small, as in Cambodia and Indonesia. Trends in consumption demand since the 1990s and 2000s, supported by the growth of the call centre industry and the large increase in OFW remittances in the country, also show evidence of this phenomenon.

Over roughly a decade, the economically secure and upper middle classes expanded even in rural areas, although not in the agriculture sector (Table 16.2, line 1), implying that social mobility has occurred in diversified occupations even beyond the country's metropolitan centres. Especially notable between the two periods was the increase in the proportion of household heads with college degrees among the economically secure (from 17% to 22%) and even more appreciably among the upper middle classes (from 48% to 58%).

The proportion of the self-employed among household heads, however, decreased in these two expenditure categories (from 40% to 24% for the middle class, and from 35% to 17% for the economically secure in the 1997–2018 period). At the same time, the proportion of those who undertake primarily wage employment decreased (from 56% to 47% for the middle class and from 62% to 45% for the economically secure), suggesting that middle-class households may have found other sources of income than self- and wage-employment, such as employment in family-owned businesses. A trend towards smaller households in the same expenditure categories is also apparent, as is an increase in the proportion of working household members.

The pervasiveness of middle-class consumption, if not incomes, has been witnessed in the country in the growth of purchases of goods and services that typically accompany the rise of upwardly mobile households, including condominium building units and other residential estate, private vehicles, outside dining, and vacation and leisure services, including foreign travel. The expansion in the use of cellular and smart phones, which also accompany the rise of online shopping and increasing time spent on social media, has been a characteristic of urban households in the metropolitan centres of the country.

3 EFFECTS OF THE CRISIS ON THE TRENDS IN WELFARE

The crisis caused by the COVID-19 pandemic has disrupted the above-discussed trends, since expectedly many of the vulnerable would have been thrust into at least transitory poverty and the poor further beaten down. Whether and how they can ultimately recover depend on how long the crisis lasts and how well-equipped they are to adapt to a period of shrunken opportunities. With regard to the current recession, however, it is reasonable to say it will not be as prolonged as the 1984–85 debt crisis, with which it is often mistakenly compared.[8] An important difference is that the current crisis is one that has been deliberately engineered and not one forced on the economy by deep structural factors (e.g., there is no foreign-exchange shortage and government finances are far from precarious levels). This implies at least the *possibility*

---

[8] GDP growth turned negative in 1984 and 1985 before turning positive again in 1986. Average growth for the whole period 1983–86 was −2.33 per cent. In the current crisis, the IMF World Economic Outlook (IMF 2021) projects average GDP growth of 2.48 per cent for the period 2019–22, with only a single year of contraction.

Table 16.2. Characteristics of the economically secure and upper middle-income class categories (1997 and 2018)

Profile	1997 Economically secure	1997 Upper middle class	2018 Economically secure	2018 Upper middle class
Proportion of households (%)				
Reside in rural areas (2000)	21.10	9.63	36.78	23.82
Undertake primarily agriculture (2006)	5.78	1.92	NA	NA
Own house and lot	67.70	75.03	72.76	79.78
Have household ownership but lease lot rent-free	9.07	2.99	11.66	3.98
Average number of household members	4.62	3.88	4.02	3.10
Proportion of household members working	40.45	47.70	46.71	56.09
Proportion of household heads (%)				
Male	80.07	73.48	73.27	63.08
Married	78.79	74.29	72.14	63.61
Not single nor married	16.03	15.53	21.51	22.58
Primarily undertake wage employment	57.09	62.84	46.13	45.42
Primarily self-employed	39.70	35.09	23.73	16.94
Finished secondary school only	45.18	36.50	42.87	30.62
Finished tertiary school	16.78	48.19	22.00	58.28
Average age of household head (years)	47.74	48.94	51.29	52.22
Proportion of household heads who are OFWs	3.38	5.58	NA	NA

Source of basic data: Family Income and Expenditure Survey (1997, 2018), PSA.

that the previous growth trajectory can be resumed if the public health situation can be resolved fairly quickly and economic scarring has not been severe in the interim.

Indeed, one may gain some insights into the persistent socio-economic trends, notwithstanding sharp economic crises, from the socio-economic transition matrix computed in the Philippine Human Development Report 2020/21 for the period 2003–9 (HDN 2020). This is still the only series available that tracks the socio-economic progress of a panel of households over many years; it fortuitously includes the crisis year 2009, when GDP growth fell to just 1.4 per cent after growth rates averaging 5.5 per cent in the previous five years. Notwithstanding the failure of growth at the time, as much as 75 per cent of the vulnerable remained in the same category or did better, although about 20 per cent were relegated to the poor. Table 16.3 shows the complete movements into and out of different socio-economic categories. Of those who were extremely poor, for example, 46.7 per cent still moved up one rung to the category of poor, while 12 per cent moved up to the vulnerable category. Moreover, a third of those who were in the poor category moved up to the vulnerable and around 7 per cent moved to the economically secure. More significant for this paper's middle-class concerns is that, notwithstanding the crisis, 74.3 per cent of the economically secure managed to remain in the same category or do even better. Among the upper middle class, this proportion was even higher (96%).

Much of the adverse welfare shocks caused by the pandemic may be expected to be non-permanent, particularly among the middle classes, although there is no denying the immediate impact on incomes and productivity owing to the lockdowns and economic contraction. This has been particularly felt by the poorest classes. A palpable indicator of the latter has been the drastic rise in the incidence of hunger during the pandemic-induced recession. Social Weather Stations, an opinion-polling firm, estimates the full-year incidence of hunger nationwide at 21.1 per cent in 2020, more than double the 9.3 per cent of the previous year and a record high in over two decades.[9]

---

[9] Hunger incidence is based on the response to the question of whether a household experienced involuntary hunger—a lack of food to eat—in the last three months. For details, see Social Weather Stations 2020.

Table 16.3. Transition matrix (2003 and 2009)

2003 category	Starting share → 2003 (%)	Proportion of households that moved/stayed in different expenditure classes					
		Extremely poor	Poor	Vulnerable	Economically secure	Upper middle	Top
Extremely poor	13.9	0.4079	0.4672	0.1179	0.0066	–	–
Poor	24.4	0.1497	0.4495	0.3343	0.0656	0.0011	–
Vulnerable	29.8	0.0268	0.2072	0.5024	0.2574	0.0062	–
Economically secure	26.8	0.0018	0.0306	0.2231	0.6372	0.1056	0.0017
Upper middle class	5.0	–	–	0.0133	0.4579	0.5113	0.0197
Top class	0.2	–	–	–	0.0608	0.5167	0.4083
	Ending share → 2009 (%)	8.8000	23.8000	31.1000	29.8000	6.4000	0.3000

Note: Shaded vertical and horizontal cells represent the starting and ending shares of socio-economic categories between 2003 and 2009, in percentage terms. The unshaded entries show the proportion of the original families in 2003 that had moved to or remained in various categories by 2009.

Source: Reproduced from HDN (2021, 34, Table 1.2) based on the Family Income and Expenditure Survey (2003 and 2009).

The pandemic has also halted, if temporarily, the gradual decline in unemployment and underemployment rates observed since the mid-2000s. The unemployment rate increased in 2020—when the brunt of the crisis was felt—by some 5 percentage points on an annualized basis to 16.3 per cent compared with the preceding year. Rates of underemployment and visible underemployment also increased by 2.4 and 1.8 percentage points, respectively, to 16.2 per cent and 9.7 per cent compared with the previous year. This means an increase in the number of unemployed workers from 2.3 million to 4.5 million, and the number of underemployed workers from 5.8 million to 6.4 million. Since then, however, the impact has moderated as the most stringent features of the lockdowns were relaxed. Rates of unemployment and underemployment as of May 2021 stood at 7.7 per cent and 12 per cent, respectively, again showing that the current crisis is due less to inevitable structural causes and more to deliberately placing the economy in "a state of hibernation"[10] to avert worse public health outcomes.

Even here, however, a more nuanced idea of the differential impact of the crisis across socio-economic classes can be obtained. Our description of the middle classes in Table 16.2 shows a great majority of household heads (i.e., 65% of the economically secure and 85% of the upper middle class) having completed at least a secondary education, with a significant proportion being college finishers. This represents a large divide between them and the poor and vulnerable, which have much lower rates of high-school graduates (and college finishers).[11] Using education level achieved as a benchmark, we divide the unemployed based on education completed, positing the completion of senior high school or better as a threshold to capture specifically middle-class employment behaviour during the crisis. This allows us to distinguish three groups: those who completed at most an elementary education (call this Group 1); those with better than an elementary completion but less than a senior high school education (Group 2); and those who completed senior high school or better, including college graduates (Group 3). We contend that those in

---

[10] This advice was made early on in the crisis in many countries. For the Philippines, an early recommendation was from Paloyo et al. (2020, 9–10).

[11] By way of comparison, in 2015 only 0.38 per cent and 1.18 per cent of household heads among the extremely poor and poor, respectively, had finished secondary school, and 34.14 per cent among the vulnerable (HDN 2020, 32, Box Table 5).

Group 3 are more likely to represent the middle-class element and, it should be noted, constitute nearly half of the unemployed, more than a third of whom are college graduates.

Figure 16.3 shows the distinctive behaviour of Group 3. When the worst of the pandemic hit, with severe lockdowns imposed beginning in March 2020 and with measured unemployment running at 17.3 per cent in April 2020, the share of Group 3 among the unemployed *fell*, while those of the first two groups rose. Subsequently, as the severe lockdown ended and restrictions on business were relaxed initially in July 2020, job seeking among Group 3 *rose*. On the other hand, unemployment of Groups 1 and 2 generally moderated or even subsided.

Figure 16.3. Shares in unemployment by attained level of education* (in %, January 2020 to May 2021)

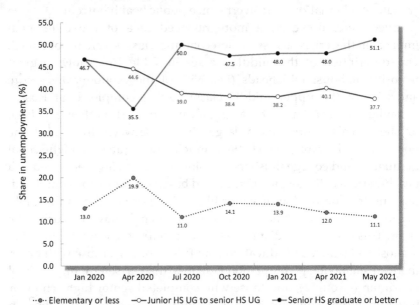

Note: *Monthly employment data became available in 2021, but data for February and March 2021 are no longer shown.

Source of basic data: Labor Force Surveys, PSA.

This divergent pattern may be explained if one considers that many among Group 3 likely left the labour force in reaction to deteriorating economic conditions. This presumption is consistent with the observation that middle-class workers—because they can draw on past savings and rely on more financially-capable social networks—are in a better position to cope with economic shocks by spending periods out of the labour or engaging in more exacting job search as needed (see, e.g., de Dios and Dinglasan 2015; Epetia 2018). This conjecture is supported in the observed drop in labour-force participation from 60.2 per cent in January 2020 to 56 per cent in April 2020. In contrast, those with lesser educational qualifications or who are poorer must respond to adverse conditions by persisting in job search and, more likely, by more readily accommodating themselves to jobs that are less remunerative and less matched to their skills (e.g., low-paying informal-sector jobs or new formal employment created by the pandemic, such as door-to-door courier businesses). One observes that as restrictions were eased in 2021 (albeit patchily and in fits and starts) and as more sectors of the economy were gradually opened, there were greater attempts at job search among the middle class. Conversely, the shares in unemployment of Groups 1 and 2 declined. Generally, therefore, labour-force participation and job seeking among the middle class have been prospectively procyclical, while those among the poorer or less educated are the opposite.

The welfare significance of aggregate indicators such as unemployment rates may thus vary across heterogeneous socio-economic groups—as will the appropriate social protection policies. In the case discussed, what seemed called for in the early days of the lockdown was an income supplementation programme focused on poor and vulnerable workers and those with fewer qualifications who had lost their employment (Groups 1 and 2); middle-class workers (Group 3), by contrast, seemed more resilient and in less need of such assistance. As economic conditions improved, however, a more general unemployment insurance scheme, together with effective job-placement and retraining programmes, would have been useful in terms of both efficiency and social welfare. The government's response in terms of directly handling the pandemic as well as managing its economic fallout unfortunately has fallen far short of what the situation requires as regards design and coverage.

All socio-economic classes, except perhaps those at the very top, have been adversely affected by the crisis. A rapid appraisal study of Philippine micro, small and medium enterprises (MSMEs) undertaken for the Asian Development Bank by Shinozaki (2020) indicates that while employment levels were gradually normalizing by the end of the third quarter of 2020, a significant number of firms reported cutting wages and working hours of employees, even as firms reporting no-wage payments have declined. The crisis in the country's mostly government-run basic education system—which is of long-standing and predates the pandemic[12]—has been also aggravated by the pandemic when normal face-to-face classes were suspended and replaced with various and invariably inferior forms of distance learning. This setback has not been limited to the poor and vulnerable, however. Luz (2020) notes that even private primary and secondary schools catering to the economically secure and upper middle-income groups achieved only half of their enrolment levels in school year 2020/2021 compared with the previous academic year. Even as the pandemic and the recession have adversely affected all social classes, their lasting or transient effects will differ depending on the people's starting human, physical, financial and social assets, and how these are deployed—as well as the effectiveness of the government's response to ameliorate the social harm. Even this early, this much is evident: that the economically secure and upper middle classes will likely weather the storm better than others and be better placed to resume the progress they were enjoying before the pandemic. The positions of the poor and the vulnerable meanwhile are prone to deteriorate and likely to suffer from the inevitable economic scarring—not to mention the intergenerational effect of their further weakened access to an already deficient education system.

The expected upshot is a wider social gulf between these groups than what existed prior to the pandemic. A sharper sensitivity to differences in social conditions, capabilities and welfare trajectories thus becomes essential if a deeper social division is to be averted.

---

[12] The Philippines scored lowest in both Grade 4 math and science among 58 countries participating in the 2019 Trends in International Mathematics and Science Study. Prior to this, the country also ranked last among 79 countries in reading and second to the last in mathematics and science in the 2018 Programme for International Student Assessment (PISA) test.

4 AN OFFICIAL BLIND SPOT

Across three administrations[13] and after a long period of scientific refinement and political legitimation, the Philippine government successfully developed programmes that directly address poverty. Balisacan (1997), Balisacan et al. (1998), Balisacan and Edillon (2003) and Balisacan (2009) document some of the anti-poverty programmes the government implemented in the 1980s and 1990s. Finding that well-designed programmes unfortunately received only modest support, thus affecting welfare outcomes of low-income groups only marginally, they recommend improvements in the targeting and evaluation of anti-poverty mechanisms. Balisacan and Fuwa (2007) also highlight the issue of vulnerability in poverty analysis and advocate the government's strengthening of its social protection net to address adverse income risks among Philippine households.

These efforts culminated in the country's comprehensive and targeted conditional cash-transfer programme (*Programang Pantawid Pamilyang Pilipino*,[14] also known as 4Ps), based on a comprehensive national census of poor households.[15] Underpinned by continuous economic growth, this sustained and targeted initiative was an important reason for the successful reduction of poverty, as discussed earlier.

In contrast to its success in poverty alleviation, however, the government still has to take official cognizance of the large shifts in the country's socio-economic composition—particularly its transformation into a minority-poor society—and the emerging importance of other classes with their peculiar progress, needs and capacities. Little, if any, of the trends described in the previous section are reflected in either the government's official plans or in pronouncements by the country's political class.[16] The country's medium-term plan for 2017–22 fails to

---

[13] Those of Gloria Macapagal-Arroyo (2004–10), Benigno Aquino, III (2010–16) and Rodrigo Duterte (2016 to the present).
[14] Literally "crossing-over programme for the Filipino family".
[15] That is, the National Household Targeting System for Poverty Reduction (NHTS-PR).
[16] It is not only the government that has failed to recognize these trends. At the other extreme, the radical Left is afflicted with the same obliviousness, with its main programme continuing to be based on support by a peasantry for an armed revolution—notwithstanding that the agricultural labour force has been reduced to a small fraction of the labour force.

mention, much less define, the middle class as a distinct socio-economic category (NEDA 2021).[17] This blind spot in official planning was confirmed in recent legislative hearings to discuss amelioration measures during the pandemic, when the country's statistical authority admitted to having no official definition of the "middle class", recognizing only the distinction between "poor" and "non-poor" (see Torregoza 2020). The singular issuance that explicitly refers to the middle class would appear to be Executive Order No. 5, s.2016. This order adopts *AmBisyon Natin 2040*, a 25-year "long-term vision" that projects the Philippines by 2040 as "a prosperous *predominantly middle-class society where no one is poor*" (emphasis supplied). Measured welfare targets in the country's medium-term plan (i.e., "headline indicators"), however, are dominated by projected trends in the incidence of total poverty and food-subsistence poverty (NEDA 2021, 1–9, Table 1.1). The more middle-class concerns, such as access to quality education, stable and productive employment, and explicit social protection, are left unmentioned or, at most, latent in aggregate indicators, such as the human development index.[18] This suggests that while the government envisions the achievement of a "middle-class society", this goal is defined primarily in terms of poverty eradication, which is still implicitly expected to dominate the country's socio-economic agenda until 2040. What such a formulation fails to recognize, however, is that specifically middle-class needs and concerns may overtake both economy and polity well before poverty is eliminated. The poor–non-poor dichotomy, which has been refined and has proved useful through the years, may now prove inadequate in addressing the needs of the majority—an inadequacy that has become especially apparent in the pandemic. The results have been under coverage in some programmes, misdirected provision and so-called "leaky buckets" in others. Overall, the effect is the creation of a dissonance between social rhetoric and implemented policy and an inadequate programme design that fails to adequately serve the poor and non-poor alike.

---

[17] Work by the Philippine Institute for Development Studies, a public think-tank, has dealt with the description and definition of the middle classes, but little of this has filtered through to official policy; see, for example, Albert, Gaspar, and Raymundo (2015) and Albert, Santos, and Vizmanos (2018).

[18] Consistent with its emerging middle-class status, the Philippines' human development index (HDI) for 2018 was 0.712, crossing the threshold for "high human development" (i.e., HDI range of 0.7–0.799) for the first time.

Okun's (1975) metaphor of a leaky bucket originally refers to the administrative waste and adverse incentive effects involved in transferring funds (mostly through taxation) from the rich to the poor. The term can also be used, however, to refer to the "leakage" that occurs when a programme intended for a defined set of beneficiaries—particularly the poor—ends up benefiting other groups or sectors that do not deserve or need the benefits of the programme.

A major example of this type of leakage is the scheme intended to provide universal health coverage under the national health insurance programme. Established in 1995, the Philhealth programme was at first paid for largely by payroll taxes; it was plagued by under coverage and underfunding. In response to criticism that Philhealth has failed to benefit the poor, the government expanded the programme through the use of national and local budgetary resources to cover annual premiums for indigents. Analysts of this programme, however, have long noted the unevenness in the utilization of the programme's benefits; the poor have been unable to avail themselves fully of the programme's benefits owing to the cumbersome requirements of filing claims and the lack of information on entitlements (Quimbo et al. 2008). One result has been that the bulk of the programme's beneficiaries have come from the non-poor. In 2018, the programme served almost 80 per cent of the richest quintile and only less than 60 per cent of the poorest quintile of households (Figure 16.4). In terms of benefits obtained, on the other hand, almost 79 per cent of total Philhealth benefits in 2016 were enjoyed by the upper 60 per cent (the middle and upper classes); the poorest quintile accounted for only 7 per cent of the total benefits paid out. This situation leads to the perverse result that government subsidies ostensibly meant to aid the poor may have actually benefited the middle classes and the rich.[19]

---

[19] To see this in simple terms, suppose government provides a subsidy to indigents amounting to sP in the expectation that the total number P of indigents will avail themselves of specified per capita benefits worth the scalar $b = s$. Then total contributions to the fund are $C = sP + wN$, where w is the mandated contribution (e.g., a payroll tax) per capita of the non-poor N. Let total benefits disbursed be $A = b(p + n)$, where the number of actual beneficiaries among indigents and non-poor are respectively $n \leq N$ and $p \leq P$. Equating $A = C$ (i.e., allowing for no surpluses or deficits) and remembering $b = s$, one obtains $b(P - p) + wN = bn$, or $n = (P - p) + (w/b)N$. Since the second term is fixed, the number of non-poor beneficiaries n is inversely related to $(P - p)$, the rate at which the poor underuse the facility.

Figure 16.4. Share of Philhealth benefits enjoyed by quintile (2016, in %)

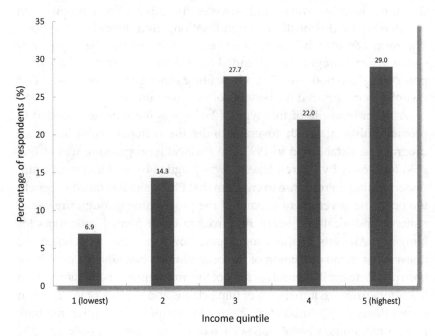

Note: From poorest = 1 to richest = 5.
Source: Solon (2019).

This regressiveness has not been ameliorated by the taxation used to finance the health premium subsidies to indigents (Solon 2019).

On the other hand, the low level of benefits covered also implies ironically that even the needs of the non-poor are not substantially met. Since current benefits are designed to meet only the minimum needs of the indigent, these are inadequate to meet the actual expenditures for healthcare among the non-poor who, though over-represented in benefit utilization, must still meet the balance of their health needs primarily through out-of-pocket expenditures (see Panelo et al. 2017, 45). What the current system does not allow is a higher degree of risk-pooling among the non-poor; this would have entailed a greater—if means-differentiated— contribution, but also a more adequate coverage of the health demands of middle-class and other non-poor households. Instead, the attempt at a universalist approach based on an assessment of minimal needs fails both progressiveness (i.e., in covering the poor) and efficiency (i.e., in even adequately serving the non-poor). A far-reaching review of the country's health system summarizes it thus: "What Philhealth has in fact managed to do is to pay a little bit of everything for all Filipinos" (Panelo et al. 2017, 43). It is a source of dissonance between enunciated policy and implemented programmes that what has been propounded as a pro-poor initiative has ended up benefiting (even if inadequately) the non-poor, particularly the middle classes.

The preceding analysis of Philhealth is symptomatic and applicable to other social programmes. The failure to recognize distinct social differences and the resort to programmes of universal but minimal provision have a crowding-out effect on the poor, but paradoxically also results in the under provision of services more relevant to the non-poor. These have been the outcomes of a change in policy direction and rationale, the reasons for which are explained below.

Proponents of universalism have pointed to the high administrative costs of targeting and applying eligibility rules, particularly given people's changing life circumstances, the incentive created for misrepresentation, possible disincentive effects on effort, and negative labelling effects encouraged by targeted programmes. On the other hand, targeted programmes do allow for higher benefits per person served, do not displace private spending, and—important for frequently budget-strapped governments—cost less per person served.[20] While the debate on the merits of each one is still ongoing in global circles of development thinking and policy,[21] no explicit debate on the issue has occurred in the Philippines. Instead, what one has witnessed is an implicit shift towards universalism owing to an easing fiscal burden and the implicit response of the political class to a growing middle-class constituency.

Government policies in past decades have moved from the one extreme of failing to provide essential economic and social services to the public, often in a targeted manner to economize on resources, to the other extreme of at times providing these services less discriminately for free or at heavily subsidized rates. In the late 1980s as well as after the Asian financial crisis in the late 1990s and early 2000s, the lack of public resources squeezed the availability of social services. This slowed down improvements in human development in the country vis-à-vis its Southeast Asian neighbours. Since the growth

---

[20] See the summary listing taken from Perlman (2012).
[21] For a flavour of recent discussions, see, e.g., Savchuk (2012) or Kidd (2016), the rejoinder by Yemtsoz (2016) and the middle ground proposed by Desai (2017).

years of the 2010s and with the resulting increase in tax revenues,[22] however, government spending in many economic and social services has increased significantly. But the incidence of such provision has not been well-defined, and while helpful in improving the welfare of some groups, it is not clear whether the provision is efficient or even effective from a targeting standpoint. Many programmes since then have drifted towards a "universalist" approach.

Among recent examples of universalist social policy legislation are the revised Universal Health Care Act (Republic Act 11223, passed in 2018), which was analysed in the preceding section; the Universal Access to Quality Tertiary Education Act (RA 10931, passed in 2017), which provides free tuition in all state colleges and universities; and the Senior Citizens Act (RA 2257, passed in 2003 and amended in 2010), which mandates, among others, a 20 per cent discount and exemption from value-added tax for all citizens aged 60 and over for the purchase of medicines, hospital and medical fees, air and land transport fare, hotel and lodging rates, as well as other miscellaneous necessities.[23] Others include the provision of free irrigation services in agricultural lands, as well as minor initiatives such as free rides for students in Metro Manila's (nationally owned) metro rail system.

In countries with fairly homogeneous class composition—such as industrial economies consisting predominantly of large middle classes or less-developed economies with predominantly poor populations—a universalist approach has its merits in being largely inclusive of the overwhelming majority of the population. In middle-income developing countries transitioning from mass poverty, however, complications arise from continuing with the implicit assessment that the great majority of the population remain homogenously poor.

The legislation providing free tuition in state universities and colleges, for example, does so, although the upper middle class and rich groups are well able to pay their own way to achieve tertiary

---

[22] Administrations began to run primary surpluses from the time of President Arroyo. The cost of borrowing has also fallen, as ultimately reflected in the investment-grade rating on the country's sovereign debt from several rating agencies beginning in 2013. See Rappler (2013).

[23] Part of the reason for the early passage of this social legislation is that it involves no direct budgetary subsidies from the government, but rather, it is left to private establishments to implement it through their preferred means of discriminatory pricing.

schooling. Among other things, it upended already established and well-functioning means-tested tuition cum subsidies in elite public institutions such as the University of the Philippines, as well as disrupted the markets for private education. Even the provision of free irrigation services in agricultural lands flies in the face of studies showing that fee-paying systems are better maintained and supported, and therefore provide better water supply to poor farmers.

Other programmes that seem motivated by universalist principles include the senior citizens' discounts (which, among others, allow even upper-income households to benefit from discounted restaurant meals which they can easily afford) and free rides for students on Metro Manila's light rail system (a national subsidy that fails to benefit poorer students in the provinces who walk or take public transportation to get to school). Indeed, some of these social programmes should be provided more properly by local authorities than by the national government. Such flaws and biases in the design of social insurance and social protection programmes have tended to be concealed under the tarp of universal provision.

The World Bank (2018c) provides a useful compilation of the benefit incidence of various social services across household income quintiles, as shown in Figure 16.5. Philhealth, which follows a universalist approach, comes out as having the largest reach even among the poorest quintiles—unsurprising considering the huge resources at its disposal. Its bias for the non-poor and even the most affluent is evident, however, since almost 80 per cent of the richest quintiles are able to avail themselves of the benefits, compared with an average reach of some 60 per cent of households among the two poorest quintiles. Even its reach among the poor is somewhat deceptive, since—based on figures suggested by Figure 16.2—the benefits they enjoy are relatively "thin" (21% of the total), against the two richest deciles that capture more than half of all benefits distributed.

By contrast, the more targeted programmes such as 4Ps, social feeding and social pension programmes show a greater bias in favour of the lower income quintiles, but these suffer from smaller budgetary resources.

Figure 16.5. Proportion of households provided with social services
(by income quintile, 2013 and 2017)

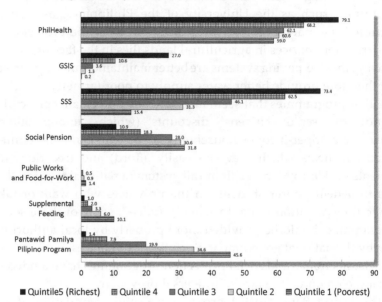

Note: GSIS – Government Service Insurance System; SSS – Social Security System
Source: World Bank (2018c, 29). Figure drawn from data in Table III.1.

What in principle should have been a major pillar of the social insurance for the middle class—the Social Security System for private-sector employees—on the surface seems to reach a decent proportion of its target audience (though again with a distinctly regressive bias). But to begin with, the system itself is far from universal, covering less than one-fourth of the country's wage and salary earners. This poor coverage is further diluted by the patchy and thin provision of benefits—in this case, sundry types of salary-based loans and indifferent retirement pay-outs. The pandemic has exposed a major deficiency of the system, however: the system is unable to provide a comprehensive system of unemployment benefits.[24] As its extraordinary response to the pandemic, for example, all the Social Security System could muster was a one-time maximum unemployment benefit of PHP20,000 over two months to 60,000 members—a measly drop in the bucket of millions unemployed.

---

[24] A proposal for an unemployment insurance system is buried on page 158 of the Philippine Development Plan 2017–2022, and has so far garnered only feeble legislative interest.

As the foregoing shows, the pandemic has exposed the inadequacy of the current social protection system. Table 16.4 shows the different disbursements made by the Department of Budget and Management to various programmes organized under the "Bayanihan Heal as One" policies of the government. By February 2021, total disbursements were reported to have reached more than half a trillion pesos. Nearly two-fifths of the spending was for cash and food subsidy programmes under the Social Amelioration Programs of the Department of Social Welfare and Development. This, in turn, has drawn flak from middle-income groups as the government has been perceived to focus its resources mostly on the poorest households, while assistance to non-poor but nonetheless affected groups has been missing (see, e.g., Venzon 2020). Wage subsidies took up almost a tenth of the allocation; a slightly higher amount went to the health sector, including allowances for health workers.

Table 16.4. *Government fund releases for programmes under the Bayanihan 1 and 2 (in million PHP)*

Programme	Agency	Bayanihan 1	Bayanihan 2
Social Amelioration Program and other social interventions	DSWD	206,487	6,000
Assistance to displaced workers	DOLE	6,335	15,900
Allocation to local governments	DOF-BTr	37,021	2,335
Food assistance programmes and agriculture stimulus programmes	DA, DOF	8,500	19,476
Repatriation programmes, assistance to nationals	DILG, DOLE, DFA	1,145	1,320
Basic and higher education learning continuity programme	DepEd, CHED	10,911	11,208
Training programmes	DTI		1,103
Support for health sector	DOH	45,718	10,044
Small business wage subsidy measure	SSS	51,000	
Contract tracing, emergency facilities	DILG, DND		18,935
Transportation measures	DoTR		1,759
Interest loan subsidy for LGUs	DOF-BTr		2,000
Assistance to small business	DOF		8,080

Table 16.4 *(continued)*

Table 16.4 *(continued)*

Programme	Agency	Bayanihan 1	Bayanihan 2
Infrastructure programmes, farm to market roads	DPWH, DA		16,869
Various lending programmes	DOF		29,973
WHO solidarity trials	DOH		384
Others		19,026	26,614
Total		386,143	172,000

Note: (1) As of February 2021.
(2) DSWD = Department of Social Welfare and Development
DOLE = Department of Labor and Employment
DOF-BTr = Department of Finance-Bureau of Treasury
DILG = Department of Interior and Local Governments
DepEd = Department of Education
CHED = Commission on Higher Education
DPWH = Department of Public Works and Highways
DA = Department of Agriculture
DOH = Department of Health
DTI = Department of Trade and Industry
SSS = Social Security System
DFA = Department of Foreign Affairs
DOTr = Department of Transportation
Source: Department of Budget and Management (2021).

Notwithstanding the magnitude of the wage and cash subsidies provided by the government during the pandemic, the absence of institutional employment insurance and the poor targeting of the national health insurance programme have meant that wage and informal sector workers have been severely affected, given the limited period and uneven scope of the programmes undertaken. The way the national government has developed and implemented social insurance and assistance programmes to address the pandemic has followed exactly the patchwork and token nature of public programmes in the country.

The aggregate distributional incidence of universalist policies in more class-heterogenous countries has been little analysed, but the Philippine experience may provide a few insights of how, owing to peculiar circumstances, universalism—ostensibly intended to benefit and cover mainly the underprivileged—may ultimately favour the economically secure and even the upper middle and top classes. At least two cases may be considered analytically. The first case is where *fixed* or *rationed benefits* are provided per beneficiary, such as in health insurance or free tuition in state tertiary education institutions. The second case is where benefits enjoyed are *open-ended and depend on the rate of usage* by individual beneficiaries. An example is the senior citizens' discount on medicines, meals and lodging, or the free irrigation to farmers regardless of farm size.

Where benefits are fixed, the crucial issue that causes distortion of benefit incidence appears to be the failure to provide comprehensive coverage, or at least the complementary inputs needed to enjoy the specified benefits. In the case of health insurance, for instance, this lack may be as simple as the failure to disseminate enough information to indigents, easing the burden of documentary requirements, or considering the cost of accessing distant health facilities—or more significantly the fact that in many cases co-payment for certain inputs is required. In education, there is the more obvious fact that tuition covers only a part of the cost of college attendance, board and lodging being more significant out-of-pocket costs that must still be borne by the would-be beneficiaries.[25] The non-inclusion of such complementary inputs degrades the value of the subsidized benefits and makes access dependent on the willingness of the would-be beneficiary to bear the private cost of such necessary inputs.[26] This tends to favour the better-off, including the middle class.[27]

On the other hand, where the size of benefits is variable and depends directly on rate of use of the subsidized service, the source of the possible distortion of benefit incidence is more easily understood, since the lack of a means-test under universal provision obviously means those with larger ladles get more access to the common pool. The benefit incidence

---

[25] This is apart from the more basic fact that the rate of secondary education completion is lower among the poor so that fewer of them qualify for college to begin with.

[26] Let the marginal utility to a person of a defined social benefit be $u(b, c)$, where b is the subsidized or free component and c is an indivisible non-free complementary input. The complementary input is essential so that $u(b, 0) = 0$. If the price of the complementary input is p and the marginal utility of income to the individual is m, then the service is worthwhile accessing if $u(b, c) - mp \geq 0$. If the marginal utility of income is assumed to decline with wealth w, i.e., $m'(w) < 0$, then for some $w \geq w^*$, the previous inequality holds, while it fails for $w < w^*$. This yields the result that better-off individuals will benefit from a universally provided service when complementary inputs are neglected.

[27] This is suggested by the fact that, among other things, poorer households spend less of their budgets than the rich on catastrophic health payments, i.e., in the face of catastrophic events "the rich draw down their wealth, the poor draw down their health" (HDN 2021, 52, Figure 1.13).

distortion here depends directly on the pre-existing distribution of wealth and incomes, becoming worse where inequality is pronounced. This is the case for free irrigation, which benefits owners of larger farms. It is also true for the senior citizens' discounts. In the latter case, the benefits largely accrue as additional consumer's surplus to already existing consumers of the subsidized service and marginally to newer users.[28]

One may also view the drift towards universalism as an implicit recognition of a shifting political landscape. That the political class has gravitated towards universalist measures suggests that it, too, has a political and electoral eye on the rising middle-class influence. After all, aside from universalist social protection programmes, a number of other initiatives have been passed that directly (if not expressly) cater to specific middle-class constituencies. These include salary increases for various categories of government employees (e.g., school teachers, the police and the military) and the tax rebracketing of compensation incomes. What keeps these and similar initiatives from being an adequate response, however, is their failure to proceed from a full analysis of needs and concerns specific to the class it seeks to benefit—in this case, specifically middle-class needs as distinct from those of the poor and the affluent. They, therefore, become reduced to piecemeal provision that at times borders on populist pandering. An example is a recent bill to provide free annual medical check-ups,[29] a measure obviously addressed and ultimately beneficial to a middle-class constituency.[30] Such a measure fails to address head-on the real issue, however, which is the need for a financially viable system of health insurance that can provide an

---

[28] Let the price-quantity demand curve $r(h)$ for a service or goods (say, restaurant meals or medicines) be the schedule of the declining reservation prices of various individuals h, assumed to be ordered according to their declining wealth or incomes, and let the unsubsidized market price be p. Then households h^+ represented by $h^+ \leq h^*$ will be buyers of the service, where h is given by $r(h^*) = p$, while households $h^0 > h^*$—the less affluent—will be out of the market. A discount of d reduces the price for the current buyers h^+ and increases their consumers' surplus while also shrinks h^0 by bringing in additional buyers, depending on the size of d. But without a cap on benefits, it is evident the number of poorer beneficiaries can be increased only by simultaneously increasing the consumers' surplus of the more affluent.

[29] As reported, e.g., in Ragasa (2021).

[30] This follows from our analysis of a fixed-benefits programme involving complementary inputs. The beneficiaries of a medical check-up are ultimately those who can afford the treatment following a diagnosis.

integrated system of care.[31] A further deficiency is the failure to account for the full distributional impact of some middle-class legislation on other social classes. As one example, the government sought to make up its revenue losses from lowering tax rates on (mostly middle-class) compensation incomes by imposing new indirect taxes, some of which hurt the poor and the vulnerable (notably the taxes on petroleum products that filter through to higher transport fares).

A major part of governance, therefore, entails the minimization of the types of leakages and under coverage discussed earlier by designing the proper types of direct social provision, social insurance and credit programmes for groups that are respectively most likely to benefit from these. This can be done through improved geographical and indicator targeting or even by designing programmes that include the beneficiaries and exclude the non-beneficiaries. At the same time, the potential for tax policy to promote mobility has been underestimated by governments that would preserve the welfare gains of the middle class. These include thinking about how tax reforms, especially among current proposals in Congress, can support the continued upward trajectory of all and not just some households.

6 MIDDLE-CLASS PLURALITY: A SHIFTING POLITICS

The rising plurality of a middle class and the relegation of the poor to a minority are bound to have an impact on the direction and character not only of policy but of politics itself. A remarkable feature of Philippine politics in recent years has been the unexpected direction in which this socio-demographic shift has taken Philippine public opinion and ultimately its electoral politics.

A commonplace in the development literature is that middle-class growth plays a role in ensuring a nation's political and economic development. Among others, countries with a larger middle class are much less politically polarized and better inclined to reach consensus

---

[31] The term "continuum of care" (Evashwick 1989) has been used to refer to "an integrated system of care that guides and tracks patients over time through a comprehensive array of health services spanning all levels of intensity of care". In the Philippines, the work of Panelo et al. (2017) analyses the effects on the access to a wide range of public health programmes by the general public caused by the devolution of health services in the country.

on policies that focus on a country's growth (Alesina 1994), including the growth of entrepreneurs that facilitate greater employment and productivity (Banerjee and Duflo 2008) and allow for more equal distribution of public goods such as health, education and infrastructure (Easterly 2001). The middle class in many countries also promote values that strengthen accumulation of human capital and savings, and also can drive the production of higher-quality consumer goods.

Among the reasons the middle class are associated with an improvement in economic growth and social policy is that they have been perceived to be agents of better institutional quality and democratization. Ferreira et al. (2012) suggest that growing middle classes have exerted, in many cases, pressure for policy reforms. In countries where a large middle class exists, there is a greater opportunity for better education and health policies to be legislated, and the quality of governance, including democratic participation and transparency, improves significantly, compared with countries where there is a small middle class and very little impetus for reform. Easterly, Ritzen, and Woolcock (2006) also show that the degree of "social cohesion" (defined as the nature and extent of social and economic divisions within a society) is important in strengthening the citizens' goodwill and trust in the government in order to advance important policy reforms.

Historically and conventionally, the rise of the middle classes elsewhere (e.g., from the rise of parliamentary power in England and since the American and French Revolutions) has been portrayed as being associated with demands for liberal political and economic values in the form of human rights, civil liberties, market competition and accountable government. It has not been too different in the Philippines' early history: the intellectual foundations for the 1896 Revolution that established the first republic in Asia were laid by an educated and economically rising middle class consisting of natives and Chinese mestizos.[32] In more recent times, the same trend of active political participation advocating democracy is noted by Bautista (2001) in her assessment of the different "People Power" mass movements that led to large regime changes. While the exact numbers are difficult to pin down, the 1986 EDSA revolution or "People Power 1" revolt that brought down the Marcos dictatorship is generally regarded as a middle class-initiated event, although its ultimate composition was broader. More distinctly,

---

[32] On the ideas and social background of the middle-class group known as the *ilustrados,* the classic reference is still Schumacher (1973).

however, the "People Power 2" that ousted Joseph Estrada and installed Gloria Macapagal-Arroyo as president in 2001 was documented to be predominantly middle class in character, going roughly by the level of education of the participants, with some 56 per cent having some college education, a figure that becomes higher if one goes beyond material standing and considers shared "work orientation and values" (Bautista 2006, 173). While the political character of this latter event is ambiguous—that is, it deposed a legitimately elected albeit scandalously corrupt government through a constitutionally infirm process— it nonetheless aligns with the conventionally understood political values that motivate the middle classes.

What tends to be overlooked is that such trends are far from universal or uniform. And often forgotten is that other historical examples exist that suggest the contrary, i.e., middle-class acquiescence in authoritarian movements and illiberal tendencies. It is generally accepted, for example, that the fascist parties in Italy and Germany found much of their support from the middle classes that yearned for order following the economic insecurity and chaos of the Weimar Republic. A glaring recent counterexample has been China, whose middle class now ranks among the largest in the world and constitutes a quarter of its population, but where no signs of democratic movement are apparent and where support for authoritarian rule has persisted. This "anomaly" has been explained as due to the dependence of the middle class on the state and party apparatus both in "institutional" (i.e., membership in the Communist Party and employment in the state sector) and in "ideational" terms (i.e., adherence to the political ideas propagated by the party and state) (Chen 2013). In Southeast Asia, the role of Thailand's urban middle classes in supporting a military coup in 2006 to replace the elected Thaksin government is also on record, although its ultimate historical significance may be unclear.[33] The spread of illiberal trends and undemocratic government elsewhere in the past decade is by now well accepted: the "democracy index" compiled by the Economist Intelligence Unit, for example, indicates that

---

[33] In many respects, this event resembles the middle-class People Power 2 (2001) revolt in the Philippines, which led to the overthrow (i.e., via construed "resignation") of the popularly elected Joseph Estrada. The two events differ, however, in that the regime change in Thailand led to a military government, while the Philippines adhered to the constitutional succession, leading to the accession of then Vice President Gloria Arroyo.

between 2015 and 2020, the proportion of the world's population living under "full" democracies decreased from 11 to 8 per cent; those under "flawed democracies" rose from 37 to 41 per cent. Some 50 per cent continued to live under authoritarian or hybrid political systems, even as the number of countries living under explicitly authoritarian systems rose from 52 to 57.[34]

Fully sorting out the causes of these global trends and their recent emergence lies beyond the scope of this paper, and there appears to be no shortage of proposed explanations. While one might assume the supply of would-be authoritarian rulers at any time to be fairly elastic, what requires explanation is their relative success in recent years. The recent trend of populism—in what are significantly middle-class societies—gravitating around conservative authoritarian leaders has been variously explained as a response of economic losers to globalization and failed "neoliberalism" (Bello 2020), or as a reaction to perceived threats to cultural values, especially in relation to immigration (Galston 2018; Gennaoili and Tabellini 2019), as well as being a phenomenon peculiar to the amplifying effects of social media (Zhuravskaya, Petrova, and Enikopolov 2020). At any rate, no comprehensive explanation appears to be in sight now, and the great differences among trends in Europe, Latin America and Asia are evident. Even a review in a more defined region concludes that "the roots and dynamics of the authoritarian project differ markedly in the three cases" (i.e., the Philippines, Thailand and Cambodia) (Bello 2021, 129).

Our more modest focus in this section is to describe how middle-class opinion in the Philippines has drifted towards own-concerns (i.e., middle-class concerns) and how the neglect of this shift has exerted a major influence on social consensus and policy, leading ironically to middle-class support for an administration with an authoritarian and illiberal agenda. The concrete expression of this trend, which has surprised many political observers, has been the broad middle-class support for President Rodrigo Duterte, both in terms of his 2016 electoral victory—at first only through a plurality—and the subsequent overwhelming majority approval he has managed to maintain throughout his term. Middle-class support for the Duterte administration—with its expressed disdain for human rights, a tolerance of opposition and an expansion of pluralist democracy—

---

[34] See Economist Intelligence Unit (2011) and compare with Economist Intelligence Unit (2020).

thus appears to fly in the face of the customary depiction of the Filipino middle class and the values they represent.

It would be a mistake, however, to regard the Duterte phenomenon as an aberration or a flash in the pan, made possible only by its leader's idiosyncratic charisma or by the insidious influence of social media campaigns. Economic growth over the past decades based on new economic sectors, combined with a gradual decline in absolute poverty, has created a middle-class stratum that has increasingly become more attuned to its own needs and that now looks beyond the issues of poverty that dominated public discussion in the past. The hypothesis we advance is that the failure of past administrations to recognize these trends provided the opportunity for an authoritarian trend to assert itself.

These shifting trends are broadly observable in public opinion data. A regular question in national public opinion surveys asks respondents to name what they consider to be the "most urgent national concerns". In the following, we use data from the polling firm Pulse Asia Research, Inc., drawn from 75 nationally representative surveys conducted over the period 2000–2019.[35] Respondents are classified using the "ABCDE" social categories used by market and opinion researchers, following Ipsos MORI conventions.[36] The category "C" is regarded as middle class, while "E" represents the poorest stratum.[37]

The time series in Figure 16.6 shows the gradual decline in the proportion of respondents— both among the middle classes and the poorest—who cite "reducing poverty" as an urgent national concern (solid and dashed black lines). Nonetheless in all periods, the middle class have consistently assigned a lower priority to this issue. The decline seems especially marked after 2010, however, after which there was a clear widening of the gap in perceptions of this issue, as between the middle and the poorest classes. In the early 2000s, the levels of concern

---

[35] Results for 2020 were excluded owing to the unusual character of the period.
[36] Rather than income, the Ipsos MORI socio-economic classification uses visible proxies of assets such as conditions of the community where the household is located, building materials used for the house, household furnishings, and ownership of house and residential lot.
[37] There can be some arguments regarding the weighting of each socio-economic category. Based on previous data cited in this article, we now believe the typical proportions used by polling firms to weight the middle class to be understated. To the extent the discussion here pertains to within-class trends through time, however, the relative importance of each class does not directly affect the conclusions as long as the sample remains representative of each class.

expressed for this problem across classes were bunched more closely around a national average response of some 35 per cent, with a smaller proportion of middle-class respondents rating the issue lower than in the poorest class. After the global financial crisis of 2008–9, however, perceptions diverged markedly, as between the poorest class ("E") and the middle class ("C"); the issue, as a whole, steadily lost ground. It cannot be a coincidence that measured poverty incidence was also on a decline since 2010. While some 30–40 per cent among the poorest still regarded the problem as urgent in the post-2008 crisis period, the proportion of the middle class sharing the same opinion declined continuously and more steeply, so that less than one-fourth of that stratum still regarded the problem as important by 2019 (solid black line in Figure 16.6).

Figure 16.6. Reducing poverty and fighting criminality as urgent national concerns* (responses by socio-economic class**, percentage of survey respondents citing, 2000–2019)

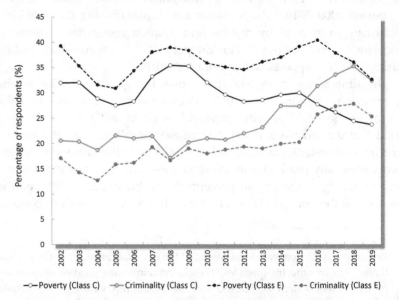

Note: * The lines represent three-year annual averages of percentage responses by socio-economic classes "C" and "E" over 75 representative national surveys conducted from 2000 to 2019. The black lines represent the proportion of respondents who cite "reducing poverty" as an urgent national concern, while the grey lines represent the proportion of respondents who cite "fighting crime" as an urgent national concern. The dashed lines represent class E respondents, while the solid lines represent class C respondents.
** Socio-economic classes are as defined by survey organizations following Ipsos MORI conventions.

Source: Pulse Asia (various years).

This trend is consistent with the observation in other studies (e.g., World Bank 2020, 103) that find weaker support among the Philippine middle class for redistribution policies and taxation of the wealthy.[38]

The opposite trend is evident for another major national concern, that of "fighting criminality". This is an issue of greater importance ex ante for the middle class, whose members are more likely to be concerned with personal safety and property protection than the poorer segments of society. Indeed, this is also borne out by Figure 16.6 (solid and dashed grey lines), which shows a consistently higher assessment of the issue during the entire period among the middle-class respondents than among the poorest. More significant, however, is the continuing rise in this issue's importance from 2010, peaking in importance around 2016–17, when a "crossover" or reversal occurred among middle-class respondents, who now had come to regard fighting crime as more urgent than reducing poverty. In contrast, no such reversal occurred for the poorest class, which continued to place a higher priority on poverty reduction.

On a national scale, the concern for poverty reduction appears to have peaked around 2008–9, coinciding with the global recession; it ranked third among the "most urgent national concerns".[39] Mirroring middle-class perceptions, it has since gradually declined in importance. On the other hand, the concern for criminality has trended upwards over two decades. There was an off-trend peak around the time of the 2016 elections, when Duterte made criminality his principal campaign issue, but the upward trend was already established prior to Duterte's electoral campaign. By 2019 the proportion of the sample population citing poverty reduction as an urgent concern had fallen to some one-third, virtually the same level as those citing criminality as urgent. In contrast to middle-class perceptions, however, fighting criminality never "crossed" poverty eradication at the national level (dashed black and grey lines in Figure 16.6).

---

[38] These trends indicated in the World Bank report are taken from the World Values Survey. A more curious characteristic is the weak support among the middle class for unemployment benefits (World Bank 2020, 103). This is more likely to be connected with opposition to additional payroll taxes, which is what unemployment insurance would entail.

[39] Perennial top urgent concerns have been "controlling inflation" and "raising the pay of workers".

An open question that remains is, to what extent the heightened concern for criminality from 2016 was due to worsening facts on the ground or the emphasis on it by the Duterte campaign. Some econometric work suggests that the change in agenda was at least partly influenced by the Duterte campaign's highlighting of the issue (Jetter and Molina 2020). At a minimum, however, the Duterte campaign was perceptive enough to tap into and amplify rising middle-class issues such as crime, graft and bureaucratic inefficiency, and go on to win the elections with a significant plurality in a divided field. This ability of the Duterte campaign to ride on rising middle-class issues has already been noted by political observers, although its long-term ramifications have not been drawn out. Bello (2021, 126) notes, for example, that "while (Duterte) draws approval from all classes, his support is most aggressively displayed among the aspiring and downwardly mobile classes" who exhibit "active" consensus behind Duterte's authoritarianism, as compared with the lower classes who display only "passive" consensus. Similarly, Teehankee (2017, 52) concludes: "The Duterte phenomenon was not a revolt of the poor but was a protest of the new middle class who suffered from lack of public service, endured the horrendous land and air traffic, feared the breakdown of peace and order, and silently witnessed their tax money siphoned by corruption despite promises of improved governance." Finally, of course, it was also class-consistent and no accident that the Duterte administration's "war on drugs"—a main pillar of its solution to criminality—ended up as a killing spree of thousands of people, mostly from urban poor communities, accused without due process of being drug users or drug dealers.[40] By contrast, drug-war victims who are middle class or affluent have been far fewer, which may partly explain

---

[40] The Philippine Drug Enforcement Agency reports that 6,011 persons died during drug operations from 1 July 2016 to 31 December 2020 (see Marquez 2021). This is likely an understatement since it refers to official anti-drug operations only. A large number of victims of the drug war were killed by unidentified vigilantes, who are suspected to have been police operatives themselves or killers contracted by the latter. Including such cases would significantly raise the number of deaths. Exact numbers are difficult to come by, but a careful study of news reports of drug-related killings between May 2016 and September 2017 found almost half (45%) were vigilante or "non-police" operations (see David et al., n.d.).

middle-class acquiescence in, if not support for, what has by all accounts been a brutal campaign.[41]

This digression into politics thus carries a similar message as the discussion of social programmes: working with accustomed political models, the political class failed to perceive the shifting class composition and the changing priorities of a large plurality of society. That failure to recognize and squarely address emerging middle-class concerns ultimately led to an electoral surprise that appeared to upend previously held notions of where middle-class values lay and provided an opening for an administration with an authoritarian agenda.

7 A MORE DIFFERENTIATED APPROACH

Thus, more and more, a government strategy to improve welfare and needs to address the concerns of its citizens should not only be focusing on reducing the numbers of those who are poor and extremely poor, but also protecting the middle class and vulnerable against downward shifts in welfare. Public policy should take into cognition that there are more distinct socio-economic categories than just poor and non-poor, and should consider the importance of ensuring that the larger majority of households move upwards on the welfare ladder. We argue that the needs and aspirations of Filipinos have become far more differentiated owing to the increasing complexity of socio-economic groups in the country.

At one level, it is possible that interests of different welfare groups may coincide. More particularly, the expansion of opportunities for upward mobility may not be inimical to poverty reduction and even extends this by protecting the vulnerable. Consider some of the policies, as noted in the experience of other countries (Birdsall 2010):

- Macroeconomic policies that protect against high levels of inflation and interest rates and overvalued exchange rates are very important to protect the purchasing power of both the middle class and the poor; public taxation reform could also provide benefit for both by protecting these classes against increases in indirect taxes for basic commodities that could

---

[41] Duterte earlier on excused better-off drug users as being less of a problem, among others, since they use cocaine and heroin, which are "less harmful" than the methamphetamine used by the poor (see Ho 2016).

have a macroeconomy-wide impact, but, at the same time, reducing income taxes and providing for social protection for the poor.
- Programmes that protect the poor against external economic or natural resource shocks tend to also reduce the number of those who are vulnerable and support those who are less economically secure; this implies a greater scope for government intervention in reducing the vulnerability of the population to rapid-onset climate-related events, such as typhoon and flooding, which occur with much regularity in the country.
- Cash transfer programmes that narrowly focus on a relatively small number of households (such as the *Pantawid Kuryente* programme for urban residents in the late 2000s) may find less support from the middle class than a better targeted programme such as the *Pantawid Pamilyang Pilipino Program*, which has reduced significantly the number of poor households in the country.

As argued earlier, however, applying a uniform approach or solution across all categories through universalist solutions fails to address the needs of an increasingly diverse society that faces different concerns and issues. A more effective approach would address the diverse issues faced by heterogeneous social groups and design nuanced interventions that ensure that the needs of the different groups are addressed. A useful framework in this regard is that outlined by the Human Development Network in responding to the long-term needs of the different socio-economic groups, but, at the same time, addressing the problems that crop up during an economic downturn, similar to the current pandemic (HDN 2021) (see Table 16.5).

Table 16.5 shows that the upper middle class and top stratum are better placed to take advantage of financial or real investment opportunities that can earn them decent returns on their savings; because of the high incomes that they earn from employment or even from returns on financial assets they own, they have practically no need for free or subsidized programmes and can typically purchase the higher-cost, higher-quality public goods. As for the middle classes, since many of the economically secure have access to regular incomes, credit and loans would be useful for them to gain access to the more expensive, quality goods and services that allow them to achieve greater economic, social and political opportunities, which they can pay for over time.

Table 16.5. Differing socio-economic groups and critical government programmes

Socio-economic status	Direct provision	Subsidies	Group insurance/ preneed	Credit/ loans	Investment opportunities
Extremely poor	Very important	Important	Less important		
Poor	Important	Very important	Less important		
Vulnerable		Less important	Very important	Important	Less important
Economically secure			Important	Very important	Important
Upper middle class			Important	Important	Very important
Top stratum				Important	Very important

Source: HDN (2021, 76).

On the other hand, direct provision of basic services, especially basic education and primary health, are most important for the extremely poor, who generate little by way of incomes and savings and, therefore, cannot finance these important aspects of human development. Indeed, providing such services to the most marginalized (e.g., indigenous peoples living in remote areas) must often be in kind and entail physically locating such facilities where they can be accessed. Cash subsidies would prove ineffective in such cases. Cash subsidies or means-tested discounts would be more useful for sections of the poor (e.g., urban poor) who participate in the cash economy and have at least physical access to establishments providing such services. Here, the caveat bears repeating: the provisions need to be targeted but comprehensive if the poor are to make full use of such subsidies. And finally, the vulnerable, who are perennially affected by health, economic and environmental risks and are susceptible to declines in welfare, may find schemes of group insurance or pre-need programmes very useful in order to reduce the threats they face.

Part of this task entails the minimization of leakages and under coverage mentioned earlier, by designing the proper types of programme mix of direct provision, subsidy and insurance for groups that are respectively most likely to benefit from these by better targeting.

This can be done through improved geographical and indicator targeting or even by designing programmes that allow the beneficiaries to gain better access to them. For instance, subsequent improvements in the implementation of the school feeding programme—by focusing the benefits not on all school children but only the undernourished— have improved its targeting efficiency (Tabunda, Albert, and Angeles-Agdeppa 2016).

This can be supplemented by tax policies that try to redistribute resources from different socio-economic groups. The child tax credit being implemented in many developed countries could provide a starting point for thinking about support for lower-income groups, which have a high dependency ratio, as well as in ensuring welfare improvement across generations. While recent tax reforms have resulted in lower taxes for the upper middle-class households and, to some extent, the economically secure, studies have shown that this may have negatively affected the lower-income households due to the higher level of commodity taxes imposed by the same reforms. Windfall taxes on real property that have increased in value due to the government's infrastructure programme and a gradual increase in inheritance and other taxes on wealth might redress the earlier situation.

Given the increasing fiscal resources that the government has achieved these past years, notwithstanding the pandemic, a differentiated programme of interventions that allow for greater access by the middle class to "care systems", especially for children, the physically and socially vulnerable and the elderly, would be important. These aspects of social protection have been given insufficient attention, even as the gains made by the middle class are strengthened through their access to greater financial gains and opportunities for occupational mobility provided by banking and infrastructure reforms.

8 CONCLUSION

The improvement of socio-economic outcomes, which has been driven by wage and employment growth especially in the past decade, and the significant strides in access to education and health services, as well as the creation of targeted social protection programmes, have pushed a significant number of households out of poverty and have broadened the middle class in the country. Although the gains in welfare most likely have suffered a setback due to the recent pandemic, the growth of the middle-income groups is expected to continue in the near future as the effects of the downturn recede.

The increasing differentiation of the socio-economic structure of the country has made more distinct the differing needs and interests of the various income groups. The issues advocated by the middle class have become more and more distinct from the concerns of the poor and the vulnerable. Unfortunately, public policy has not caught up with this changed environment. The challenge for policymakers, therefore, is to target interventions not only to equalize opportunities but to better achieve outcomes that are relevant to the concerns and needs of these different groups. As recent developments have shown, ignoring these large socio-economic changes risks not only distorting welfare outcomes but may also put in peril the country's political future.

ACKNOWLEDGEMENTS

This paper owes a great deal to research the authors undertook in preparing the *Philippine Human Development Report 2020/2021* (HDN 2021). We are grateful to the Human Development Network for providing the research opportunity, and thank Paolo Adriano and Rene Marlon Panti for valuable research assistance. This piece is dedicated to Arsenio M. Balisacan, who served as president of the Human Development Network. All views expressed and any remaining errors are solely of the authors.

REFERENCES

Albert, J. R., R. Gaspar, and M. J. Raymundo. 2015. "Why Should We Pay Attention to the Middle Class". *PIDS Policy Notes*, no. 2015–13. Manila: Philippine Institute for Development Studies. https://serp-p.pids.gov.ph/publication_detail?id=5574.

Albert, J. R., A. G. Santos, and J. F. Vizmanos. 2018. "Defining and Profiling the Middle Class". *PIDS Policy Notes*, no. 2018–18. Manila: Philippine Institute for Development Studies. https://serp-p.pids.gov.ph/publication_detail?id=6725.

Alesina, A. 1994. "Political Models of Macroeconomic Policy and Fiscal Reforms". In *Voting for Reform: Democracy, Political Liberalization, and Economic Adjustment*, edited by Stephan Haggard and Steven Webb. New York, NY: Oxford University Press.

Balisacan, A. M. 1997. "In Search of Proxy Indicators for Poverty Targeting toward a Framework for a Poverty Indicator and Monitoring System". Report prepared for a UNDP-assisted Project: Strengthening Institutional Mechanisms for the Convergence of Poverty Alleviation Efforts. Pasig City: National Economic and Development Authority.
―――. 2001. "Poverty in the Philippines: An Update and Re-examination". *Philippine Review of Economics* 38, no. 1: 15–52.
―――. 2009. "Poverty Reduction: Trends, Determinants and Policies". In *Diagnosing the Philippine Economy: Toward Inclusive Growth*, edited by D. Canlas, M. Khan, and J. Zhuang. London, UK: Anthem Press.
Balisacan, A. M., R. Alonzo, T. Monsod, G. Ducanes, and P. J. Esguerra. 1998. "Conceptual Framework for the Development of an Integrated Poverty Monitoring and Indicator System". Report prepared for the UNDP-assisted Project: Strengthening Institutional Mechanisms for the Convergence of Poverty Alleviation Efforts. Pasig City: National Economic and Development Authority.
Balisacan, A. M., and R. Edillon. 2003. "Poverty Targeting in the Philippines". In *Poverty Targeting in Asia*, edited by J. Weiss. Cheltenham, UK: Edward Elgar.
Balisacan, A. M., and N. Fuwa. 2007. "Poverty and Vulnerability". In *Reasserting the Rural Development Agenda: Lessons Learned and Emerging Challenges in Asia*, edited by A. M. Balisacan and N. Fuwa. Singapore: ISEAS Publishing.
Banerjee, A., and E. Duflo. 2008. "What is Middle Class about the Middle Classes around the World?". *Journal of Economic Perspectives* 22, no. 2: 3–28.
Bautista, C. 2001. "Middle Class Politics and Views on Society and Government". In *Exploration of the Middle Classes in Southeast Asia*, edited by M.H. Hsiao, pp. 208–65. Taipei: Center for Asia-Pacific Area Studies.
―――. 2006. "Beyond the EDSA Revolts: The Middle Classes in Contemporary Philippine Development and Policies". In *The Changing Faces of the Middle Classes in Asia-Pacific*, edited by M. H. Hsiao, 167–86. Taipei: Center for Asia-Pacific Area Studies.
Bello, W. 2021. "Neoliberalism, Contentious Politics, and the Rise of Authoritarianism in Southeast Asia". In *The Global Rise of Authoritarianism in the 21st Century*, edited by B. Berberoglu, pp. 115–32. New York and London: Routledge.
Birdsall, N. 2010. "The (Indispensable) Middle Class in Developing Countries; or the Rich and the Rest, Not the Poor and the Rest". In *Equity and Growth in a Globalizing World*, edited by M. Spence and R. Kanbur. Washington, DC: World Bank.
Chen, J. 2013. *A Middle Class Without Democracy: Economic Growth and the Prospects for Democratization in China*. Oxford: Oxford University Press.
Clarete, R., E. Esguerra, and H. Hill, eds. 2018. *The Philippine Economy: No Longer the East Asian Exception?* Singapore: ISEAS-Yusof Ishak Institute.

David, C. C., R. U. Mendoza, J. M. L. Atun, R. Cossid, and C. l Soriano. n.d. "Building a Dataset of Publicly Available Information on Killings Associated with the Antidrug Campaign". *The Drug Archive.* https://drugarchive.ph/post/14-antidrug-dataset-public-info-killings.

Desai, R. 2017. "Rethinking the Universalism Versus Targeting Debate". In: *Brookings.* https://www.brookings.edu/blog/future-development/2017/05/31/rethinking-the-universalism-versus-targeting-debate (accessed 31 May 2021).

De Dios, E., and K. Dinglasan. 2015. "Just How Good is Unemployment as a Measure of Welfare? A Note". *Philippine Review of Economics* 52, no. 2: 243–54.

DBM (Department of Budget and Management). 2021. "Status of COVID-19 Releases". Updated 27 July 2021. https://www.dbm.gov.ph/index.php/programs-projects/status-of-covid-19-releases#bayanihan-2.

Easterly, W. 2001. "The Middle-Class Consensus and Economic Development". *Journal of Economic Growth* 6, no. 4: 317–35.

Easterly, W., J. Ritzen, and M. Woolcock. 2006. "Social Cohesion, Institutions, and Growth". *CDC Working Paper 94.* Washington, DC: Center for Global Development.

Economist Intelligence Unit. 2020. "Democracy Index 2020: In Sickness and in Health?". *The Economist.* https://www.eiu.com/n/campaigns/democracy-index-2020/.

———. 2011. "Democracy Index 2011: Democracy Under Stress". *The Economist.* https://thecubaneconomy.com/wp-content/uploads/2012/01/Democracy_Index_Final_Dec_2011.pdf.

Epetia, M. C. 2018. "Overeducation among College Graduates in the Philippine Labor Market." PhD dissertation, University of the Philippines.

Evashwick, C. 1989. "Creating the Continuum of Care". *Health Matrix* 7, no. 1: 30–39.

Ferreira, F., H. J. Messina, J. Rigolini, L. F. López-Calva, M. Lugo, R. Vakis, and L. F. Ló. 2012. *Economic Mobility and the Rise of the Latin American Middle Class.* Washington, DC: World Bank.

Galston, W. A. 2018. "The Populist Challenge to Liberal Democracy". *Journal of Democracy* 29, no. 2: 5–19.

Gennaioili, N., and G. Tabellini. 2019. "Identity, Beliefs, and Political Conflict". *CESifo Working Paper No. 7707.* http://dx.doi.org/10.2139/ssrn.3300726.

Ho, A. 2016. "Duterte Explains: Why the Rich Are Beyond Reach of Drug War". *CNN Philippines,* 24 August 2016, updated 25 August 2016. https://cnnphilippines.com/news/2016/08/24/Duterte-why-rich-beyond-reach-drug-war.html.

HDN (Human Development Network). 2021. 2020/21 *Philippine Human Development Report: Socioeconomic Mobility and Human Development.* Quezon City: HDN.

IMF (International Monetary Fund). 2021. "World Economic Outlook: Managing Divergent Recoveries". Washington, DC: International Monetary Fund. April. https://www.imf.org/en/Publications/WEO/Issues/2021/03/23/world-economic-outlook-april-2021 (accessed 16 June 2021).

Jetter, M., and T. Molina. 2020. "Persuasive Agenda-Setting: Rodrigo Duterte's Inauguration Speech and Drugs in the Philippines". IZA *(Institute of Labour Economics) Discussion Paper, no. 13027* (March). http://ftp.iza.org/dp13027.pdf.

Kidd, S. 2016. "Social Protection: Universal Provision is More Effective than Poverty Targeting". In *iD4D*. https://ideas4development.org/en/social-protection-universal-provision-is-more-effective-than-poverty-targeting/ (accessed 30 May 2021).

Luz, M. 2020. "Too Many Children Not Enrolled This School Year Is a Major Concern". *Rappler*, 19 November 2020. https://www.rappler.com/voices/ispeak/analysis-too-many-children-not-enrolled-this-school-year-major-concern.

Macaraeg, P. 2020. "Sariling Diskarte: The Heavy Impact of Lockdown on Micro, Small Businesses". *Rappler*, 7 April 2020. https://www.rappler.com/newsbreak/in-depth/heavy-impact-coronavirus-lockdown-micro-small-medium-enterprises.

Marquez, Consuelo. 2021. "Drug War Death Toll Reaches 6,011 as of December 2020—PDEA". *Inquirer.net*, 30 January 2021. https://newsinfo.inquirer.net/1390134/drug-war-death-toll-reaches-6011-as-of-december-2020-pdea.

Muyrong, M. 2020. "#StayAtHome #Bayanihan: Understanding the Profile of Displaced Workers Due to ECQ". *Policy Brief, no. 2020–03*. Quezon City: Economics Department, Ateneo de Manila University.

NEDA (National Economic and Development Authority). 2020. *Addressing the Social and Economic Impact of the Pandemic*. Pasig: NEDA: https://www.neda.gov.ph/wp-content/uploads/2020/03/NEDA_Addressing-the-Social-and-Economic-Impact-of-the-COVID-19-Pandemic.pdf.

———. 2021. *Updated Philippine Development Plan 2017–2022* (prepublication copy). Pasig: NEDA. http://pdp.neda.gov.ph/wp-content/uploads/2021/02/20210218-Pre-publication-copy-Updated-Philippine-Development-Plan-2017-2022.pdf.

Nishimori, A. N. 2021. "IT-BPM Sector Posts 2020 Growth Despite Pandemic Pinch". *ABS-CBN News*, 24 April 2021. https://news.abs-cbn.com/business/04/24/21/it-bpm-sector-posts-2020-growth-despite-pandemic-pinch.

Okun, A. 1975. *Equality and Efficiency: The Big Trade-off*. Washington, DC: Brookings Institution.

Panelo, C., O. Solon, R. Ramos, and A. Herrin. 2017. *The Challenge of Reaching the Poor with a Continuum of Care: A 25-Year Assessment of Philippine Health Sector Performance*. Quezon City. http://www.upecon.org.ph/wp-content/uploads/2018/03/HSR_061818.pdf.

Paloyo, A., C. Magno, K. Jandoc, L. Escresa, M.C. Epetia, M.S. Gochoco-Bautista, and E. de Dios. 2020. "A Philippine Social Protection and Economic Recovery Plan". *UPSE Discussion Paper 2020–02* (March). Quezon City: School of Economics, University of the Philippines. https://econ.upd.edu.ph/dp/index.php/dp/article/view/1525/1007.

Perlman, M. 2012. "Targeted vs. Universal Programs". *Atlas of Public Management*. https://www.atlas101.ca/pm/concepts/targeted-vs-universal-programs/.

PSA (Philippine Statistics Authority). various years. Family Income and Expenditure Survey. Quezon City: Philippine Statistics Authority.

———. various years. Labor Force Survey (quarterly). Quezon City: Philippine Statistics Authority.

Pulse Asia. various years. *Ulat ng Bayan National Surveys*. Quezon City: Pulse Asia.

Quimbo, S., J. Florentino, J. Peabody, R. Shimkada, C. Panelo, and O. Solon. 2008. "Underutilization of Social Insurance among the Poor: Evidence from the Philippines". *PLoS One* 3, no. 10: e3379–ff.

Ragasa, F. Y. 2021. "Angara Files Bill Seeking Free Annual Medical Check-ups for Filipinos". *Inquirer.net*, 2 July 2021. https://newsinfo.inquirer.net/1454494/angara-files-bill-seeking-free-annual-medical-check-ups-for-filipinos.

Rappler. 2013. "A First: Investment Grade Rating for PH". *Rappler.com*, 27 March 2013. https://www.rappler.com/business/economy/a-first-investment-grade-rating-for-ph.

Schumacher, J. 1973. *The Propaganda Movement: 1880–1895*. Manila: Solidaridad.

Social Weather Stations. 2020. "Fourth Quarter 2020 Social Weather Survey: Hunger Eases to 16.0% of Families in November". *Social Weather Stations*, 16 December 2020. https://www.sws.org.ph/swsmain/artcldisppage/?artcsyscode=ART-20201216145500.

Solon, O. 2019. "Who Pays and Who Benefits from Philhealth Premium Subsidies from Tobacco Taxes?" Working Paper, School of Economics, University of the Philippines.

Savchuk, K. 2012. "Why Universalism Trumps Targeting in Social Policy". In *Polis*. https://www.thepolisblog.org/2012/05/why-universalism-trumps-targeting-in.html.

Shinozaki, S. 2020. "COVID-19 Impact on Micro, Small, and Medium-Sized Enterprises and Post–Crisis Actions: Six-Month After the Outbreak in the Philippines". Presentation at the Asian Impact Webinar: Asia's SMEs Beyond the COVID-19 Crisis, 28 October 2020. https://www.adb.org/sites/default/files/event/648436/files/covid-19-impact-msme-post-crisis-actions-philippines.pdf.

Tabunda, A., J. R. Albert, and I. Angeles-Agdeppa. 2016. "Results of an Impact Evaluation Study on DepEd's School-Based Feeding Program". *PIDS Discussion Paper Series, no. 2016–05*. Quezon City: Philippine Institute for Development Studies. https://dirp3.pids.gov.ph/websitecms/CDN/PUBLICATIONS/pidsdps1605.pdf.

Teehankee, J. 2017. "Was Duterte's Rise Inevitable?". In *A Duterte Reader: Critical Essays on Rodrigo Duterte's Early Presidency*, edited by N. Curato, pp. 37–56. Quezon City: Bughaw (Ateneo de Manila University Press).

Torregoza, H.. 2020. "'Simplify Socio-economic Classes', Senators Urge NEDA". *Manila Bulletin*, 17 September 2020. https://mb.com.ph/2020/09/17/simplify-socio-economic-classes-senators-urge-neda/.

Venzon, Cliff. 2020. "Duterte's Cash Aid for Poor Filipinos Draws Middle Class Pushback". *Nikkei Asia*, 17 April 2020. https://asia.nikkei.com/Economy/Duterte-s-cash-aid-for-poor-Filipinos-draws-middle-class-pushback.

Virola, R. A., J. O. Encarnacion, B. B. Balamban, M. B. Addawe, and M. M. Viernes. 2013. "Will the Recent Robust Economic Growth Create a Burgeoning Middle Class in the Philippines?". Paper presented during the 12th National Convention on Statistics (NCS), Mandaluyong City. Metro Manila, Philippines.

World Bank. 2018a. "Philippine Economic Update: Investing in the Future". In *Macroeconomics, Trade and Investment Global Practice, East Asia and Pacific Region*. Washington, DC: World Bank.

———. 2018b. *Riding the Wave: An East Asian Miracle for the 21st Century*. Washington, DC: World Bank. https://www.doi.org/10.1596/978-1-4648-1145-6.

———. 2018c. *Philippines: Social Protection Review and Assessment. East Asia and Pacific Region*. Washington, DC: World Bank.

———. 2020. *Braving the New Normal: Philippine Economic Update*. Manila: World Bank.

Yemtsov, R. 2016. "Social Protection: Universal & Poverty Targeting Approaches Are Not in Contradiction". In *ID4D*. https://ideas4development.org/en/social-protection-universal-poverty-targeting-approaches-are-not-in-contradiction. (accessed 30 May 2021).

Zhuravskaya, E., M. Petrova, and R. Enikopolov. 2020. "Political Effects of the Internet and Social Media". *Annual Review of Economics* 12: 415–38.

17 Redistributive Preferences and Prospects for Intergenerational Mobility in Southeast Asia

Joseph J. Capuno

1 INTRODUCTION

Does the expectation of upward mobility influence an individual's preference for government redistribution? We investigate the relevance of the *prospects of upward mobility* (POUM) hypothesis in the context of eight Southeast Asian countries to explain individual attitudes towards redistribution. As originally expounded in Benabou and Ok (2001), the POUM hypothesis suggests that when people expect redistributive policies not to change for some time, those with income below the mean but who anticipate better fortunes may not support such policies. The reason is that the upwardly mobile people, though currently poor, foresee themselves subjected to progressive taxes that would be difficult to amend. Such attitudes towards government redistribution may be reinforced by insights from older family members whose own efforts proved more important than exogenous factors (such as government aid) in their social advancements (Picketty 1995). Contrary to the median voter theorem that relates redistributive preferences to current income status (Meltzer and Richard 1983), the POUM hypothesis relates them instead to future income status, thereby explaining why a redistributive policy may not be supported by some of its intended beneficiaries (Alesina and La Ferrara 2005).

The POUM hypothesis builds on the assumptions that policies are stable and individuals, including the poor, are not too risk averse.[1] Most studies on this hypothesis are about developed countries where policies and institutions are fairly durable. Using US survey data to construct both objective and subjective measures of mobility, Alesina and La Ferrara (2005) find some corroborating evidence. Similarly, Alesina and Giuliano (2011) report a negative relationship between preference for redistribution and several social mobility indicators in the United States. Alesina, Stantcheva, and Teso (2017) show broadly similar findings based on both survey and experimental data from France, Italy, Sweden, United Kingdom and the United States. Whereas earlier studies use employment or occupational status to proxy risk attitudes, Cojocaru (2014) use a direct measure and find evidence consistent with the POUM hypothesis in countries belonging to the European Union (EU), but not in countries outside the EU. Investigating the possible mediating effect of political ideology on mobility expectations in Dutch households, Lemeris, Garretsen, and Jong-A-Pin (2018) find that only right-wing individuals conform to the POUM hypothesis, while left-wing individuals prefer redistribution regardless of their expectations of upward income mobility. Using data from the British Cohort Study, Gregg, Macmillan, and Vittori (2019) find a "J-shaped" association between parental childhood income and son's adult lifetime earnings, with greater effect when coming from an affluent family. Also using subjective measures of intergenerational mobility, Gugushvili (2016) finds greater support for income differences among the upwardly mobile individuals and less support among the downwardly mobile. That such attitudes may come from an acculturation process is suggested by findings based on several waves of European Values Surveys (Jaime-Castillo and Marques-Perales 2019).

Relatively fewer studies on redistributive preference focus on East Asian or Southeast Asian countries. Among them are Yamamura (2012, 2014), whose findings in Japan underscore the importance of trust in government and social capital in one's community. Based on the third wave of the Asian Barometer Survey, Chang (2018) reports that

---

[1] Arguably, a low-income, risk-averse individual will prefer a small but sure post-transfer income to a large but uncertain tax-free income, *ceteris paribus*.

traditional Asian norms—particularly, self-determination, self-reliance and filial duty—are negatively correlated with support for redistributive policies. It is noted that while he ascribes these results to Asian beliefs about the potency of hard work and frugality to achieving a better life, his preference indicator includes dimensions of democracy. Testing the median voter model in developing countries, including those in Asia, Haggard, Kaufman, and Long (2012) find income to be a relatively unimportant factor. Using survey data, Abad (1997) compares trends in the Philippines and other countries. Interestingly, Tohyama (2019) reports that Asians' attitudes towards redistribution may diminish as market opportunities widen. However, none of these studies examine the POUM hypothesis per se.

The present study helps fill this gap by exploring the hypothesis in the cases of Cambodia, Indonesia, Malaysia, Myanmar, the Philippines, Singapore, Thailand and Vietnam. These countries have adopted various policies and programmes to alleviate poverty and reduce income inequalities. Besides their welfare impacts, whether these initiatives also reflect the demands, needs or aspirations of the local population may interest policymakers, development scholars and other stakeholders. Using nationally representative survey data, overall, we find no strong support for the POUM hypothesis. Instead, we find that those who expect their children to overtake them in socio-economic status tend to favour government redistribution. This behaviour is especially notable among the poor, which we take to be consistent more with aspirational than real prospects for social advancement of one's children.

2 SETTING

The period 2013–17 (i.e., around the time of the surveys) witnessed important developments in the eight Southeast Asian countries (Table 17.1). As their populations rose, so did their nominal per capita gross domestic product (GDP). Economic growth in all countries was robust, though comparatively higher in Cambodia, Indonesia, Myanmar, the Philippines and Vietnam. The unemployment rate was consistently low in Vietnam and in the relatively well-off countries of Singapore, Malaysia and Thailand, but was high—upwards of 5.5 per cent—in Indonesia and the Philippines.

Table 17.1. Selected development indicators (2013–17)

Country / Indicator	2013	2014	2015	2016	2017
Cambodia					
Population (in million)	14.68	14.88	15.09	15.30	15.52
Per capita GDP (KHR '000, at current prices)	4,178.55	4,865.03	5,308.54	5,788.41	6,893.88
Annual GDP growth (%)	7.36	7.14	7.03	7.02	6.84
Gini Index	n.a.	n.a.	n.a.	n.a.	n.a.
Unemployment rate	0.16	0.29	0.18	0.10	0.10
Health, education & social protection (%)[a]	3.77	3.95	4.16	4.42	4.72
Indonesia					
Population (in million)	248.82	252.17	255.46	258.71	261.89
Per capita GDP (IDR '000, at current prices)	38,365.90	41,915.90	45,119.60	47,937.70	51,891.20
Annual GDP growth (%)	5.56	5.01	4.88	5.03	5.07
Gini Index	40.00	39.40	39.70	38.60	38.1
Unemployment rate (%)	6.17	5.94	6.18	5.61	5.50
Health, education & social protection (%)[a]	4.15	4.09	4.65	6.55	5.27
Malaysia					
Population (in million)	30.21	30.71	31.19	31.63	32.02
Per capita GDP (MYR, at current prices)	33,713.70	36,030.50	37,739.3	39,505.50	42,833.80
Annual GDP growth (%)	4.69	6.01	5.09	4.45	5.74
Gini Index	41.30	n.a.	41.1	n.a.	n.a.
Unemployment rate	3.10	2.90	3.10	3.40	3.40
Health, education & social protection (%)[a]	7.25	7.12	6.81	6.30	6.27

Table 17.1 (continued)

Table 17.1 (continued)

Country / Indicator	2013	2014	2015	2016	2017
Myanmar					
Population (in million)	51.45	51.99	52.45	52.92	53.39
Per capita GDP (MMK '000, at current prices)	1,127.60	1,255.30	1,386.30	1,402.50	1,549.00
Annual GDP growth (%)	8.43	7.99	6.99	5.86	5.75
Gini Index	n.a.	n.a.	38.10	n.a.	30.70
Unemployment rate (%)	n.a.	4.01	0.78	n.a.	1.57
Health, education & social protection (%)[a]	3.08	3.51	3.98	3.96	3.85
Philippines					
Population (in million)	98.20	99.88	101.56	103.24	104.90
Per capita GDP (PHP '000, at current prices)	123.23	132.98	138.29	147.59	158.94
Annual GDP growth (%)	6.75	6.35	6.35	7.15	6.93
Gini Index	46.50[b]	n.a.	44.6	n.a.	42.30[c]
Unemployment rate (%)	7.10	6.60	6.30	5.40	5.70
Health, education & social protection (%)[a]	5.64	3.78	4.88	5.26	6.84
Singapore					
Population (in million)	5.40	5.47	5.54	5.61	5.61
Per capita GDP (US$, at current prices)	71,283.00	72,938.00	76,503.00	78,508.00	84,115.00
Annual GDP growth (%)	4.84	3.94	2.99	3.24	4.34
Gini Index	n.a.	n.a.	n.a.	n.a.	n.a.
Unemployment rate (%)	2.60	2.60	2.60	2.80	2.90
Health, education & social protection (%)[a]	5.90	6.30	6.82	6.55	5.92

Table 17.1 (continued)

Table 17.1 (continued)

Country / Indicator	2013	2014	2015	2016	2017
Thailand					
Population (in million)	67.16	67.57	67.98	68.24	68.89
Per capita GDP (THB '000, at current prices)	192.31	195.81	202.17	213.83	224.82
Annual GDP growth (%)	2.69	0.98	3.13	3.40	4.10
Gini Index	37.80	37.00	36.00	36.90	36.50
Unemployment rate (%)	0.72	0.84	0.88	0.99	1.18
Health, education & social protection (%)[a]	7.28	7.33	7.41	7.56	7.38
Vietnam					
Population (in million)	90.19	91.20	92.23	93.25	94.29
Per capita GDP (VND '000, at current prices)	39,740.60	43,176.50	45,461.60	48,286.30	53,093.60
Annual GDP growth (%)	5.42	5.98	6.68	6.21	7.08
Gini Index	n.a.	34.8	n.a.	35.30	35.70[b]
Unemployment rate (%)	1.71	1.86	2.11	3.02	2.01
Health, education & social protection (%)[a]	n.a.	n.a.	n.a.	n.a.	n.a.

Note: [a] Share of government expenditures on health, education and social protection in GDP.
[b] 2012
[c] 2018

Sources: Gini Indexes are from the World Bank (https://data.worldbank.org/indicators). All other indicators are from the Asian Development Bank (*Key Development Indicators for Asia and the Pacific 2020*, https://kidb.adb.org).

The pro-poor orientation of public policies in these countries may be inferred from their outlays for health and education services, and social protection programmes. The average annual GDP share of these outlays ranges from about 3.7 per cent in Myanmar and 4.2 per cent in Cambodia to 4.9 per cent in Indonesia and 5.28 per cent in the Philippines, 6.3 per cent in Singapore and 6.75 per cent in Malaysia, and 7.4 per cent in Thailand. Notable among the anti-poverty programmes recently implemented in these countries are those on social health insurance (Vietnam, Thailand, Indonesia and the Philippines) and conditional cash transfer (Indonesia and the Philippines).

Over the same period, income inequality (i.e., Gini index) also improved much in Indonesia and the Philippines, but only slightly in Thailand; it somewhat worsened in Malaysia and Vietnam. Based on the World Bank's poverty threshold of US$1.90/day, the proportion of poor people was around 6 per cent in Indonesia in 2017, 8 per cent in the Philippines in 2015, 6 per cent in Myanmar in 2015, and 2 per cent in Vietnam in 2016 (World Bank 2021). These varied accomplishments suggest that factors other than growth could be at play.

To be sure, the eight countries differ in governance institutions, including those that impel their governments to be responsive and accountable to their citizens. Based on the 2015 Democracy Index of the Economist Intelligence Unit (2016), Vietnam is an "autocracy"; Thailand, Cambodia and Myanmar are "hybrid regimes"; and the other four are "flawed democracies".[2] Ostensibly, these differences in the countries' governance quality and provisions for social services shape, if not reflect, their citizens' views towards redistribution and visions for social advancement.

3 DATA

3.1 Source and description

We use the data for the eight SEA countries included in the fourth wave of the Asian Barometer Survey (ABS) conducted along with

---

[2] For 2016, Polity V characterizes the political regimes in Singapore, Vietnam and Thailand as autocracies, Cambodia and Malaysia as weak democracies, and the three other SEA countries as institutionalized democracies (Marshall and Elzinga-Marshall 2017).

local institutions under the Asian Barometer Project (2013–2016).[3] Like previous ABS rounds, the fourth wave adopted the same basic sampling design and method (particularly, face-to-face interviews), and survey instrument in all countries. The country samples were randomly selected and nationally representative. The standard questionnaire has several modules, including economic evaluation, trust in institution, social capital and socio-economic background. The fourth wave added new modules on redistribution and social mobility. The surveys were conducted in Malaysia, the Philippines, Singapore and Thailand in 2014, and in Cambodia, Myanmar and Vietnam in 2015. The Indonesian survey was completed in 2016.

Cambodia, the Philippines, Thailand and Vietnam each have 1,200 samples. Myanmar has 1,620 samples, Indonesia 1,550, Malaysia 1,207 and Singapore 1,039. The share of urban samples is 100 per cent in Singapore, 57 per cent in Malaysia and the Philippines, and around 50 per cent in Indonesia. Cambodia, Thailand, Myanmar and Vietnam have largely rural samples (Figure 17.1).

Figure 17.1. Total samples (by country)

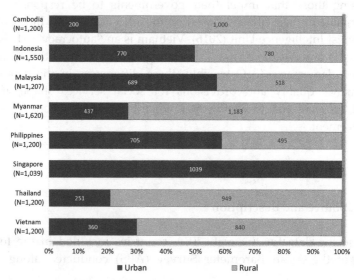

Source of raw data: Asian Barometer Survey (4th wave).

---

[3] The Asian Barometer Project (2013–2016) was co-directed by Professors Fu Hu and Yun-han Chu. It received support from Taiwan's Ministry of Education, Academia Sinica and National Taiwan University.

3.2 Government responsibility to reduce income differences

The survey respondents were each asked whether they strongly agree, agree, disagree or strongly disagree with the following statement: "It is the responsibility of the government to reduce the difference between people with high income and those with low income." Figure 17.2 shows the distribution of the responses, including those who declined to answer.

Over 80 per cent of the samples in Indonesia, Malaysia, Myanmar, Singapore and Vietnam said they strongly agree or agree with said statement, as well as around 75 per cent in Thailand and Cambodia and around 60 per cent in the Philippines. However, the proportion of those who said they strongly agree with the statement is less than 20 per cent in the Philippines and Indonesia; around 26 per cent in Cambodia, Singapore and Thailand; 39 per cent in Malaysia and 45 per cent in Myanmar.

Figure 17.2. Distribution of respondents in their views about government's role to reduce income differences between people with high income and those with low income (by country)

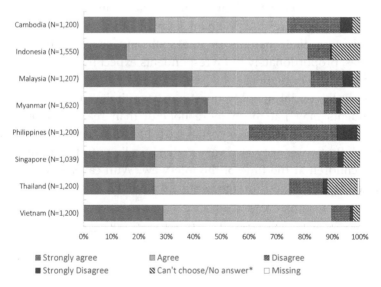

Note: Based on answers to the question "Do you agree or disagree with the following statement: It is the responsibility of the government to reduce the differences between people with high income and those with low incomes." Possible responses are "strongly agree", "agree", "disagree", "strongly disagree", "do not understand the question", "can't choose", or "decline to answer". The last three possible responses are lumped under "Can't choose/No answer" in the figure.

Source of raw data: Asian Barometer Survey (4th wave).

The distribution of the responses weakly correlates with poverty and inequality. The high proportion of "strongly agree" or "agree" in Vietnam and Indonesia may be associated with their poverty reductions, and in Malaysia with its worsened income inequality. Yet, in Myanmar, where inequality improved, many claimed to be pro-redistribution. Moreover, the significant gains in alleviating destitution and inequality in the Philippines did not elicit strong pro-redistribution responses from its citizens.

3.3 Social mobility

In the social mobility module, the respondents were asked to imagine a ten-step staircase, where the poorest people are in the lowest rung and richest ones in the top rung, and then to indicate on which steps they would put themselves and their parents and where they expect their children would be. Figure 17.3 show the summary of responses per country.

Most respondents assigned themselves and their parents on the middle steps (usually the fifth). Proportionately more respondents in Indonesia, Singapore and Vietnam than in other countries assigned themselves or their parents on the sixth and seventh steps. In all countries, proportionately more respondents expect their children to be on the fifth step or higher.[4]

Surely the social mobility questions have limitations. For one, the respondents may had been more hopeful than realistic about their children's prospects. Probably, they also had different time horizons in mind. Responses may also vary systematically with the number and age of children at the time of the interview. With caveats, we use the reported steps to assess intergenerational mobility.

---

[4] According to the few extant studies on social mobility or income mobility in Southeast Asia, in general upward mobility is less for the low-income population than the upper income, particularly in Vietnam (Lam and Cuong 2017), Indonesia (Pattinasarany 2015) and the Philippines (Dacuycuy 2018).

Figure 17.3. Distribution of respondents by self-assessed socio-economic status (by country)

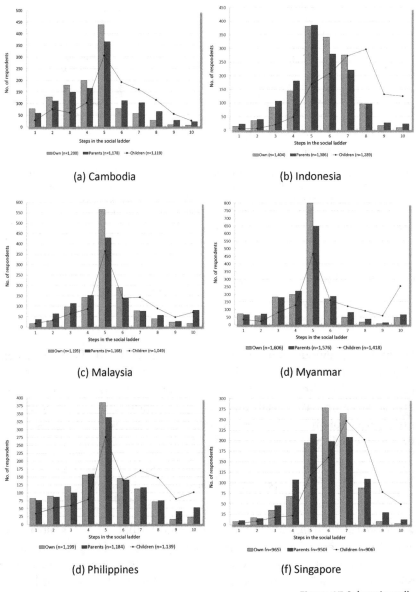

(a) Cambodia

(b) Indonesia

(c) Malaysia

(d) Myanmar

(d) Philippines

(f) Singapore

Figure 17.3 (continued)

Figure 17.3 *(continued)*

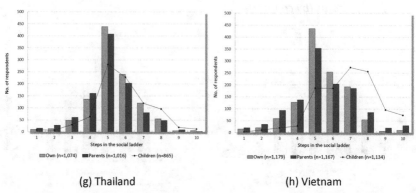

(g) Thailand   (h) Vietnam

Note: These figures are based on responses to the question "Imagine a staircase with 10 steps where the poorest people are on the first step and the richest on the tenth step. Where would you put yourself on this staircase? Where would you put your parents on this staircase? Where do you think your children will be on this staircase?"

Source of raw data: Asian Barometer Survey (4th wave).

4   EMPIRICAL METHODS

4.1   Estimating equation

Following previous studies (e.g., Alesina and La Ferrara 2005; Cojocaru 2014), the unobserved preference for redistribution is assumed to be related to the survey response concerning the redistributive role of the government. Specifically, let R_i^* be individual i's underlying preference for redistribution, which is linked with the observed preference indicator (*Redistribution*), as follows:

$$Redistribution_i = \begin{cases} 1 \ if \ R_i^* > 0 \\ 0 \ if \ R_i^* \leq 0 \end{cases}$$

where *Redistribution$_i$* takes the value of 1 if individual i's reply is "strongly agree" or "agree" to statement "It is the responsibility of the government to reduce the difference between people with high income and those with low income", and 0 otherwise. To test the POUM hypothesis, we construct also from the ABS data two additional key variables: prospects for upward mobility (M) and risk aversion (Z). Also adjusting for other covariates (included in the vector X), we then estimate equations of the following form:

$$R_i^* = \alpha + \beta Z_i + \gamma(Z_i \times M_i) + \varphi M_i + X_i'\theta + \varepsilon_i, \quad (1)$$

where α, β, γ, φ and θ are parameters to be estimated and ε_i is the error term, which is assumed to be $\varepsilon_i \sim N(0,1)$. The key hypothesis is that high prospects for upward mobility lead to lower preference for redistribution, controlling for risk aversion and other factors. That is, $H_0: \hat{\gamma} Z_i + \hat{\varphi} < 0$, which can be evaluated at the mean level of risk aversion ($\bar{Z}$). Given the distributional assumption about ε_i, the distribution of *Redistribution$_i$* conditional on (Z_i, M_i, X_i) is specified as a probit model:

$$P(Redistribution_i = 1 | Z_i, M_i, X_i) = \Phi(\alpha + \beta Z_i + \gamma(Z_i \times M_i) + \varphi M_i + X_i'\theta), \quad (2)$$

where $\Phi(\cdot)$ is the standard normal distribution function (Wooldridge 2002).

Two POUM indicators are constructed based on the respondents' *current* socio-economic status and their children's expected *future* socio-economic status. The variable *own status lower than children's* takes the value of 1 if the respondent's own step in the ten-step staircase is lower than that of the children, and 0 otherwise. The indicator *own status same as children's* takes the value of 1 if the respondent's own step is same as that of the children, and 0 otherwise. Thus, both variables pertain to the children's prospects.

Since there is no direct survey question about risk attitude, a proxy for risk aversion is derived based on the item, "The following is a hypothetical question: If you were unfortunate enough to lose your main source of income, how serious would it be for you and your family?" Specifically, *serious income loss* takes the value of 1 if the response is "It would be serious, and we would have difficulty coping", and 0 otherwise.[5] Notwithstanding its limitations, *serious income loss* is assumed correlated with risk aversion. Presumably, someone increasingly vulnerable to destitution loses appetite for risk.

The specific POUM hypotheses to be tested are: *ceteris paribus*, (i) an increase in risk aversion (i.e., from *serious income loss* = 0 to *serious income loss* = 1) will intensify redistributive preferences (i.e., $\Delta P(Redistribution = 1 | .) > 0$); (ii) when children are expected to be upwardly mobile (i.e., from *own status lower than children's* = 0 to *own status lower than children's* = 1), it will dampen redistributive preferences;

---

[5] The other possible answers are: "It would be serious, but we could deal with it", "We could manage just fine", "Do not understand the question", "Can't choose", and "Decline to answer".

and (iii) when children are expected to attain the same socio-economic status (i.e., from *own status same as children's* = 0 to *own status same as children's* = 1), it will lead to greater or lower redistributive preferences.[6] The third hypothesis allows for the possibility that a high-status parent will not back redistributive policies and for a low-status parent to support them when both expect their children's status to be the same as theirs. Clearly, this last hypothesis hinges on the parent's current status. So, an additional variable is introduced: *own status higher than parents'*, which equals 1 if the respondent's step in the ten-step staircase is higher than the parents' step, and 0 otherwise. Following Piketty (1995), this variable allows for past experiences of social mobility to bear on current redistributive preferences.

4.2 Model specifications and covariates

To obtain robust results, five model specifications are estimated. All specifications use the key POUM variables and a common set of covariates (X). They vary only in a few additional variables that in previous studies were found correlated with redistributive preferences. Table 17.2 presents the regression variables and their summary statistics.

For the baseline model ([1]), the probit model (2) is estimated without the interaction between the risk aversion and mobility variables to show only their respective direct effects. Model [2] includes an interaction term to show also their indirect effects. Extending model [2], model [3] includes two trust variables: *trust in national government* and *trust most people*. Following others (e.g., Yamamura 2012, 2014), the trust variables allow for the possibility that individuals' attitudes towards redistribution depend on their trust in government institutions (e.g., not to be corrupt) or in other members of society (e.g., to be fair). Model [4] extends model [3] by adding the dummy variables *income distribution is fair* and *more opportunities than parents*. The idea behind these two variables is that individuals who believe their society to be just may develop a more sanguine view of government redistribution (see, e.g., Alesina and La Ferrara 2005; Cojocaru 2014). Finally, model [5] adds two more dummy variables — *wealth is due to fate* and *religious* — to capture the individuals' sense of self-agency or control over their lives (see, e.g., Alesina and Angeletos 2005; Alesina, Stantcheva, and Teso 2017).

---

[6] The change in probabilities or marginal probabilities is computed here as average marginal effects using STATA.

Table 17.2. Regression variables: definitions and summary statistics (N = 7943)

Variable name	Definition	Mean	SD
Redistribution	= 1 if strongly agree or agree with the statement: "It is the responsibility of the government to reduce the difference between people with high income and those with low income", 0 otherwise	0.835	0.371
Serious income loss	= 1 if loss of main income would be serious and coping would be difficult for family, 0 otherwise	0.402	0.490
Own status lower than children's	= 1 if own step in an imaginary 10-step staircase is lower than children's, 0 otherwise	0.564	0.496
Own status same as children's	= 1 if own step in an imaginary 10-step staircase is same as children's, 0 otherwise	0.360	0.480
Own status higher than parents'	= 1 if own step in an imaginary 10-step staircase is higher than parents', 0 otherwise	0.247	0.431
Trust in national government	= 1 if has quite a lot or great deal of trust in the national government, 0 otherwise	0.635	0.481
Trust most people	= 1 if most people can be trusted, 0 otherwise	0.209	0.406
Income distribution is fair	= 1 if current family income is very fair or fair, 0 otherwise	0.433	0.496
More opportunities than parents	= 1 if has more opportunities now than parents' generation, 0 otherwise	0.692	0.462
Wealth is due to fate	= 1 if strongly agree or agree to the statement that "wealth and poverty, success and failure are all determined by fate", 0 otherwise	0.573	0.495
Religious	= 1 if very religious or moderately religious, 0 otherwise	0.727	0.446
Common covariates			
Income quintile1	= 1 if first income quintile, 0 otherwise	0.231	0.421
Income quintile2	= 1 if second income quintile, 0 otherwise	0.294	0.456
Income quintile3	= 1 if third income quintile, 0 otherwise	0.254	0.435

Table 17.2 *(continued)*

Table 17.2 *(continued)*

Variable name	Definition	Mean	SD
Income quintile4	= 1 if fourth income quintile, 0 otherwise	0.130	0.336
Income quintile5	= 1 if fifth income quintile, 0 otherwise	0.092	0.289
Age	Age in years	41.74	13.71
Female	= 1 if female, 0 otherwise	0.495	0.500
College	= 1 if finished at least college, 0 otherwise	0.119	0.323
Employed	= 1 if employed, 0 otherwise	0.704	0.456
In_union	= 1 if married or living in with a partner, 0 otherwise	0.762	0.426
Divorced	= 1 if divorced, separated or widowed, 0 otherwise	0.058	0.234
Household size	Number of household members	4.718	2.016
Single generation	= 1 if single-generation household, 0 otherwise	0.266	0.442
Biggest ethnic group	= 1 if belongs to the biggest ethnic group in the country, 0 otherwise	0.672	0.469
Buddhist	= 1 if religion is Buddhism, 0 otherwise	0.426	0.495
Christian	= 1 if religion is Christianity, 0 otherwise	0.187	0.390
Hindu	= 1 if religion is Hindu, 0 otherwise	0.021	0.144
Islam	= 1 if religion is Islam, 0 otherwise	0.217	0.412
Megacity	= 1 if capital or mega city, 0 otherwise	0.170	0.375
Major city	= 1 if regional centre or major city, 0 otherwise	0.233	0.423
Urban	= 1 if urban, 0 otherwise	0.422	0.494
Cambodia	= 1 if country is Cambodia, 0 otherwise	0.134	0.341
Indonesia	= 1 if country is Indonesia, 0 otherwise	0.143	0.350
Malaysia	= 1 if country is Malaysia, 0 otherwise	0.119	0.324
Myanmar	= 1 if country is Myanmar, 0 otherwise	0.157	0.364
Philippines	= 1 if country is Philippines, 0 otherwise	0.139	0.346
Singapore	= 1 if country is Singapore, 0 otherwise	0.080	0.271
Thailand	= 1 if country is Thailand, 0 otherwise	0.091	0.287
Vietnam	= 1 if country is Vietnam, 0 otherwise	0.137	0.344
Y2014	= 1 if year is 2014, 0 otherwise	0.426	0.495

Note: All variables, except age and household size, are dummy variables.

4.3 Country-level analysis

Of the total 10,216 observations, only 78 per cent are used here due to incomplete information. The proportion of valid sample is about 90 per cent each for Cambodia, the Philippines and Vietnam; 79 per cent for Malaysia; 77 per cent for Myanmar; 73 per cent for Indonesia; 61 per cent for Singapore and 60 per cent for Thailand. Since the skewed distribution of valid samples may affect the overall results, we regressed the same models for each country. The key results are reported below.[7]

5 MAIN RESULTS

5.1 Pooled analysis

Table 17.3 shows the marginal effects of the key POUM variables (*serious income loss, own status lower than children's* and *own status same as children's*) and selected covariates based on the full sample ($N = 7{,}943$). Note that the marginal effects of each POUM variable already incorporate its direct and indirect effects. In all models, *serious income loss* is positive — ranging from 2.01 percentage points to 2.62 percentage points — and highly significant at $p < 0.05$. Also, both *own status lower than children's* and *own status same as children's* are consistently positive (at around 3 percentage points) and significant (although at the 10% level only for most estimates). The sign of *serious income loss* is as expected, while the signs of the two mobility variables are inconsistent with the POUM hypothesis. Note that the results for the POUM variables are largely unaffected when new variables are added (in models [3], [4] and [5]).

To further examine the rather puzzling results of the POUM variables, we ran the same five regression models on a subsample comprising those in the 1st and 2nd income quintiles ($N = 4{,}165$), and on another subsample comprising those in the 3rd–5th income quintiles ($N = 3{,}778$).[8]

---

[7] The complete results are available from the author upon request.
[8] Since the respondents declared their own income quintiles, this resulted in an unequal number of observations across quintiles.

Table 17.3. Marginal effects of selected covariates of preference for redistribution (full sample, N = 7,943)

Covariate	Model				
	[1]	[2]	[3]	[4]	[5]
Serious income loss	0.0201**	0.0204**	0.0212**	0.0262***	0.0262***
	(0.0090)	(0.0090)	(0.0087)	(0.0089)	(0.0089)
Own status lower than children's	0.0331*	0.0324*	0.0331**	0.0300*	0.0300*
	(0.0173)	(0.0170)	(0.0165)	(0.0160)	(0.0160)
Own status same as children's	0.0326*	0.0318*	0.0297*	0.0265*	0.0265*
	(0.0172)	(0.0171)	(0.0161)	(0.0160)	(0.0161)
Trust in national government			0.0485***	0.0368***	0.0364***
			(0.0080)	(0.0076)	(0.0078)
Trust most people			0.0481***	0.0415***	0.0418***
			(0.0131)	(0.0120)	(0.0120)
Income distribution is fair				0.0558***	0.0554***
				(0.0091)	(0.0093)
More opportunities than parents				0.0348***	0.0349***
				(0.0133)	(0.0127)
Wealth is due to fate					0.0051
					(0.0128)
Religious					0.0058
					(0.0157)
Own status higher than parents'	0.0113	0.0116	0.0119	0.0080	0.0080
	(0.0091)	(0.0091)	(0.0088)	(0.0085)	(0.0085)

Table 17.3 (continued)

Table 17.3 (continued)

Covariate	Model				
	[1]	[2]	[3]	[4]	[5]
Other covariates[a]	YES	YES	YES	YES	YES
Pseudo-R^2	0.0990	0.0994	0.1073	0.1166	0.1167
Joint test of significance					
All coefficients					
Wald χ^2	1,623.48	1,726.19	1,808.08	6,321.74	8,162.22
Prob>χ^2	0.00	0.00	0.00	0.00	0.00
Mobility coefficients[b]					
Wald χ^2	7.68	9.84	11.57	13.55	13.59
Prob>χ^2	0.0530	0.0800	0.0412	0.0187	0.0184

Note: (1) [a]Age, Female, College, Employed, In_union, Divorced, log Household size, Single generation, Biggest ethnic group, Buddhist, Christian, Hindu, Islam, Megacity, Major city, Urban, Income quintile2, Income Quintile3, Income quintile4, Income quintile5, Cambodia, Indonesia, Malaysia, Myanmar, Singapore, Thailand, Vietnam, Y2014.
(2) [b]H_0: Serious income loss = Own status lower than children's = Own status same as children's = Serious income loss × Own status lower than children's = Serious income loss × Own status same as children's = 0.
(3) Figures in parentheses are robust standard errors adjusted for region clustering.
(4) * $p < 0.1$, ** $p < 0.05$, and *** $p < 0.01$

The idea behind this exercise is to show whether current socio-economic status is linked with expectations of children's prospects and attitudes towards redistribution.[9] The respective results are shown in Tables 17.4 and 17.5.

In Table 17.4, *serious income loss* is again consistently positive in all models, but significant only in models [4] and [5]. Both *own status lower than children's* and *own status same as children's* remain positive and significant in all specifications. In Table 17.5, all three key POUM variables are no longer significant, though positive, across models. From these two sets of results, we may deduce that the puzzling POUM-related results are true more for the poor than non-poor respondents in the sample.

While the POUM variables are individually significant, their joint significance is established here by applying Wald χ^2 tests. As reported in the bottom row of Table 17.3, the null that the key POUM variables are simultaneously equal to zero cannot be rejected at $p < 0.10$ in models [1] and [2] and at $p < 0.05$ in models [3]–[5]. The results in Table 17.4 suggest the same hypothesis can also be rejected at the 5 per cent level but not at the 10 per cent level. The results in Table 17.5 imply that all key POUM variables are all likely to be jointly equal to zero even at $p < 0.10$.

5.2 Other variables

In Table 17.3, most of the additional variables are systematically associated with redistributive preferences. Specifically, the two trust variables are consistently positive and highly significant. Both bigger in size than *serious income loss*, *trust in national government* and *trust in most people* are consistent with previous findings on the role of social capital, which include trust in people fulfilling their civic duties (Yamamura 2012, 2014). Consistently positive and highly significant also are *income distribution is fair* and *more opportunities than parents*. The positive sign of *income distribution is fair* may partly reflect the views of current beneficiaries of redistribution programmes among the respondents.

---

[9] Of the 4,165 observations in the bottom (poorest) two income quintiles, only 6.3 per cent have college education, 70 per cent are employed and 34.2 per cent live in urban areas. Of the 3,778 observations in the upper three income quintiles, on the other hand, 18 per cent have college education, 71.3 per cent are employed and 51 per cent live in urban areas.

Table 17.4. Marginal effects of selected covariates of preference for redistribution (1st & 2nd income quintiles, N = 4,165)

Covariate	Model				
	[1]	[2]	[3]	[4]	[5]
Serious income loss	0.0201	0.0208	0.0220	0.0277**	0.0278**
	(0.0142)	(0.0142)	(0.0138)	(0.0139)	(0.0139)
Own status lower than children's	0.0442*	0.0427*	0.0451**	0.0391*	0.0386*
	(0.0228)	(0.0227)	(0.0222)	(0.0210)	(0.0208)
Own status same as children's	0.0495**	0.0487**	0.0483**	0.0428**	0.0425**
	(0.0216)	(0.0213)	(0.0206)	(0.0200)	(0.0199)
Trust in national government			0.0426***	0.0273***	0.0273***
			(0.0112)	(0.0097)	(0.0102)
Trust most people			0.0612***	0.0525***	0.0525***
			(0.0130)	(0.0126)	(0.0123)
Income distribution is fair				0.0691***	0.0693***
				(0.0136)	(0.0138)
More opportunities than parents				0.0417**	0.0409**
				(0.0172)	(0.0164)
Wealth is due to fate					−0.0019
					(0.0144)

Table 17.4 (continued)

Table 17.4 (continued)

Covariate	Model				
	[1]	[2]	[3]	[4]	[5]
Religious					0.0159
					(0.0212)
Own status higher than parents'	0.0120	0.0129	0.0138	0.0116	0.0115
	(0.0131)	(0.0131)	(0.0129)	(0.0130)	(0.0129)
Other covariates[a]	YES	YES	YES	YES	YES
Pseudo-R^2	0.1144	0.1153	0.1223	0.1342	0.1345
Joint test of significance					
All coefficients					
Wald χ^2	4,381.99	4,425.03	5,066.56	5,285.94	15,691.69
Prob > χ^2	0.00	0.00	0.00	0.00	0.00
Mobility coefficients[b]					
Wald χ^2	7.55	12.31	14.00	13.90	13.87
Prob > χ^2	0.0564	0.0307	0.0156	0.0162	0.0165

Note: (1) [a] Age, Female, College, Employed, In_union, Divorced, log Household size, Single generation, Biggest ethnic group, Buddhist, Christian, Hindu, Islam, Megacity, Major city, Urban, Income quintile2, Cambodia, Indonesia, Malaysia, Myanmar, Singapore, Thailand, Vietnam, Y2014.
(2) [b] H_0: Serious income loss = Own status lower than children's = Own status same as children's = Serious income loss × Own status lower than children's = Serious income loss × Own status same as children's = 0.
(3) Figures in parentheses are robust standard errors adjusted for region clustering.
(4) * $p < 0.1$, ** $p < 0.05$, and *** $p < 0.01$

Table 17.5. Marginal effects of the covariates of preference for redistribution (3rd–5th income quintiles, N = 3,778)

Covariate	Model				
	[1]	[2]	[3]	[4]	[5]
Serious income loss	0.0168	0.0171	0.0172	0.0214	0.0213
	(0.0149)	(0.0152)	(0.0147)	(0.0143)	(0.0144)
Own status lower than children's	0.0125	0.0135	0.0122	0.0125	0.0126
	(0.0209)	(0.0209)	(0.0204)	(0.0205)	(0.0205)
Own status same as children's	0.0072	0.0079	0.0034	0.0030	0.0030
	(0.0205)	(0.0206)	(0.0198)	(0.0206)	(0.0208)
Trust in national government			0.0549***	0.0471***	0.0465***
			(0.0096)	(0.0103)	(0.0106)
Trust most people			0.0371**	0.0324*	0.0328*
			(0.0189)	(0.0176)	(0.0177)
Income distribution is fair				0.0452***	0.0441***
				(0.0134)	(0.0134)
More opportunities than parents				0.0205	0.0211
				(0.0145)	(0.0143)
Wealth is due to fate					0.0155
					(0.0177)
Religious					−0.0042
					(0.0170)
Own status higher than parents'	0.0089	0.0086	0.0083	0.0042	0.0048
	(0.0111)	(0.0111)	(0.0115)	(0.0115)	(0.0117)

Table 17.5 (continued)

Table 17.5 (continued)

Covariate	Model				
	[1]	[2]	[3]	[4]	[5]
Other covariates[a]	YES	YES	YES	YES	YES
Pseudo-R^2	0.0841	0.0851	0.0953	0.1019	0.1025
Joint test of significance					
All coefficients					
Wald χ^2	1,128.79	3,257.00	4,050.36	10,811.78	11,1024.19
Prob>χ^2	0.00	0.00	0.00	0.00	0.00
Mobility coefficients[b]					
Wald χ^2	1.30	5.29	5.73	6.07	6.00
Prob > $\chi 2$	0.7289	0.3821	0.3331	0.2994	0.3058

Note: (1) [a] Age, Female, College, Employed, In_union, Divorced, log Household size, Single generation, Biggest ethnic group, Buddhist, Christian, Hindu, Islam, Megacity, Major city, Income quintile4, Income quintile5, Cambodia, Indonesia, Malaysia, Myanmar, Singapore, Thailand, Vietnam, Y2014.
(2) [b] H_0: Serious income loss = Own status lower than children's = Own status same as children's = Serious income loss × Own status lower than children's = Serious income loss × Own status same as children's = 0.
(3) Figures in parentheses are robust standard errors adjusted for region clustering.
(4) * $p < 0.1$, ** $p < 0.05$ *** $p < 0.01$

That is, their beneficiary status justifies their support for government interventions. On the other hand, the positive sign of *more opportunities than parents* may reflect the frustrations of some who may have failed to take advantage of their options. That such "failures" may be driven by an underlying fatalistic attitude or sense of helplessness finds weak support in model [5]. Here, *wealth is due to fate* and *religious* are both positive and insignificant, while both *income distribution is fair* and *more opportunities than parents* remain positive and significant. *Own status higher than parents* is consistently positive and insignificant across models.

In Tables 17.4 and 17.5, the two trust variables and *income distribution is fair* remain positive and significant, while *wealth is due to fate* and *religious* still show no effect. *More opportunities than parents* are significant only in Table 17.4.

5.3 Country-level analysis

Figures 17.4 and 17.5 show country-level estimates of the marginal effects and the corresponding 90 per cent confidence interval of the POUM variables for each of the five model specifications.[10] As shown in Figure 17.4(a), all three key POUM variables are positive but insignificant for Cambodia. All estimates for Indonesia (Figure 17.4(b)) and Singapore (Figure 17.4(c)) are likewise insignificant. Interestingly, in the case of Myanmar (Figure 17.4(d)), *serious income loss* is positive and both *own status is lower than children's* and *own status is same as children's* are negative. While the signs in this case are consistent with the POUM hypothesis, none of the estimates is significant.

Also somewhat aligned with the POUM model predictions are the results for Malaysia (Figure 17.5(a)) and Vietnam (Figure 17.5(d)). In Malaysia's case, the two mobility indicators are consistently negative, although only *own status lower than children's* is significant (in models [2], [3] and [4]). In Vietnam's case, both mobility variables are negative and significant in models [2]–[5]. In both country, *serious income loss* is insignificant.

---

[10] To avoid multicollinearity, the following covariates are excluded: *Hindu* and *Islam* in the Vietnam analysis; *Hindu*, *Buddhist* and *Islam* in the Philippines; *Christian* and *Hindu* in Cambodia; *Buddhist* in Indonesia; *major city*, *Hindu*, *Buddhist*, *Christian* and *Islam* in Thailand; and *urban*, *megacity* and *major city* in Singapore.

Figure 17.4. Marginal effects *of* serious income loss, own status lower than children's *and* own status same as children's *(Cambodia, Indonesia, Myanmar and Singapore)*

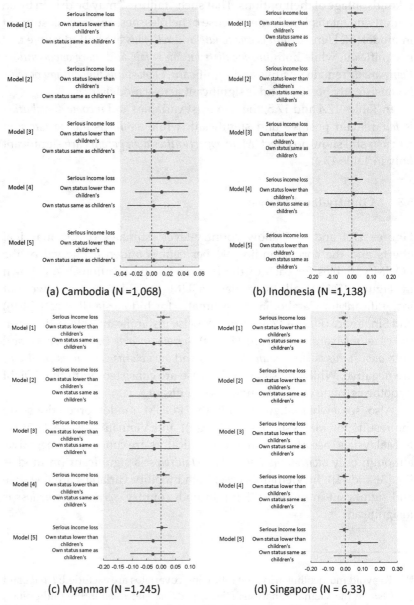

(a) Cambodia (N =1,068)
(b) Indonesia (N =1,138)
(c) Myanmar (N =1,245)
(d) Singapore (N = 6,33)

Note: (1) Figures show the marginal effects and the 90 per cent confidence interval.
(2) As those reported in Table 17.2, models [1]–[5] here have same specifications, except for the country dummy variables and a few covariates to avoid multicollinearity. (See footnote #10)

Figure 17.5. Marginal effects of serious income loss, own status lower than children's *and* own status same as children's *(Malaysia, the Philippines, Thailand and Vietnam)*

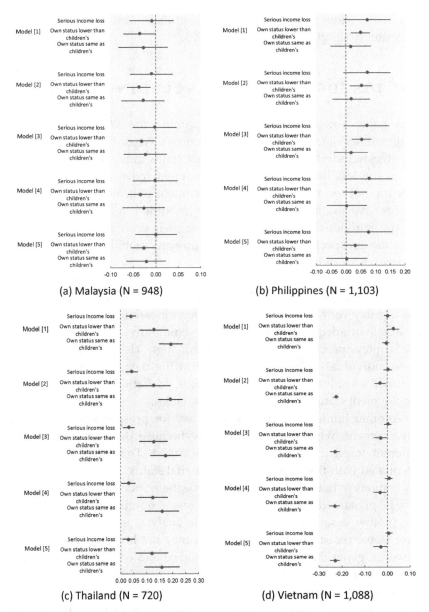

Note: (1) Figures show the marginal effects and the 90 per cent confidence interval.
(2) As those reported in Table 17.2, models [1]–[5] here have same specifications, except for the country dummy variables and a few covariates to avoid multicollinearity. (See footnote #10)

In contrast, the estimates of the key POUM variables are positive in the cases of the Philippines (Figure 17.5(b)) and Thailand (Figure 17.5(c)). In the Philippines' case, only *own status lower than children's* is significant (but only in models [2] and [3]). In Thailand's case, *serious income loss, own status lower than children's* and *own status same as children's* are consistently significant, mostly at $p < 0.05$.

6   DISCUSSION AND CONCLUDING REMARKS

This paper sought to empirically examine the POUM hypothesis using survey data from eight SEA countries. According to the POUM hypothesis, individuals who expect their status in life to advance in the future are less likely to support government redistribution, provided they are not too risk averse and government policies do not abruptly change. We examined here a slightly modified version: Controlling for the individuals' own assessment of their economic vulnerability, does the prospect of their children's upward mobility diminish their preference for redistribution?

Before we summarize and discuss the results, it is important to note the data limitations. First, in lieu of a direct measure of risk attitude, we use a proxy variable based on economic vulnerability. This proxy may be less than adequate, however, since some individuals face potential bankruptcy precisely because of their high risk tolerance. While these individuals cannot be identified in the data, their behaviour is assumed accounted for by age, civil status, educational attainment, sex, employment status and other control variables.

Another limitation concerns the proxy for prospects for children's advancement, which may vary simply because the respondents had different implicit time horizons when asked. This problem may be attenuated with the controls for age, marital status, household size and generations of household members, since the respondents' expectations may be presumed correlated with the age and number of children.

Another assumption underlying the analysis is that the countries have stable redistributive policies. This may not hold for all countries, however, given their changing sociopolitical and economic conditions. Moreover, there could be country-specific factors like cultural norms, ethnic tensions and conflict situations that shape attitudes towards government redistribution. Hopefully, the effects of these factors are partly captured by the dummy variables for countries and years.

With these caveats, the main findings are: (1) controlling for other factors, those who anticipate difficulty in coping if they lose their source of income tend to express greater preference for redistribution; and (2) there is greater preference for redistribution among those who expect their children to overtake them in social status someday. While the first finding is consistent with the POUM hypothesis, the second is not.

Apparently, the overall results reflect more the attitudes of the less well-off respondents. In a subsample comprising the poorest two income quintiles, a greater preference for redistribution is found among those who will find it hard to cope with income losses and those who foresee social advancement in their children. In the subsample comprising the richest three income quintiles, on the other hand, redistributive preferences are found independent of risk aversion or prospects for children's upward mobility. Unlike the poor, the well-off perhaps think their own resources are adequate to secure their offspring's future.

How then to square the findings on the poor with the POUM hypothesis? The positive and statistically significant relationship between *own status same as children* and redistributive preferences is easier to explain. Poor parents who foresee no better future for their children without external support will obviously want the government to help. But poor parents who favour government redistribution and expect their children to advance in life (i.e., *own status lower than children*) may be simply expressing hopes or aspirations. While any parent can be expected to wish the best for an offspring, an indigent parent would fear that without government intervention or luck, such wishes would be unrealized. Put differently, such aspirations are to be expected among the poor in countries with high poverty incidence or income inequality, controlling for governance regimes and other factors.

Only the results for Vietnam strongly support the POUM hypothesis, although those for Malaysia and, somewhat, Myanmar appear consistent with the hypothesis also. On the one hand, this may indicate that the Vietnamese on their own increasingly partake in their economy's growth, given Vietnam's fairly stable government. On the other hand, that the robust economic growth in Myanmar and Malaysia has only muted effect may be due to the fragile political situations therein.

In contrast, the results for Cambodia, Singapore, Thailand, the Philippines and, to a certain extent, Indonesia are somewhat inconsistent with the POUM hypothesis. Yet, even in Singapore and Thailand where the living standards are comparatively higher and prospects for mobility more realistic than in other countries, their citizens' redistributive preference correlates with their children's prospects. That such attitude towards government redistribution holds even after controlling for trust in government or other members of the society, the role of luck or self-efficacy, or fairness of the income distribution only further underscores the inadequacy of the simple POUM hypothesis. Such attitude makes sense, however, if the prospects are aspirational and especially in the context of expanding pro-poor fiscal spending (as in the Philippines and Thailand.)

If aspirational upward mobility drives support for government redistribution, this has some policy implications. For one, redistributive policies based on objective indicators of income or wealth status will be inadequate. Even if incomes were already equitably distributed, dissimilarities in aspirations may lead to other redistributive policies. People with both low aspirations and low income will probably need more than just income infusion to improve their lives. Thus, government redistribution programmes should address both the extrinsic (i.e., wealth or income) and the intrinsic (i.e., hope, aspirations) constraints facing individuals.[11] The government's task will be more complicated and difficult, however. Since one's aspirations cannot be limited or directly observed by another, declared aspirations can be unrealistic or too costly to attain, even with government support. The challenge facing the governments in these eight SEA countries then is how to encourage their citizens to hope and aspire realistically and to take responsibility for improving their lives, even as their governments work to ensure that everyone attains some minimum capability to do so.

ACKNOWLEDGEMENT

I gratefully acknowledge the Philippine Center for Economic Development for supporting an earlier study (Capuno 2019) from which this paper draws, the Asian Barometer Project Office for the survey data, Julian Thomas Alvarez and Jan Chael Laude Pon-An for excellent research assistance, and the editors for thoughtful comments.

---

[11] The importance of hope, aspirations and other psychological motivations of the poor is attracting more attention in economics (e.g., Dalton, Ghosal, and Mani 2014; Lybbert and Wydick 2018).

REFERENCES

Abad, R. G. 1997. "Attitudes towards Welfare and Inequality". *Philippine Studies* 45, no. 4: 447–76.

Alesina, A., and G.-M. Angeletos. 2005. "Fairness and Redistribution". *American Economic Review* 95, no. 4: 960–80.

Alesina, A., and P. Giuliano. 2011. "Chapter 4 - Preferences for Redistribution". In *Handbook of Social Economics*, Volume 1, edited by J. Benhabib, M. Jackson, and A. Bisin, pp. 93–131. Amsterdam, the Netherlands: Elsevier.

Alesina, A., and E. La Ferrara. 2005. "Preferences for Redistribution in the Land of Opportunities". *Journal of Public Economics* 89, no. 5–6: 897–931.

Alesina, A., S. Stantcheva, and E. Teso. 2017. "Intergenerational Mobility and Preferences for Redistribution. *NBER Working Paper* 23027. National Bureau of Economic Research, Cambridge, MA. http://www.nber.org/papers/w23027.

Asian Development Bank. 2020. "Key Development Indicators for Asia and the Pacific 2020". https://kidb.adb.org (accessed 14 March 2021).

Benabou, R., and E. A. Ok. 2001. "Social Mobility and the Demand for Redistribution: The POUM hypothesis". *Quarterly Journal of Economics* 116, no. 2: 447–87.

Capuno, J. J. 2019. "Preferences for Redistribution in Southeast Asia". Final research report submitted to the Philippine Center for Economic Development, Quezon City, Philippines.

Chang, A. C. 2018. "How Do Asian Values Constrain Public Support for Redistribution?". *Journal of Behavioral and Experimental Economics* 77: 139–50.

Cojocaru, A. 2014. "Prospects for Upward Mobility and Preferences for Redistribution: Evidence from the Life in Transition Survey". *European Journal of Political Economy* 34: 300–14.

Dacuycuy, L. 2018. Social Mobility in the Philippine Labor Market". *Philippine Review of Economics* 55, no. 1&2: 1–40.

Dalton, P., S. Ghosal., and A. Mani. 2014. "Poverty and Aspirations Failure". *Economic Journal* 126: 165–88.

Economist Intelligence Unit. 2016. "Democracy Index 2015: Democracy in an Age of Anxiety". https://www.eiu.com/public/topical_report.aspx?campaignid=DemocracyIndex2015 (accessed 14 March 2021).

Gregg, P., L. MacMillan, and C. Vittori. 2019. "Intergenerational Income Mobility: Access to Top Jobs, the Low-Pay No-Pay Cycle and the Role of Education in a Common Framework". *Journal of Population Economics* 32: 501–28.

Gugushvili, A. 2016. "Intergenerational Objective and Subjective Mobility and Attitudes towards Income Differences: Evidence from Transition Societies." *Journal of International and Comparative Social Policy*. https://doi.org/10.1080/216999763.2016.1206482.

Haggard, S., R. R. Kaufman, J. D. Long. 2012. "Income, Occupation, and Preferences for Redistribution in the Developing World". *Studies in Comparative International Development* 48, no. 2: 113–40.

Jaime-Castillo, A. M., and I. Marques-Perales. 2019. "Social Mobility and Demand for Redistribution in Europe: A Comparative Analysis". *British Journal of Sociology* 70, no. 1: 138–65.

Lam, N. T., and N. V. Cuong. 2017. "Intragenerational and Intergenerational Mobility in Viet Nam". *ADBI Working Paper Series* no. 722. Tokyo: Asian Development Bank Institute.

Laméris, M. D., H. Garretsen, and R. Jong-A-Pin. 2018. "Political Ideology and the Intragenerational Prospect of Upward Mobility". *CESifo Working Paper* no. 6987. Munich: Center for Economic Studies and Ifo Institute.

Lybbert, T. J., and B. Wydick. 2018. "Poverty, Aspirations, and the Economics of Hope". *Economic Development and Cultural Change* 66, no. 4: 709–53.

Marshall, M. G., and G. Elzinga-Marshall. 2017. *Global Report 2017. Conflict, Governance, and State Fragility*. Vienna, VA: Center for Systemic Peace.

Meltzer, A.H., and S. F. Richard. 1983. "Test of Rational Theory of the Size of Government". *Public Choice* 41, no. 3: 403–18.

Pattinasarany, I. R. I. 2015. "Stimulating Upward Mobility in Indonesia". *Global Dialogue*. https://globaldialogue.isa-sociology.org/stimulating-upward-mobility-in-indonesia/ (accessed 4 April 2021).

Piketty, T. 1995. "Social Mobility and Redistributive Politics". *Quarterly Journal of Economics* 110, no. 3: 551–84.

Tohyama, H. 2019. "How Does a Liberalizing Market Structure Influence a Synergy between Redistribution Preference and Social Preferences in Asian Socio-economies?". *Evolutionary and Institutional Economic Review* 16, no. 2: 455–77.

Yamamura, E. 2012. "Social Capital, Household Income, and Preferences for Income Redistribution". *European Journal of Political Economy* 28, no. 4: 498–511.

———. 2014. "Trust in Government and Its Effect on Preferences for Income Redistribution and Perceived Tax Burden". *Economics of Governance* 15: 71–100.

Wooldridge, J. M. 2002. *Econometric Analysis of Cross Section and Panel Data*. Cambridge, MA: MIT Press.

World Bank. 2021. World Bank Open Data. https://data.worldbank.org/indicators/GINI (accessed 4 March 2021).

PART 5

Competition Law and Policy

18 Adopting and Adapting Competition Policy: Asian Illustrations

Majah-Leah V. Ravago, James A. Roumasset and Arsenio M. Balisacan

1 INTRODUCTION

Competition disciplines firms to subjugate other objectives to the pursuit of profits, thereby enhancing market efficiency. In his *Wealth of Nations*, Adam Smith (2008) describes competition as the "exercise of allocating productive resources to their most highly valued uses and encouraging efficiency". Competition can also incentivize product variety and prices, thus enhancing consumer welfare. Moreover, it plays an important role in encouraging innovation, increasing productivity and propelling growth, thereby promoting a country's sustained economic development.

Effective competition does not necessarily follow from the mere existence of many competing firms, however. Inappropriate government policies and firm conduct can impair competition and hinder its role in economic development. Weak institutions and rent-seeking by special interests may inhibit competition-enhancing reforms, restrict opportunities for innovation and diminish consumer welfare. This is where competition policy plays a role. Competition policy encompasses competition advocacy as well as laws and regulations concerning anticompetitive behaviour and production structures (Motta 2004).

Competition law is a set of enforceable legal rules designed to prevent the abuse of market dominance and anticompetitive behaviour and to break down barriers to entry. Competition advocacy promotes a culture of competition as well as consumer interests (Clark 2005; Rakić 2018). Since effective competition can improve income distribution as well as innovation and productivity, competition policy can be critical in achieving inclusive growth and sustained development.

To investigate the impact of the adoption of competition law on long-term economic growth, we constructed a cross-country data set from 1975 to 2015. Countries may choose to adopt—or not adopt—competition law depending on their circumstances, including level of economic development, institutions and geography. Considering endogeneity and self-selection, we employ an endogenous switching regression, allowing for the interdependence of economic growth and adoption of competition law. Our analysis shows that adoption increased the growth rates in adopting countries but would have decreased growth in non-adopting countries.

In addition to correcting the abuses of anticompetitive behaviour, competition policy should be designed to promote innovation and productivity growth and be well coordinated with trade and domestic policies. We review these arguments, focusing on Asian countries. While the design and organization of competition authorities in Asia vary according to each country's historical and economic situation, we focus on South Korea, Thailand and the Philippines to capture the characteristics of the competition law and authorities at various stages of maturity.

The next section outlines the role of competition in economic development and explains the need for competition policies to play a complementary role to other policy instruments. Section 3 describes the evolution of competition policy, its institutional aspects and political economy considerations. Section 4 presents an empirical investigation of the role of economic development in competition policy adoption and contributors to the effectiveness of competition policies. Section 5 discusses competition policies in South Korea, Thailand and the Philippines. The last section concludes.

2 COMPETITION AND DEVELOPMENT

2.1 Competition policy and the promotion of welfare

The role of government with respect to the economy is to promote the general welfare by constructing an infrastructure of cooperation. This includes rules and standards of property and contracting, including competition policy, such that bilateral exchange leads to competitive markets. The centrepiece of neoclassical economics is the fundamental theorem of welfare economics, a formalization of Adam Smith's *invisible hand* proposition that, under ideal circumstances, competitive markets can eliminate waste and achieve economic efficiency. Ensuring freedom of entry and other preconditions for competition is thus an integral part of the infrastructure of cooperation. The metaphor of the invisible hand captures the central irony that the purpose of competition is to promote coordination of economic activities for promotion of the common good. Beyond the neoclassical model are the benefits of competition for specialization and innovation.

Competition policy promotes the general welfare through both behavioural and organizational means. Competition renders abusive behaviours (e.g., price-fixing) unprofitable. It also selects (through entry and exit) firms that reduce costs and improve product quality and variety. The infrastructure of economic cooperation also includes complementary functions where bilateral exchange is insufficient for efficiency. Thus, in the case of natural monopolies, public goods and incomplete markets, the role of government extends to facilitating multilateral cooperation, including market regulation and provision of public goods.

Should competition policy promote total welfare or focus more narrowly on consumer welfare? Kaplow (2013) argues that the objective of competition policy should be total economic welfare on the grounds that distributional consequences can be offset by redistributive instruments. The choice between consumer and total welfare may be a false dichotomy, however. In one of his most famous passages, Adam Smith (2008) notes: "People of the same trade seldom meet together, even for merriment and diversion, but the conversation ends in a conspiracy against the public, or in some contrivance to raise prices." Arrow (1969) alludes to a formalization of Smith's conspiracy theory when he states: "It is not the size of transaction costs but their bias that is important." That is, while people of the same trade can easily collude, it is much more difficult for consumers to form a coalition to block those efforts, such as by temporary boycotts. Indeed, regulation of potentially anticompetitive agreements, organizations and behaviour can be viewed as an *administered contract* (Goldberg 1976) by government on behalf of consumers to confer *countervailing power* (Galbraith 1952) on consumers. That is, the ideal regulator offsets the bias in bargaining power that threatens the ability of markets to deliver the promise of maximizing public welfare (Balisacan 2019).

In other words, government should not be viewed as a benevolent despot, eager to do the bidding of the metaphorical economist who prescribes how to correct market failures associated with externalities, public goods and market power.[1] From a political economy perspective, that would be futile.[2] Given the nature of the political equilibrium, total welfare may be best pursued by promoting consumer welfare, particularly by acting as a countervailing force against the restraint of trade, orchestrated by commercial elites and enabled by misguided public policy.[3] More generally, the perceived trade-off between total and consumer welfare may result from partial equilibrium diagrams depicting net welfare as the sum of producer and consumer surplus. But in general equilibrium, it is consumer welfare that is maximized, including the returns to shareholders of private business.[4]

We regard the purpose of competition policy as *making markets work for economic development*. By combating collusion and rent-seeking, competition policy facilitates the ability of bilateral exchange to efficiently promote the general welfare. By blocking anticompetitive

---

[1] See, e.g., Brennen and Munge (2014) on Knut Wicksell and James Buchanan's aversion to "modeling government as if it were a benevolent despot" and pursuing public policy as if all the economist needs do is whisper in the despot's ear.

[2] Politicians determine, via selection, official economic views, not the other way around (Blinder 1987).

[3] Once lobbying of the competition agency and the endogeneity of merger applications are considered, it is also possible that assigning a consumer welfare objective to the competition agency will increase total welfare more than assigning a goal of total welfare in the first place (Nevin and Röller 2005; Besanko and Spulber 1993).

[4] Moreover, to the extent that competition eliminates excess profits, shareholders are reimbursed only for their costs. Despite the continuing controversy, the consumer-welfare perspective has mostly dominated in the United States since a Supreme Court ruling to that effect in 1979 (Wright and Ginsburg 2013).

agreements and behaviour among elite producers and providing an equal playing field for small and medium-sized enterprises, it promotes vertical equity as well. Competition policy also promotes horizontal equity, since equality under the law includes freedom from price and other forms of commercial discrimination and equal opportunity to engage in economic exchange.

2.2 Competition, growth and development

To the extent that Asian countries have borrowed competition policies from the West (Ravago, Roumasset, and Balisacan 2021; McEwin and Chokesuwattanaskul 2021) where static considerations have dominated discussions, Asian competition policy can benefit from understanding the role of government in the dynamics of growth and development, especially regarding specialization, innovation and investment coordination. What does growth and development theory tell us about said dynamics?

In the dismal science of Malthus and Ricardo, adding increasing quantities of labour to a fixed resource base is self-limiting, with the economy heading to a stationary state with subsistence wages. Neoclassical growth theory is somewhat more optimistic: by adding capital faster than the rate of population growth, per capita income increases. But eventually the rate of growth slows to the rate of technical change. In this view, the government needs only to promote the infrastructure of cooperation described above.

Endogenous growth theory is even more optimistic. Due to the economies of human capital and specialization, growth need not slow down. In this view, an additional role of government is implied—the promotion of knowledge spillovers, especially by way of education and R&D.

Economic development is economic growth modified by structural change. In particular, structural transformation is characterized by the decline of the share of agriculture in the economy, the growth and subsequent decline of the share of industry, and the growth of the services sector. On an efficient development path, productivity growth in agriculture stimulates industrialization via supply and demand linkages. Further productivity growth in agriculture combined with even faster growth in industry raises real wages and per capita incomes.

At the early stages of development, capital accumulation and innovation in agriculture barely surpass diminishing labour productivity from population pressure (Boserup 1965, 1981; Lucas 1993; Roumasset 2008). Even with modest growth of productivity relative to population, the relatively low income elasticity of demand for food and the supply-side linkages of savings and low-cost labour eventually lead to the emergence of industrialization and to increasing shares of output and employment contributed by manufacturing (Jorgenson 1961).

Greater rates of specialization and capital formation, especially in manufacturing, spur faster productivity growth in the economy and provide a further impetus to wage growth. This process also increases the returns to human capital formation, lowering fertility and further contributing to the virtuous circle of rising productivity (Lucas 1993, 2001). Along with this transformation, manufactured products increase as a proportion of exports, and both exports and imports grow relative to total production.

The fact that average productivity tends to be higher in industry than in agriculture does not imply that government policy should artificially promote the transition, such as by taxing agriculture and subsidizing import-substituting manufacturing through tariff protection (Bautista, Power, and Associates 1979). Productivity growth leads to structural transformation, not the other way around (Jorgenson 1961; Felipe and Estrada 2018).

In the final stage of structural transformation, the services sector modernizes and grows relative to industry; it is sometimes seen as an increasingly important source of growth and poverty alleviation "due to its complementarity with manufacturing, criticality in the global value chain, and rising tradability" (World Bank Thailand 2016). As Wallis and North (1986) have detailed, the modern services sector is largely composed of the *transaction sector* (especially transportation, communication, finance and the digital economy). This facilitates specialization and the continued escalation of productivity. The size of the transaction sector grows even as *unit transaction costs* (e.g., transport cost per ton-kilometre) fall.[5]

Specialization is a key engine of growth. The falling costs of communication and transportation facilitate more and more transactions, more complex economic organization and further specialization in the

---

[5] The stylized facts of structural transformation are described by Clark (1940), Kuznets (1966), Chenery and Syrquin (1975) and Timmer (1988). For a more detailed discussion of the nature of structural transformation, see Roumasset (2008) and Ravago and Balisacan (2016).

virtuous circle that grows the transaction sector (modern services). Horizontal and vertical specialization promote innovation and learning. To illustrate, think of the first rifle that was ever made. It would have been made by a blacksmith who created all the parts—lock, stock and barrel. But as demand grew, artisans began horizontally specializing in different rifles, vertically specializing in parts, and later horizontally specializing in different parts. At first, the components had to be standardized. There is a scene in the movie, "The Good, the Bad, and the Ugly", in which Tuco puts together a gun from several different models. We see that the components from different brands (during the time of the Civil War) were made to be interchangeable. Specialization in intermediate goods (lock, stock and barrel) was *limited by the size of the market* (Stigler 1951). As demand grew further, specialized producers emerged for the differentiated components for Remington, Winchester, Colt, Smith-Wesson and other brands.

For specialization to be only limited by the size of the market, vertical coordination (and its concomitant governance costs) must be increased, facilitated by ever falling unit transaction costs. The increased total transaction costs are warranted by the greater value added from the external and internal economies[6] and the improved fit of production with diverse preferences. Given the increasing complexity of economic organization, some flexibility in competition policy is needed, lest regulation restricts the evolution of efficient organizational forms.

As economic development proceeds, companies develop new institutions to lower coordination costs. Consider *parallel sourcing*, for example. Toyota typically uses only one supplier of each component for each of its models (i.e., one supplier of steering wheels for Corolla, another for Cressida and so on). Each is a monopolistic supplier to a particular model, but there is competition across models, so Toyota gets the best of both worlds. The use of one supplier improves inter-firm relationship, making it conducive to product quality, while competition motivates suppliers to specialize and innovate at reasonable costs (Richardson and Roumasset 1995). This case illustrates that competition need not displace intra- and inter-firm relationships. Rather competition and firm relationships can be complementary. It is easy to see how

---

[6] The internal economies of scale occur in the production of the intermediate product. In a competitive environment, these result in lower costs (and/or quality improvements) of rifle production, known as *Marshallian external economies* (Stigler 1951).

rules-based competition policy could be carried too far and undermine efficient institutions.

In the neoclassical paradigm, specialization becomes complete as transaction costs, eventually shrinking to zero in what might be viewed as the *Omega Point*[7] of development, wherein the economy is well represented by the Arrow-Debreu general equilibrium model of supply and demand (e.g., Debreu 1959). This view is contradicted by the facts, however, since the transaction sector and the importance of internal governance grow with specialization. At any point in time, specialization is limited only by the trade-off between the economic gains it affords and the increased costs needed to govern it. But as *unit* transaction costs decline, both horizontal and vertical specialization increase further. Competition policy for economic development therefore needs to facilitate competition without impairing the extra-market coordination needed for increased specialization.

The canonical excess-burden graph for a monopoly seems to suggest that the more monopoly power is reduced, the more welfare will increase, and that competition authorities should seek to reduce monopoly power wherever they can. That generalization may be counterproductive, however. For example, if you have two industries and made the less monopolistic one even more competitive, that would typically worsen the inefficiency. Monopoly pushes resources out of the monopolistic sector, making them less socially productive. Pulling even more resources into the relatively less competitive sector by making it more competitive makes those resources even less productive. One must be accordingly careful about piecemeal attempts to make individual sectors more competitive.

2.3 Role of trade, competition and industrial policy in economic development

Economic development thinking in the last thirty years has shifted from a *letting-markets-work* viewpoint focused on the static efficiency properties of competitive markets to a perspective of *helping markets work*

---

[7] Coined by Pierre Teilhard de Chardin and rooted in the metaphysics of Aristotle, this refers to the belief that everything is moving towards a final point of divine unification.

with physical and institutional infrastructure[8] and a greater focus on dynamics-productivity growth and structural transformation for increased levels of living.

In the late 1980s and early 1990s, the predominant view of economic development policy, labelled the Washington Consensus (Williamson 1990), focused largely on static efficiency losses (e.g., Krueger, Schiff, and Valdez 1988, 1991–92). The philosophy was to reduce market distortions associated with taxes, subsidies and barriers to competition both domestically and from international trade. In this view, economic regulation and other market interventions are only needed to correct for externalities and guard against anticompetitive forces. This view subsequently lost favour due to the mixed success of static-focused policy reforms and because incentives for enhancing investment and productivity were given short shrift (Rodrik 2006).

A more comprehensive view was fomented by the *East Asian Miracle* (Roumasset 1992; World Bank 1993), in which investment coordination and productivity growth were key. The "miracle" countries succeeded by dramatically growing manufactured exports. Manufacturing provides almost limitless opportunities for both horizontal and vertical specialization, and specialization appropriates external economies from knowledge, learning and networks (Yang 2003).

One key to export promotion is lower tariff and non-tariff barriers to imports. These promote economic development via multiple channels, all involving increased competition and engagement with international markets. First, the gains from trade provide an immediate boost to levels of living. Second, removing import protection spurs industrial development, especially via manufactured exports, inasmuch as tariff protection discriminates against exports via an appreciated exchange rate (Power 1972). The concomitant specialization leads to further growth through learning-by-doing, network externalities and outward-oriented innovation (Lucas 1993). A third mechanism lies in the ability of international competition to retard domestic rent-seeking (e.g., Oman 1996).

---

[8] This begins with the rule of law and includes a legal system for the enforcement of rights and contractual exchange, consistent with the Smithian view of *public institutions* and broadly construed *standards and measures* (Besley and Ghatak 2006).

Another key to export promotion in the "miracle" countries was the selective assistance for domestically successful firms to transition to the export market, through such tools as subsidized credit, government certification of product quality and investment coordination. Competition and cooperation were intertwined in this channel. First, domestic competition provided a mechanism to select the most successful firms. Many of the successful firms then formed conglomerates (the Keiretsus and Chaebols of Japan and Korea, respectively) that facilitated cooperation between firms, banks and governments in coordinating investments. This enabled firms to initially succeed in international competition and to sustain their success through innovation in product quality and production methods (Halberstram 1986; Roumasset 1992).

2.4 Innovation

Productivity growth is central to economic development, and innovation is a key factor in increasing productivity. How should competition policy be adapted to promote innovation? Schumpeter (1942) famously proposes that too much price-lowering competition can destroy the competition that really matters—competition to develop new technologies, products and organizational forms, and new sources of supply. This inverse relationship between innovation and competition was formally derived by Romer (1990), Grossman and Helpman (1991) and Aghion and Howitt (1992), but empirically rejected by Nickell (1996) and Blundell, Griffith, and van Reenen (1999), who found a positive relationship instead. This led Aghion et al. (2005) to synthesize the theory of an inverted U-shaped relationship between innovation and competition,[9] which they confirmed using a panel of firms listed on the London Stock Exchange. The results are shown in Figure 18.1, wherein the maximum effect of competition, given by one minus the Lerner index, occurs at a price-cost margin of around 15 per cent.[10]

---

[9] For an alternative derivation based on a model of monopolistic competition with directed technical change, see Acemoglu (2016).

[10] The average competition index for the United States is around 0.85 (Hall 2018). On average, further increases in competition could undermine innovativeness.

Figure 18.1. Competition promotes innovation up to a point

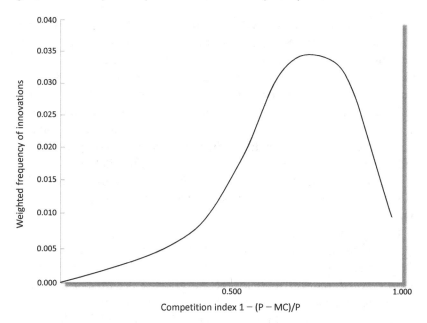

Source: Adapted from Agion et al. (2005).

The humped-shaped relationship between R&D effort and competition is thought to be the result of opposing forces. On the one hand, firms have positively sloped reaction functions to the innovative efforts of competitors. On the other hand, at high levels of competition, this is overcome by falling individual returns to innovation (Acemoglu 2009).[11]

Patent law may be seen as a device to incentivize innovation without conferring a surfeit of excess profits to producers. In effect, the innovator becomes a temporary monopolist over the innovation. The patent system has some disadvantages, however, notably restricting use of what is essentially a public good, imposing a rather arbitrary patent duration, and requiring disclosure of technical information that may have been costly for a firm to acquire (Konan et al. 1995).

---

[11] Acemoglu (2016) derives this result in a model of monopolistic competition and directed technical change. See Chernyshev (2016) for a review and theoretical synthesis of this literature.

2.5 Investment coordination

The most prominent growth externality involves interdependent investments (Stiglitz 1996). Suppose that a manufacturer and its supplier are considering an expansion such that a win-win outcome is realized if both parties invest. There is an *assurance problem* in that both players stand to lose if they invest but their counterpart does not.[12] Inasmuch as static spot markets are not well suited to the dynamic coordination of investments, competition that disrupts efficient mechanisms of coordination may be welfare reducing. Relatedly, competition that undermines internal governance structures that facilitate coordination in the value chain may also be harmful. As a result, competition, in the absence of forward markets, needs to be supplemented by extra-market mechanisms.

One approach to the coordination of investments is to correct market signals by Pigouvian price adjustments, typically through tax incentives. The problem with this approach is that those special interests with the best lobby efforts will tend to get the greatest tax breaks. The most promising approach to coordinating investments may be through economic cooperation. In the Keiretsu-Chaebol model followed by Japan and South Korea, for example, cooperative investment has been encouraged by means of conglomerates and *deliberation councils* (Lee and Naya 1988).[13] While direct coordination through conglomerates and deliberation councils can internalize coordination externalities, they also risk encouraging rent-seeking. Competition policy can potentially curb these excesses without undermining the warranted coordination (Shin 2018). While there remains a risk that the competition authority can be captured by the very industries it is meant to regulate (Stigler 1971), this risk is mitigated by the quasi-judicial nature of competition agencies and by the orientation of these authorities to the whole economy instead of a particular industry.

---

[12] In game theory, the win-win outcome is said to be *pay-off dominant*, whereas the no-invest Nash equilibrium is *risk dominant*. Adopting a strategy of cooperation without assurances of cooperation by the other players is said to be a "sucker move", and "nobody likes to be a sucker" (Suzor 2014).

[13] For a more extensive discussion of the investment coordination problem and the pros and cons of alternative remedies, see Roumasset (1992) and Stiglitz (1993, 1996).

As anticipated by Adam Smith, the role of the state also includes the facilitation of public works, now known as *public goods,* such as transportation infrastructure and education. Public goods are *non-rival* in consumption, thereby conferring positive consumption externalities on non-providers. State facilitation of public goods also takes a variety of forms, including *provision, procurement* and *incentives* (e.g., through vouchers or public-private partnerships). Since "government failure may be as important as market failure" (Besley and Ghatak 2006), competition policy also embodies regulation of the public sector, be it a public utility, a public procurement process or a public agency providing private goods such as a grain-marketing parastatal.

In summary, focusing competition policy on economic development calls for greater orientation to the dynamics of investment, innovation, specialization and coordination. In addition to the need for the rule of law, especially market-friendly institutions for contracting, there must be balance between the coordination of interdependent investments and anticompetitive regulations that limit the scope for rent-seeking. A dynamic perspective puts more weight on productivity-enhancing innovations than squeezing out the last drop of excess profits. This will be enhanced by policies that improve free entry and by avoiding unnecessary protectionist efforts to keep existing businesses afloat.

Modifying competition policy for economic development requires an understanding of its possible drawbacks. We review arguments from public choice and transaction cost economics regarding possible negative effects. We also discuss how the single-minded pursuit of competition in isolation from the complex nature of economic development will not always advance the common good. As we have seen, competition needs to be supplemented by extra-market institutions. A few additional problems with common generalizations about competition policy help to illustrate the danger of following simple rules of thumb.

2.6 Pitfalls: Views from public choice and transaction cost economics

The *public choice* school of economics seeks to *explain,* rather than *prescribe,* economic policy. In particular, the *third-best level of analysis* explains public policy as the non-cooperative outcome of competition between opposing interest groups (Becker 1983; Balisacan and Roumasset 1987; Dixit 1999). From this perspective, economic regulation may lower public welfare via regulatory capture (Stigler 1971), according to which regulated industries tend to divert the actions of regulatory authority from what may have been their original purpose. According to Olson's law of large groups (Olson 1971), a small number of industry players with high stakes are more motivated to invest in influencing the regulator than many consumers with small individual stakes.[14] Some authors contend that anticompetitive forces even shaped the original antitrust legislation in the United States (e.g., Boudreaux, DiLorenzo, and Parker 1995; Ekelund, McDonald, and Tollison 1995).

Politically motivated case selection can actually lower competition and welfare. Long, Schramm, and Tollison (1995) present evidence that preventing consumer welfare losses had little to do with the antitrust case selection in the United States. Nor does the advent of antitrust law necessarily decrease the number of mergers. Bittingmayer (1995) shows that the Sherman Act caused the Great Merger Wave in the United States, as firms substituted mergers for cartels, which, in turn, led to the Clayton Act. Moving to macroeconomic effects, Shughart and Tollison (1995) contend that antitrust enforcement had a negative effect on employment in the United States by actually raising prices and lowering output.

Can mergers improve efficiency? Even before his contributions to *transaction cost economics* (TCE), Oliver Williamson (1968) used the framework shown in Figure 18.2 to answer in the affirmative. Suppose that the merger lowers production costs from MC_1 to MC_2 through redeployment of assets, avoidance of duplication and incentive for innovation. The merger confers market power that increases the price from P_1 to P_2. Consumers lose $A_1 + A_3$ while producers gain $A_2 + A_3$ in excess profits. Since area A_3 is an offsetting loss and gain, this leaves a net gain of $A_2 - A_1$, which, as shown by Williamson (1968), is positive unless the demand elasticity is very high.[15] Kaplow (2013) argues (for the US case) that the hypothetical merger shown should be allowed because the negative distributional effects can be offset with distributional instruments such as a negative income tax.[16]

---

[14] For formalization of Olson's law in the context of agricultural protection, see Balisacan and Roumasset (1987) and Gardner (1987).
[15] Williamson (1968) characterizes his model as "naïve", however. If we were not starting with perfect competition or distortions exist in other markets, the analysis would be more complicated.
[16] See also Kaplow and Shavell (2002).

Figure 18.2. The Williamson trade-off: Should efficiency-enhancing mergers be allowed?

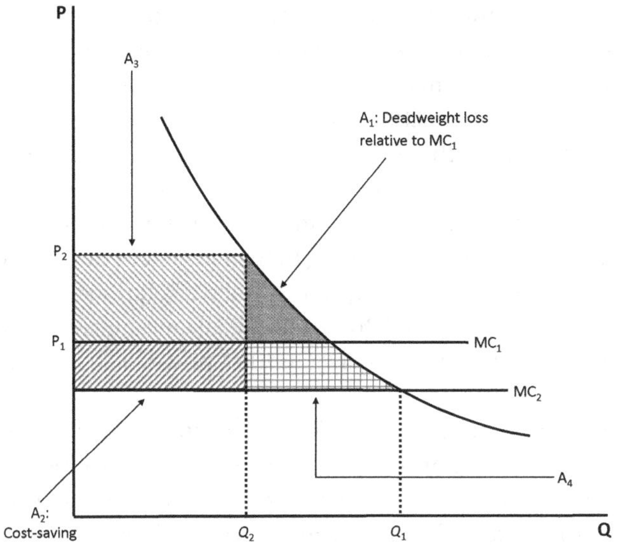

[Figure: Williamson trade-off diagram showing price P on vertical axis and quantity Q on horizontal axis. Demand curve slopes downward. Horizontal line MC_1 at price P_1 and MC_2 below it. Pre-merger equilibrium at (Q_1, P_1); post-merger price rises to P_2 with quantity Q_2. A_1: Deadweight loss relative to MC_1 (shaded triangle). A_2: Cost-saving rectangle. A_3 arrow indicating price increase. A_4 along MC_2.]

Source: Adapted from Williamson (1968)

But said transfers would be difficult to arrange, face moral hazard problems of their own and create horizontal inequity by discriminating against consumers of a particular product. The solution would also be highly inefficient, leaving a large excess burden triangle $A_1 + A_4$.[17]

Before the heyday of TCE, it was widely presumed that the purpose of vertical mergers was to restrain trade. As Coase argues in his 1937 *Nature of the Firm*, however, firms will tend to acquire a supplier when what are now called the "agency costs" of internal governance are less than

---

[17] One possibility for appropriating the potential efficiency gains without these adverse effects would be to allow a conditional merger with conditionalities (e.g., price caps) in order to limit consumer losses. Exactly how to determine and enforce the conditions can be elusive, however (Kaplow 2013). For example, a producer can decrease quality to comply with a price cap, which when set too low can potentially lower welfare by inducing shortages. For example, rice retailers in the Philippines have been known to lower rice quality in order to comply with a price cap on National Food Authority rice so they can sell at an equilibrium price (Roumasset 2000).

the contracting costs of dealing with the external firm. This efficiency rationale for vertical mergers became widely appreciated due to the *new institutional economics* (e.g., Williamson 1975, 1985, 2000), including the clarification that contracting costs include the governance costs and residual losses associated with opportunistic behaviour such as the "hold-up" problem. The efficiency rationale for vertical mergers is now widely recognized in the practice of competition policy.

These examples show that the single-minded pursuit of competition instead of consumer welfare can be counterproductive. Accordingly, modern competition policy seeks to understand the causes of mergers and other practices instead of assuming that all apparent deviations from competition are conspiracies against the public.[18] Rather than basing merger cases on market share, for example, econometric studies are sometimes done to determine whether market power will unacceptably raise prices.

Increasing competition one market at a time can also decrease economic welfare. Attracting more resources into one sector may pull resources away from a sector that is even less competitive, thereby increasing the total excess burden of monopolistic forces. To the extent that a competition authority passively responds to complaints and requests for approval, piecemeal reforms can easily miss the larger picture. This implies the need to actively review markets and find out where the distortions are greatest, including sectors with major state-owned enterprises.

Awareness of the interdependence of trade and industrial policies has stimulated a discussion on whether these policies are substitutes or complements. For example, Palim (1998) interprets Friedman and Friedman (1979) as suggesting that freer trade can be used as a substitute for competition law, and purports to have rejected that hypothesis. More generally, trade liberalization and competition policy may be complements in one situation and substitutes in another. And the fact that import competition inhibits some monopoly power does not imply that competition law is any less important. Indeed, removing some trade barriers can make domestic monopoly power even more distorting, just as lowering tariffs increases the dead-weight loss from non-tariff

---

[18] As Coase once said before TCE was understood, "if an economist finds something—a business practice of one sort or other—that he does not understand, he looks for a monopoly explanation" (Shapiro 2010 quoting Williamson quoting Coase).

barriers (Clarete and Roumasset 1990). The notion that liberalized trade policy provides adequate domestic competition would only follow if there were no non-traded goods and no impediments to domestic trade (including transportation costs, communication costs and domestic policy distortions). Such transaction costs and distortions can isolate local domestic prices from world prices. Development policy therefore requires a balancing of trade, industrial and competition policies, not a substitution of one for another.

Competition policy is best seen as an instrument for promoting economic welfare and development, not promoting competition as an end in itself. Given the complex nature of economic development and the growth needed by the transaction sector to facilitate it, competition policy needs to be seen as one part of pro-market interventionism, whereby markets are both facilitated and complemented by extra-market institutions. The competition authority should play an active role beyond responding to complaints and requests for approval, particularly by conducting market and economy-wide reviews, including reviews that prioritize sectors needing reform and of government monopolies. Competition policy should be seen as complementary to other development and trade policies, providing an integrated reform package. In general, public policies should respect the Hippocratic maxim: first do no harm.

3 EVOLUTION OF COMPETITION POLICY

Competition policy evolved from the antitrust policy in the United States, which can be traced to the Sherman Antitrust Act enacted in 1890.[19] By this time, railways had dramatically extended throughout the United States, along with the expansion of telegraph and telephone services. This revolution in transportation and communication moved domestic trade closer to a single US market, allowing firms to take advantage of economies of scale and scope. Technological advancements in other fields (e.g., metallurgy, chemicals and energy), the growth of capital markets and the development of new managerial methods also tended to increase firm size through expansion and

---

[19] See Motta (2004, chapter 1) for an extensive account of the history of competition policy.

mergers. While increased firm size brought cost advantages, it also heightened market concentration, thereby inviting anticompetitive behaviour.

The Sherman Antitrust Act addressed price-fixing, market-sharing agreements between two independent firms and monopolization practices of single firms. With mergers increasingly substituting cartels, the US Congress passed the Clayton Antitrust Act in 1914, providing for merger regulation and prohibiting price discrimination and tie-in sales (*abuses of dominance*). The Federal Trade Commission was established at the same time, sharing enforcement responsibilities with the Department of Justice and establishing consent decrees as an alternative enforcement mechanism. By the mid-1980s, the "Chicago School" critique of antitrust intervention in the 1960s and 1970s—big is not necessarily bad (e.g., Demsetz 1973; Brozen 1974; Baumol, Panzer, and Willig 1982)—had reoriented enforcement to the documentation of harm, not just industry concentration.

In Europe, competition law evolved from its practice in Germany. Originally, competition and price warfare were viewed as destabilizing, such that price-fixing agreements by cartels were allowed. By 1923, however, the proliferation of cartels and price agreements were seen as contributing to Germany's hyperinflation. This led to the introduction of Germany's Cartel Law. But lacking sharp teeth, the law had little impact, and the number of cartels continued to increase. Cartels were viewed as helping to avoid bankruptcy during the Great Depression and as promoting "national champions" during the Nazi period (Motta 2004). It was only in 1957 when Germany passed a strict competition law, establishing the Federal Cartel Office to enforce rules against price-fixing agreements and other anticompetitive behaviour (Motta 2004).

A series of pro-competitive measures was adopted by France, Germany, Holland, Belgium, Luxembourg and Italy in 1951, including the European Coal and Steel Community to guard against economic domination by Germany and to make essential inputs accessible to other countries. Buoyed by the role of competition in the US economic success, the 1951 Treaty of Paris founded competition law on the principles of market efficiency and European market integration, including non-discrimination on the basis of national product origin/destination (Motta 2004).

The United Kingdom introduced the Profiteering Act of 1919, also motivated by inflation. After World War II, unemployment concerns led to the Monopolies and Restrictive Practices (Inquiry and Control) Act of 1948; however, specific objectives and enforcement tools remained vague. In 1998, the passage of the Competition Act aligned the competition law of the United Kingdom with that of the European Union.

Overall, the European system places somewhat more emphasis on consumer and worker welfare, whereas the US system is commonly viewed as focusing more on economic efficiency, including producer welfare. The European system is also oriented to limiting economic power from spilling over into the political system.

Around the world, the number of countries adopting and enforcing competition law has rapidly increased, with the country's development stage influencing the maturity and modernity of its competition policy. The widespread adoption of competition policy after 1990 was part of the global movement towards greater economic and political liberalization (Palim 1998). It can be partly attributed also to the rise of trade liberalization, as indicated, for example, by the advent of the World Trade Organization (WTO).

In addition to the relationship between competition policy adoption, trade liberalization and development stage, pressure from multilateral organizations may also help explain the rapid adoption of competition law after 1990. For instance, member countries of the Association of Southeast Asian Nations (ASEAN) are required to adopt competition law, regardless of their level of development.

4 COMPETITION POLICY AND ECONOMIC DEVELOPMENT: SOME EMPIRICS

4.1 Role of competition policy in development: Previous results

There is substantial empirical literature on the development effects of competition and competition policies. Ma (2011) shows a positive relationship between effective enforcement of competition law (proxied by "government effectiveness") and productivity growth, although the relationship is insignificant for developing countries. Voigt (2009) finds that the independence of a competition agency is decisive. De facto independence is most significant, explaining the variation in total factor productivity.

Petersen (2013) finds that the introduction of antitrust law has a positive effect on the level of gross domestic product (GDP) per capita and economic growth after ten years. Romero et al. (2016) show also a significant and positive correlation between competition law and per capita GDP worldwide, but not for the subgroup of Latin American countries. Dalkir (2015) finds that effectiveness varies significantly across countries according to level of development, experience (years) with competition law and EU status, even after controlling for budget allocation. Gutmann and Voigt (2014) show that the presence of competition law and the duration of its operation help explain growth, foreign direct investment (FDI) and productivity growth. Clougherty (2010), using data from 32 antitrust bodies, finds that a nation's budgetary commitment to competition policy plays a significantly positive role in economic growth.

Overall, these studies suggest that competition and competition policies affect economic development, albeit by varying degrees. Some of the differences may be due to premature adoption, especially in developing countries. Variations across studies may be due to differences in variables and estimation methods. A particular challenge is dealing with reverse causation (endogeneity). On the one hand, the level of a country's per capita income plays a role in adoption and the nature of competition policy. On the other hand, the general purpose of competition policy is to increase productivity and economic growth.

Notably, Borrell and Tolosa (2008) and Buccirossi et al. (2013) are studies that controlled for endogeneity issues. Using cross-country data for 52 countries in 2003, Borrell and Tolosa (2008) find a positive and statistically significant impact of antitrust enforcement on total factor productivity. The measure of effectiveness comes from the World Economic Report survey on anti-monopoly policies, which ranks countries according to policy effectiveness. Borrell and Tolosa's study treats anti-monopoly policies and openness to international trade as policy variables affecting productivity. Thus, there is simultaneity bias because the policy variables are endogenous. To address this issue, they estimated the productivity and policy equations jointly using three-stage least squares (3SLS), which requires a set of instruments. In this case, the instruments are institutional factors that determine the policy variables but are not significantly correlated with productivity.

These include latitude, regional dummies, percentage of English speakers, and dummy variables for federalism, colonial origins and corruption. The study finds that treating antitrust policy as exogenous overestimates the impact of competition on productivity by as much as 18 per cent and underestimates the impact of trade openness on productivity by 37 per cent.

Buccirossi et al. (2013), using cross-country panel data for 22 industries in 12 OECD countries from 1995 to 2007, created Competition Policy Indices based on measures of antitrust infringement, merger control processes, institutional features and enforcement features of each jurisdiction. To address endogeneity issues, their study used several instruments related to governmental stance towards competition and regulation. These include government's pro-regulation attitude, its limitations of the welfare state, the need for economic planning, and the extent of pro-EU attitude of government. After controlling for endogeneity issues, Buccirossi et al. (2013) find that their aggregate and individual indices of competition policy have positive and significant effects on total factor productivity growth. Institutions and antitrust law have the strongest and most significant impacts, compared with enforcement effort and merger control effects.

As Waked (2008) notes, many studies may overestimate the effect of competition policy on measures of economic performance by attributing to competition policy what may have resulted from economic liberalization and other reforms. Recall that before 1990, competition policy adoption was correlated with per capita income, but the contributions of different causal pathways were difficult to determine. Controlling for other contributing factors and confronting the endogeneity problem tend to reduce the estimated impact of competition policy on economic performance.

4.2. Effect of competition policy on growth: New estimates

In what follows, we contribute to the discussion in the literature by comparing the economic growth of countries that adopted competition law with those that did not. We constructed cross-country data from 1975 to 2015 to investigate the effect of competition law adoption on economic growth. In the spirit of Barro's (2003) growth regressions, we focus on decadal average growth rates of countries for the periods 1975–84, 1985–94 and 1995–2015, each period roughly corresponding to a particular regime. The first period, 1975–84, is characterized by the post-World War II wave of competition law (Edwards 1974 as cited by Palim 1998). The second period, 1985–94, was the decade leading to the creation of the WTO in 1995. The fall of the Berlin Wall in 1989 also paved the way for the proliferation of more liberal market policies in formerly centrally planned economies (Palim 1998). The third period, 1995–2015, experienced two major shocks, the 1997 Asian financial crisis and the 2008–9 global economic crisis. We collated information on countries with competition law from Palim (1998), Voigt (2009), Armoogum (2016) and recent country reports.

Table 18.1 gives the number of countries with and without competition policies at the start of each decade under consideration. Our sample is composed of 205 countries, 89 of them adopting competition law by 1995. An examination of the average economic growth of countries using a simple t-test (done prior to conducting a formal analysis) reveals that the mean average growth rate of adopting countries is higher at 2.62 than that of non-adopting countries, and that the difference is significant using a two-tailed test (Table 18.2). Economic growth is captured by the decadal average growth rate of GDP per capita.

Table 18.1. Number of countries that adopted competition law in our data

Period	Adopted		Not adopted	
	Number	Percentage	Number	Percentage
1975–84	14	7%	191	93%
1985–94	69	34%	136	66%
1995–2015	89	43%	116	57%

Note: Total number of countries = 205
Sources of basic data: Palim (1998); Voigt (2009); Armoogum (2016).

Table 18.2. Average growth rates of GDP per capita (1975–2015)

Group	Obs	Mean	Std. Err.	SD	[95% Conf. Interval]	
Not adopt: 0	395	1.52	0.22	4.34	1.09	1.95
Adopt: 1	170	2.62	0.15	1.94	2.33	2.91
diff		−1.10	0.26	0.00	−1.62	−0.58

Note: (1) Diff = mean (0) − mean (1); $t = -4.15$
(2) Two-tailed test: Pr $(T > t) = 0.0000$
(3) Satterthwaite's degrees of freedom = 562.29

We estimate a Barro and Sala-i-Martin (2004) economic growth model to investigate the impact of competition law adoption on a country's long-term economic growth. Our dependent variable is decadal average growth rates of GDP per capita for the periods 1975–84, 1985–94 and 1995–2015. A simple approach in examining the difference in economic growth between adopters and non-adopters of competition law is to include a dummy variable equal to 1 for adopting countries, and then apply panel fixed effects (i.e., representing country characteristics as constant within each decade). This approach would give a biased estimate, however.

In estimating the impact of competition law adoption on economic growth, we recognize that adoption is endogenous (reverse causality). That is, countries may choose to adopt—or not adopt—competition law, depending on their circumstances such as level of economic development, institutions and geography. This suggests a potential self-selection problem in our data, specifically since some determinants of adoption may also contribute to economic growth. The idea is illustrated in Figure 18.3, with the log of GDP per capita in the y-axis and time on the x-axis.

Figure 18.3. Income growth and adoption of competition law

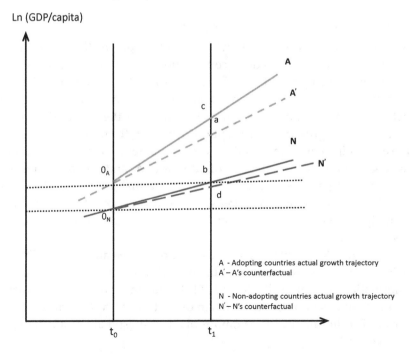

Thus, the slope of the line gives the growth trajectory of the two groups of countries, adopters (A) and non-adopters (N). The solid lines represent the observed or actual growth trajectories, and the dashed lines are counterfactuals. Before the time of adoption, A and N are on different growth paths. Adopting countries adopted because doing so increases growth. However, had non-adopting countries adopted, it would have decreased growth. To address this issue of self-selection based endogeneity problem, we employ an endogenous switching regression (Lee and Trost 1978), allowing for the interdependence of economic growth and adoption of competition law.

We test the hypothesis that competition law increases growth rates in adopting countries. The following model consists of the switching equation determining adoption and two growth equations for adopting and non-adopting regimes (Maddala 1983, 223–24; Di Falco, Veronesi, and Yesuf 2011).

Switching equation:

$$I_i^* = \gamma Z_i + \eta_i \text{ with } I_i = \begin{cases} 1 \text{ if } I_i^* > 0 \\ 0 \text{ otherwise} \end{cases} \quad (1)$$

Regime equations for economic growth:

Adopting $\quad y_{Ai} = \beta_0 + Y_{At0} + \beta_A X_{Ai} + \varepsilon_{Ai} \quad (2)$

Non-adopting $\quad y_{Ni} = \beta_0 + Y_{Nt0} + \beta_N X_{Ni} + \varepsilon_{Ni} \quad (3)$

where I_i^* is a latent variable (inferred, not observed) that determines a country's decision to adopt competition law, and Z_i is a vector of factors influencing adoption. We cannot estimate equation (1) directly because I_i^* is not directly observed. The hypothesized relationship between I_i^* and I_i is that I_i is equal to 1 whenever the expected benefits (i.e., economic growth) with adoption is positive, 0 otherwise. This gives the estimating equation, $I_i = \delta Z_i + \mu_i$. The variables y_{Ai} and y_{Ni} are decadal average economic growth rates of adopting (A) and non-adopting (N) countries, respectively. Y_{At0} and Y_{Nt0} are the initial per capita GDP. X_i is a vector of explanatory variables that influence long-term economic growth. The vector of parameters is $\beta_0, \beta_A, \beta_N$ and γ. The error terms are $\varepsilon_A, \varepsilon_N$ and η.

We estimate a switching regression model (Lee and Trost 1978) by using the logarithmic likelihood function. β and γ are estimated via full information maximum likelihood (FIML) to simultaneously fit binary and continuous parts of the model in order to yield consistent standard errors. The simultaneous maximum likelihood estimation of equations

(1) to (3) corrects for selection bias in the estimates of regime equations for economic growth. This approach relies on joint normality of the error terms in the binary and continuous equations (Lokshin and Sajaia 2004). The model is appropriate when adoption (akin to treatment) would affect coefficient estimates by rotating the regression line (Clougherty, Duso, and Muck 2016).

Following Barro and Sala-i-Martin's (2004) empirics, our vector of explanatory variables, X_i, is categorized into two groups, initial-condition variables and time-varying variables. The initial-condition variables reflect the values of variables at the beginning of the period (i.e., at t_0). The time-varying variables are differences between values at the ending and beginning years of a decade. Tables 18.3 and 18.4 provide our summary statistics and data sources for all countries and for the two groups of countries, respectively. Initial-condition variables include per capita GDP level (in logs) at the beginning of the period. The coefficient of this variable is the rate of convergence from the neoclassical model and convergence theory of Barro and Sala-i-Martin (2004, chapters 1 and 2), which states that long-term growth of real per capita GDP is inversely related to the initial level of per capita GDP. The other initial conditions include the stock of human capital (represented by health capital), fertility rates (in logs) and the total average years of education completed among people over age 15. Health capital is proxied by the log of the reciprocal of life expectancy at age one (roughly the average probability of dying) (Barro 2003). Fertility affects population growth. In turn, population growth negatively affects the steady-state ratio of capital to effective workers. Moreover, in the neoclassical growth model, higher fertility rates negatively affect economic growth.

The time-varying variables include the change in economic freedom and its square (*EF_ch and EF_ch_sq*), government effectiveness (*GEE_ch*), government expenditure (% of GDP, *GovExp_ch*), inflation (*Inflation_ch*), political freedom (*PF_ch*), regulatory quality (*RQE_ch*) and trade openness (trade as a % of GDP, *TradeOpen_ch*). The degree of economic freedom is a composite index capturing the size of government, the legal system and property rights, sound money, freedom to trade internationally and regulation (Fraser Institute 2016). Political freedom serves as a proxy for good governance, taken as the average of political rights and civil liberty indices (Freedom House 2016). Regulatory quality captures perceptions of the ability of government to formulate and implement sound policies and regulations that permit and promote private-sector development (Worldwide Governance Indicator 2020).

Table 18.3. *Summary statistics for all countries*

Description	Source	Variable name	All countries		
			Obs	Mean	Std. Dev.
Ave. growth of GDP per capita	WDI, World Bank (2020)	*GrGDPcap*	568	1.85	3.80
Initial-condition variables					
Log of GDP per capita	WDI, World Bank (2020)	*Lgdpcap*	521	8.33	1.53
Log of 1/(life expectancy)	WDI, World Bank (2020)	*LOneLife*	567	-4.18	0.16
Log of fertility rates at birth	WDI, World Bank (2020)	*Lfertility*	567	1.14	0.55
Total years of schooling	WDI, World Bank (2020)	*Schl15Tot*	429	6.93	2.89
Time-varying variables					
Economic freedom	Fraser Institute (2016)	*EF_ch*	477	3.25	6.78
Economic freedom square	Fraser Institute (2016)	*EF_ch_sq*	477	56.43	117.74
Gov. effectiveness	Worldwide Governance Indicator (2020)	*GEE_ch*	609	0.00	0.29
Gov. expenditure (% of GDP)	WDI, World Bank (2020)	*GovExp_ch*	543	-0.01	4.82
Inflation	WDI, World Bank (2020)	*Inflation_ch*	540	-37.06	562.82
Political freedom	Freedom House (2016)	*PF_ch*	585	0.19	1.09
Regulatory quality	Worldwide Governance Indicator (2020)	*RQE_ch*	609	0.00	0.31
Trade as % of GDP	WDI, World Bank (2020)	*TradeOpen_ch*	570	3.24	31.94

Table 18.3 *(continued)*

Table 18.3 (continued)

Description	Source	Variable name	All countries		
			Obs	Mean	Std. Dev.
Effectiveness of anti-monopoly policies	World Economic Forum (2020)	Antitrust_ch	285	−0.07	0.34
Regional and multinational pressure	Authors' calculation	RegMPr_ch	618	26.10	22.17
Adoption of competition law (CL)	Palim (1998), Voigt (2009), Armoogum (2016)	Adoption	615	0.28	0.45

Note: (1) Scores of economic freedom are 1 to 10, low to high.
(2) Gov. effectiveness index ranges from −2.5 to 2.5, low to high.
(3) Political freedom is measured on a 1–7 scale, low to high (we reversed the scale from the original source for comparability with other indices and easier interpretation).
(4) Regulatory quality index ranges from −2.5 to 2.5, low to high.
(5) Effectiveness of anti-monopoly policies at ensuring fair competition ranges from 1 (not effective) to 7 (extremely effective).

Table 18.4. Summary statistics for adopting vs non-adopting countries

Description	Variable name	Countries that adopted CL				Countries that did not adopt CL			
		Obs	Mean	Min	Max	Obs	Mean	Min	Max
Ave. growth of GDP per capita	GrGDPcap	170	2.62	-1.71	9.69	395	1.52	-37.00	37.99
Initial-condition variables									
Log of GDP per capita	Lgdpcap	170	9.04	5.91	11.53	348	7.96	5.13	11.88
Log of 1/(life expectancy)	LOneLife	170	-4.26	-4.41	-3.77	394	-4.14	-4.40	-3.44
Log of fertility rates at birth	Lfertility	170	0.76	0.07	1.92	394	1.31	-0.13	2.18
Total years of schooling	Schl15Tot	160	8.74	1.57	12.86	266	5.81	0.61	11.71
Time-varying variables									
Economic freedom	EF_ch	168	3.70	-18.08	26.80	306	3.02	-25.90	27.70
Economic freedom square	EF_ch_sq	168	62.90	0.00	718.08	306	53.39	0.00	767.29
Gov. effectiveness	GEE_ch	171	0.06	-0.99	0.84	435	-0.02	-1.28	1.28
Gov. expenditure (% of GDP)	GovExp_ch	169	0.18	-15.81	10.11	371	-0.09	-28.24	29.42
Inflation	Inflation_ch	163	-14.55	-691.24	94.66	374	-47.17	-11,741.77	1,849.90
Political freedom	PF_ch	172	0.13	-2.50	3.50	410	0.21	-3.00	5.50
Regulatory quality	RQE_ch	171	0.04	-1.23	1.52	435	-0.02	-1.30	1.22
Trade as % of GDP	TradeOpen_ch	169	5.24	-90.96	110.59	398	2.34	-345.26	220.19
Effectiveness of anti-monopoly policies	Antitrust_ch	165	-0.12	-1.80	1.16	117	0.01	-0.34	0.59
Regional and multinational pressure	RegMPr_ch	172	44.98	2.08	70.69	443	18.63	0.00	70.69

Government effectiveness captures perceptions of the quality of public services, the quality of the civil service and the degree of its independence from political pressures, the quality of policy formulation and implementation, and the credibility of the government's commitment to such policies (Worldwide Governance Indicator 2020). We recognize that these economy-wide measures of governance effectiveness mask considerable heterogeneity in governance quality within a country.

Given that competition law adoption does not necessarily mean that implementation of the law across countries would be the same, we include the variable *Antitrust_ch* in the growth equation. This variable captures the change in the effectiveness of anti-monopoly policies at ensuring fair competition. Data were obtained from the Global Competitiveness Report of the World Economic Forum, which presents the results of a survey among executives on their perception of the business environment in their country.

Our variables for the selection equation of adopting or not adopting competition law include the initial level of per capita GDP (in logs) at the beginning of the period, economic freedom, political freedom, regulatory quality, government effectiveness and trade openness. We include the variable regional and multinational pressure (*RegMPr_ch*), which serves as a proxy for peer pressure from multilateral organizations and from neighbouring countries. The variable *RegMPr_ch* is the proportion of countries in the World Bank's regional grouping with competition policies in a given year. The inclusion of this variable follows from the discussion in section 4.1.

4.3. Discussion of results

Table 18.5 presents our estimates using panel fixed effects and an endogenous switching regression model estimated by FIML. Our dependent variable is the decadal average growth rates of GDP per capita for the periods 1975–84, 1985–94 and 1995–2015. *Adoption* is equal to 1 if the country adopted competition law before or at the starting year of the three decadal period, 0 otherwise. We first apply the simple approach, the panel fixed effects. The estimated parameter for *Adoption* is positive as expected and significant at the 5 per cent level (column 1). This result can be interpreted as adoption increases decadal average growth rates of GDP per capita by 0.67 relative to countries that did not, holding other things constant.

Table 18.5. Parameter estimates of adoption of competition law and growth equations

Description	Variable	(1) Panel FE	(2) Adoption (1/0)	(3) Adoption = 0 Gr. GDP/cap	(4) Adoption = 1 Gr. GPD/cap
Initial-condition variables					
Log of GDP per capita	Lgdpcap	-4.461***	0.258***	-1.396***	-0.864***
		(0.749)	(0.086)	(0.186)	(0.153)
Log of 1/(life expectancy)	LOneLife	-1.235		0.209	-2.280
		(2.688)		(2.745)	(1.564)
Log of fertility rates at birth	Lfertility	-4.143***		-4.914***	-1.801***
		(0.764)		(0.617)	(0.477)
Total years of schooling	Schl15Tot	0.263		-0.019	0.090
		(0.181)		(0.126)	(0.079)
Time-varying variables					
Economic freedom	EF_ch	0.070**	0.027	0.067**	-0.006
		(0.028)	(0.018)	(0.028)	(0.031)
Economic freedom square	EF_ch_sq	-0.003**		-0.004***	0.003
		(0.001)		(0.001)	(0.002)
Gov. effectiveness	GEE_ch	0.304	-0.196	1.713	0.328
		(0.386)	(0.562)	(1.049)	(0.499)

Table 18.5 *(continued)*

Table 18.5 (continued)

Description	Variable	(1) Panel FE	(2) Adoption (1/0)	(3) Adoption = 0 Gr. GDP/cap	(4) Adoption =1 Gr. GPD/cap
Gov. expenditure (% of GDP)	GovExp_ch	-0.000		-0.084	-0.081*
		(0.024)		(0.056)	(0.043)
Inflation	Inflation_ch	0.000*		0.000	0.011***
		(0.000)		(0.001)	(0.004)
Political freedom	PF_ch	-0.115	0.068	-0.532***	0.073
		(0.073)	(0.100)	(0.144)	(0.129)
Regulatory quality	RQE_ch	1.018***	-0.056	0.147	1.091**
		(0.374)	(0.526)	(0.855)	(0.481)
Trade as % of GDP	TradeOpen_ch	-0.009	-0.006	0.016**	0.002
		(0.005)	(0.005)	(0.008)	(0.005)
Adoption of CL	Adoption	0.666**			
		(0.322)			
Effectiveness of anti-monopoly policies	Antitrust_ch			0.370	1.069***
				(1.437)	(0.319)
Regional and multinational pressure	RegMPr_ch		0.081***		
			(0.012)		
Constant	Constant	36.563***	-3.709***	19.773*	1.173
		(11.972)	(0.836)	(11.447)	(6.396)

Table 18.5 (continued)

Table 18.5 (continued)

Description	Variable	(1) Panel FE	(2) Adoption (1/0)	(3) Adoption = 0 Gr. GDP/cap	(4) Adoption = 1 Gr. GPD/cap
Observations		353	241	241	241
Number of countries		126			
R^2		0.499			
Ins				0.439***	0.297***
				(0.092)	(0.060)
r				−0.842***	0.278
				(0.325)	(0.264)

LR test of independence equations: $chi^2(2) = 8.65$ | Prob > $chi^2 = 0.0132$

Note: (1) Dependent variable is decadal average growth of GDP per capita, 1985–94, 1995–2004, 2005–15.
(2) Robust se in parentheses.
(3) *** $p < 0.01$, ** $p < 0.05$, * $p < 0.1$

However, since this approach assumes that adoption of competition law is exogenously determined, the estimates may be biased and inconsistent. The approach is limited inasmuch as differences in growth rates of country groups are not accounted for.

We estimate an endogenous switching regression specification using Stata's "*movestay*" command (Lokshin and Sajaia 2004, 2008) to estimate the parameters of the model. Column (2) presents the estimated coefficients of switching equation (3) (i.e., choosing either to adopt or not adopt competition law). The switching equation results show that the variables log of GDP per capita and regional and multinational pressure are positive and significant at 1 per cent level. These results are consistent with the findings of Ravago, Roumasset, and Balisacan (2021) that there are other factors influencing adoption, in addition to level of development. These also support the observation that pressure from multilateral organizations and neighbouring countries and the condition of having a competition policy imposed on being a member of regional agreements are important determinants of adoption.

The *Rho* values are the correlation coefficients between the error term (η_i) in the selection equation and the error terms (ε_{Ai} and ε_{Ni}) in the growth equations (1) and (2). These are reported using the transformation of the correlation (r). *Rho* accounts for the endogenous switching in the growth equations. Only the r for the non-adopters is significant and negative. Thus, the hypothesis of absence of sample selectivity bias may be rejected among the non-adopters. Moreover, the switching regression is more appropriate than the panel fixed effects regression. The likelihood ratio test of independence of the selection and outcome equations indicates that we can reject the null hypothesis of no correlation between adoption and the growth equation.

We now turn to effect of adoption on long-term growth. The coefficient estimates in Table 18.5 columns (3) and (4) pertain to the growth equations for non-adopters and adopters, respectively. The estimates of the log of real per capita GDP are −1.396 for non-adopters and −0.864 for adopters. These results are consistent with conditional convergence reported in many studies (Barro 2003 1991; Mankiw, Romer, and Weil 1992). The estimated coefficients of the log of fertility rates are also negative and significant as expected.

Among the time-varying variables, change in economic freedom and its square are positive and negative, respectively; both are significant in the growth equation for non-adopters but not for adopters. These results imply that increases in economic freedom stimulate growth, but the positive influence diminishes as economic freedom increases. This also explains why economic freedom is insignificant in the growth equation of adopters. The change in the political freedom variable is negative and significant, and the change in the trade openness variable is positive and significant for the growth equation for non-adopters. On the other hand, the change in government expenditure variable is negative and significant, and the change in inflation and change in regulatory quality variables are positive and significant in the growth equation for adopting countries.

While economic development influences the adoption of competition law, once adopted and enforced, competition law may affect the trajectory of economic development (Borrell and Tolosa 2008; Voigt 2009; Clougherty 2010; Ma 2011; Petersen 2013; Buccirossi et al. 2013). We include the variable *Antitrust_ch* in the growth equation to capture the effectiveness of anti-monopoly policies in ensuring fair competition after considering endogeneity in the decision whether or not to adopt competition policy. The estimated coefficient of this variable (1.07) is significant for adopting countries, as expected, but not for non-adopting countries.

We now compare the income growth of adopting and non-adopting countries by examining the conditional expectation, treatment effects and heterogeneity effects (see Di Falco et al. 2011 for econometric specification). Table 18.6 reports the corresponding predicted values. The expected average growth rates of GDP per capita of the adopting countries and non-adopting countries are 2.45 and 2.33, respectively.

Table 18.6. *Conditional expectation, treatment and heterogeneity (average decadal growth of GDP per capita as dependent varible)*

Subsample	Decision stage		Treatment effects	
	Adopt	Not adopt		
Adopt	[a] 2.45	[c] 2.32	TT	0.14
Not adopt	[d] 1.92	[b] 2.33	TU	−0.42
Heterogeneity effects	BH_A 0.54	BH_N −0.02	TH	0.55

Note: (1) [a] and [b] represent the observed expected value of average growth of GDP per capita. [c] and [d] represent the counterfactual expected value.
(2) Being observed to adopt CL is like being treated, with adoption as the treatment. TT is the treatment effect on the treated. TU is treatment effect on the untreated.
(3) The heterogeneity effect is the effect of base heterogeneity for countries that adopted and those that did not. TH = TT-TU is the transitional heterogeneity.

By comparing the actual growth of adopting countries with counterfactual growth without adoption (cells [a] vs. [c]), we see that adoption increased growth in those countries by 0.14. On the other hand, comparing the actual growth of non-adopting countries with the counterfactual of adoption (cells [b] vs. [d]) shows that estimated growth would have been lower by 0.42 had they chosen to adopt. These results suggest that pressuring countries to adopt competition law may be counterproductive. First of all, a country may have little interest in enforcing the law, as seems to be the case in Bhutan (UNCTAD 2015). Second, to the extent that enforcement attempts are made, they may do more harm than good.

The last row of Table 18.6 adjusts for potential heterogeneity in the sample—that is, accounting for differences in the characteristics of countries in the sample. Adopting countries have higher growth than countries in the counterfactual case (c), even when accounting for heterogeneity and vice versa. If the two groups include countries with diverse characteristics, the effect of the treatment is different among the countries that differ between the two groups. This implies that other factors are at play, hence the growth of adopting countries are higher than the non-adopting countries.

The *endogenous switching regression model* employed addresses self-selection and dual causation relating to competition law adoption and levels of development. Nonetheless, scholars still face the enormous challenge of judging the consequences of competition policy for development due to the difficulty of measuring the effectiveness of implementation and the many confounding variables that influence development. Our efforts will hopefully motivate further studies for creation of measures that capture the effectiveness of competition laws and policy.

5 DESIGN AND ORGANIZATION OF COMPETITION AUTHORITIES IN ASIA

5.1 The long road to competition in Asia

The first instance of competition law in Asia occurred in the Philippines in 1925 as part of its legal framework under US occupation (Lin 2005). Japan formally introduced competition policy legislation with the Anti-monopoly Law of 1947. South Korea and New Zealand enacted competition laws in the 1980s, and Thailand and Indonesia in the 1990s (Figure 18.4). More countries in Asia and the Pacific followed suit in the current millennium. The latest additions include the Philippines, Brunei Darussalam, Lao PDR and Myanmar. As of 2020, twenty countries in Asia and the Pacific, including Australia and New Zealand, have competition laws in place. Cambodia and Afghanistan have drafted theirs. Bhutan adopted a competition policy instead of a competition law after considering its enforcement capacity (UNCTAD 2015; Royal Government of Bhutan 2020). Spearheaded by the Ministry of Economic Affairs, Bhutan's national competition policy provides a framework for ensuring coherence in public policy—promoting efficiency, competitiveness and consumer welfare. The Office of Consumer Protection is responsible for its implementation (Royal Government of Bhutan 2020).

While competition law and policies have evolved rapidly in Asia as reflected by actions of competition authorities and court decisions (Zhang 2015), tension exists between pro-growth industrial policies and consumer-oriented competition policies. Like in the United States and Europe, the evolution of competition policies in Asia have been intertwined with economic and political history. While competition policies in the Asian region had been largely borrowed from the United States and Europe, Asian nations have their unique government systems, legal systems, business practices, institutions and culture. We review below the experience of South Korea, Thailand and the Philippines. These countries were chosen to illustrate the spectrum of influence and force of competition laws in Asia.

South Korea has long been considered a model of economic cooperation because of the strong relationship between government policy and the family-owned industrial conglomerates or chaebols, such as Samsung, Hyundai, LG Electronics and SK Holdings (Roumasset and Barr 1992; World Bank 1993).[20] Following the assassination of President Park Chung-hee in 1979, the new ruling elite enacted a competition law as part of sweeping economic and social reforms and in recognition of the particular need to correct and complement industrial policies for development (Lee 2015). The law was put in place in 1980 (when per capita income was only US$1,598), followed by the creation of the Korean Fair Trade Commission (KFTC) in 1981.

---

[20] Heavy and chemical industries (HCI) were also supported, although their growth performance has been relatively sluggish.

Figure 18.4. Timeline of enactment of competition law in Asia

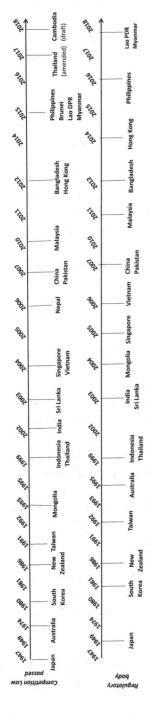

Note: Southeast Asia = 9 countries with competition law, 1 with draft (Cambodia), 1 no competition law (Timor Leste)
East Asia = 5 countries + HK with competition law, 1 no competition law (North Korea)
South Asia = 5 countries with competition law, 1 draft (Afghanistan), 1 competition policy (Bhutan), 1 no competition law (Maldives)

However, it had limited success during most of the 1980s when industrial policy continued to favour selected industries, retarding new entry and suppressing the exit of incumbents. From 1987 to 1997, the competition law was refined and, with its additional enforcement mechanisms, is now regarded as one of the strongest in Asia. The KFTC has had notable success in building technical capacity, adapting procedures for timely enforcement, winning the trust of the public through competition advocacy, and securing its independence (Chang and Jung 2005). It has secured a number of convictions, notably of Choi Soon-Sil in 2017 for corruption during the Park administration.

Until recently, Thailand has been at the other end of the spectrum. Its Trade Competition Act BE 2542 was legislated upon the initiative of the Ministry of Commerce in 1999 after the 1997 "People's Constitution" took effect, calling for "free and fair competition". Thailand's Trade Competition Commission (TCC) was responsible for implementing the law. Despite the relatively high industry concentration[21] and receiving more than 100 complaints, the TCC had failed to punish a single violator (Thanitcul 2015; Nikomborirak 2005, 2006). The failure stemmed largely from the TCC's lack of independence; its chair, a politician, is also the Minister of Commerce. This lack of independence removes a potential check on rent-seeking, whereby political support is exchanged for the promotion of special interests (Lowi 1969; Olson and Zeckhasuer 1966).

The Philippines has only recently enacted its competition law after four decades of attempts. The Philippine Competition Act (PCA) of 2015 also created the Philippine Competition Commission (PCC), an independent quasi-judicial body mandated to promote and maintain market competition by regulating anticompetitive conduct. The PCC is seen as a model for young competition agencies (Global Competition Review 2018), and hopes are high for it to become one of the strongest in the region. The PCA provided a transitory period of two years (2016–18) to allow businesses and industries to make voluntary adjustments and reforms in the way they conduct business. The law took full effect in August 2018.

The two-year transitory period was not entirely smooth sailing for the PCC as businesses raced to consummate transactions prior to the release of the PCA's implementing rules and regulations (IRR). The PCC got its baptism by fire in the case involving the potential duopoly control of the

---

[21] The soap, detergent, vegetable oil and instant noodle industries have about 8–15 firms, while the cement, beer, soda, mirrors and glass industries have about 2–6 firms each (Thanitcul 2015).

telecommunications industry. The two leading telecom companies in the country have argued that their acquisition and sharing of a broadband spectrum from a third company is consistent with a "deemed approved" provision of the transitory merger rule, which was in place before the PCA's IRR took effect in June 2016. The case was still pending resolution by the Supreme Court as of September 2021.

The timeline for South Korea, Thailand, the Philippines and other Asian countries generally conforms to Palim's (1998) finding that competition policy adoption is correlated with per capita income and economic reforms. Trade liberalization and competition policies in OECD countries were greatly stimulated by the pro-market revolution in economics during the 1980s that co-evolved with the Reagan-Thatcher administrations. Lower income countries adopted competition policies later, especially in the 1990s and the new millennium.

The formation of a competition authority is a crucial step in the implementation of competition law. The bottom panel of Figure 18.4 shows the timeline when competition authorities in Asia were formed after countries adopted competition laws. Mongolia, which passed the law in 1993, formed its commission in 2004 only. The Competition Commission Act of India was enacted in 2002 but the Competition Commission of India[22] became fully operational only in 2009 (Zhang 2015). The Myanmar Competition Commission and the Lao PDR Business Competition Commission were both established in 2018.

Competition authorities in Asia are evolving rapidly due to the rise of Asia in global markets. Their organizational structures vary according to the countries' historical and economic situations. We return to South Korea, Thailand and the Philippines to capture the characteristics of the authorities at various stages of maturity.

5.2. South Korea

The Monopoly Regulation and Fair Trade Act (MRFTA) of 1980 prevents abuse of dominance and unfair practices of cartels, including price, product and quota fixing, resale price maintenance, refusal to sell and discriminatory pricing. The law also stipulates

---

[22] India is in the curious position of having had a competition law for many years, but one that has been widely held to be inadequate in both its rules and implementation.

prior consultation with the trade enforcement agency when enacting competition-restricting regulation.

Established under the Economic Planning Board in 1981 as a ministerial-level agency under the office of the Prime Minister, the KFTC functions as an independent, quasi-judiciary body for the enforcement of competition policies. The KFTC does not directly participate in trade policy, but can be involved in trade-related regulatory reforms. Organizationally, it consists of a committee and a secretariat, which function as the decision-making body and a working body, respectively. The chairperson and the vice chairperson are recommended by the Prime Minister and appointed by the President. The other seven commissioners are recommended by the chairperson and appointed by the President. The KFTC deliberates and decides on competition and consumer protection issues. Its secretariat drafts and promotes competition policies, investigates antitrust issues, presents cases before the committee, and carries out the committee's decisions.

While the KFTC was created by the MRFTA, it also enforces 11 additional laws, including the Fair Subcontract Transactions Act of 1984. Since its inception, the KFTC has grown, and its law enforcement has evolved with the economic environment and demand for competition enforcement (Hur 2006). The specific economic and business environment in Korea has led to some differences in enforcement operations in an advanced jurisdiction. The KFTC pursues its competition advocacy by influencing government's decisions and regulations, with the goal of building a more competitive market structure and fostering competitive conduct in the business sector in accordance with agreements with other regulatory agencies.

Hur (2006) identifies two main reasons for the strength and successes being enjoyed by the KFTC today. First, the KFTC faithfully and strongly enforces the MRFTA in the traditional antitrust areas of mergers, cartels and other unfair trade practices. Second, its consumer advocacy has enhanced its reputation with the general public and with other parts of the government.

5.3. Thailand

Thailand initially created a competition law and the TCC in 1999, which prohibited unlawful market dominance, mergers that allow unfair competition, collusion to restrict competition, and other unfair trade practices. The TCC was charged with promoting competition, but its power and duties were limited to creating and overseeing a subcommittee that investigated violations. The TCC's composition included senior executives from the Ministries of Commerce and Finance and the Department of Internal Trade. Its secretariat was a bureau established within the Department of Internal Trade, Ministry of Commerce. It was responsible for studying, analysing, examining and verifying facts before passing them on to the TCC. Due to its lack of independence from the Ministry of Commerce, the TCC had been unable to exact even a single penalty for any alleged violation (Thanitcul 2015; Nikomborirak 2005, 2006).

A widespread recognition of the TCC's ineffectiveness led to Thailand's passing of a new Trade Competition Act (TCA) in 2017. The new TCA created a new TCC, consisting of a chairperson, a vice chairperson and five other commissioners. The extensive vetting and selection process make the new TCC less immune to regulatory capture. The new TCA established a new Office of the Trade Competition Commission (OTCC), which is independent from the other parts of the government's executive branch. These two changes have given the new competition authority independence—a crucial element for the effective enforcement of competition law. For a detailed discussion of the structure, conduct and scope of competition policy in Thailand, see Ravago, Roumasset, and Balisacan (2021).

5.4. Philippines

The Philippine Competition Act (PCA) of 2015 is "enforceable against any person or entity engaged in any trade, industry, or commerce", including international trade that has direct, substantial and reasonably foreseeable effects on Philippine markets. It prohibits two forms of anticompetitive agreements: *per se* violations and those subject to the "rule of reason". *Per se* prohibited are price fixing and bid rigging involving competitors in the market. All other agreements involving competitors, as well as between and among entities in the supply chain, are subject to the rule of reason— that is, the balance of evidence showing that these prevent, restrict or lessen competition. The PCA also prohibits anticompetitive mergers and acquisitions, and abuse of dominance (e.g., predatory pricing, exclusive dealings and bundling of unrelated products) by companies.

The PCA established the Philippine Competition Commission (PCC), an independent quasi-judicial body, to implement the national competition policy. The PCC is composed of a chairperson (department secretary rank) and four commissioners (undersecretary rank) who serve for seven years (without reappointment) and hold security of tenure. It has primary jurisdiction in the enforcement and regulation of all competition-related issues. While it has also jurisdiction over cases involving both competition and non-competition issues, the PCC, before making its decision, is mandated to consult the concerned sector regulator, affording the latter the opportunity to submit its opinion. The PCC's decisions may be challenged at the Court of Appeals and the Supreme Court.

In October 2021, President Rodrigo Duterte issued Administrative Order (AO) no. 44, directing all government agencies, including local government units and government-owned and controlled corporations, to adopt and implement the national competition policy. The AO mandates these agencies to ensure that all government policies, rules and regulations support the national competition policy and foster a culture of competition.

For a detailed discussion of the structure, conduct and scope of competition policy in the Philippines, see Balisacan (2019) and Ravago, Roumasset, and Balisacan (2021).

6 CONCLUSION

The engine of economic development and structural transformation is productivity growth spurred by specialization, innovation and investment coordination. Specialization requires a deeper external governance (growth of the transaction sector) as well as internal governance (agency costs). The challenge for competition policy is to curb anticompetitive behaviour, agreements and organizations without impinging on extra-market governance that promotes specialization, innovation and coordination of investments. In addition, competition policy must be coordinated with the other instruments of economic development, including infrastructure, trade and sectoral policies. The perceived tension between the pursuit of consumer welfare versus total economic welfare is largely illusory. Due to the bias in transaction costs, suppliers can easily "conspire against the public", while consumers have a great difficulty in forming blocking coalitions. The *raison d'etre* of competition agencies is therefore to act on behalf of consumers to exercise the missing countervailing power.

We provide a preliminary exploration into the nature, causes and consequences of competition policy. Historically, competition law has evolved in tandem with globalization, although with somewhat of a lag. This may indicate a degree of complementarity. For example, falling import barriers in other countries increase the efficiency losses from domestic distortions, thwart potential comparative advantage and retard the process of specialization.

As competition policy has diffused throughout the world, its determinants have changed. Before the 1990s, per capita income mostly determined a country's decision to adopt competition law, indicating that the law's importance in the infrastructure of economic cooperation grows with economic development. In recent years, however, pressure from multilateral organizations and neighbouring countries have become more important, including requirements for being a member of economic unions such as the ASEAN. Our switching-regression results indicate that adoption increased the growth rates in adopting countries but would have tended to decrease growth in most non-adopting countries. Adopting countries have higher growth rates than non-adopters, partly because of adoption and partly because of other factors.

The formation of competition authorities follows closely the adoption of competition law. The design and organization of competition authorities in Asia vary according to each country's historical and economic situation. South Korea, Thailand and the Philippines serve as case studies to capture the characteristics of the authorities at various stages of maturity. South Korea is one of the oldest authorities and a relatively strong one. The young authority in the Philippines appears poised to become strong relative to its cohort. Despite its intermediate tenure, the old authority in Thailand was perceived to be weak, prompting the country to amend the law. The new authority has become an important part of Thailand's economic environment.

Some countries may not be ready for competition law. Since adoption can negatively affect growth, countries should not be pressured to prematurely adopt competition law. To the extent that international pressure and requirements are relaxed in the future, there still may be need for more limited international or regional agreements, especially regarding coordination of competition policies towards multinational corporations. As Rodrik (2020) observes, however, international coordination need not involve policy uniformity. Harmonization cannot be achieved by everyone playing the same note (see also Uy's chapter 25 in this volume).

Competition policy can potentially complement trade and sectoral policies in facilitating economic development. Limitations include the risk of regulatory capture (potentially offset by the independence of the competition agency), budget allocations and verdict challenges (e.g., via a Supreme Court). The official and implicit mandates of competition authorities also vary by country. For example, the Crown Property Bureau in Thailand and Indonesia's state-owned enterprises may be exempted from the purview of the competition authorities.

ACKNOWLEDGEMENT

J. Roumasset and M. Ravago acknowledge the support of the Asian Development Bank. M. Ravago conducted her research for this project under the Research and Creative Work Faculty Grant through the Ateneo de Manila University Research Council. The authors also thank Renzi Frias, J. Kathleen Magadia, Jestoni Olivo and Danilo Atanacio for research assistance. The views and findings in this paper are of the authors. Any errors of commission or omission are the authors' sole responsibility and should not be attributed to any of the above, the Philippine Competition Commission, or the authors' respective institutional affiliations.

REFERENCES

[data] Fraser Institute. 2016. "Economic Freedom of the World". https://www.fraserinstitute.org/studies/economic-freedom (accessed 1 October 2019).
[data] Freedom House. 2016. "Freedom World in the World 2016". https://freedomhouse.org/sites/default/files/FH_FITW_Report_2016.pdf (accessed 1 October 2019).
[data] World Bank. 2020. World Development Indicators. https://databank.worldbank.org/source/world-development-indicators (accessed 1 June 2020).
[data] World Economic Forum. 2018. "Global Competitiveness Report 2018". http://www3.weforum.org/docs/GCR2018/05FullReport/TheGlobalCompetitivenessReport2018.pdf.
[data] Worldwide Governance Indicator. 2020. https://info.worldbank.org/governance/wgi/.
Acemoglu, D. 2009. *Introduction to Modern Economic Growth*. Princeton: Princeton University Press.
———. 2016. "Competition, Policy and Technological Progress". PowerPoint presentation. Massachusetts Institute of Technology. http://economics.mit.edu/files/11962 (accessed March 2018).

Aghion, P., and P. Howitt. 1992. "A Model of Growth through Creative Destruction". *Econometrica* 60, no. 2: 323–51.
Aghion, P., N. Bloom, R. Blundell, R. Griffith, and P. Howitt. 2005. "Competition and Innovation: An Inverted-U Relationship". *Quarterly Journal of Economics* 120, no. 2: 701–28.
Armoogum, K. 2016. "Assessing the Comparative Performance of Competition Authorities". PhD dissertation, University of East Anglia.
Arrow, K. 1969. "The Organization of Economic Activity: Issues Pertinent to the Choice of Market versus Non-market Allocations". In *Analysis and Evaluation of Public Expenditures: The PPP System*, pp. 47–64. USA: Joint Economic Committee of Congress.
Balisacan, A. 2019. "Toward a Fairer Society: Inequality and Competition Policy in Developing Asia". *Philippine Review of Economics* 56, no. 1&2: 127–47. https://doi.org/10.37907/7ERP9102JD.
Balisacan, A., and J. Roumasset. 1987. "Public Choice of Economic Policy: The Growth of Agricultural Protection". *Weltwirtschafliches Archiv* 123, no. 2: 232–48.
Barro, R. J. 1991. "Economic Growth in a Cross Section of Countries". *Quarterly Journal of Economics* 106, no. 2: 407–43.
Barro, Robert. 2003. "Determinants of Economic Growth in a Panel of Countries". *Annals of Economics and Finance* 4: 231–74.
Barro, R. J., and X. Sala-i-Martin. 2004. *Economic Growth*. Cambridge, MA: MIT Press. Second edition.
Baumol, W. J., J. C. Panzar, and R. D. Willig. 1982. *Contestable Markets and the Theory of Industry Structure*. New York: Harcourt Brace Jovanovich.
Bautista, R., J. Power, and Associates. 1979. *Industrial Promotion Policies in the Philippines*. Manila: Philippine Institute for Development Studies.
Becker, G. 1983. "A Theory of Competition among Pressure Groups for Political Influence". *Quarterly Journal of Economics* 98, no. 3: 371–400.
Besanko, D., and D. Spulber. 1993. "Contested Mergers and Equilibrium Antitrust Policy". *Journal of Law, Economics & Organization* 9, no. 1: 1–29.
Besley, T., and M. Ghatak. 2006. "Public Goods and Economic Development". In *Understanding Poverty*, edited by A. Banerjee, R. Bénabou, and D. Mookherjee. Oxford: Oxford University Press.
Bittingmayer, G. 1995. "Did Antitrust Policy Cause the Great Merger Wave?". In *The Causes and Consequences of Antitrust: The Public Choice Perspective*, edited by F. McChesney and W. Shughart II, chapter 8. Chicago: University of Chicago Press. https://press.uchicago.edu/ucp/books/book/chicago/C/bo3645637.html.
Blinder, A. 1987. *Hard Heads, Soft Hearts: Tough-Minded Economics for a Just Society*. New York: Basic Books.
Blundell, R., R. Griffith, and J. van Reenen. 1999. "Market Share, Market Value and Innovation in a Panel of British Manufacturing Firms". *Review of Economic Studies* 66, no. 3: 529–54.

Borrell, J., and M. Tolosa. 2008. "Endogenous Antitrust: Cross-Country Evidence on the Impact of Competition-Enhancing Policies on Productivity". *Applied Economics Letters* 15, no. 11: 827–31.

Boserup, E. 1965. *The Conditions of Agricultural Growth*. London: Allen & Unwin.

———. 1981. *Population and Technological Change: A Study of Long-Term Trends*. Chicago: University of Chicago Press.

Boudreaux, D., T. DiLorenzo, and S. Parker. 1995. "Antitrust Before the Sherman Act". In *The Causes and Consequences of Antitrust: The Public Choice Perspective*, edited by F. McChesney and W. Shughart II, chapter 15. Chicago: University of Chicago Press.

Brennan, G., and M. Munge. 2014. "The Soul of James Buchanan?". *Independent Review* 18, no. 3: 331–42.

Brozen, Y. 1974. "Concentration and Profits: Does Concentration Matter?". *Antitrust Bulletin* 19: 381–99.

Buccirossi, P., L. Ciari, T. Duso, G. Spagnolo, and C. Vitale. 2013. "Competition Policy and Productivity Growth: An Empirical Assessment". *Review of Economics and Statistics* 95, no. 4: 1324–36.

Chang, S. W., and Y. Jung. 2005. "Republic of Korea". In *Competition Policy and Development in Asia*, edited by D. Brooks and S. Evenett. London: Palgrave Macmillan.

Chenery, H., and M. Syrquin. 1975. *Patterns of Development: 1950–1970*. New York: Oxford University.

Chernyshev, N. 2016. "The Inverted-U Relationship between R&D and Competition: Reconciling Theory and Evidence". Working paper, University of St. Andrews.

Clarete, R., and J. Roumasset. 1990. "The Relative Welfare Cost of Industrial and Agricultural Policies". *Oxford Economic Papers* 42: 462–72.

Clark, C. 1940. *The Conditions of Economic Progress*. London: MacMillan.

Clark, J. 2005. "Competition Advocacy: Challenges for Developing Countries". *OECD Journal: Competition Law and Policy* 6, no. 4: 69–80.

Clougherty, J. 2010. "Competition Policy Trends and Economic Growth: Cross-National Empirical Evidence". *International Journal of the Economics of Business* 17, no. 1: 111–27.

Clougherty J. A., T. Duso, and J. Muck. 2016. "Correcting for Self-Selection Based Endogeneity in Management Research: Review, Recommendations and Simulations". *Organizational Research Methods* 19, no. 2: 286–347. https://doi.org/10.1177/1094428115619013.

Dalkir, S. 2015. "A Quantitative Evaluation of Effectiveness and Efficacy of Competition Policies across Countries". In *Politics Triumphs Economics? Political Economy and the Implementation of Competition Law and Regulation in Developing Countries*, edited by P. Mehta and S. Evenett. New Delhi: CIRC.

Debreu, G. 1959. *The Theory of Value: An Axiomatic Analysis of Economic Equilibrium*, Cowles Foundation for Research in Economics. New Haven and London: Yale University Press.

Demsetz, H. 1973. "Industry Structure, Market Rivalry, and Public Policy". *Journal of Law and Economics* 16: 1–10.

Di Falco, S., M. Veronesi, and M. Yesuf. 2011. "Does Adaptation to Climate Change Provide Food Security? A Micro-Perspective from Ethiopia." *American Journal of Agricultural Economics* 93, no. 3: 829–46. https://doi.org/10.1093/ajae/aar006.

Dixit, A. 1999. *The Making of Economic Policy*. Cambridge, MA: MIT Press.

Ekelund, R., M. McDonald, and R. Tollison. 1995. "Business Restraints and the Clayton Act of 1914: Public- or Private-Interest Legislation?". In *The Causes and Consequences of Antitrust: The Public Choice Perspective*, edited by F. McChesney and W. Shughart II, chapter 16. Chicago: University of Chicago Press.

Edwards, C. D. 1974. "The Future of Competition Policy: A World View". *California Management Review* 16, no. 4: 112–26. https://doi.org/10.2307/41164535.

Felipe, J., and G. Estrada. 2018. "Why Has the Philippines' Growth Performance Improved? From Disappointment to Promising Success". *ADB Economics Working Paper 542*. Manila: Asian Development Bank. https://www.adb.org/publications/philippines-growth-performance-improved.

Friedman, M., and R. Friedman. 1979. *Free to Choose*. San Diego: Harcourt.

Galbraith, J. K. 1952. *American Capitalism: The Concept of Countervailing Power*. Boston: Houghton Mifflin.

Gardner, B. 1987. "Causes of U.S. Farm Commodity Programs". *Journal of Political Economy* 95, no. 2: 290–310.

Global Competition Review. 2018. "Emerging Enforcers 2018, Philippine Competition Commission." Available at https://globalcompetitionreview.com/guide/emerging-enforcers/emerging-enforcers-2018/article/philippine-competition-commission (accessed on 20 May 2020).

Goldberg, V. P. 1976. "Regulation and Administered Contracts". *Bell Journal of Economics* 7: 426–48.

Goulder, L., and R. Williams. 2003. "The Substantial Bias from Ignoring General Equilibrium Effects in Estimating Excess Burden and a Practical Solution". *Journal of Political Economy* 111, no. 4: 898–927.

Grossman, G. M., and E. Helpman. 1991. *Innovation and Growth in the Global Economy*. Cambridge, MA: MIT Press.

Gutmann, J., and S. Voigt. 2014. "Lending a Hand to the Invisible Hand? Assessing the Effects of Newly Enacted Competition Laws". SSRN. http://ssrn.com/abstract=2392780 (accessed January 2017).

Halberstam, D. 1986. *The Reckoning*. New York: Morrow.

Hall, R. 2018. "Using Empirical Marginal Cost to Measure Market Power in the US Economy". *NBER Working Paper 25251*. Cambridge, MA: National Bureau of Economic Research.

Hur, J. S. 2006. "Korea". In *Competition Regimes in the World, A Civil Society Report*. CUTS International. http://www.competitionregimes.com/toc.htm (accessed January 2018).

Jorgenson, D. 1961. "The Development of a Dual Economy". *Economic Journal* 71, no. 282: 309–34.

Kaplow, L. 2013. *Competition and Price-Fixing*. Princeton: Princeton University Press.

Kaplow, L., and S. Shavell. 2002. *Fairness vs. Welfare*. Cambridge: Harvard University Press.

Konan, D. E., S. J. La Croix, J. A. Roumasset, and J. Heinrich. 1995. "Intellectual Property Rights in the Asian-Pacific Region: Problems, Patterns, and Policy". *Asian-Pacific Economic Literature* 9, no. 2.

Krueger, A., M. Schiff, and A. Valdez. 1988. "Agricultural Incentives in Developing Countries: Measuring the Effect of Sectoral and Economy-wide Policies". *World Bank Economic Review* 2, no. 3: 255–72.

———, eds. 1991–92. *The Political Economy of Agricultural Pricing Policy: Volumes I–V*. Baltimore: The Johns Hopkins University Press.

Kuznets, S. 1966. *Modern Economic Growth: Rate, Structure and Spread*. New Haven: Yale University Press.

Lee, C., and S. Naya. 1988. "Trade in East Asian Development with Comparative Reference to Southeast Asian Experiences". *Economic Development and Cultural Change* 36, no. S3: S123–S152.

Lee, H. 2015. "Development of Competition Laws in Korea". *Discussion Paper 2015–78*. Economic Research Institute for ASEAN and East Asia.

Lee, L.-F., and R. P. Trost. 1978. "Estimation of Some Limited Dependent Variable Models with Application to Housing Demand". *Journal of Econometrics* 8, no. 3: 357–82. https://doi.org/https://doi.org/10.1016/0304-4076(78)90052-0.

Lin, P. 2005. "The Evolution of Competition Law in East Asia". In *Competition Policy in East Asia*, edited by E. M. Medalla. London: Routledge.

Lokshin, M., and Z. Sajaia. 2004. Maximum Likelihood Estimation of Endogenous Switching Regression Models. *Stata Journal* 4, no. 3: 282–89. https://doi.org/10.1177/1536867X0400400306.

———. 2008. MOVESTAY: Stata Module for Maximum Likelihood Estimation of Endogenous Regression Switching Models. https://econpapers.repec.org/RePEc:boc:bocode:s456710.

Long, W., R. Schramm, and R. Tollison. 1995. "The Economic Determinants of Antitrust Activity". In *The Causes and Consequences of Antitrust: The Public Choice Perspective*, edited by F. McChesney and W. Shughart II, chapter 6. Chicago: University of Chicago Press. https://press.uchicago.edu/ucp/books/book/chicago/C/bo3645637.html.

Lowi, T. J. 1969. *The End of Liberalism: The Second Republic of the United States*. New York: Norton.

Lucas, R. 1993. "Making A Miracle". *Econometrica* 61, no. 2: 251–72.

———. 2001. *Lectures on Economic Growth*. Cambridge: Harvard University Press.

Ma, T. C. 2011 "The Effect of Competition Law Enforcement on Economic Growth". *Journal of Competition Law and Economics* 7, no. 2: 301–34.

Maddala, G. S. 1983. *Limited-Dependent and Qualitative Variables in Econometrics*. Cambridge: Cambridge University Press.

Mankiw, N. G., D. Romer, and D.N. Weil. 1992. "A Contribution to the Empirics of Economic Growth". *Quarterly Journal of Economics* 107, no. 2: 407–37.

McEwin, I., and P. Chokesuwattanaskul. 2021. "What is an 'Effective' ASEAN Competition Law? A Methodological Note". *Singapore Economic Review* 0 0: 0, 1–41 https://doi.org/10.1142/S0217590821430013.

Motta, M. 2004. *Competition Policy: Theory and Practice*. Cambridge: Cambridge University Press.

Nevin, J., and L. Röller. 2005. "Consumer Surplus vs. Welfare Standard in a Political Economy Model of Merger Control". *International Journal of Industrial Organization* 23, no. 9&10: 829–48.

Nickell, S. J. 1996. "Competition and Corporate Performance". *Journal of Political Economy* 104, no. 4: 724–46.

Nikomborirak, D. 2005. "Thailand". In *Competition Policy and Development in Asia*, edited by D. Brooks and S. Evenett. London: Palgrave Macmillan.

———. 2006. "Political Economy of Competition Law: The Case of Thailand". *Northwestern Journal of International Law & Business* 26, no. 3: 597–618.

Olson, M. (1965) 1971. *The Logic of Collective Action: Public Goods and the Theory of Groups*, Cambridge, Massachusetts; London, England: Harvard University Press. Second printing with a new preface and appendix. https://doi.org/10.2307/j.ctvjsf3ts.

Olson Jr., M., and R. Zeckhauser. 1966. "An Economic Theory of Alliances". *Review of Economics and Statistics* 48, no. 3: 266–79.

Oman, C. 1996. "Introductory Session: The Contribution of Competition Policy to Economic Development". In *OECD Competition Policy: 1994 Workshop with the Dynamic Non-Member Economies*. Paris: OECD.

Palim, M. 1998. "The Worldwide Growth of Competition Law: An Empirical Analysis". *Antitrust Bulletin* 43: 105.

Petersen, N. 2013. "Antitrust Law and the Promotion of Democracy and Economic Growth". *Journal of Competition Law & Economics* 9, no. 3: 593–636.

Power, J. H. 1972. "The Role of Protection in Industrialization Policy with Particular Reference to Kenya." *Eastern Africa Economic Review* 4, no. 2.

Rakić, I. 2018. "The Role of Competition Advocacy: The Serbian Experience". In *Competition Authorities in South Eastern Europe. Contributions to Economics*, edited by B. Begović and D.Popović. Cham, Switzerland: Springer. https://doi.org/10.1007/978-3-319-76644-77.

Ravago, M. V., and A. M. Balisacan. 2016. "Agricultural Policy and Institutional Reforms in the Philippines: Experiences, Impacts, and Lessons". *Southeast Asian Agriculture and Development Primer*. Los Baños, Philippines: SEARCA.

Ravago, M. V., J. Roumasset, and A. M. Balisacan. 2021. "What Influences Adoption of Competition Law? The Case of ASEAN Economies". *Singapore Economic Review*. https://doi.org/10.1142/S0217590821430049.

Richardson, J., and J. Roumasset. 1995. "Sole Sourcing, Competitive Sourcing,

Parallel Sourcing: Mechanisms for Supplier Performance". *Managerial and Decision Economics* 16, no. 1: 71–84. https://doi.org/10.1002/mde.4090160109.

Rodrik, D. 2006. "Goodbye Washington Consensus, Hello Washington Confusion?". *Journal of Economic Literature* 44: 969–83.

———. 2020. "A Patchwork Planet". *Prospect Magazine*, June 2020. United Kingdom.

Romer, P. 1990. "Endogenous Technological Change". *Journal of Political Economy* 98, no. 5: S71–S102.

Romero, C., D. Petrecolla, E. Greco, and J. Martinez. 2016. "Competition Policy and Growth: Evidence from Latin America". In *Competition Law in Latin America: A Practical Guide*, edited by J. Pena, and M. Calliari. USA: Wolters Kluwer.

Roumasset, J. 1992. "The Role of Government in Economic Cooperation". In *The Economics of Cooperation: East Asian Development and the Case for Pro-Market Intervention*, edited by J. Roumasset and S. Barr. Boulder: Westview Press.

———. 2000. "Black-Hole Security". *Working Paper no. 00-5*, University of Hawaii. https://www.economics.hawaii.edu/research/workingpapers/005.pdf.

———. 2008. "Population and Agricultural Growth". In *The New Palgrave Dictionary of Economics*, edited by S. Dulauf and S. Blume. London: MacMillan Publishing. Second edition.

Roumasset, J., and S. Barr. 1992. *The Economics of Cooperation: East Asian Development and the Case for Pro-Market Intervention*. Boulder: Westview Press.

Royal Government of Bhutan. 2020. National Competition Policy 2020. https://www.gnhc.gov.bt/en/wp-content/uploads/2020/03/National-Competition-Policy-2020.pdf (accessed 17 May 2021).

Schumpeter, J. 1942. *Capitalism, Socialism and Democracy*. New York: Harper and Brothers.

Shapiro, C. 2010. "A Tribute to Oliver Williamson: Antitrust Economics". *California Management Review* 52, no. 2:138–46.

Shin, J. 2018. "Korea Needs to Change Ways of Reforming Chaebol: FTC Chief". *Korea Herald*, 18 Dec 2018.

Smith, A. 2008. *An Inquiry into the Nature and Causes of the Wealth of Nations*. Oxford World's Classics. London, England: Oxford University Press.

Shughart II, W., and R. Tollison. 1995. "The Employment Consequence of the Sherman and Clayton Acts". In *The Causes and Consequences of Antitrust: The Public Choice Perspective*, edited by F. McChesney and W. Shughart II, chapter 10. Chicago: University of Chicago Press. https://press.uchicago.edu/ucp/books/book/chicago/C/bo3645637.html.

Stigler, G. 1951. "The Division of Labor is Limited by the Extent of the Market". *Journal of Political Economy* 59, no. 3: 185–93.

———. 1971. "The Theory of Economic Regulation". *Bell Journal of Economics and Management Science* 2, no. 1: 3–21.

Stiglitz, J. 1993. *Whither Socialism?* Cambridge, MA: MIT Press.

———. 1996. "Some Lessons from the East Asian Miracle". *World Bank Research Observer* 11, no. 2: 151–77.

Suzor, N. P. 2014. "Free-Riding, Cooperation, and 'Peaceful Revolutions' in Copyright". *Harvard Journal of Law and Technology* 28, no. 1.

Thanitcul, S. 2015. "Competition in Thailand". *CPI Antitrust Chronicle*. https://www.competitionpolicyinternational.com/assets/Uploads/ThailandAug-151.pdf (accessed 12 January 2018).

Timmer, C. 1988. "The Agricultural Transformation". In *Handbook of Development Economics, vol. 1*, edited by H. Chenery, and T. Srinivasan. Amsterdam: North Holland.

UNCTAD. 2015. "Bhutan Finalise National Competition Policy, with UNCTAD Assistance". https://unctad.org/news/bhutan-finalise-national-competition-policy-unctad-assistance (accessed 17 May 2020).

Voigt, S. 2009. "The Effects of Competition Policy on Development – Cross-Country Evidence Using Four New Indicators". *Journal of Development Studies* 45, no. 8:1225–48.

Waked, D. 2008. "Competition Law in the Developing World: The Why and How of Adoption and Its Implications for International Competition Law". *Global Antitrust Review* 1: 69.

Wallis, J., and D. North. 1986. "Measuring the Transaction Sector in the American Economy, 1870–1970". In *Long-Term Factors in American Economic Growth*, edited by S. Engerman and R. Gallman. Chicago: University of Chicago Press.

Williamson, J. 1990. "What Washington Means by Policy Reform". In *Latin American Adjustment: How Much Has Happened*, pp. 90–120. Washington, DC: Peterson Institute of International Economics.

Williamson, O. 1968. "Economies as an Antitrust Defense: The Welfare Tradeoffs". *American Economic Review* 58, no. 1: 18–36. http://www.jstor.org/stable/1831653 (accessed 13 June 2021).

———. 1975. *Markets and Hierarchies: Analysis and Antitrust Implications*. New York: The Free Press.

———. 1985. *The Economic Institutions of Capitalism*. New York: Macmillan

———. 2000. "The New Institutional Economics: Taking Stock, Looking Ahead". *Journal of Economic Literature* 38, no. 3: 595–613.

Wright, J., and D. Ginsburg. 2013. "The Goals of Antitrust: Welfare Trumps Choice". *Fordham L. Rev.* 81, no. 5: 2405–23.

World Bank. 1993. *The East-Asian Miracle: Economic Growth and Public Policy*. Oxford: Oxford University Press. http://documents.worldbank.org/curated/en/322361469672160172/Summary.

World Bank Thailand. 2016. "Services as a New Driver of Growth". In *Thailand Economic Monitor 2016*. Thailand: World Bank Group.

Yang, X. 2003. *Economic Development and the Division of Labor*. Hoboken: Blackwell.

Zhang, V. 2015. *Competition Policy in Asia: Essays on Recent Development*. Boston, MA: Competition Policy International.

19 Competition and Employment Growth in the Philippines: A Baseline Assessment[1]

Stella A. Quimbo, Meg L. Regañon,
Eina Izabela Z. Concepcion and Cara T. Latinazo

1 BACKGROUND

In theory, employment growth is one of the dynamic gains expected from increased competition in markets. The basic intuition is that with increased competition, factor productivity increases, prices of goods and services are lower and, consequently, demand for goods, services and labour is higher (Nickell 1999; Layard, Nickell, and Jackman 1991; Hay and Liu 1997; OECD 1997). Firms could also dynamically respond to competition that could increase output and demand for labour, such as introduce new and improved products and processes that will require or result in the hiring of more workers (Aghion et al. 2005; Pianta 2005). In the short run, however, competitive pressures could force firms to undertake cost-cutting measures, including retrenching employees. Hence, an important concern among economic managers is whether competition kills or creates jobs (OECD 2015).

The concern is particularly relevant in countries where antitrust law is relatively new. In the Philippines, the competition law came to force in

---

[1] Portions of this research were done while the authors were affiliated with the Philippine Competition Commission.

2015, after over two decades of congressional deliberations. The Philippine Competition Act (PCA) prohibits anticompetitive agreements, abuse of dominant position, and anticompetitive mergers and acquisitions in all sectors of the economy (Republic Act No. 10667, An Act Providing for a National Competition Policy Prohibiting Anti-Competitive Agreements, Abuse of Dominant Position and Anti-Competitive Mergers and Acquisitions, Establishing the Philippine Competition Commission and Appropriating Funds Therefor).

Scholars have characterized the Philippine economy, particularly the manufacturing sector, as highly concentrated (Medalla 2003). Aldaba (2008) points to historical factors causing such concentration, particularly the protectionist policies in the 1950s up to the early 1980s, when removal of tariff and non-tariff barriers was initiated. Further, barriers to trade combined with heavy government regulation, as well as government-tolerated collusive practices, have contributed to the oligopolistic structure of the Philippine manufacturing industry. Protectionism also stems from several highly restrictive economic provisions in the Philippine Constitution. According to Sicat (2005):

> "The economic provisions of the Constitution are the barriers that make us into a high-cost economy, thereby burdening the country with loss of competitive capacity. The country has reached a point that requires the relaxation of these limitations on foreign capital so that we can raise the level and quality of national economic performance. Foreign direct investment will provide the quickest way to generate more capital to raise the economy's overall performance."

To be sure, the Philippine economy grew moderately in the period following the trade reform programme in the early 1980s: economic growth rose from 1.7 per cent in the 1980s to 2.8 per cent in the 1990s (Aldaba 2008). However, a casual inspection of long-term trends in employment growth, covering the 1950s up to 2015, does not present a clear relationship between increased foreign trade through the years and employment growth (Figure 19.1). Observers suggest that the limited impact of market-oriented reforms on economic performance could be due to other structural factors such as regulatory and behavioural barriers to competition (Aldaba 2008; Clarete 2005). For example, while Republic Act No. 11203, which liberalized rice importation in 2019 by lifting all quantitative import restrictions, caused rice imports to increase substantially, the incentives for local rice farmers to improve farming methods as they face tougher competition from cheaper imports could have been weakened tremendously by the substantial drop in farm-gate rice prices following the surge in rice imports.

Figure 19.1. Employment growth and import growth (Philippines, 1957–2016)

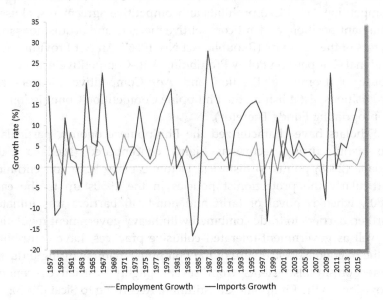

Balie, Minot, and Valera (2020) find that the policy led to a reduction of rice prices for consumers and producers, which benefits most households as net rice consumers, but negatively impacts domestic rice farmers. The substantial drop in farm-gate prices may have been caused by monopsony power exercised by traders and other middlemen, among others. In the absence of anticompetitive elements in the rice supply chain, farm-gate prices would perhaps not have dropped as much.

Hence, a testable hypothesis worth pursuing is whether more intense competition—among domestic firms or from foreign firms—could drive employment growth. The much-anticipated passage of the Philippine Competition Act is expected to bring about the needed structural change for a sustained inclusive growth, or an alternative trajectory to "jobless growth" (Balisacan 2019). Meanwhile, there is a pending legislative measure as of mid-2021, the Resolution of Both Houses No. 2 (RBH2), which aims to give Congress the power to amend select economic restrictions in the Constitution via the regular procedure of legislative amendments. This would be in lieu of the more tedious route undertaken for Constitutional amendments, which must be proposed through either (a) the creation of a constitutional commission, a constitutional assembly or a people's initiative or (b) a vote of three-fourths of all members of Congress and ratification through a national plebiscite. The economic provisions to be amended through RBH2 pertain to restrictions on foreign ownership for entities engaged in the following: exploration and utilization of natural resources; lease of land; management and operation of public utilities, educational institutions, mass media or advertising; and other economic investments. Specifically, RBH2 proposes to add the phrase "unless otherwise provided by law" to these provisions in order to allow Congress to relax or otherwise qualify them through legislation, thereby introducing greater flexibility to the country's policies on foreign participation in these markets. Relaxed regulations on foreign participation can facilitate the entry of foreign direct investments, potentially reducing market concentration and spurring competition in these key sectors.

We therefore ask: can baseline economic conditions predict if increased competition in Philippine industries can bring about a more inclusive economic growth through the employment pathway? The objective of this paper is to assess, at baseline, the possible effects of increased competition on employment growth. We use census data prior to the passage of the PCA and attempt to predict industry-level effects of reduced industry concentration on employment growth. Regression results indicate that increased competition in markets predicts higher employment growth.

2 COMPETITION PATHWAYS TO EMPLOYMENT GROWTH

The theoretical literature suggests a tight link between competition and employment. We cite three pathways: efficiency channels, innovation and wage dynamics. As discussed below, these three pathways taken together tend to favour a positive relationship, which we seek to validate using Philippine data.

2.1 Efficiency channels

Stronger competition faced by domestic firms from foreign firms through trade liberalization can spur firm productivity and expansion and, thus, employment growth.

Classical trade theory explains that trade between different countries facilitates specialization according to each one's comparative advantage (Bernard et al. 2007). Comparative advantage can be based on differences in technology (Ricardian theory) or differences in factor supplies

(Hecksher-Ohlin theory). If the source of a country's comparative advantage is abundant labour supply, as is the case in many developing countries, then specialization can facilitate increased employment.

Under classical theory, specialization occurs in the context of "inter-industry" trade. In the 1980s, new trade theory was developed to explain how economies of scale and consumers' preferences for variety can facilitate intra-industry trade (Krugman 1980; Helpman 1981). This provides a closer depiction of observed trading patterns, where there is two-way trade within industries (Bernard et al. 2007). Under new trade theory, international trade expands the market and allows more firms with differentiated products to thrive and take advantage of economies of scale. To the extent that operations are labour intensive, we can expect such expansion to result in increased employment.

More recent theory explores the gains from trade, given heterogeneous firms—specifically, firms within the same industries that vary in size and profitability (Melitz and Trefler 2012). In this case, increased competition from trade facilitates a shift in labour and capital to better-performing firms and away from worse-performing firms, thus, improving overall industry efficiency. Better performers can expand internationally, while worse performers contract and may even shut down in the face of foreign competition. With this mix of positive and negative effects on job creation, we can expect the overall impact on employment to vary, depending on firm processes, the extent of shifts in firm market share, and labour market conditions in each specific industry.

International experience shows that countries that are more open to trade and foreign competition have indeed chalked up greater growth and development than those that are not (OECD et al. 2010). The Organisation for Economic Co-operation and Development (OECD), in its assessment of G-20 countries, concludes that this facilitates increases in employment, particularly when part of the proper policy framework.

Empirical studies also support the observation that trade reallocates resources to better-performing firms, improving average industry productivity. For example, Pavcnik (2002) finds that the greater survival and growth of higher-productivity firms contributed two-thirds of the increased aggregate productivity in Chile following the country's trade liberalization. Further, the literature shows that reallocation of labour following trade liberalization tends to take place within industries rather than between different industries (OECD et al. 2010; Bernard et al. 2007). This supports the assertion that changes in employment due to trade are driven by job shifts, generation and loss within industries, particularly due to firm heterogeneity.

However, evidence on the net effect of this reallocation on employment in the short term appears mixed. Felbermayr, Prat, and Schmerer (2009), studying various developed and developing countries, find that a 10 per cent increase in trade openness is associated with a 1 per cent reduction in unemployment. Meanwhile, Tybout (2003), in a comprehensive review, shows that while there is evidence to support the expansion of exporting firms, there is also evidence of notable firm contraction due to trade (at least in the short term), sometimes leading to a reduction in employment. A study using evidence from Brazil finds that although firm productivity improved in response to increased foreign competition, market share did not increase enough, resulting in reduced employment overall (OECD et al. 2010).

While trade may lead to mixed employment and wage effects in the short run, there appear to be clearer benefits in the longer term. Dutt, Mitra, and Ranjan (2009) find that while trade liberalization may be immediately followed by a spike in unemployment, this effect is more than offset by gains in the longer run, with unemployment ultimately declining by 3.5 per cent three years after liberalization. Bernard and Jensen (1999) also find significantly more employment growth among exporters than non-exporters over several time periods. The evidence on economic reforms undertaken by Thailand and Malaysia also shows that increased economic openness can be a pathway to inclusive growth through job creation (Mirza and Giroud 2004). On the other hand, OECD et al. (2010) emphasize the need for complementary policies to help workers navigate disruptions and adjust to competition so they can take advantage of the gains of trade, and to facilitate improvements in employment outcomes in the long run.

Generally, since stronger competition can incentivize improved efficiency at the firm level (Hay and Liu 1997) and help reallocate resources to more productive sectors (World Bank 2021), the efficiency effects discussed above can also be triggered by increased domestic competition alone.

2.2 Innovation

Competition may also impact employment through its effects on innovation. That is, to the extent that new technologies require additional complementary labour or promote output expansion through increasing labour, competition may have an innovation pathway to employment growth. The available literature on competition and employment growth is largely indirect: studies typically establish the link either between competition and innovation or between innovation and employment.

With respect to competition and innovation, ideas stemming from the seminal work of Schumpeter (1939, 1976) propose that imperfect competition provides a more stable platform for innovation, as monopoly profits are necessary to form the sufficient incentive and ability to undertake innovation. However, Arrow (1962) argues that competition spurs innovation, as firms are incentivized to innovate when there is strong rivalry and contestability in the market.

Aghion et al. (2005) propose an inverted-U relationship between competition and innovation, where innovation is least likely among monopolies and highly competitive markets and most likely among moderately competitive markets. They argue that competition may increase the incentive to innovate for the technologically capable (i.e., the "escape-competition effect") but may also reduce the incentive to innovate for those who are already considered laggards; the changes in the relative balance between these two effects at low and high levels of competition are what explains the inverted-U relationship. Empirically, they find that this inverted-U relationship peaks at a competition level of around 95 per cent (equivalent to a Lerner Index of 5%). Consistent with the findings of Aghion et al., Lee (2009) finds that the impact of competition on a firm's incentive to invest in research and development (R&D) varies, depending primarily on its technological competence; that is, firms with more technological capability respond to stronger competitive pressure with higher R&D efforts. Meanwhile, Cohen (2010), in his survey of existing literature, argues that the relationship between market structure and R&D remains inconclusive due to mixed evidence, and that there is a need to further understand how industry-specific factors might affect this relationship.

With respect to the impact of innovation on employment, findings vary, depending on whether innovations are product innovations (introducing a new product or technology into the market) or process innovations (improvements in production processes). Evidence points to a strong positive relationship between product innovation and job creation, as tested in a variety of settings (Piva and Vivarelli 2005; Benavente and Lauterbach 2008; Crespi and Tacsir 2011; Harrison et al. 2014; OECD 2015). The relationship is not as straightforward for process innovations; employment may be negatively impacted if the process is labour saving instead of labour inducing. However, evidence suggests that process innovations can be net positive for employment if they help improve the competitiveness of an existing product or the firm, increasing demand for the product and, thus, promoting job creation over time (Horbach and Rennings 2013; Harrison et al. 2014).

2.3 Wage dynamics

Increased competition can lead to higher employment levels via wage formation (OECD 2015). When product prices are reduced with increased competition, output expands, real wages increase and the quantity of labour supplied rises. At the same time, the income effect of the increase in real wages induces further output expansion alongside an increase in the demand for labour. Available evidence suggests that increased competition also leads to greater productivity, higher real wages and greater employment (OECD 2015). However, this impact may be diminished when labour markets are inflexible (World Bank 2021). Gersbach (2000) finds that product market reforms—lowering markups, fostering productivity and inducing rapid expansion of a firm's product mix—can help reduce unemployment in most circumstances, unless workers are immobile. Hollweg et al. (2014) observe that the presence of labour market frictions, which increase mobility costs for workers, may reduce the gains from competition on employment, as workers are slower to transition in response to changes in real wages. The impact of these labour adjustment costs varies across industries and countries. Thus, in certain contexts, labour market reforms can play a role in facilitating the benefits of competition on employment.

Overall, based on the theoretical and empirical literature, stronger competition can positively impact employment through several pathways. We examine below whether Philippine data support this relationship, and how various firm and industry characteristics may enhance it.

3 METHODOLOGY

3.1 Empirical model

We estimate the following employment growth model, which directly follows standard models of demand for labour:

$$E_i = e_i(w_i, r_i, Q_i, C_i, X_i) \qquad (1)$$

where i is the industry subclass, E_i is the logarithm of the number of employees, w_i is a measure of labour cost, r_i measures the cost of capital, Q_i refers to output or scale, C_i is a measure of competition and X_i is a vector of other characteristics, including capital-to-labour ratio, number and age of establishments, investments and R&D expenditure.

The reduced form allows flexibility to test the various pathways to employment growth. We interact the competition measure with variables that could indicate pathways for employment growth given a change in competition levels, as suggested by the review of literature. These variables include wage, average profits, capital-to-labour ratios, investments, R&D expenditure and industry fixed effects. While wage endogeneity could introduce a bias in the estimated coefficient of wages, we note that our central variables of interest are the measures of competition. Hence, our results can still provide useful insights on the competition-employment gradient.

We use ordinary least squares to estimate the model at the industry subclass level using the five-digit Philippine Standard Industrial Classification (PSIC) codes. The industry subclass level allows us to group establishments producing similar goods and services, and therefore form relevant markets. We estimate three sets of regression models, one for each measure of competition: the Herfindahl-Hirschman Index (HHI), the top four concentration ratio (CR4) and the Lerner Index or Price Cost Margin (PCM), as discussed below. Possible heteroskedasticity is addressed by using the robust option in STATA.

We then use the regression estimates to simulate employment effects under various scenarios of increased competition, as measured by the HHI. The HHI is computed as the sum of the squared market shares of each establishment[2] and can take a value between 0 and 10,000. Following the US benchmarks for HHI, we define markets as very competitive (HHI of at most 1,400), somewhat competitive (HHI of at most 2,000) and less

---

[2] To compute for the market concentration measures, we replicated the population of more than 200,000 establishments that the 2012 CPBI sample of 46,000 establishments represented, based on the weights provided by the PSA. Observations with weights in decimal form were rounded off to facilitate construction of the said data set. To illustrate, an establishment with a weight of 2.5 was taken to represent 3 establishments with similar characteristics.

competitive (HHI of at most 2,600).[3] We then calculate, for each subclass, the reduction in HHI needed to achieve the various levels of increased competition (if applicable) and, using the regression coefficients, to determine the number of additional employees hired under each scenario.

3.2 Data

The main data set used for the analysis is the 2012 Census of Philippine Business and Industry (CPBI). Conducted by the Philippine Statistics Authority (PSA) annually, the CPBI is a nationwide survey of formal businesses in the country, such as corporations, partnerships, cooperatives and single proprietorships.[4] The data set provides detailed information on businesses in the country, such as their levels of employment, revenues, expenditure, PSIC code and other characteristics.

Confined to the formal sector of the economy, the 2012 CPBI covered 46,302 establishments to represent 219,201 establishments. These are (a) all establishments with 10 or more employees and (b) all establishments with fewer than 10 employees, except those organized as single proprietorships and single establishments. Based on the 2012 List of Establishments, there were 945,000 establishments in the country; 262,800 of these made up the formal sector.

Each establishment is tagged with a five-digit PSIC code to indicate the industry subclass to which the establishment belongs. Overall, there were a total of 1,006 industry subclasses spread out among 18 major industries in the 2012 CPBI.

3.2.1 Dependent variable

The main dependent variable in the regression models is the logarithm of total employment at the industry subclass level. This includes both paid and unpaid employees of the establishments as of November 2012.

---

[3] Based on the US Thresholds (US DOJ and FTC 2010), industries with HHIs above 2,500 are considered highly concentrated; industries with HHIs between 1,500 and 2,500 are moderately concentrated; and industries with HHIs below 1,500 are unconcentrated.

[4] The CPBI is done every six years while the Annual Survey of Philippine Business and Industry (ASPBI) is conducted in the intervening years. The main difference between them is the former's larger sample size.

Paid employees "are all full-time and part-time employees who receive regular pay ", while unpaid workers are "working owners who do not receive regular pay, apprentices and learners without regular pay, and persons working for at least 1/3 of the normal working time without regular pay".

The establishments covered in the 2012 CPBI generated a total of 5.4 million employees, of which 98 per cent were paid employees. This total accounts for only about 15 per cent of the 37.7 million employed Filipinos as of October 2012 (PSA 2012). This is likely because the CPBI excludes employment generated by the informal sector of the economy and certain industries.[5] The analysis presented in this paper thus pertains only to competition effects on formal employment.

3.2.2 Main independent variables of interest

For the main independent variables, we constructed two measures of market concentration: HHI and CR4, computed as the revenue share of the top four establishments in the total revenue of the industry subclass.

One major data limitation in using the 2012 CPBI is that the survey's unit of observation is an establishment. Establishments are classified according to economic organization: single establishment, main office only, branch office only, main office and branch office with other branches elsewhere, and ancillary unit. This poses a problem when computing for measures of market concentration because we may be treating related establishments as competitors. The data set does not allow the aggregation of establishments that in reality may be all part of a single enterprise. Therefore, the computed CR4 and HHI could be understated for some industry subclasses.[6]

---

[5] The following industries are not included in the 2012 CPBI: public administration and defense; compulsory social security (O), activities of households as employers; undifferentiated goods- and services-producing activities of private households for own use (T), and activities of extraterritorial organizations and bodies (U).

[6] Since the data set does not allow us to account for foreign competition and competition from the informal sector, the computed concentration measures could also be overstated.

Hence, we also utilize an alternative measure of market concentration—the Lerner Index or PCM, defined as the markup between price and marginal cost over price. The higher the market PCM, the higher the likelihood of market power. Given the available data, we approximate the Lerner Index or PCM as the profit margin of an industry subclass. The profit margin is computed as total revenue minus total cost (which includes total compensation) over the total revenue of each industry subclass. As shown by a World Bank Group assessment of the state of competition in Philippine markets, HHI and PCM have a significant positive correlation, at least for manufacturing and wholesale/retail sectors (Miralles Murciego et al. 2018).

3.2.3 Other independent variables

To proxy for labour cost, we compute the average wage as total compensation over total employment. Total compensation is composed of gross salaries and wages, separation/retirement/terminal pay, and gratuities and employer's contribution to the Social Security System (SSS) or Government Service Insurance System (GSIS).

To proxy for capital stock, we use the book value of the tangible fixed assets of the subclasses. Tangible fixed assets refer to physical assets such as land, buildings, transport, machinery equipment and others.

To control for output and productivity of each subclass, we compute for value added using the factor-income approach, particularly as the sum of labour compensation, depreciation expenses and profit. The alternative measures of scale are number of establishments and average firm size in a subclass. Average firm size is calculated as total employment over the number of establishments.

Employment pathway variables include (a) average profits, defined as total revenues minus total costs over the number of establishments; (b) total investments, defined as the subclass's expenditure on new tangible and intangible assets, where tangible assets refer to physical assets as previously defined and intangible assets refer to non-physical assets such as purchased patents, trademarks, franchises, computer software and databases, and entertainment, literary and artistic originals; (c) total R&D expenditure, defined as the subclass's spending on any systematic, scientific and creative work undertaken to use the added knowledge generated to create new or improved products, processes, services and other applications; and (d) capital intensity or capital-to-labour ratios, defined as capital stock per employee. Average wage, value added and industry fixed effects (generated using the alpha character of the PSIC codes) are also used as employment pathway variables.

Another industry characteristic that could explain employment growth is the average age of establishments in years, computed using information provided by the survey respondents.

Table 19.1 presents the summary statistics of the industry subclass variables generated from the 2012 CPBI. Overall, both CR4 and HHI (simple averages) suggest that Philippine industries are concentrated according to US standards. We also note that 124 subclasses have negative PCMs.

Table 19.1. Summary statistics: Subclass variables

Variable	Obs	Mean	Std. dev.	Min	Max
Total employment	1,006	5,393	17,869	1	319,428
C4	1,006	67	31	1	100
HHI	1,006	3,100	3,080	4	10,000
PCM	1,006	7	31	(513)	76
Average wage	1,006	237,209	356,911	0	8,068,234
Total assets	1,006	4,220,000,000	19,800,000,000	0	398,000,000,000
Total value added	1,006	3,550,000,000	17,400,000,000	(3,100,000,000)	329,000,000,000
Total establishments	1,006	218	672	1	6,801
Average profits	1,006	64,100,000	499,000,000	(3,900,000,000)	11,300,000,000
Capital to labour ratio	1,006	1,263,781	6,033,337	0	125,000,000
Total investments	1,006	467,000,000	2,300,000,000	0	43,500,000,000
Total &D expenses	1,006	5,698,097	40,600,000	0	838,000,000
Average firm age	1,005	15	11	0	212
Average firm size	1,006	95	292	1	4,636

Note: Variables corresponding to monetary terms are in Philippine Peso.

Table 19.2 shows the weighted average CR4 by categories of the industry subclasses. The data suggest that high levels of concentration characterize many parts of the Philippine economy. Concentration is particularly high in the industry sector (i.e., mining and quarrying, water supply and waste management, manufacturing) and lowest in the services sector (i.e., accommodation and food service activities, wholesale and retail trade, repair of motor vehicles).

Table 19.2. Average top four concentration ratio (CR4) for major industries

	Major industry	C4
Agriculture		
A	Agriculture, forestry and fishing	83
Industry		
B	Mining and quarrying	90
C	Manufacturing	77
D	Electricity, gas, steam and air conditioning supply	57
E	Water supply; sewerage, waste management and remediation activities	79
F	Construction	57
Services		
G	Wholesale and retail trade; repair of motor vehicles and motorcycles	38
H	Transportation and storage	80
I	Accommodation and food service activities	27
J	Information and communication	76
K	Financial and insurance activities	72
L	Real estate activities	46
M	Professional, scientific and technical activities	63
N	Administrative and support service activities	73
P	Education	41
Q	Human health and social work activities	55
R	Arts, entertainment and recreation	63
S	Other service activities	45

4 RESULTS

Tables 19.3, 19.4 and 19.5 present the regression results using each measure of competition—HHI, CR4 and PCM, respectively. The fit of all models is good, given high r-squared values. Overall, we find significant negative coefficients ($p < 0.05$) for competition measures, suggesting possible employment expansion with reduced concentration of markets due to the new competition law. Using the full model (model 5) and predicting at the means, the estimates shown in Table 19.3 suggest that a 10 per cent decrease in HHI predicts a 1.8 per cent increase in employment. These results are similar in direction and magnitude to other studies (Griffith et al. 2006; Ebell and Haefke 2009; Feldman 2012; Dierx et al. 2016). Using CR4 as an alternative measure of competition in Table 19.4, we find that a percentage point reduction in CR4 is associated with a 0.6 per cent increase in employment (model 5). Finally, estimates in Table 19.5 suggest that a percentage point reduction in PCM predicts a 3.1 per cent increase in employment (model 5).

In unreported PCM regressions, wherein we exclude subclasses with negative PCMs, we find broadly similar results in terms of the sign and significance of the variables as in Table 19.5.

For each table, Models 4 and 5 present indicators of non-linearities in the employment effects of competition. Indeed, these models suggest that employment effects could be either enhanced or mitigated by other firm or industry outcomes or behaviour as shown in Table 19.6. Following increased competition, employment growth appears more pronounced with increased profitability, productivity, investments and R&D spending. Moreover, employment effects, as expected, would be mitigated with increased capital intensity and higher average wages.

We also note varying employment effects across industries. For example, the regressions that include industry dummy variables interacted with measures of competition (model 5 of Tables 19.3–19.5) suggest that in certain large and capital- or technology-intensive industries, wherein the minimum efficient scale is presumably high, increased competition predicts reductions in employment levels.

Table 19.3. Regression results using HHI
Dependent variable: Log total employment

Parameter	Model 1	Model 2	Model 3	Model 4	Model 5
Log HHI	-0.8617	-0.2042	-0.1998	-1.0486	-1.2074
	(0.0333)****	(0.0376)****	(0.0340)****	(0.5296)***	(0.5033)***
Log average wage		-0.6300	-0.5782	-1.2235	-1.3633
		(0.1199)****	(0.1126)****	(0.3500)****	(0.3454)****
Log assets		0.1119	0.1239	0.1153	0.1211
		(0.0233)****	(0.0229)****	(0.0221)****	(0.0221)****
Log value added		0.6843	0.6249	0.6623	0.7049
		(0.0438)****	(0.0417)****	(0.0904)****	(0.0971)****
Capital-to-labour ratio			-3.65e-08	-2.06e-07	-1.67e-07
			(0.0000)****	(0.0000)****	(0.0000)***
Log investments			0.0131	0.0189	0.0205
			(0.0038)****	(0.0235)	(0.0239)
Log R&D expenses			0.0092	0.0473	0.0308
			(0.0028)****	(0.0142)****	(0.0202)*
Total establishments			0.0001	-0.0000	0.0001
			(0.0000)***	(0.0000)	(0.0000)***
Average firm age			0.0001	-0.0004	0.0008
			(0.0026)	(0.0019)	(0.0019)
Average firm size			0.0003	0.0003	0.0003
			(0.0001)****	(0.0001)***	(0.0001)***

Table 19.3 (continued)

Table 19.3 *(continued)*

Parameter	Model 1	Model 2	Model 3	Model 4	Model 5
Log HHI * Log average wage				0.0776	0.0986
				(0.0518)*	(0.0506)**
Log HHI * Log average profits				-1.23e-11	-7.73e-12
				(0.0000)	(0.0000)
Log HHI * Log value added				-0.0019	-0.0093
				(0.0123)	(0.0131)
Log HHI * Capital-to-labour ratio				2.12e-08	1.65e-08
				(0.0000)***	(0.0000)**
Log HHI * Log investments				-0.0007	-0.0009
				(0.0031)	(0.0031)
Log HHI * Log R&D expenses				-0.0051	-0.0030
				(0.0020)***	(0.0027)
With industry dummy variables					Yes
With industry dummy variables interacted with log HHI					Yes
Constant	13.0721	0.3538	0.4027	7.2423	8.3436
	(0.2403)****	(0.7296)	(0.7593)	(3.6646)***	(3.5085)***
R^2	0.3900	0.9100	0.9300	0.9300	0.9400
N	1,006	977	976	976	976

Note: (1) * $p < 0.15$, ** $p < 0.1$, *** $p < 0.05$, **** $p < 0.01$
(2) Numbers in parentheses are standard errors.

Table 19.4. Regression results using CR4
Dependent variable: Log total employment

Parameter	Model 1	Model 2	Model 3	Model 4	Model 5
CR4	-0.0394	-0.0091	-0.0083	-0.0267	-0.0334
	(0.0017)****	(0.0018)****	(0.0015)****	(0.0207)	(0.0208)*
Log average wage		-0.6351	-0.5734	-0.8170	-0.8576
		(0.1219)****	(0.1147)****	(0.1081)****	(0.1121)****
Log assets		0.1143	0.1260	0.1276	0.1344
		(0.0239)****	(0.0235)****	(0.0221)****	(0.0221)****
Log value added		0.6853	0.6212	0.7022	0.7005
		(0.0446)****	(0.0428)****	(0.0406)****	(0.0447)****
Capital-to-labour ratio			-3.62e-08	-1.96e-07	-1.78e-07
			(0.0000)****	(0.0000)****	(0.0000)****
Log investments			0.0134	0.0131	0.0134
			(0.0038)****	(0.0086)*	(0.0090)*
Log R&D expenses			0.0081	0.0223	0.0159
			(0.0028)****	(0.0057)****	(0.0093)**
Total establishments			0.0001	0.0000	0.0001
			(0.0000)****	(0.0000)	(0.0000)****
Average firm age			0.0001	0.0004	0.0013
			(0.0025)	(0.0018)	(0.0018)
Average firm size			0.0003	0.0003	0.0003
			(0.0001)****	(0.0001)***	(0.0001)***

Table 19.4 (continued)

Table 19.4 (continued)

Parameter	Model 1	Model 2	Model 3	Model 4	Model 5
CR4 * Log average wage				0.0030	0.0038
				(0.0021)	(0.0022)**
CR4 * Average profits				-1.49e-12	-1.07e-12
				(0.0000)**	(0.0000)
CR4 * Log value added				-0.0009	-0.0010
				(0.0006)*	(0.0006)**
CR4 * Capital-to-labour ratio				1.75e-09	1.55e-09
				(0.0000)****	(0.0000)***
CR4 * Log investments				-7.31e-06	-5.04e-06
				(0.0001)	(0.0001)
CR4 * Log R&D expenses				-0.0002	-0.0001
				(0.0001)***	(0.0001)
With industry dummy variables					Yes
With industry dummy variables interacted with CR4					Yes
Constant	9.3969	-0.5385	-0.5485	0.7003	1.1192
	(0.1209)****	(0.8819)	(0.8848)	(1.1360)	(1.1437)
R^2	0.3800	0.9100	0.9300	0.9300	0.9400
N	1,006	977	976	976	976

Note: (1) * $p < 0.15$, ** $p < 0.1$, *** $p < 0.05$, **** $p < 0.01$
(2) Numbers in parentheses are standard errors.

Table 19.5. Regression results using PCM
Dependent variable: Log total employment

Parameter	Model 1	Model 2	Model 3	Model 4	Model 5
PCM	0.0076	−0.0310	−0.0276	−0.0348	−0.0981
	(0.0016)****	(0.0020)****	(0.0018)****	(0.0325)	(0.0410)**
Log average wage		−0.8284	−0.7503	−0.7839	−0.8619
		(0.1131)****	(0.1197)****	(0.0807)****	(0.0595)****
Log assets		−0.0009	0.0300	0.0489	0.0609
		(0.0313)	(0.0321)	(0.0294)**	(0.0344)**
Log value added		0.9239	0.8525	0.8571	0.8384
		(0.0393)****	(0.0419)****	(0.0363)****	(0.0434)****
Capital-to-labour ratio			−2.48e−08	−5.36e−08	−5.34e−08
			(0.0000)****	(0.0000)****	(0.0000)****
Log investments			0.0040	9.73e−06	0.0054
			(0.0033)	(0.0048)	(0.0041)
Log R&D expenses			0.0062	0.0091	0.0115
			(0.0026)***	(0.0031)****	(0.0034)****
Total establishments			0.0001	0.0001	0.0001
			(0.0000)****	(0.0000)****	(0.0000)****
Average firm age			−0.0020	−0.0005	0.0004
			(0.0020)	(0.0025)	(0.0024)
Average firm size			0.0001	0.0002	0.0002
			(0.0000)**	(0.0001)****	(0.0001)****

Table 19.5 (continued)

Table 19.5 (continued)

Parameter	Model 1	Model 2	Model 3	Model 4	Model 5
PCM * Log average wage				0.0042	0.0084
				(0.0037)	(0.0051)**
PCM * Average profits				-1.30e-12	-3.39e-12
				(0.0000)*	(0.0000)****
PCM * Log value added				-0.0025	-0.0015
				(0.0016)*	(0.0014)
PCM * Capital-to-labour ratio				6.33e-10	7.03e-10
				(0.0000)****	(0.0000)****
PCM * Log investments				0.0003	-0.0003
				(0.0003)	(0.0003)
PCM * Log R&D expenses				-0.0002	-0.0003
				(0.0002)	(0.0002)
With industry dummy variables					Yes
With industry dummy variables interacted with PCM					Yes
Constant	6.7052	-0.9406	-1.1790	-1.1637	-0.2416
	(0.0630)****	(1.1015)	(1.1568)	(0.8976)	(0.5715)
R^2	0.0100	0.9400	0.9500	0.9500	0.9600
N	1,006	977	976	976	976

Note: (1) * $p < 0.15$, ** $p < 0.1$, *** $p < 0.05$, **** $p < 0.01$
(2) Numbers in parentheses are standard errors.

Table 19.6. Employment effects of increased competition via different pathways

	Parameter	Reductions in		
		HHI	CR4	PCM
	Productivity			
	Average profits	+	+	+
	Value added	+	+	+
For high levels of...		(211.34)***	(207.69)***	(214.83)***
	Capital-to-labour ratio	−	−	−
		(16.82)***	(8.28)***	(13.46)***
	Innovation			
	Investments	+	+	+
		(7.54)***	(6.47)***	(0.90)
	R&D expenditure	+	+	+
		(3.59)**	(2.78)*	(6.67)***
	Wage			
	Average wage	−	−	−
		(137.60)***	(94.33)***	(243.49)***

Note: (1) "+" refers to a factor that enhances competition's effect on employment while "−" refers to a factor that mitigates competition's effect on employment
(2) The numbers in parentheses are F-statistics when testing the joint significance of the variable (e.g., log value added) and its interaction with a measure of competition (e.g., log HHI * log value added).
(3) The p values are referred to as follows: * $p < 0.1$, ** $p < 0.05$, *** $p < 0.01$.

The estimated coefficients of the other independent variables suggest robustness of estimates (model 5 of Tables 19.3–19.5). The positive coefficients for firm size and R&D expenditure suggest that larger scales of business (as measured by firm size) and increased R&D spending predict higher employment. Meanwhile, the negative coefficient of average wage suggests that lower labour costs predict higher employment. Similarly, negative coefficients for capital-to-labour ratio suggest that increased capital relative to labour predicts lower employment.

Table 19.7 provides simulation results of employment effects under various scenarios of increased competition, as measured by HHI. The predicted total increase in employment following increased competition in concentrated subclasses ranges from 26,000 to 68,000 workers, with the services and industry sectors expected to reap the most employment gains.

Table 19.7. Predicted employment effects under increased competition scenarios

Major sector	Total employment	Scenario 1: Very competitive markets	Scenario 2: Somewhat competitive markets	Scenario 3: Less competitive markets
Agriculture	164,706	2,897	2,131	1,460
		(1.8%)	(1.3%)	(0.9%)
Industry	1,532,044	38,209	20,868	13,519
		(2.5%)	(1.4%)	(0.9%)
Services	3,728,823	26,679	15,939	10,592
		(0.7%)	(0.4%)	(0.3%)
TOTAL	5,425,573	67,784	38,939	25,571
		(1.2%)	(0.7%)	(0.5%)

Note: Under scenario 1 (very competitive markets), all subclasses have HHIs of 1,400 and below; under scenario 2 (somewhat competitive markets), all subclasses have HHIs of 2,000 and below; and under scenario 3, all subclasses have HHIs of 2,600 and below.

5 DISCUSSION

Estimates of the multivariate regression models suggest significant employment effects: enhanced competition predicts higher employment growth. Our results lend support to the theoretical literature, where increased competition predicts overall increases in employment. Moreover, we find that the employment effects are non-linear, varying with firm and industry characteristics. The positive competition effects are more pronounced with lower wages and among more profitable firms, and are less pronounced in capital-intensive industries. Increased competition could allow the more efficient firms within an industry to take advantage of economies of scale, which also lends support to newer trade theory. The results also suggest that the employment effects of increased R&D expenditure are larger among firms in more competitive industries.[7]

---

[7] Taking the derivative of the dependent variable on R&D, we find that increased employment will follow increased R&D for sufficiently low levels of HHIs and C4.

To secure potential employment gains from enhanced competition, it is important for the PCA to be effectively enforced. Indeed, studies have shown that the presence of a competition authority increases growth and output in the OECD countries (Clougherty 2010; Taylor 2002; Dierx et al. 2016). Experience from various jurisdictions suggests, however, that setting up and building the capacity of competition authorities could take time, and therefore, projected employment gains could come with a lag. For example, the Competition Commission of Singapore adjudicated its first abuse of dominance case in 2009, about five years after Singapore passed its competition law (O'Melveny & Myers LLP 2010).

Are the predicted employment effects substantial? By comparing the predicted total effects (26,000–68,000 workers) with the target number of jobs to be created for the Philippine economy, we argue that such effects are non-trivial. The Updated Philippine Development Plan (2017–2022) indicates a target of 2.4 million to 2.8 million jobs generated in 2021 and 1 million to 1.2 million in 2022. The predicted competition effects account for at most 3 per cent of the target for 2021 and at most 7 per cent for 2022.

An important limitation of this research is that we focus only on increased competition within the same product markets. To the extent that there are possible vertical effects of competition, our estimates of employment effects could be understated. Specifically, we are unable to measure the impact of increased competition on input markets for a particular output or product market. There could be situations, for example, where improved competition enforcement would allow access to input markets that were previously foreclosed. Further research that considers input-output linkages is needed.

6 CONCLUSION

This study is a first attempt at predicting industry-level employment effects of potential enhanced competition in the marketplace, following the passage of a competition law in the Philippines. The Philippine experience confirms that competition has a positive impact on employment. Increased competition improves efficiency and induces output expansion. Moreover, for a given level of competition, whether weak or strong, increased firm profitability, R&D expenditure and investments also promote output expansion. Under these circumstances, employment is expected to increase, particularly, when labour requirements of production technologies are larger. The PCA, if effectively enforced, has the potential to generate employment growth. Another important legislative measure, the RBH2, which seeks to amend the highly restrictive economic provisions of the Philippine Constitution, can also play a role in employment generation. Relaxing the 40 per cent limit on ownership of equity by foreign entities is expected to facilitate entry of foreign investors, particularly in markets that tend to be highly concentrated. Our findings suggest that reduced market concentration following increased participation by foreign firms in the Philippine economy will create jobs. Considering that this baseline study was conducted under current restrictive rules on entry, the simulation results can be interpreted as minimum, rather than average effects of relevant amendments to the Constitution. Hence, further studies are needed to determine the extent of employment creation resulting from easing restrictions of entry by foreign firms in the Philippine economy.

REFERENCES

Aghion, Philippe, Nick Bloom, Richard Blundell, Rachel Griffith, and Peter Howitt. 2005. "Competition and Innovation: An Inverted-U Relationship". *Quarterly Journal of Economics* 120, no. 2: 701–28.

Aldaba, Rafaelita M. 2008. "Assessing Competition in Philippine Markets". *PIDS Discussion Paper Series* No. 2008-23. Manila: Philippine Institute for Development Studies.

Arrow, Kenneth J. 1962. "Economic Welfare and the Allocation of Resources for Invention". In *The Rate and Direction of Inventive Activity: Economic and Social Factors*, pp. 609, 619–20. USA: National Bureau of Economic Research.

Balie, J., N. Minot, and H. Valera. 2020. "Distributional Impacts of the Rice Tariffication Policy in the Philippines". *Economic Analysis and Policy* 69: 289–306.

Balisacan, Arsenio M. 2019. "Toward a Fairer Society: Inequality and Competition Policy in Developing Asia". *Philippine Review of Economics* 56, no. 1&2 (June–December): 127–47.

Benavente, J., and R. Lauterbach. 2008. "Technological Innovation and Employment: Complements or Substitutes?". *The European Journal of Development Research* 20: 318–29.

Bernard, Andrew B., and J. Bradford Jensen. 1999. "Exceptional Exporter Performance: Cause, Effect, or Both?". *Journal of International Economics* 47, no. 1: 1–25.

Bernard, Andrew B., J. Bradford Jensen, Stephen J. Redding, and Peter K. Schott. 2007. "Firms in International Trade". *Journal of Economic Perspectives* 21, no. 3: 105–30.

Clarete, Ramon. 2005. "Effects of Trade Liberalization in the Philippines: Ex-ante Versus Post Trade Reform Assessment". Paper presented at the 4th PEP Research Network General Meeting, Colombo, Sri Lanka, 13–17 June 2005.

Clougherty, Joseph A. 2010. "Competition Policy Trends and Economic Growth: Cross-National Empirical Evidence". *International Journal of the Economics of Business* 17, no 1: 111–27.

Cohen, W. 2010. "Fifty Years of Empirical Studies of Innovative Activity and Performance". In *Handbook of the Economics of Innovation Volume I*, edited by B. Hall and N. Rosenberg, pp. 129–213. Oxford, UK: Elsevier.

Crespi, Gustavo, and Ezequiel Tacsir. 2011. "Effects of Innovation on Employment in Latin America". *MPRA Paper Series No. 35429*. Germany: University Library of Munich.

Dieppe, Alistar, ed. 2021. *Global Productivity: Trends, Drivers, and Policies*. Washington, DC: World Bank.

Dierx, Adriaan, Fabienne Ilzkovitz, Beatrice Pataracchia, Marco Ratto, Anna Thum-Thysen, and Jannos Varga. 2016. "Distributional Macroeconomic Effects of the European Union Competition Policy—A General Equilibrium Analysis". In *A Step Ahead: Competition Policy for Shared Prosperity and Inclusive Growth*, pp. 153–82. Washington, DC: World Bank.

Dutt, P., D. Mitra, and P. Ranjan. 2009. "International Trade and Unemployment: Theory and Cross-National Evidence". *Journal of International Economics* 78, no. 1: 32–44.

Ebell, Monique, and Christian Haefke. 2009. "Product Market Deregulation and the U.S. Employment Miracle". *Review of Economic Dynamics* 12, no. 3 (July): 479–504.

Felbermayr, G., J. Prat, and H. J. Schmerer. 2009. "Trade and Unemployment: What Do the Data Say?". *IZA Discussion Papers* No. 4184. Bonn: Institute for Study of Labor.

Feldmann, Horst. 2012. "Product Market Regulation and Labor Market Performance around the World". *Review of Labour Economics and Industrial Relations* 26, no. 3: 369–91.

Gersbach, Hans. 2000. "Promoting Product Market Competition to Reduce Unemployment in Europe: An Alternative Approach?". *Kyklos*, 53 no. 2: 117–33.

Griffith, Rachel, Elena Huergo, Jacques Mairesse, and Bettina Peters. 2006. "Innovation and Productivity across Four European Countries". *Oxford Review of Economic Policy* 22, no. 4: 483–98.

Hay, Donald A, and Guy S. Liu. 1997. "The Efficiency of Firms: What Difference Does Competition Make?". *The Economic Journal* 107, no. 442 (May): 597–617.

Harrison, R., Jordi Jaumandreu, Jacques Mairesse, and Bettina Peters. 2014. "Does Innovation Stimulate Employment? A Firm-Level Analysis Using Comparable Micro-Data from Four European Countries". *International Journal of Industrial Organization* 35: 29–43.

Helpman, Elhanan. 1981. "International Trade in the Presence of Product Differentiation, Economics of Scale, and Monopolistic Competition: A Chamberlin-Heckser-Ohlin Model". *Journal of International Economics* 11, no. 3: 305–40.

Hollweg, C.H., Daniel Lederman, Diego Rojas, and Elizabeth Rupert Bulmer. 2014. "Sticky Feet: How Labor Market Frictions Shape the Impact of International Trade on Jobs and Wages". In *Directions in Development—Trade*. Washington, DC: World Bank Group.

Horbach, J., and Klaus Rennings. 2013. "Environmental Innovation and Employment Dynamics in Different Technology Fields—an Analysis Based on German Community Innovation Survey 2009". *Journal of Cleaner Production* 57: 158–65.

Krugman, Paul. 1980. "Scale Economies, Product Differentiation, and the Pattern of Trade". *American Economic Review* 70, no. 5: 950–59.

Layard, Richard, Stephen Nickell, and Richard Jackman. 1991. "Unemployment: Macroeconomic Performance and the Labour Market". *OUP Catalogue*. Oxford University Press, no. 9780198284345 (December).

Lee, Chang-Yang. 2009. "Competition Favors the Prepared Firm: Firms' R&D Responses to Competitive Market Pressure". *Research Policy* 38: 861–70.

Medalla, Erlinda M. 2003. "Philippine Competition Policy in Perspective". *PIDS Perspective Paper Series* no. 4. Manila: Philippine Institute for Development Studies.

Melitz, M., and D. Trefler. 2012. "Gains from Trade When Firms Matter". *Journal of Economic Perspectives* 26, no. 2: 91–118.

Miralles Murciego, Graciela, Roberto Martin Nolan Galang, Sara Nyman, Tilsa Guillermina Ore Monago, and Leandro Deambrosio Zipitria. 2018. *Fostering Competition in the Philippines: The Challenge of Restrictive Regulations* (English). Washington, DC: World Bank Group. http://documents.worldbank.org/curated/en/478061551366290646/Fostering-Competition-in-the-Philippines-The-Challenge-of-Restrictive-Regulations (accessed 4 July 2021).

Mirza, H., and A. Giroud. 2004. "Regional Integration and Benefits from Foreign Direct Investment in ASEAN Economies: The Case of Viet Nam". *Asian Development Review* 21, no. 1: 66–98.

NEDA (National Economic and Development Authority). 2021. Updated Philippine Development Plan 2017–2022, Chapter 4: Philippine Development Plan 2017-2022 Overall Framework. http://www.neda.gov.ph/wp-content/uploads/2013/09/CHAPTER-1.pdf (accessed 26 December 2016).

Nickell, Stephen. 1999. "Product Markets and Labour Markets". *Labour Economics* 6: 1–20.

OECD (Organisation for Economic Co-operation and Development). 1997. *Competition Policy in OECD Countries 1994–1995*. Paris, France: Organisation for Economic Co-operation and Development. p. 259.

———. 2015. "Does Competition Kill or Create Jobs? A Discussion on the Links and Drivers between Competition and Employment". 2015 Global Forum on Competition. Paris, France, 29–30 October 2015.

OECD, ILO, World Bank, and WTO. 2010. "Seizing the Benefits of Trade for Employment and Growth: Final Report". Prepared for submission to the G-20 Summit. Seoul, Korea, 11–12 November 2010.

O'Melveny & Myers LLP. 2010. "Is South East Asia's Young Competition Regime Ready to Claim Its Place on the Global Antitrust Stage? A Review of the Competition Commission of Singapore's Decisions in 2009". *Alerts and Publications*. O'Melveny. https://www.omm.com/resources/alerts-and-publications/publications/a-review-of-the-competition-commission-of-singfapores-decisi/?sc_lang=zn-CN (accessed 26 December 2016).

Pavcnik, Nina. 2002. "Trade Liberalization, Exit, and Productivity Improvement: Evidence from Chilean Plants". *Review of Economic Studies* 69, no. 1: 245–76.

PSA (Philippine Statistics Authority). 2012. *Labor Force Survey 2012*. October Results. Manila: Philippines Statistics Authority.

———. 2015. *Yearbook of Labor Statistics 2015*. Manila: Philippine Statistics Authority.

———. 2016. National Accounts—Data Series. http://psa.gov.ph/nap-press-release/data-charts.

Pianta, M. 2005. "Innovation and Employment". In *Handbook of Innovation*, edited by J. Fagerberg, D. Mowery, and R.R. Nelson. Oxford: Oxford University Press.

Piva, M., and M. Vivarelli. 2005. "Innovation and Employment: Evidence from Italian Microdata". *Journal of Economics* 86: 65–83.

Schumpeter, Joseph A. 1939. *Business Cycles: A Theoretical, Historical, and Statistical Analysis of the Capitalist Process*. New York: McGraw-Hill Book Company Inc.

———. (1942) 1976. *Capitalism, Socialism and Democracy*. London: George Allen & Unwin.

Sicat, G. 2005. "Reform of the Economic Provisions of the Constitution: Why National Progress is At Stake". *UPSE Discussion Paper Series* no. 2005–10. Quezon City, Philippines: School of Economics, University of the Philippines Diliman.

Taylor, J. E. 2002. "The Output Effects of Government Sponsored Cartels during the New Deal". *Journal of Industrial Economics* 50, no. 1: 1–10.

Tybout, James R. 2003. "Plant- and Firm-Level Evidence on the 'New' Trade Theories". In *Handbook of International Trade*, edited by E. Kwan Choi and James Harrigan. Oxford: Basil Blackwell.

US Department of Justice and Federal Trade Commission. 2010. *Horizontal Merge Guidelines*. Washington, DC, USA.

20 Buyer Power and Late Payment Behaviour in the Shoe Capital of the Philippines

Tetsushi Sonobe

1 INTRODUCTION

Many developing countries have adopted competition law in the recent few decades. There are more than 130 competition law regimes in the world today (Cheng 2020). Competition agencies in developing countries tend to emphasize that their competition policies aim at contributing to economic development and social inclusion (Evenett 2005). For example, Arsenio M. Balisacan, the first chairperson of the Philippine Competition Commission (PCC), stresses that "the PCC, a young competition agency, has to quickly develop its enforcement capacity, in light of expectations for enforcement to contribute to sustaining rapid economic development and achieving inclusive development" (Balisacan 2020, 13).

The competition agencies of Korea and Japan have traditionally acted against late payment by large firms to small and medium enterprises (SMEs) in retailing and wholesaling, as well as subcontracting. In 2011, the European Commission (EC) strengthened its Late Payment Directive by including a provision that if firms do not pay their invoices within 60 days, they will be forced to pay interest and reimburse the reasonable recovery costs of the creditor. The policy was adopted because a number of SMEs have gone bankrupt each year while waiting for their invoices to be paid and because late payment deprives jobs and stifles entrepreneurship (European Commission 2011). The government of the United Kingdom has been intensifying its efforts to bring about a culture change in payment practice.[1] Few studies have been conducted on payment practices in the developing world, however, and the competition agencies and governments in these countries seem not to be determined to combat late payment to enhance inclusive development.

This chapter presents the case of late payment practices in the shoe industry in the Philippines circa 2000, using interview materials and survey data of shoemakers. In those days, shoemakers did not have the option of using digital platforms to sell goods directly to customers; their direct buyers were retailers and wholesalers. Although none of these buyers dominated the entire domestic market for shoes, it seems that they had buyer power, allowing some of them to delay payment to shoemakers for an extended period, which could be more than a year. The financial burdens and time costs due to long delays in payment could affect creditors' growth, longevity, employment and investment. The economics literature has only a few empirical studies on late payment, however. Little is known about the power balance between debtor and creditor, the impact of late payment on the creditor, and which measures are effective in preventing late payment.

I conducted personal interviews with scores of shoemakers, some shoe material traders and several wholesalers in Marikina, Metro Manila, the shoe industry's national centre, and with a smaller cluster of shoemakers in Biñan, Laguna province in 1997 and late 2003. Based on the results of these unstructured interviews, a questionnaire was developed and used to conduct a small survey with a random sample of 58 shoemakers in Marikina and 40 in Biñan in early 2004 in collaboration with the Philippine Institute for Development Studies. Although the survey collected recall data on production and sales in 1998, 2001 and 2003, former shoemakers who had exited the market prior to the survey were not included in the sample. Moreover, data

---

[1] For example, the Small Business, Enterprise and Employment Act 2015 requires the UK's largest firms to report biannually on their payment practices, policies and performance.

on the survival of the sample shoemakers are not available because the survey has not had its second wave.

Indeed, the industry was rapidly declining and having a high incidence of exits in the late 1990s and the early 2000s due to intense import competition. From the data, we cannot know whether late payment and bankruptcy are associated. The lack of information on exits and the small sample size of the survey are the major weaknesses of the study.

Despite these weaknesses, the data together with interview materials provide some useful information. They show that relatively large shoemakers manufacturing products popular with urban consumers were more likely to deal with department stores, despite the latter's high incidence of late payments with considerably long delays. Increases in such late payment are associated with decreased sales revenues and equipment investment. On the other hand, increases in transactions with department stores are associated with greater sales revenues and higher margin rates as long as there was no late payment. These findings are consistent with the view that the large sales floor spaces occupied by department stores are a source of buyer power vis-à-vis large shoemakers, and that their late payment to shoemakers was abuse of this power.

The next section briefly presents the history of the shoe industry and its situation around the turn of the twenty-first century. Section 3 describes sales routes and payment practices. The final section summarizes the findings and discusses their implications, given recent developments in Marikina.

2 MARIKINA AND BIÑAN

The shoe industry in the Philippines has a long history, dating back to the late nineteenth century. It used to export its products to the developed-country markets in the 1960s and 1970s. Its centre, Marikina, a city along the eastern border of Metro Manila, had become home to over three thousand workshops, including 513 registered factories. It became known as the shoe capital of the country. The industry retreated from the export markets, however, presumably due to lack of mechanization and capacity for mass production. And then came the era of import competition. In the 2000s, imported products from China and other developing countries flooded the Philippine shoe market. By 2010, the number of registered shoemakers had fallen to 126.

Footwear industrial clusters are ubiquitous in time and space. Northampton was known as a cluster of shoemakers already in the seventeenth century. There are famous clusters in Milan, seven large cities in India, Sinos Valley in Brazil, Wenzhou in China and Addis Ababa in Ethiopia (e.g., Schmitz 1995; Sonobe et al. 2009). Marikina in its heyday ranked as one of these major clusters in the world.

An industrial cluster is born and grows because enterprises producing or providing similar goods or services benefit from being located near each other—that is, the benefit of localization economies, a category of agglomeration economies. In the cluster, trade secrets are not a secret but are "in the air", to borrow Alfred Marshall's expression. Also, a pool of workers with special skills is available in the cluster. Geographical proximity and human network in the cluster facilitate trust between transacting parties because rumours of cheating, shirking and other opportunistic behaviour spread rapidly. Social ostracism can be used as a punitive measure against such behaviour. Trust relationship reduces transaction costs and facilitates the division of labour and specialization.

The division of labour may be limited by the size of market as well as transaction costs (Stigler 1951). In Marikina, for example, even micro-sized workshops can use expensive specialized machinery, such as a skiving machine that shaves the surface of leather, by either renting the machine on hourly basis or contracting out the process to the machine owner, who invested in it in expectation of a large demand.[2] Since shoemakers did not have to invest in expensive equipment, the cost of new market entry was low in the cluster.

The upper part of Table 20.1 presents data on product prices in the two clusters in 1998 and 2003. The average price here is the ratio of revenue divided by the number of pairs sold, whether the material is leather or synthetic. It was much higher in Marikina than in Biñan because about 50 per cent of sample shoemakers in Marikina specialized fully in leather shoes, which were much more expensive than synthetic

---

[2] See Sonobe and Otsuka (2006). While a manufacturer here means a firm or a self-employed artisan that assembles parts to produce finished shoes, material suppliers are either factories producing or trading firms dealing in materials such as leather and thread. Traders dealing in finished products include retailers and wholesalers.

shoes. In comparison, all sample shoemakers in Biñan specialized fully in synthetic shoes. The data on prices shown here are not deflated. Since the Philippine consumer prices increased by 21 per cent between 1998 and 2003, the real price decreased for both leather and synthetic shoes, but the real price of leather shoes declined much less than that of synthetic shoes. The average price of synthetic shoes was 20–30 per cent higher in Marikina than in Biñan, but the difference was not statistically significant because of the large variance within clusters. Relatively high-priced products in Biñan tended to be labelled "Marikina Style", indicating Marikina shoes' appeal among consumers.

Table 20.1. Price, quantity, margin and machinery (1998, 2003)

Parameter		(1) Marikina	(2) Biñan	(3) t-statistics H_0: (1) − (2) = 0
Average price (PHP)[1]	1998	360.300 (187.300)	86.900 (38.300)	10.30***
	2003	414.100 (208.700)	93.200 (49.800)	11.20***
Leather shoes price (PHP)[2]	1998	470.100 (172.600)	na	na
	2003	535.500 (172.600)	na	na
Synthetic shoes price (PHP)[3]	1998	118.600 (83.500)	86.900 (38.300)	1.19
	2003	114.900 (83.500)	93.200 (49.700)	0.82
No. of pairs sold[4]	1998	22,940.000 (22,429.000)	14,402.000 (15,686.000)	2.14**
	2003	20,609.000 (30,049.000)	9,901.000 (10,396.000)	2.50**
Profit margin $(p-c)/p$[5]	1998	0.303 (0.152)	0.191 (0.091)	4.28***
	2003	0.268 (0.157)	0.186 (0.086)	3.22***

Table 20.1 (continued)

Table 20.1 (continued)

Parameter		(1) Marikina	(2) Biñan	(3) t-statistics H_0: (1) − (2) = 0
No. of sewing machines for uppers	1998	3.090 (3.440)	2.260 (2.660)	1.30
	2003	4.100 (3.840)	2.290 (3.060)	2.30**
No. of obs	1998	53.000	38.000	
	2003	58.000	38.000	

Note: (1) [1] The average price of various types of shoes made by a sample firm was obtained by dividing total sales revenue by the number of all types of shoes sold. Data on sales revenue by type of shoes are not available. This row shows the mean value of the average price among the sample firms within the respective clusters.
[2] The leather shoe price was obtained by taking the mean of the average prices for the firms that produced only leather shoes. There were 28 such firms in Marikina in 2003. Although men's leather shoes were more expensive than women's and children's, the sheer lack of data prevented estimating the average prices of these categories separately.
[3] This price was obtained by taking the mean of the average prices in the above sense for the firms that produced only synthetic shoes. There were 11 such firms in Marikina. In Biñan, all firms in the sample produced and sold only synthetic shoes.
[4] The number includes leather and synthetic shoes.
[5] This is the average gross profit margin. In the formula, p is the average price and c is the unit cost, i.e., the total production cost divided by the number of shoes sold. The total production cost consists of material cost, subcontracting cost, labour cost, utility cost and transportation cost.
(2) Numbers in parentheses are standard deviations.

Table 20.1 also shows data on quantity sold, margin rate and equipment. The quantity sold includes both leather and synthetic shoes. The standard deviation of this variable relative to its mean is even greater than that of the price, reflecting the large diversity of firm sizes and firm dynamics. The reduction in quantity was much smaller in Marikina than Biñan. In the Marikina sample, 24 of the 53 firms in operation in 1998 experienced more than 20 per cent reduction in sales quantity in 2003, but 10 firms increased their sales quantity by more than 20 per cent. In addition, five firms in the sample entered the market after 1998. In Biñan, 27 of the 38 firms (with usable quantity data) similarly experienced decreased sales quantity of more than 20 per cent, while 2 firms increased their sales quantity during the same period. None of the Biñan sample firms entered the market after 1998.

The margin rate is the ratio of the price-unit cost margin to the price. The number of sewing machines for uppers is an important determinant of production capacity in the busy season. Its average and median in Marikina increased from 3 to 4 and from 2 to 3, respectively, in five years; neither increased in Biñan. The margin rate was higher in Marikina than Biñan, and so was the rate of capital accumulation.

When I interviewed the shoemakers, the prevalent view among them was that their industry was declining due to the flood of cheap synthetic shoes imported from other developing countries. Consistent with this view, the intense import competition hit Biñan harder; in Marikina, shoemakers shifted from synthetic to leather shoes. Data on exits are missing in Table 20.1. Presumably, Biñan had a high incidence of exits, but even in Marikina, many shoemakers ceased production, leaving room for some firms to expand.

One of the difficulties in the shoe manufacturing business is the large seasonal fluctuation in demand. Table 20.2 shows that the busy season lasted for only three months in Biñan and 4.5 months in Marikina. Both the number of workers employed and the number of hours worked hugely differed between the busy and slack seasons in both clusters, but more so in Biñan. To meet the high demand in the busy season, shoemakers tried to secure a sufficient number of highly skilled workers and paid them on a piece-rate basis to give them a strong incentive to produce large quantities of shoes.[3]

Table 20.2. Employment and wage (2003)

Parameter		(1) Marikina	(2) Biñan	(3) t-statistics H_0: (1) – (2) = 0
No. of busy months in a year		4.52 (1.51)	2.97 (1.37)	5.19***
No. of piece-rate workers	Busy season	20.50 (21.20)	6.76 (8.22)	4.46***
	Slack season	14.70 (17.70)	3.05 (2.96)	4.92***

Table 20.2 (continued)

---

[3] The average hourly wage rate of high- and low-skilled workers, as shown towards the bottom of Table 20.2, was on parity with the minimum wage in Metro Manila in 2003. However, considering that many workers were jobless during the slack season, wage rates were not high even in Marikina.

Table 20.2 *(continued)*

Parameter		(1) Marikina	(2) Biñan	(3) t-statistics $H_0: (1) - (2) = 0$
Hours worked by a typical piece-rate worker per week	Busy season	48.70 (11.60)	73.40 (16.70)	−6.95***
	Slack season	20.00 (11.50)	14.90 (11.80)	2.06**
No. of time-rate workers	Busy season	7.43 (16.80)	0.00	3.36***
	Slack season	0.79 (2.42)	0.00	2.50**
Hours worked by a typical time-rate worker per week	Busy season	21.80 (23.80)	na	na
	Slack season	15.90 (20.00)	na	na
Total person-hours[1]		38,667.00 (50,252).00	9,915.00 (15,931.00)	4.06***
Average wage per hour[2]		35.40 (54.20)	19.70 (21.60)	1.94*

Note: (1) [1] The total person-hours here is the number of busy months times four weeks a month times the number of hours worked by a typical piece-rate worker per week in the busy season times the number of piece-rate workers in the busy season plus the corresponding figure in the slack season plus the corresponding figures for time-rate workers. Although piece- and time-rate workers in Marikina differ in skills and jobs, their labour inputs are mixed in the calculation of the total person-hours.

[2] The average wage per hour here is the labour cost divided by the total person-hours. Since data on labour cost are available only for the sum of labour cost for piece- and time-rate workers, their wage rates are mixed in the calculation of this average wage per hour.

(2) Numbers in parentheses are standard deviations.

Table 20.3 presents data on the attributes of the entrepreneurs.[4] Although Marikina has a longer history than Biñan, the two clusters share almost the same average number of years of establishment. This may be because second and third generations did not necessarily succeed their parents' workshops, and if they did, they might have changed their firms' status from unregistered to registered. What is striking in Table 20.3 is the high level of educational attainment of entrepreneurs in Marikina compared with entrepreneurs of small and medium light-manufacturing enterprises in developing Asia.[5] A high proportion of respondents in Marikina had attended business training programmes geared for shoe business provided by the association of shoemakers.

Table 20.3. Attributes of entrepreneurs

Parameter	(1) Marikina	(2) Biñan	(3) t-statistics H_0: (1) – (2) = 0
Year of firm establishment	1,985.900	1,985.100	0.40
	(10.577)	(9.079)	
Founder (yes = 1/no = 0)[1]	0.741	0.902	–2.16**
	(0.442)	(0.300)	
Age	47.710	47.74	–0.02
	(9.915)	(8.867)	
Educational attainment (years)	12.200	9.510	4.33**
	(2.600)	(3.260)	
Participation in a footwear business training programme (yes = 1/no = 0)	0.708	0.195	5.89***
	(0.459)	(0.401)	

[1] Entrepreneurs who are not founders are either a child, spouse, relative or former employee of the founder.

Note: During the period 1998–2003, no entrepreneurs in the sample were replaced, hence, the attributes of the sample entrepreneurs remained unchanged.

---

[4] The entrepreneur here is the most important decision-maker of the firm.
[5] Sonobe and Otsuka (2006, 2011) report, for example, that entrepreneurs who founded electric fittings manufacturing firms in Wenzhou, China between 1995 and 2000 had 10.9 years of schooling; those operating firms manufacturing knitwear and steel construction materials near Hanoi, Vietnam during the same period had 7.2 and 9.8 years, respectively.

3 SALES ROUTES AND LATE PAYMENT

The number of weeks a pair of shoes stays on a retail shop shelf is random, and the variance of waiting time becomes smaller as sales volume increases, according to the law of large number. This is a source of scale economies in retailing, which gives advantage to large-scale retailers or department stores occupying large sales floor spaces on a busy street. The reason why wholesalers try to deal with many small retail shops must be similar. These scale economies give rise to market power in the retail/wholesale sector.[6]

Shoemakers skilled at making shoes that appeal to urban consumers wished to receive orders from department stores, even though the latter tended to prefer relatively large producers rather than dealing with scores of smaller producers to save on transaction costs. This confers at least a small amount of marketing scale economies on larger producers. The other sales routes include boutiques, consignment, and retailing at own workshop or own retail shops. Shoemakers may also work as subcontractors.

The upper part of Table 20.4 presents data on sales routes as percentage of sales revenue. Retailers here mean department stores for the Marikina sample and smaller-scale retailers for the Biñan sample.

Table 20.4   Sales routes and payment practices as percentage of revenue (2003)

Parameter	(1) Marikina	(2) Biñan	(3) t-statistics H_0: (1) − (2) = 0
% of sales revenue from			
Retailers[1]	27.50	24.10	0.41
	(38.80)	(40.0)	
Wholesalers[2]	29.80	69.30	−4.55***
	(40.70)	(41.90)	

Table 20.4 *(continued)*

---

[6] According to the World Bank (2018, 2), "Philippine markets are relatively concentrated" and "a notable proportion of markets would be classified as highly concentrated, …close to 50 per cent in wholesale/retail, …according to standard Herfindahl–Hirschman Index (HHI) thresholds used by competition agencies."

Table 20.4 *(continued)*

Parameter	(1) Marikina	(2) Biñan	(3) t-statistics $H_0: (1)-(2) = 0$
Boutiques and other small shops[3]	16.10 (29.90)	1.30 (8.10)	3.55***
Subcontracting[4,5]	14.30 (31.20)	2.60 (16.20)	2.38**
% of sales revenue from			
Advance payment	0.53 (2.92)	11.30 (21.20)	−2.81***
Immediate cash payment	10.30 (21.2)	28.50 (37.90)	−2.27**
Immediate post-dated cheque	78.90 (33.80)	38.60 (46.30)	4.73***
Late payment by buyers	10.30 (23.40)	21.60 (37.70)	−1.65
Percentiles			
50th	0.00	0.00	
75th	10.00	35.00	
90th	30.00	100.00	
95th	50.00	100.00	
100th	100.00	100.00	
% of material cost			
Late payment to suppliers	49.50 (42.80)	50.50 (43.60)	0.11
Percentiles			
25th	0.00	0.00	
50th	50.00	50.00	
75th	100.00	100.00	
No. of weeks until payment of suppliers	5.69 (5.30)	2.36 (2.64)	3.97***

Note: (1) [1] For the Marikina sample, retailers here mean large-scale retail stores. For the Biñan sample, retailers mean smaller retail shops.
 [2] Wholesalers purchased shoes from producers in bulk and sold them to retail shops across the country, including distant regions.
 [3] Boutiques here mean retail stores selling fashionable items.
 [4] Subcontracting refers to the production of footwear products based on product design and specifications given by the buyer.
 [5] Sales routes other than large-scale retailer, wholesaler, boutique, consignment and subcontracting are selling a product directly to consumers at the producer's premises and selling to small-scale retailers.
(2) Numbers in parentheses are standard deviations.

While wholesalers were the dominant sales route in Biñan, they were not as important in Marikina, where shoemakers used boutiques, consignment and own retail outlets. The percentage of boutiques and consignment increased during the 1998–2003 period, but these increases are not statistically significant.[7]

The second part of Table 20.4 presents data on the timing of payment relative to the delivery or pickup of shoes. The buyers' most common mode of payment was to issue a post-dated cheque, which also serves as a request made by the payer to the recipient to wait until the written date. This mode accounted for nearly 80 per cent of the shoemaker's revenue in Marikina and 40 per cent in Biñan. On receiving a post-dated cheque, shoemakers often encashed it before the indicated date at a discounted value because they needed cash to buy materials and pay workers.

If a buyer pays in advance, it is a credit the buyer gives the seller. Late payment is a credit given by the seller to the buyer. These trade credits, with or without a written consent, are common across the business world. Late payment, however, should be condemned as abusive or exploitative if the delay is remarkably long. To see how late is remarkably late, it is useful to refer to provisions on late payment. As mentioned earlier, the Late Payment Directive 2011/7/EU of the European Parliament entitles the creditor to payment of interest and compensations for recovery costs incurred due to late payment — that is, payment made more than 60 days after receipt of the invoice or the goods or services.[8] In Korea, the Act on Fair Transactions in Subcontracting and the Act on Fair Transactions in Large Retail Business require large-scale retailers to pay their suppliers the fees within 60 days after receipt of the goods, if the retailers entrust the suppliers with manufacturing, and the proceeds from consignment sales within 40 days after the monthly closing date, if the retailers are entrusted with the sale of goods by suppliers and receive and manage sales proceeds.

Payment delays were much longer in Marikina. According to my personal interviews with relatively large shoemakers there, they had to frequently visit their debtors' offices for three months to more than a year before getting paid. The median delay is around six months.

---

[7] Neither the survey data nor my interview materials provide any information on the reason why the producers or consumers did not shift from large-scale retailers or wholesalers to these sales routes.

[8] The interest rate is 8 per cent plus the European Central Bank base rate.

Moreover, when they were paid, the payment was not in cash but post-dated cheques that take another 3–6 months to maturity. Because they needed cash to pay their workers and material suppliers, they would immediately encash the cheques at a discount. The time costs and financial burdens caused by late payment were substantial in Marikina. In Biñan, the delays were much shorter, from one week to three months, with the median at around one month.

Unlike these unstructured interviews, the survey using a questionnaire with many other questions was unable to elicit in-depth information about late payment. It only obtained data on the amount of late payment as a percentage of annual revenue. Table 20.4 presents the mean and percentiles of the percentage of revenue representing late payment. In both clusters, the majority of shoemakers managed to avoid late payment from their buyers, but some shoemakers received all payments late. Interestingly, the mean was much lower in Marikina, where the incidence of remarkably late payment was high. One possible reason is sample selection bias, as mentioned earlier, due to the possibility that the shoemakers who suffered more from remarkably late payment may have already exited the market. Another possible reason is that large-scale retailers might have restrained themselves from making more late payments so as not to lose their reliable suppliers.

Another interesting observation is that the majority of shoemakers in both clusters also habitually made delayed payments to their suppliers of materials. Table 20.4 shows that the majority in both clusters paid material suppliers late more than half of the time (based on their invoices). The delays averaged 5.69 weeks and 2.36 weeks in Marikina and Biñan, respectively.

Tables 20.5 and 20.6 summarize some statistical associations between the variables discussed. Table 20.5 looks at static relationships between variables by regressing the mean of the dependent variable over the three points of recall data (i.e., 1998, 2001 and 2003) on the means of the explanatory variables over the three data points. In other words, the between estimator is employed. In the first two columns, the dependent variable is the logarithm of annual revenue, and the explanatory variables include percentage of sales to retailors, percentage of sales from leather shoes, year of firm establishment and entrepreneur's educational and occupational backgrounds.

Table 20.5. Regression summarizing the data (between estimator) (1998, 2001, 2003)

Parameter	ln(revenue)		Late payment %	
	Marikina	Biñan	Marikina	Biñan
	(1)	(2)	(3)	(4)
Sales to retailer (% of revenue)	0.011**	-0.001	0.214***	0.208
	(0.004)	(0.005)	(0.070)	(0.156)
Leather shoes (% of revenue)	0.015***		0.126	
	(0.005)		(7.542)	
Year of establishment	0.013	-0.003	-0.051	1.015
	(0.018)	(0.025)	(0.289)	(0.848)
Founder (0 or 1)	0.049	1.030	-13.020*	-28.750
	(0.411)	(0.651)	(6.503)	(22.050)
Age	0.010	0.015	-0.121	2.232**
	(0.019)	(0.027)	(0.300)	(0.910)
Years of schooling	0.057	0.043	-0.656	-1.948
	(0.088)	(0.055)	(1.387)	(1.854)
Business training (0 or 1)	0.845**	0.296	-4.000	-38.760**
	(0.362)	(0.506)	(5.733)	(17.140)
Experience of shoe business (0 or 1)	-0.005	-0.699*	-12.170**	-31.540**
	(0.355)	(0.376)	(5.625)	(12.750)

Table 20.5 (continued)

Table 20.5 (continued)

Parameter	ln(revenue)		Late payment %	
	Marikina	Biñan	Marikina	Biñan
	(1)	(2)	(3)	(4)
Constant	−13.130	17.610	137.000	−2,034.000
	(36.540)	(50.010)	(578.000)	(1,694.000)
R-squared	0.455	0.291	0.320	0.276
Observations	163.000	116.000	163.00	116.000
Number of firms	56.00	40.00	56.00	40.000

Note: (1) The between estimator is used.
(2) Numbers in parentheses are standard errors.
(3) ***, ** and * indicate statistical significance at the 1, 5 and 10 per cent levels, respectively.

Column (1) confirms that larger shoemakers in Marikina dealt more with department stores. The statistically significant coefficient on the share of sales to retailers suggests that Marikina shoemakers dealing only with large-scale retailers have about 110 per cent larger revenues than those without any transaction with large-scale retailers. Shoemakers producing leather shoes only have 150 per cent greater revenue than those producing shoes using synthetic materials only. Shoemakers with prior participation in a business training programme have 84 per cent greater revenue than those who had not participated in such a programme. In Biñan (see column (2)), revenue is not associated with sales route, but it is associated weakly and negatively with prior experience in shoemaking. Presumably, the negative relationship indicates that those who used to be employees of shoemakers tended to have smaller initial investments in equipment and smaller amounts of working capital than those who switched from another occupation to shoemaking after accumulating initial capital. In columns (3) and (4), the dependent variable is percentage of annual revenue paid late. Column (3) confirms that late payment and large-scale retailers are associated in Marikina. No association between late payment and sales route is found in the Biñan data. A new finding is that late payment is associated with lack of experience on the side of shoemakers, as represented by age, prior participation in a business training programme and experience in shoe business.

Table 20.6 shows the results of the application of the within (or fixed effect model) estimator to the regression, which compares the change in the dependent variable over time with the over-time changes in the explanatory variables. In the Marikina sample (see column (1)), an increase in late payment is negatively associated with revenue. If the dependent variable is replaced by the logarithm of the quantity sold, the result is qualitatively the same as that reported in column (1). If the dependent variable is the logarithm of unit price, the coefficient on late payment is close to zero and insignificant. Thus, the negative association between late payment and revenue is driven by the negative association between late payment and quantity sold. There are three possible explanations for this finding. First, an increase in long delays increases the amount of money that could not be received by the end of year. Second, if revenue reduction results from decreased product appeal to consumers, the department store would expect the product to take a long time to sell and become reluctant to pay the shoemaker.

Table 20.6. Regressions summarizing the data (fixed-effects estimator) (1998, 2001, 2003)

Parameter	ln(revenue)		Margin rate (%)		Growth in no. of sewing machines (%)	
	Marikina (1)	Biñan (2)	Marikina (3)	Biñan (4)	Marikina (5)	Biñan (6)
Late payment (% of revenue)	-0.012** (0.005)	0.001 (0.004)	-0.105 (0.086)	0.151** (0.074)	-0.083*** (0.028)	0.002 (0.010)
Sales to retailer (% of revenue)	0.021* (0.012)	0.001 (0.005)	0.498** (0.212)	0.133 (0.101)	0.033 (0.021)	0.036*** (0.013)
Leather shoes (% of revenue)	0.778** (0.356)		-1.389 (6.135)		-0.078 (0.302)	
Year dummy 2001	-0.095 (0.084)	-0.087 (0.068)	-2.452* (1.471)	2.214 (1.467)	0.081 (0.051)	-0.115 (0.090)
Year dummy 2003	-0.120 (0.086)	-0.272*** (0.070)	-3.287** (1.496)	-0.952 (1.516)		
Constant	14.15*** (0.447)	13.48*** (0.186)	0.176** (0.078)	0.124*** (0.041)	-0.351 (0.686)	-0.730** (0.317)
R-squared	0.146	0.183	0.133	0.139	0.261	0.226
Observations	165.000	116.000	162.000	109.000	85.000	68.000
Number of firms	57.000	41.000	56.000	39.000	46.000	35.000

Note: (1) The fixed effects (or within) estimator is used.
(2) Numbers in parentheses are standard errors.
(3) ***, ** and * indicate statistical significance at the 1, 5 and 10 per cent levels, respectively.

Third, an increase in late payment jeopardizes the shoemaker's financial stability, making it difficult to secure labour and materials, thereby leading to substantial decreases in output and revenue. In Biñan (see column (2)), revenue is not closely associated with late payment. One possible explanation is that the delays were much shorter in Biñan than in Marikina. Column (2) confirms that revenue decreased substantially in 2003.

In columns (3) and (4), the dependent variable is margin rate—that is, the proportion of revenue minus material, labour, subcontracting, utility and transport costs to revenue. In Marikina (see column (3)), margin rate is not associated with late payment, but it is positively and closely associated with share of sales to retailers. This close association with margin rate, together with a marginally significant coefficient on the share of sales to retailers in column (1), seems to explain why shoemakers wanted to deal with retailers despite the higher risk of exploitative delay in payment associated with retailers. In Biñan (see column (4)), increases in late payment are associated with increases in the margin rate. Here, causality seems to run from margin rate to late payment. That is, if a shoemaker in Biñan shifts from a simple product to a fancier product and puts a "Marikina Style" label without increasing the unit cost much, the price and margin rate would go up, but wholesalers and retailers would expect it would take them a longer time to sell the product to rural retail shops.

In columns (5) and (6), the dependent variable is the difference in the number of sewing machines between the current and the next data points divided by the number of sewing machines held at the current data point. This variable is intended to capture equipment investment. The highly significant and negative coefficient on late payment in column (5) confirms that increase in late payment is closely associated with decrease in equipment investment in Marikina. On the other hand, such relationship is missing in Biñan, where late payment was not as exploitative.

4 CONCLUSION

Large-scale retailers that occupied large sales floor spaces in busy districts tended to be late or bad payers, and their creditors tended to be relatively large shoemakers manufacturing products popular with urban consumers. Delays in payment between them were much longer than late payment in other sale routes of shoemakers, as well as in transactions between shoemakers and material suppliers. Increases in remarkably late payments reduced sales revenues and equipment investment. Still, large shoemakers continued to deal with large-scale retailers, possibly because increases in transactions with large-scale retailers were associated with greater sales revenues and higher margin rates. In all likelihood, buyer power arose from the scarcity of sales floor in busy districts, and large-scale retailers abused this power vis-à-vis large shoemakers.

Late payment negatively affects liquidity and complicates financial management. It forces creditors to cancel or postpone planned investments in equipment and research and development, and even leads some of them into bankruptcy (European Commission 2015). It is possible that unfair payment practices inhibit the incentive for and financial ability of industries to innovate, hence, negatively impacting consumers' benefits and job creation. Evidence is missing in the literature, however. This chapter presents suggestive evidence (albeit weak) that increases in late payment are associated with decreases in equipment investment. In this respect, it is noteworthy that the shoe industry in Marikina has recently been revived after a prolonged stagnation (Tupas 2019; Endo 2019). Marikina shoemakers have been increasing in number and sales has been growing in recent years. This reinvigoration is driven by their use of digital platforms, such as Instagram, Facebook Market Place, Lazada and Shopee, which have made it possible for them to sell their products directly to consumers even beyond the national border. They are no longer constrained by sales floor spaces in busy districts occupied by large-scale retailers. This anecdote is indicative of the grave consequences that buyer power has for SMEs, industrial development and job creation.

The European Commission's (2015) report on the implementation of the Late Payment Directive 2011/7/EU finds that buyer power is so deeply rooted that SMEs are reluctant to exercise their right to claim payment of interest and other compensation due to late payment by their buyers. Policy measures to induce both SMEs and large firms to change payment culture are important, but it may be difficult to produce the desired results through these measures alone. Given such difficulty and the solution provided to SMEs by digital markets, the efforts of competition agencies to protect and promote competition and fair-trade practices in digital markets have become all the more important.

ACKNOWLEDGEMENT

With thanks to Fernando Aldaba, Arsenio Balisacan, Brian Aldrich Chua, Noel P. de Guzman, Cielito Habito, Karl Jandoc, Stella Quimbo, Jose Adlai Tancangco, Irish Joy Yparranguirre and other participants of a seminar at the Ateneo de Manila University held in March 2021 for their valuable comments. Thanks to the editors for very helpful comments and suggestions. Thanks also to Roehlano Briones and Arsenio Balisacan for encouraging and helping me to study the Philippine economy and its SME sector. The survey of shoemakers was financially supported by the National Graduate Institute for Policy Studies.

REFERENCES

Balisacan, Arsenio M. 2020. "Toward a Fairer Society: Inequality and Competition Policy in Developing Asia". *Philippine Review of Economics* 56, no. 1&2: 127–46.

Cheng, Thomas. 2020. *Competition Law in Developing Countries*. UK: Oxford University Press.

Endo, Jun. 2019. "Philippines' Shoe Industry Has a New Spring in Its Step: Metro Manila's Marikina Revives with Help from Net-Savvy Salespeople". *Nikkei Asia*, 14 January 2019. https://asia.nikkei.com/Business/Business-trends/Philippines-shoe-industry-has-a-new-spring-in-its-step.

European Commission. 2011. "Directive 2011/7/EU of European Parliament and the Council of 16 February 2011 on Combating Late Payment in Commercial Transactions". European Commission, L48/2011. https://eur-lex.europa.eu/legal-content/EN/TXT/?uri=CELEX:32011L0007.

———. 2015. "Ex-post Evaluation of Late Payment Directive". ENTR/172/PP/2012/FC-LOT14. https://op.europa.eu/en/publication-detail/-/publication/400ecc74-9a54-11e5-b3b7-01aa75ed71a1.

Evenett, Simon J. 2005. "What Is the Relationship between Competition Law and Policy and Economic Development?". In *Competition Policy and Development in Asia*, edited by Douglas H. Brooks and Simon J. Evenett, pp. 1–26. London: Palgrave Macmillan.

Schmitz, Hubert. 1995. "Small Shoemakers and Fordist Giants: Tale of Super Cluster". *World Development*, 23, no. 1: 9–28.

Sonobe, Tetsushi, and Keijiro Otsuka. 2006. *Cluster-Based Industrial Development: An East Asian Model*. New York: Palgrave Macmillan.

———. 2011. *Cluster-Based Industrial Development: A Comparative Study of Asia and Africa*. New York: Palgrave Macmillan.

Sonobe, Tetsushi, John Akoten, and Keijiro Otsuka. 2009. "An Exploration into the Successful Development of the Leather-Shoe Industry in Ethiopia". *Review of Development Economics* 13, no. 4: 719–36. https://doi.org/10.1111/j.1467-9361.2009.00526.x.
Stigler, George J. 1951. "The Division of Labor Is Limited by the Extent of Market". *Journal of Political Economy* 59, no. 3: 185–93.
Tupas, Emanuel. 2019. "Marikina Shoe Industry Still Thriving, Is Worth P1 Billion". *One News Ph*, 11 September 2019. https://www.onenews.ph/marikina-shoe-industry-still-thriving-is-worth-p1-billion.
World Bank. 2018. *Fostering Competition in the Philippines: The Challenge of Restrictive Regulations*. Washington, DC: World Bank.

21 Regulation, Market Evolution and Competition in the Philippine Microfinance Sector

Jan Carlo B. Punongbayan, Gilberto M. Llanto and Emmanuel F. Esguerra

1 INTRODUCTION

The Philippine microfinance sector encompasses banks, non-governmental organizations (NGOs) and various non-bank financial intermediaries (e.g., cooperatives and credit unions) providing financial services[1] to customers that most mainstream financial institutions deem too costly or risky. The sector has transformed over the years, both in terms of the number of institutions providing microfinance services and the number of clients served. From the late 1980s when NGOs and similar not-for-profit institutions used to dominate microlending, the sector has steadily grown, attracting commercial players, chiefly banks of varying orientations (e.g., rural, thrift and cooperative banks), encouraged by the business potential of tapping a large, hitherto underserved, market. The microfinance clientele has similarly grown from a few thousands to several millions (MCPI 2016).

---

[1] These services include loans, deposits, payment services, money transfers and insurance products, although not all microfinance institutions (MFIs) provide the full range. At the minimum, all MFIs engage in microlending.

The growth of the sector can be traced in part to a wider acceptance of the view that broadening access to finance is an effective strategy for poverty alleviation.[2] The pessimism that grew out of the failed subsidized credit programmes of an earlier period has given way to a more sanguine view of "banking with the poor", based on the celebrated successes of models like the Grameen Bank and the Association for Social Advancement (ASA) of Bangladesh and BancoSol of Bolivia. A key element in these successful experiments has been the application of sound banking principles emphasizing financial sustainability, challenging microfinance institutions (MFIs) to rely less on government or donor subsidies while serving more of the poor.

At the institutional level, the creation of a policy environment more hospitable to financial inclusion supported the paradigm shift from one of subsidy dependence to financial sustainability. This included the adoption of microfinance standards for NGOs as well as the encouragement given banks to get involved in microfinance. In 1997, the Philippines rolled out the National Strategy for Microfinance (NSM) to provide the framework for the promotion of microfinance as a sustainable activity. The strategy called for government policies directed at enlarging the role of private MFIs in financial services provision for low-income groups. It also provided the basis for subsequent laws and issuances on financing poverty alleviation measures.[3] Executive Order (EO) 138, promulgated in 1999, explicitly disallows participation of non-financial government agencies in direct lending. Moreover, in acknowledging the non-collateralized feature of microlending and granting clout to the monetary authority to institute rules and regulations to govern the practice of microfinance among banks,[4] the General Banking Act of 2000 effectively laid the groundwork for greater bank participation in microfinance. At its peak in 2007, more than 200 thrift, rural and cooperative banks were involved in varying degrees in microfinance. That number has come down since to around 150 in 2020.

---

[2] Empirical evidence on the poverty-reducing effects of microfinance remains mixed at best, however (Roodman and Morduch 2009).
[3] These are identified in Alindogan (2005).
[4] A unit was established within the Bangko Sentral ng Pilipinas (BSP) to handle microfinance-related matters.

Against this backdrop, this paper revisits[5] the Philippine microfinance sector from the perspective of competition economics. This comes from the recognition that, unlike regular banks, MFIs strive to achieve a "double bottom line"—that is, to attain financial self-sufficiency (defined as the ability to continue to profitably do business free of subsidies) while keeping to the original mission of reaching out to the poor and unbanked segment of society. The idea that competition maximizes economic welfare by driving firms to behave efficiently is widely accepted. However, the framing of competition policy when "public interest" considerations (e.g., distributional equity) are involved can be quite problematic (Balisacan 2019). Some studies suggest that competition tends to undermine the original mission of microfinance. For example, Cull, Demirgüç-Kunt, and Morduch (2007) show that the poorest borrowers are crowded out of MFIs' portfolios; Schicks and Rosenberg (2011) observe a general decline in MFIs' outreach and loan portfolio performance. The relationship between competition and the performance of MFIs has in fact been the subject of theoretical and empirical research (McIntosh and Wydick 2005; Kar and Swain 2014; Kar 2016; Navin and Sinha 2019).

This paper's objectives are more modest. We inquire about the status of competition in the Philippine microfinance sector following the changes in the regulatory environment, which opened up the sector to for-profit institutions. Specifically, we assess the level of competition in the Philippine microfinance sector and its evolution during the period 1999–2018 using three available measures of competition: the Herfindahl-Hirschman Index (HHI), the Panzar-Rosse method or PRH index and the Boone indicator.

The next section describes the policy setting in which microfinance activity grew, throwing the spotlight on actions taken by the government to mainstream microfinance in banking and enforce performance standards on microfinance NGOs. The third section provides an overview of how competition in microfinance markets has been analysed in the literature in light of MFIs' "double bottom line". The fourth section describes the Philippine microfinance market using institution-level data available from the Microfinance Information eXchange (MIX). We use this data set to generate measures of competition for the Philippine microfinance market in the fifth section. The sixth section concludes.

---

[5] For earlier studies, see Esguerra (2012) and Llanto (2015).

2 EVOLUTION OF MICROFINANCE POLICY

The unprecedented growth in microfinance in many developing countries has been attributed to several factors. Kar (2016) cites profit-making opportunities to be made in this lively market and subsidized funding from governments and development agencies. High repayment rates by microcredit clients and availability of commercial fund sources have attracted mainstream financial institutions to the microfinance market (Navin and Sinha 2019). In the past, NGOs relied on grants and subsidized loans from government to finance microlending.

The Philippine microfinance market reflects this phenomenal growth. In the late 1980s, a handful of microfinance NGOs attempted to provide micro-borrowers with access to credit. A microfinance NGO with 2,000–5,000 borrowers was the envy of its peers, but now (as indicated in section 4 below) it has become only one of the foremost players in the market. Banks, mostly rural banks, have also entered this market, sensing tremendous profit-making opportunities in many unbanked and underserved areas.[6]

Much of this phenomenal growth in the microfinance market is due to the policy and regulatory environment for microfinance, which has had a profound impact on MFIs. Regulation has made entry easy and microfinance operation very attractive for for-profit players in this market. This involved two phases: fixing the policy environment and issuing specific regulations governing microfinance operations.

First, the government fixed the policy environment. The subsidized credit programmes in the 1970s through the 1990s proved to be unsustainable and had to be stopped. Huge fiscal costs, closure of many rural banks and high loan defaults and arrears of many borrowers undermined this policy intervention. By 1997, as many as 86 government-subsidized credit programmes were being implemented by government line agencies, government non-bank financial institutions, government-owned and controlled corporations and government financial institutions. The initial fund allocation for 63 of these programmes amounted to almost 2 per cent of the gross domestic product (GDP) in 1996. Twenty-four of these programs reported reaching

---

[6] A leading microfinance rural bank, the CARD Rural Bank reports over a million borrowers. Commercial banks have established savings banks (e.g., BPI Direct BanKo, Inc.) or bought rural banks (e.g., BDO Unibank bought One Network Bank, Inc.).

a total of 67,821 borrowers and around 685,794 indirect beneficiaries.[7] Around half of the 86 subsidized credit programmes registered an average repayment rate of 82.6 per cent. For 42 reporting programmes by agency type, the average repayment rate in 1995–96 was 76 per cent for line agencies, 91.7 per cent for non-bank financial institutions, 89.8 per cent for government financial institutions and 67.2 per cent for government-owned and controlled corporations (Llanto, Geron, and Tang 1999).

That the subsidized credit programmes in the Philippines failed is not unique. Braverman and Guasch (1986) show that subsidized credit programmes fail spectacularly in achieving the many objectives behind them, namely, to increase agricultural output or improve rural income distribution and to alleviate poverty. Mere removal of credit subsidies, however, failed to ease the credit constraint as private commercial banks and even MFIs continued to avoid smallholder agriculture for its riskiness and high transactions cost (Balisacan and Sebastian 2006). Thus, the government undertook a major shift in its overall credit policy by issuing EO 138 (s.1999) and the National Strategy for Microfinance and by enacting the General Banking Law of 2000 (Republic Act 8791). The latter formally recognized microfinance as part of mainstream banking and finance, enabling the Bangko Sentral ng Pilipinas (BSP) to configure appropriate regulation and supervision of banks engaged in microfinance. EO 138 prohibits government non-financial agencies from providing credit and encourages private-sector participation in the microfinance market (Llanto 2018). In the rural sector, this policy shift found expression in the reforms instituted under the Agriculture and Fisheries Modernization Program (Ravago, Balisacan, and Sombilla 2018).

These policy issuances provided the basic legal framework for a new regulatory stance on microfinance. The BSP adopted light-touch regulation—some prefer to call it "proportionate" regulation (Banal-Formoso and Bolido 2020, 43)—and risk-based supervision; this twin approach has enabled microfinance banks to be flexible in designing innovative loan products and adroit in managing low-income, asset-deficient microfinance clients.[8]

---

[7] From 24 of the 63 subsidized credit programmes. The listed borrower could be a cooperative, which in turn re-lends to members (indirect beneficiaries here).

[8] Rule 2 (n) of the implementing rules and regulations (IRR) of the Microfinance NGOs Act of 2015 defines "low income" as "income of individuals or families

The very first circular on microfinance was BSP Circular No. 272 (2001), which provides the operating guidelines on implementing the provisions of the General Banking Law regarding microfinance. It recognizes cash-flow based lending as a peculiar feature of microfinance, defines microfinance loans and provides for the exemption of microfinance loans from rules and regulations issued regarding unsecured loans. Twenty years ago, this was a revolutionary approach to bank lending, especially regarding unsecured loans, which brought microfinance banks to mainstream finance. Circular 272 and subsequent circulars issued by the BSP have triggered the eventual growth of microfinance portfolios and outreach. Box 1 lists the various BSP circulars fostering microfinance.

Box 21.1. BSP regulations fostering microfinance

Particulars	Circular issued and purpose
Loan Products	Circular 678 (2010) provides rules and regulations that govern the approval of banks' housing microfinance products.
	Circular 680 (2010) provides rules and regulations on the approval of banks' micro-agri loans.
	Circular 683 (2010) provides rules and regulations in the marketing, sale and servicing of micro-insurance products by banks.
	Circular 744 (2011) defines microenterprise loan plus or "microfinance plus", which ranges from PHP150,001 to PHP300,000 and caters to the growing business of microfinance clients.
	Circular 950 (2017) and Circular 1022 (2018) allow covered institutions to implement reduced Know-Your-Customer rules for certain low-risk accounts and use technology for face-to-face contact requirements; they update the rules on validating client identity by accepting the national ID (PhilSys).

Box 21.1 *(continued)*

---

that fall below the low-income threshold, which is defined by the National Economic and Development Authority as twice the official national poverty threshold".

Box 21.1 *(continued)*

Particulars	Circular issued and purpose
Loan Products *(continued)*	Circular 992 (2018) introduces the framework for basic deposit accounts to meet the need of the unbanked for a low-cost, no-frills account (low opening amount capped at PHP100, no maintaining balance, no dormancy charges, simplified identification requirements).
Loan Regulations	Circular 272 (2001) recognizes cash flow-based lending as a peculiar feature of microfinance, defines microfinance loans and provides for the exemption of microfinance loans from rules and regulations issued regarding unsecured loans.
	Circular 364 (2003) reduces to 75 per cent the risk weight applicable to small and medium enterprises (SMEs) and microfinance loan portfolios that meet prudential standards.
	Circular 409 (2003) provides the rules and regulations for the portfolio-at-risk (PAR) and the corresponding allowance for probable losses, which depends on the number of days of missed payment.
Rediscounting	Circular 282 (2001) opens a rediscounting facility for rural banks/cooperative rural banks engaged in microfinance.
	Circular 324 (2002) opens a rediscounting facility for thrift banks engaged in microfinance.
Accessibility	Circular 273 (2001) provides partial lifting of the moratorium on establishment of new banks as long as the new banks are microfinance oriented.
	Circular 340 (2002) provides the rules and regulations concerning the establishment of branches or loan collection and disbursement points (LCDPs).
	Circular 365 (2003) liberalizes select provisions of Circular 340.

Box 21.1 *(continued)*

Box 21.1 *(continued)*

Particulars	Circular issued and purpose
Accessibility *(continued)*	Circular 505 (2005) revises branching guidelines by allowing qualified microfinance-oriented banks and microfinance-oriented branches of regular banks to establish branches anywhere in the Philippines.
	Circular 608 (2008) revises the rules on acceptable identification cards, lessening the requirement from two to one valid identification card and widening the range of acceptable IDs.
	Circular 624 (2008) amends branching policy and guidelines governing the establishment of branches, extension offices and other banking offices (OBOs).
	Circular 649 (2009) provides guidelines on the issuance of electronic money (e-money) and the operations of electronic money issuers (EMIs) in the Philippines.
	Circular 669 (2009) allows the servicing of limited withdrawals by microfinance/Barangay Micro-business Enterprises (BMBEs) clients in LCDPs and OBOs of microfinance-oriented banks/branches.
	Circular 694 (2010) allows for the establishment of micro-banking offices (MBOs) and defines microfinance products.
	Circular 727 (2011) amends the guidelines on branching and voluntary closure/sale/acquisition of branches/other banking offices.
	Circular 728 (2011) allows for phased lifting of branching restriction in the eight "restricted areas" of Metro Manila.
	Circular 759 (2012) amends the branching policy and guidelines under the Manual of Regulations for Banks.

Box 21.1 *(continued)*

Box 21.1 *(continued)*

Particulars	Circular issued and purpose
Accessibility *(continued)*	Circular 777 (2012) amends the subsection on the Manual of Regulations for Banks (MORB) regarding the opening of approved but unopened branches.
	Circular 783 (2013) amends the regulations on relocation and voluntary closure/sale of branches/OBOs.
	Circular 808 (2013) provides guidelines on information technology risk management for all banks and other BSP-supervised institutions.
	Circular 847 (2014) amends pertinent MORB provisions, specifically on the application of special licensing fees on relocation of head offices, branches/OBOs and approved but unopened branches/OBOs to restricted areas.
	Circular 868 (2015) expands the range of services that can be delivered in MBOs and waives the collection of processing fee for banking offices that will be established in unbanked cities and municipalities.
	Circular 940 (2017) allows banks to serve clients through ubiquitous retail outlets such as cash agents, which can accept and disburse cash on behalf of the bank.
	Circular 980 (2017) adopts the National Retail Payment System framework to promote interoperability, allowing digital transactions to be sent from any account to any account, whether held in a bank or e-money issuer.
	Circular 987 (2017) allows the establishment of branch lite units to provide a wide range of products and services, depending on the market needs of a specific area or locality.

Source: BSP (2021)

Banks responded with appropriate loan products, such as educational loans, working capital loans, housing microfinance, micro-agri loans, micro-insurance and basic deposit accounts. Liberalized branching regulations, including the establishment of micro-banking offices (later formalized into branch lite units or BLUs), enabled the expansion of outreach to more and more unbanked and underserved areas of the country.[9]

Meanwhile, with light-touch regulation, it was a short step to having regulations that foster financial inclusion; these have resulted in an even greater outreach by microfinance banks. Since 2000, the BSP has issued over sixty circulars to foster financial inclusion. These circulars facilitated e-banking for small-scale clients, covering electronic payment transactions, small value transfers and remittances. These have resulted in a wider range of inclusive financial products and services, lowered barriers to customer on-boarding and enhanced financial consumer protection.[10]

The BSP has moved away from traditional supervision to risk-based supervision and examination. Risk-based supervision places greater emphasis on risk management, internal control systems including internal audits, adequate provisioning for expected credit losses, external independent auditors, management information systems, and information disclosure. A complementary move was the establishment of the BSP Micro-SME Finance Group for effective risk-based supervision and examination of microfinance banks through Monetary Board Resolution No. 1012 issued in 2006. With these decisions, the BSP's regulatory and supervisory stance balances the requirements for safe and sound banking practices with an understanding of the unique characteristics and risks of microfinance markets, calling for a nuanced approach to supervision.

---

[9] See Appendix Figures 21A and 21B for growth in the number of banks with microfinance operations and the corresponding expansion in loans and client outreach over time. In 2019, there were 2,248 BLUs in 871 local government units (LGUs); 195 of these LGUs were being served solely by BLUs. The number of touchpoints through agents has continued to multiply, bringing the total number of cash agents to 17,000 and e-money agents to over 43,000 in 2019 (Fonacier 2020).

[10] We are indebted to Mynard Bryan Mojica of the BSP for this information.

The second strand of the regulatory environment for microfinance is the regulation of microfinance NGOs. Microfinance NGOs generated much public attention in the 1980s because of their willingness to support or expand microenterprises, which generally had failed to access bank loans. However, many of them had problems of outreach and, most of all, sustainability (Llanto 2018). Reform initiatives in the mid-1990s to improve performance came from the Coalition for Performance Standards and the Credit Policy Improvement Project (CPIP), a technical assistance project funded by the US Agency for International Development (USAID). The community of practicing microfinance NGOs agreed to adhere to performance standards introduced by the Coalition and CPIP. The Coalition later morphed into the Microfinance Council of the Philippines, Inc., which advocates sustainable and client-responsive solutions to poverty in the Philippines.[11]

It took around 18 years for a formal regulatory structure for microfinance NGOs to be established. The Microfinance NGOs Act of 2015 (Republic Act 10693) created the Microfinance NGO Regulatory Council. The Council is chaired by the Securities and Exchange Commission (SEC) and has the following members: Departments of Finance, Social Welfare and Development, and Trade and Industry as permanent members, and three appointive members from the microfinance NGO sector.

Microfinance NGOs are required to obtain accreditation from the Council. The criteria for accreditation include sound and measurable standards of financial performance, social performance and governance.[12] Accreditation and good performance measured against standards are preconditions for accessing certain incentives provided by the Act, such as a preferential tax of 2 per cent based on gross receipts from microfinance operations in lieu of all national taxes; support programmes consisting of operational and capacity-building grants, low-interest loans and guarantee funds; and technical assistance. The Microfinance NGO Regulatory Council can revoke accreditation

---

[11] The MCPI was registered with the Securities and Exchange Commission as a non-stock corporation in June 1999. It has grown to comprise 59 institutions, including 46 practitioners, 2 regional councils and 11 support institutions. It is estimated that MCPI members account for at least 75 per cent of the total active outreach of the microfinance sector in the Philippines (MCPI 2021).

[12] Rule 3, Section 2 of the IRR of the Microfinance NGOs Act of 2015.

and impose corresponding administrative sanctions for violations of the Act and its rules and regulations.

The Council serves as an oversight body for microfinance NGOs. Registration and accreditation with the SEC work for microfinance NGOs. These provide them with a sense of legitimacy as formal lending institutions. Accreditation signals good standing with an oversight body and the microfinance community. Microfinance NGOs are not allowed to mobilize savings from the public, thus, they are dependent on cheap loans, donations or grants and reflows from their existing portfolios to expand microfinance operations. Moreover, donors and lenders are more comfortable dealing with microfinance NGOs that are monitored by some oversight body like the Council.

In sum, the regulatory environment for microfinance has provided a supportive platform for MFIs' financial sustainability and outreach. The market orientation of credit policies, ease of entry and flexibility to design innovative loan products and services are critical for financial self-sufficiency. Client outreach has been reinforced by liberal branch banking, establishment of branch lite units and incentives (for microfinance NGOs). Meanwhile, the BSP has issued circulars designed to protect consumers from risks and misconduct by lenders in the world of digitalized banking, even as microfinance banks and microfinance NGOs start to embrace new technologies (e.g., e-money, electronic payment mechanisms) for greater client outreach and efficient operations. A detailed examination shows that regulations have not been a barrier to entry. The rules have not been designed to enable dominance in the market or favour or protect a particular type of institution. It seems that regulations so far issued can help microfinance institutions achieve their double bottom line of financial sustainability and outreach. With this supportive platform, microfinance NGOs and microfinance banks have entered a competitive market. Data show many have fallen by the wayside while a few have become strong competitive market players. However, given the vast microfinance market, attractive profit-making opportunities, and a strong sense of service to the bottom of the pyramid, many new players, microfinance NGOs and banks continue to try their lot in this dynamic market.

3 RELATED LITERATURE

Early in the days when financial sustainability became a buzzword in the microfinance movement, dissenting voices warned against "mission drift", or the tendency to focus less on the poor, as MFIs pursue commercial viability. This sparked a debate on whether a trade-off exists between financial sustainability and depth of outreach. Although this strand of the microfinance literature does not explicitly mention competition, the analyses are invariably based on models of a microfinance market where socially motivated and profit-oriented MFIs co-exist. In a study of 124 MFIs in 49 countries, Cull, Demirgüç-Kunt, and Morduch (2007, F131) show evidence of a negative association between loan sizes and average costs, suggesting a trade-off between profitability and outreach given that larger average loan sizes have been interpreted as implying less outreach to the poor. For Ghosh and Van Tassel (2008), mission drift occurs because MFIs previously catering to the poorest clients adjust to commercialization by entertaining more of the "better-off" poor to balance financial return and poverty reduction while maximizing their impact on poverty. Armendariz et al. (2011) explain mission drift as resulting from subsidy uncertainty, which was found to be associated with higher interest rates. Increased commercialization causes incumbent MFIs dependent on and competing for limited concessional funds to combine lending to the poor with catering to better-off clients in order to demonstrate some measure of financial sustainability and guard against the possibility of subsidies being withdrawn. In another paper, Armendariz and Szafarz (2011) explain why it is difficult for empirical researchers to distinguish between mission drift and cross-subsidization.

Theoretical and empirical research on the effect of competition on the performance of MFIs has also drawn from studies on the banking sector. One point of view is that competition brings stability to the sector. According to the competition-stability view (Boyd and de Nicolo 2005), increased market power that gives rise to high interest rates in loan markets can worsen moral hazard and adverse selection, making repayment more difficult. The competition-fragility view (Berger, Klapper, and Turk-Ariss 2008), on the other hand, posits that higher concentration favours stability in the sense that lenders have a lower risk exposure. Competition reduces the lender's profit margin, leading it to take on greater risks to boost returns. This suggests a positive association between competition and loan portfolio risk as measured by the share of loans at risk of default.

McIntosh and Wydick (2005) show how, as a result of competition, MFIs lose the ability to cross-subsidize clients and asymmetric information on borrower quality worsens. In this model, rents are competed away as interest rates are reduced due to Bertrand-type competition and client-maximizing behaviour. This pressures MFIs to direct their attention away from the poorest clients towards the more profitable segment of the market. Moreover, profitable borrowers of socially motivated MFIs are encouraged to migrate to the profit-oriented MFIs that are bent on attracting more prosperous clients with larger loans (Navajas, Conning, Gonzalez-Vega 2003; Vogelgesang 2003; McIntosh and Wydick 2005). The portfolio quality of the socially motivated MFIs thus deteriorates as they lose their cross-subsidization possibilities. Meanwhile, competition leads "impatient borrowers" to access multiple loans, increasing their indebtedness and making defaults a near certainty.

Kar and Swain (2014) explain further how increased competition among MFIs affects the industry and its clients. More MFIs competing for the same clients leads to a weakening or loss of credit discipline otherwise enforceable when MFIs are fewer by making future access to credit contingent on prompt repayment of previous loans. This also tends to exacerbate information asymmetry regarding clients' risk profiles and encourages multiple loans or "double dipping" by borrowers. As a result, portfolio quality suffers[13] and excessive borrowing leads to higher non-repayment rates of MFIs.

The negative impact of competition on outreach is also discussed in Hartarska and Nadolnyak (2007) and Hermes, Lensink, and Meesters (2011). According to Assefa, Hermes, and Meesters (2013), intense competition is negatively correlated with MFI outreach, profitability, efficiency and repayment rates. In intensely competitive markets, MFIs strive to preserve their client base and reduce their costs by relaxing lending standards or reducing screening efforts, thereby resulting in higher default rates due to adverse selection.

---

[13] The deterioration of portfolio quality due to asymmetric information in multi-lender markets is discussed in Broecker (1990) and Marquez (2002) as cited in Kar and Swain (2014).

4 THE PHILIPPINE MICROFINANCE LANDSCAPE

We analyse the microfinance sector of the Philippines using the MIX database. Launched in 2002 and freely downloadable from the World Bank, MIX contains panel data on financial service providers and MFIs from about 100 developing country markets.[14] A study conducted in 2006 benchmarked Philippine MFIs with those in Asia and the rest of the MIX sample (MIX and MCPI 2006 as cited in Esguerra 2012). It notes that local MFIs are older, smaller based on loan portfolio size, less dependent on concessional sources for their loanable funds, cover fewer borrowers, and tend to cater more to small borrowers (i.e., have more depth of outreach) than their international peers. While showing a higher financial revenue ratio, Philippine MFIs also incur a higher cost of delivering financial services compared with non-Philippine MFIs. This probably explains why interest rates and other fees charged on loans by Philippine MFIs are about 8 per cent higher than those by Asian and other MFIs. Philippine MFIs also have a riskier loan portfolio. In this paper, we restrict our analysis to annual Philippine data from 1999 to 2018 (quarterly data are available for some years).

Figure 21.1 shows the number of Philippine MFIs by type in the MIX database. We treat banks and rural banks as one group (labelled "banks"); "others" includes credit unions/cooperatives, non-bank financial institutions (NBFIs), as well as those categorized as "unknown". The third group is composed of microfinance NGOs. The number of rural banks steeply rose in the early to mid-2000s, coinciding with the period after the enactment of the General Banking Law of 2000. NGOs came in a close second. But in the 2010s, NGOs started to outnumber rural banks, whose rank dwindled fast—possibly due to reporting issues, but more likely due to a real decline in participation for various reasons as indicated by the BSP data (see Appendix Figure 21A). For one, the period after 2010 was marked by some closures as well as mergers and consolidations among banks. Some banks may have also changed strategies, deciding to opt out of microfinance. In 2018, 60.9 per cent of the top MFIs were NGOs while 26.1 per cent were rural banks.

---

[14] MIX collects data from MFIs around the world and standardizes these for comparability. The voluntary nature of participation in the data exchange suggests that the MFIs in MIX are likely to be the better financial performers in their respective countries.

Figure 21.1. Philippine MFIs by last known legal status (1999–2018)

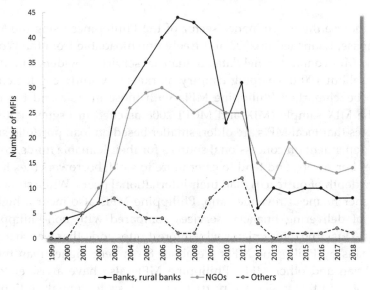

Source of data: MIX.

Table 21.1 shows the top MFIs by gross loan portfolio (million PHP). On top is ASA Philippines, followed by CARD Bank and CARD NGO. These three institutions alone controlled 56.7 per cent of the market in 2018 in terms of total assets. Considering that CARD Bank and CARD NGO belong to one company, one can argue that in fact CARD is the biggest MFI in the Philippines, garnering 33.9 per cent of market share, followed by ASA Philippines at 22.8 per cent.

Figures 21.2–21.4 show a pronounced increase in the number of active borrowers, gross loan portfolios and assets of NGOs and rural banks starting in 2005. This trend is largely driven by the top three players: ASA Philippines (NGO), CARD NGO and CARD Bank (rural bank). Essentially all MFIs provide the same services. But, unlike banks, NGOs do not have a reserve requirement and are lightly regulated (through the Microfinance NGOs Act of 2015; NGOs are regulated by the Microfinance NGO Regulatory Council). This may account for the noticeable rise of NGO players like ASA Philippines and CARD NGO. Meanwhile, rural banks have not only become fewer, but—except for CARD Bank and 1st Valley Bank—also did not experience high growth in business compared with ASA Philippines and CARD. However, the fact that banks generally have larger loan portfolios and fewer borrowers than NGOs (Table 21.2) indicates smaller average loan sizes for the latter MFI type.

Table 21.1. Top MFI players in 2018

MFI name	Last known legal status	Gross loan portfolio (million PHP)	Market share in terms of assets (%)	Market share (assets) in subgroup (%)	Debt-equity ratio	Cost per borrower (PHP)	Portfolio at risk, > 30 days (%)	Portfolio at risk, > 90 days (%)
ASA[1] Philippines	NGO	17,660	22.81	41.63	1.96	1,949.17	0.38	0.00
CARD[2] Bank	Rural Bank	10,300	18.39	43.82	3.10	2,386.05	1.87	1.61
CARD NGO	NGO	8,216	15.49	28.26	1.05			
1st Valley Bank	Rural Bank	6,965	11.11	26.46	3.55	13,303.92	8.72	7.09
NWTF[3]	NGO	3,286	5.49	10.01	1.53	2,283.69	1.50	1.28
GM Bank	Rural Bank	2,680	4.74	11.30	8.47	23,296.72	9.88	8.49
Bangko Kabayan	Rural Bank	1,901	3.77	8.97	5.02	17,484.78	0.63	0.58
TSKI[4]	NGO	1,746	3.16	5.77	6.42	1,940.64	0.58	8.67
TSPI[5]	NGO	1,722	2.62	4.79	1.95	4,761.44	22.41	19.22
One Puhunan[6]	NBFI	1,720	2.48	100.00	5.86	3,381.68	4.60	3.36
KMBI[7]	NGO	1,045	1.62	2.96	1.55	3,485.70	2.27	0.95
ASHI[8]	NGO	980	1.35	2.46	3.66	3,493.30	1.37	0.99
RB Camalig	Rural Bank	878	1.69	4.03	3.78	7,241.68	5.70	5.36
Bangko Mabuhay	Rural Bank	588	2.27	5.41	5.38	15,255.91	26.92	13.81
CEVI[9]	NGO	474	0.71	1.29	1.73	2,792.62	4.93	2.48
ECLOF – PHL[10]	NGO	262	0.45	0.82	16.38	4,635.25	11.82	9.81

Table 21.1 (continued)

Table 21.1 (continued)

MFI name	Last known legal status	Gross loan portfolio (million PHP)	Market share in terms of assets (%)	Market share (assets) in subgroup (%)	Debt-equity ratio	Cost per borrower (PHP)	Portfolio at risk, > 30 days (%)	Portfolio at risk, > 90 days (%)
RPMI[11]	NGO	257	0.56	1.02	1.28	2,679.66	3.35	1.94
OK[12] Bank	Bank	242	0.42	55.44	3.25	17,336.85	7.79	5.26
Dungganon Bank	Bank	204	0.33	44.56	1.16	4,475.68		
Kazama Grameen	NGO	195	0.27	0.50	4.91	2,591.82	5.47	4.94
JMH[13] Microfinance	NGO	128	0.22	0.39	2.71	2,473.17	0.68	0.41
Joyful Development	NGO	19	0.03	0.05	-3.60	6,370.30	16.07	12.32
JVOFI[14]	NGO	13	0.03	0.05				

Note:
1 Association for Social Advancement
2 Center for Agricultural and Rural Development
3 Negros Women for Tomorrow Foundation
4 Taytay sa Kauswagan, Inc. (meaning Bridge to Progress)
5 Tulay sa Pag-unlad, Inc. (meaning Bridge to Development)
6 Also known as CreditAccess Phils. (Puhunan means capital or investment)
7 Kabalikat para sa Maunlad na Buhay, Inc. (meaning Partner for a Progressive Life)
8 Ahon Sa Hirap, Inc. (meaning Rise from Poverty)
9 Community Economic Ventures, Inc.
10 Ecumenical Church Foundation – Philippines
11 Rangtay sa Pagrang-ay Microfinance, Inc. (meaning Bridge to Prosperity)
12 Opportunity Kauswagan Bank (Kauswagan means progress)
13 Formerly J. M. Honrado Foundation
14 Jaime V. Ongpin Foundation, Inc.

Source of data: MIX.

Figure 21.2. Average number of active borrowers by MFI type

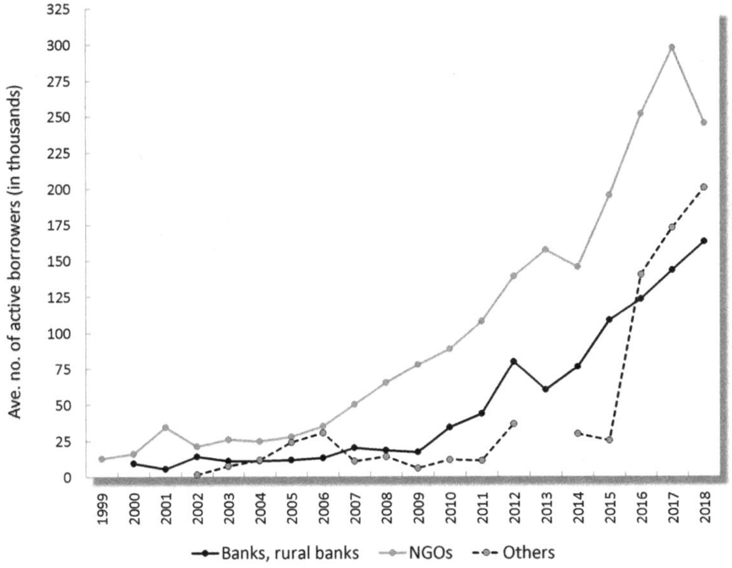

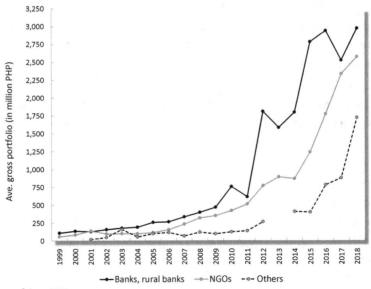

Source of data: MIX.

Figure 21.3. Average gross loan portfolio (in million PHP) by MFI type

Source of data: MIX.

Figure 21.4. Average assets (in million PHP) by MFI type

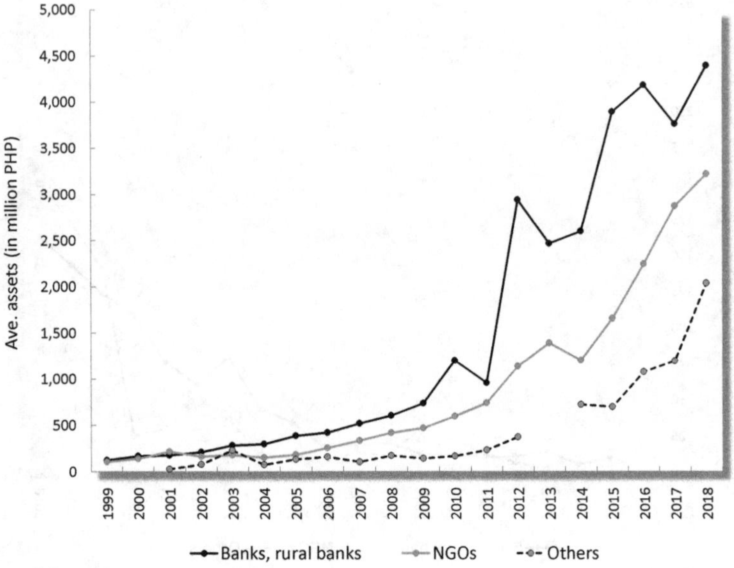

[Line chart showing average assets from 1999 to 2018 for Banks/rural banks, NGOs, and Others]

Source of data: MIX.

Table 21.2. Selected MFI indicators (2018)

Parameter	Banks	NBFIs	NGOs	Rural banks
No. of active borrowers (in '000)	7.51	200.67	245.18	214.89
Gross loan portfolio (million PHP)	223.18	1,720.24	2,571.59	3,885.24
Assets (in million PHP)	308.76	2,038.27	3,220.46	5,755.57
Efficiency (%)	30.43	47.53	42.16	19.93
Cost per borrower (in PHP)	10,906.26	3,381.68	3,288.06	13,161.51
Portfolio at risk, > 30 days (%)	7.79	4.60	6.66	8.95
Portfolio at risk, > 90 days (%)	5.26	3.36	5.25	6.16
Debt-equity ratio	2.21	5.86	3.19	4.88
Return on assets (%)	0.94	1.93	4.15	2.59
Return on equity (%)	4.41	11.65	20.91	12.24
Real yield on gross portfolio (%, 2016)	38.31		46.74	20.59

Note: Data on real yield on gross portfolio stopped in 2016.
Source of data: MIX.

Figure 21.5 shows that average efficiency, defined as operating expenses divided by average gross loan portfolio, has generally remained stable for rural banks and NGOs. Meanwhile, the cost per borrower of banks and rural banks has risen significantly from 2016 (Figure 21.6). In general, the average cost per borrower is higher for banks than for NGOs. This can be explained by the higher overhead expenses normally incurred by banks relative to NGOs and the fact that the latter have more borrowers than the former.

Figures 21.7 and 21.8 show portfolio-at-risk greater than 30 days (PAR > 30) and greater than 90 days (PAR > 90), respectively. For PAR > 30, the average PAR fluctuated between 5 and 15 per cent for both banks and NGOs. For PAR > 90, the average PAR fluctuated within a narrower range for NGOs than for banks; the NGOs' average PAR also appears to be slightly lower. In both cases, the ratio averaged less than 10 per cent for the period under consideration, which is within the acceptable range.

Figure 21.5. Average efficiency (%) by MFI type

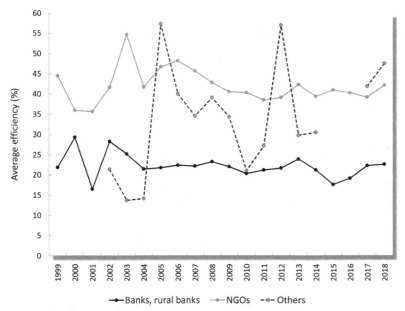

Note: Efficiency means operating expenses/average gross loan prtfolio.
Source of data: MIX.

Figure 21.6. Average cost per borrower (PHP) by MFI type

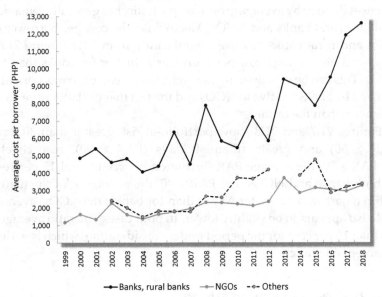

Source of data: MIX.

Figure 21.7. Average portfolio at risk, > 30 days (%) by MFI type

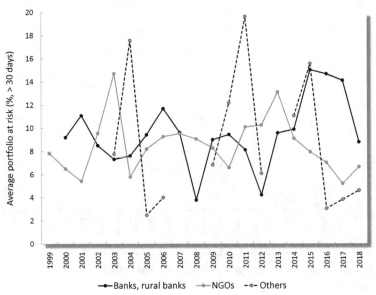

Source of data: MIX.

Figure 21.8. Average portfolio at risk, > 90 days (%) by MFI type

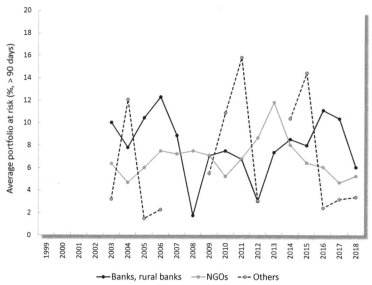

Source of data: MIX.

Banks generally have a higher debt-equity ratio than NGOs (Figure 21.9). But the average debt-equity ratio for NGOs registered a significant rise after 2015, a development due to one NGO, before dropping again. With respect to return on assets (Figure 21.10), banks in general have been able to keep this at positive levels throughout, while NGOs experienced negative returns in some years. Almost the same pattern is observed with return on equity (Figure 21.11).

Finally, the average real yield on gross portfolio, which is a measure of the effective interest rate charged by MFIs on microcredit, declined for both banks and NGOs from levels seen in the early 2000s (Figure 21.11). But interest rates charged by NGOs were nearly double those charged by banks. The higher cost of servicing small loans accounts for this, as MFIs focused on lending to poorer clients report an operational expense ratio more than double that reported by MFIs catering to a wider clientele (Esguerra 2012). In contrast, banks' loan portfolios tend to be more diversified.

Figure 21.9. Average debt-equity ratio by MFI type

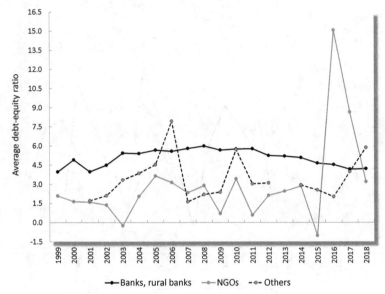

Source of data: MIX.

Figure 21.10. Average return on assets (%) by MFI type

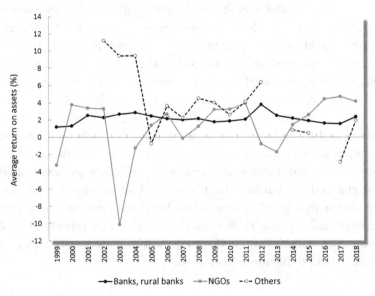

Source of data: MIX.

Figure 21.11. Average return on equity (%) by MFI type

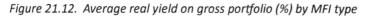

Source of data: MIX.

Figure 21.12. Average real yield on gross portfolio (%) by MFI type

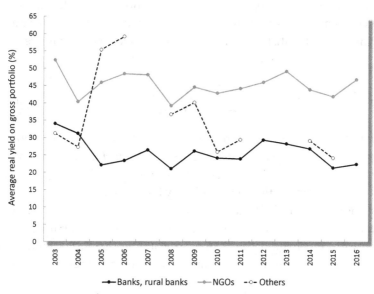

Source of data: MIX.

5 MEASURING COMPETITION IN THE PHILIPPINE MICROFINANCE MARKET

Following the traditional structure-conduct-performance (SCP) approach, the HHI may be computed from the market shares of individual MFIs. As the SCP approach is said to lack support from microeconomic theory, other researchers have used instead non-structural approaches that look directly at the firms' observed behaviour. Examples are the Lerner index, which measures the price-cost margin, and the Panzar-Rosse model, which checks if input and output prices move proportionately or not.

Navin and Sinha (2019) use the Panzar-Rosse model to estimate competition among Indian MFIs. This model, which is particularly apt in markets that are contestable, measures competition from the way a change in factor input prices is reflected in equilibrium revenues. MFIs are deemed as profit-maximizing firms with a homogeneous product, so cost structure is assumed to be homogeneous. As usual, profit is maximized when marginal revenues equal marginal costs, thus:

$$R'_i(y_i, n, v_i) - C'_i(y_i, w_i, q_i) = 0 \qquad (1)$$

where y_i is total output for firm i, w_i is a vector of factor prices, n is the total number of MFIs and v_i, q_i are exogenous variables affecting revenues and costs, respectively. Let R_i^*, C_i^* denote the equilibrium levels of revenues and costs for firm i. Competitiveness is measured using the PRH index (or H-statistic), which is the sum of elasticities of the revenue of firm i with respect to each of the m input prices:

$$PRH = \sum_{x=1}^{m} \frac{\partial R_i^*}{\partial w_{i_x}} \frac{w_{i_x}}{R_i^*}. \qquad (2)$$

The H-statistic ranges from negative infinity to 1: if $H = 0$, there is a monopoly; if $H = 1$, there is perfect competition; if H is between 0 and 1, there is monopolistic competition. Useful as it is, the H-statistic is static and measures competition at the industry level only, not at the firm level.

In contrast, Kar (2016) uses the Boone model, which is said to be less data intensive than competition measures in the literature before it. The intuition behind the Boone indicator is that MFIs with lower marginal costs are more efficient and thus enjoy a higher market share and greater profits.

The indicator ignores differences in MFI types (e.g., banks, NGOs) as well as in product quality and design, among others (Leuvensteijn et al. 2011 as cited in Kar 2016). The Boone indicator is estimated using the following equation:

$$\ln \pi_{it} = \alpha + \sum_{t=1}^{T} \beta_t \ln (MC_{it}) + \sum_{t=1}^{T-1} \alpha_i d_t + \mu_{it} \quad (3)$$

where π_{it} is the profit of MFI i at year t, MC is the marginal cost, β is the Boone indicator and d_t is the time dummy. MC is estimated using a separate translog cost function, and MC here is simply the first derivative of the cost function with respect to output, which is proxied by gross loan portfolio. MFIs with lower MC gain higher profits, so $\beta < 0$. Hence, a more negative Boone index denotes a higher level of market competition. A positive value may denote the presence of collusion or competition in quality. Ordinary least squares may be used to estimate parameters of the cost function, but Kar (2016) uses a stochastic frontier model instead. One may also add time-dependent interaction terms using the Boone index and time dummies to capture year-specific factors, and therefore get a yearly Boone index to trace the pattern of competition across years.

Several papers have looked at competition among MFIs. Kar (2016) uses the Boone indicator to measure competition in 10 countries, including the Philippines. He finds that between 2003 and 2010, competition was most vibrant in India and Nicaragua. Although competition was steady in most of the economies, MFI competition significantly declined in Bangladesh and Bolivia primarily due to consolidation and the predominance of "giant" players. Meanwhile, Navin and Sinha (2019), looking at the Indian microfinance sector from 2005 to 2017 and using the MIX database, find heightened concentration in recent years. Yet they find no evidence to suggest that such concentration had led to exploitation of customers by the biggest players.

Except for Kar (2016), no study has specifically looked at competition among Philippine MFIs in recent years, and none with data from the 2010s. We fill this gap using available data in the MIX database.

First, Figure 21.13 shows the HHI for all MFIs as well as the HHI for banks (including rural banks) and microfinance NGOs. Note that there has been increasing concentration for MFIs in general starting in 2011, driven largely by the increasing concentration among NGOs and banks following the decline in their numbers at the time.[15]

Second, as used in Navin and Sinha (2019), we estimate the H-statistic using the Panzar-Rosse model. We modify it and estimate the following equation:

$$\ln(FR)_{it} = \alpha_0 + \alpha_1 \ln w_{l,it} + \alpha_2 \ln w_{f,it} + \alpha_3 \ln w_{v,it}$$
$$+ \beta_1 \ln PAR30_{it} + \beta_2 \ln TA_{it} + \beta_3 \ln CA_{it} \qquad (4)$$
$$+ \gamma GDP_t + \ln(FR)_{i(t-1)} + \epsilon_{it}$$

where FR_{it} is the financial revenue for MFI i in year t, w_l is the personnel expenses-assets ratio, w_f is the interest expenses-deposits ratio, w_v is the administrative expenses-assets ratio, PAR30 is the portfolio-at-risk (unpaid for more than 30 days), TA is total assets, CA is equity-assets ratio and GDP is the GDP growth rate (Table 21.3). The H-statistic is the sum of the coefficients for the factor inputs. Owing to the addition of lagged dependent variable, $\ln(FR)_{i(t-1)}$, as an independent variable, we use the generalized method of moments à la Arellano-Bond to estimate the above equation.

Figure 21.13. HHI values across banks (including rural banks), NGOs and all types

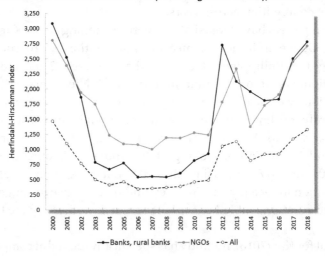

Note: Banks include rural banks. Other categories were omitted due to too few players in some years, which distort the graph.
Source of data: MIX.

---

[15] Credit unions/cooperatives and NBFIs were excluded from the analysis because of large changes in the number of reporting units from one year to the next.

Table 21.3. Summary statistics

Parameter	Variable name	N	Mean	Std. dev.	Min	Max
Financial revenue (in million PHP)	FR	749	230.166	563.791	0.000	6,649.685
Personnel expenses-assets ratio (%)	w_l	591	11.297	7.940	0.423	55.881
Interest expenses-deposits ratio (%)	w_f	560	3.199	3.946	0.000	51.791
Admin. expenses-assets ratio (%)	w_v	599	8.128	5.045	0.551	50.698
Portfolio at risk (> 30 days) (%)	$PAR30$	608	9.089	10.096	0.000	72.720
Total assets (in million PHP)	TA	790	852.273	1,805.373	3.473	18,769.310
Total costs (in million PHP)	TC	749	154.792	366.728	0.011	3,418.600
Equity-asset ratio (%)	CA	790	23.459	17.608	−93.488	100.000
Return on assets (%)	ROA	629	2.121	8.147	−95.630	22.930
Gross loan portfolio (in million PHP)	q	811	595.891	1,392.420	1.333	17,660.090
GDP growth (%)	GDP	822	5.233	1.668	1.448	7.334

Source: MIX database

Table 21.4 shows that for the entire sample from 1999 to 2018, the PRH statistic is at 0.509, which indicates monopolistic competition among Philippine MFIs. We then split the sample between periods pre- and post-2010 to see what effect, if any, the observed decline in the number of MFIs after 2010 might have had on competition. The results show a reduction in the PRH statistic from 0.575 in 1999–2010 to 0.512 in 2011–18, which indicates a weakening of competition in more recent years. This corroborates the insight from the HHI values earlier.

Table 21.4. PRH statistic; dependent variable = log of financial revenue

Parameter	(1) 1999–2018	(2) 1999–2010	(3) 2011–18
Financial revenue ($t-1$)	0.156***	0.237***	0.015
	(0.040)	(0.051)	(0.085)
Personnel expenses-assets ratio (w_l)	0.208***	0.327***	0.159***
	(0.031)	(0.058)	(0.049)
Interest expenses-deposits ratio (w_f)	0.013	0.015	0.005
	(0.010)	(0.011)	(0.028)
Admin. expenses-assets ratio (w_v)	0.288***	0.233***	0.348***
	(0.035)	(0.045)	(0.067)
Portfolio at risk (> 30 days)	– 0.003	– 0.007	– 0.011
	(0.007)	(0.007)	(0.025)
Total assets	0.792***	0.686***	0.879***
	(0.050)	(0.066)	(0.090)
Equity-assets ratio	0.056**	– 0.007	0.087**
	(0.023)	(0.049)	(0.036)
GDP growth	– 0.006	– 0.003	– 0.015
	(0.004)	(0.004)	(0.010)
Constant	1.337***	1.979***	2.341*
	(0.472)	(0.580)	(1.296)
PRH statistic	0.509	0.575	0.512
Observations	248	159	89
Number of MFIs	57	50	29

Note: (1) Standard errors are in parentheses.
(2) ***$p < 0.01$, **$p < 0.05$, *$p < 0.1$.
(3) PRH statistic is the sum of coefficients of w_l, w_f and w_v.

Third, following Kar (2016) we also estimate the Boone indicator. We start by estimating the translog cost function (equation 5). In this formulation, total cost of MFI i at time t (TC_{it}) is proxied by total expenditures over total assets, MFI output q_{it} is represented by its gross loan portfolio, w denotes prices for the j inputs and ε_{it} is an error term. The input prices (and their respective proxies) are cost of labour (personnel expenses-total assets ratio), cost of funds (interest expense-deposits ratio) and cost of capital (administrative expenses-total assets ratio).

$$TC_{it} = \alpha_0 + \delta_0 \ln q_{it} + \frac{\delta_1}{2}(\ln q_{it})^2 + \sum_{j=1}^{3} \alpha_j \ln w_{jit} + \ln q_i \sum_{j=1}^{3} \alpha_j \ln w_{jit} + \frac{1}{2}\sum_{j=1}^{3}\sum_{k=1}^{3} \alpha_{j,k} \ln w_{jit} \ln w_{kit} + \sum_{t=1}^{T-1} \alpha_t d_t + \epsilon_{it} \quad (5)$$

Assuming linear homogeneity in input prices, we use the price of physical capital to normalize total costs and the two other input prices. The estimation results are reported in Table 21.5.

Table 21.5. Translog cost function estimation

Parameter	Dependent variable: Log of total costs
Log of output (q_{it})	−0.051**
	(0.025)
0.5*(Log of q_{it})²	0.003**
	(0.001)
Log of price of labour (w_l)	0.486***
	(0.041)
Log of price of funds (w_f)	0.021
	(0.018)
0.5*(Log of w_l)²	0.190***
	(0.005)
0.5*(Log of w_f)²	0.002***
	(0.001)
Log of w_l*Log of w_f	−0.004***
	(0.001)
Log of w_l*Log of q_{it}	0.000
	(0.002)
Log of w_f*Log of q_{it}	−0.000
	(0.001)

Table 21.5 (continued)

Table 21.5 (continued)

Parameter	Dependent variable: Log of total costs
Constant	1.260***
	(0.240)
Observations	476
Number of MFIs	98
R^2	0.989

Note: (1) Standard errors are in parentheses.
(2) *** $p < 0.01$, ** $p < 0.05$, * $p < 0.1$.
(3) w_l is personnel expenses-total assets ratio, whereas w_f is interest expenses-deposits ratio. Total costs, price of labour and funds are normalized using price of capital (w_k) or administrative expenses-total assets ratio.

The estimated coefficients from the translog cost function are then used to derive marginal cost as follows:

$$MC_{it} = \frac{\partial TC_{it}}{\partial q_{it}} = \frac{TC_{it}}{q_{it}} \left(\delta_0 + \delta_1 \ln q_{it} + \sum_{j=1}^{3} \alpha_j \ln w_{j,it} \right) \quad (6)$$

Finally, to obtain the Boone indicator, we estimate the following equation:

$$\ln \pi_{it} = \alpha_0 + \sum_{t=1}^{T} \beta_t d_t \ln(MC_{it}) + \sum_{t=1}^{T-1} \alpha_t d_t + \mu_{it} \quad (7)$$

using OLS and, alternatively, a fixed effects model to account for possible endogeneity since performance and costs are solved simultaneously. The Boone indicator is the coefficient β_t and it changes over time; d_t denotes year dummies. Values of β_t below zero denote competition, and above zero indicate collusion (because of the positive correlation between marginal costs and profits).

Table 21.6 shows the Boone scores over time and Figure 21.14 plots them. First, we note that except for 2013 all yearly values of the Boone indicator, including previous estimates by Kar (2016), are not statistically different from zero. Second, compared with Kar's estimates, which averaged −0.0081 for 2003–10, indicating that the microfinance market is competitive, our estimates for the longer period 2003–18 suggest otherwise. The average fixed effects Boone indicator is 0.0015, while the OLS estimate is 0.0042. Third, yearly Boone scores take on positive and negative values, implying that competition levels change over time though with fewer negative values observed among the OLS estimates than the fixed effects estimates.

Table 21.6. Boone scores for Philippine MFIs

Year	Kar (2016)	New estimates	
		OLS	FE
2003	− 0.0130	0.0027	− 0.0008
2004	0.0010	0.0104	0.0084
2005	− 0.0080	0.0008	− 0.0032
2006	− 0.0090	0.0062	0.0001
2007	− 0.0090	− 0.0014	− 0.0013
2008	− 0.0020	− 0.0003	− 0.0015
2009	− 0.0110	0.0032	0.0021
2010	− 0.0140	0.0020	− 0.0003
2011		0.0048	0.0027
2012		0.0079	− 0.0105
2013		− 0.0157***	− 0.0134**
2014		0.0028	0.0096
2015		0.0176	0.0056*
2016		0.0117	0.0182
2017		0.0044	− 0.0028
2018		0.0106	0.0116

Note: ***$p < 0.01$, **$p < 0.05$, *$p < 0.1$.

Figure 21.14. Boone indicator over time

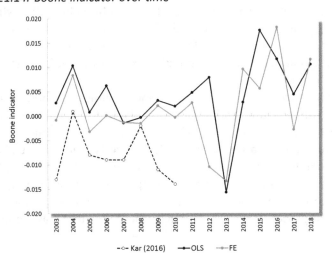

Note: Values below zero denote competition; values above zero denote collusion/lack of competition.
Source of data: MIX.

For both sets of estimates, the occurrence of more positive than negative values in the latter years is particularly notable. This indicates a weakening of competition especially after 2010, which is consistent with the observed increase in HHI and the decrease in the PRH statistic. Several factors may have contributed to this development: the decline in the number of participating banks due to closures and consolidation in the industry and the continued growth of leading MFIs such as ASA Philippines, CARD Bank and CARD NGO. Yet this tendency towards consolidation may have been also tempered by competition induced by measures to liberalize branching after 2010 and make financial services more accessible, such as permitting the use of various retail outlets to accept and disburse cash for banks as well as the establishment of branch lite units in 2017. This suggests that the predominance of large MFIs is not permanent, and that the microfinance market is contestable.

6 CONCLUSION

This paper examines the status of competition in the Philippine microfinance sector in light of changes in the regulatory environment that opened up the sector to commercialization in the late 1990s. Specifically, it assesses the level of competition during the period 1999–2018 using three measures of concentration: the Herfindahl-Hirschman Index (HHI), the Panzar-Rosse method or PRH index and the Boone indicator. We generally observe a weakening of competition after 2010, while the preceding years were characterized by steady to increasing competition. We view this development as less the result of regulation and more of industry dynamics, which may better explain the increase in market shares of certain MFIs.

Microfinance is inherently risky and complex; without subsidies only the more astute and financially viable MFIs will survive and be able to sustain operations. Over the years, Philippine MFIs have increasingly moved away from a purely poverty lending focus because of sustainability concerns. As subsidies dried up, they realized that to stay in the game they would have to adopt a financial systems approach to reach low-income clients, not necessarily the poorest that the poverty lending approach targets.[16] As such, the MFIs that have effectively

---

[16] More than a decade ago, Arun and Hulme (2008) observed a widespread global shift by MFIs from poverty lending to financial services provision.

utilized this new approach have also successfully increased their market shares.

Although the microfinance industry may not be unambiguously competitive as suggested by the empirics, this is not necessarily a permanent state. Rising concentration among a few major players could itself be a consequence of competition. What is important is that the regulatory environment safeguards contestability.

This paper serves to break ground for further research on the microfinance industry. We mention a few: with better data, research on the effect of competition on MFI performance; MFI competition in product quality; the impact of the entry of new players (e.g., fintech firms with innovative underwriting practices and loan screening techniques) on competition; and the effect of new technologies on competition and financial inclusion of the poor and the underbanked.

APPENDIX

Figure 21A. Number of banks with microfinance operations

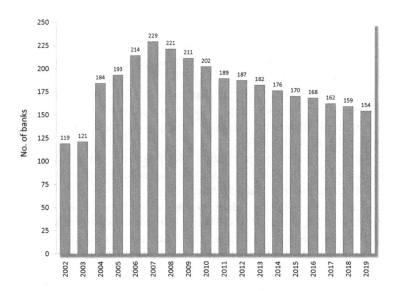

Figure 21B. Amount of microfinance loans and number of borrowers

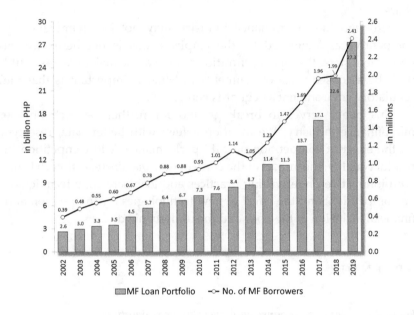

REFERENCES

Alindogan, A. 2005. "Microfinance: Focusing on Our Nation's Wealth". In *The Bangko Sentral and the Philippine Economy*, edited by V. Valdepeñas. Manila: Bangko Sentral ng Pilipinas.

Armendariz, B., B. D'Espallier, M. Hudon, and A. Szafarz. 2011. "Subsidy Uncertainty and Mission Drift". *CEB Working Paper No. 11/104*. Brussels: Centre Emile Bernheim, Research Institute in Management Sciences, Universite Libre de Bruxelles.

Armendariz, B., and A. Szafarz. 2011. "On Mission Drift in Microfinance Institutions". In *The Handbook of Microfinance*, edited by B. Armendariz and M. Labie. Singapore: World Scientific.

Arun, T., and D. Hulme. 2008. "Microfinance – a Way Forward". *BWPI Working Paper No. 54*. UK: Brooks World Poverty Institute, University of Manchester.

Assefa, E., N. Hermes, and A. Meesters. 2013. "Competition and the Performance of Microfinance Institutions". *Applied Financial Economics* 23, no. 9: 767–82.

Balisacan, A. M. 2019. "Toward a Fairer Society: Inequality and Competition Policy in Developing Asia". *Philippine Review of Economics* 56, no. 1&2: 127–47.

Balisacan, A. M., and L. S. Sebastian. 2006. "Challenges and Policy Directions: Overview". In *Securing Rice, Reducing Poverty: Challenges and Policy Directions*, edited by A. M. Balisacan, L. S. Sebastian, and Associates. Los Baños: Southeast Asian Regional Center for Graduate Study and Research in Agriculture.

Banal-Formoso, Cielo, and Linda Bolido, eds. 2020. *No One Left Behind: The Philippine Financial Inclusion Journey*. Manila: Bangko Sentral ng Pilipinas.

Berger, A., L. Klapper, and R. Turk-Ariss. 2008. "Bank Competition and Financial Stability". *World Bank Policy Research Working Paper No. 4696*. Washington, DC: World Bank.

Boyd, J. H., and G. De Nicolo. 2005. "The Theory of Bank Risk Taking and Competition Revisited". *Journal of Finance* 60, no. 3: 1329–43.

Braverman, Avishay, and J. Luis Guasch. 1986. "Rural Credit Markets and Institutions in Developing Countries: Lessons for Policy Analysis from Practice and Modern Theory". *World Development* 14, no. 10/11 (October/November): 1253–67.

Broecker, T. 1990. "Credit-Worthiness Tests and Interbank Competition". *Econometrica* 58, no. 2: 429–52.

Cull, R., A. Demirgüç-Kunt, and J. Morduch. 2007. "Financial Performance and Outreach: A Global Analysis of Leading Microbanks". *Economic Journal* 117 (February): F107–33.

Esguerra, E. F. 2012. "Truth in Microlending: Is Microfinance Overrated?" *UP-BSP Professorial Chair Lecture*, 12 November 2012. Manila: Bangko Sentral ng Pilipinas.

Fonacier, Chuchi. 2020. "Reshaping the Future of Banking through Financial Inclusion". Introduction. In *No One Left Behind: The Philippine Financial Inclusion Journey*, edited by Cielo Banal-Formoso and Linda Bolido. Manila: Bangko Sentral ng Pilipinas.

Ghosh, S., and E. Van Tassel. 2008. "A Model of Mission Drift in Microfinance Institutions". *Working Paper No. 08003*. USA: Department of Economics, College of Business, Florida Atlantic University. http://home.fau.edu/vantasse/web/MDDec11.pdf.

Hartarska, V., and D. Nadolnyak. 2007. "Do Regulated Microfinance Institutions Achieve Better Sustainability and Outreach? Cross-Country Evidence". *Applied Economics* 39, no. 10:1207–22.

Hermes, N., R. Lensink, and A. Meesters. 2011. "Outreach and Efficiency of Microfinance Institutions". *World Development* 39, no. 6: 938–48.

Kar, A. K. 2016. "Measuring Competition in Microfinance Markets: A New Approach". *International Review of Applied Economics* 30, no. 4: 423–40. https://doi.org/10.1080/02692171.2015.1106445.

Kar, A. K., and R. B. Swain. 2014. "Competition in Microfinance: Does It Affect Performance, Portfolio Quality, and Capitalization?". In *Microfinance Institutions: Financial and Social Performance*, edited by R. Mersland and R. O. Strom. London: Palgrave Macmillan.

Leuvensteijin, M. van, J. Bikker, A.V. Rixtel, and C.K. Sorensen. 2011. "A New Approach to Measuring Competition in the Loan Markets of the Euro Area". *Applied Economics* 43, no. 23: 3155–67.

Llanto, Gilberto M. 2015. "Financial Inclusion, Education, and Regulation in the Philippines". *ADBI Working Paper No. 541*. Tokyo: Asian Development Bank Institute. http://www.adb.org/publications/financial-inclusion-education-and-regulation-philippines.

———. 2018. "Using Policy Research and Policy Windows: Some Story to Tell". In *From Evidence to Policy: Celebrating 40 Years of Policy Research*, edited by Gilberto Llanto, Vicente Paqueo, and Aniceto Orbeta, chapter 7. Quezon City: Philippine Institute for Development Studies.

Llanto, Gilberto, Ma. Piedad Geron, and Christine Tang. 1999. "Directed Credit Programs: Issues and Framework for Reform". Technical report submitted to the Credit Policy Improvement Project, National Credit Council, Department of Finance, Manila, Philippines.

Marquez, R. 2002. "Competition, Adverse Selection, and Information Dispersion in the Banking Industry". *Review of Financial Studies* 15, no. 3: 901–26.

McIntosh, C., and B. Wydick. 2005. "Competition and Microfinance". *Journal of Development Economics* 78: 271–98.

MCPI (Microfinance Council of the Philippines, Inc.). 2016. "Social Performance Country Report 2016". Pasig: MCPI. www.microfinancecouncil.org.

———. 2021. "History". About MCPI. https://microfinancecouncil.org/history (accessed 30 April 2021).

MIX (Microfinance Information eXchange). https://datacatalog.worldbank.org/dataset/mix-market.

MIX (Microfinance Information eXchange) and MCPI. 2006. "Benchmarking Philippine Microfinance 2005". A report from the Microfinance Information Exchange, Inc. (November).

Navajas, S., J. Conning, and C. Gonzalez-Vega. 2003. "Lending Technologies, Competition and Consolidation in the Market for Microfinance in Bolivia". *Journal of International Development* 15, no. 6: 747–70.

Navin, N., and P. Sinha. 2019. "Market Structure and Competition in the Indian Microfinance Sector". *Journal for Decision Makers* 44, no. 4: 167–81.

Ravago, M. V., A. M. Balisacan, and M. A. Sombilla. 2018. "Current Structure and Future Challenges of the Agricultural Sector". In *The Future of Philippine Agriculture: Scenarios, Policies, and Investments under Climate Change*, edited by M. W. Rosegrant and M. A. Sombilla. Singapore: ISEAS.

Roodman, D., and J. Morduch. 2009. "The Impact of Microcredit on the Poor in Bangladesh: Revisiting the Evidence". *Working Paper No. 174*. Washington, DC: Center for Global Development.

Schicks, J., and R. Rosenberg. 2011. "Too Much Microcredit? A Survey of the Evidence on Over-Indebtedness". *Occasional Paper No. 19*. Washington, DC: Consultative Group to Assist the Poor.

Vogelgesang, U. 2003. "Microfinance in Times of Crisis: The Effects of Competition, Rising Indebtedness, and Economic Crisis on Repayment Behavior". *World Development* 31, no. 13: 2085–2114.

22 Tariffication and Market Structure: The Case of the Philippine Rice Industry

Ramon L. Clarete

1 INTRODUCTION

The Philippine government liberalized rice imports in 2019, ending the import monopoly of the National Food Authority (NFA) and lowering the effective tariff on imported rice. Earlier studies had generally suggested lifting this privilege of the NFA and allowing private sector importation at lower tariffs, among other reforms (Balisacan, Clarete, and Cortes 1992; Roumasset 1999; David 2003; Balisacan and Sebastian 2006; Dawe, Moya, and Casiwan 2006; Sombilla, Lantican, and Beltran 2006; Clarete 2008; David, Intal, and Balisacan 2009; Briones 2018.) While the proposed reform had long been pushed, Philippine lawmakers in several Congresses had consistently considered it not a priority. Not even the country's obligation to tariffy all quantitative import restrictions under the World Trade Organization's (WTO) Agreement on Agriculture in 1996 nor a structural adjustment programme with the Asian Development Bank[1] at the turn of the century had pushed lawmakers to reform the NFA's role in the rice industry. What finally persuaded legislators to pass the Rice Tariffication Law (RTL) in 2019 was the high food price inflation in 2018, which analysts traced to the NFA.

---

[1] This structural adjustment lending was called the Grains Sector Development Program.

As soon as the RTL went into effect in the first quarter of 2019, private-sector importers started to import unprecedentedly large quantities of rice. To a price-taking open economy with perfect competition, the domestic price of rice is expected to fall by the percentage reduction of the import tariff rate. However, wholesale prices of rice fell significantly lower than expected in 2019. Furthermore, consumer rice prices dropped by less than that of wholesale rice prices. To top it all, the farmers bore the largest adjustment to rice import liberalization—that is, farm-gate prices of palay plunged the most in percentage terms.

Accordingly, reform opponents claim that the domestic rice market is imperfectly competitive and has remained that way despite import liberalization. With the NFA no longer providing a countervailing check to keep retail prices down, large importers and traders control not only the local supply but also the volume of imported rice.

The policy divide surrounding the RTL has spilled into competing claims on the incidence of gains and losses from the reform. One group claims society is better off because of it and the other provides estimates to claim the opposite. These one-year ex post analyses on the gains and losses from the RTL accounted the net benefits for key stakeholders, anchoring their estimates on observed rice price movements. Other impact studies of the RTL were ex ante analyses using economic models that are straightforward applications of trade theory and regard the rice market as perfectly competitive.

This paper focuses on the ex post price movements. It describes an analytical partial equilibrium model of a small open economy with two types of traders/importers, and uses the model to explain the observed rice price movements following the RTL. One type of traders/importers faces increasing cost-to-scale from importing rice, while the other group, made up of smaller firms, is assumed to have constant import cost, except that the members have large entry cost into the import business. When the RTL opened up the local rice market to imports, the first group settles with a desired imported volume lower than what is expected under constant unit import costs and succeeds in keeping price higher in the absence of competition from the other group.

The following section summarizes the reforms enabled by the RTL. Section 3 documents the variations of rice prices in 2019 following the implementation of the RTL. Section 4 describes an analytical partial equilibrium model with two heterogeneous representative groups of rice importers. The model is used to analyse the impact of lowering the import rice tariff on wholesale and retail rice prices. Section 5 traces the transmission of rice prices through a multilevel domestic marketing system to explain why farm-gate prices of palay fell more than that of wholesale rice prices. The implication on competition policy is taken up in the concluding section.

2   RICE TARIFFICATION REFORMS

When the Philippines became a member of the WTO in 1995, the country had to convert all its agricultural import quantity restrictions (QRs) into tariff protection, except on rice. It availed of the special treatment provision in the WTO agriculture accord for rice, postponing for ten years the implementation of its legal commitment to tariffy its QR on rice.

Rice tariffication was deferred because rice farmers were unprepared for import competition. When the ten-year period lapsed in 2005, the Philippines secured from the WTO a seven-year extension of special treatment to 2012. In 2012, the Philippines could no longer get another extension of its special treatment from the WTO. Instead, it applied and obtained (after two years of negotiation) a three-year waiver of its rice tariffication legal obligation, from 2014 to 2017. The rice waiver expired in 2017, but the rice QR continued for another two years until the Rice Tariffication Law (Republic Act 11203) was enacted in February 2019.

The rice QR was a non-tariff measure in the form of the NFA's import monopoly on rice. Presidential Decree no. 4 issued in 1972 created the NFA and assigned to it the task of solely importing rice but only when needed to do so. The NFA decided each year how much the country should import, calibrating the quantity to be imported to a level that stabilizes rice prices and striking a balance between boosting farm-gate rice prices for the benefit of farmers and making rice affordable for the country's poor.

Spanning nearly half a century, the rice QR had severely impacted the economy. With it, the country had to put up with ineffective and incompetent import monopoly, making the population vulnerable to food insecurity and waste, if not graft and corruption in public spending on rice imports.

This became clear in 2008 when world rice prices spiked. The NFA mistakenly imported a large volume of rice apparently for food security, but ended up helping push world rice prices up (Slayton 2009) and wasting rice.[2] Because the NFA was the only importer, its "panic buying" became the country's mistake as well, which likely could have been avoided with a decentralized rice import arrangement.

Import quantity decisions were discretionary and accorded trade protection to rice producers, millers and traders, at the expense of consumers. The quantities of imported rice were low and at times delayed, resulting in price spikes. With rice making up about 10 per cent of the consumer basket, higher rice prices feed overall inflation. According to PhilRice (2019), rice prices contributed one full percentage point to inflation at its peak in 2018.

2.1 Rice tariff rate

The most favoured nation (MFN) tariff rate on imported rice ranges from 40 to 50 per cent. The Tariff Commission, tasked by law to set the tariff equivalent rate of the rice QR, prescribed to slap a 40 per cent tariff on imported rice up to the minimum access volume of 350,000 metric tons, and 50 per cent in excess of that quota.

But because the Philippines is a member of the Association of Southeast Asian Nations (ASEAN) economic community, the effective tariff rate is the preferential rate of 35 per cent on rice coming from other ASEAN members. Thus, the RTL did not only liberalize rice importation, it also reduced the tariff protection of rice producers.

The three-year moving average of the annual tariff equivalent rates of the rice QR was 48.33 per cent in 2018 (Table 22.1); it unexpectedly rose to 52.32 per cent in 2019, the first year of RTL implementation, which is 50 per cent higher than the expected ASEAN tariff rate of 35 per cent. The spike may be traced to the fall in world rice prices in 2019. Holding world prices at the same level as in 2018, the moving average implicit tariff protection would have fallen to 45.68 per cent, reflecting the RTL's effect.

---

[2] A local news daily reported on rotted rice (GMA News 2010).

Table 22.1. Estimated implicit tariff protection on rice production (2015–19)

Parameter	2015	2016	2017	2018	2019
CIF (US$/kg)[1]	0.40	0.45	0.40	0.43	0.37
Average peso exchange rate (PHP/US$)[2]	45.50	47.49	50.40	52.66	51.80
CIF (PHP/kg)	18.27	21.36	20.25	22.77	18.93
Plus: port handling (PHP/kg)[3]	1.83	1.83	1.97	2.13	2.30
Landed cost (PHP/kg)	20.10	23.18	22.22	24.89	21.23
Plus: transportation to first warehouse (PHP/kg)[4]	0.33	0.38	0.36	0.41	0.35
Storage cost (PHP/kg)[5]	0.49	0.57	0.54	0.61	0.52
Handling cost (PHP/kg)[6]	0.09	0.10	0.10	0.11	0.09
In situ warehouse cost (PHP/kg)	21.01	24.23	23.23	26.02	22.19
Average Manila wholesale price (PHP/kg)[7]	36.31	33.99	35.89	39.08	33.79
Implicit rice tariff (%)[8]	72.82	40.27	54.52	50.19	52.26
Three-year moving average implicit tariff			55.87	48.33	52.32

Note: [1,7] Philippine Statistics Authority
[2] Bangko Sentral ng Pilipinas
[3] Based on 1999 percentage of Manila Port handling cost to landed cost = 0.0133875
[4] Based on 1995–99 average percentages of transportation cost to in situ warehouse cost = 0.0156165
[5] Based on 1995–99 average percentages of storage cost to in situ warehouse cost = 0.0234023
[6] Based on 1995–99 average percentages of handling cost to in situ warehouse cost = 0.0042292
[8] ((Average Manila wholesale price divided by in situ warehouse cost)−1) * 100 per cent

2.2 Other reforms

The rice reforms did more than simply convert the rice QR to tariff protection. It also removed the NFA's regulatory powers. Clarete (2008), which documents the various changes in the NFA's mandate, shows that the following basic elements of the mandate had persisted through the years: "buying high and selling low",[3] maintenance of rice buffer stocks and import monopoly on rice. The NFA provided palay price support and distributed rice at official and below market prices (Clarete 2019). In response to the price crisis of 2008, Balisacan, Sombilla, and Dikitanan (2010) suggest limiting the NFA's role on effective buffer stock management, a reform that the RTL has enabled on top of liberalizing import rice policies.

The rice subsidy programme designed for the poor had been costly and had a significant leakage to the non-poor. Jah and Mehta (2008) estimate that the operational cost of the NFA rice subsidy programme, including price stabilization and targeted rice distribution programmes, is 2.5 per cent of the Philippines' gross domestic product (GDP). Using survey data, the World Bank's "Filipino Report Card on Pro-poor Services" has a similar observation: only 15 per cent of the respondents reported buying NFA rice (World Bank 2001).

3 RICE PRICE PUZZLE

The policy divide during the RTL's enactment has spilled into the determination of the reforms' gains and losses. One group of analyses, which conducted ex ante simulation studies on the impact of tariffication, indicated that rice consumers gain and rice farmers lose from rice tariffication (Balié and Valera 2020; Perez and Pradesha 2019; Cororaton and Yu 2019; Briones 2018). The studies were

---

[3] "Buying high and selling low" refers only to the NFA's commercial transactions for local rice. "Buying high" confers palay price support to farmers, which ordinarily, on account of low palay procurement quantities, has negligible effect on market prices of palay at the farm gate. "Selling low" influences market prices of rice, the extent of which depends on the NFA's rice inventory in a given lean season. Ordinarily since the NFA sells below market price, it accords price subsidy to its buyers.

straightforward applications of trade theory using models that regard the rice market as perfectly competitive and its intermediation system as efficient.

Another group of studies comprised ex post assessments of the economic welfare of stakeholders. The analyses were anchored on rice price movements, quantifying gains or losses using production or consumption data and related statistics. It is generally accepted that the liberalization of rice import policies benefits rice consumers, particularly the poor. Balisacan (2000) notes that the bottom two deciles of the population were net rice consumers; thus, high rice prices would hurt the poorest of the poor in the Philippines. The more interesting question is: does the RTL benefit the rice farmers who are both rice producers and consumers?

PhilRice (2019) estimates that around 1.6 million or 55 per cent of rice farming households are smallholders, growing rice on fields smaller than a hectare. This implies that although over half of the country's farmers might have lost from lower farm-gate prices during harvest because of the reform, they nonetheless gain as rice consumers during the rest of the year. Balié and Valera (2020) estimate that 80 per cent of households in the Philippines are net rice buyers. Only less than 10 per cent of households are net rice sellers. These figures suggest that overall the gains of rice farm households from the RTL as consumers may have exceeded their losses as farmers.

After-a-year estimates of the gains and losses from the RTL in 2019 are mixed (Table 22.2), keeping alive the discourse on the appropriateness of the reform. The Federation of Free Farmers (FFF), which opposes the rice reform, estimated that rice farmers lost PHP68 billion or twice the PHP34 billion gain of rice consumers. Its estimates were largely based on the fact that farm-gate rice prices plunged significantly more than retail rice prices. IBON Foundation, which also opposes the reform, had a larger estimate of farmers' income losses—PHP85 billion—but presented no estimate of the rice consumers' gains.

Montemayor (2020) later revised the FFF estimates, reducing farm income losses to PHP40.34 billion and the rice consumers gains to only PHP0.23 billion. The adjustment factored in estimates of the income gains of rice traders and millers. According to the FFF, most of the reforms' gains went instead to importers and traders, amounting to PHP57.54 billion, not to consumers. Millers even lost PHP0.23 billion.

Table 22.2. Comparison of the estimated trade-off gains and losses from the Rice Tariffication Law (in billion PHP)*

Market Player	FFF version 1 (FFF 2020)	IBON Foundation (2020)	PIDS	DOF	Montemayor (2020) FFF version 2	Adriano, Adriano and Adriano (2020): Recalculation using FFF methodology
Farmers	−68.00	−85	−38.4	−32.70	−40.34	−38.15
Traders/Millers					−0.23	
Importers					14.25	
Wholesalers-Retailers					43.29	26.00
Consumers	34.16			64.30**	0.23	4.12

Note: (1) DOF = Department of Finance
FFF = Federation of Free Farmers
PIDS = Philippine Institute for Development Studies
(2) * Blanks mean the source did not specify any values.
** Value corrected as specified in http://www.bsp.gov.ph/downloads/Publications/2020/WPS202006.pdf

The FFF's inclusion of traders and millers in its analysis brings in an interesting viewpoint on the incidence of gains and losses from the reform. While its estimates can be independently reviewed, the numbers indicate that traders/importers have the largest gain from the reform, not the rice consumers as claimed by reform proponents.

The FFF's analysis ties up with that of Jandoc and Roumasset (2018) who observe that the larger share of the higher price that consumers pay for rice goes to traders and millers, not to rice farmers. They estimate that about three-fourths of the price, which the rice QR kept high supposedly to boost rice farm incomes, went not to rice farmers but to rice traders and millers, as well as to defraying the cost of an inefficient rice milling and trading in the country. A fall in the rice price disproportionately hit rice farmers more than it does rice traders and millers.

3.1 Rice price changes

Ex post analyses on the gains and losses from the RTL were anchored on rice price movements. The FFF held on to its position that not even rice consumers benefited from the reform, but rather the higher income rice traders and importers. Wholesale rice prices did not go down as expected. Rice retail prices did not fall by as much as wholesale rice prices. Farm-gate palay prices had the deepest reduction in percentage terms. This section examines this price puzzle as it may suggest imperfect competition in rice marketing.

The price puzzle has three elements. One, wholesale rice prices in the National Capital Region (NCR) dropped in 2019 from 2018 by less than what was expected based on the reduction of import tariff to 35 per cent. Two, retail rice prices in the NCR fell by an even significantly lower proportion than that of the wholesale price. Three, the reduction in the average farm-gate price of palay in the whole country correlated more closely with the variation in the wholesale price, but was deeper than that of the wholesale price. In perfectly competitive markets, changes in all three prices following a policy change are expected to be highly correlated with each other.

Annual retail rice prices in the NCR fell by only 4.4 per cent in 2019 from 2018 (Figure 22.1). In contrast, wholesale rice prices in the region dropped by more than 14.55 per cent, while farm-gate prices of palay plunged by 17.43 per cent.

Figure 22.1. Annual rice and palay prices (National Capital Region and Philippines, 2000–2019, in PHP/kg)

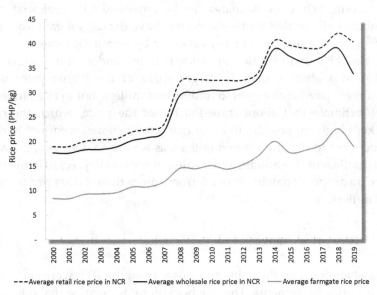

--- Average retail rice price in NCR —— Average wholesale rice price in NCR —— Average farmgate rice price

Source of basic data: Philippine Statistics Authority.

The above changes in rice prices at the retail, wholesale and farm-gate levels in the two crucial years of 2018 and 2019 are apparently supported by variations in their standard deviations and correlation coefficients. These variations are between the standard deviations of prices in 2000–2018 (before RTL) and in 2000–2019 (post RTL). Besides standard deviations, correlation coefficients among these prices were computed for the two periods and compared to examine if the RTL had left its imprint on prices.

Table 22.3 shows that the correlation of yearly price fluctuations of wholesale and retail prices significantly weakened: from 0.98 in 2000–2018 to 0.94 in 2000–2019. The difference suggests that in 2019 retail price fluctuations weakly followed those of wholesale prices. On the other hand, the correlation strengthened for wholesale rice and farm-gate palay price fluctuations. The corresponding correlation coefficients changed from 0.79 to 0.85. These numbers mirror the observed closer movements of wholesale and farm-gate prices from 2018 to 2019 (Figure 22.1). In contrast, those of wholesale and retail prices for the same period were far apart.

Table 22.3. Standard deviations and correlation coefficients of rice prices and their yearly fluctuations (2000–2019, in PHP/kg)

Year/Indicator	Wholesale price	Yearly fluctuation	Retail price	Yearly fluctuation	Farm-gate price	Yearly fluctuation
2000–2018						
Standard deviation	7.79	7.36	8.09	7.86	4.21	7.94
Correlation coefficients						
Wholesale rice	1.00	1.00	1.00	0.98	0.98	0.79
Retail rice	1.00	0.98	1.00	1.00	0.98	0.76
Farm-gate palay	0.98	0.79	0.98	0.76	1.00	1.00
2000–2019						
Standard deviation	7.71	8.32	8.22	7.90	4.24	9.27
Correlation coefficients						
Wholesale rice	1.00	1.00	0.99	0.94	0.98	0.85
Retail rice	0.99	0.94	1.00	1.00	0.98	0.76
Farm-gate palay	0.98	0.85	0.98	0.76	1.00	1.00

Source of basic data: Philippine Statistics Authority.

Except for the wholesale rice prices in NCR, which displayed lower volatility following the RTL, retail and farm-gate rice prices became less stable. The standard deviations of retail prices are 8.09 in 2000–2018 and 8.22 in 2000–2019. The corresponding numbers for farm-gate prices of palay are 4.21 and 4.24. Yearly fluctuations of these prices show more volatility: wholesale rice price, 7.36 to 8.32; retail rice price, 7.86 to 7.9; and farm-gate price of palay, 7.94 to 9.27. Price fluctuations of wholesale rice and farm-gate palay are sharper than those of retail rice prices. This may show the adjustments that went on in 2019 as market players adjusted to the RTL.

3.2 Actual and simulated price change in retail rice price

As Figure 22.1 shows and supported by changes in the correlation coefficients, retail rice prices fell by a significantly lower proportion than wholesale rice prices in the NCR. Suppose the change in rice consumption in the Philippines (2018 vs. 2019) is divided by an estimated price elasticity of demand for rice, how large must the retail rice price fall to be consistent with rice use change? This simulation is done to help validate the observed reduction in retail prices.

In estimating the price elasticity of demand, a linear approximation of an Almost Ideal Demand System (LA/AIDS) model is done on rice and sixteen other commodities deemed as complements to or substitutes for rice. The estimation procedure uses a quarterly data set from 1991 to 2019.

Table 22.4 shows the average estimated income and own-price elasticities of rice in 2018 and 2019. Annual estimates were obtained because the analysis of variance (ANOVA) test results suggest that these variables vary yearly. Applying an ANOVA test with Bonferroni correction suggests that the 2018 and 2019 estimates do not differ from each other. Thus, the Marshallian price elasticities of the two years were averaged and used in predicting retail price changes between 2018 and 2019.

Table 22.5 shows the predicted year-on-year changes in quarterly retail prices of rice in 2019. The retail prices used in computing these variations are of regular-milled and well-milled rice. In the first quarter, the percentage change in retail price was 3.04. The average quarterly retail price decreased by 2.80 per cent in the second quarter of 2019 (when the RTL took effect) from its 2018 level, and by 11.19 per cent and 12.39 per cent in the third and fourth quarters, respectively.

Table 22.4. Estimated average income and own-price elasticities of rice (2018 and 2019)

Commodity	2018			2019		
	Income elasticity	Own-price elasticity		Income elasticity	Own-price elasticity	
		Marshallian	Hicksian		Marshallian	Hicksian
Rice	0.246	−0.759	−0.692	0.23	−0.769	−0.705

Source: Author's calculation

Table 22.5. Actual versus predicted year-on-year changes in rice retail price in 2019

Qtr	Actual quarterly retail price change (%)	Estimated retail price change* (%)	
		Using quarterly rice consumption data as residuals in the 2018 and 2019 supply utilization accounts	Using hypothetical rice consumption data for 2019**
Q1	3.04	−16.41	−26.71
Q2	−2.80	−13.52	−37.92
Q3	−11.19	7.36	−16.21
Q4	−12.39	−20.23	−26.30
(Simple) Average	−5.84	−10.70	−26.79

Note: * Used Marshallian price elasticity estimates
 ** Estimated based on simulated inventory for 2019 using the average proportions of rice inventory to gross supply in the quarterly supply utilization accounts for rice, 1991–2018

The average year-on-year change is −5.84 per cent, which compares closely with the change in annual retail rice prices (−4.4%) for the same years.

Predicted percentage changes in quarterly retail prices are shown also in Table 22.5. There are two sets of estimates. The first set makes use of rice consumption as a residual in the quarterly rice supply utilization accounts of the country. Rice use as food reported in these accounts is a residual, the result of subtracting use of rice for inventory, wasted rice or rice fed to animals, for seeds in next season's planting and for processing from the period's gross supply. The latter is composed of the current local rice output during the quarter, arrivals of imported rice and rice inventory at the beginning of the quarter.

The predicted percentage change in retail price for the quarter is the percentage change of rice consumption divided by the price elasticity of demand. Except for the third quarter, the predicted percentage changes in retail rice prices are negative, implying higher rice consumption of the country in these periods. As for the third quarter, the consumption must have gone down to generate a positive change in retail rice prices. The average predicted year-on-year percentage change in retail rice prices is −10.7 per cent.

The estimate (−5.84%, see Table 22.5) is significantly larger than the −4.4 per cent estimated change in retail rice prices in NCR between 2018 and 2019. One possible explanation is that 2019 was a transition year. It was the year when the government allowed the private sector to import rice, which the latter substantially did. It is possible that the prevailing estimates of rice inventory by those who assembled the rice supply and use tables might not have reflected yet the possible increase in inventory. When the inventory is underestimated, the consumption residual becomes larger than actual, resulting in a larger estimate of the percentage decline in retail prices.

This point is pursued further in the second set of results in Table 22.5. If one takes the pre-RTL behaviour of market players on how much rice they were going to stock up, it can be shown that there had been a large increase in the residual in the supply use tables. Suppose one uses the average rice inventory as a proportion of gross rice supply from 2000 to 2018 and applies that to 2019 to predict the rice inventory in 2019, the result would be that the residual spikes as well as consumption. As Table 22.5 shows, the average quarterly year-on-year percentage changes in retail rice prices in 2019 turned out to be −26.79.

The rice policy changed from a marketing system dominated by a few traders and the NFA to one that likely involves the same number of traders in 2019 but sans the NFA. A few questions remain though. Why did wholesale rice prices go down by less than the extent policymakers expected them to fall? Why did retail prices drop by only about a third of the rate of decline in wholesale prices? Why did farm-gate palay prices plummet the deepest of the three?

The following three sections explain these three price puzzles in 2019.

4 A SMALL OPEN ECONOMIC MODEL WITH HETEROGENEOUS IMPORTERS

The following describes a small open partial equilibrium model of the rice market with heterogeneous rice importers; this is used to explain why wholesale rice prices did not fall as expected. Unlike Melitz (2003), the importers are not distinguished from each other in terms of firm-specific productivities, nor are they continuously distributed around a productivity parameter.

The model's importers comprise two groups. One group is made up of relatively large enterprises with significant experience in local trading and importing rice. Their size and experience enable them to attain scale economies and face relatively lower transaction costs from importing. The second group comprises a potentially larger group but made up of relatively small firms that may be engaged in local trading but are inexperienced in the import business. The small firms, while having constant unit import costs, face large entry costs relative to the first group. They may import rice at relatively low scale, since the rice import business does not require lumpy fixed cost. They face stiffer entry costs because they lack import experience and must learn to navigate the non-tariff measure of phytosanitary import license.

In contrast, the larger firms are assumed to have more experience in importing rice, and thus have lower import entry costs. Some of these traders may already have partnered with farmers' cooperatives, aggregating in a limited way the import requirements of farmers' associations.[4] However, their import storage capacities may be limited, having emerged from an import policy regime dominated by the NFA, and their storage capacities are dedicated to local rice procurement. Not only do they have diminishing returns on import because of limited storage capacities, but they also face supply search costs, which may rise with volume.

Each group is assumed to be made up of homogeneous firms and is represented by a collective firm with the same characteristics as each of the firms in the group.

---

[4] In early 2000, then President Gloria Arroyo instructed the NFA to allow farmers' cooperatives to import rice. The NFA allocated part of the country's rice import requirement for the year to farmers' cooperatives. In practice, the cooperatives, not having experience in the import business, partnered with rice traders who imported for the farmers their assigned allocations.

The rice market is represented with a small open partial equilibrium model, with gross supply made up of domestic and imported rice. The local supply curve for rice can be represented by a total price inelastic supply curve. On the import side, the country is assumed to be a price taker in the world rice market. However, the import supply functions of each group reflect their respective transactions costs from importing.

Without these costs, the foreign rice supply would simply be represented with a perfectly price elastic curve at the going price of rice in the world market. The transaction cost acts like a specific tax and shifts up uniformly above the landed cost of rice by the amount of the transaction cost. However, the less experienced importers face a higher transaction cost, such that in equilibrium it is possible that they will decide not to import rice.

4.1 Basic model

The supply and demand functions are linearly dependent on domestic rice price and some other variables. Equations 1 and 2 represent respectively the total domestic demand and local supply of rice:

$$Q^D = A + \alpha P \qquad (1)$$

$$P = B + \beta Q^L \qquad (2)$$

where Q^D, Q^L and P are the rice quantity demanded and supplied, and the local rice price, respectively. Parameters A and B are the constant terms for the demand and supply functions, and α and $1/\beta$ are the corresponding price coefficients.

In a conventional small open market model with a large group of homogeneous importers not facing transactions cost in importing rice, the import supply function is infinitely price elastic at the landed price of imported rice, gross of the import tariff. Imported rice is assumed to be qualitatively identical to local rice.[5] The gross total supply of rice is the horizontal sum of both the local and imported supply functions. At low quantities, rice demand can be fully met with locally produced

---

[5] In future research, this assumption may be relaxed to accommodate an Armington feature of the model, in that imported rice is qualitatively different from locally produced rice. See Setboonsarng, chapter 25, this volume on recent trends of global rice trade.

rice, and with local and imported rice in the case of larger requirement. The equilibrium price is

$$P = B + \beta Q^L \quad \text{at} \quad P < \bar{P}(1+t)$$
$$= \bar{P}(1+t) \quad \text{otherwise,} \tag{3}$$

where $\bar{P}$ is the landed cost of imported rice and t is the tariff rate on imported rice. The typical quantity bought by buyers is larger and is supplied with local rice up to the quantity, $\frac{\bar{P}(1+t)-B}{\beta}$ and imported rice: $M = [A + \alpha(\bar{P}(1+t))] - \left(\frac{\bar{P}(1+t)-B}{\beta}\right)$. The equilibrium local price is $\bar{P}(1+t)$.

4.2 Heterogeneous importers

The group of large importers with lower import transactions cost (group 1) has an import supply function:

$$P_1^M = \frac{\bar{P}(1+t)}{\lambda_1} + \mu_1 Q_1^M \qquad \lambda_1 = 1; \ \mu_1 > 0. \tag{4}$$

The members of group 1 have rising marginal costs to import rice, reflected in a positive μ_1. The group is assumed not to invest in larger imports capability given the thinness in the world's rice trade and the uncertainty on the policy for liberal rice importation. Accordingly, increasing their quantities of imported rice is met with diminishing returns.

The other group comprises smaller importers with no or meager experience in importing rice. Its members have the following import supply function:

$$P_2^M = \frac{\bar{P}(1+t)}{\lambda_2} + \mu_2 Q_2^M \qquad 0 < \lambda_2 < 1, \qquad \mu_2 < \mu_1, \tag{5}$$

The import productivity parameter, λ, reflects the capability of importers belonging to a particular group to import rice. It can be interpreted as their respective entry costs into the import business. In equation (4), $\lambda_1 = 1$ indicates that the group of large importers has zero entry cost into the import business. However, they face diminishing returns.

The group of small importers faces entry cost, as shown with a λ_2 being less than 1 in equation (5). However, because of their small-scale importations, the members of this group do not encounter rising marginal cost as much as the first group, $\mu_2 < \mu_1$.

There are two equilibrium scenarios in this model.

In the first equilibrium, the domestic price of rice is equal to the price gross of the first group's import transactions cost, shown in equation (5). The second group of importers is unable to overcome its entry cost and decide not to import the commodity. This scenario occurs if the marginal cost of importing rice for the second group of importers exceeds the equilibrium price, $P = P_1^M < P_2^M$.

The equilibrium quantity is:

$$Q^D = A + \alpha P_1^M$$
$$= \frac{A + \alpha(\bar{P}(1+t))}{(1-\alpha\mu_1)},$$

since local production is assumed to be zero, $Q^D = Q_1^M$. If group 1 faces constant marginal cost from importing, the equilibrium quantity reduces to one at the landed cost of rice, gross of the import tariff.

In the other equilibrium, the other group of importers overcomes its entry cost due to the higher equilibrium price, P_2^M, as shown in equation (6). The equilibrium quantity is equal to

$$= \frac{A + \alpha(\bar{P}(1+t))}{\lambda_2(1-\alpha\mu_2)}.$$

This scenario applies if local demand for rice is large and requires more imports. Since the first group's marginal cost from importing increases, it becomes exposed to competition from the other group with lower import transactions cost.

4.3 Local production

With local rice supply considered in the model with its supply equation given by equation (2), total rice supply is still the sum of local and imported rice supplies, with imports being provided by either group 1 importers or both groups. The equilibrium price is equal to:

$$P = B + \beta Q^L \quad \text{for} \quad P < \bar{P}(1+t) + \mu_1 Q_1^M$$
$$= \bar{P}(1+t) + \mu_1 Q_1^M \quad \text{for} \quad B + \beta Q^L < P \leq \frac{\bar{P}(1+t)}{\lambda_2} + \mu_2 Q_2^M \quad (6)$$
$$= \frac{\bar{P}(1+t)}{\lambda_2} + \mu_2 Q_2^M \quad \text{otherwise.}$$

Local supply is relatively price inelastic, its quantity determined less by the market price and more by exogenous factors such as the weather.

Figure 22.2 shows the rice market equilibrium. Equilibrium is established at P^* and Q^*. The quantity is supplied by local rice supply and imported rice of group 1. The other group stays out of the import business. At the vertical intercept, P_1^M, the price is equal to the landed cost gross of the import tariff. Equilibrium price however reflects group 1's transactions cost from importing.

The vertical intercept for the second group, P_2^M, exceeds P_1^M because of the import entry cost of the group members. Its members however do not encounter rising import marginal cost because of the low quantity of their respective import supplies. The third vertical intercept is simply the landed cost of rice without the import tariff.

Figure 22.2. Equilibrium in the rice market with heterogeneous importers

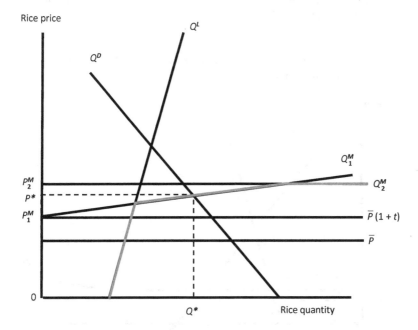

4.4 Liberalizing the import market

Transaction cost limits the effect of liberalizing the import market of rice (see Figure 22.3). Suppose the tariff is removed. Both import functions shift down, say from Q_1^M to $Q_1^{M'}$. The price of rice goes down to $P^{*'}$, which still exceeds $\bar{P}$ due to rising cost to import encountered by group 1 members.

Although the supply function for imported rice of the other group shifts down to $Q_2^{M'}$, the group is still unable to overcome its entry cost into the import business. Liberalization of the import market has no impact at all on their decision not to import rice. Figure 22.3 shows $Q^{*''}$, which is the expected quantity of rice to be imported as a result of the removal of the import tariff.

Proposition. In a market with two types of importers, one facing rising costs with the quantity of the imported commodity and the other facing significant entry costs into the import business such that its group members have not been importing, liberalizing the import market of a commodity reduces its wholesale price by less than the extent of the reduction of import restrictions.

Figure 22.3. Equilibrium without tariff distortions in the rice market with heterogeneous importers

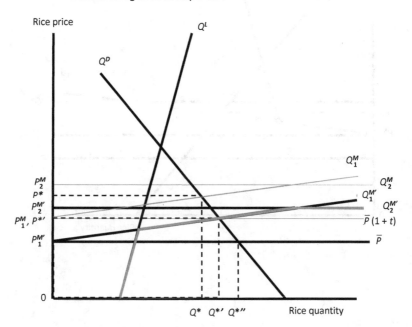

From Table 22.1, the in situ warehouse cost of a kilogram of imported rice is PHP22.19 in 2019. At the effective import tax of 35 per cent, the local rice price in the NCR must be PHP29.96/kg. The prevailing wholesale rice price in the region in 2019 was PHP33.79/kg, giving therefore a margin of PHP3.83/kg. The gap may not be enough to induce new importers to enter the import business if this was their first time to import rice. When import costs are negligible to all potential importers, economic theory predicts that the price of rice in the NCR must be PHP29.96/kg.

But why did existing importers fail to take advantage of the additional profits by importing a larger volume? One possible explanation is they may have higher profits as a group by limiting the quantity they import. The group has an effective market-price-making power, given that the other group faces entry costs and may not pose any competition at all.

4.5 Rice inventory and retail price change

The second element of the price puzzle is that retail rice prices fell by a much lower extent than wholesale rice prices, 4.4 per cent for the former compared with 14.55 per cent for the latter. This was also observed in Table 22.3, indicating a weakening of yearly price fluctuations of wholesale and retail prices.

Varying rice stocks influences the level of retail prices because of their relationship with rice consumption. In a supply utilization table, the total gross supply of rice is made up of the beginning of the year stock of the country, the quantity of local rice output and the imported rice. On the utilization side, the total demand comprises the use of rice for planting in the next season and the amount of rice for processing, exports, animal feeds, inventory and consumption. To attain balance of supply and demand, consumption is estimated as a residual.

The country does not export rice. Except for rice inventory and consumption, all other uses of rice are not large and are fairly constant, their sum being at a little over 7 per cent of production. Rice inventory is estimated independently. Hence, as inventory increases, consumption (estimated as the residual in the supply and use table) falls, and vice versa. Since the decline in rice consumption is accompanied by an increase in retail price, inventory variations influence retail prices.

This is the plausible reason why retail rice prices did not fall as much as wholesale prices. Figure 22.4 displays the rice stocks held by households, commercial establishments and the NFA from 1990 to 2019. Household stocks are relatively predictable, their changes ordinarily not taken as a factor to price movements.

However, commercial and NFA stocks are regarded as highly determining retail rice prices. In 2019, both commercial and NFA stocks increased, pulling up the total stocks. Private-sector traders had imported significant amounts of rice in 2019. If those stocks were injected in the rice market, retail rice prices could have plummeted by more than 4.4 per cent. This may be gleaned from Table 22.5. A hypothetical stock-taking behaviour of both commercial establishments and the NFA (as indicated by the average proportion of rice stocks to gross supply from 2000 to 2018) was predicted to potentially reduce retail rice prices by −26.79 per cent.

The RTL helped propped up retail rice prices by removing from the NFA the function of stabilizing rice prices. The NFA historically had been juxtaposing its rice injections to the local market with that of commercial traders. If the latter raise prices by holding more rice stocks,

Figure 22.4. Rice stocks, by market players (1991–2019, in thousand mt)

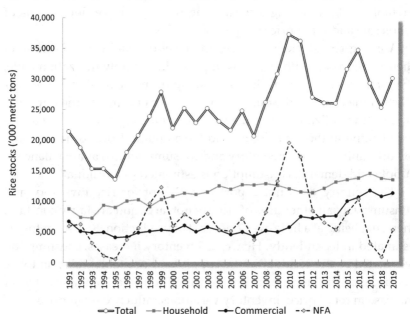

the NFA releases more rice into the market. On the other hand, if commercial traders are unloading their rice stocks, the NFA reduces its rice supplies to the local market. In 2019, with the NFA no longer empowered to undertake this role due to the RTL, the local market became a traders' market, which may have dampened the fall of retail rice prices, suggesting an imperfect competition story in the wholesale and retail price variations.

5 RICE MARKET MODEL WITH INTERMEDIARIES

The third dimension of the price puzzle is that the reduction of the average farm-gate price of palay in the whole country, while relatively correlated more closely with variations in the wholesale price, dropped more than the wholesale price did. Wholesale rice prices in the NCR dropped by 14.55 per cent in 2019 from 2018, while farm-gate prices of palay plunged by 17.43 per cent.

In perfectly competitive and efficient markets, both changes following a policy change must be perfectly correlated with each other.

In this section, the partial equilibrium model of the rice and palay markets is extended to consider intermediaries, traders and millers. Unmilled rice or palay is traded from farms to higher level traders. In the process, it gets milled into rice, stored and gets sold in the market to final consumers.

The model shows that with efficient trading and milling, the percentage changes in wholesale and farm-gate prices are identical. This is done using the implicit tariff and nominal protection rate. Implicit tariff is the penalty wholesalers pay due to prevailing taxes and policies. In this case, if import rice policies were changed to allow private-sector imports, subject to an import tariff, implicit tariff on rice indicates such a penalty. In the absence of the tariff or any other related policy distortions in a small open market model of rice, implicit tariff is zero. On the other hand, the nominal protection rate is the proportionate increase in palay price from its level if there were no such policy distortions.

The discussion that follows suggests that palay prices fell by an even deeper proportion than the wholesale price because of inefficiencies (technical or policy-related such as imperfect competition) in the supply chain.

CASE 1. *Consider a supply chain with product transformation and the respective operating costs of millers and two market intermediaries for palay and rice, respectively.*

Let that commodity be rice. The commodity starts in the supply chain as palay and ends up as rice at the wholesaler's warehouse. In the supply chain, palay becomes rice, where a kilogram of palay is converted to rice.

Rice milling involves splitting the primary commodity into rice and bran, a feedstuff. The palay trader procures palay at the farm and sells it to the rice trader. The latter gets palay milled, pays the miller its milling toll and transports the rice to the wholesaler's warehouse. The miller is a service provider, not in the business of procuring palay and selling it as rice to the rice trader or the market. The miller is compensated with a milling fee and the bran. The miller is assumed to sell the bran without any transport cost.

The operating cost of the rice trader involves buying palay from the palay trader, paying the milling toll net of the value of bran, packaging the rice and transporting the commodity to the wholesaler. The operating cost of the palay trader covers the cost of procuring palay, packing and transporting it to the rice trader.

The margins are assessed on different versions of the product: the palay trader's margin is on the price of palay, while that of the rice trader is on rice price.

Suppose that only the cost of milling is involved. Let μ be the conversion rate of a kilogram of palay to that of rice, $0 < \mu < 1$.

$$P_P = \mu P_R$$

with subscripts P and R denoting palay and rice, respectively.

The free trade (FT) price of palay is

$$P_{P,FT} = \mu P_{R,FT}.$$

$$NPR_P = \left[\frac{P_P}{P_{P,FT}}\right] - 1$$

$$= \left[\frac{\mu P_R}{\mu P_{R,FT}}\right] - 1$$

$$= IT_R.$$

The *NPR* on palay and *IT* on rice are identical.

Let subscripts *MG* and *W* denote millgate and first warehouse from the border, respectively. Consider the following definitions:

$P_{R,MG} = \dfrac{P_{R,W}}{(1+t_{RT})}$, where t_{RT} is the efficient ad valorem operating cost of the rice trader.

$P_{R,FT}$ is the free trade price of rice at the first warehouse from the border.

$P_{R,MG,FT} = \dfrac{P_{R,FT}}{(1+t_{RT})}$ is the free trade price of rice at the millgate.

$P_{P,FG} = \dfrac{P_{P,MG}}{(1+t_{PT})}$, where t_{PT} is the efficient ad valorem operating cost of the village trader.

Given these definitions, the relationship between the prices of palay and rice at the miller's gate is:

$$P_{P,MG} = \mu P_{R,MG}.$$

To calculate the NPR,

$$NPR_P = \left[\dfrac{P_{P,FG}}{P_{P,FT}}\right] - 1$$

$$NPR_P = \left[\dfrac{P_{P,FG}}{\dfrac{\mu(P_{R,FT}/(1+t_{RT}))}{(1+t_{PT})}}\right] - 1$$

$$= \left[\dfrac{\mu(P_{R,MG}/(1+t_{PT}))}{\dfrac{\mu(P_{R,FT}/(1+t_{RT}))}{(1+t_{PT})}}\right] - 1$$

$$= \left[\dfrac{(P_{R,MG}/(1+t_{PT}))}{\dfrac{(P_{R,FT}/(1+t_{RT}))}{(1+t_{PT})}}\right] - 1$$

$$= \left(\dfrac{P_{R,W}}{P_{R,FT}}\right) - 1$$

$$= IT_R.$$

The *NPR* on palay and *IT* on rice are identical.

CASE 2. *Suppose now that the domestic margin exceeds some efficient margin for transporting and milling rice.*

Let *t* remain to be the efficient ad valorem operating cost of the rice or palay trader, but then the domestic marketing margin is less efficient, and τ be the ad valorem domestic operating cost of the same traders.

$$\tau = \delta t$$

where $\delta > 1$.

Let the milling conversion ratio be efficient.

$$P_{R,MG} = \frac{P_{R,W}}{(1+\tau_{RT})},$$

where τ_{RT} is the less efficient ad valorem domestic operating cost of the rice trader. Consider these definitions:

$P_{R,MG,FT} = \frac{P_{R,FT}}{(1+t_{RT})}$, where t_{RT} is the efficient ad valorem operating cost of the rice trader.

$P_{R,FT}$ is the free-trade price of rice at the first warehouse from the border. Given these, the free trade price of palay is:

$$P_{P,FG} = \frac{P_{P,MG}}{(1+\tau_{PT})}$$

where τ_{PT} is the less efficient ad valorem domestic operating cost of the palay trader.

$$P_{P,MG} = \mu P_{R,MG}.$$

To calculate the NPR,

$$NPR_P = \left[\frac{P_{P,FG}}{P_{P,FT}}\right] - 1$$

$$NPR_P = \left[\frac{P_{P,FG}}{\frac{\mu(P_{R,FT}/(1+t_{RT}))}{(1+t_{PT})}}\right] - 1$$

$$= \left[\frac{\mu(P_{R,MG}/(1+\delta t_{PT}))}{\frac{\mu(P_{R,FT}/(1+t_{RT}))}{(1+t_{PT})}}\right] - 1$$

$$= \left[\frac{(P_{R,MG}/(1+\delta t_{PT}))}{\frac{(P_{R,FT}/(1+t_{RT}))}{(1+t_{PT})}}\right] - 1$$

$$= \left[\frac{(1+t_{PT})/(1+\delta t_{PT})(P_{R,MG})}{(P_{R,FT}/(1+t_{RT}))}\right] - 1$$

$$= \left[\left(\frac{(1+t_{PT})}{1+\delta t_{PT}}\right)\left(\frac{P_{R,W}}{P_{R,FT}}\right)\right] - 1$$

$$= \alpha\left[\left(\frac{P_{R,W}}{P_{R,FT}}\right) - 1\right] + (\alpha - 1)$$

$$= \alpha\, IT_R + (\alpha - 1)$$

where $\alpha = \left(\frac{(1+t_{PT})}{(1+\delta t_{PT})}\right).$

<u>Proposition</u>: The less efficient is domestic rice intermediation, the lower is NPR on palay compared with the IT on rice.

$$NPR_p = \alpha\, IT_R + (\alpha - 1) \leq IT_R$$

<u>Proposition</u>: If domestic rice intermediation cost approaches the efficient benchmark cost for identical intermediation, the NPR and IT are identical.

$$\lim NPR = IT, \text{ as } \delta \to 1.$$

The observed deeper penalty on palay farmers following the RTL — that is, they lost trade protection relative to the percentage loss of traders — is traced to the inefficiencies in the supply chain. This result ties up with a similar finding by Jandoc and Roumasset (2018), who document that about a fourth of the trade protection margin of retail rice prices went to rice farmers. The residual was appropriated by traders and millers either as excess profits or to pay for marketing and milling inefficiencies (Dawe et al. 2008). Policy distortions such as market interventions of the NFA in the marketing sector, which displace private transportation, storage and handling, contribute to making the palay and rice intermediation sector less competitive and efficient (Roumasset 1999).

6 CONCLUDING REMARKS

It is well known that the rice marketing structure in the Philippines before the RTL was far from being perfectly competitive. The few traders at the top of the rice supply chain have a dominant position in the market and can set the price, if the NFA did not exercise a countervailing influence on rice prices to check possible abuse by the few traders of their dominant market position. If rice prices increase, the NFA injects more rice into the market.

However, there had been times in the past when the NFA had low rice stocks, preventing it from performing effectively its price stabilization role. This happened two years before the RTL enactment, which significantly increased rice prices and overall inflation in 2018. Through the RTL, policymakers removed that role from the NFA and replaced the marketing regime with one that is more open to imported rice.

Import liberalization is expected to provide competition among existing market players. However, as the ex post assessment of rice price movements in 2019 indicates, the RTL's strategy for promoting competition failed to meet expectation. Wholesale prices fell by less than the import tariff rate. Retail prices, which should move *pari pasu* with wholesale prices, and farm-gate prices, whose changes correlated more with those of wholesale prices, plunged more than wholesale prices.

The analytical model described in this paper may explain why the reduction in wholesale prices was less than that of the import tariff rate. Rice importers face increasing costs from importing. The resulting price margin could not be competed away by the other group of rice importers due to significant entry barriers in the import business. The other pieces of the price puzzle may be explained by the insufficient arrival of imported rice and the inefficiency of intermediation in the rice supply chain.

It may be said that the RTL left behind a marketing system dominated by a few traders, without the effective import competition that it statutorily enabled due to possible entry costs for new importers. Instead of reversing to pre-RTL market policies for rice, the options of policymakers include enforcing or facilitating import competition to induce competition as well in rice intermediation. Both are usually implemented imperfectly.

Enforcing competition entails costs, and the amount of additional rice that may be flushed out from warehouses and injected into the market is limited by the optimal importation of the first group of importers, who face rising costs with imported quantity. In contrast, facilitating competition, which may entail finding out the nature of import barriers faced by the other type of importers and potential entrants to the import business and helping such potential entrants hurdle such costs, has the potential of bringing in more rice to the market, causing rice prices to drop. Facilitating competition may even include helping the first group of importers expand their fixed capacities to mitigate their increasing costs in importation.

One important area of facilitating competition is trade facilitation. The proper use of sanitary and phytosanitary (SPS) measures, which are necessary non-tariff measures, and the streamlining of compliance process are a good start. SPS measures are automatic import licensing regulations. If the imported rice meets the phytosanitary conditions, the importer bringing the rice in should be given the import license. At the border, customs clearance processes implemented by both the Bureau of Plant Industry and the Bureau of Customs may inadvertently impose additional trade cost to importing.

Facilitating competition may be regarded as an integral part of opening local markets to import competition in order to promote the public interest. Balisacan (2019) points out that in countries like China, India and South Africa, the structural and institutional characteristics of their respective economies carried more weight in framing their competition policies. Market concentration is accommodated in local industries with small domestic markets. However, Balisacan stresses that an open trade policy is important to effectively restrain any abuse of market dominance in such concentrated markets. In support of that, facilitating the entry of firms in the import business following the statutory lifting of import restrictions is important to make import competition more effective.

In sum, promoting more competition would drive farm-gate prices even lower. However, in the analysis done in this paper, reducing the inefficiencies in market intermediation can pull up the prices received by rice farmers. It may improve the reader's understanding of the issues taken up here if future research introduces realistic features of the marketing system such as space and time, as well as differential quality of imported and locally produced rice.

The transactions costs highlighted in this paper are by no means permanent features of the import marketing system. In due time, traders will gain experience and adjust their capacities to reduce their diminishing returns on importation. However, without competition from new entrants, they have the dominant market position. And without the NFA to perform an implicit countervailing function to their attempts at exploiting any supply shortages and set the price against the interests of consumers—a solution shown to be grossly costly for the country, the sensible option left to policymakers is to enforce competition in the sense of Balisacan (2019). Otherwise, the Philippines may be in a worse situation than before the RTL.

REFERENCES

Adriano, F. 2020. "RTL, Short-Term Impacts and the Modern-Day Luddites". *Manila Times*, 6 August 2020.

Adriano, F., L. Adriano, and K. Adriano. 2020. "Philippine Rice Tariffication Law - a Year and a Half Later: Challenges and Opportunities". ADB paper. Unpublished.

Balié, J., and Harold Glenn Valera. 2020. "Domestic and International Impacts of the Rice Trade Policy Reform in the Philippines". *Food Policy*. https://doi.org/10.1016/j.foodpol.2020.101876 (accessed December 2020).

Balisacan, A. M. 2000. "Growth, Inequality and Poverty Reduction in the Philippines: A Re-examination of Evidence". Discussion Paper. Quezon City: University of the Philippines.

———. 2019. "Toward a Fairer Society: Inequality and Competition Policy in Developing Asia". *Philippine Review of Economics* 56, no. 1&2 (June-December): 127–47.

Balisacan, A. M., R. Clarete, and A. Cortez. 1992. "The Food Problem in the Philippines". Unpublished.

Balisacan, A. M., and L. S. Sebastian. 2006. "Challenges and Policy Directions: Overview". In *Securing Rice, Reducing Poverty: Challenges and Policy Directions*, edited by A. M. Balisacan, L. S. Sebastian, and Associates, pp. 1–19. Los Baños: Southeast Asian Regional Center for Graduate Study and Research in Agriculture.

Balisacan, A. M., M. A. Sombilla, and R. Dikitanan. 2010. "Rice Crisis in the Philippines: Why Did It Occur and What Are Its Policy Implications?". In *The Rice Crisis: Markets, Policies, and Food Security*, edited by D. Dawe, pp. 123–42. Rome: FAO and Earthscan.

Briones, R. 2018. "Scenarios for the Philippine Agri-food System With and Without Tariffication: Application of a CGE Model with Endogenous Area Allocation". *Discussion Paper Series*, no. 2018-51. Quezon City: Philippine Institute for Development Studies.

Clarete, R. 2008. "Options for National Food Authority Reforms in the Philippines". In *From Parastatals to Private Trade: Lessons from Asian Agriculture*, edited by S. Rashid, A. Gulati, and R. Cummings Jr. Baltimore: Johns Hopkins University Press.

Clarete, R. 2019. "Rice Reserves, Policies and Food Security: The Case of the Philippines". In *How Can Food Reserves Best Enhance Food and Nutrition Security in Developing Countries? Case Studies*. A report prepared by Centre de Coopération Internationale en Recherche Agronomique pour le Développement (CIRAD) and DAI Europe, Ltd. for the European Commission.

Cororaton, C., and K. Yu. 2019. "Assessing the Poverty and Distributional Impact of Alternative Rice Policies in the Philippines". *DLSU Business & Economics Review* 28, no. 2: 1.

David, C. C. 2003. "Agriculture". In *The Philippine Economy: Development, Policies and Challenges*, edited by A. M. Balisacan and H. Hill, pp. 175–218. New York: Oxford University Press and Quezon City: Ateneo de Manila University Press.

David, C. C., P. Intal, and A. M. Balisacan. 2009. "The Philippines". In *Distortions to Agricultural Incentives in Asia*, edited by K. Anderson and W. Martin, pp. 223–54. Washington, DC: World Bank.

Dawe, D., P. Moya, and C. Casiwan, eds. 2006. *Why Does the Philippines Import Rice: Meeting the Challenge of Trade Liberalization*. Los Baños, Philippines: IRRI and PhilRice.

Dawe, D., P. Moya, C. Casiwan, and J. Cabling. 2008. "Rice Marketing Systems in the Philippines and Thailand: Do Large Numbers of Competitive Traders Ensure Good Performance?". *Food Policy* 33, no. 5: 455–63.

FFF (Federation of Free Farmers). 2020. "Farmers Lose P68 Billon from Rice Tariffication Law". https://www.philstar.com/business/2020/02/22/1995025/farmers-lose-p68-billion-rice-tariffication-law.

GMA News. 2010. "Aquino: Rice Rotted in NFA Warehouses". GMA News, 26 July 2010. http://www.gmanetwork.com/news/story/197016/economy/aquino-rice-rotted-in-nfa-warehouse (accessed 30 March 2013).

IBON Foundation, Inc. 2020. "Farmers Lose PHP85 Billion during First Year: Peasant Livelihoods Destroyed, Food Insecurity Worsened by Rice Liberalization". IBON Media & Communications, 14 February 2020. https://www.ibon.org/farmers-lose-php85-billion-during-first-year-peasant-livelihoods-destroyed-food-insecurity-worsened-by-rice-liberalization/.

Jandoc, K., and J. Roummaset. 2018. "Rice Tariffication and Its Role in Reducing Rice Prices". Unpublished.

Jha, Shikha, and Aashish Mehta. 2008. "Effectiveness of Public Spending: The Case of Rice Subsidies in the Philippines". *ADB Economics Working Paper Series*, no. 138. Manila: ADB.

Melitz, M. J. 2003. "The Impact of Trade on Intra-Industry Reallocations and Aggregate Industry Productivity". *Econometrica* 71, no. 6: 1695–1725.

Montemayor, R. 2020. "Winners and Losers from the Rice Tariffication Law". Inquirer.net, 6 September 2020. https://newsinfo.inquirer.net/1332019/winners-and-losers-from-the-rice-tariffication-law#ixzz6bxAEpGm4.

PhilRice (Philippine Rice Research Institute). 2019. Rice Tariffication Law (Republic Act 11203). *FAQs Rice Competitiveness Enhancement Fund (RCEF) Series*, no. 2. https://wwwphilricegov.ph/wp-content/uploads/2019/09/RCEF_FAQ02-RiceTariff.pdf.

Perez, N., and A. Pradesha. 2019. "Philippine Rice Trade Liberalization: Impacts on Agriculture and the Economy, and Alternative Policy Actions". *NEDA-IFPRI Policy Studies*, commissioned by the National Economic Development Authority. Washington, DC: International Food Policy Research Institute. https://doi.org/10.2499/p15738coll2.133371.

Roumasset, J. 1999. "Market Friendly Food Security: Alternatives for Restructuring NFA". A report commissioned by the USAID-supported AGILE project for the National Food Authority.

Setboonsarng, S. 2022. "Transformation of the Global Rice Market". In *Agriculture, Poverty, and Competition Policy in the Philippines and East Asia*, edited by H. Hill, M. V. Ravago, and J. Roumasset. Singapore: Institute for Southeast Asian Studies.

Slayton, T. 2009. "Rice Crisis Forensics: How Asian Governments Carelessly Set the World Rice Market on Fire". *Working Paper No. 163*. Washington, DC: Center for Global Development.

Sombilla, M. A., F. A. Lantican, and J. C. Beltran. 2006. "Marketing and Distribution". In *Securing Rice, Reducing Poverty: Challenges and Policy Directions*, edited by A. M. Balisacan, L. S. Sebastian, and Associates, pp. 213–38. Los Baños, Laguna, Philippines: Southeast Asian Regional Center for Graduate Study and Research in Agriculture.

World Bank. 2001. "Philippines: Filipino Report Card on Pro-poor Services". *Report No. 22181–PH*, Wash B. Environment and Social Development Sector Unit, East Asia and Pacific Region. Manila: World Bank.

23 The Role of Government Subsidies in Philippine Agricultural Competition

Arlene B. Inocencio and Agnes C. Rola

1 INTRODUCTION

Government subsidies have been used to pursue legitimate public interests when markets do not deliver optimal outcomes for society. They are used to promote priority sectors and establish growth areas that are aligned with the government's development goals (Administrative Order No. 59, Rationalizing the Government Corporate Sector, issued on 16 February 1988 by President Corazon C. Aquino). In the Philippines, the reasons commonly cited for subsidizing the agriculture sector include the need for market stability and food security, as well as to help low-income farmers and aid rural development.

The Philippine agriculture sector has received substantial subsidies over time. Figure 23.1 shows the subsidies to the sector from 2010 to 2015, which averaged PHP3.36 billion annually. The subsectors receiving sizeable subsidies in 2014 were papaya growing, perennial trees (with edible nuts) growing, operation of irrigation systems through non-cooperatives and seaweed farming; it was dairy farming in both 2013 and 2014. The subsectors of *operation of irrigation systems through cooperatives* and *services to establish crops, promote their growth and protect them from pests and diseases, n.e.c.* received subsidies for most years between 2010 and 2015.[1] Such support for the agriculture sector

---

[1] n.e.c. means "not elsewhere classified".

is provided through government-owned and controlled corporations (GOCCs).

The government enacted the Philippine Competition Act (Republic Act 10667) in 2015. Despite the passage of this law, however, the competition environment in the country remains weak because there are other existing laws deemed inconsistent with this Act. For instance, GOCCs have charters providing for both proprietary and regulatory functions. Some of these corporations receive subsidies that affect competition in two ways (Neven and Veroudin 2008). One, they influence the behaviour of competitors as a response to that of the recipient. Two, firms behave relative to how the government reallocates rent via subsidies. These non-neutral policies distort the market. Limited competition slows down economic development and job creation in key sectors (Miralles Murciego et al. 2018). There has been no empirical study that estimates the effects of government subsidies on firms' behaviour and the business environment. This study bridges this gap by examining the market structure and power of agriculture subsectors that receive government subsidies.

Figure 23.1. Subsidies to the agriculture sector (2010–15)

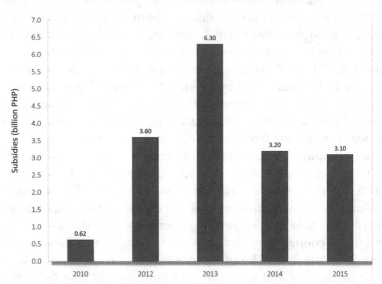

Sources: CPBI and ASPBI, PSA (2010–15).

This chapter heavily draws from a scoping paper and data collected on Philippine subsidies to the agriculture and manufacturing sectors (Inocencio, Inocencio, and Barnedo 2019) commissioned by the Philippine Competition Commission in 2019. It is structured as follows: Section 2 contains the study framework and methodology. Section 3 estimates the Philippine government subsidies to the agriculture sector. Section 4 discusses the state of competition. Section 5 presents the assessment of impacts of subsidies on competition in agriculture. Section 6 provides deeper insights through selected GOCC cases. The last section concludes and offers some recommendations.

2   FRAMEWORK AND METHODOLOGY

To achieve the objectives in this chapter, we first define subsidies and the measures for competition and market power. Then we provide a framework for assessing the impacts of subsidies on market competition. This section ends with a brief discussion of the data.

2.1   Defining subsidies

A subsidy is a financial contribution by government or any public body within the territory of the government, and it confers a benefit. Specifically, subsidies can be an income or price support and can take any of the following forms: (1) a direct transfer of funds such as grants, loans and equity infusion, or potential direct transfers of funds or liabilities (e.g., loan guarantees); (2) government revenue that is otherwise due is forgone or not collected (e.g., fiscal incentives such as tax credits); (3) provision of goods or services other than general infrastructure; and (4) payments to a funding mechanism, or a private body is directed to carry out one or more of the other three types of functions, which would normally be vested in the government.

2.2   Measures of competition and market power

Inocencio, Inocencio, and Barnedo (2019) characterize competition in terms of widely accepted measures of market concentration and market power. Two market concentration measures are used: the Herfindahl-Hirschman Index (HHI) and the top-four-firm concentration ratio (CR4), defined as:

$$HHI = \sum_{i=1}^{N} d_i^2 \qquad (1)$$

$$CR4 = \sum_{i=1}^{4} d_i \qquad (2)$$

where d_i is the per cent market share of the i-th enterprise and N is the total number of enterprises in the subsector for HHI. CR4 takes the values of 0 to 100 per cent, while HHI, 0 to 10,000. The higher the HHI and CR4, the greater the opportunities for oligopolistic behaviour.

A high concentration value is a necessary but not sufficient condition for market power to exist. The extent to which a firm has market power may be revealed by the margin between price and marginal cost. The price-cost margin (PCM) is calculated as price less the marginal cost divided by price. A firm with market power can charge a price substantially above marginal cost while that without will charge a price close to marginal cost. Market power allows firms to set prices above those in competitive conditions, leading to excessive economic profits. A zero PCM indicates competitive behaviour, while a positive value indicates market power. However, the magnitude is not sufficient to determine the extent of market power.[2] Spierdijk and Zaouras (2017) argue that a negative PCM could entail either a competitive or uncompetitive market. In this case, there is a need to gather additional information on market contestability and barriers to entry and exit.

2.3 Assessing the impacts of subsidies

To assess the impact of subsidies on market power, Inocencio, Inocencio, and Barnedo (2019) followed the method of Chen and Yu (2019). With the computed PCM as the dependent variable, the following was estimated:

$$PCM_{jt} = \alpha_0 + \alpha_1 s_{jt} + \alpha_2 (s_{jt} * GOCC_j) + \alpha_3 n_{jt} + \alpha_4 p_{jt} + v_j + u_{jt} \qquad (3)$$

where s is subsidy of the jth 5-PSIC level subsector at time t, $s*GOCC$ is the interaction variable for subsidy given to GOCCs, n is number of establishments, p is labour productivity, v_j is the sector specific term and u_{jt} is the idiosyncratic error term.

The GOCC dummy takes the value of 1 for a subsector in the 5-PSIC level where at least one GOCC operates and 0 otherwise. The interaction

---

[2] The PCM measure indicates presence or absence of market power, so it is deemed a one-sided test.

term for subsidy and GOCC provides an additional information for sub-sectors with at least one existing GOCC.

We interpret α_1 and α_2 as follows (Chen and Yu 2019):

$\alpha_1 > 0$ implies that government subsidy empowers oligopolistic players and promotes less competition in the market.

$\alpha_1 < 0$ means that subsidies do not enable market power that results in excessive profits.

For state-owned and controlled corporations, the marginal effect of subsidies would be $\alpha_1 + \alpha_2$:

$\alpha_1 + \alpha_2 > 0$ implies that government subsidies through GOCCs enable more market power and excessive profits.

$\alpha_1 + \alpha_2 < 0$ means that government subsidies do not enable firms to gain market power and extract excessive rents.

2.4 Methodology and data sources

The industry data collected by the Philippine Statistics Authority (PSA) include subsidies, which are defined as "all special grants in the form of financial assistance or tax exemption or tax privilege given by the government to aid and develop an industry". Using PSA data—specifically the Census of Philippine Business and Industry (CPBI) for 2012 and the Annual Surveys of Philippine Business and Industry (ASPBI) for 2010, 2013–15—we estimated market concentration, market power and impact of subsidies on competition. We used the 5-digit Philippine Standard Industry Classification (PSIC) for the subsectoral analyses and followed Medalla's (2018) calculation of PCM, which includes the cost of raw materials, total compensation and other variable costs such as utilities, fuel and industrial services done by others. Then we carried out quantitative analyses.

3   AGRICULTURAL SUBSIDIES

Agricultural subsidies from 2010 to 2015 were largely captured by a few subsectors. In 2010, the *services to establish crops, promote their growth and protect them from pests and diseases, n.e.c.* subsector accounted for 94 per cent of total subsidies from the government. This was followed by *hog farming*, which accounted for only 3 per cent of the total. Table 23.1 presents the agriculture subsectors (at the 5-PSIC level) in 2012,

Table 23.1. Subsidy, ratios to value added and concentrations of subsidy (2012)

PSIC	Industry description	No. of firms	Subsidy ('000 PHP)	Ratio of subsidy to value added (%)	Concentration of subsidy sHHI	sCR4
A01121	Growing of paddy rice, lowland, irrigated	33	6,827	1.04	9,898	100
A01140	Growing of sugarcane, including muscovado sugar-making in the farm	309	5,838	0.42	5,101	100
A01172	Growing of fruit-bearing vegetables, such as tomato, eggplant, cucumber, ampalaya, squash, gourd and other fruit-bearing vegetables, n.e.c.	12	592	0.50	10,000	100
A01211	Growing of banana, cavendish	153	450	0.02	10,000	100
A01250	Growing of papaya	10	19,211	*	3,940	100
A01282	Growing of plants used primarily in medical/pharmaceutical purposes, such as lagundi, banaba, ginseng, oregano	s	s			
A01292	Growing of perennial trees with edible nuts, e.g., pili nuts, cashew nuts	s	21,937	*	10,000	100
A01296	Growing of oleaginous fruits, except coconut	17	200	0.15	10,000	100
A01442	Goat farming	s	s			
A01450	Hog farming	397	500	0.02	10,000	100
A01511	Operation of irrigation systems through cooperatives	77	4,865	27.33	4,239	
A01512	Operation of irrigation systems through non-cooperatives	4	2,306,349	68.67	10,000	

Table 23.1 (continued)

Table 23.1 (continued)

PSIC	Industry description	No. of firms	Subsidy ('000 PHP)	Ratio of subsidy to value added (%)	Concentration of subsidy sHHI	Concentration of subsidy sCR4
A01534	Services to establish crops, promote their growth and protect them from pests and diseases, n.e.c.	6	1,182,757	1493.00	10,000	
A01571	Preparation of crops for primary markets, i.e., cleaning, trimming, grading, disinfecting, threshing, bailing and related services	21	1,429	*	8,834	
A03121	Catching fish, crabs and crustaceans in inland waters	s	s			
A03130	Support service activities incidental to fishing	s	s			
A03251	Culture of freshwater crustaceans (except prawns), bivalves, and other mollusks	11	116	0.02	10,000	
A03261	Pearl culture	6	229	0.10	10,000	
A03271	Seaweed farming	s	s			
Total	**Agriculture, Forestry & Forestry**	**2,461**	**3,555,643**			

Note: (1) * = value-added calculations turn out negative following the PSA formula
(2) s = suppressed. PSA does not give firm-level data which can be directly linked to a company. Given the nature of the sector, we infer that A01512 is likely National Irrigation Administration (NIA); A01534, Philippine Coconut Authority (PCA); A02110, Philippine Forest Corporation (PFC) and A03130, Philippine Fisheries Development Authority (PFDA). A01442 and A01450 are possibly National Dairy Administration (NDA) or Philippine Carabao Center (PCC).

Source: Inocencio, Inocencio, and Barnedo (2019).

of which 14 subsectors were subsidized. *Operation of irrigation systems through non-cooperatives* received 65 per cent of total subsidies while *services to establish crops, promote their growth and protect them from pests and diseases, n.e.c.* got 33 per cent.

These 2012 top two subsectors likewise accounted for 99 per cent of the subsidies in 2013 and 2014, which totalled PHP6.3 billion and PHP3.2 billion, respectively. While subsidies to the other subsectors were nominal relative to their value added, *seaweed farming* got more than 20 per cent in 2013–2014. It was the same case in 2012 for *growing of perennial trees with edible nuts, e.g., pili nuts, cashew nuts* and *growing of other tropical fruits, e.g., jackfruit, guavas, avocados, lanzones, durian, rambutan, chico, atis, mangosteen, makopa*. In 2015, 94 per cent of the subsidies went to *services to establish crops, promote their growth and protect them from pests and diseases, n.e.c.* and 4 per cent to *operation of irrigation systems through non-cooperatives* (Table 23.2).

Most of the subsidies given from 2010 to 2015 went to a single firm in each subsector, as indicated by the subsidy concentration measures (sHHI and sCR4). In sum, except for three or four subsectors, the subsidies were below 7 per cent of the value added. Moreover, only two subsectors consistently got the bulk of the subsidies in most years.

4 COMPETITION IN AGRICULTURE

There are 55 subsectors (at the 5-PSIC level) with HHIs of at least 2,500, six of which received support from the government. We find that about 95 subsectors (58%) in agriculture are highly concentrated.[3] The estimates of concentration of subsidies (based on the HHI and CR4 measures) indicate that in six of the ten agriculture subsectors, subsidies went to a single firm only. Consistently in all years, the *services to establish crops, promote their growth and protect them from pests and diseases, n.e.c.* subsector is found to be a highly concentrated market with a negative PCM. This result is inconclusive, however, and will require further investigation of the subsector to clearly establish market power (Medalla 2018; Spierdijk and Zaoras 2017). The subsector of *operation of irrigation systems through non-cooperatives*, which receives a relatively high subsidy, is highly concentrated also.

---

[3] There are 152 subsectors in agriculture (crops and livestock) and forestry and fishing at 5-PSIC level. Not all of them receive subsidies.

Table 23.2. Subsidy, ratios to value added and concentrations of subsidy (2015)

PSIC	Industry description	No. of firms	Subsidy ('000 PHP)	Ratio of subsidy to value added (%)	Concentration of subsidy	
					sHHI	sCR4
A01512	Operation of irrigation systems through non-cooperatives	s	121,390	5.30	10,000	100
A03130	Support service activities incidental to fishing	s	29,622	7.34	10,000	100
A01581	Growing of paddy rice for seed purposes	5	228	2.79	10,000	100
A01130	Growing of corn, except young corn (vegetable)	7	33	0.00	10,000	100
A01121	Growing of paddy rice, lowland, irrigated	34	28,365	2.85	10,000	100
A01534	Services to establish crops, promote their growth and protect them from pests and diseases, n.e.c.	3	2,911,117	*	10,000	100
A01511	Operation of irrigation systems through cooperatives	90	29	0.22	10,000	100
Total	**Agriculture, Forestry & Forestry**	**2,646**	**3,090,783**			

Note: (1) * = the value-added calculations turn out negative following the PSA formula
(2) s = suppressed

Source: Inocencio, Inocencio, and Barnedo (2019).

Table 23.3 shows that 11 agriculture subsectors are highly concentrated in 2012. Based on the four-firm concentration ratios, the biggest four firms in each of these subsectors account for 83–100 per cent of the market. In 2015, six subsectors, which received subsidies, account for 95 to 100 per cent of the market (Table 23.4). These estimates indicate less competition and some degree of market power in several subsectors in agriculture, which in principle can be exploited to the disadvantage of consumers.

Looking into market concentration and market behaviour summarized at the 2-PSIC level, we find the subsectors of *crop production, hunting and related service activities* and *fishing and aquaculture* as moderately concentrated with positive PCMs, suggesting monopolistic behaviour. The *forestry and logging* subsector is highly concentrated with a negative PCM, implying that the incumbent firms appear not to be enjoying abnormal profits.

5 IMPACT OF SUBSIDIES ON COMPETITION IN AGRICULTURE

With market concentration variables as dependent variables, Table 23.5 shows the impact of subsidies on competition, which accounted for time-invariant omitted-variable bias in the model. All the models are specified as random effects (RE) given the results of the Hausman tests. The results of the Breusch-Pagan Lagrange multiplier tests are consistent with those of the Hausman tests: the RE model specification is deemed more appropriate than the OLS specification. Year dummies were added as the joint tests suggest that there are time effects. Except for models 2 and 6, all the year dummy variables are statistically significant at varying levels. The negative relationship with market concentration indicates that the agriculture sector is becoming less concentrated over the study period.

The results show some negative impacts of PCM on HHI market concentration (columns 1 and 5 in Table 23.5), but the coefficients are not statistically significant. A negative impact indicates that a low PCM provides a disincentive to new entrants or drives out less efficient firms, thus the higher degree of concentration.

Table 23.3. Market concentrations of agriculture subsectors (2010–15)

PSIC	Industry description	2010 HHI	2010 CR4	2012 HHI	2012 CR4	2013 HHI	2013 CR4	2014 HHI	2014 CR4	2015 HHI	2015 CR4
High concentration (HHI > 2,500)											
A01121	Growing of paddy rice, lowland, irrigated			3,251	84			5,978	99	4,655	95
A01130	Growing of corn, except young corn (vegetable)					3,570	99			5,439	100
A01172	Growing of fruit-bearing vegetables, such as tomato, eggplant, cucumber, ampalaya, squash, gourd and other fruit-bearing vegetables, n.e.c.			3,423	89						
A01240	Growing of mango			4,173	100						
A01291	Growing of other tropical fruits, e.g., jackfruit, guavas, avocados, lanzones, durian, rambutan, chico, atis, mangosteen, makopa			3,377	96						
A01292	Growing of perennial trees with edible nuts, e.g., pili nuts, cashew nuts			10,000	100						

Table 23.3 (continued)

Table 23.3 (continued)

PSIC	Industry description	2010 HHI	2010 CR4	2012 HHI	2012 CR4	2013 HHI	2013 CR4	2014 HHI	2014 CR4	2015 HHI	2015 CR4
A01296	Growing of oleaginous fruits, except coconut			4,555	83						
A01512	Operation of irrigation systems through non-cooperatives	9,984	100	9,968	100	9,998	100	9,996	100	10,000	100
A01534	Services to establish crops, promote their growth and protect them from pests and diseases, n.e.c.	4,953	100	3,471	100	4,692	100	4,399	100	4,436	100
A01550	Rental of farm machinery with drivers and crew					6,803	99				
A01571	Preparation of crops for primary markets, i.e., cleaning, trimming, grading, disinfecting; threshing, bailing and related services	9,785	100	8,169	98						
A01581	Growing of paddy rice for seed purposes									6,401	100

Table 23.3 (continued)

Table 23.3 *(continued)*

PSIC	Industry description	2010 HHI	2010 CR4	2012 HHI	2012 CR4	2013 HHI	2013 CR4	2014 HHI	2014 CR4	2015 HHI	2015 CR4
A02110	Growing of timber forest species (e.g., gemelina, eucalyptus), planting, replanting, transplanting, thinning and conserving of forest and timber tracts	4,049	100								
A02400	Support services to forestry					6,684	100				
A03130	Support service activities incidental to fishing									10,000	100
A03251	Culture of freshwater crustaceans (except prawns), bivalves, and other mollusks			4,292	97						
A03261	Pearl culture	3,203	97	2,919	97						
A03271	Seaweed farming					9,474	100	5,854	100		
Moderate concentration (2,500 > HHI > 1,500)											
A01430	Dairy farming					2,195	80	2,336	81		
Unconcentrated (HHI < 1,500)											
A01140	Growing of sugarcane, including muscovado sugar-making in the farm	132	11	99	12						

Table 23.3 (continued)

Table 23.3 (continued)

PSIC	Industry description	2010 HHI	2010 CR4	2012 HHI	2012 CR4	2013 HHI	2013 CR4	2014 HHI	2014 CR4	2015 HHI	2015 CR4
A01211	Growing of banana, cavendish			586	42						
A01212	Growing of other bananas			2,224	88						
A01220	Growing of pineapple	1,390	69								
A01293	Growing of rubber tree	1,010	52					1,621	66		
A01450	Hog farming	300	25	365	27						
A01511	Operation of irrigation systems through cooperatives			539	34	1,707	75	2,348	85	2,350	82
A03111	Ocean fishing, commercial (using vessels over 3 tons)	824	50								

Sources: CPBI, PSA (2012) and ASPBI, PSA (2010, 2013–15).

Table 23.4. Price-cost margin by market concentration (2010–15)

Industry description	2010	2012	2013	2014	2015
High concentration (HHI > 2,500)					
Growing of paddy rice, lowland, irrigated		0.24		0.61	0.52
Growing of corn, except young corn (vegetable)			0.18		0.34
Growing of fruit-bearing vegetables, such as tomato, eggplant, cucumber, ampalaya, squash, gourd and other fruit-bearing vegetables, n.e.c.		0.32			
Growing of mango		3.02			
Growing of other tropical fruits, e.g., jackfruit, guavas, avocados, lanzones, durian, rambutan, chico, atis, mangosteen, makopa		1.02			
Growing of perennial trees with edible nuts, e.g., pili nuts, cashew nuts		7.55			
Growing of oleaginous fruits except coconut		0.25			
Operation of irrigation systems through non-cooperatives	0.56	−1.11	−0.17	0.16	0.19
Services to establish crops, promote their growth and protect them from pests and diseases, n.e.c.	−0.56	−0.25	−0.16	−0.92	−1.20
Rental of farm machinery with drivers and crew			0.30		
Preparation of crops for primary markets, i.e., cleaning, trimming, grading, disinfecting; threshing, bailing and related services	0.11	−0.12			
Growing of paddy rice for seed purposes					0.36
Growing of timber forest species (e.g., gemelina, eucalyptus), planting, replanting, transplanting, thinning and conserving of forest and timber tracts	−0.16				

Table 23.4 (continued)

Table 23.4 (continued)

Industry description	2010	2012	2013	2014	2015
Support services to forestry			0.38		
Support service activities incidental to fishing					0.19
Culture of freshwater crustaceans (except prawns), bivalves, and other mollusks		0.19			
Pearl culture	−2.62				
Seaweed farming		0.36	0.22	0.18	
Moderate concentration (2,500 > HHI > 1,500)					
Dairy farming			−0.06	0.30	
Unconcentrated (HHI < 1,500)					
Growing of sugarcane, including muscovado sugar-making in the farm	0.23	0.12			
Growing of banana, cavendish		0.05			
Growing of other bananas		−0.14			
Growing of pineapple	0.13				
Growing of rubber tree	0.01			−0.36	
Hog farming	0.17	0.42			
Operation of irrigation systems through cooperatives		0.07	0.51	0.50	
Ocean fishing, commercial (using vessels over 3 tons)	0.18				−0.49

Sources: CPBI, PSA (2012) and ASPBI, PSA (2010, 2013–15).

Table 23.5. Impact of subsidies on market concentration

Variable	(1) HHI	(2) CR4	(3) HHI	(4) CR4	(5) HHI	(6) CR4
PCM	−88.60	0.0222			−87.63	0.0289
	(85.83)	(0.418)			(85.92)	(0.4190)
Subsidy			1.38e−07	9.42e−10	1.26e−07	9.46e−10
			(3.86e−07)	(1.89e−09)	(3.86e−07)	(1.89e−09)
Y2012	−1,427.00***	−7.821***	−1,421.0***	−7.879***	−1,434.00***	−7.8750***
	(300.60)	(1.457)	(301.4)	(1.459)	(301.50)	(1.4620)
Y2013	−751.20**	−3.399**	−764.1**	−3.490**	−763.20**	−3.4900**
	(300.50)	(1.456)	(303.0)	(1.466)	(302.90)	(1.4680)
Y2014	−1,075.00***	−2.698*	−1,081.0***	−2.748*	−1,082.00***	−2.7480*
	(295.10)	(1.430)	(296.0)	(1.432)	(295.90)	(1.4340)
Y2015	−604.10**	−1.552	−582.2*	−1.607	−610.10**	−1.5980
	(299.60)	(1.452)	(299.1)	(1.448)	(300.30)	(1.4560)
Constant	7,114.00***	93.420***	7,112.0***	93.440***	7,116.00***	93.4400***
	(389.30)	(2.0750)	(390.3)	(2.076)	(390.50)	(2.0790)

Table 23.5 (continued)

Table 23.5 (continued)

Variable	(1) HHI	(2) CR4	(3) HHI	(4) CR4	(5) HHI	(6) CR4
Observations	367	367	367	367	367	367
Number of id	97	97	97	97	97	97
sigma_u	3,133	17.39	3,145	17.41	3,150	17.45
sigma_e	1,630	7.868	1632	7.868	1,633	7.881
rho	0.787	0.830	0.788	0.830	0.788	0.831
Wald Chi^2	26.75	36.24	25.78	36.53	26.83	36.45

Note: (1) Standard errors in parentheses
(2) *** $p < 0.01$, ** $p < 0.05$, * $p < 0.1$

Source: Inocencio, Inocencio, and Barnedo (2019).

The current data do not support this argument, however. Subsidy is found to be positively correlated with market concentration but not statistically significant, as shown in models (3) to (6). So, the results do not support the argument that subsidies contribute to market concentration. These results are intuitive as only a few subsectors in agriculture received subsidies, which are deemed small relative to their value added. On the other hand, substantial subsidies were poured into subsectors where GOCCs are operating to deliver support services. Over the years, the subsidized programmes for the agriculture sector have been rationalized to reduce the risks or negative externalities brought about by calamities and pest infestations, and to help farmers.

Table 23.6 presents the impact of subsidies on market power.[4] The positive and statistically significant coefficient for subsidies indicates that subsidies empower oligopolistic players in the agriculture sector. However, the coefficient for the interaction term for subsidy and GOCCs is statistically significant and negative. This finding suggests that agricultural subsidies dispensed through the GOCCs do not appear to enable the recipients to abuse their market power and extract excessive rents. This seemingly unintuitive result actually makes sense. In markets where state-enabled monopolies operate, the market concentrations may be high, but there is no evidence of abuse of market power.

6 AGRICULTURAL LAWS, SUBSIDIES AND THE PHILIPPINE COMPETITION POLICY: CASES OF GOCCs

Given the empirical results above, this section deep dives into understanding the context of agricultural subsidies affecting market competition. At least five laws (Fabella, Bacani, and Palacios 2020) affect market competition in the agriculture and fisheries sector of the Philippines (Table 23.7). For instance, the Magna Carta of Small Farmers of 1992 (Republic Act No. 7607) aims to empower small farmers by providing incentives via physical infrastructure, access to vital services and capacity building to improve their economic performance. Farmers can form organized groups for more market power. Market power is enhanced through increased volume of purchase of inputs and disposal of outputs through farmer cooperatives.

---

[4] The Hausman test indicates random effects (RE) as the appropriate model.

Table 23.6. Impact of subsidies on market power

Variable	PCM
Subsidy	5.18e−05**
	(2.04e−05)
Subsidy*GOCC	−5.20e−05**
	(2.04e−05)
No. of establishment	0.000861
	(0.001520)
Labour productivity	0.000154
	(0.000172)
Constant	−0.117000
	(0.131000)
Observations	367
R-squared	
Number of id	97
sigma_u	0.977
sigma_e	1.112
Rho	0.436
FStat	
Wald Chi²	7.978

Note: (1) Standard errors in parentheses
(2) *** $p < 0.01$, ** $p < 0.05$, * $p < 0.1$

Source: Inocencio, Inocencio, and Barnedo (2019).

The same is true with the Agriculture and Fisheries Modernization Act (AFMA) of 1997 (Republic Act No. 8435) as the policy instrument for agricultural modernization and global competitiveness (Aquino et al. 2013). AFMA aims to build the competitive capabilities of farmers by providing input subsidies, training programmes and irrigation facilities, among others. Its trade and fiscal incentives aim to raise the competitive edge of Philippine agricultural products in both domestic and global markets. The government also tries to protect local farmers by creating barriers to agricultural imports such as higher tariffs and embargoes.

Table 23.7. Laws and provisions affecting market competition in the agriculture and fisheries sector of the Philippines

	Law	Provision
(1)	Magna Carta of Small Farmers of 1992 (RA No. 7607)	Government provides incentives to small farmers' cooperatives, i.e., provision of infrastructure and other physical assets, access to vital agricultural services, capacity building to improve small farm productivity
(2)	Agriculture and Fisheries Modernization Act of 1997 (RA No. 8435)	The State shall adopt the market approach in assisting the agriculture and fisheries sectors, without neglecting the welfare of the consumers, especially the lower income groups. The State shall promote market-oriented policies in agricultural production to encourage farmers to shift to more profitable crops. Government will enable more equitable access to assets, income, basic and support services and infrastructure.
(3)	Philippine Fisheries Code of 1998 (RA No. 8550)	Government will provide support to the fisheries sector, through appropriate technology and research, adequate financial, production, construction of post-harvest facilities, marketing assistance, and other services.
(4)	Agricultural and Fisheries Mechanization Law of 2013 (RA No. 10601)	Government will strengthen support services such as credit facilities, research, training and extension programmes, rural infrastructure, post-harvest facilities and marketing services and to deliver integrated support services to farmers, fisherfolk and other stakeholders, and assist them to be able to viably operate and manage their agricultural and fisheries mechanization projects.
(5)	Agricultural Tariffication Act of 1996 (RA No. 8178)	The State will adopt the use of tariffs in lieu of non-tariff import restrictions to protect local producers of agricultural products, with exception of rice. To effect the constitutional mandate of protecting Filipino firms against unfair trade, the State will employ anti-dumping and countervailing measures to protect local producers from unfair trade practices, rather than use quantitative import restrictions.

Sources of data: Provisions of the various laws (Republic Acts) stated above.

The government must adhere to the provisions of these laws by giving the necessary funding (Aquino, Lim, and Ani 2013) via subsidies. As mandated by these laws, GOCCs are often the providers of government goods and services. This section discusses three GOCCs dealing with crop insurance, the coconut industry and the dairy industry. These GOCCs received the highest government subsidy in 2015–18 (see Table 23.8), excluding rice trading and irrigation, two areas that have been written copiously in the literature.

6.1   Philippine Crop Insurance Corporation (PCIC)

The PCIC, created in 1978 and attached to the DA, aims to provide insurance protection to farmers against agricultural crop losses arising from natural calamities, plant diseases and pest infestations. It also provides protection against damage to/loss of non-crop agricultural assets (PCIC 2021a). The insurance programmes are for rice, maize, high-value crops, livestock, fisheries and non-crop assets (PCIC 2021b).

Government subsidy to the PCIC from 2015 to 2018 amounted to PHP7.704 billion (Table 23.8). This was for the full insurance premiums of subsistence farmers and fisherfolk to cover crops, livestock, fisheries and non-crop agricultural assets. In 2019, a big-time subsidy of PHP3.5 billion was given to the PCIC, enabling it to increase the number of insured farmers and the number of beneficiaries of the *free insurance* of special programmes (PCIC 2019). The PCIC links with the local government units in rolling out its programme. Vulnerable farmers who are in the hinterlands are not easily reached by this programme. Earlier studies show low participation rates due to lack of information, poor communication strategies, lack of field personnel and lack of technical persons to assess crop damage (Rola, Rola, and Aragon 2015; Rola and Querijero 2017). A very small percentage of farmers were covered through micro insurance and were willing to pay the premium. Further studies on impact of crop insurance on market concentration and market power could provide insights as to incentives for private micro insurance to enter the industry. On the other hand, Wright (2015) asserts that crop insurance as a policy needs more critical analysis in terms of the theory supporting this, the high transactions cost accompanying its implementation as a government programme and the factors affecting low demand by farmers, among others.

Table 23.8. Amounts and nature of subsidies to GOCCs in agriculture (2015–18, PHP million)

GOCC	2015	2016	2017	As of Sept 2018	Nature of subsidy
National Irrigation Administration	11,677	20,270	30,163	28,780	**Operating and programme subsidy** for Irrigation System Restoration/Repair/Rehabilitation and Improvement, which shall be used for operating requirements of NIA, procurement of heavy equipment, Agrarian Reform Program, national irrigation systems and communal irrigation systems, payment of agri-agra bonds, payment of non-power component-irrigation share cost of the San Roque Multi-purpose Project and other irrigation projects
National Food Authority	4,250	4,250	5,105	7,000	**Programme subsidy**, i.e., Buffer Stocking Program
National Dairy Authority	171	190	200	471	**Operating and programme subsidy** for Dairy Industry Development Program, which shall be used for dairy herd build-up, dairy enterprise development, dairy regulation, dairy market development and milk feeding
Philippine Coconut Authority	71*	1,251	1,425	1,375	**Operating and programme subsidy** for Coconut Industry Development Program and Oil Palm Industry Development, which shall be used for Coconut Planting/Replanting Project, Coconut Fertilization Project, KAANIB Intercropping Project, KAANIB Community/Household Level Coconut Processing Project, Smallholders Palm Plantation Development Project, Seed Farm Development Project and Coconut Hybridization Project.

Table 23.8 (continued)

Table 23.8 (continued)

GOCC	2015	2016	2017	As of Sept 2018	Nature of subsidy
Philippine Crop Insurance Corporation	1,329	1,600	2,500	2,275	**Programme subsidy** for Crop Insurance Program, specifically for the full insurance premiums of subsistence farmers and fisherfolk to cover crops, livestock, fisheries and non-crop agricultural assets.
Philippine Fisheries Development Authority	27	162	94	111	**Programme subsidy** for Fisheries Infrastructure Development Program, which shall be used for construction, rehabilitation and improvement of fish ports.
Philippine Sugar Corporation	–	–	–	192	**Programme subsidy** for Credit Financing Assistance Program for sugarcane planter's cooperatives/federations/associations and sugar mills/refineries
Sugar Regulatory Administration	–	601	1,138	113	**Programme subsidy** for Sugar Industry Development Program, which shall be used for block farms as start-up capital.

Note: * This figure is inconsistent with the figure from PSA, which indicates that the subsector where this GOCC belongs received about PHP2.9 billion in 2015.

Sources: BTr (2021); DBM (2021); GCG (2021).

6.2 Philippine Coconut Authority (PCA)

The PCA is tasked to develop the coconut industry by promoting the rapid integrated development and growth of the coconut and other palm oil industry (Revised Coconut Industry Code, Presidential Decree no. 1468 s.1978, Article 1, Section 2). Coconut farmers—mostly tenants and lessees (Castillo and Ani 2019)—are also among the poorest in the country, due to low productivity of coconuts and the very volatile price of copra. On the other hand, coconut products are significant dollar earners for the Philippines; it earned US$1.519 billion in exports in 2017 (Castillo and Ani 2019). This high level of export earnings may be the motivation for government subsidies to the industry, at least to maintain production, such as in 2014 when there was an outbreak of *cocolisap*.[5] This outbreak affected as many as 2.1 million coconut trees in the provinces of Cavite, Laguna, Batangas, Rizal and Quezon, as well as in parts of Mindanao (Cinco 2015). The subsidies protected the industry through pest control research and other tactics.

Subsidies from 2015 to 2018 reached PHP4.122 billion (Table 23.8). PSA (2019) data indicate no significant improvement in the coconut industry, despite a boom in export (Ani and Aquino 2016; Castillo and Ani 2019) and government subsidies to the PCA. However, as a result of research done on the management of *cocolisap*, significant production losses seem to have been avoided (PCA 2021).

6.3 National Dairy Authority (NDA)

The NDA, which is also attached to the DA, was created in 1995 to facilitate the development of the country's dairy industry. Its mandate covers both policy directions for the sector and programme implementation (NDA 2021). It is also required to have a base of dairy smallholders and/or farmer organizations and/or cooperatives operating dairy production units and participating as co-owners and beneficiaries in processing and marketing cooperative enterprises (Republic Act No. 7884, National Dairy Development Act 1995, Implementing Rules and Regulations). Available reports show positive impacts of NDA's programmes on

---

[5] *Cocolisap* (*Aopidiolus rigidus*) is a bug that feeds on the sap of coconut trees, causing the leaves to dry up and turn brown, then wither.

the household level (Lumanta 2021); the evidence on impact at the community level is scanty.

Compared with other GOCCs, the NDA had lower levels of subsidy in 2015–18, totalling PHP1.032 billion only. COA (2020) reports that despite the implementation of the herd programme and carabao development programmes, the reported increase in dairy herd was not enough to warrant the attainment of the desired milk sufficiency level. PSA data show a very little increase in both dairy inventory and annual dairy production (PSA 2019). Local milk production remained at 1.3 per cent of the country's dairy requirement based on 2019 data; the bulk was supplied by imports. Government subsidy to NDA will have insignificant effect on the dairy industry due to its relatively small contribution to the sector.

Several reasons have been cited for the dairy industry's failure to attain its objectives. These include lack of coordination between the NDA and the Philippine Carabao Center, absence of well-defined roles and responsibilities of NDA's stakeholders, difficulties of the NDA and the Philippine Carabao Center in importing dairy animals due to lack of funds, and high cattle and buffalo mortality rates (COA 2020).

The above cases suggest that market power and market competition have been maintained as a result of government subsidies to the GOCCs, supported by laws aimed at promoting agricultural competitiveness. These laws, which mandate direct provision of goods and services by government entities and protection of favoured market players, should be re-examined in the context of the national competition policy (Fabella, Bacani, and Palacios 2020).

7 CONCLUSIONS AND RECOMMENDATIONS

We find that government subsidies are mostly channelled through two key agriculture subsectors: *services to establish crops, promote their growth and protect them from pests and diseases, n.e.c.* and *operation of irrigation systems through non-cooperatives*. Moreover, market concentrations of agriculture subsectors receiving government subsidies are decreasing over time. Market power does not enhance market concentration. We also find that the agriculture subsidies through the GOCCs do not enhance market power. However, even if the subsidies do not lead to market power, the subsectors being subsidized are very highly concentrated and have low incentives for the private sector to invest, given higher risks and low incomes in such subsectors. Given the significant resources poured into these subsectors and the national competition policy, a review of the decision-making processes, governance structures, transparency and accountability, and benefits to consumers is warranted.

Agricultural subsidies have not influenced market power in their respective subsectors. As Balisacan (2020) aptly says, "Many sectors that have significant impact on consumer welfare and economic development are still characterized by high levels of market concentration and barriers to entry. Consequently, the full benefits of competition—lower prices, better quality, and wider variety of goods and services—are yet to be felt by most Filipinos." Under the Philippine Competition Act, the PCC, acting on behalf of consumers, "has the power to make markets work better so consumers reap the full benefit of vigorous competition" (Balisacan 2019).

In the long term, there is a need to study more the impacts of government subsidies on competition, especially on the creation of a level playing field. The laws underpinning such subsidies have had a long history of evolution and, hence, call for a more in-depth study, not discounting the possibility of having new laws, to be in harmony with the current national competition policy.

ACKNOWLEDGEMENT

We would like to thank the Philippine Competition Commission (PCC) for allowing us to publish from a study it commissioned in 2019. We also acknowledge the excellent research assistance of Emmanuel Barnedo in the conduct of the PCC study.

REFERENCES

Ani, P. A. B., and A. P. Aquino. 2016. "The Long Climb towards Achieving the Promises of the Tree of Life: A Review of the Philippine Coco Levy Fund Policies". *FFTC Agricultural Policy Platform*. Food and Fertilizer Technology for the Asian and the Pacific Region. https://ap.fftc.org.tw/article/1008 (accessed 13 January 2021).

Aquino, A. P., V. A. A. Lim, and P. A. B. Ani. 2013. "Republic Act 7607: Empowering Small Farmers in Their Economic Endeavors". *FFTC Agricultural Policy Platform*. Food and Fertilizer Technology for the Asian and the Pacific Region. https://ap.fftc.org.tw/article/600 (accessed 1 Feb 2021).

Aquino, A. P., A. G. Tidon, P. A. B. Ani, and M. A. Festejo-Abeleda. 2013. "The Agriculture and Fisheries Modernization Act of 1997: A Collective Approach to Competitiveness". *FFTC Agricultural Policy Platform*. Food and Fertilizer Technology for the Asian and the Pacific Region. https://ap.fftc.org.tw/article/514 (accessed 1 February 2021).

Balisacan, Arsenio M. 2019. "Toward a Fairer Society: Inequality and Competition Policy in Developing Asia". *Philippine Review of Economics* 56, no. 1-2: 127–47. https://doi.org/10.37907/7ERP9102JD.

———. 2020. "2020: Towards a More Robust Competition Regime". Competition Matters. *Business Mirror*, 15 January. https://businessmirror.com.ph/2020/01/15/2020-toward-a-more-robust-competition-regime/ (accessed 28 January 2021).

BTr (Bureau of Treasury). 2021. "Annual Cash Operations Report: National Government Subsidy", https://www.treasury.gov.ph/?page_id=4221 (accessed 15 January 2021).

Castillo, M. B., and P. A. B. Ani. 2019. "Philippine Coconut Industry: Status, Policies, and Strategic Directions for Development". *FFTC Agricultural Policy Platform*. Food and Fertilizer Technology for the Asian and the Pacific Region. https://ap.fftc.org.tw/article/1382 (accessed 13 January 2021).

Chen, Y., and X. Yu. 2019. "Do Subsidies Cause a Less Competitive Milk Market in China?". *Agricultural Economics* 50. https://doi.org/10.1111/agec.12485.

Cinco, Maricar. 2015. "Agency Warns of Return of 'Cocolisap'". http://www.pestnet.org/SummariesofMessages/Crops/Plantationcrops/Coconutoilpalm/Insects/Scaleoutbreak(cocolisap),Philippines.aspx (accessed 17 January 2021).

COA (Commission on Audit). 2020. "Herd Build Up and Carabao Development Program". Performance Audit Report. PAO-2019-02-CDP.pdf, Quezon City.

DBM (Department of Budget and Management). 2021. General Appropriations for 2018. https://www.dbm.gov.ph/index.php/budget-documents/2018/general-appropriations-act-fy-2018 (accessed 15 January 2021).

Fabella, R. V., S. C. Bacani, and A. Palacios. 2020. "Competition Policy and Inclusion in the Philippines". *Public Policy Monograph Series* 2020-05. Diliman, Quezon City: Center for Integrative and Development Studies, University of the Philippines.

GCG (Governance Commission for Government Owned or Controlled Corporations). 2021. List of GOCCs as of 7 January 2020. https://icrs.gcg.gov.ph/files/UM2bsQhenyb0hbePyv2K.pdf (accessed 15 January 2021).

Inocencio, Arlene B., A. D. Inocencio, and E. Barnedo. 2019. "Scoping Paper on Philippine Subsidies and State-Owned Enterprises in Agricultural and Manufacturing Sectors". Final report submitted to the Philippine Competition Commission. Quezon City.

Lumanta, C. 2021. "PNDZP Showcases Dela Roca Farm". https://nda.da.gov.ph/index.php/en/vetbud1.htm (accessed 13 January 2021).

Medalla, Erlinda. 2018. "Competition in Philippine Markets: A Scoping Study of the Manufacturing Sector". Philippine Competition Commission, Quezon City, Philippines. (unpublished paper).

Miralles Murciego, Graciela, Roberto Martin Nolan Galang, Sara Nyman, Tilsa Guillermina Ore Monago, and Leandro Deambrosio Zipitria. 2018. "Fostering Competition in the Philippines: The Challenge of Restrictive Regulations". Washington, DC: World Bank Group. http://documents.worldbank.org/curated/pt/478061551366290646/pdf/134949-Revised-Fostering-Competition-in-the-Philippines.pdf.

NDA (National Dairy Corporation). 2021. "NDA Mandate". https://nda.da.gov.ph/index.php/en/about-us (accessed 13 January 2021).

Neven, D., and V. Verouden. 2008. "Towards a More Refined Economic Approach in State Aid Control". In *EU Competition Law – Volume IV: State Aid*, edited by W. Mederer, N. Pesaresi, and M. Van Hoofs. http://ec.europa.eu/dgs/competition/economist/economic_approach_sa_control.pdf (accessed January 2019).

PCA (Philippine Coconut Authority). 2021. "About Us". https://pca.gov.ph/index.php/about-us/programs (accessed 14 January 2021).

PCIC (Philippine Crop Insurance Corporation). 2019. *Annual Report 2019*. https://pcic.gov.ph/wp-content/uploads/2020/12/PCIC-2019-ANNUAL-REPORT.pdf (accessed 13 January 2021).

———. 2021a. "About Us". https://pcic.gov.ph/about-us/ (accessed 13 January 2021).

———. 2021b. "Insurance Products". https://pcic.gov.ph/insurance-products-2/ (accessed 13 January 2021).

PSA (Philippine Statistics Authority). 2010. *Annual Survey of Philippine Business and Industry*. Quezon City: Philippine Statistics Authority.

———. 2012. *Census of Philippine Business and Industry*. Quezon City: Philippine Statistics Authority.

———. 2012. "Explanatory Text". *Census of Philippine Business and Industry*. Quezon City: Philippine Statistics Authority.

———. 2012. "Subsidies". *Census of Philippine Business and Industry*. Philippine Statistics Authority. https://psa.gov.ph/content/subsidies (accessed February 2019).

———. 2013. *Annual Survey of Philippine Business and Industry*. Quezon City: Philippine Statistics Authority.

———. 2014. *Annual Survey of Philippine Business and Industry*. Quezon City: Philippine Statistics Authority.

———. 2015. *Annual Survey of Philippine Business and Industry*. Quezon City: Philippine Statistics Authority.

———. 2019. *Selected Statistics on Agriculture*. Quezon City: Philippine Statistics Authority.

Rola, Armand C. C., W. R. Rola, and C. T. Aragon. 2015. "Loss Reduction Effects of Rice Farmers' Participation in Crop Insurance Program". *Philippine Journal of Crop Science* 40, no. 2 (August): 45–58.

Rola, Armand C. C., and N. J. V. Querijero. 2017. "Efficiency and Effectiveness of the Philippine Crop Insurance Corporation's Rice Crop Insurance Program: The Case of Laguna Province, Philippines". *The Journal of Public Affairs and Development* 4: 29–48.

Spierdijk, Laura, and Michalis Zaouras. 2017. "The Lerner Index and Revenue Maximization". *Applied Economic Letters* 24, no. 15: 1075–79. https://doi.org/10.1080/13504851.2016.1254333.

Wright, Brian. 2015. "The Role of Agricultural Economists in Sustaining Bad Programs". In *Sustainable Economic Development: Resources, Environment, and Institutions*, edited by Arsenio M. Balisacan, Ujjayant Chakravorty, and Majah-Leah V. Ravago, pp. 239–45. USA and UK: Elsevier, Inc.

PART 6

International Dimensions

24 Modernization of the Global Rice Market

Suthad Setboonsarng

1 INTRODUCTION

Since 2012, India has been the top exporter of rice in the world market, taking over from Thailand and Vietnam. At the same time, China has become the number one importer of rice, overtaking the Philippines and Indonesia.[1] Factors that have caused these changes will define the future environment for the rice market in the twenty-first century.

Rice and its products will continue to contribute significantly to the nutritional needs of a large proportion of the world population for decades to come. Rice will continue to generate employment for a significant number of workers around the world throughout its production, processing and marketing value chain. It will remain one of the most politically sensitive products for most governments.

The rice value chain has undergone a major transformation in the past decade, embracing automation and digital technology. New business models have emerged, reorganizing the industry in both domestic and international markets. The existing system and policy environment of the twentieth century may need to be adjusted to the requirements of the future. A market-based cooperative solution may be more effective and efficient in achieving rice security and environmental sustainability for each country and the global market.

---

[1] Global rice trade is about 6–7 per cent of the total production.

The availability of staple foods such as rice is a global issue that needs a global solution. This modernized market is an opportunity to reduce the sensitivity of rice supply by strengthening the production and delivery system and by making separate arrangements for emergency situations.

The next section highlights some key changes in the rice market. Section 3 tackles the main drivers of these changes that will continue to shape the future of the rice market. Section 4 discusses possible reforms for the rice market in the twenty-first century. It attempts to broadly follow the nature-cause-and-consequence paradigm for policy analysis suggested by Roumasset (2015).

2 CHANGES IN THE GLOBAL RICE MARKET

Some changes in the structure of the global rice market have become more evident since the turn of the millennium. These changes may continue into the future and redefine the landscape of the global rice market.

2.1 Changing structure of the international rice trade

Since 2012, China and India, the two largest producers and consumers of rice,[2] have become the largest importer and exporter, respectively (Figures 24.1 and 24.2). The medium-sized importers (1–2 million tons) from the Middle East have continued to increase their imports. On the export side, India has overtaken Thailand as top exporter since 2012, even with the decline in exports since 2018.

Rice production in India has increased faster than in China, although the latter's rice yield has increased faster than that of India. Relatively higher wages in the non-agriculture sector have drawn labour from the agriculture sector in most countries. However, India's higher population growth rate has provided a large pool of labour, so that wages have increased slower than in China.

---

[2] China produces 148 million tons (about 29% of world production in 2020) and consumes 144 million tons (or about 30% of world consumption in 2020). India produces 115 million tons (22% of world production) and consumes 100 million tons (20% of world consumption). Together they produce 51 per cent of world production and account for 50 per cent of world consumption.

Figure 24.1. Top ten rice-importing countries

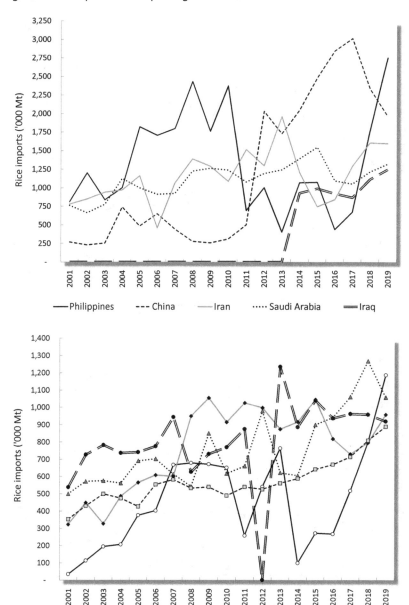

Source: Trade Maps database (https://www.trademap.org/Index.aspx).

Figure 24.2. Top ten rice-exporting countries

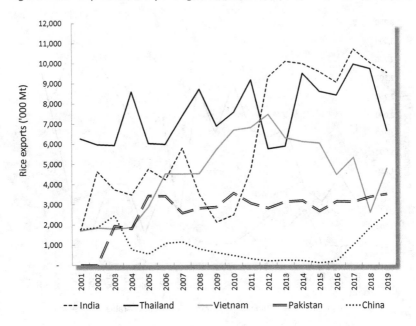

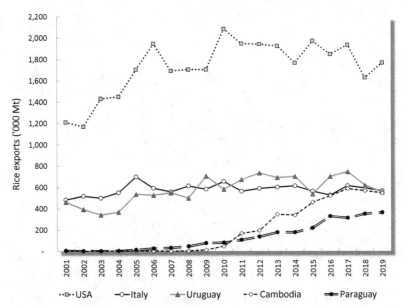

Source: Trade Maps database (https://www.trademap.org/Index.aspx).

A similar phenomenon can be seen in other countries. High and increasing labour costs in Thailand have increased rice production cost, causing the country to move to higher quality rice. In Vietnam, the rapid growth in the manufacturing sector has drawn farm labour into the sector, increasing the cost of rice production. Newcomers, especially Myanmar and Cambodia, still have low wages and available water and land, which make them cost competitive. With better infrastructure to access the market, they could become the new top rice exporters, provided competitive conditions can be maintained.

2.2 High global rice stock

Global rice stocks have been increasing steadily, reaching 184 million tons (130 days of consumption) in 2021. This is much higher than the three-month or ninety-day consumption guideline suggested by the United Nations Food and Agriculture Organization (FAO). High stocks usually reflect either surplus production or reduced demand. They may increase global food security, but also reflect a growing concern over rice security.

The top four countries—China, India, Thailand and Indonesia—hold almost 90 per cent of the global rice stock (Figure 24.3). China, the largest producer and importer, holds about 55 per cent of the global rice stock (117 million tons of the total of 184 million tons). It accounts for 68 per cent of total domestic utilization.[3] Given the uncertainty of the global trading environment facing China, a high stock level for food security may carry an important strategic function.

India, the second largest producer and largest exporter, holds only about 35 million tons or about 33 per cent of total domestic utilization. It reflects the supply increase, which also drives the increase in export. Indonesia, a net importer, used to carry as much as 8 million tons of stock during good harvest years, but currently has only 4.5 million tons, or 12 per cent of domestic utilization. Thailand, an exporter, carries a relatively high level of stock (an average of about 40–45% of domestic utilization), partly reflecting the uncertainty of global demand.

---

[3] Although the temporary stock scheme was abolished in 2014, the public stock in China has continued to be used as a tool to manage supply and price fluctuations in the country. Pu and Zheng (2018) suggest that adjusting the minimum price bands can be a more efficient way to achieve market stability.

Figure 24.3. Ending stocks of rice

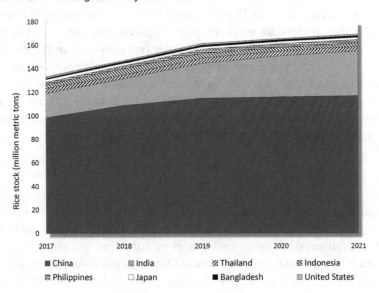

Source: Compiled from the World Market and Trade database, USDA (https://usda.library.cornell.edu/concern/publications/zs25x844t?locale=en).

2.3 Yield increase

In the past decade, global rice output increased from 463 million tons in 2010/2011 to 508 million tons in 2020/2021 (about 9.7% growth), while rice harvested area increased from 160 million hectares to 162 million hectares only (about 1% increase). The difference is accounted for by the increase in yield (from 4.34 t/ha to 4.7 t/ha). This yield increase is quite an achievement considering the deterioration of the production environment, such as depletion of soil nutrients, stronger pests and diseases, and rising sea level in key production areas. This is a contribution from both agricultural and non-agricultural sciences.

The United States, Japan and China have the highest rice yields (Figure 24.4). Japanese rice farms are small and intensive, while rice farms in the United States are large.[4] Both countries mechanize land

---

[4] The United States has about 1.2 million hectares of rice cultivation and Japan has 1.54 million hectares. The former has only about 5,000 rice farmers (Childs, Skorbiansky, and McBride 2020) and the latter has about 2 million. (The number of Japanese rice farmers was derived from the average farm size reported in https://ricepedia.org/japan.)

Figure 24.4. Five-year moving average of rice yields in major production areas

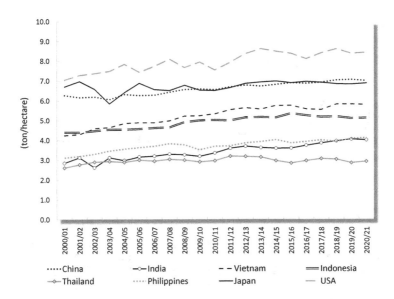

Source: Agricultural Market Information System (AMIS) database (http://www.amis-outlook.org/amis-monitoring/monthly-report/en/).

preparation and harvesting. They also use high levels of fertilizers, pesticides and other agricultural inputs. Good road systems allow them to easily move their output to the market at a low cost. Rice farmers in both countries are also well organized and carry substantial political power.

2.4 Relatively low rice price index

Although rice is a very important staple food, its price has been kept relatively low (Figure 24.5). There was a spike in 2008, but since 2010 the rice price index has been at its lowest, compared with that of other cereals.

Figure 24.5. Grains price index

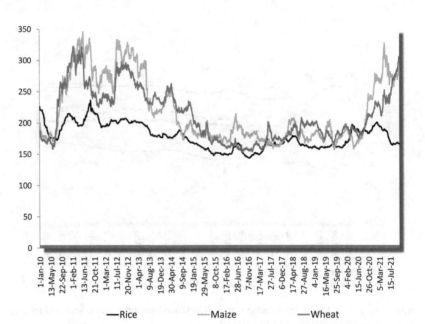

Source: International Grains Council as reported in AMIS (http://www.amis-outlook.org/index.php?id=40182).

The low price of rice has been due to various forms of farm subsidies given to reduce farmers' production costs so they can sell their products at a low price. Aside from distorting the price of rice, such measures also create distortions in the input markets and make rice farmers dependent on them. The situation has become a vicious cycle as the inefficiency perpetuates subsidies (Setboonsarng 2014), as shown by some economic analyses (e.g., Wright 2015).

2.5 Modernization of the rice value chain

There have been many changes throughout the value chain of rice, from production to delivery to the final consumer. New business arrangements have evolved to take advantage of the better transport and communication systems, thus improving the efficiency of bringing rice from the farm to processing and finally to the table.

2.5.1 Marketing channels and logistics systems

During the past decade, more rice has been distributed through the modern marketing channel, convenience stores and especially through e-commence. Rice e-commerce value was estimated at US$53 billion in 2020 and growing at 49 per cent per annum.[5] E-commerce can reduce the labour cost and increase the flexibility and service level of the rice market (Yang and Hu 2016). While still important, the traditional rice marketing channel needs improvement. Having an efficient logistic system has improved the efficiency, speed and precision of moving rice from growers to consumers.

Being able to get closer to the final consumers has improved the bargaining power of rice growers. Retnoningsih (2019), for example, finds that with proper marketing management, the share of farmers in the final value of rice can increase from 40 to 73 per cent. Moreover, the use of social media has also opened up innovative marketing strategies in articulating specific characteristics of rice that farmers produce. There are over 1,000 varieties/locations of rice selling on the internet, while a grocery store can carry only a few selections. Better information on rice characteristics helps the market match rice types with diverse consumer preferences, thereby adding value.

2.5.2 Processing and packaging

Improvements in harvesting, post-harvest management, processing and storage have reduced losses and increased rice quality. The share of rice in convenient packaging has increased in all markets. About half of Thai rice exports, especially the premium-grade aromatic rice, is put in retail packaging and shipped using containers.[6] The development of retail packaging has improved rice quality, particularly its cleanliness and weight precision. Retail packaging has become an additional service offered by rice millers because packaging equipment and materials have become cheaper and readily available.[7]

---

[5] https://www.iiec.edu.in/product/agriculture/rice-e-commerce-business/
[6] The shortage of containers in the last quarter of 2020 reduced Thailand's rice export (Econotimes.com 2021).
[7] A simple rice milling plus packaging machine processing 10 metric tons a day costs less than US$6,000. https://www.alibaba.com/product-detail/Super-

It is also a means for entrepreneurs to differentiate products and create brands. The international standard on rice packaging has had a spillover effect on the standard of rice trade in the domestic market.[8]

Despite the changes in the rice value chain in the domestic and global markets, the global average rice consumption per capita remained almost unchanged (around 54 kg) in 2000–2020. This has been influenced by the steady consumption per capita in both India and China, the two largest rice consumers. While rice consumption has significantly declined in Vietnam and Indonesia, it has increased in some countries such as the Philippines and Nigeria (Figure 24.6).

Figure 24.6. Rice consumption per capita in major consuming countries

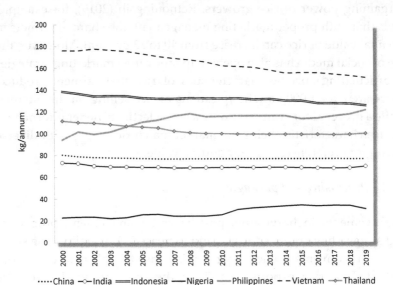

Source: AMIS database.

---

quality-Rice-mill-packing-machine_1600260656318.html?spm=a2700.7724857.normal_offer.d_image.6a4912d2dkjREG

[8] The Standard and Poor's (S&P) guideline specification on rice packaging is "new single white woven polypropylene bags, each of 50 kg net shipped weight, with buyer's marks. Minimum tare weight of 110 g 2% empty bags to be loaded at seller's cost" (https://www.spglobal.com/platts/PlattsContent/_assets/_files/en/our-methodology/methodology-specifications/global-rice.pdf).

There is a rapidly growing new market segment for high-quality rice, which is taking advantage of modern marketing and distribution channels, especially e-commerce. Social networks help spread information on specific rice qualities to consumers, and modern delivery systems allow products to move from various locations to the buyers. Even in poorer countries like Bangladesh, there is evidence of increased consumption of higher quality rice (Minten, Murshid, and Reardon 2011).

A study conducted in 2013–14 in South and Southeast Asia shows that consumers prefer different characteristics of rice and that these two regions have significantly different preferences (Figure 24.7). The quality characteristics include nutrition (including minerals), cooking quality (soft/hard/sticky, etc.), physical appearance (size, colour/whiteness, long/short, whole/broken, etc.), impurities and time used for cooking (Custodio et al. 2019; Velasco et al. 2015).

Figure 24.7. Consumer preference for the different characteristics of rice

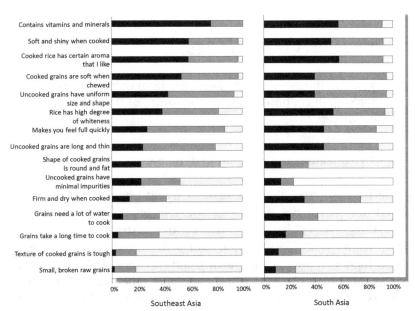

Note: Perception of premium, good and poor-quality rice of urban consumers based on a survey in 24 cities in selected Southeast and South Asian countries in 2012–14, based on a single-answer question with 15 pre-defined statements. For each statement, respondents were asked to indicate which of the three quality levels they associated with the statement.
Sources: Custodio et al. (2019); Velasco et al. (2015).

Results show that consumers in Southeast Asia give more weight to the minerals in rice than consumers in South Asia, who care more about the shape and size of cooked rice. Competition is expected among rice sellers as they use new strategies to market specific rice characteristics to meet consumer demands. An example is the market for rice with low glycemic index,[9] which has grown rapidly through the use of social media. Its distribution has been facilitated also through supermarkets and hypermarkets. It is predicted that this market will increase from US$3 billion in 2020 to US$4.7 billion in 2027.

In summary, these five phenomena—new structure of the international rice market, high level of ending stocks, low price of rice (compared with other cereals), modernization of the rice value chain, and expansion of quality rice market—reflect the evolution of the rice market from its traditional setting to the modern environment. More changes are coming and at a faster speed. A better understanding of the drivers of these changes will help the stakeholders, both in the public and private sectors, to shape a desired and efficient rice market.

3   KEY DRIVING FORCES

The changes in the global rice market have been driven by many forces. These forces will continue to shape the future of this market, together with new drivers.

3.1   Urbanization and population dynamics

In the next 20 years, the difference in world population growth will change the global rice market. Of the 1.45 billion increase in global population, 748 million (53%) will be from Africa and 531 million (38%) from Asia. Urban population will increase by 1.56 billion (larger than total population growth), and rural population will decline by 144 million (Table 24.1), which will affect the availability of farm workers. Meanwhile, the number of rice consumers will increase in the urban areas.

---

[9] Glycemic index is the level of glucose in the blood measured two hours after consumption of the food (https://glycemicindex.com/gi-search/&?food_name=rice+thai).

There are differences between China and India, the two largest rice-producing and consuming countries. China's total population will decline slightly in the next 20 years, and its rural population will decrease by over 215 million. In comparison, India's total population will grow from 1.38 billion to 1.6 billion (an increase of about 212 million people), while its rural population will decline by only 39 million. Thus, India will have a comparative advantage in rice production, which will still be a labour-intensive product. Its average yield is also lower than China's (see Figure 24.3), which means it has more room to improve its yield (see Box 24.1 for more discussion). This will affect other countries, especially those in the ASEAN that also have slow population growth and reduction in rural workers.

The urban condition and environment affect rice purchases, storage and consumption behaviour. As more rice consumers congregate in urban areas, the rice market responds quickly, embracing new technologies and changing the management of the value chain system. Consumption per capita in urban areas usually declines. Table 24.2 shows the results of regressing urbanization on per capita consumption of major rice-consuming countries. Urbanization reduces per capita consumption of rice in most countries, except Nigeria where the growth of rice consumption per capita is increasing rapidly (see Figure 24.4).

The decline in per capita consumption of rice in urban areas could arise from the low income of a large number of urban dwellers and higher price of rice. The impact of urbanization is low (−0.48) for China, which has a lower urban poverty, compared with the Philippines (−10.61), which has a high urban poverty. On the other hand, the concentration of population in the urban areas could improve the efficiency of the distribution, storage and consumption system.

Changes in the rice supply chain are expected to meet the demands of the growing urban consumers. The population forecast shows that 81 per cent of the population in Eastern Asia will be in urban areas by 2050. However, with the rapid expansion and improvement of infrastructure, by 2030 more than 80 per cent of the population may already be living in what is defined now as an urban environment (e.g., with access to public utilities, electricity, transportation and communication networks).

Table 24.1. Population growth and urbanization

Region	Total population (millions)				Urban population (millions)				Rural population (millions)		
	2020	2040	Change	%	2020	2040	Change	%	2020	2040	Change
World	7,795	9,210	1,415	100%	4,379	5,938	1,559	100%	3,416	3,272	-144
Asia	4,623	5,154	531	38%	2,361	3,177	815	52%	2,262	1,978	-284
ASEAN	668	769	101	7%	334	469	135	9%	334	300	-34
East Asia	1,664	1,649	-15	-1%	1,078	1,286	208	13%	585	362	-223
China	1,425	1,417	-7	-1%	875	1,083	208	13%	549	334	-215
Japan	126	115	-11	-1%	116	108	-8	-1%	10	7	-3
Korea	52	52	1	0%	42	44	2	0%	10	8	-1
Other East Asia	61	64	3	0%	45	51	6	0%	16	13	-3
South Asia	1,936	2,284	348	25%	709	1,087	378	24%	1,226	1,197	-29
India	1,383	1,605	222	16%	483	744	261	17%	900	861	-39
Bangladesh	170	196	27	2%	65	102	38	2%	105	94	-11
Pakistan	208	277	69	5%	77	127	50	3%	131	150	19
Other Asia	357	453	96	7%	240	334	94	6%	117	119	2

Table 24.1 (continued)

Table 24.1 (continued)

Region	Total population (millions)				Urban population (millions)				Rural population (millions)		
	2020	2040	Change	%	2020	2040	Change	%	2020	2040	Change
Africa	1,353	2,100	748	53%	588	1,125	537	34%	765	975	210
Sub-Saharan	1,107	1,777	670	47%	459	933	474	30%	648	844	196
Southern Africa	68	81	13	1%	44	59	16	1%	24	21	−3
Other Africa	178	243	64	5%	85	133	47	3%	93	110	17
Europe	743	729	−15	−1%	557	587	31	2%	187	141	−45
America	1,218	1,395	177	13%	983	1,192	209	13%	235	203	−32
North	369	417	48	3%	305	363	58	4%	64	55	−10
Latin America	664	757	93	7%	539	650	110	7%	125	107	−18

Source: Source: UN population forecast.

Box 24.1. Why India's rice export increases despite a fast population growth, and China's rice import increases despite a slowing population growth: The supply side story

For India, population expansion has increased labour supply. The slower growth of the manufacturing sector cannot absorb the additional labour, slowing down the growth in wage rates of rural labour. The lower wages and availability of labour keep the cost of rice production in check, making exports from India competitive. Having better logistics and access to the market, Indian farmers have the incentive to adopt new technologies and improve yield, thus increasing total rice production. With the competitive cost and relatively constant per capita consumption of rice, the increase in production allows India to increase rice export. For example, in July 2021, the export price of rice from India was quoted at US$368 per ton, while the standard world price was US$405.

For China, the rapid growth of the non-agriculture sector attracts rural farm workers, which drives up farm wages. Hence, the cost of rice production goes up. The gains from the rapid adoption of new technologies, such as hybrid rice and farm mechanization, have only partially compensated for the high labour cost. In 2020, the minimum purchase price programme was RMB 2,540 per ton of paddy (or about US$393); a ton of milled rice will cost US$576 (assuming that 10 kg of paddy can get 6.8 kg of milled rice). With the import price of rice at US$405 per ton, every ton of imported rice can save the government US$171 (minus import expenses). However, it should be noted that the import is only less than 3 per cent of the total supply and that imported rice adds to the diversification of supply.

Table 24.2. Effects of urbanization and income on per capita rice consumption

Parameter		China	t-Test	India	t-Test	Indonesia	t-Test	Nigeria	t-Test	Philippines	t-Test	Vietnam	t-Test	Thailand	t-Test
	Intercept	95.6400	47.52	144.79000	14.06	173.19	12.87	17.050000	0.59	577.51000	7.79	229.08	15.03	162.19000	36.21
Urbanization	%	−0.4800	−8.75	−2.70000	−7.23	−0.87	−2.73	0.120000	0.14	−10.61000	−6.47	−2.07	−3.37	−2.00000	−10.65
Per capita income	Local currency	0.0001	7.19	0.00012	6.24	0.00	0.57	0.000017	0.83	0.00022	11.00	−0.00	−0.50	0.00016	7.04
	F–Stat	4.5989		38.0239		69.62		38.612200		61.25930		287.15		309.54218	

3.2 Rising middle-income class

As economies grow, the proportion of the middle-income class will increase and form the majority of the global population.[10] Their behaviour will define the future of the rice market. Increased incomes may induce consumers to substitute rice with other foods (e.g., meats); consumers may also prefer higher quality rice.

Middle-class buyers are more conscious of the cleanliness, safety and weight precision of the rice they purchase for their family. They usually buy conveniently packed rice from local grocery stores and hypermarkets, which is cleaner and has accurate weight labels. Packaging in differently sized bags with quality labels provides product information that differentiates rice from various suppliers.

The market is responding to this new pattern of demand by incorporating many new characteristics into rice products, including aroma, texture, nutrition and health value, as well as cultural and other less tangible characteristics. New technologies are expected to be deployed to accommodate the new demands.

In the coming decade, the relative size of middle-income populations will increase faster in South Asia because it is starting from a lower base. Although the pandemic has slightly pushed back growth rates, the region will be the major contributor to the growth of the middle class. Kochhar (2021) estimates that the COVID-19 pandemic will push 62 million people (about 3%) of the global middle class back to the poor income group.

These two trends—population dynamics and the growing middle-income class—will play significant roles in shaping the future of the global rice market, especially in Asia.

3.3 Digital transformation in the rice value chain

The use of big data carries a big promise for rice cultivation. Digital technology has been modifying the value chain of the agriculture sector—rice, in particular. The direct benefit of applying

---

[10] The number of middle-class people will increase from about 4 billion in 2021 to 5.3 billion in 2050, accounting for about 54 per cent of the total global population.

digital technology in precision agriculture may be large, but the bigger benefit may come indirectly from the improved organization and management of farm inputs and outputs by reducing transaction costs and inducing innovative management processes and procedures. One example is the use of social media to arrange for farming services, such as tractors, combine harvesters and transportation services. It enhances the adoption of farm mechanization.

The possibility of accessing the consumer market opens up new opportunities for each rice farmer. At the minimum, the availability of improved information in the market offers a choice of buyers and increases the farmers' bargaining power.

The impact is also substantial on the demand side. Consumers are becoming more knowledgeable and developing preference for different rice characteristics, such as aroma, look, texture and stories. For example, Google Trend shows that worldwide search for Basmati and Jasmin rice is growing steadily (see Figure 24.8).

Figure 24.8. Google search index for Basmati and Jasmin rice

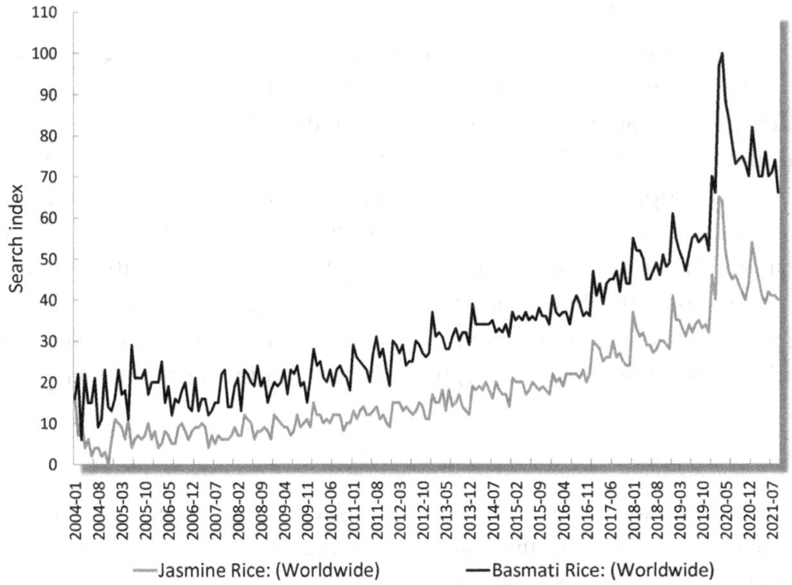

Source: Google Trends.

As mentioned in section 2.5, rice sale via e-commerce is growing rapidly. Although the COVID-19 pandemic may have contributed to this growth, this new marketing channel is expected to become dominant in the future. This is evidenced in the boom of Basmati rice sales in the international market, especially to developed countries.

Digital transformation will improve the overall efficiency of the rice market. It is a blessing for some farmers, logistic operators and consumers, but a curse for those who will be disadvantaged by this technology, especially older generation farmers and those who do not have access to the internet (Ravago, Balisacan, and Chakravorty 2015).

3.4 Climate change and good governance

Climate change affects rice production and marketing. The rise in sea levels directly affects prime rice production areas in the deltas, such as the Mekong River Delta, Ganges Basin, Chao Phya and even coastal areas in the United States (Teng, Caballero-Anthony, and Lassa 2016). At the same time, rice cultivation is both an important sequester of carbon dioxide from the atmosphere and source of greenhouse gas emission (e.g., methane and nitrite oxide).

There are many possible mitigation measures, including research into more climate-resilient varieties, better irrigation and farming practices.[11] The Sixth Assessment Report of the Intergovernmental Panel on Climate Change (IPCC 2021, 451), released in August 2021, concludes that with proper mitigation the residual impact of climate change on rice production is not significant. However, a recent study shows that the mitigation measures are not being implemented sufficiently because of inadequate implementation systems.[12] Mitigation is seen as the responsibility of the government, and indeed governments are taking the lead in these projects. However, from the standpoint of good governance

---

[11] There are many suggestions such as the ones found in the Rice and Climate Change Research of the International Rice Research Institute (http://climatechange.irri.org/projects/mitigation).

[12] Monitoring of the greenhouse gas (GHG) project implementation shows that efforts are limited and not pervasive (https://ccafs.cgiar.org/research/projects/ghg-mitigation-rice-evidence-based-concepts-adoption-scale).

of public policies,[13] it is suggested that governments should confine their role to providing policy direction and developing the incentive structure that allows all stakeholders to participate in these mitigation efforts. The private sector in the rice industry should play an active role in these mitigation efforts.

3.5 Lessons from the COVID-19 pandemic

A survey of rice farmers and stakeholders in South and Southeast Asia by the International Rice Research Institute shows that the COVID-19 pandemic has had some limited impact on rice cultivation activities. It identifies four main needs post-pandemic: mechanization, digital agriculture, improved value of rice output and improved supply chain management (Balie and Valera 2020). Rice farmers are looking for opportunities to take advantage of the new technology to access the market.

However, the management of the pandemic and vaccination poses a bigger question on the fairness and efficiency of global crisis management. What would happen if there was a rice crisis or food famine now? How should the limited stock of rice be distributed? The possible scenario is horrible. There is thus an urgent need to repair the trust and build cooperation among countries to create a reliable system to ensure the resilience of rice.

3.6 Changing focus of government strategy

Given the rapid changes in technology and the rice value chain, as well as the growing environmental issues, governments are focusing on modernizing the farming sector, especially the rice-based agricultural system. The strategy is to build an enabling environment instead of

---

[13] The 2013 Consultation Draft of the proposed International Public Sector Governance Framework provides guidelines on implementing good governance principles. One of these is "determining the intervention necessary to optimize the intended outcome", which suggests that the point of intervention and options to intervene given the capacity of the organization should be considered (https://www.ifac.org/system/files/publications/files/Good-Governance-in-the-Public-Sector.pdf).

providing direct interventions such as input subsidies and trade barriers, which were found to be inefficient and have repercussions on the rest of the economy through the exchange rate.[14] Figure 24.9 shows that rice has the highest import duty rate among cereals.[15] This new strategy implies that farmers have to stay competitive and need to embrace the global issues.[16]

Figure 24.9. Import tariff of wheat, rice and soybean (2012–15)

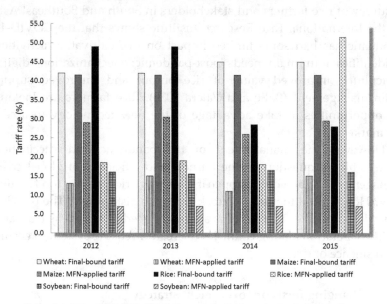

Source: Policy Database, AMIS (http://statistics.amis-outlook.org/policy/index.html).

---

[14] For example, see Siamwalla and Setboonsarng (1989) and Anderson (2015). These measures are not allowed by the World Trade Organization (WTO). However, some subsidy measures are acceptable to the WTO, such as research and development and environmental protection.

[15] Bounded rate is the maximum import tariff rate of a product that a country commits under the WTO.

[16] In the past, farm subsidy rested on the premise that rice farmers are "poor" and need help to get out of poverty. This was the start of a vicious cycle. Politicians came in to help farmers fight for more subsidies. Reducing farm subsidies became politically unpopular and almost impossible. After many decades of subsidies, farmers have remained poor, or became even poorer, and need even more subsidies. The new premise is that farmers are not "competitive" with the world market and need to embrace new technologies.

This new strategy will also support the need for an open global food market, which is a more efficient way to manage future food security problems as industrialization will draw away more farm workers and reduce food supply (Anderson 2015). Regional and multilateral trade arrangements are necessary to address future food security problems.

Governments also seek to reduce price fluctuations, especially to control prices during nationwide shortages. Hawe (2015) notes that it is very costly or inefficient to eliminate price fluctuations because doing so kills the appropriate market signals. Some degree of price fluctuation is healthy as it gives a signal to all stakeholders. A combination of some degree of price fluctuations, stock holding for emergencies and open international trade may be the optimum strategy.

In summary, the six drivers discussed above will define the future of the global rice market. They are not mutually exclusive but interact with each other throughout the rice value chain. The impact also varies across geographical locations. Table 24.3 summarizes the impacts of these key drivers.

4. TRANSFORMING THE GLOBAL RICE MARKET

The modernization and integration of the global rice market, especially in terms of information management, present more efficient opportunities to ensure food security and address future challenges. A more enabling operation environment is needed to take advantage of such opportunities.

Table 24.3. *Summary of the impacts of key drivers*

Driver	Supply	Demand	Marketing and distribution
Population dynamics	*	****	***
Middle-income class	*	****	****
Digital economy	**	****	****
Physical environment	**	*	**
COVID-19 pandemic	*	**	***
Government policies	****	**	***

4.1 Accountability of the private sector for food security

The public sector has assumed the responsibility for food security as it is a matter of national security. Rice supply particularly is an important national security issue, receiving similar treatment as an armament in many countries. This is understandable during war but not in normal times.

The private sector, being the stakeholder of the food market, should be incentivized to play a bigger role in providing food security to the general public.[17] During a crisis, the rice business community should be tasked to ensure the provision of appropriate supply at a fair price. The role of the government will be to ensure that the private sector delivers its promise and ensure competition in the market while protecting the consumers and general public. For example, in Singapore, the private sector is already involved in the national rice security scheme. Rice traders are required to hold a certain level and grade of rice as part of the national security reserve.[18]

The integration of the rice market (e.g., through e-commerce) allows consumers to buy a specific quality of rice they want from anywhere in the world. Under such an environment, the security of rice supply can be markedly increased if rice is allowed to move freely across borders. For disaster relief, which is usually location specific, if rice can be bought online and sent to the disaster area, the rice supply chain can play a great role in mitigating the food security risk. This may open up opportunities for innovative mechanisms so that the private sector can be more involved in times of crisis (see section 4.4 for further discussion).

4.2 Role of the public sector

In the context of a more integrated global rice market, the role of the public sector is to ensure that all stakeholders act to create a resilient

---

[17] The private sector is the agent of the market and the stakeholder of food security. Alavi et al. (2012) suggest that the private sector should be incentivized to participate in creating food security.
[18] Under Singapore's Price Control Act, rice importers are required to participate in the Rice Stockpile Scheme, which serves as the national emergency reserve (https://www.enterprisesg.gov.sg/e-services/rice-stockpile-scheme/rice-stockpile-scheme).

supply of rice in a sustainable manner, and that farmers are fairly rewarded. Food security should be achieved by strengthening the rice market through international cooperation in production, distribution, investment and trade. Private businesses in the rice market should be given a conducive and competitive environment.

To have a new generation of smarter and proactive rice farmers and rice business entrepreneurs, they should be equipped with the appropriate skill set—from data and knowledge management, compliance with legal requirements to financial management and human resource management. Public investment will need to be diverted from the traditional education system to an intensive education and training programme for these skills.

The modernization of the rice market will also require the use of different scientific areas. The public sector should increase investment in rice research beyond production, covering the whole rice value chain, from plant breeding and water management to understanding the needs of the growing urban poor and middle class, access to the market and availability of healthy and safe rice. The target of public sector research should be to create global public goods that enable efficient rice production and trade. For example, the establishment of an international rice quality and safety standard and certification system can increase consumer confidence and rice trade both domestically and internationally.

4.3 Expansion of the scope of rice research

In the coming years, rice farmers will have to use more knowledge and technology to operate their business. To survive the uncertainties of the production environment, comply with environmental regulations and manage the value chain, a rice farmer should be equipped with the appropriate skill set, including the use of a computer, compliance with legal requirements, financial management and human resource management.

Rice research has to expand beyond plant breeding and agronomy; it should encompass the whole value chain of rice, including understanding the needs of the growing urban poor, their consumption behaviour, access to the market and ability to pay. Food security issues have changed.

4.4 Building confidence and trust: Emergency rice reserve

The pre-United Nations Food Summit System 2021 underscores that food security is a joint global effort—no single country can do it alone. The current atmosphere of distrust and animosity among countries has cast a shadow on cooperative activities. Regaining the cooperative spirit and building constructive activities should be given attention.

The occurrence of natural disasters around the world is becoming more frequent. It is thus critical that food and water are available to feed the victims and rescue personnel. Rice is one important item. However, because rice is a strategic and security product for many countries, there are rules and regulations associated with rice buying and selling, import and export, and quality. These regulations limit or even prevent rice from being used in emergency situations. It is suggested that countries be allowed to buy, sell and move rice across borders at appropriate quantities during emergency situations, without need for the usual formalities. The modern global rice delivery system can be deployed to assist in such situations.

Currently, the ASEAN Plus Three Emergency Rice Reserve (APTERR)[19] aims at providing rice to its members for emergency relief. APTERR could be improved to increase the flexibility of securing and dispatching an agreed appropriate quantity of rice to affected areas with no or minimum formalities. It should also be expanded to include other countries, especially in South Asia, Middle East and Africa. It should consider involving the private sector in the acquisition and distribution systems.

4.5 Liberalization of high-quality rice

Recent developments in the rice market have seen the rapid expansion of a new market segment for higher quality rice. This segment caters to the higher-income consumer who can afford to pay for specific quality aspects of rice and its products. It opens up ample opportunities for rice farmers to innovate and develop rice with new characteristics. The expansion of such market will also generate employment for the

---

[19] ASEAN plus China, Japan and Korea (https://www.apterr.org/).

skilled and semi-skill work force, not just in rice production but also in marketing and management.

This market segment should be separate from the general market and not subject to any trade restriction. In most countries, this may require a special exemption. A "sandbox" facility can be created to try out this opportunity. The role of government includes information provision and fraud protection to ensure the enforcement of contracts and promote consumer welfare.

4.6 Remote-sensing information and smart farming

Weather uncertainty is a challenge for both farmers and policymakers. The availability of climate data, access to satellite imagery and advances in remote-sensing technology make crop forecasting more accurate and change uncertainties to risks. Together with crop modelling, crop forecasting has become more accurate, enabling farmers to make better decisions on input investment, marketing and financial planning. It can also assess rice-based greenhouse gas emission and availability of agricultural services in rice-growing areas. Moreover, it can help decision-makers in planning and managing natural disasters.[20]

At the farm level, smart farming embraces remote-sensing technology to improve production planning and execution. Artificial intelligence (AI) will make rice production more predictable and use more equipment and less labour.

A new generation of farmers is expected to emerge and takeover from the existing generation. These new farmers will be equipped with the ability to process and make use of information from remote-sensing technology, so that information asymmetry between them and business operators is minimized, if not avoided. No longer just focused on farming, they will understand the changes occurring in the market and care for the global environment.

The six measures above are not comprehensive, but they can be stepping stones to building a new governance system for the global rice market.

---

[20] https://www.irri.org/mapping

5 CONCLUSION

New market environments are shaping the future of the global rice market. China and India, the two largest producers of rice, are now also its top importer and exporter, respectively. The rice value chain has been modernized, resulting in an increased proportion of rice being sold through e-commerce. The traditional self-sufficiency strategy, which had previously dominated government policies in many countries, is no longer relevant.

The urban population is expected to account for 81 per cent of the total population by 2050. But given the rapid improvement in transport, telecommunication and digital technologies, that date can be shortened to 2030. Most of the growth of the middle-income class will mainly occur in urban areas. This means that most rice consumers will be in these areas, where a sizeable proportion of the population will have money to buy high-quality rice. On the other hand, the environmental challenge for rice is big and will become even bigger with climate change. However, the rice value chain will be upgraded through improvements in information management. These parameters are changing the nature of food security management.

A new governance system for rice security is needed, for which there must be international cooperation. However, the current mood of global politics has reduced the level of trust and spirit of constructive cooperation among countries. To move forward, the following action points are recommended:
    a.   Make the private sector accountable for food security.
    b.   Confine the role of the public sector to providing direction, information/data and research.
    c.   Expand the scope of rice research to cover the whole value chain, not just projection.
    d.   Build confidence and trust in international cooperation.
    e.   Liberalize the high-quality rice market.
    f.   Promote smart farming – utilization of remote sensing information.

REFERENCES

Anderson, Kym. 2015. "Trends and Fluctuations in Agricultural Price Distortions". In *Sustainable Economic Development*, edited by Arsenio M. Balisacan, Ujjayant Chakravorty, and Majah-Leah V. Ravago, pp. 293–309. Academic Press. https://doi.org/10.1016/B978-0-12-800347-3.00017-0.

Alavi, Hamid, Aira Htenas, Ron Kopicki, Andrew W. Shepherd, and Ramon Clarete. 2012. "Trusting Trade and the Private Sector for Food Security in Southeast Asia". *Discussion Paper*. Washington, DC: World Bank.

Balie, Jean, and Harold G. Valera. 2020. "Is COVID-19 a Threat to Stability of Rice Price and Supply?". International Rice Research Institute. https://www.irri.org/news-and-events/news/covid19-threat-stability-rice-price-and-supply.

Childs, Nathan, Sharon Raszap Skorbiansky, and William D. McBride. 2020. "US Rice Production Changed Significantly in the New Millennium, but Remained Profitable". *Amber Waves, 4 May 2020*. https://www.ers.usda.gov/amber-waves/2020/may/us-rice-production-changed-significantly-in-the-new-millennium-but-remained-profitable/.

Custodio, Marie Clare, Rosa Paula Cuevas, Jhoanne Ynion, Alice G. Laborte, Maria Lourdes Velasco, and Matty Demont. 2019. "Rice Quality: How Is It Defined by Consumers, Industry, Food Scientists, and Geneticists?". *Trends in Food Science & Technology* 92: 122–37. https://www.sciencedirect.com/science/article/pii/S0924224417306131.

Econotimes.com. 2021. "Thailand's Rice Exportation Hampered by Shipping Container Shortage". *Econotimes*, 6 January 2021. https://www.econotimes.com/Thailands-rice-exportation-hampered-by-shipping-container-shortage-1599599.

Hawe, D. 2015. "Options to Manage Rice Price Volatility: Stock and Trade". UN Food and Agriculture Organization. https://www.slideshare.net/FAOoftheUN/options-for-managing-rice-price-volatility-stock-and-trade-policies?from_action=save.

Kochhar, Rakesh. 2021. "The Pandemic Stalls Growth in the Global Middle Class, Pushes Poverty Up Sharply". Report. Pew Research Institute. https://www.pewresearch.org/global/2021/03/18/the-pandemic-stalls-growth-in-the-global-middle-class-pushes-poverty-up-sharply/.

Minten, Bart, K. A. S. Murshid, and Thomas Reardon. 2011. "The Quiet Revolution in Agrifood Value Chains in Asia: The Case of Increasing Quality in Rice Markets in Bangladesh". *IFPRI Discussion Paper 01141*. Washington, DC: International Food Policy Research Institute. https://www.researchgate.net/publication/254417046.

Pu, M., and F. Zheng. 2018. "Evaluating Public Grain Buffer Stocks in China: A Stochastic Simulation Model". Paper presented at the 30th International Conference of Agricultural Economists, International Association of Agricultural Economists (IAAE), Vancouver, Canada, 28 July–2 Aug 2018.

Ravago, Majah-Leah V., Arsenio M. Balisacan, and Ujjayant Chakravorty. 2015. "The Principles and Practice of Sustainable Economic Development: Overview and Synthesis". In *Sustainable Economic Development*, edited by Arsenio M. Balisacan, Ujjayant Chakravorty, and Majah-Leah V. Ravago, pp. 3–10. Academic Press. https://doi.org/10.1016/B978-0-12-800347-3.00001-7.

Retnoningsih, Dwi. 2019. "Analysis of Rice Distribution Channel in Ngawi Regency, East Java Province of Indonesia". *Russian Journal of Agricultural and Socio-Economic Sciences* 89, no. 5: 247–55. https://doi.org/10.18551/rjoas.2019-05.31.

Roumasset, James, A. 2015. "Reflections on the Foundations of Development Policy Analysis". In *Sustainable Economic Development*, edited by Arsenio M. Balisacan, Ujjayant Chakravorty, and Majah-Leah V. Ravago, pp. 11–45. Academic Press. https://doi.org/10.1016/B978-0-12-800347-3.00002-9.

Setboonsarng, Suthad. 2014. "Agriculture in ASEAN Economic Community (AEC): Is Win-Win Possible". Paper presented at the 2nd International Conference on Agriculture and Rural Development in Southeast Asia, Manila, Philippines, 12 November 2014.

Siamwalla, Ammar, and Suthad Setboonsarng. 1989. "Exchange Rate, Trade (Political Economy of Agricultural Trade Policies)". Paper, World Bank, Washington, DC.

Teng, P. S., M. Caballero-Anthony, and J. A. Lassa. 2016. "The Future of Rice Security under Climate Change". *NTS Report No. 4*. Singapore: S. Rajaratnam School of International Studies, Nanyang Technological University. https://www.rsis.edu.sg/wp-content/uploads/2016/10/NTS-Report4-July2016-ClimateChangeAndRice.pdf.

IPCC (Intergovernmental Panel on Climate Change). 2021. *The Sixth Assessment Report of Intergovernmental Panel on Climate Change*. Geneva: IPCC.

Velasco, M. L., M. C. Custodio, A. G. Laborte, and N. Suphanchaimat. 2015. "Rapid Value Chain Assessment and Rice Preferences of Consumers, Farmers and Other Rice Value Chain Actors in Thailand". MRT Report. Los Baños, Philippines: International Rice Research Institute.

Yang, M., and S. Hu. 2016. "Research on the e-Business Platform of Agricultural Products and Rice Marketing Channel Based on Network Big Data". *Rev. Tec.Ing. Univi.Zulia*, 39, no. 12: 258–65. https://pdfs.semanticscholar.org/8c2f/3c91d2258ce5a702e2c5db37109f73d6538c.pdf

Yansui Liu, Fang Fang, and Yuheng Li. 2020. "Key Issues of Land Use in China and Implications for Policymaking". *Journal of Land Use Policy* (November). https://www.researchgate.net/publication/262642011_Key_issues_of_land_use_in_China_and_implications_for_policy_making.

Wright, Brian. 2015. "The Role of Agricultural Economists in Sustaining Bad Programs". In *Sustainable Economic Development*, edited by Arsenio M. Balisacan, Ujjayant Chakravorty, and Majah-Leah V. Ravago, pp. 239–45. Academic Press. https://doi.org/10.1016/B978-0-12-800347-3.00014-5.

25 International Cooperation for Development: Learning from Trade and Tax Policies

Marilou Uy

1 INTRODUCTION

Effective international cooperation can bring enormous benefits to developing countries, such as by providing access to markets and facilitating technology transfer and investments for development. With much deeper global economic integration, there is an even greater need for coordinated policy actions by countries to avoid beggar-thy-neighbour policies and adverse spillovers and, instead, create conditions to lift global welfare. Achieving international cooperation that serves development, however, is not always forthcoming nor easy to promote in existing international forums. A key challenge for policymakers in developing countries is to extend their attention beyond implementing national policies to also finding the means to influence support for international measures that serve their respective countries' interests.

This paper explores the interplay of national policies and international regimes in the areas of trade policy and corporate tax policies to illustrate how international cooperation has shaped their impact on development. It draws on the substantial body of analytical work on these areas to highlight some key challenges faced by developing countries in reflecting their interests to influence international rules and practices. The first part discusses lessons from the rules-based international trading system. The second part reflects on the challenges of reforming the international corporate tax system, especially from the perspective of developing countries. The third part considers other policy areas where international cooperation will be important for developing countries.

2 LESSONS FROM A RULES-BASED INTERNATIONAL TRADING SYSTEM

The textbook economic case for international trade—the law of comparative advantage—says that two or more countries can gain from specialization and trade of goods. Free trade also offers dynamic benefits, such as from the pressure on companies to be more productive to be able to compete internationally. History shows, however, that countries also have incentives to limit imports to protect local production in specific sectors, gain terms of trade advantage and/or raise fiscal revenues. Countries have used trade agreements as mechanisms to seek reciprocal commitments to reduce barriers to trade and provide greater access to markets.

Evidence shows that the world has benefited from the rules-based international trading system.[1] In assessing the "arbiter of cooperation in international policy" role of the World Trade Organization (WTO), established in 1995 to succeed the General Agreement on Trade and Tariffs (GATT), Deardorff (1996) frames the problems of international trade as a prisoners' dilemma and shows how the WTO's rules-based mechanisms contribute to resolving these problems. He points to the creation of a forum for countries—developed and developing[2]—to exchange information and negotiate constraints on trade policy actions of member governments, while also providing exceptions for

---

[1] Anderson (2016), among others, demonstrates the welfare-enhancing effect of the three WTO rules. Tang and Wei (2009) estimate that acceding to the WTO boosts a developing country's growth rate by 2 per cent a year for five years after joining.

[2] Developed and developing countries participated in the GATT and are now members of the WTO. The GATT had 128 member countries; the WTO has 159 member countries now.

prescribed reasons, and a mechanism for settling trade disputes among members. The basic principle of non-discrimination among foreign suppliers and between foreign and domestic suppliers underpins the workings of the GATT and the WTO, and forms the basis for ensuring fairness and promoting economic welfare. Stiglitz (2006) regards the first step towards the creation of a rules-based trading system as the greatest achievement of the Uruguay Round. He notes, however, that the system is imperfect since the rules are a product of negotiations, wherein the powerful countries tend to dominate, and that enforcement is asymmetric since a threat of retaliation from a small developing country does not elicit the same response as one coming from a major developed country.

Agreements reached under the GATT and subsequently the WTO have led to a major decline in average tariff rates and strong growth of exports and trade globally. When negotiations under the Doha Round stalled, countries entered into bilateral and regional preferential trade agreements, or simply liberalized unilaterally, which pushed tariffs even further down. Between 1990 and 2006 when tariffs declined the most, average tariff rates fell from 6 per cent to 2.4 per cent in developed countries and remarkably from 37.8 per cent to 10 per cent in developing countries.[3] World trade, in turn, increased dramatically and more rapidly than overall economic growth (Figure 25.1). A large proportion of the growth in world trade can be explained by improvements in transportation technology and specialization (Krugman 1995).[4] Multinationals have played an increasingly important role, accounting for nearly two-thirds of global trade by 2016 (De Backer, Miroudot, and Rigo 2019).

As trading opportunities opened, a number of developing countries, especially in East Asia, pursued export-oriented development strategies and saw significant increases in their exports to the world and growth in per capita incomes. For many other developing countries, however, trade liberalization did not necessarily come with increased exports or significant increases in economic growth. According to Rodrik (2002),

---

[3] Non-tariff barriers also protect imports, but their tariff equivalents are not reported here.
[4] Kei Mu Yi (2000) shows that 70 per cent of the growth in world trade can be explained by vertical specialization in manufacturing. Mattoo (2018) documents major increases in cross-border trading of intermediate goods.

Figure 25.1. Average growth of trade and GDP

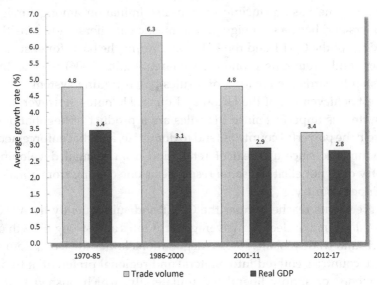

Note: Trade growth is the average of import and export growth rates.
Sources: World Development Indicators, World Bank, and G-24 staff calculations.

inadequate domestic infrastructure and reforms and the lack of liberalization of agricultural imports have hampered the ability of developing countries to compete. The developed countries' high import barriers for agricultural products and their enormous subsidies to farmers have remained, and attempts to reduce them have largely failed.[5] Escalating tariffs (the tendency to levy higher tariffs on intermediate goods than on raw materials and higher still on final goods) further protect developed countries from greater competition from processed agriculture in developing countries.[6] Eliminating the subsidies and opening up agricultural markets will benefit more people in the developing world, who rely on agriculture for livelihood. Krueger (2021) discusses the continued importance of reviving multilateral efforts to meet future challenges of governing agricultural policies.

---

[5] The Philippines, for example, was one of the developing countries that urged greater attention to agricultural trade barriers from the WTO and the United Nations System (see Binswanger and Lutz 2000).

[6] Escalating tariffs also exacerbate inequality by increasing the wage premium on skilled labour (e.g., Guha-Khasnobis 2004).

Developing countries, using the dispute resolution system as a means to pursue unfair trade practices in an orderly legal manner, have had notable successful cases against developed countries (Krist 2013). They have increasingly participated in the WTO processes and negotiations. But in contrast to the well-resourced developed countries, many developing countries have much less resources, constraining their ability to advance their interests during negotiations. In assessing the politics of trade agreements, Krist (2013) recommends that the US government develop institutional arrangements to assess the impact of trade proposals on developing countries.

Under the WTO, rules were expanded to include those governing the flow of investments, intellectual property rights and services[7] presumably to facilitate the transfer of technology, and direct foreign investment by multinational corporations, which have been major drivers of trade and cross-border investments. The rules put in place, however, were often benchmarked against the standards used in advanced countries, thus do not reflect the institutional realities and capacity of the institutions in developing countries. Some studies (e.g., Gallagher, Sklar, and Thrasher 2019) have shown that some provisions in the trade and investment agreements actually do harm by constraining the policy space of developing countries.[8] Another important example is the set of rules governing intellectual property rights that do not necessarily encourage innovation or respond to development concerns, but serve to ensure intellectual property rights for multinationals (Finger and Schuler 2002). Many in the developing countries, however, are unable to afford high monopoly prices charged by, say, pharmaceutical companies. This was highlighted in the late 1990s when Brazil and South Africa explored the idea of compulsory licenses to broaden access to technology to lower the cost of AIDS medicines. But the effort failed. It was resisted by developed countries, which were home to the major pharmaceutical companies. The same debate resurfaced recently when South Africa and India, with widespread support from developing countries, sought waivers to

---

[7] Unlike the GATT, which allowed for special and differential treatment of developing countries, the WTO requires all member countries to adhere to all agreements, except for government procurement (Krist 2013).

[8] Gallagher, Sklar, and Thrasher 2019 show that a large proportion of trade agreements include rules that constrain a country's policy space from deploying, when needed, appropriate measures to manage volatile capital outflows.

patent protection under the WTO's Trade Related Aspects of Intellectual Property Rights (TRIPS) to boost the supply of affordable vaccines and medicines to combat COVID-19. Developed countries' support of the proposed waiver on vaccines, which is currently under consideration, will constitute a strong signal of enlightened international cooperation under the aegis of the WTO. This recurring issue reveals the need to re-examine the effectiveness of the framework on intellectual property protection under TRIPS in enabling technology transfer, and how it should be shaped to respond better to future pandemics.

Preferential trade agreements have been increasing and deepening and associated with greater global value chain (GVC)-related trade (Figure 25.2) (World Bank 2020; Hofmann, Osnago, and Ruta 2017). Participants in GVCs are increasingly resorting to agreements that not only reduce trade barriers but also protect intellectual property rights, ensure regulatory certainty and advance trade regulation in services. Lowering the cost of services, such as finance, transport and human resources, can further stimulate GVC trade, which has intensive coordination costs. Some agreements include provisions to implement competition policies consistently across

Figure 25.2. Increasing and deepening trade agreements

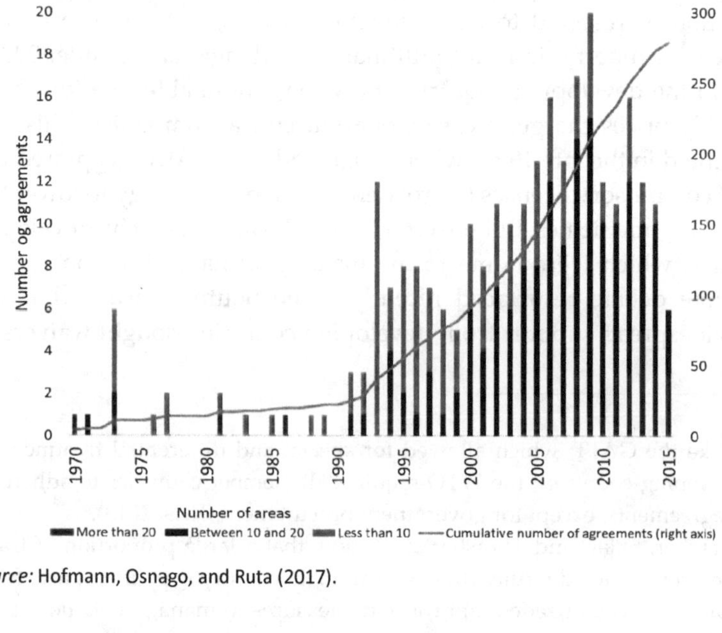

Source: Hofmann, Osnago, and Ruta (2017).

trading partners to avoid anticompetitive behaviour by GVC firms. These investment-related areas are bridging gaps in existing WTO policies (World Bank 2020; Roy 2019). In this dynamic context, the task ahead for developing countries is to build capacity to advance their development interests in broad-based trade and investment agreements if they are to participate in GVCs, which are increasingly advancing due to technological change.

A stronger rules-based trade system remains crucial to development in the face of new and emerging challenges. Recent trade tensions between and among countries and national protectionist reactions in some advanced countries, however, threaten the future of the rules-based trading system. Going forward, the willingness of the WTO member countries, especially those with major economies, to strengthen the rules-based trading system will depend on shared interests and incentives within the system. To strengthen the likelihood that countries follow existing rules and to lower the propensity of some countries to use trade policy towards specific countries as an instrument of foreign policy, new enforcement mechanisms might have to be considered. Unlike proposals to enforce climate change commitments, for example, the governing body to execute improved enforcement—the WTO—is already in place.[9]

There are positive steps that may be taken in the interim. Groups of WTO members—developed and developing—have shown a willingness to cooperate plurilaterally, in lieu of achieving consensus among all members, on new rules and regulatory practices, such as on e-commerce and digital trade and actions to facilitate investment (Hoekman and Zedillo 2021). These positive steps could provide a way forward to identify cooperative policies to promote trade and development, wherein producers and consumers are much more interlinked by GVCs facilitated by technological change and digitization and where digital trade is expected to be increasingly important in a post-COVID-19 pandemic world. There could also be more reflections on how trade policy would be affected as countries seek to improve resilience to and preparedness for future pandemics.

---

[9] To enforce international cooperation on greenhouse gas emissions, Nordhaus (2015) suggests the formation of climate clubs to impose trade sanctions on non-cooperating countries. In the case of furthering cooperation on trade, the club already exists.

3 THE CHALLENGE OF INTERNATIONAL TAX COOPERATION

It is now well-recognized that the existing century-old architecture for taxing multinationals needs fundamental reform.[10] There is strong evidence that governments have used tax policies (e.g., corporate income taxes) to attract investments. Tax competition, in turn, has led to reductions in tax rates in one or a few countries, triggering the same in other countries. When tax competition happens among subnationals, as in the United States, national governments can set rules to apportion profits derived from each state. In the absence of a world government,[11] however, tax competition among countries have led to beggar-thy-neighbour policies and loss in overall welfare (Hebous 2021).[12]

While the extent and impact of tax competition is not fully known, Figure 25.3 clearly shows the secular decline in corporate tax rates globally in the past few decades. Between 1985 and 2018, the global average statutory corporate tax rate fell by about half, from 49 per cent to 24 per cent. Corporate tax rates declined in advanced countries and in all regions of the developing world. Beyond reducing corporate tax rates, developing countries have also provided generous tax incentives to promote foreign investments, resulting in significant forgone tax revenues (Crivelli et al. 2015).[13]

Multinationals have been able to avoid taxes also by shifting profits from higher to lower tax jurisdictions. Profit shifting has been facilitated by several reasons, such as transfer pricing practices.

---

[10] De Mooij, Klem, and Perry (2021) provide a comprehensive analysis of the pressures confronting the existing international corporate tax system.

[11] Tanzi (1999) advocates the creation of a World Tax Organization.

[12] The race to the bottom from tax competition can be represented by positively sloped reaction functions: a tax reduction by one country results in another country's reduction below what would be optimal to attract productive investments, leading to a further reduction in the first country and so on. In the Nash Equilibrium outcome of the race, both countries lose welfare.

[13] See also Keen and Simone (2004), who studied the spread of different types of tax rate reductions and incentives in a sample of 40 developing countries between 1990 and 2000. During this decade of the largest reduction in tax rates, tax revenues fell by 20 per cent on average among developing countries, and even more so among low- and lower middle-income countries.

Figure 25.3. Statutory corporate tax rates (1980–2020)

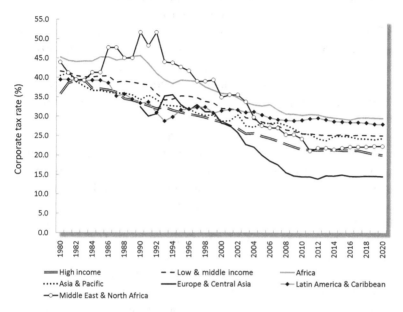

Sources: Corporate Tax Rates around the World 2020, Tax Foundation, OECD Database on Statutory Corporate Income Tax Rates and G-24 Secretariat staff calculations.

Hence, multinationals that operate with substantial intangible assets can more easily shift their profits to different locations (Auerbach et al. 2017). Increased use of digital technology has further enabled multinationals to avoid taxes on profits earned in markets where they are not physically present, which is the rule that currently determines whether they are taxed or not. Tørsløv, Wier, and Zucman (2018) estimate that close to 40 per cent of multinational profits globally are shifted to tax havens, and the location of corporate profits changes if all countries adopt the same effective corporate tax rate. Further, Saez and Zucman (2019) estimate that US multinationals book 60 per cent of their profits abroad in low tax jurisdictions, without evidence that production has shifted to these countries. The absolute amounts of tax revenues lost[14] are clearly

---

[14] Crivelli, De Mooij, and Keen (2015) estimate that annual tax revenue losses globally due to profit shifting amount to around US$100 billion to US$240 billion, or equivalent to 4–10 per cent of global corporate tax revenues. Long-run average revenue losses are estimated at US$650 billion globally.

much larger for advanced countries, but developing countries lose disproportionately more given their greater dependence on corporate tax revenues and their more limited tax base.

Bilateral tax treaties have been a central feature and the only form of "hard law" in the international tax system. They define and limit the ability to tax cross-border earnings of multinationals in countries where the owners reside (residence) and where the income is generated (source). Investment promotion has motivated participation in bilateral treaties, in order to avoid double taxation of the same incomes in both residence and source countries and to ensure tax certainty. The impact on investments and the fairness of the limitations these treaties impose on taxing rights of developing countries have been often questioned, however.[15] While there is little analytical evidence that tax treaties have enhanced foreign investment, their abuse has been a major problem, leading to substantial tax revenue losses for developing countries. For example, Beer and Loeprick (2018) estimate that, without notable increases in investment, the ability of multinational companies to exploit favourable treaty arrangements has led to a significant loss— 15 per cent—of corporate tax revenues in Sub-Saharan Africa.

On the other hand, Hearson (2021b), comparing tax treaties signed by 26 developing countries[16] over time, shows encouraging improvements in the taxing rights of source countries and provisions to prevent treaty abuse in new and renegotiated treaties. This is partly due to the impact of the OECD Base Erosion and Profit Shifting (BEPS) initiative's efforts to raise awareness of and contain treaty abuse (discussed below). The study further shows that with the same treaty partner, some developing countries do better than others in increasing their taxing rights (Figure 25.4). Although there could be legitimate reasons for the differences, these suggest that developing countries could learn more from each other about strengthening analytical and negotiating capabilities.

---

[15] The IMF's 2014 Report on spillovers of the international tax system notes that developing countries "...would be well-advised to sign treaties only with considerable caution". See also Hearson (2021a).

[16] These are members of the G-24, an intergovernmental grouping of developing countries. Hearson (2021b) used a database of tax treaties signed by 118 middle-income and low-income countries to compare specific treaty provisions and amalgamated the treaty content into an index to indicate trends in the balance of taxing rights.

Figure 25.4. Source taxing rights with common treaty partners

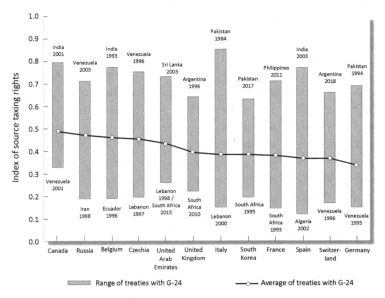

Source: Hearson (2021b).

Developing countries could also do more to address remaining constraints to source taxing rights and systematically improve their treaty arrangements.

Several multilateral initiatives in recent years have focused on countering tax avoidance practices of corporations. These have been carried out through the BEPS initiative started in 2015. The OECD Inclusive Framework, which has both developed and developing member countries, has been charged with the implementation of this initiative. The initiative has led to measures that curtail "treaty abuse", better country reporting by multinationals and automatic exchange of information. The successful implementation of the Multilateral Instrument (OECD 2016) put in place under BEPS will systematically improve the taxing rights of participating developing countries, especially their protection against tax treaty abuse. The BEPS initiative has been an important step in tax cooperation. Hence, developing countries continue to urge more efforts to better tailor the initiative's standards and measures to the capacity levels of developing countries so they can realize the potential revenues from these measures.

At this point, there are important efforts towards more fundamental reforms to mitigate tax competition through a global minimum tax rate, address profit shifting and allocate taxing rights more equitably between exporter countries (residence of multinationals) and importers (source countries) of capital and investments. The reform momentum has been largely driven by political pressures brought about by the minimal taxes paid by highly profitable multinationals and the challenges of taxing the digital economy, which have prompted some source countries to impose unilateral tax measures. The forces for change further increased when the United States and other G7 countries[17] — the group of the largest developed countries — expressed strong support for the introduction of a minimum global corporate tax of at least 15 per cent and the sharing of a portion of the residual profits of multinationals with market countries (where sales have been made), which are profits above the margin of 10 per cent (see the G7 Communiqué, US Department of Treasury 2021b). As of this paper's writing, 136 countries in the G20/OECD Inclusive Forum, where negotiations for reforms have been going on since 2019, have agreed on a package of reforms, which includes a global minimum tax and revised profit allocation rules (see OECD 2021). The global reforms are expected to be implemented in 2023.

Achieving the necessary multilateral cooperation to change the existing tax architecture has been difficult, possibly more so than in the area of international trade. There is a wide divergence of interests between the major economies, which are the residence of multinationals, and many developing countries, which are largely source countries. Advanced countries are mainly interested in reforms to prevent profit shifting to low tax jurisdictions and stop tax competition. Many developing countries share these concerns, but would also like deeper changes so that multinationals pay their fair share of taxes in line with their real activities and economic presence in these countries. In addition, they prefer a simpler system of allocating taxable income to the existing complex arms-length rules, which have been difficult to implement given their limited administrative capacity. Notably, a number of leading economists have concluded that the reforms recently agreed upon largely benefit advanced countries and can only be seen as an interim solution for developing countries (ICRICT 2021).

---

[17] The G7 consists of Canada, France, Germany, Italy, Japan, United Kingdom and United States.

The discussion below elaborates on the proposed reforms on a global minimum corporate tax and the allocation of taxing rights to address the digital economy, with particular attention on how to better serve the interests of developing countries.

3.1 Global minimum corporate tax and taxing rights allocation in a digital economy

Putting in place a global minimum corporate income tax has obtained strong support from the United States (United States Treasury 2021a) and other G7 nations, as mentioned earlier. Tax experts have long advocated having a meaningful global minimum tax to tackle tax competition and profit shifting by multinationals.[18] The agreed minimum tax will be 15 per cent on incomes of outward investments by residence countries alongside the rate and scope of intragroup payments prone to base erosion that source countries can tax.[19] The global corporate minimum tax is intended to facilitate coordinated action by willing governments to prevent a race to the bottom. Investors themselves will also be discouraged from seeking tax incentives in source countries since they will be taxed at their countries of residence.

A global minimum tax is expected to raise tax revenues globally and has the potential to do so meaningfully for developing countries (IMF 2019). For most developing countries, a higher minimum rate will help. For example, according to Barake et al. (2021), a global minimum tax of 15 per cent is expected to raise EUR100 million for Indonesia, but raising the minimum to 21 per cent will triple revenues. Many developing countries have tax rates in the range of 20–25 per cent, so there is concern that a lower global minimum rate will not discourage profit shifting. In addition, requiring recipient countries to revise their tax treaties in order to apply the minimum tax will put them in a disadvantageous position since partner countries will likely not accept such revisions to the tax treaties. Therefore, it is important that the reform involves mechanisms that will enable developing countries to

---

[18] ICRICT (2016) proposes a global minimum tax rate of 25 per cent. See also Picciotto (2016).
[19] The "subject to tax rule" minimum rate to apply to interest, royalties and a defined set of other payments prone to base erosion will be 9 per cent (OECD 2021).

implement the minimum tax regime on multinationals, as appropriate, at source. With a global minimum tax, many developing countries will also need to revisit their domestic investment regimes, with the view to balancing their objectives of raising tax revenues and attracting direct foreign investment.

Increased digitalization of the economy has made obsolete the existing rule of using physical establishment or production to determine the right of a source country to tax a multinational's affiliate. In this context, several developing countries—mostly source countries—have proposed that taxable presence be determined by a multinational's significant economic presence in a country, using factors such as sustained revenues, user base and volume of data content, even where it is not physically present (see, e.g., G-24 2019). This method acknowledges the value contributed by the consumer demand, in addition to the supply side of the product's value chain. There is widespread support for using the concept of economic presence, but views have differed on how to allocate the taxing rights between residence and source countries.

The complexity of and scope for profit shifting from transfer pricing practices and the taxation challenges of digitization have revitalized interest in more formulary methods of apportioning profits of multinationals across countries, which tax experts and think tanks have been advocating for some time (ICRICT 2016; Picciotto 2016).[20] These methods have been used to apportion incomes among subnationals, such as in the United States, Canada, Germany and Japan (IMF 2014). However, they have not been part of existing international tax rules that attribute profits based on arms-length pricing of transactions within a company. Under a global formulary method, the profits of the affiliates of a multinational are consolidated worldwide and then apportioned across jurisdictions based on a formula that considers demand and supply factors.[21] This will substantially reduce the ability of multinationals to shift taxes to low

---

[20] In 2019, the Group of 24 proposed a similar method it termed as fractional apportionment in its response to the public consultations conducted by the OECD.

[21] Auerbach et al. (2017) discuss the option of a destination-based sales tax, in which taxing rights are based on final sales or consumption in each jurisdiction, which will remove incentives to shift profits to avoid taxes. This is not currently regarded as one of the reform options.

tax jurisdictions, thus raising global tax revenues and allocating profits more equitably between residence and source countries. A formulary approach will also simplify the administration of attributing taxable profits, benefiting the more capacity-constrained developing countries.

The multilateral approach agreed upon in October 2021 by the OECD Inclusive Forum is a more incremental solution, in which 25 per cent of the residual profits—defined as profits in excess of the pre-determined routine profits of 10 per cent of revenues—of the largest multinationals would be apportioned among countries where the sales are made. The taxing rights over routine profits will continue to be based on existing tax rules (OECD 2019). The distribution of tax bases under this reform will be different from that under the current system, but will not yield a large increase in global tax revenues, especially since it will be applied only to the largest multinationals. While the major economies are expected to gain from the reforms and tax havens and low tax jurisdictions will lose significant tax revenues, most developing countries will not gain materially from this incremental approach (Cobham, Faccio, and FitzGerard 2019). Developing countries have been seeking a greater share of both routine and residual profits for source countries,[22] especially since the digital technology has led to scale economies in transaction costs that confer opportunities to earn significant economic rents. These differences in views suggest that adjustments will be needed in order for developing countries to expect benefits to meaningfully exceed the costs of implementation of the new rules, especially since they are also asked to forgo the use of unilateral taxation measures, such as digital services tax, on all companies under the multilateral approach.

That said, developing countries have a lot at stake in the reform of international tax rules to improve their ability to mobilize fiscal resources without jeopardizing their ability to attract productive foreign investments. Existing governance arrangements of the global tax system, however, are perceived as still lacking in putting adequate weight on the concerns and circumstances of developing countries and in identifying and shaping the options for reforms (Christensen, Hearson, and Randriamanalina 2020; see also Uy 2019). This sentiment was reflected in the support from many developing countries during

---

[22] The African Tax Administration Forum stresses this principle. See G-24 (2021).

the 2015 Addis Ababa Conference on Financing for Development for the failed proposal to upgrade the UN Committee of Experts on International Cooperation on Tax Matters to an intergovernmental body. The OECD Inclusive Framework was subsequently created to broaden participation; it has 139 member countries now. While it is still uncertain if developing countries are participating on an equal footing in the Inclusive Framework's tax standard-setting process, developing countries need to find ways to work around their capacity constraints to understand the potential consequences of various proposals so they can advance their interests in the reform process. Collaborative efforts among like-minded countries could help. For example, Christensen, Hearson, and Randriamanalina (2020) document how the African Tax Administration Forum, a regional tax body, and the Group of 24, an intergovernmental group of developing countries, have articulated their members' shared concerns to propose alternative policy options for consideration during the negotiations towards a multilateral approach in the OECD Inclusive Framework.

It is evident that a more inclusive approach to multilateral cooperation is needed to deal with the spillovers of harmful tax practices (IMF 2014). Enhancing ways for the UN to further catalyse changes in tax practices that benefit developing markets could be further explored. For example, the UN Tax Committee agreed in 2014 to include a new article in the UN Model Double Taxation Convention[23] to provide host countries the right to tax technical services fees paid by a foreign affiliate in their state, despite strong opposition by the OECD countries. Many developing countries has since used this new article in their tax treaties. The UN Tax Committee subsequently approved in 2021 the inclusion of a new article in the UN Model that grants additional taxing rights to countries where customers of automated digital services are located, which supports source countries. Collaborative efforts by the UN, the World Bank Group and the IMF, which have broader country membership, have led to a useful guidance to contain tax avoidance practices that are of particular concern to developing countries but are not covered in the work of the OECD.

---

[23] Treaties are guided by either the OECD Model Double Taxation Convention or the UN Model Tax Convention between Developed and Developing Countries. While the majority of countries have used the OECD convention, the UN model is associated with providing more taxing rights to source countries.

4 COOPERATION BEYOND TRADE AND TAX POLICIES

Given the greater cross-border economic activity, cooperative policy solutions have increasingly become an important part of policymaking in many areas. In infrastructure, for example, each country cannot fully internalize the full benefits of investments that lower the cost of trade and will most likely underinvest (World Bank 2020). Coordinated investments by importing and exporting countries would lead to larger gains in trade. China's Belt and Road Initiative is a recent example of such multi-country cooperation. Wider connectivity could stimulate increased economic activity from many more participants and connect more prosperous regions with lagging ones to foster more equitable development. Another notable effort is the 2017 WTO Trade Facilitation Initiative, which both advanced and developing countries supported and have implemented.

Regulatory arrangements will also need to respond to the surge of cross-border flows of data, which now drive the most dynamic exports of developing countries (see World Bank 2021). Data-driven trade in the Philippines, for example, now matches the amount of manufacturing exports and is twice that of agricultural exports. Policy coordination will be necessary to balance concerns around data protection and privacy of importing countries and the need for access to their markets by developing countries. Shaping cross-border agreements on data flows that support development, especially with the expected continued strong growth of digital services post-COVID-19, is an important emerging issue for policymakers in developing countries.

Competition policy is another area where international cooperation will be increasingly sought. International tax reforms to contain profit shifting will partly improve market competition, since these "practices fundamentally distort competition, leading to higher effective tax rates for companies that operate within national borders than for MNEs", according to OECD Secretary General Angel Gurria in his 2014 speech on taxation and competition policy. Connor (2014, as cited in World Bank 2020), who examined 1,530 cartel cases across five regions in the world, shows an average overcharge of at least 49 per cent. Citing specific cases, World Bank (2020) illustrates the need for cooperation between national competition agencies in detecting and undoing these anticompetitive practices that affect the distribution of gains within global value chains. National competition agencies in countries that are negatively impacted are likely unable to enforce their competition laws on violating firms that are not located domestically.

Notable institutional arrangements for cooperation among national competition agencies in developing countries have recently emerged. The ASEAN Competition Enforcers' Network was established in 2018 to facilitate cooperation in competition cases and operate as a platform to address cross-border cases.[24] The potential for regional cooperation has been recognized with deepening trade and services liberalization (Lee and Fukunaga 2014). Recent efforts to coordinate more systematically have in fact been driven by concerns of competition agencies in the Asian region regarding the anticompetitive impact of several visible mergers of large companies that deliver digitally enabled services across countries. Facilitating information exchange, encouraging research and pooling relevant expertise will further build the capacities of national competition agencies. Large emerging markets have also created the BRICS Competition Law and Policy Center[25] to stimulate research and build knowledge of competition policy issues that need to be addressed to serve development better. Developing the framework for cooperation on enforcement will be an important subject for future work.

5   CONCLUSION

It is evident that the rise of cross-border trade, the digital economy, and global enterprises and value chains have made policy spillovers a more important consideration. International cooperation—most likely in all the areas discussed above and more—is essential to guard against adverse spillovers and promote greater gains from trade and investment. There is much to learn from the experience in a rules-based trading system, which has led to important development gains but continues

---

[24] Developing effective competition policies has been a key element of the ASEAN Economic Community Framework. Within this framework, member countries have developed their national regulatory capacities at different paces. Before the creation of the ASEAN Competition Enforcers' Network, the ASEAN Economic Ministers endorsed a Regional Cooperation Framework to provide a set of principles, guidelines and possible areas of cooperation in relation to the development and enforcement of competition laws.

[25] BRICS is composed of Brazil, Russia, India, China and South Africa.

to confront developing countries with major challenges that need to be addressed to better capture the opportunities and benefits of the system. The ongoing process of reforming the international tax system illustrates the difficulty of achieving international cooperation and the challenge developing countries face in getting their development interests factored into the design of reforms. The importance of collective solutions is also increasingly evident in complementary areas beyond trade and tax policies, such as in investing in infrastructure, managing cross-border data flows and containing anticompetitive practices. Furthermore, the economic fallout due to the COVID-19 pandemic and the necessity of securing a resilient global recovery bring to the fore the need for collective actions in an even wider range of areas.

For developing countries, a key goal is to promote international cooperation in a changing world in ways that meet their development imperatives. This is not easy to do when stakeholders have diverging interests and bargaining strength often determines the agenda and negotiation outcomes. The discussion above makes a case for developing countries to build their institutional capacity and expertise to understand better the benefits and costs of policy actions so they can collectively advance their development interests in the evolving international discussions in a timely way. In this regard, collaborative efforts among like-minded countries within or across regions would be useful to bridge differences in existing capacities. There is also value to doing more analytical work on effective mechanisms and incentives to foster broader participation across countries and to ensure compliance to sustain collective actions that improve global welfare.

ACKNOWLEDGEMENT

My sincere thanks to James Roumasset for his valuable support throughout the preparation of this paper.

REFERENCES

Anderson, K. 2016. "Contributions of the GATT/WTO to Global Economic Welfare". *Journal of Economic Surveys* 30, no. 1:56–92.

Auerbach, A., M. Devereux, M. Keen, and J. Vella. 2017. "International Tax Planning under the Destination Based Cash Flow Tax". *National Tax Journal* 70, no. 4: 783–802.

Barake, M., T. Neef, P. E. Chouc, and G. Zucman. 2021. "Collecting the Tax Deficit of Multinational Companies: Simulations for the European Union". Paris: EU Tax Observatory.

Beer S., and J. Loeprick. 2018. "Too High a Price? Tax Treaties with Investment Hubs in Sub-Saharan Africa". *International Tax and Public Finance* 28, no. 1: 113–53.

Binswanger, H., and E. Lutz. 2000. "Agricultural Trade Barriers, Trade Negotiations and Developing Country Interests". High-Level Roundtable on Trade and Development: Directions for the 21st Century, UNCTAD, Bangkok, Thailand, 12 February 2000.

Christensen, R., M. Hearson, and T. Randriamanalina. 2020. "At the Table, Off the Menu: Assessing the Participation of Lower-Income Countries in Global Tax Negotiations". *ICTD Working Paper No. 115.* https://www.ictd.ac/publication/at-table-off-menu-assessing-participation-lower-income-countries-global-tax-negotiations/.

Cobham, A., T. Faccio, and V. FitzGerard. 2019. "Global Inequalities in Taxing Rights: An Early Evaluation of the OECD Tax Reform Proposals". Tax Justice Network. Draft.

Connor, J. M. 2014. "Cartel Overcharges". In *Research in Law and Economics, Volume 6: The Law and Economics of Class Actions,* edited by J. Langenfeld, pp. 249–387. Bingley, UK: Emerald Publishing.

Crivelli, R., R. De Mooij, and M. Keen. 2015. "Base Erosion, Profit Shifting and Developing Countries". *IMF Working Paper.* Washington, DC: International Monetary Fund.

Deardorff, A. V. 1996. "An Economist's Overview of the World Trade Organization". *Discussion Paper No. 388.* Research Seminar in International Economics. Ann Arbor, Michigan: School of Public Policy, University of Michigan.

De Backer, K., S. Miroudot, and D. Rigo. 2019. "Multinational Enterprises in the Global Economy: Heavily Discussed, Hardly Measured". https://voxeu.org/article/multinational-enterprises-global-economy.

De Mooij, R., A. Klemm, and V. Perry. 2021. *Corporate Income Taxes under Pressure: Why Reform Is Needed and How It Could Be Designed.* Washington, DC: International Monetary Fund.

Finger, M., and P. Schuler. 2002. "Implementation of WTO Commitments: The Development Challenge". In *Development, Trade and the WTO: A Handbook,* edited by B. Hoekman, A. Mattoo, and P. English, pp. 293–503. Washington, DC: World Bank.

G-24 (Group of Twenty-Four). 2019. "Proposal for Addressing Tax Challenges Arising from Digitalization". January 2019. https://www.g24.org/wp-content/uploads/2019/03/G-24_proposal_for_Taxation_of_Digital_Economy_Jan17_Special_Session_2.pdf.

———. 2021. "Comments to Pillar One and Pillar Two Proposals Being Discussed by the G20/OECD Inclusive Framework on BEPS". 17 May 2021. https://www.g24.org/wp-content/uploads/2021/06/Comments-G-24-to-BEPS-IF-SG-May-2021_FINAL.pdf

Gallagher, K., S. Sklar, and R. Thrasher. 2019. "Quantifying the Policy Space for Regulating Capital Flows in Trade and Investment Treaties". Working Paper of the G-24. https://www.g24.org/wp-content/uploads/2019/03/Gallagher_Capital_Flows_and_Treaties.pdf.

Guha-Khasnobis, B. 2004. "Who Gains from Tariff Escalation?". *Journal of Economic Integration* 19, no. 2 (June): 416–24.

Hearson, M. 2021a. "Imposing Standards: The North-South Dimension to Global Tax Politics". In *Cornell Studies in Money*, edited by E. Helleiner and J. Kirshner. Ithaca and London: Cornell University Press.

———. 2021b. "Tax Treaties of G-24 Countries: Analysis Using a New Dataset". Working Paper of the Intergovernmental Group of Twenty-Four (G-24). https://www.g24.org/wp-content/uploads/2021/06/G24-treaties-WP_Final.pdf.

Hebous, S. 2021. "Has Tax Competition Become Less Harmful?". In *Corporate Income Taxes under Pressure: Why Reform Is Needed and How It Could Be Designed*, edited by R. De Mooij, A. Klemm, and V. Perry, pp. 87–106. Washington, DC: International Monetary Fund.

Hoekman, B., and E. Zedillo. 2021. *Trade in the 21st Century: Back to the Past*. Washington, DC: Brookings Institution Press.

Hofmann, C., A. Osnago, and M. Ruta. 2017. "Horizontal Depth: A New Database on Preferential Trade Agreements". *Policy Research Working Paper No. 7981*. Washington, DC: World Bank.

ICRICT (International Commission for the Reform of International Corporate Taxation). 2016. "Four Ways to Tackle Tax Competition". https://www.icrict.com/icrict-documentsfour-ways-to-tackle.

———. 2021. ICRICT Open Letter to G20 Members: "A Global Tax Deal for the Rich." https://www.icrict.com/press-release/2021/10/12/icrict-open-letter-to-g20-leaders-a-global-tax-deal-for-the-rich.

IMF (International Monetary Fund). 2014. "Spillovers in International Corporate Taxation". *IMF Policy Paper*. Washington, DC: International Monetary Fund.

———. 2019. "Corporate Taxation in the Global Economy". *IMF Policy Paper*. Washington, DC: International Monetary Fund.

Keen, M., and A. Simone. 2004. "Is Tax Competition Harming Developing Countries More Than Developed?". https://www.taxjustice.net/cms/upload/pdf/Keen_TNI_copyright_tax_competition_developing.pdf

Kei Mu Yi. 2000. "Can Vertical Specialization Explain the Growth of World Trade". *Staff Report No. 96*. New York: Federal Reserve Board of New York.

Krist, W. 2013. *Globalization and America's Trade Agreements*. Washington, DC: Woodrow Wilson Center Press with Johns Hopkins University Press.

Krueger, A. 2021. "The Agricultural Challenge in the Twenty-First Century". In *Trade in the 21st Century: Back to the Past?*, edited by B. Hoekman and E. Zedillo. Washington, DC: Brookings Institution Press.

Krugman, P. 1995. "Growing World Trade: Causes and Consequences". *Brookings Papers on Economic Activity* 1: 1995.

Lee, C., and Y. Fukunaga. 2014. "ASEAN Regional Cooperation on Competition Policy". *Journal of Asian Economics* 35: 77–91.

Mattoo, A. 2018. "Trade and Cooperation in an Age of Insecurity". Presentation at the G-24 Technical Group Meeting, Colombo, Sri Lanka, February 2018.

Nordhaus, W. 2015. "Climate Clubs: Overcoming Free-Riding in International Climate Policy". *American Economic Review* 105, no. 4: 1339–70.

OECD (Organisation for Economic Co-operation and Development). 2014. "Taxation and Competition Policy". Speech delivered by Angel Gurria, OECD Secretary-General. https://www.oecd.org/about/secretary-general/taxation-and-competition-policy.htm.

———. 2016. "The Multilateral Convention to Implement Tax Treaty Related Measures to Prevent BEPS". https://www.oecd.org/tax/treaties/multilateral-convention-to-implement-tax-treaty-related-measures-to-prevent-beps.htm.

———. 2019. "Programme of Work to Develop a Consensus Solution to the Tax Challenges Arising from the Digitalization of the Economy". OECD/G20 Inclusive Framework on BEPS. Paris: OECD.

———. 2021. "Statement on a Two-Pillar Solution to Address the Tax Challenges Arising from the Digitalisation of the Economy". https://www.oecd.org/tax/beps/statement-on-a-two-pillar-solution-to-address-the-tax-challenges-arising-from-the-digitalisation-of-the-economy-october-2021.pdf.

Picciotto, S. 2016. "Taxing Multinational Enterprises as Unitary Firms". Working Paper No. 53. International Centre for Tax and Development. Brighton, UK: Institute of Development Studies.

Rodrik, D. 2002. "Trade Policy Reform as Institutional Reform". In *Development, Trade and the WTO: A Handbook*, edited by B. Hoekman, A. Mattoo, and P. English. Washington, DC: World Bank.

Roy, M. 2019. "Elevating Services: Services Trade Policy, WTO Commitments and Their Role in Economic Development and Trade Integration". Working Paper of the G-24. https://www.g24.org/wp-content/uploads/2019/02/Roy_G24_paper__Jan_2019.pdf.

Saez, E., and G. Zucman. 2019. *The Triumph of Injustice: How the Rich Dodge Taxes and How to Make Them Pay*. New York, NY: W.W. Norton & Company, Inc.

Stiglitz, J. 2006. *Making Globalization Work*. New York and London: W.W. Norton and Company, Inc.

Tang, M.-K., and Wei Shang-Jin. 2009. "The Value of Making Commitments Externally: Evidence from WTO Accessions". *Journal of International Economics* 78, no. 2: 216–29.

Tanzi, V. 1999 "Is There a Need for a World Tax Organization". In *The Economics of Globalization: Policy Perspectives from Public Economics*, edited by A. Razin and E. Sadka. Cambridge: Cambridge University Press.

Tørsløv, T., L. Wier, and G. Zucman. 2018. "The Missing Profits of Nations". *NBER Working Paper*. Cambridge, MA: National Bureau of Economic Research.

US Department of Treasury. 2021a. "The Made in America Tax Plan". https://home.treasury.gov/system/files/136/MadeInAmericaTaxPlan_Report.pdf.

———. 2021b. "G7 Finance Ministers & Central Bank Governors Communiqué". Press Releases, 5 June 2021. https://home.treasury.gov/news/press-releases/jy0215.

Uy, M. 2019. "The G-24 Proposal and the Challenges of the Inclusive Framework". Presentation at the Tax Justice Network Virtual Conference. December 2019. https://www.taxjustice.net/wp-content/uploads/2019/12/Marilou-Uy.pdf.

World Bank. 2020. "Trading for Development in the Age of Global Value Chains". World Development Report. Washington, DC: World Bank.

———.2021. "Data for a Better World". World Development Report. Washington, DC: World Bank.

Index

A

agricultural employment, 102–04, 118–19, 190–91, 203–05, 228–29, 234, 236, 241–42, 283, 288, 568
agricultural exports, 202, 293–94, 296–98
agricultural incentives, 6, 78–92, 300, 547, 690
agricultural insurance, 212–13, 686–88
agricultural investments, 209–213
agricultural productivity
    labour productivity, 104–112, 121–22, 126–27, 130, 499–500
    labour productivity growth, 104–08, 118, 121–22, 126–27, 130
    relationship with farm size, 133–152, 225
agricultural protectionism, 76–8, 85, 91, 635, 633, 635–38, 652, 661, 690
agricultural subsidies, 13, 16, 84, 86, 160, 170, 182–83, 206–08, 212–13, 638, 665–691, 704, 718, 730
agricultural R&D, 159, 182, 208–212
agricultural technologies, 198–201, 209–10, 212, 215
agricultural transformation
    in China, 118–130
    inclusiveness of, 122–130
    productivity, 117, 120–22
    role in rural poverty reduction, 7, 116–131
    in Southeast Asia, 118–130
    trends of, 118–122
    typology of, 127–29
agriculture sector
    comparative advantage of, 134–35, 142–46, 150
    importance in economic growth, 6, 95–112

global rice market, 697–724
    share in GDP, 100–02, 107, 118–19, 190, 226–27, 280, 290, 293–94, 400–01, 499
    share in employment, 102–04, 226, 228–29, 234, 236, 241–42, 290, 293–94
    share in exports, 293–94, 296–97
Agriculture and Fisheries Modernization Act (AFMA), 19–20, 158–59, 164, 684–85
Ambisyon Natin, 8, 10, 22, 29, 316–17
anticompetitive behaviour, 14–6, 76–8, 292–94, 495–98, 501–08, 510–12, 532, 535–36, 547–49, 633, 635–38, 661
antitrust, 508, 511–15, 521–23, 525, 528–29, 533–34
anti-monopoly policies, 512–14, 521–23, 525, 528–29, 533
Aquino (Benigno) administration, 41, 55, 166
Aquino (Corazon) administration, 39, 165, 252
Arrow-Debreu general equilibrium model, 502
Arroyo (Gloria Macapagal) administration, 41, 56, 167, 444
ASEAN performance
    export performance, 43–4, 296–97
    food security, 302–04
    GDP growth, 32–7, 92–112, 116–17, 462–66
    governance, 58–9, 466
    income inequality, 463–66
    internet penetration, 60–1
    per capita GDP, 463–66
    trade openness, 298–99
    unemployment, 463–66
    public expenditure on health, education and social protection, 463–65

Asian Barometer Survey, 466–71
Asian financial crisis, 9, 34, 40, 53, 223, 280, 284, 434, 516
Asia's miracle, 95–7
automotive industry, 255, 248, 255, 501, 530

B

Belt and Road Initiative, 300, 743
Boone indicator, 597, 620–21, 625–28
business process outsourcing (BPO), 43–9, 59–60, 415–16
buyer power, 575–76, 592

C

cash transfer programme, 24, 65–6, 184, 213, 340, 367, 430, 436, 451, 466
climate change, 88, 190–217, 716, 724
climate models, 191–192, 197, 198, 216
competition and competition policy
　economic growth and development, 496–529
　evolution of, 13, 496, 511–13
　innovation, 495–97, 499, 501, 503–05, 507–08, 536, 551–54, 560–69
　in Asia, 529–533, 537
　in Philippines, 535–37
　in South Korea, 533–34, 537
　in Thailand, 534–35, 537
　specialization, 497, 499–503, 507, 536–37
　trade, competition and industrial policy, 502–04
competitive equilibrium model, 363–65, 368–370, 383
computable general equilibrium (CGE), 192, 202, 216–17, 284, 286
COVID–19, 2, 10, 48–66, 68–9, 108, 176, 214, 226, 237, 281, 305, 316, 329–30, 332, 414–17, 420, 422–31, 437–39, 451–53, 714, 716–17, 719
credit market, 339–54, 384–86, 595–630
crop models, 191–95, 198, 209, 216, 723

D

Decision Support System for Agro-technology Transfer (DSSAT), 192–93, 202, 216
demographic dividend, 10, 311–34
demographic transition, 10, 311–19, 322, 326–27, 329, 331, 333–34
digital economy, 11–2, 46, 59–62, 63, 65, 90–1, 500, 719, 738–42, 740, 744
distributive justice, 11–2, 361–86
Duterte (Rodrigo) administration, 168, 170, 172–75, 237, 330, 445, 448–49, 536

E

economic growth and development, Asia
　comparative ASEAN, 32–7, 116–17, 462–66
　comparative Asia, 32–7, 92–112, 116–17, 462, 499–502, 515–29
economic growth and development, Philippines, 2, 4–6, 9, 12, 14, 22, 30, 32–53, 68, 95, 223–24, 226–27, 250, 253, 280–85, 305, 311–34, 361, 385, 390–92, 414–16, 547
economic openness, 52–6, 87, 79, 91, 281–88, 294–96, 298, 302–03, 305–06
economic performance
　agricultural performance, 288–89, 296, 302
　comparative Asia, 32–7
　export performance, 43–4, 254–65, 275, 296–97
　manufacturing performance, 225–26, 233, 236, 242–43
　trade and investment performance, 288–90, 305
economic regulation, 497–98, 501, 503, 507, 512, 515, 519, 533–34, 536
education
　literacy, 36, 60, 96, 393–94, 396, 398, 407, 409, 411
　public expenditure in, 12, 64, 407–10, 438–39, 465–66
　Universal Access to Quality Tertiary Education Act of 2017, 435–36
electronics industry, 43–5, 248, 249–53, 256, 260, 265, 267–70, 275, 288, 290

employment
  educational attainment, 366, 368, 372, 377, 379–82, 384, 426–28, 435, 440, 444
  employment growth, 14, 37, 415, 546–54, 558, 560, 568, 570
  employment rate, 10, 48–51, 378
  in formal sector, 9, 37, 224–26, 237
  in informal sector, 224–25, 237
  job creation and opportunities, 237–38, 283, 290, 293–94, 305–06, 415, 551–53
  minimum wage, 37–8, 79, 253, 258
exports, 9, 43–4, 247–50, 254–63, 274–75, 282–83, 288–91, 293–94, 296–98, 503–04
export processing zone (EPZ), 9, 250–54, 256, 268, 274
external debt, 3, 37–8, 40, 288–89

F

Family Income Expenditure Survey (FIES), 20, 48, 223, 228–31, 235, 292, 327, 362, 373–75, 417–19, 420–21, 423, 425
farm size and productivity
  inverse relationship, 133–35, 137–42, 146, 150
  large farms, 137–39, 142, 150–52
  small farms, 133–35, 140–51
  U-shaped relationship, 136–40, 142
fertility rate, 317–20, 327–29, 333–34
fertility reduction
  female labour participation, 324–25, 327–31
  health of children, 326–29
financial inclusion, 12, 341–42, 355, 366, 381–82, 384–86, 595–630
financial market, 364–66, 368, 371, 380–82, 385–86
financial sector
  formal sector, 339, 342, 345–46, 384–86, 595–630
  informal sector, 339–54
fiscal incentives, 250–51, 254–55, 258, 268, 274
fiscal stimulus, 49, 51, 53, 59–60
foreign investments, 46–7, 55, 248, 250–54, 271–72, 281, 286–88, 290, 293, 298, 305, 730, 734
foreign direct investments (FDI), 55, 248, 250–54, 272, 283, 286–90, 298, 305, 730
foreign and development aid, 286–88
food security and self-sufficiency, 85–90, 135, 144–46, 157–59, 160–63, 170–71, 196, 205, 210, 215, 302–04, 701, 719–22

G

Gini index, 361–62, 373–74, 385, 463–66
General Agreement on Tariffs and Trade (GATT), 89, 281, 728–29, 731
global manufacturing value chains (GMVC)
  buyer-driven production networks, 248–49, 260, 262, 264
  export performance, Philippines, 254, 256–65, 275
  global production network, 43, 249, 252, 255, 260, 271, 274–75
  GMVC exports, 256–57, 259–63, 275
  GMVC participation, 265–74
  history in Philippines, 249–56
  producer-driven production networks, 9, 246–75
global production sharing, 9, 246–48, 253, 257–59, 265, 268, 270–71, 274–75
Global Trade Analysis Project (GTAP) model, 84, 88
government-owned and controlled corporation (GOCC), 16, 598–99, 666–69, 683–90
government redistribution, 150, 152, 448, 460–62, 466–69, 471–74, 477, 479–82, 487–89, 497
government subsidies, 13, 16, 160, 170, 182–83, 206–08, 212–13, 432, 436, 438–40, 451–52, 596–99, 628, 638, 665–91, 704, 730
globalization, 46, 75, 187, 246, 253, 275, 281–287
global rice market, 697–724
Grain Sector Development Program, 165–68
growth accounting method, 95, 98–9, 106

H

healthcare system
  health insurance, 63, 432–41
  public expenditure in, 432–33, 438–39
health indicators
  child and infant mortality, 12, 62, 301–02, 326–29, 393–94, 399–400, 407, 409, 411
  life expectancy, 63, 286, 393–94
  mortality rate, 62, 314, 326–29, 393, 399, 407, 690
  hunger and malnutrition, 195–96, 301–02, 304, 424

Herfindahl–Hirschman Index (HHI), 14–15, 554–58, 560–62, 567–68, 597, 620–22, 624, 628, 667–82
household income, 11, 88, 224, 227–228, 231, 283, 366, 373, 375, 436
Human Development Index (HDI), 12, 392–96, 400, 409, 411, 431
hunger and malnutrition, 195–96, 301–02, 304, 424
hyperbolic discounting, 341, 355

I, J

IMF rescue programme, 38–9, 53, 165
imports
    import competition, 576–77, 580, 635, 660–61
    import control, 15–16, 157–58, 160, 165, 172–87, 547–48, 633, 635–38, 652, 661
    import cost, 634, 647–53, 660–61
    import tax, 634–35, 641, 648–52, 655, 660
income distribution, 283–84, 368, 372–73, 377, 381, 473–74, 479–82, 484, 489, 496
income growth, 90, 126, 215, 315, 322 327–28, 366, 372, 517–18, 528
income inequality, 11, 283–85, 361–62, 364–68, 372–77, 381, 383, 385–86, 473–74, 463–66, 479–82, 484, 489
industrialization, 32, 36–7, 45, 88, 130, 224, 246–50, 259, 268, 274–75, 280–81, 362, 499–500, 502–04, 510–11, 530, 532, 719
industrial policy, 37, 96, 246–75, 502–04, 510–11, 530, 532
infant and child mortality, 12, 62, 301–02, 326–29, 393–94, 399–400, 407, 409, 411
innovation, 495–97, 499, 501, 503–05, 507–08, 536, 551–54, 560–69
institutions and governance, 56–9
intergenerational mobility, 12, 461, 469–74, 476–77, 479, 485–87
international tax cooperation
    corporate tax, 728, 734–36, 738–42
    tax treaties, 736–37, 739, 742
    taxing rights, 736–42
international tax and trade cooperation, 727–45

International Model for Policy Analysis of Agricultural Commodity and Trade (IMPACT), 192–93, 202, 216–17
investment climate, 247, 251–52, 256, 259, 271–72, 274–75
job creation and opportunities, 237–38, 283, 290, 293–94, 305–06, 415, 551–53

L

labour force participation, 96, 99, 111–12, 231–36, 241–43, 324–25, 328–31, 376–79, 428
labour market, 46, 136–38, 147, 202, 207, 311–12, 324–26, 331–32, 334–36, 366–68, 372, 375–77, 379–80, 383–86, 553
labour productivity, 97, 99, 104–08, 112–14, 121–22, 126–27, 130, 499–500
land reform, 133–35, 143, 149–52, 159, 284, 362
land reform policies and programmes, 133–35, 150–52, 159
late payment behaviour, 574–92
Late Payment Directive, 574, 585, 592
Laurel-Langley Agreement, 250–51
Lerner index (price cost margin), 552–54, 557–58, 560, 565–67, 668–69, 672, 674, 681, 684
liberalization, 39, 54–6, 157–58, 165, 172–87, 280–306, 510–11, 547, 549–51, 722–24, 729
life expectancy, 63, 286, 393–94
literacy, 12, 36, 60, 96, 393–94, 396, 398, 407, 409, 411

M

manufacturing employment, 225–26, 233, 236, 242–43, 266–68, 283, 290, 293–94
manufacturing export, 247, 254–55, 256–58, 260
manufacturing performance, 225–26, 233, 236, 242–43
manufacturing protectionism, 76–7, 81
manufacturing sector
    employment in, 225–26, 233, 236, 242–43, 266–68, 283, 290, 293–94
    share in employment, 225–26, 233, 236, 242–43, 293–94
    share in export, 293–94
    share in GDP, 43–5, 224, 227, 258, 290, 293–94

Marcos (Ferdinand) administration, 37–8, 170, 250, 252
market concentration, 512, 549, 554, 556–57, 570, 661, 667–75, 677, 679–81, 683, 686, 690–91
market intermediation, 639, 655–59, 660–61
market power, 14–6, 554–58, 560–62, 565–68, 597, 607, 620–22, 624, 667–84, 686, 690–91
mechanization, 134–35, 137, 141–42, 144, 146, 148–52, 176–77, 576, 685, 702, 712, 717
microfinance industry, Philippines
    competition in, 15, 597, 607–08, 620–29
    evolution of, 596–606
    policies in, 596–606, 610, 628
    regulatory environment in, 15, 597–99, 604–06
microfinance institutions (MFIs), 339, 345–46, 368, 595–99, 606–30
minimum wage, 11, 365, 367–68, 382–84, 386
minimum wage legislation, 135, 500, 553, 560
monopoly, 165, 501–02, 504–05, 510–14, 521–23, 552, 620, 624, 635
mortality
    child and infant mortality, 12, 62, 301–02, 326–29, 393–94, 399–400, 407, 409, 411
    mortality rate, 62, 314, 326–29, 393, 399, 407, 690
multinational enterprise (MNE), 731, 734–41

N, O

Neoclassical growth model, 497, 499, 502, 519
nominal rate of assistance (NRA), 78–84
OFW remittances, 10, 46–7, 49, 223, 258, 282, 284, 287, 295, 305, 415–17, 421

P

Pantawid Pamilyang Pilipino Program (4Ps), 66, 430, 436–437, 451
Panzar-Rosse method (PRH index), 15, 597, 620, 624, 628
partial equilibrium model, 634, 647–55
Philippine Competition Act, 22, 55, 532, 535, 547–49, 569–70, 666, 691

Philippine Competition Commission, 13, 22–3, 55–6, 179, 532, 535–36, 546–47, 667, 691
Philippine Dynamic Computable General Equilibrium Model (PhilDCGE), 192, 202, 216–17
Philippine Health Insurance Corp. (PhilHealth), 432–37
Philippine Standard Industry Classification (PSIC), 265, 267, 554–55, 558, 668–78
Plaza Accord, 39, 252
population
    population age structure, 231, 311–16, 327–29, 331, 334
    population density, 1, 393–97
    population growth, 99, 121, 143, 160, 190, 314, 317, 321–22, 328, 499, 698, 708–09, 712
    population management, 317, 319, 321–26, 330, 334
    population projection, 10, 316, 321–22, 709
    rural population, 37, 123, 708–11
    urban population, 116–17, 708, 710–11, 724
poverty
    factors affecting, 283–86
    poverty and inequality, 3–4, 6, 76, 86, 231, 282, 306, 462, 469
    poverty rate and incidence, 30–42, 48, 117, 124–27, 224–28, 233–34, 236, 250, 281, 295–96, 315, 317, 319–20, 367, 431, 466, 488
    poverty reduction, 41, 116–30, 283–84, 286–87, 296, 301–02, 305–06, 311, 315, 362, 414–415, 430, 446–48, 462, 469, 500, 596, 599, 605, 607
price distortion, 80–4, 87–8
privatization, 165, 172, 280–81
productivity growth
    between sector, 98–9, 107, 113
    constraints to, 366, 372, 375, 380–82
    sources of, 98–9, 549, 553, 560
    within sector, 98, 106, 107, 113
profit-shifting, 734–36, 738–40
prospects of upward mobility (POUM) hypothesis, 460–62, 471–73, 476, 479, 484, 487–89
protectionism, 15–6, 36, 76–8, 85, 91, 285, 288, 292–94, 305, 547–49, 633, 635–38, 652, 661
protection rate, 78, 285, 288, 655

Index   755

R

Ramos (Fidel) administration, 39–40, 54–5, 165, 166, 252–53
Ranis-Fei model, 224–26, 231–36
recession, 9, 30–1, 34, 37, 39, 40, 41, 47–52, 53, 288, 305, 416–17, 420, 422, 424, 429, 448
redistribution
  redistributive preferences, 460–62, 471–73, 479–82, 487–88
  redistributive policies and programs, 57, 133, 150–52, 386, 448, 460, 462, 473, 479, 487, 489, 497
Rice Tariffication Law (RTL), 6, 15–6, 172–86, 205, 213–14, 547, 633–39, 641–46, 654–55, 659–61
Regional Comprehensive Economic Partnership (RCEP), 89, 300
relative rate of assistance (RRA), 78–82
rent-seeking, 14, 495, 498, 503, 506–07, 532
replacement fertility rate, 317–20, 333
Reproductive Health Law of 2012, 317, 321–22
research and development (R&D), 159, 182, 208–12, 552, 554, 560–69
rice industry
  governance institutions in, 163–64, 167–71
  rice imports, 157–58, 160–64, 172–75, 178–79, 182–84, 633–36, 639, 647–55, 660, 699
  rice prices, 120, 163–65, 168, 172–74, 178–85, 214, 547, 634–36, 638–47, 653–55, 660–61, 703–04
  rice programmes, 165–68, 170–71, 179, 182–84
rice-exporting countries, 163–64, 697, 704–09, 714–16, 719, 721, 724
rice-importing countries, 699, 697–99, 701, 709, 724
rice value chain, 697, 704–09, 714–16, 719, 721, 724
rice trade liberalization, 172–87, 205, 213–14, 547, 633–34, 636, 639, 652–53, 660, 722–24
rural transformation, 117, 120–30

S

Sangla ATM (debit card pawning), 10, 339–354
services sector
  employment in, 283, 288, 290, 292–94
  share in employment, 102–04, 225–26, 228–29, 236, 241–42, 290, 292–94, 400–01, 568
  share in exports, 293–94
  share in GDP, 42, 100–02, 107, 224, 226–27, 280, 290, 293–94
shoe manufacturing, 574–92
small and medium enterprises (SMEs), 14–5, 251, 285, 414, 574–92
social differentiation, 12, 414–54
social mobility, 12–3, 64, 421, 460–62, 467, 469–74, 476–77, 479, 481–89
social safety net
  cash transfer, 24, 65–6, 184, 213, 340, 367, 430, 436, 451, 466
  employment protection, 11, 383–84
  financial inclusion, 12, 381–82, 384–86
  insurance, 213, 432–37, 439–41
  minimum wage legislation, 11, 365, 367–68, 382–84, 386
  public expenditure, 432–33, 435, 438–39
  senior citizen's discount, 435–36, 441
  social pension, 436–37, 439
socio-economic class
  middle class, 415–29, 431–54
  by per cent share of population, 419–20
  by number of households, 420–21
  by educational attainment, 426–27, 444
spatial inequality, 12, 60, 390–411
structural transformation, 5–9, 88, 97–114, 116–31, 190–91, 213–14, 246–47, 499–500, 503, 536, 548, 620

T

technical change, 96, 98, 110–12
total factor productivity, 134, 139–40
total fertility rate, 317–20, 327–29, 333–34

trade agreements
  ASEAN Free Trade Area (AFTA), 281, 300
  Belt and Road Initiative, 300, 743
  Doha Round, 729
  General Agreement on Tariffs and Trade (GATT), 89, 281, 728–29, 731
  Laurel-Langley Agreement, 250–251
  Plaza Accord, 39, 252
  Regional Comprehensive Economic Partnership (RCEP), 89, 300
  Uruguay Round, 85–86, 729
  World Trade Organization (WTO), 728–33, 743
trade liberalization, 9–10, 39, 55, 86, 160, 172–87 205, 252, 280–306, 510, 513, 533, 549–51
trade protectionism, 76–8, 85, 91, 285, 288, 292–94, 305, 633, 635–38, 652, 661, 727–28, 730, 734
trade in value (TiVA), 268–69
trade policy reforms, 77–8, 84–6, 88–91
trade reduction index (TRI), 80–2
trade and welfare effects, 77–9, 80–2

U

unemployment, 10–11, 48, 102, 231, 280, 294, 316, 325, 329–34, 366–68, 376–80, 382–85, 426–28, 462–65, 551–53
unemployment rate, 10–1, 281, 316, 329–33, 368, 377–80, 426–28, 463–65, 462–65
urbanization, 116–17, 130, 190, 708–14
Uruguay Round, 85–86, 729

W

wage
  minimum wage, 11, 365–68, 382–84, 386
  minimum wage legislation, 365, 367–68, 382–84, 386
  wage growth, 135, 500, 553, 560
Water, Nutrient and Light Capture in Agroforestry Systems (WaNuLCAS), 192, 216
welfare, 415–17, 422–31, 435, 442, 450, 452–54, 495, 497–99, 502, 506–11, 513, 530, 536
welfare reduction index (WRI), 80–2
World Governance Indicators, 57–9